Decision Making without Algorithms

Prentice-Hall, Inc., Englewood Cliffs, New Jersey

To Ann and Katharine

Library of Congress Cataloging in Publication Data

Eppen, Gary D (Date)
  Quantitative concepts for management.

  Bibliography: p.
  Includes index.
    1. Management—Mathematical models. I. Gould,
Floyd Jerome, (Date)   joint author. II. Title.
HD30.25.E66   658.4′03   78-10337
ISBN 0-13-746602-1

QUANTITATIVE CONCEPTS FOR MANAGEMENT

Decision Making without Algorithms

Gary D. Eppen | F. J. Gould

Permission acknowledgments on page xx

Editorial and production supervision: *Joyce Fumia Perkins*
Editorial assistance: *Mary Helen Fitzgerald*
Interior and cover design: *Hersch Wartik*
Drawings: *Hersch Wartik Inc.*
Manufacturing coordination: *Nancy J. Myers*

PRENTICE-HALL INTERNATIONAL, INC., *London*
PRENTICE-HALL OF AUSTRALIA PTY. LIMITED, *Sydney*
PRENTICE-HALL OF CANADA, LTD., *Toronto*
PRENTICE-HALL OF INDIA PRIVATE LIMITED, *New Delhi*
PRENTICE-HALL OF JAPAN, INC., *Tokyo*
PRENTICE-HALL OF SOUTHEAST ASIA PTE. LTD., *Singapore*
WHITEHALL BOOKS LIMITED, *Wellington, New Zealand*

Contents

14 Special Topics: Integer Programming, Network Models, Multiple Objectives, and Goal Programming

370

Part 2 *Decisions under Uncertainty*

15 Probability and Expected Utility: A Basic Model for Decisions under Uncertainty

409

16 Extending the Basic Model: Conditional Probabilities and Decision Trees   446

17 Forecasting   473

18 Simulation Models   499

19   Simulation and Sample Statistics   532

20   Stochastic Inventory Management and Queuing Problems   571

Appendixes **Supplementary Mathematical Topics**

1 **Notation of Sums**

2 **Plotting Point Sets, Equalities, and Inequalities**

3 **The Language of Linear Algebra**

Foreword

"A great university," Garfield noted, "was a student at one end of a log and Mark Hopkins on the other." Mark Hopkins has, of course, long since departed the halls of learning for even more illustrious and eternal halls. The log likely has gone from academe also, or at best, its wood is the now-yellowed pages of an erudite manuscript. Today's universities have few of the stature to equal Mark Hopkins. Rather, it is the log, after being transformed into the pages of a text, that has become the more widespread means of learning.

Past and present, however, sometimes unite and a text appears that captures a portion of the vigorous spirit Mark Hopkins must have emanated. In management science, although thousands of books have appeared since the field's inception only a few have achieved such stature. This book, I submit, is among them.

The instruction of management science has continually been confounded by a perplexing question. How can one teach a student with, say, a classical Greek background to discover happiness, truth, and beauty within the intricacies of the simplex method? To the advanced student or expert there is indeed a beauty and elegance which underlies the methodology and algorithms of management science. And the quest of virtually every textbook author is how to transmit these notions of simplicity, elegance, and practicality to the new student. Martin Fischer might have interpreted the dilemma as a question of teaching students wisdom rather than knowledge. Fischer observed, "Knowledge is a process of building up facts; wisdom lies in their perception and simplification." The Eppen and Gould book, in my judgment, not only tries to transmit knowledge and fact but also attempts the wisdom.

One of the book's techniques is to involve the student immediately in lifelike examples. PROTRAC is a mythical manufacturer of heavy equipment with an international market. Throughout the book, the student grapples with PROTRAC's problems in marketing, finance, capital budgeting, production, and other areas, and soon feels him- or herself at the right arm of PROTRAC's chief executive. The examples, moreover, are not, as in so many texts, mere afterthoughts contrived to illustrate the use of an algorithm or a technique. Instead, the examples serve to illustrate basic concepts, both simple and subtle, and these concepts arise naturally out of the example. No longer is an algorithm the final product of management science. Rather, the final product here is a point of view stressing model formulation and problem analysis.

Numerous examples are employed throughout the text. Some are subtle like the track team's high hurdler who mistakenly turns out to be a King Kong creature. Some are ancient such as Joseph and the Pharaoh of Egypt, while recent history unfolds with France and the Maginot line. A fashion-conscious student can try his or her luck as head buyer for Bloomingdale's. The student will even determine the probability that Shakespeare wrote the King James Version of the Bible and thereby be introduced to decision trees. And who said you can't compare apples and oranges? Multiple objective functions are called upon to solve that seeming paradox.

The concepts are motivated by examples, while the underlying mathematics is illuminated by diagrams and pictures. The presentation of linear programming is especially noteworthy in this regard. Excellent pictures are given not only for the graphical solution but for duality, sensitivity, and parametric programming. For instance, complete diagrams depict how the LP problem changes as its constraints, parameters, and other features are changed. Due to such pains-taking visual portrayals of the fundamentals, even our student of classical Greek may find the mathematics enlightening.

The usual topics expected in an introductory texts are covered, of course, including the full menu of deterministic and stochastic models. However, the emphasis throughout is not on technique or algorithms but on motivation, understanding, and appreciation. The emphasis is on analyzing the problem, developing the model, data usage, plus interpretation and implementation, rather than on the algorithms. Most texts discuss algorithms almost exclusively, which, of course, trains technicians. Instead of that, this book's objective is to create a sophisticated and perceptive utilizer of management science and operations research.

To me, and despite my observations about the presentation, examples, and lucidity of expression, the underlying clue to the book lies elsewhere. The secret is that management science is treated with a bit of humor—with an insightful, sometimes even elegant usage of fun. For many students management science seems the drudgery of adding columns of numbers made even more difficult because various algorithmic rules must be followed. Certainly the best examples, diagrams, and presentation lighten the load markedly. Yet, as in life, also required is the seasoning of a few perceptive and intelligent jests. The King Kong creature previously mentioned, a biblical creator of linear programming, "feathering your own nest" as the lead into suboptimization, the "divide and conquer" means of forecasting, and numerous other examples very pleasantly reveal this secret.

Management science itself is exciting. Unfortunately, many of its presentations are much the opposite. I am delighted to discover a text that conveys what management science truly is, a useful field that is creative, exciting, and fun.

To adapt Colton, the study of management science, like the giant redwood, starts in minuteness and ends in magnificence. This book, I hope, will speed that growth.

W. I. ZANGWILL

Preface

In many organizations both in industry and in government, it is clear that decision making is becoming more and more a quantitative process. Planners are trained to look at all the alternatives and seek as much data as possible in determining how to effectively allocate scarce resources under their control. The widespread use of management science and operations research reflects the belief that an informed use of quantitative models can lead to better planning. The pervasiveness of this belief, not only among practitioners but even in academia, is supported by the following statement:

. . . a new element has entered the picture in recent years—the adoption of methods of modern economic analysis by private business. I have in mind the fast spreading use of advanced methods of Operations Research and of so-called Systems Analysis . . . While academic theorists are content with the formulation of general principles, corporate Operations Researchers and practical Systems Analysts have to answer questions pertaining to specific real situations . . .[1]

In summary, the use of models is currently commonplace in many large, complex organizations. Moreover, with the continuing development of computers, and the continuing academic interest in socioeconomic applications of mathematics, it seems reasonable that this trend toward formalism is likely to continue.

For these reasons, most programs in management education have at least one required basic course that is oriented to the teaching of formal models. Such courses are called "An Introduction to Management Science" or "An Introduction to Quantitative Models," and so on. In our opinion, although such courses have existed for 10 or 15 years, the question of how to teach about models at the *introductory* level remains unresolved. We strongly feel that such a course should be oriented toward the *nonspecialist* and should serve at least three main purposes:

1 The course should provide terminal students (that is, those who are not management science majors) with an appreciation for the use of quantitative models in practical situations.

2 It should provide students with some specific new skills—in particular, by giving the student some expertise in the use of quantitative models in a computer-assisted environment.

3 Finally, the course should provide introductory perspectives for students who may wish to continue with additional study in management science but who nevertheless at this point are still in the nonspecialist category.

This leads to the question of whether a text exists that is suitable for such a course. Not surprisingly, a number of books have been written especially for this introductory models (or introductory "quant methods") course. The available texts vary substantially in the level of quantitative sophistication they assume, ranging from those that are clearly appropriate for undergraduate courses up through those that contain at least some material that is typically considered in more advanced courses.

Despite these quite different quantitative levels, the available books are remarkably similar in the overall approach. They purport to emphasize the relevance and applications

---

1 W. Leontief, presidential address, American Economic Association, Detroit, December 1970.

of models and of management science, but in fact they devote a major amount of time to the detailed study of algorithms and a pencil-and-paper type of number crunching. Even the most elementary texts follow a cookbook organizational structure, more or less as follows:

1 A class of models is introduced, such as linear programming models, network models, integer programs, dynamic programs, inventory models, and so on.

2 The class of models is illustrated in formulation problems that tend to be artificial textbook examples.

3 An algorithm is presented for solving the class of problems.

4 There are simple numerical "hand applications" illustrating the use of the algorithm and then numerous exercises in which the algorithm must be employed.

The available texts clearly offer an adequate to excellent treatment of this type of approach, and thus additional efforts in this "chapter-by-chapter, model-by-model" direction hardly seem worth the effort. Even more to the point, it is our opinion that the described approach makes management science seem like a classroom game. The assumptions in the simple models are unrealistic. Most discourse on the problems of applying models in real situations is relegated to a first or last chapter. The formulation problems are often trivial. Consequently, students who want to understand the relevance of models to themselves as future managers typically are left unenlightened.

Moreover, almost without exception the currently available texts devote well over half the textual material to the teaching of algorithms, and one obtains a solid impression that the learning of these various algorithms is an important part of management education. We take sharp exception to this point of view. We believe that the advantages in studying quantitative models, *at the introductory level,* have little to do either with trivial examples or with the learning of algorithms. We believe that the real advantages are twofold:

1 Whether or not a student will become a quantitative expert—or, as we like to describe it, a *producer* of quantitative models and results—he or she will, as a modern manager, quite probably become a *consumer* of quantitative work. Quantitative studies and computer analyses are important inputs to many management decisions. An introductory course should provide students with enough in the way of *facility, concepts,* and *"new intuition"* to enable them to interact more effectively with the quantitative specialists and, in summary, to make them *more mature consumers.* This implies much more than the conventional study of algorithms. This conventional study does indeed provide facility, but it is a facility for doing very little that is useful. The real problems are always solved on a computer—never by hand. It is much more important to understand the role of the model (as opposed to the solution technique) clearly and to develop a facility for reading, understanding, and analyzing the computer output associated with a solution to a model. Students should learn enough in the way of concepts to enable them to scrutinize applied quantitative work and to ask the right questions. This type of maturity does not emerge from the algebraic study of algorithms.

2 The study of formal models can implicitly have an advantageous effect on students in their own decision-making processes. The ability to think as a constrained optimizer, to express oneself in terms of functions, constraints, tradeoffs between variables, and similar concepts can have a substantial influence on the way one approaches, organizes, and analyzes all varieties of decision problems.

We suspect that other authors would not disagree with the goal of making the student a more mature consumer of quantitative work. The question is, how do you effectively achieve this goal? Most writers argue that the teaching of algorithms gives insight into the models and thereby serves to enhance maturity. We disagree. We consider this to be a rationalization for doing what comes naturally. To us, the situation is analogous to the problem faced by an instructor who has one quarter or one semester to teach French to American business executives moving to Belgium. One approach is to analyze in excruciating detail the basic rules of grammar (algorithms) and insure that the student will recognize specific forms such as the subjunctive (a shortest-route network model) when they occur. Another approach is to cover fewer of the rules in order to emphasize the use of the language, the objective being to enable students to get around, to communicate at a rudimentary level, to ask intelligent questions, to understand answers, to know when they are being led astray, and to enable them to appreciate the potential effect that the new language can have on their achievement. We strongly prefer this latter approach.

As a result of our growing dissatisfaction with the usual cookbook approach, we were prompted to redesign our "Introductory Models Course" at Chicago, but a suitable text did not exist. In spite of the number of purportedly model-oriented texts that are currently available, we feel that they all leave a void between quantitative techniques and applications. That void has to do with the failure to convey clearly those concepts of management science that are of great practical importance—and with the failure to properly interpret quantitative techniques in a real decision-making environment. It is our hope that the present text will fill that void. Our emphasis is on the *use* of methods rather than on the methods themselves. The book is built from the bottom up for the prospective user of models, not for the professional model builder.

For the sake of realism and specificity, a portion of the exposition and many of the examples and problems relate to "cases" concerning a hypothetical firm called PROTRAC, a producer of heavy farm machinery and related products. This has the advantage of helping to minimize the number of different word problems and artificial scenarios that students have to digest in order to apply the concepts they are studying. Some of the PROTRAC-related material emphasizes the different functions of models at different levels in the organizational hierarchy, as well as the concepts of suboptimization and centralized versus decentralized planning. At the outset, model formulation is treated in detail. Constrained and unconstrained models are compared, and various real-world "justifications" for the use of constraints are discussed in terms of uncertainty, short-term technological limitations, the handling of nonlinearities, expediting the search, and even nest-feathering. The notion that a model is an abstract approximation of reality is developed from different points of view, and the use of simulation models is compared with optimization models, emphasizing the fact that in business problems there really are no optimal solutions. We also consider the role of judgment in the construction of the model and in its use. We emphasize that the model is only a tool for problem analysis, and a very imperfect tool. That is, limitations are stressed. The student learns about models and tradeoffs in a hands-on environment by analyzing a wealth of computer output which is provided in the text, and by developing an appreciation for the fact that the analysis only begins, rather than ends, with the computer output for a particular problem. A number of specific problems are presented and solved. Then, constraints are modified. New considerations are introduced, and sensitivity questions are considered in detail. It is shown in specific examples that the optimal solution is often only a starting point and perhaps the least interesting part of the overall analysis. There is a recurring emphasis on the role of models as a mechanism for communication and as only one of many inputs in the overall decision-making process.

Organization

The material leading up to and through Chapter 12 should significantly increase the student's ability to think quantitatively and correctly about tradeoffs and interactions within the context of a given model. In particular, this training in analytics culminates with the activity analysis discussion in Chapter 12, in which students are challenged to explain, for example, how an extra unit of a resource availability would actually impact on the model in terms of how the optimal activity levels (that is, decisions) will adjust.

In treating decisions under uncertainty, the concepts of probability and expected returns are introduced in an elementary way. Our basic decision model, for treating events with uncertain outcomes, is developed from the viewpoint of expected utility maximization. This basic model is then extended in two directions: updating with new information via Bayes' theorem; sequential decision analysis via decision trees. The treatment of uncertainty includes a chapter on forecasting and two especially important chapters on simulation. All of the exposition is cast in terms of specific examples.

A number of chapters deal with special topics such as inventory control and project scheduling, integer programming and network models, goal programming, multiple objectives, forecasting, and queuing.

The text is organized in two parts: "Deterministic Decisions under Constraints" (Chapters 3 through 14), and "Decisions under Uncertainty" (Chapters 15 through 20). Chapters 1 and 2 are introductory general discussions of models. The chapter-network-diagrams in Figures P1.1 and P1.2 provide the prerequisite relationships for the various chapters in the book. This can be used to suggest various routes through the text and corresponding courses for which the book may be used.

It is our belief that any use of the book should include Chapters 1, 3, and 18. They discuss in broad terms the general notion of a model and the two major types of models: constrained optimization and simulation.

Chapters 3, 4, 5, and 6 provide a minimal introduction to constrained optimization models in terms of formulation, computer analysis, and geometric interpretation. These chapters are prerequisite to all the following chapters in the first part of the book. Chapter 7 deals with the simplex method and the formal duality theory of linear programming. The simplex discussion is included for completeness—for the benefit of the instructor who is reluctant to part completely with tradition, as well as for mathematically oriented students who want a more detailed look at the inside of the black box they are learning to use. Chapters 8 and 9 elaborate on sensitivity analysis in more detail, and in mastering this material the reader becomes an unusually knowledgeable user of linear programming. The coverage of sensitivity analysis is unified by treating the topic from the perspective of pertubation functions, an approach that is, to the best of our knowledge, unique for a text of this type. Chapters 11 and 12 present a reasonably large LP model and illustrate realistic applications of dual pricing and parametric analysis. In Chapter 12 activity analysis is discussed and illustrated with several examples. Chapters 10, 13, and 14 cover special topics such as nonlinearity, suboptimization, decentralized planning, integer programming applications, network models, inventory control and project scheduling,

Figure P1.1   *Precedence Relationships for Part 1, "Deterministic Decisions under Constraints"*   **Figure P1.2**   *Precedence Relationships for Part 2, "Decisions under Uncertainty"*

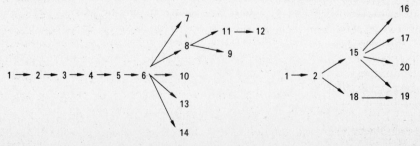

goal programming, and multiple objectives. Chapter 15 begins Part 2 on decisions under uncertainty with an introduction to concepts of probability, sample spaces, return, risk, and expected return, and a discussion of the model for maximizing expected utility. In Chapter 16, conditional probabilities, Bayes' theorem, and decision trees are introduced and then used to extend the basic model. Chapter 17 presents several commonly used forecasting models, and Chapters 18 and 19 cover simulation. The material on simulation is treated in several contexts. In Chapter 18, a simulation model is used as a planning tool at the highest level in the hierarchy of the firm. This model is used to assist the corporate president in strategic long-range corporate planning in the face of future economic uncertainty. Another section of this chapter considers simulation of past data to develop confidence in a model's future performance. In the spirit of hands-on experience in the learning process, a simple hand simulation is also presented for a specific problem. In Chapter 19, a particular simulation study is developed in considerable detail. The analysis requires the introduction of a number of statistical concepts including random variables, expected values, populations, samples, and confidence intervals. Other topics in this chapter include independence, initialization, grouping of data, and differencing of data. Chapter 20 presents a brief and conceptual treatment of queuing and stochastic inventory models.

Calculus is not used anywhere in the text, and the only formal prerequisite is what is normally called "high-school algebra." In our experience, most of the material in the text is readily accessible to students with backgrounds varying from Romance languages to the hard sciences. Several of the chapters are more demanding than the others with respect to the student's maturity in terms of the ability to handle notation and logical detail. There is ample material to allow an instructor to select at the appropriate level for any introductory class. In order to help a student gauge his or her progress, there are numerous example problems with their solutions, as well as exercises, all of which constitute an important part of the material. More difficult problems or sections of the text are identified as such.

   Clearly, the book contains more material than can probably be presented in a one-quarter or one-semester course. The instructor is therefore able to use the book in a number of different patterns in order to suit specific curricular needs. For example, our introductory one-quarter course minimally covers the constrained optimization material in Chapters 1 through 6, 8, 11 and 12, plus Chapters 15, 18, and 19. In addition, varying amounts of material from other chapters are selected, with the mix determined by the individual instructor's preferences. We do not intend to suggest that this course is optimal for all environments. Other instructors may prefer to organize the material in other ways. The appropriate use will depend upon the instructor's objectives and tastes and the desired balance between depth and breadth in his or her particular course.

Acknowledgements

We are indebted to the many students at the University of Chicago's Graduate School of Business who have participated in the class-testing of this material during its development. Their suggestions have substantially contributed to the product. We are also indebted to the following for their constructive comments, criticisms, and encouragement: Robert Abrams, University of Chicago; John P. Evans, University of North Carolina at Chapel Hill; Marshall Fisher, University of Pennsylvania; Linus Schrage, University of Chicago; David Rubin, University of North Carolina at Chapel Hill; and Ralph Steuer, University of Kentucky.

The Graduate School of Business at the University of Chicago has provided a stimulating and supportive atmosphere for this project. We appreciate the tangible support and encouragement of Dean Richard Rosett and gratefully acknowledge our debt to our colleagues who have profoundly affected our thinking about management education. The faculty secretarial staff, and especially Nerissa Walton and Vicky Longawa, provided important help with typing and proofreading. A very special expression of gratitude goes to Marjorie Walters for her help with the final manuscript and to Clairmarie Slaveck who for three years handled the typing and retyping of draft after draft in a seemingly endless pattern of revisions. Without her skill and dedication this book would not have been completed.

The material for this text has passed through an extensive review process, and we have profited from the insights it has provided. We wish to thank in particular: John J. Bernardo, University of Kentucky; Robert L. Childress, University of Southern California; Marvin Jay Karson, University of Alabama; Charles H. Kriebel, Carnegie-Mellon University; Irwin Kruger, University of Miami; John ReVelle, University of Nebraska at Omaha; Mitchell L. Slotnick, Loyola University of Chicago; Harvey M. Wagner, University of North Carolina at Chapel Hill; and Willard I. Zangwill, University of Illinois at Urbana-Champaign. Each has read and commented on at least part of the material. We are also indebted to Professor Zangwill for writing the Foreword.

We are grateful to the Literary Executor of the late Sir Ronald A. Fisher, F.R.S., to Dr. Frank Yates, F.R.S., and to Longman Group Ltd., London, for permission to abridge Table III from their book *Statistical Tables for Biological, Agricultural and Medical Research* (6th edition, 1974).

Certain examples and problems have been adapted from the following sources, all with the permission of the publishers. Ex. 6, 12, 3, prob. 19, pp. 70, 79, 83, 98: Adapted from Harvey M. Wagner, *Principles of Operations Research*, 2nd ed. (Englewood Cliffs, N.J.: Prentice-Hall, Inc., 1975), pp. 66, 62, 61, 64. Prob. 1, p. 91: Adapted from Henri Theil, John C. G. Boot, and Teun Kloek, *Operations Research and Quantitative Economics* (New York: McGraw-Hill, Inc., 1965), p. 4, Prob. 8, p. 93: Adapted from Frederick S. Hillier and Gerald J. Lieberman, *Operations Research*, 2nd ed. (San Francisco: Holden-Day, Inc., 1974), p. 204. Prob. 15, p. 96: Adapted from Daniel Teichrow, *An Introduction to Management Science* (New York: John Wiley & Sons, Inc., 1964), p. 433. Prob. 18, p. 97: Adapted from R. W. Metzger and R. Schwarzbek, "A Linear Programming Application to Cupola Charging," *J. Indus. Engr.* **12**, no. 2, part 1 (March–April 1961), 87–93, © 1961 by the American Institute of Industrial Engineers, Inc.

While all these individuals share in the credit for bringing forth this text, the authors assume the sole responsibility for all errors. Of course errors can be corrected, but nothing much can be done about our attempts at humor. Unfortunately, there is here a quality that is irrevocable and must speak for itself.

GARY D. EPPEN

F. J. GOULD

1 *An Introduction to Models*

This is an introductory chapter on what models are and why and where they are used. The student is introduced to the concept of a formal model and to some of the nuances of model formulation. A rationale is presented for the existence and use of models in real-world applications.

1.1 Models, Computers, and Planning

Facing today's economic upheavals and the uncertainties of the future, companies are scrambling for new and better planning techniques. They are relying more and more on the use of computers and quantitative models. At the same time, they are becoming more knowledgeable about what models can do. It is unclear to what extent the planning function will ultimately entail the use of formulas and computers, but one thing is certain: computer printouts are becoming as common as pencils and paper, and the combination of modeling and computer analysis is here to stay.

Whether a modeler's recommendations are accepted or rejected, they must be questioned and understood. If they are accepted, it had better be on grounds other than blind faith. If they are rejected, forceful and equally quantitative arguments may be required to contradict the modeler's analysis. No matter what surprises the future holds in store, the planner who utilizes computers and formulas must be reckoned with. Whether his or her recommendations are implemented or shelved, they must be clearly interpreted in the proper perspective and context.

Although computers and models are separate entities conceptually, in terms of use they usually go hand in hand. Managers are seldom interested either in models or computers, per se. In today's managerial setting, no one uses a model without a computer, and anyone who uses a computer is familiar with at least some kind of model.

This book is about the model part of the picture. We shall refer to computer analyses, and we shall examine and discuss computer printouts. At times, it will be informative to state the power and limitations of the computer as related to model building. In order to keep models in perspective, it will sometimes be appropriate to consider computer speed, costs, and capacities. Since models tend to be sterile without the use of machines for computation, such computer-related considerations are obviously important. But for our purposes, the computer is treated as a given tool that can be used without much requisite knowledge or skill in the same way that you can use the telephone without understanding the complexities of the Bell system.

The emphasis in future chapters is on the role of models in the decision-making context. But in order to work in detail with models, you must understand some of the basic concepts and tools of mathematics. It is assumed that you approach this text with a solid background in elementary algebra. By *elementary*, we mean algebra at the level commonly taught in high school. Specifically, you should be able to use summation notation, to plot sets of points, to represent geometrically points satisfying equalities and inequalities, and to work with variables, functions, contours, and simultaneous linear equations.

1.2   Different Types of Models

In our world, many kinds of models are associated with many kinds of activities. Engineers build model airplanes, urban planners build model cities, designers make model dresses, and stage managers make model sets. Physicists construct models of the universe, and economists build models of the economy. Business managers and corporate planners work with models of their own particular environments. Such an environment may be a complex multinational corporation or it may simply be a one-room shop where three products are assembled on four machines.

Despite the diversity of these models, they have one aspect in common. They are all idealized and simplified representations of reality. Another way of saying the same thing is that

A model is a selective abstraction of reality.

An artist looks at reality, filters it, and creates a selective representation. A modeler does the same thing. Based on observation and experimentation, Galileo stated that a falling body, no matter what its mass, falls a distance of

$$D = \frac{gt^2}{2}$$

feet in t seconds, where g is the so-called constant of acceleration. This statement is a selective representation of reality that explicitly describes the quantitative relation between distance, D, and time, t. This equation, $D = gt^2/2$, is an excellent example of a model. It states an idealized numerical relationship. It is idealized and simplified because it ignores everything else that is happening in the world and focuses only on a particular relationship between the two distinguished entities, D and t. Although the relationship set forth in the model is not *exactly* satisfied in any real situation (because of air friction and other variable factors) the model is certainly useful, important, and simple. Its very simplicity represents a level of achievement often sought but seldom realized, for unquestionably the best models are the simplest ones—those that are easiest to use and understand.

In economics, a well-known model describes the equilibrium price of a given commodity. Namely, in equilibrium, the price of that commodity is such that the amount suppliers are willing to bring to market is exactly equal to the amount consumers are willing to purchase. Thus we have the concise model

Supply = demand

This simple model is certainly a selective representation of reality. It ignores most of the world and describes only three entities of interest: price, quantity supplied, and quantity purchased. The model is also an idealization, for the world we live in is never truly in equilibrium. There are constant shocks and perturbing factors. There are spatial effects. Consumer prices in Chicago and New York are different. However, the model has been found to be useful in various contexts and is considered to be important by economists.

The model *Supply = demand* has several features in common with the model $D = gt^2/2$. Both are extremely simple. Both are quantitative. That is, both models describe a *quantitative relationship* between entities of interest.

In the business environment, models are also quantitative in nature. Unfortunately, they are usually much more complicated than $D = gt^2/2$ or *Supply = demand*. Although models used in business may become simpler in the future, it is notable that computation costs have been historically decreasing and that the current trend in model building is toward greater complexity.

In addition to complexity, another important difference exists between management models and the type we have been discussing. The models of interest to management are what we call **decision models,** and these models are the main subject of this book. Every decision model contains **decision variables.** It will be seen that selecting a decision amounts to determining numerical values for decision variables. In other words, from the perspective of modeling, decisions are numbers. Every decision model also contains **objectives.** As simple illustrations, consider the following examples:

---

1   *Salesforce allocation model*   The decisions (that is, decision variables) might be how many salespeople to assign to each territory. Alternative objectives might be to minimize costs, to make sure that the best salespeople get the best accounts, and so on.

2   *Job-shop scheduling model*   The decisions (decision variables) might be how many hours to schedule given parts on given machines, and in what sequence. Alternative objectives might be to minimize costs, to minimize the total completion time for all parts, to minimize tardiness on deliveries, and so on.

3   *Cash-management model*   The decision variables might be the amount of funds to be held in each of several categories (cash, treasury bills, bonds, stocks) each month. Alternative objectives might be to minimize the opportunity cost of holding more liquid assets, to minimize the probability of short-term debt given other constraints, and so on.

It is not difficult to think of many other types of decision models. For example, consider policy-planning models that attempt to forecast GNP, unemployment, or inflation under assumptions about various government policies. Or consider a corporate-planning model where the problem is whether to invest in oil from the North Sea or in synthetic fuels.

All these examples of decision models fit into a general framework that we are beginning to establish. Namely:

Decision models selectively describe the environment.

Decision models designate decision variables.

Decision models designate objectives.

We shall discuss these three points in more detail in the following pages and in other chapters. For now, let us summarize the focus of this text. In the business environment, the models we are concerned with are called *quantitative decision models.* Many models satisfy this description. In Figure 1.1, 13 different kinds of models are listed, all of which are used in real-world quantitative decision problems. The list is not exhaustive; it will simply give you an idea of the breadth of the field of quantitative modeling. Figure 1.1 also shows the type of mathematics employed for different models. From this information, it should be apparent that even professional model builders have to specialize.

Figure 1.1 *Decision models by class, type, and mathematical discipline*

Class	Model Type	Mathematical Discipline			
		Linear Algebra	Functions and Calculus	Probability and Statistics	Computer Science
Optimization	Linear programming	●			●
	Integer programming	●			
	Dynamic programming		●	●	
	Stochastic programming		●	●	
	Nonlinear programming		●		●
	Game theory	●		●	
	Network theory	●			●
	Inventory and production	●	●	●	
	Scheduling	●	●	●	
	Optimal control		●	●	
Simulation	Queuing			●	●
	Difference equation		●	●	●
	Econometric	●	●	●	●

In this book, we shall consider two broad classes of quantitative decision models. One class, called *optimization models,* includes the first ten types in Figure 1.1. The other class, called *simulation models*, often, but not exclusively, includes the last three types in Figure 1.1.

1.3 Model Building

Whether a model is simple or complex, it is a representation that idealizes, simplifies, and selectively abstracts reality, and this representation is something that is built, or constructed, by individuals. Unfortunately, there are no easy rules or automatic methods for model building. Model building involves art and imagination as well as technical know-how.

In a business environment, model building usually involves the quantification of interactions between many variables. That is, the problem must be stated in the language of mathematics. We shall see many examples of model building in the chapters to follow. Do not be misled by the specific examples in the text, for in the complexity of real-world problems there is usually no single "correct way" to build a model. Different models may address the same situation in much the same way that paintings by Picasso and Van Gogh would make the same field look different.

As an overall guide, we can break down the process of building a decision model into three steps:

The environment is studied.

A selective representation of the problem is formulated.

A symbolic expression of the formulation is constructed.

The first of these three steps, a study of the environment, is often undervalued by those new to modeling. The stated problem is often not the real problem. A variety of factors, including organizational conflicts, a difference between personal and organizational goals, and the complexity of the situation, may stand between the modeler and a clear understanding of the problem. Experience is probably the most essential ingredient for success—experience in building models and a working experience in the environment to be studied.

The second step, formulation, involves basic conceptual analysis, in which crucial assumptions and simplifications may have to be made. During the formulation phase, pertinent relationships are conceptualized in much the same way that Galileo thought about the interactions among distance, time, and the rate of acceleration due to gravity in the falling-object problem. The process of formulation also requires the model builder to isolate from the total environment those aspects of reality relevant to the problem scenario. Since the problems we are concerned with involve decisions and objectives, these must be explicitly identified and defined. In future chapters it will become apparent that there are many applications in which the definition of the decision variables and the objective is a major task in itself. There may be various ways to define the decision variables, and the most appropriate definition may not be apparent initially. For example, it may be unclear whether a certain model should include amounts produced of every product or of only some subset of products. To keep the model suitably small for computational purposes, it may even be desirable to "aggregate" all products into one idealized or abstract product. Moreover, the objectives may be unclear. Even the most capable managers may not know precisely what results they want to achieve. Equally problematic, there may be too many objectives to be satisfied, and it may be necessary to choose one out of many. (It will become evident that it is usually impossible to optimize two different objectives at the same time, and thus, generally speaking, it is nonsensical to seek to obtain "the most return for the least investment.")

Once a model is formulated, it must be constructed. In a sense, formulation and construction are integrated processes, with formulation the conceptual aspect and construction the actual representation of the conceptual relationships. All models are constructed of some medium. A dress designer constructs models out of fabric. The model city is made of clay. The conceptual formulation (a compact radial city with inner and outer hubs, underground parking, moving sidewalks, and so on) takes on a physical representation in the clay model. The conceptual relationships among distance, time, and acceleration due to gravity are represented via the medium of mathematical symbols in the statement $D = gt^2/2$.

In a decision-making environment, models are usually constructed in the symbolic language of mathematics. Also, construction may involve a good deal of data collection and computer programming. The construction of the model may, however, be less critical than the formulation. The reason is this: formulation requires analysis, selectivity, and decisions about relevance and objectives, whereas construction is usually a more technical process, involving a translation into mathematics and the adaptation and use of known tools.

The interactions between formulation and construction are usually critical. For example, the formulation of a corporate-planning model may involve a decision on whether to look three, five, or ten years into the future. It may involve judgments on which divisions and subsidiaries to include. It may then turn out that the model as formulated is far too complex to be constructed in a way that can be useful. Perhaps the required data simply do not exist. Or perhaps the data can be found, but it turns out that with existing techniques it would take three days to run the model on the computer. This embarrassment can make the cost of using the model outweigh any potential gain. Unemployed management scientists can testify to the fact that, all too often, models are formulated that simply cannot be built.

Does this process of model building sound like too much for one person to accomplish? Often, it is. When operations research began, during World War II, logistic models were built by teams of mathematicians, statisticians, economists, physicists, engineers, and generalists. Today, the picture is not much different, except that econometricians, computer scientists, and management scientists have been added. Usually, management scientists train in the *theory* and *development* of models. They are also concerned with the development of *algorithms*, which are techniques for solving models. Thus, models are frequently built by heterogeneous and interdisciplinary teams of experts from various fields. A management scientist working alone has a very limited repertoire and limited capabilities.

1.4 Using Models

Models are used in as many ways as there are people who build them. They can be used to sell an idea or a design, to order optimal quantities of nylon hosiery, to better organize our knowledge of the universe, or to better organize an economy or a firm.

In the firm, models are increasingly synonymous with executive planning. Planning models are used to forecast the future, to explore alternatives, to develop multiple-contingency plans, to increase flexibility and reaction time—in short, to provide planners with all sorts of data. No model can ever give a high-level planner the "best decision." No model can ever tell a decision maker what to do, for the future remains forever uncertain, and forecasts are imperfect. In fact, models are all the more important precisely because we do not know how to forecast.

In any case, no model is a surrogate for executive judgment and intuition. But models do provide interesting data for executives to evaluate. This is important. All decisions, at least to some extent, are based on an evaluation of data.

Decisions are numbers.

Decisions are based on data.

Models provide additional data.

Models often do no more than take crude data and refine them for special use. In fact, the outputs of some models may be used as the inputs for other models. It is not atypical for models to be linked together, as illustrated in Figure 1.2. Notice, for example, that the marketing model has as its output a forecast of next year's demand, and this forecast is an input to the production model.

Figure 1.2   *Analysts use models as inputs to other models*

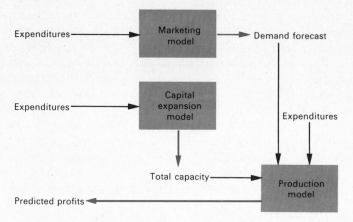

In the following chapters, you will see that models play different roles at different levels of the firm. At the top levels, models provide data and information. They are useful as strategic planning tools. At lower levels, models are actually used to make decisions. In many plants, for example, assembly-line operations are completely computerized. Decisions are produced by a model of the operation.

Models have different uses at different levels of the firm for a number of reasons. At progressively lower levels of an organization, alternatives and objectives are apt to become clearer. Interactions are easier to specify quantitatively. Data are often more available and the future environment more certain. For example, at the bottom of the hierarchy a decision may concern the scheduling of a particular machine. We know the products that will be run on it and the costs of changing the machine from the production of one product to any other product. The goal of the model is to find a schedule that produces the necessary amounts by the due dates and minimizes changeover and storage costs.

Contrast the clarity and explicitness of that problem with a multibillion-dollar, top-management decision between "invest and grow" and "produce and generate current earnings." Models can certainly be applied to such broad and fuzzy problems, but the models themselves are loaded with assumptions and uncertainties. In such cases, the validity of the model may be as difficult to determine as the desired decision.

In spite of these different uses of models at different levels of the firm, a few generalities apply to all quantitative decision models. All such models provide a framework for logical and consistent analysis. More specifically, models are widely used for at least four reasons:

Models force managers to be explicit about objectives.

Models force managers to identify and record the types of decisions (decision variables) that influence objectives.

Models force managers to identify and record pertinent interactions and tradeoffs between decision variables.

Models force managers to record constraints (limitations) on the values that the variables may assume.

It follows from these features that a model can be used as a *consistent tool* for evaluating different policies. That is, each policy or set of decisions is evaluated by the same objective according to the same formulas for describing interactions and constraints. Moreover, models can be explicitly adjusted and improved with historical experience.

A final point: models provide the opportunity for a systematic use of powerful mathematical methods. They can handle a large number of variables and interactions. The mind is capable of storing only so much information. Models allow us to use the power of mathematics hand in hand with the storage and speed of computers.

1.5 Summary of Key Concepts

In terms of use, computers and models go together. (Section 1.1)

*A model is a selective abstraction of reality. **(Section 1.2)***

*The current trend in model building is toward greater complexity. **(Section 1.2)***

*Decision models contain decision variables and objectives. **(Section 1.2)***

*Two broad classes of quantitative decision models are optimization models and simulation models. **(Section 1.2)***

*Model building involves the following: (1) a study of the problem environment; (2) formulation, which means defining decision variables, objectives, interactions between variables, and making pertinent assumptions or necessary simplifications about the real environment; and (3) construction of symbolic expression of the formulation, usually in mathematical terms or in computer language. **(Section 1.3)***

*Algorithms are techniques for solving models. **(Section 1.3)***

*Decisions, in the context of models, are numbers. **(Section 1.4)***

*Decisions in the real world are based on data. **(Section 1.4)***

*Models provide additional data. **(Section 1.4)***

*Four important reasons for the use of models are: (1) models force managers to be explicit about objectives; (2) models force managers to identify and record the types of decisions (decision variables) that influence objectives; (3) models force managers to identify and record pertinent interactions and tradeoffs between decision variables; (4) models force managers to record constraints (limitations) on the values that the variables may assume. **(Section 1.4)***

1.6   Problems

A major goal of this text is to give you an appreciation for what models do and how they are made. The following questions are intended to provoke discussion and to help pull together the ideas we have introduced in Chapter 1. Most of these questions do not have clear-cut answers, but with a certain amount of thought and imagination, they can be interesting for you to pursue, especially in group discussions. As the course develops, your perspective will expand, and you will find it worthwhile to reapproach some of these problems.

1   Suppose that you want to become a managerial decision maker but your special abilities and interests are far from the quantitative field. What is the point to your studying an introductory quantitative-modeling text?

2   List several specific ways in which the use of models might be superior to a more conventional kind of reasoning.

3   List decision problems that involve a choice between only two or three discrete alternatives rather than a choice among a continuous spectrum of alternatives.

4   List several kinds of corporate-planning decisions. Compare these with specific operational decisions.

5   What reasons can you think of to explain the fact that many models are built and never implemented? Does the absence of implementation mean that the entire model-development activity was a waste?

6   What is your interpretation of the phrase, "a successful application of a model"?

7   "Different models are often applied to the same situation." Give several interpretations to this assertion. What makes one model different from another?

8   What do you think it means to "solve" a model?

9   Suppose a model has been constructed to represent a specified segment of the firm's activity. Discuss how the type of activity might be related to the number of times the model is used. That is, think about kinds of models that might be used on a regular schedule, such as hourly, daily, weekly, or monthly, versus kinds of models that might be used on a very sporadic basis.

10   Try to imagine some ways in which existing models might have to be up-dated, as opposed to not tampered with.

11   Do you have any specific ideas why interdisciplinary teams might be an asset in building models? Can you think of specific instances that might draw on different disciplines?

12   What is your understanding about the ways in which models might be used at different levels in the firm?

13   To many people the terms *management science, operations research,* and *systems analysis* all mean the same thing. Are you aware of any different connotations that, at least to some extent, distinguish these professions?

14   What is a decision? How are decisions made? Consider a model designed to help determine whether a new facility should be located in Philadelphia or Pittsburgh. How might such a decision be represented in the model as a decision variable and as a number?

2 Data and Models

This chapter considers the role of data in decision making and in the construction and use of models. Particular emphasis is given to the sources and representation of data. Tables and plots are treated as embryonic forms of quantitative models in realistic scenarios. An example is presented that uses total, average, and marginal costs, and revenues.

2.1 Introduction

In most enterprises, decisions are based to a large extent on the evaluation and interpretation of data. Models provide a way to evaluate and interpret data consistently. Models can also be used to generate data, and a certain amount of data is usually required to build a model. In fact, it is not exceptional for the success or failure of a modeling effort to be data-related. Because of these intimate and varied linkages, a great deal of attention centers on the subject of data in the practical use of models. In this chapter, we introduce some of the considerations pertinent to the use of data in model building. In particular, we discuss forms and sources of data, along with the related topics of aggregation, refinement, and data display. We apply the use of data tables, plots, and graphs—each a vehicle for data display—to problems involving marginal, average, and total cost functions.

Data tables, plots, or graphs are the simplest types of models managers work with. Consequently, we devote a substantial portion of this chapter to illustrating the use of tables, plots, and graphs in a business environment. The scenario for this discussion, and others in this book, is a hypothetical firm called *PROTRAC*.

2.2 PROTRAC: Historical Sketch

PROTRAC started in the late 1800s as a partnership between a blacksmith and a financier. The site was a two-story, 80-by-100-foot factory in Chicago. The firm employed about 100 men in the manufacture of a narrow line of harvesting equipment. The business developed on principles of product quality, aggressive marketing, and efficient distribution. For example, PROTRAC was one of the first firms to issue money-back guarantees, the first to advertise standard as opposed to bartered prices, and it assured quick deliveries at harvest time by locating storage agencies at key distribution points throughout the country.

By 1916, PROTRAC's net income (total earnings minus all expenses, depreciation, interest) was $4,932,024.72 from a product line that had expanded to include manure spreaders, lime and fertilizer sowers, hay loaders, corn shellers, grain elevators, hillside plows, hay stackers, corn binders, cotton and corn planters (two-row and single-row), beet lifters, four-row beet and bean planters, walking cultivators, light tractor disc plows, walking gang plows, and self-dumping hay rakes.

These products were manufactured in 14 factories, located as follows: 6 in Moline, Illinois; 1 in Horicon, Wisconsin; 1 in Syracuse, New York; 1 in Ottumwa, Iowa; 1 in Welland, Ontario; 1 in Fort Smith, Arkansas; 1 in St. Louis, Missouri; 1 in Waterloo, Iowa; and 1 in Malvern, Arkansas. In addition to these assets, the company owned hardwood timber lands in Arkansas and Louisiana.

PROTRAC's major sales activities were conducted through offices in 24 U.S. cities and 5 Canadian cities. Its export business was handled through a special office in Moline, with a forwarding office in New York; the amount of export outside Canada was negligible.

Since 1916, growth has been substantial. In the past year, PROTRAC had record net sales of $1.03 billion; net income was $62.3 million. The product line has diversified, now including over 200 items distributed among farm machinery, industrial and construction machinery, chemical products, and lawn and garden equipment. The main source of revenue is the sale of machine tools for agriculture, construction, forestry, landscaping, earthmoving, and materials handling.

For the most part, these products are made in the same 14 factories. There are now only 14 sales offices in U.S. cities, still 5 in Canada. However, foreign business has grown considerably. There are now 45,434 employees throughout the world, 32,414 in the U.S. and Canada.

In analyzing the success of PROTRAC, two factors deserve considerable weight. One is enlightened management. The other is the gradual but significant increase in demand for its products caused by the growth in population.

Considering the future, it is estimated that world population will double by the year 2000. This growth will create additional demand for food, clothing, and housing. In addition, increasing affluence will cause more people to want better food, clothes, and housing.

2.3   Data as a Model: An Example

As is the case in most firms, decisions in PROTRAC are based to a large extent on available information, that is, on the evaluation and interpretation of data. In Chapter 1, we stated that, from the modeling point of view, a decision is defined to be a number. Keep this very precise definition in mind. We also want you to be very clear on what we mean by *data*. For our purposes, the word *data* also means "numbers."

To see how numbers and models become intimately connected, consider a PROTRAC management decision on how much money to allocate to European marketing. Before making such a decision, management may want to have some idea of the effect of this allocation on total European sales. Therefore, an executive requests data on European marketing expenditures and total European sales for a 12-year period. These data are presented in Figure 2.1.

Figure 2.1   *PROTRAC European marketing expenditures and sales, 1963–74 (in thousands of dollars)*

Year	Marketing Expenditures	Sales
1963	0	0
1964	50	400
1965	100	750
1966	200	1,200
1967	150	1,000
1968	250	1,390
1969	400	1,800
1970	300	1,565
1971	350	1,715
1972	450	2,025
1973	500	2,140
1974	550	2,200

This table is simply one means of conveying the requested data. The format of the table is purely a matter of convenience; it is not intended to connote any special relationship between the various numbers. However, suppose that after studying the data in Figure 2.1, the executive hypothesizes some relationship between marketing expenditures and sales. He may feel, for example, that the total sales in a given year depend directly on the marketing expenditure in that year. (The words "depend directly" imply that a higher expenditure on marketing leads to higher sales.) Thus, the executive may feel that sales of $1.8 million in 1969 were significantly related to the marketing expenditures of $400,000 in 1969. Alternatively, he may feel that the 1969 sales are more truly related to the marketing expenditure in 1967. Or, he may hypothesize that 1969 sales depend equally on the 1967, 1968, and 1969 marketing expenditures.

Numerous possible relationships could be hypothesized. The appropriate relationships would obviously depend on many factors associated with the actual PROTRAC environment. Also, we have phrased the hypothesized relationships, or interactions, in vague, semiquantitative language. That is, we hypothesized that 1969 sales "depended directly" on 1969 marketing expenditures, but we did not hypothesize a specific quantitative relationship. We could make a specific quantitative statement: actual sales in 1969 are 4.5 times the marketing expenditure in the same year. This means that in 1969, there were, *on the average*, 4.5 dollars of sales for each dollar of marketing. However, this fact *by itself* certainly does not permit us to conclude that a $600,000 marketing expenditure in 1969 *would have* led to a $2.7 million level of sales. Furthermore, does the 1969 factor of proportionality have any bearing on the current decision? In 1974, for example, the factor of proportionality was 4.0, not 4.5. How do the 1974 data relate to the 1969 data? Are current PROTRAC marketing techniques more like they were in 1974 than in 1969? Or has the operation basically remained unchanged between 1969 and 1974?

And what about other relevant factors, such as general economic conditions? If we hypothesize some causal relationship between marketing and sales in each year t, then the data reveal that *on the average* each dollar expended on marketing in 1969 was more effective than in 1974. What real-world factors might lie behind these different degrees of effectiveness in the different years? That is, what real-world interactions are reflected by the data? There could be differences in advertising techniques, differences in market softness and demand that, in turn, could be due to different economic conditions, weather, government policies, and so on.

The manager must consider these kinds of questions as soon as he begins to "interpret" the data in the table. But the point of the present discussion is this: as soon as the manager begins to hypothesize even a semiquantitative relationship between the numbers in Figure 2.1, he is beginning to formulate a model. He is beginning to interpret the data as a reflection of important interactions. Figure 2.1 takes on a special significance to the manager: it becomes a selective representation of reality. As such, the table of data fits one of our earlier definitions of a model. It is important to emphasize that the numbers by themselves do not represent the model. In fact, the numbers by themselves don't mean anything aside from records of fact (for example, in 1969, total European sales were $1.8 million). It is only when some relationship or interaction is ascribed to the numbers that a model, at least in embryonic form, exists.

2.4 Data-related Considerations

2.4.1 Forms of Data

These numbers, which we call data, may be encoded on a magnetic tape or stored in coded form in a computer. They may be recorded on punched cards or in tables like the phone book or the almanac. The numbers may be in pounds or tons, francs or dollars. Questions of units are often important in working with data. For example, in what currency should PROTRAC management measure European sales? If the answer is dollars, what exchange rates should be used to convert foreign currencies into dollars? These rates vary from time to time, and the effect of these variances could be insignificant wrinkles in our calculations, or they could cause the world to look significantly different.

2.4.2 Sources of Data

Data may come from records of the past. Data may be generated by making direct observations or estimates in the present. In particular, the data may be produced by a model that requires certain decisions as inputs. Or, finally, data can be produced by making forecasts of the future.

2.4.3 Planning and Data

It is difficult to say which comes first, quantitative planning or the gathering of data. Certainly, data are required for effective planning. Efforts toward better planning often lead to the acquisition and storage of new types of data. The existence of data increases the potential for the use of models. One of the characteristics of advanced civilization, at least in terms of technology, seems to be the acquisition and use of data.

2.4.4 Aggregation of Data

One of the key considerations in using data is the degree of aggregation desired. For example, does a model require data on total yearly sales over the past five years, or on total yearly sales per country over the past five years, or on total yearly sales per plant over the past five years, or on total yearly sales per plant per product over the past five years? This list of requirements describes data in increasingly *disaggregated* form. Disaggregated data are more detailed and are generally more difficult to obtain. However, they are also more valuable because they contain more information. Furthermore, it is possible to aggregate disaggregated data, but it is not possible to go the other way. Thus, if total yearly sales per plant per product are known, it is possible to obtain total sales per product per country, or total sales per country, or total sales per product, or total sales per plant. However, it is clearly not possible to go from the aggregated down to the disaggregated numbers.

Although disaggregated data are desirable because they contain much information, it is also true that data may be too disaggregated for an individual decision maker's use. In terms of a decision on whether or not to build new plants in Europe, PROTRAC executives may want to compare a small select collection of aggregated data. That is, their decision may be based on a "mental model" in which they selectively represent reality with a few chosen numbers.

It should be obvious that more information can only lead to better decisions. (If this is not obvious, at least it should be clear that more information cannot lead to worse decisions.) However, it is also true that the degree of disaggregation an individual decision maker can digest is limited. Models and computers can work with much more detail than an individual; this is a major reason for their use. As activities become more complex and sophisticated, *details* become increasingly important. However, the sword is double-edged. Though models typically like to have disaggregated data, sometimes the disaggregation itself creates insurmountable problems. Disaggregation may create too many decision variables, thus making the model too large and impossible to use. In this respect, the balance is between the ideal of using the most information available (highly detailed, disaggregated data) and the practical matter of implementation.

2.4.5 Refinement of Data

The term *refinement* is often used synonymously with disaggregation. Thus *highly refined data* (often called *highly structured*) refers to highly disaggregated data. However, refinement has another meaning. A considerable amount of data may be available. The data may be relevant to the problem under study but they may not be in the correct form. We may have yearly data on total sales volume and yearly data on total number of plants operating, but for our model we may require average sales per plant in each year. It is possible to obtain the figures we need by performing some simple algebraic manipulations on the existing data. This process of manipulating or "massaging" data is also termed *refining* the data. Such refinements can be quite extensive, depending on what is available and what is needed. The refining of data is usually a job relegated to computers and, in fact, computers can be reasonably described as powerful "data refineries."

2.4.6 Storing and Displaying Data

All data, once accumulated, must be stored. In order to examine data, they must be displayed. Most data are stored on paper, on magnetic tapes, in magnetic discs, or in computers. For our purposes, the storage is less important than the display.

The same numbers can be displayed in various alternative ways. Numbers can be displayed in tables, by plots, or by graphs. The choice may be dictated by convenience or the reasons may be more basic. For example, a table is a display of a finite amount of data. A graph is a display of an infinite amount of data. In the remainder of this chapter, we discuss various displays and their uses in the decision process.

2.5 Plots and Graphs

Tables, plots, and graphs provide alternative ways of displaying data. You have already seen a tabular representation in Figure 2.1. Let us return to these data to demonstrate the use of plots and graphs. Recall that these data represent a historical record of marketing expenditures and sales over time. The name for data that represent observations over time is a *time series.*

Suppose PROTRAC's manager believes that neither marketing techniques nor product demand has changed in any significant way during the period over which the data were recorded. As a result, the manager considers the time element to be of minor importance in terms of capturing the interaction between marketing and sales. He hypothesizes that there is some direct relationship between marketing expenditures in year t and total sales in year t. He does not know exactly what the relationship is, but he feels that it is reflected by the numbers in Figure 2.1. However, he also feels that the appropriate relationship does not depend on the year. For example, he may have a rough idea that sales volume should be "*about* four times" marketing expenditures, regardless of the year. This factor of proportionality, 4, is hypothesized to be *independent* of time. We use the phrase "about four times" because the manager knows that the factor may be somewhat less than 4 in some years and somewhat greater than 4 in others, because of random events. In this linguistic sense, of course, the factor does depend on time. However, from the viewpoint of mathematics, the words *dependent* and *independent* have special and important meanings. In the mathematical sense, the hypothesis that the factor of proportionality is "independent of time" means that time has no consistently recognizable or identifiable influence.

Suppose, however, that the manager feels that marketing efficiency has been improving year by year, because of such factors as new knowledge, shifting tastes leading to increased product demand, greater sales potential because of government policies, and so on. Many of these influences are difficult to measure and quantify directly, and the manager may therefore lump them together into a single factor or influence he thinks of as "time." Thus, time becomes a surrogate for other quantities not explicitly in the model. In that case, the factor of proportionality between marketing and sales would depend explicitly on the year. In other words, the relationship between marketing and sales would be *dependent* on time.

Let us return to our original scenario. The manager has hypothesized that the factor of proportionality is "about four." In order to pin the value down more closely, or, as we sometimes say, in order to get a better feeling for the data, it is often convenient to *plot* the numbers, as in Figure 2.2. Explicit reference to time is deliberately omitted because we are operating under the manager's assumption that the essential quantitative relationship is independent of time.

Figure 2.2   *PROTRAC European sales versus marketing expenditures*

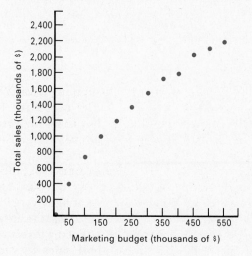

The information presented in data tables, or the plots associated with them, is *discrete* rather than *continuous*. In other words, in Figure 2.2 the value of total sales is given for only a selected number of values of the marketing budget.

In some cases, the discreteness of the data is a conceptual necessity dictated by the type of phenomenon being considered. After all, the phone company has few alternatives to listing its subscribers and their phone numbers. Similarly, data on crawler tractor production must occur in discrete units, since fractions of tractors are not produced.

In many other cases, however, there is no conceptual problem with having a very large number of possible values for the quantities considered, and indeed with having an infinite number or a continuum of values. For example, there is no conceptual reason why a refinery manager cannot think of processing 156.984215 barrels of crude oil per day.

Although there is no conceptual problem with a relationship between two continuous quantities or variables, there are substantial practical problems in determining such relationships. Many textbooks on quantitative methods are devoted to deriving "optimal" decisions assuming that we are given various quantitative relationships, but the truth is that in many applied situations the most difficult problem is knowing the precise quantitative form of those relationships. The problem of deriving relationships from data cannot be "assumed away." Moreover, in real problems relevant data often do not exist, or, when data are available, they may not reveal anything meaningful or causal about the particular relationship of interest to management.

The present scenario provides a case in point. Let's review the logic:

1   The data in Figure 2.1 provide a historical record. That much is clear and indisputable.
2   It seems reasonable to feel that there are interactions of a causative nature between marketing expenditures and total sales. These interactions may or may not be deduced from the data in the table.
3   Now the manager makes several big assumptions. He does not actually "believe" these assumptions, but he considers them to be at least reasonable "first approximations." First, he assumes that the interactions *can* be deduced from the numbers in Figure 2.1. Second, he assumes that sales in year *t* depend only on marketing efforts in year *t*, and not on past marketing expenditures. (In technical language, he assumes that *lags* are unimportant.) Third, he assumes that the relevant interaction between sales and marketing is independent of time.

Given this logic, an important question for our purposes is, How is it possible to compute the total sales anticipated with a marketing budget of $324,579.36? Before you read on, try to answer this question. Consider how you would go about getting a specific number from Figure 2.2. You cannot read this number directly from the figure. You will have to do a certain amount of reasoning and "fudging."

There are two reasonable approaches to this problem. The first approach is very intuitive and simple. Take a ruler and draw a straight line "close" to all the points. This straight line, called a *graph*, provides a means for representing continuous data. The equation of the line can be computed, and from then on it is fairly easy to obtain the total sales associated with the marketing expenditure of $324,579.36. Figure 2.3 shows this approach. The straight line in this figure is a model for the relationship between marketing expenditure and sales.

The equation of the line in Figure 2.3 is

Sales = 4 × marketing + 200

Therefore, the total sales associated with a marketing value of $324,579.36 is $1,498,317.44.

Obviously, we could draw other straight lines or graphs that would be close to the points in Figure 2.2. The study of which line is "best" is a separate topic that lies in the domain of statistics and is called *linear regression analysis*. In the empirical analysis of data, regression is a very important topic, but at this point it is too technical for us to delve into. Some discussion of the topic will appear in Chapter 17.

The data could also be approximated by a curve rather than a straight line. This topic of curve-fitting is called *nonlinear regression*. The equation

Figure 2.3 *Straight-line approximation*   **Figure 2.4** *Piecewise linear approximation*

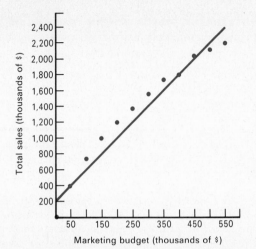 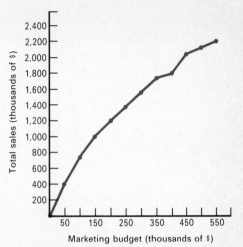

of a curve is often difficult to compute, and the statistical theory becomes much more complicated. This does not mean that curved graphs are not used in practice. Quite to the contrary, they are often essential in representing nonlinear phenomena.

But for our present purposes, it is sufficient to draw any straight line that looks close to the points on the plot. After all, we have already acknowledged the existence of random disturbances from year to year, and we are seeking only a reasonable first approximation to the interaction between marketing and sales.

The second intuitive approach we can use for continuous estimation in this situation is simply to connect each data point with a straight line. The result, which is linear in segments, is shown in Figure 2.4. This type of graph is called a *piecewise linear approximation*.

Using this method, we can compute the total sales associated with the marketing value of $324,579.36 from the particular linear segment that connects the marketing expenditures of 300 and 350 to the appropriate sales, 1,565 and 1,715. The equation of this segment is

Sales = 3 × marketing + 665

Consequently, the total sales associated with a marketing value of $324,579.36 is $1,638,738.08. The piecewise linear approximation differs from the straight-line approximation value by $140,420.64, which is certainly not an insignificant amount. It is important for the manager to be aware of the possibility of *alternately plausible estimates*.

The fact is, in this example the two approaches may not be equally plausible, and the second estimate may be preferable to the first. Look at Figure 2.4 again. Notice that between the marketing expenditures of 0 and 400 the linear segments decrease in steepness. At the marketing level 400 the steepness sharply increases, but then the decreasing pattern continues.

Decreasing steepness in a piecewise linear graph is sometimes called *decreasing* (or diminishing) *returns to scale*. It reflects real-world phenomena of concern to management. For example, in the present scenario, decreasing returns to scale could be explained by market saturation, meaning that most of the market has already been captured. An additional dollar spent on advertising must convince ever more reluctant customers and consequently yields a smaller amount of revenue than the last dollar spent. Also, market saturation may mean that financial incentives such as lower payments and carrying charges may have to be offered to attract more customers.

Since the number 324,579.36 is in an area of decreasing returns to scale, it may mean that some of the foregoing phenomena are at work at that level of marketing. In other words, if the manager "believes" the decreasing returns pattern, then Figure 2.4 should be used to represent the interactions of interest.

The key consideration is the manager's interpretation of the shapes of the graphs. If he believes that the quantitative relationship is basically linear and that the deviations from the straight line (in Figure 2.3) are due to random factors such as bad weather, then Figure 2.3 should be accepted. If he believes that Figure 2.4 reflects a real-world operational phenomenon in the form of decreasing returns in the budget region of interest, then Figure 2.4 should be accepted. His interpretation and judgment are crucial in his use of these graphs as tools.

2.6　An Example: PROTRAC Annual Production Decisions

PROTRAC utilizes a matrix type of organization. For example, the large crawler tractor (LCT) manager in the Moline plant reports both to the LCT manager in corporate headquarters and to the Moline plant manager. The LCT manager in corporate headquarters is responsible for recommending an overall annual level of LCT production to the corporate vice-president.

Let us consider the corporate LCT manager's problem. Although there are really three different LCT types, the P–7, P–8, and P–9, for purposes of determining the general level of activity they are treated as a common "unit of production." Also, in short-term planning (planning for next year) the capacity is considered to be more or less fixed within a given range. In other words, expanding capacity by capital investment (new plant and equipment) requires more than a year. Moreover, LCT production is sufficiently specialized so that it is impossible to sublet any significant part of the process. As a result of these considerations, there are relatively inflexible upper limits to which next year's capacity can be extended. The allowable variations are controlled by

1　determining the number of shifts the assembly line will work;
2　allowing workers to work overtime; and
3　increasing the speed of the assembly line, which entails hiring additional assemblers and material handlers.

In attempting to recommend a desirable annual level of production, the corporate LCT manager has gathered some data on the historical relations

Figure 2.5 *Data on PROTRAC totals*

Quantity Produced	Total Revenue (millions of $)	Total Cost (millions of $)	Profit (millions of $)
0	0	14[a]	−14
500	60	36	24
1,000	120	58	62
1,500	166	80	86
2,000	200	103	97
2,500	224	134	90
3,000	243	165	78
3,500	255	196	59
4,000	265	227	38
4,500	273	262	11
5,000	280	297	−17

[a]Cost of producing 0 units at $14 million represents the fixed costs to the firm of maintaining plants, equipment, and so on.

Figure 2.6 *Total and marginal graphs for PROTRAC revenue and cost*

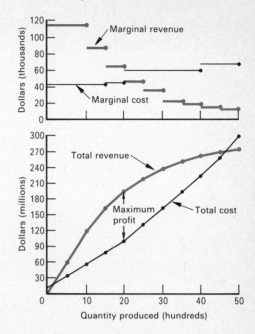

between *quantity produced, total revenue, total cost, profit, average revenue, average cost, average profits, marginal revenue,* and *marginal cost.* The definitions of these quantities are:

$$\text{Average revenue} = \frac{\text{total revenue}}{\text{quantity produced}}$$

$$\text{Average cost} = \frac{\text{total cost}}{\text{quantity produced}}$$

$$\text{Profit} = \text{total revenue} - \text{total cost}$$

$$\text{Average profit} = \text{average revenue} - \text{average cost}$$

$$\text{Marginal revenue} = \text{additional revenue from last unit produced}$$

$$\text{Marginal cost} = \text{additional cost from last unit produced}$$

The data on total revenue, total cost, and profit are presented in Figure 2.5. In Figure 2.6, the data for total revenue and total cost are plotted against quantity produced, and then the points are connected by straight lines to obtain piecewise linear graphs of total revenue and total cost.

Note that this method of connecting points creates a number of corners on the graphs. Remember that these graphs are only approximations. A truer picture of the underlying relationships could conceivably be smooth and without corners.[1] However, for the present problem the question of which method to use to connect the points should be considered in the perspective that a certain

---

1 In mathematics, this terminology is redundant, for the word *smooth* means "without corners."

amount of uncertainty and imprecision in the underlying real-world relationships is inevitable. From this point of view, it is relatively unimportant whether we use straight lines, as in Figure 2.6, or whether we sketch a smooth graph through or near the points, as with the regression type of approximation we mentioned in Section 2.5. For the present purpose, we can obtain marginal information very easily from a piecewise linear approximation; therefore, it is convenient to use this method. These marginal data derived from the total cost and total revenue curves are also displayed in Figure 2.6. For example, the marginal revenue obtained from producing unit 2,200 is equal to the steepness, or *slope*, of the total revenue graph at the same point. Reading from Figure 2.5, this slope is

$$\frac{224(10^6) - 200(10^6)}{500} = \frac{24}{5}(10^4) = 48,000$$

This calculation shows that the revenue added by unit 2,200 is \$48,000. All the marginal figures can be obtained from the slope of the total graphs in this way. At the corners, the *slope from the left* is used to define the marginal data; for example, the marginal revenue at 1,500 units is \$9,200.

In analyzing these data, it is important to note that marginal revenue is nonincreasing and marginal cost is nondecreasing. At all production levels less than 2,000 units, marginal revenue is greater than marginal cost. This means that the return on each unit is greater than the cost of producing that unit. Consequently, for each of the first 2,000 units produced, a profit results. For each unit of production after the first 2,000, marginal revenue is less than marginal cost and hence a loss results from each such unit. This implies that the maximum profit occurs at the quantity 2,000. You can verify this from either Figure 2.5 or from the graphs in Figure 2.6.

As a final comment on marginal data, recall our earlier discussion that the graphs on totals could have been sketched as smooth curves rather than as piecewise linear approximations. Regardless of which choice had been made, the graphs would have looked more or less the same. However, this statement is not true for the graphs on marginal data. Explanations for this phenomenon go beyond our scope and intent. It is enough to say that if the totals had been graphed as smooth curves, then the marginal curves[2] would look very different from those in Figure 2.6. Marginal revenue would be a continuous decreasing graph, and marginal cost would be a continuous increasing graph. However, these two graphs would cross over somewhere near a production level of 2,000, and this cross-over point, where marginal revenue equals marginal cost, would give the quantity at which maximum profit is indicated by the smoothed total curves.

Data on averages are displayed in Figure 2.7 and plotted in Figure 2.8. Note that according to our analysis, although total profit is maximized at a production level of 2,000 units with a corresponding profit of \$97 million, the average profit is maximized at a production level of 1,000 with the total profit at only \$62 million. Although production of 1,000 units produces the largest

---

2   In the language of calculus, the marginal curve is the first derivative of the total.

Figure 2.7 *Data on PROTRAC averages*

Quantity Produced	Average Revenue ($)	Average Cost ($)	Average Profit ($)
500	120,000	72,000	48,000
1,000	120,000	58,000	62,000
1,500	110,666	53,333	57,333
2,000	100,000	51,500	48,500
2,500	89,600	53,600	36,000
3,000	81,000	55,000	26,000
3,500	72,857	56,000	16,857
4,000	66,250	56,750	9,500
4,500	60,666	58,222	2,444
5,000	56,000	59,400	−3,400

Figure 2.8 *PROTRAC average revenue, cost, and profit graphs*

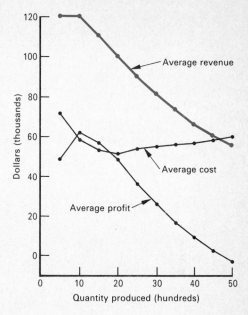

profit per unit, most firms are interested in obtaining a maximum level of total profit, even though the profit per unit may be smaller. The corporate LCT manager's view is consistent with overall profit maximization, and he therefore recommends a production level of 2,000 units.

Suppose, however, that the firm's objective is not to maximize profit, but rather to capture as much of the market as possible without losing money. Thus, the objective is to sell as many units as possible without taking a loss. The solution can be found with the aid of either Figure 2.6 or Figure 2.8. The appropriate point in Figure 2.6 is the one where the totals curves cross over, namely at a production level of about 4,700 units. At this point, total revenue equals total cost, and profit is zero. The same point is found from Figure 2.8 by determining the production level at which average profit equals zero (for this clearly implies that total profit must also be zero). Again, you can see that the solution is approximately 4,700 units. This is clearly a sales volume much larger than the profit-maximizing quantity of 2,000.

2.7 Summary of Key Concepts

Decisions are based on the evaluation and interpretation of data. (Section 2.1)

Data tables, plots, and graphs are the simplest types of models for interpreting data. (Section 2.1)

Data appear in many forms and come from many sources. (Section 2.4)

Disaggregated data contain more information than aggregated data. (Section 2.4.4)

Tabular representations are for discrete data, plots and graphs for continuous data. (Section 2.5)

Two ways to estimate continuous relationships are regression fits and piecewise linear approximation. (Section 2.5)

2.8 Problems

1   What is the relationship between data and models?

2   Define the terms *decision* and *data*.

3   At what point do entries in a data table, such as Figure 2.1, begin to take on the role of a model?

4   List some of the forms and sources of data.

5   What is the advantage of having disaggregated data? What is the advantage of aggregated data?

6   What is the distinction between a time-dependent relationship and one that is time independent?

7   Name some types of data that are conceptually discrete as opposed to continuous. Name two quantities that are inherently continuous. Is money continuous or discrete?

8   What is meant by "diminishing returns to scale"? What type of data might exhibit such a phenomenon, and how might it be explained?

9   What is the relationship between the shape of the marginal graph and a total graph that exhibit the following characteristics?

   a Diminishing returns to scale
   b Increasing returns to scale

10   Does *profit maximization* generally mean the same thing as *maximize average profit*?

Part

Deterministic Decisions under Constraints

1

3 Constrained Optimization Models

This chapter introduces constrained optimization models. The symbolic form of these models is discussed and interpreted in terms of decision variables, objective functions, and constraints. Some discussion as to the importance of this class of models and the art of converting real decision problems into constrained optimization models is included. Distinctions are drawn between two views of the world: constrained versus unconstrained. Numerous examples illustrate the justification and relevance for the constrained approach to real-life problems.

3.1 Introduction

Most people make many of their personal and professional decisions in situations where the set of allowable decisions has been restricted in some way. In the language of modeling, a restriction on the set of allowable decisions is called a *constraint*. Constraints may be self-imposed or dictated by others. A person with a strict budget must buy groceries for the week without spending too much money. A production manager must plan production schedules without exceeding the capacity of plant and equipment. A speculator is constrained in his or her trading by the amount of margin on deposit with a broker. A parent of three teenagers can let only one of them take the family car Saturday night. A plant superintendent can assign only unoccupied maintenance crews to unanticipated repairs. A member of Alcoholics Anonymous declines an invitation for cocktails. The list is endless. It is perhaps not surprising, therefore, that *constrained optimization,* which means achieving the best possible result considering the restrictions, has been the most active area of management-science research. Indeed, one of the most commonly employed management-science tools, linear programming, is a special model for carrying out constrained optimization.

In this chapter, we consider the concept of constrained optimization and the language used in constrained optimization models. Chapter 3 opens a 12-chapter sequence on deterministic decisions under constraints. With so many pages devoted to constrained optimization, it is obvious that we think the subject is important. Indeed, we believe that constrained optimization models capture the essence of management decision making, and much of this chapter is devoted to explaining this belief. At the outset, however, we want to delineate our position carefully, and this calls for some precautionary comments.

Constrained optimization models, when solved, provide what are called *optimal,* or best, *decisions,* but this statement calls for the strongest possible caveat. Optimization models produce the optimal answer to a mathematical problem posed by a model. This may or may not be a good (to say nothing of optimal) answer in the real context. Whenever we use words like "real" or "true" we are referring to the real-world problem that underlies the mathematical model. The term *optimality* is a theoretical (that is, mathematical), as opposed to a real-world, concept. The truth is that there are no optimal decisions for the complicated problems of business, and one of the worst mistakes a manager can make is to blindly allow a model to make his decisions. In fact, in management problems, two plus two do not always equal four. Rather than seeking the quantitatively superior solution, the mature manager will often be more concerned with the optimal political solution. This, however, does not by any means imply that quantitative models do not play an important role in the overall decision-making process. In order to appreciate this role, it is necessary to appreciate some of the relationships between the real problem, the problem analyst, the decision maker, and the model.

And so, let us begin to explain the assertion that the complicated problems of business (and even more so, of government) have no optimal solution. There are always considerations that cannot be built into the model, for to include everything would complicate the model enormously and make it impossible to solve. What do we mean by "complicate the model"? This will become clearer as we proceed. For now, it suffices to mention two major complicating factors: (1) form, or mathematical structure, and (2) size. For example, in terms of form it is often important to keep all expressions in the model linear. But it simply may not be possible to capture some of the interactions with linear expressions, and consequently such interactions may not be included. In terms of size, models with too many constraints and too many variables cannot be solved even on high-speed computers. This consideration can also lead to simplifications, and a limited and incomplete representation of the real problem may result. These facts help to amplify our assertion in Chapter 1 that models are selective representations of reality. In any realistic application, the ultimate effect of this selectivity is the following truth:

What is optimal in the model may not be optimal in reality.

Consequently, the decision maker has to blend the output of the model with his own personal interests and his own perceptions about the nature and credibility of the model and its correspondence with the real problem.

In fact, you will see that one of the most important applications of models is to provide reinforcement for the intuition of the decision maker. This reinforcement can be positive. It can provide quantitative support for the decision maker's preconceived notions. It can bolster his confidence in his own intuition. It can show him explicitly how to go about implementing his preferred policy (regardless of the motivation for that policy) and what results, in quantitative terms, might be expected. On the other hand, the model's reinforcement can be negative. The results can challenge the intuition. Previously hidden or overlooked relations may become apparent. The decision maker may be forced to choose between his intuition and the model. The better and more credible the model, the more difficult the choice.

We will illustrate these and related ideas in the context of specific applications. However, before getting into applications, it is useful to know what we are actually going to apply. To proceed effectively, you must develop a good grasp for the form and the explicit meaning of a constrained optimization model.

3.2 Mathematical Formulation and Interpretation

The terms *constrained optimization* and *mathematical programming* are often used to describe the same general model. Although the explicit meaning of this model can be described in words, the symbolic or mathematical representation is the most unambiguous way to depict all that it says. In symbolic form, the constrained optimization model is

Maximize (or minimize) $f(x_1, x_2, \ldots, x_n)$

subject to the constraints that

$$g_1(x_1, x_2, \ldots, x_n) \quad \begin{array}{c} \leq \\ = \\ \geq \end{array} \quad b_1$$

$$g_2(x_1, x_2, \ldots, x_n) \quad \begin{array}{c} \leq \\ = \\ \geq \end{array} \quad b_2$$

$$\vdots \qquad\qquad \vdots$$

$$g_m(x_1, x_2, \ldots, x_n) \quad \begin{array}{c} \leq \\ = \\ \geq \end{array} \quad b_m$$

When all the functions in this model are linear, we have the important special case of a *linear programming model.* Ultimately, we will pay specific attention to linear programs, but for now the discussion of this model is quite general.

The function f is called the *objective function,* or the *payoff function,* or simply the *return.* The model states that the problem is to make the value of this function as large (or as small) as possible, provided that the *constraints,* or restricting conditions, are also satisfied. The value of the objective function is often measured in quantities like dollars of profit (in a maximization problem) or dollars of cost (in a minimization problem). The variables x_1, x_2, $\ldots$, x_n are called *decision variables.* Recall our earlier definition that, for our purposes, decisions are numbers. The numerical values of the decision variables represent actions or activities to be undertaken at various levels. The decision maker has the values of these variables under his direct control. Any choice of these values indirectly assigns a numerical value to the objective function. The functions $g_1, \ldots, g_m$ are called *constraint functions.* Any selection of numerical values for the decision variables also indirectly assigns values to the constraint functions. The model requires that each of these constraint function values must satisfy a condition expressed by a mathematical inequality or an equality. The first constraint, for example, is one and only one of the following conditions:

$$g_1(x_1, x_2, \ldots, x_n) \leq b_1$$
$$g_1(x_1, x_2, \ldots, x_n) = b_1$$
$$g_1(x_1, x_2, \ldots, x_n) \geq b_1$$

where b_1 is a parameter with a specified numerical value. The numbers b_i, $i = 1, 2, \ldots, m$ taken together are called the *right-hand sides* (abbreviated, RHS). The number b_1 is called the right-hand side of the first constraint, and so on. The set of all m of the constraints taken together, that is, the group of relations

$$g_i(x_1, x_2, \ldots, x_n) \overset{\leq}{\underset{\geq}{=}} b_i \qquad i = 1, \ldots, m$$

indirectly restricts the values that can be assigned to the decision variables.

For example, suppose the model contains the requirement that

$$g_1(x_1, x_2, \ldots, x_n) \leq b_1$$

Consider a vector $x = (x_1, \ldots, x_n)$ of decisions that imply that

$$g_1(x_1, x_2, \ldots, x_n) > b_1$$

This choice of decisions will be forbidden by the model since it violates one of the constraints. The model will consider only those decisions that satisfy *all* the constraints.

3.3 The Hyde Park Police Captain

The problems of the captain of the Hyde Park police force will help to illustrate the meaning of the constrained optimization model. The police captain wants to penetrate one of the city's most pernicious dope rings. His tactic is to select a patrolman to impersonate a hurdler on the University of Chicago track team. Since he has neither the time nor the inclination to interview each patrolman individually, he will ask the personnel department to screen the employee files. Recalling from the Olympics that most hurdlers are young and tall, he instructs the personnel department to send to his office the tallest patrolman between the ages of 20 and 28. His selection procedure is described by the following constrained optimization model:

Find an x that maximizes $f(x)$

subject to

$$20 \leq g_1(x) \leq 28$$

where the decision variable x represents a patrolman and

$f(x)$ = the height of patrolman x

$g_1(x)$ = the age of patrolman x

Note that the constraint $20 \le g_1(x) \le 28$ is equivalent to two constraints in standard form, namely, $g_1(x) \le 28$ and $-g_1(x) \le -20$. This problem is illustrated by the lineup in Figure 3.1. As this figure shows, although there are points where the objective function $f(x)$ takes on larger values, the captain has limited the search to those values of x for which $g_1(x)$, the patrolman's age, is between 20 and 28. Among those constrained values of x he seeks one that maximizes his objective function. The optimal solution to the model is provided by the patrolman with badge number 34. When the personnel department sends the optimal solution to his office, the captain is disappointed to discover that the man weighs 310 pounds and looks more like King Kong than a hurdler. Although the solution is optimal in terms of the model, the captain's intuition tells him it is far from optimal in terms of his real problem. Rather than reject his intuition, he decides to reject his model. He decides that it must be an inaccurate portrayal of his problem. One of his management consultants suggests that they modify the instructions to the personnel department so as to find the tallest man between the ages of 20 and 28 who *also* weighs between 150 and 180 pounds (that is, the tallest man who satisfies *two* conditions). The new model is

Find an x that maximizes $f(x)$

subject to

$20 \le g_1(x) \le 30$

$150 \le g_2(x) \le 180$

Figure 3.1   *Selecting a hurdler: the model with one decision variable and one constraint*

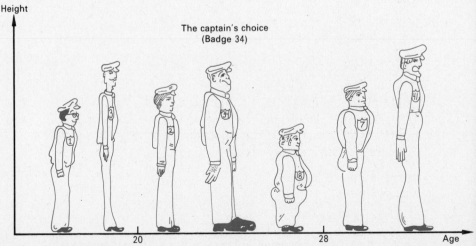

Height

The captain's choice
(Badge 34)

20   28   Age

Drawing by Elaine M. Reichart

Figure 3.2 *Selecting a hurdler: the model with one decision variable and two constraints*

Drawing by Elaine M. Reichart

where x, $f(x)$, and $g_1(x)$ are defined as before and $g_2(x)$ is the weight of patrolman x. This problem is illustrated in a three-dimensional portrayal in Figure 3.2. In this figure, height is represented vertically above the two-dimensional plane representing age and weight. In the new model, number 34 has been rejected; he does not satisfy *both* constraints. The new optimal solution is number 2.

If we now generalize f and g_1 to be functions defined on, say, all nonnegative numbers x, then a generalized version of Figure 3.1 will provide a reasonable geometric representation of a constrained optimization problem with one decision variable x and one constraint. Figure 3.3 illustrates the following generalized problem and the solution, x^*.

Maximize $f(x)$

subject to

$g_1(x) \geq b_1$

$x \geq 0$

In Figure 3.3, you can see the numerical values of x at which the value $g_1(x)$ is not less than b_1. These are the *constrained*, or *allowable values* of x. Considering all these allowable values of x, the value $f(x^*)$ is the largest objective value. This means that x^* is the optimal value of x (the solution) for the given model. Let us now complicate the model by adding a second constraint, say $g_2(x) \leq b_2$. The model becomes

Maximize $f(x)$

subject to

$g_1(x) \geq b_1$

$g_2(x) \leq b_2$

$x \geq 0$

Figure 3.3 *A constrained optimization problem with one
variable and one constraint*

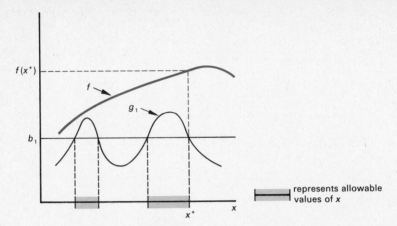

represents allowable
values of x

This problem is shown along with the new solution, $\hat{x}$, in Figure 3.4. You
can see that the set of x values that satisfy both constraints is a subset of
the x values that satisfy either constraint individually. You can also note that
in the problem with two constraints, the solution is not "as good"—that is,
$f(\hat{x}) < f(x^*)$—as it was for the problem with a single constraint. In other
words, adding a constraint to a problem can "hurt" the objective. But don't
forget the Hyde Park police captain. Adding a constraint to his model did,
in fact, hurt the model's objective (to maximize height), but it actually improved
the decision maker's objective (to find the best impersonator of a hurdler).
Thus, adding a constraint served to make the model more credible. We shall
return to this point later in this chapter. For now, you have some idea of
what a model looks like (symbolically and geometrically) and what it says.

Figure 3.4 *A constrained optimization problem with one
variable and two constraints*

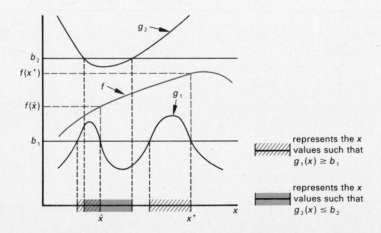

represents the x
values such that
$g_1(x) \geq b_1$

represents the x
values such that
$g_2(x) \leq b_2$

3.4   Decision Variables, Parameters, Constants, and Data

Constrained optimization models are constructed from elements that we classify as decision variables, parameters, and constants. We define and illustrate these quantities in terms of the following model.

Objective function

Maximize $5{,}000E + 4{,}000F$

subject to

constraints

$$
\begin{aligned}
E + F &\ge 5 \\
10E + 15F &\le 150 \\
20E + 10F &\le 160 \\
150 - (30E + 10F) &\le 15 \\
E - 3F &\le 0 \\
E, F &\ge 0
\end{aligned}
$$

The decision variables in a constrained optimization model represent the actions to be taken or the decisions to be made. They are the entities that the decision maker can control directly. The decision variables can thus be thought of as the unknowns in the model. They are represented by the usual symbols for variables, such as E and F in the foregoing example. The decision variables *implicitly* stand for numbers. The model specifies that these numbers must satisfy certain algebraic conditions, called the *constraints*. These decision variables are *not* part of the data of a problem.

Except for the decision variables, everything else in the constrained optimization model is an explicitly stated number. All these *explicit* numbers constitute the data of the model. In general, the data consist of two parts, parameters and constants. *Parameters* are entities whose values remain fixed during the current solving of the problem but whose values are not forever fixed by some immutable law. The coefficients in the objective function of the model are an example. The coefficients 5,000 and 4,000 represent the profit from selling one unit of E and F, respectively. These numbers depend on the current sales prices and costs. If management were to increase the sales price of E and the cost were to remain the same, the coefficient of E would increase from its current value of 5,000 to a new level, perhaps 5,500. This change might change the optimal values of the decision variables (the solution of the model) and hence the optimal value of the objective function. In fact, the optimal value of the objective function in a constrained optimization problem can be thought of as the output of a function machine where the input is the parameters in the model and the function is the algorithm that produces a solution. This notion is illustrated in Figure 3.5.

Thus, parameters are numbers that remain fixed for the current execution of the solution procedure but whose values are, at least conceptually, subject to change. In the next chapter, we shall pose problems where the parameters are quantities like the demand in the next month for a specific product or the quantity of labor available in a certain week. In such examples, we will

Figure 3.5 *A function machine for producing optimal decisions from parameters*

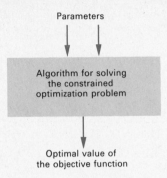

Parameters

Algorithm for solving
the constrained
optimization problem

Optimal value of
the objective function

see that management is often interested in the solution to the "same" problem but with a number of different parameter values.

Constants are numbers that are forever fixed. Quantities such as π or e (the base of the natural logarithm) are good examples of constants. Consider a designer who wants to select the radii for four circles. Among other constraints is the fact that the total area determined by these circles must be no greater than 100. The constraint

$$\pi r_1^2 + \pi r_2^2 + \pi r_3^2 + \pi r_4^2 \leq 100$$

must be included in the model. The symbols r_1, r_2, r_3, and r_4 are the decision variables, 100 is a parameter, and π is a constant. It will never change. Or, consider a designer of a chemical process. As an intermediate part of the process, she wants to use water to produce hydrogen and oxygen. Let w be the number of water molecules admitted to the process per second and assume that she needs at least 10^{23} hydrogen atoms per second. The constraint

$$2w \geq 10^{23}$$

must be added to the problem. The number 2 is a constant since it is a physical law that each water molecule consists of 2 atoms of hydrogen and 1 atom of oxygen. The symbol w is a decision variable, and 10^{23} is a parameter.

Let us summarize the important concepts in this section:

A constrained optimization (or mathematical programming) model is formed with two components: an objective function and a set of constraints.

Each component is constructed from decision variables and data.

The data consist of parameters and constants.

3.5 Applications of Constrained Optimization Models

Constrained optimization models were first used in decision making in the 1940s. Among the major applications were logistic problems in World War II. The fields of operations research and management science arose from these early defense applications.

Now, applications of constrained optimization models range across all sorts of planning activities in both the public and private sectors. Applications in government are frequent. They currently include modeling efforts in the areas of defense, health planning, transportation, energy planning, and resource allocation, to name only a few. In the private sector, applications vary from long-term planning to daily, or even hourly, scheduling of activities. Specific applications in long-term planning include capital budgeting, plant location, long-range marketing strategy, and long-range investment strategy. Shorter-term applications include production and work-force scheduling, inventory management, machine scheduling, aircraft routing, chemical blending, product design, media selection, statistical estimation, feed-mix blending, tanker scheduling, waste disposal, site selection, and project scheduling in the construction of nuclear submarines or major shopping centers. The list could go on and on.

In all these applications, there are decisions to be made in order to carry out an activity or collection of activities optimally according to some criterion (such as minimizing cost, time, waste, or delay, or maximizing profit or total amount shipped). Also, in all these applications, there are limitations imposed either by scarce resources that must be allocated or by certain requirements that must be satisfied, or a combination of both. These limitations or requirements place constraints on the decisions that can be made. Other constraints may exist in the form of logical relations or physical laws that must be satisfied by the decision variables. Thus, decisions must be found that optimize the objective subject to all the constraints.

3.6 The Faculty Candidate Problem and Multiple Objectives

You have seen that constrained optimization problems have two major components: an objective function and a set of constraints. You have learned that the conceptual procedure for the solution technique is to determine values for the decision variables that produce the largest (or smallest) possible value for the objective function subject to the condition that none of the constraints are violated. With a good algorithm (or mathematical procedure) for solving constrained optimization problems, you are now in a position to help make some important management decisions, right?

Well, not quite. The preceding statement is true, but unfortunately it is only part of the story. Taking a real-world decision problem and stating it as a constrained optimization model can be an enormous challenge in itself. One difficulty is that in many real-world problems the planner has numerous objectives he or she wants to satisfy simultaneously, whereas the constrained optimization model requires the identification of a single objective.

Let us illustrate this difficulty in the following context. A great deal of discussion at faculty meetings concerns the hiring of new professors and the criteria for selecting among candidates. Typically, there are two important criteria: teaching and scholarship (research). Let us imagine that each of these criteria can be measured quantitatively in some generally acceptable way. For example, teaching might be measured by an average score obtained on student rating forms over the past five years, and scholarship might be measured by the number of published papers. Let us also imagine the quite reasonable possibility of finding out that no single candidate dominates all others in *both* teaching and research. The best teacher is not the best scholar, and the best scholar is not the best teacher. How shall we tackle this problem?

The difficulty here is that we appear to have a problem with two objectives. It looks as though we want to maximize both teaching and scholarship simultaneously, but in the present situation this is clearly not possible. One plausible suggestion is simply to decide which is more important, teaching or research. Then you can use the more important criterion as an objective and include the other in the model as a constraint. Let us pursue this suggestion. Suppose you agree that, in the final analysis, scholarship is really more important and that a teaching rating of, say, 2.5 is acceptable. Accordingly, you formulate the following constrained optimization model:

Maximize   Scholarship

subject to

Teaching $\geq$ 2.5

Suppose, for simplicity, that only individuals A and B satisfy the constraint but that A is the better scholar. Consequently, A wins the job.

Alternatively, your colleague in the next office may feel that teaching is more important but that any candidate should have published at least 31 papers. In that case, the appropriate model is

Maximize   Teaching

subject to

Scholarship $\geq$ 31

You then learn that both A and B have published at least 31 papers. Since you already know that A is the better scholar and no candidate is superior in both measures, it must follow that B is the better teacher. Hence, by the second formulation, B is the winner.

So far, it all seems simple. You must only decide which is more important, teaching or scholarship. Then the corresponding model is formulated and the solution obtained. According to this procedure you prefer A, your neighbor prefers B.

However, let us now suppose that you gain some additional information the model did not provide. You learn that although A and B both satisfy your teaching constraint, it turns out that candidate B is a ten-times better teacher than A. In fact, she materializes objects in the classroom, heals the sick, and people come from distant lands to hear her speak. Moreover, although A is a better scholar, he is only slightly better. He has published 35 papers whereas B has published 31. Upon gaining this additional information, you might very well think, "Well, even though I feel that scholarship is more important, the candidates are so close in that respect and B is so superior in teaching, I will reverse my vote. I agree that candidate B should get the job." Thus, you can see the possibility that merely deciding on what is most important in terms of objective versus constraint may not provide you with the decision you actually would prefer.

The difficulty with this example is that teaching and scholarship are both true objectives, or at least it is more correct to think of them both as objectives than to think of one as an objective and the other a constraint. In fact, you found out that "Which is more important?" was actually a meaningless question. You finally became aware that the importance of one, in your own mind, depended on the level of the other. Of course, situations exist in which there is a clear distinction between objectives and constraints in the real problem. In such cases, it is easy to reflect the proper distinction in the model. If, for example, you really do not care how good a teacher the candidate is as long as he or she satisfies the 2.5 condition, then "teaching" is truly a constraint. The first of the foregoing models is appropriate, and A is indeed the correct choice. As it turned out, though, the problem was not so simple because it had multiple objectives.

Before developing a more satisfactory analysis of cases with multiple objectives, let us look at another example. Consider a corporate president who has set the following goals for the next three years:

1 Maximize the present value of the near-term stream of yearly profits.
2 Maximize market share existing *at the end* of year 3.
3 Minimize deterioration of existing plant and facilities during the three-year period.

At first glance, it appears that he has three objectives to be optimized simultaneously. A little thought, however, will convince you that the tradeoffs in the problem are such that this is not possible. For example, decisions that maximize near-term (three-year) profits will tend to channel funds into current production (such as the cost of labor and material resources) at the expense of activities that tend to have a longer-range payoff (such as marketing, product research, and investment in new plant and equipment). Thus, any policy that maximizes near-term profits, as specified in item 1, will certainly not serve the objectives in items 2 and 3. There is a tradeoff between production, research, and investment. Expenditures in the latter categories are aimed at enhancing profits further down the line at the expense of profits obtained by increasing the current production budget.

In attempting to attack his problem with a constrained optimization model, the president might decide on one single objective and incorporate the other conditions as constraints. He could, for instance, decide that profit maximization is the single most important consideration but that he does not want to achieve profit with all caution thrown to the wind on marketing, research, and investment. He could decide that at the end of three years, in order to play it safe, the firm should have about one-third of the total market share and 200 million square feet of top-grade industrial floor space. Conceptually, he could structure his problem as

Maximize   Present value of three-year profit stream

subject to

Market share at end of year 3 $\geq$ $\frac{1}{3}$ total market

Top-grade industrial floor space at end of year 3 $\geq$ 200,000,000 sq ft

Of course, he might structure the problem differently. He might decide instead to maximize market share while including a minimum threshhold of three-year profits as a constraint. The important point here is that either of these formulations can lead to the same inconsistency encountered in the teaching-and-research discussion. The president truly has multiple objectives, and the above procedure may yield a solution that is not the most preferable.

In order to better analyze these multiple objective situations, at least in a conceptual way, let us return to the faculty-candidate problem. Suppose there are many individuals in our universe of candidates and that you solve the problem as follows. You first look at all candidates who satisfy a very low teaching level requirement, say 1.0, and find the best scholar by solving

Maximize   Scholarship

subject to

Teaching ≥ 1.0

You then look at all candidates who satisfy a higher level of teaching ability, say 1.5, and find the best scholar. This candidate is found by solving

Maximize   Scholarship

subject to

Teaching ≥ 1.5

Continuing in this way, you would generate a table as shown in Figure 3.6.

Figure 3.6   *Generating numerical values for faculty candidates*

Scholarship (number of papers)	Minimal Teaching Level (rating)
40	1.0
39	1.5
38	2.0
35	2.5
31	3.0
26	3.5
17	4.0

You then locate a row in this table with the following properties:

1   Any increase in scholarship (teaching level) is accompanied by an unacceptable decrease in teaching (scholarship).

2   Any decrease in scholarship (teaching level) more than offsets the accompanying increase in teaching level (scholarship).

It seems reasonable that the candidate identified with such a row is your most preferred choice.[1]

The corporate president's problem might be solved, at least *conceptually*, in the same way. That is, he could use the model

Maximize   Present value of three-year profit stream

subject to

Market share at end of year 3 $\geq M$

Top-grade industrial floor space at end of year 3 $\geq C$

to *generate* a three-column data table, the entries being maximum profit corresponding to a sequence of specified minimal levels, M and C, for market share and industrial floor space, respectively. The president then faces the problem of selecting the row in this table that he prefers. Although this problem is certainly more difficult than the preceding one with only two columns in the table, it is not insurmountable. It is not unusual for a manager to face the problem of having to select one of several alternative actions, where each action has different levels of at least three desiderata.

Let us now make several additional observations.

---

1 It is not necessarily true that two different corporate presidents would choose the same row, nor is it necessarily the case that two different faculty members will prefer the same mix of teaching and scholarship. Moreover, these examples are quite simple. In many important real-world decision problems, there are numerous criteria of interest, not just two or three, and this makes it even less likely that individuals will agree on "the best mix." This observation points out some of the difficulty inherent in group decision making and underscores the role of individual judgment. In other words, the individual's taste is very important in the decision-making process.

2 The constrained optimization model played an important role in creating a rational solution procedure for the multiple-objective problem. Although a single run of the model was not very informative, the model was employed sequentially to construct a data table. The data table, as noted in Chapter 2, can be interpreted as yet another model. In other words, the model was used to produce particularly useful data, which is the primary purpose of any quantitative decision model. The decision is based on the eventual model output—in this case, the data in the table.

3 The problem of multiple objectives is often called the problem of apples and oranges, derived from the question, "How do you add apples and oranges?" The point is, how do you combine quantities that are incommensurate? If there is some common denominator, such as dollars, then the problem can be eliminated by expressing the different objectives in the same unit and optimizing the sum. This can often be accomplished in business problems. For example, a manager may want to find a new plant location that minimizes labor costs and also minimizes transportation costs. These two objectives can be combined into the single objective of minimizing total cost. However, in many socioeconomic and public-sector problems the various objectives are incommensurate. They cannot be explicitly added. Students sometimes will suggest that the objectives be indexed on a common scale and then added, or that an average or

---

[1] Students of economics will note that in constructing this table, you have defined the hull of the opportunity set and its frontier, and in technical terms you have found a point, or particular values for (teaching, scholarship), at which this frontier is tangent to an indifference contour of your subjective utility function.

a different weighted sum be optimized. In general, however, it is extremely difficult to give a credible interpretation to the quantities that result from such explicit weighting schemes. Nevertheless, these schemes come quite close to the point, for the procedure described in the text provides a way to add up the various objectives *implicitly*. The data table makes it possible for the decision maker *subjectively* to combine the results of various alternative actions.

4   Finally, it should be emphasized that the foregoing discussion is conceptual. It points out the role of models as a rational mechanism for attacking problems with multiple objectives. This topic is of considerable importance in applications, and some of the recent research in management science has produced new and promising techniques for handling such problems efficiently. We discuss the issue of problems with multiple objectives from several other perspectives in Sections 14.5 and 14.6.

3.7   Constrained versus Unconstrained Optimization

Most professionals in management science or operations research believe the statement we made in Section 3.1 that constrained optimization models capture the essence of management decision making. Others do not. One dissident group adheres to what is sometimes labeled the *economist's*[2] or the *price theorist's* point of view. This point of view was most succinctly put forth by a former colleague at Chicago who emphatically stated, "There is no such thing as a truly constrained optimization problem."

The disputed issue concerns the role of parameters in the decision-making process. In the constrained optimization approach, the right-hand-side (RHS) parameters play a role in defining the constraints in the model, and values for these parameters are viewed as being temporarily fixed. The modeler seeks to find the best decision (for example, the one that maximizes the objective function) within the limits prescribed by these parameters. We shall see that he or she may want to explore the effects of varying these parameters, but in a single execution of the model they are fixed. For example, in a production-planning model it might be specified that the capacity of a certain department or production facility is fixed, and the goal would be to maximize profits within that limit.

In the price theorist's view, constraining parameters simply do not exist. For example, in a box-manufacturing plant, the capacity of the printing department is not considered fixed. It is "always" possible to purchase additional printing capacity. Perhaps we can hire more workers or work another shift or send boxes out to another printer. Symbolically, the difference between these points of view is expressed as follows. Suppose $g_4(x_1, x_2, ..., x_n)$ is the printing time required if we produce x_1 units of product 1, and so on, and let b_4 be an RHS parameter whose value is the capacity of the printing department. Then, instead of employing a constraint $g_4(x_1, x_2, ..., x_n) \leq b_4$, the price theorist prefers to use a function

$$C_4[g_4(x_1, x_2, ..., x_n)]$$

---

2   In this context, we cheerfully acknowledge the inaccuracy of this label since many economists have a deep interest in constrained optimization. For example, Tjalling Koopmans, a Nobel Prize winner in economics, was one of the first developers of linear programming.

that yields the cost to the firm of obtaining $g_4(x_1, x_2, ..., x_n)$ hours of printing time. This term along with many similar terms makes up a profit function to be used as the objective for the firm. There are no constraining parameters in the model. The value of the objective function is maximized without constraints; this is thus called an *unconstrained optimization model.* The assumption in such a model is that anything can be had at the right price.

In summary, the two approaches can be compared as follows:

The constrained optimizer imposes conditions that irrevocably rule out some decisions and then optimizes.

The unconstrained optimizer allows the potential for any decision to occur at an appropriate cost.

In the abstract, the unconstrained model is rational and it may be conceptually satisfying, for there are probably few things in life that cannot be changed at some price. However, the empirical fact is that many problems in reality are solved either formally or informally as constrained optimization problems.

Why is there this seeming paradox between the unconstrained view of decision making and what many people actually do? We believe that the answer is this:

Although the unconstrained model has theoretical appeal, it frequently cannot be implemented in practice.

More precisely, the unconstrained approach is frequently *uneconomical* to implement in practice. In the following section, you will learn why the constrained approach, on the other hand, offers a pragmatic alternative. You will also see cases where the unconstrained approach is even theoretically invalid.

3.8 Why Constraints Are Imposed

The analyst confronts a real-world problem. His or her apparent goal is to construct a quantitative optimization model. A more correct description is: the analyst's goal is to provide some quantitative rationale and support in the decision-making process. In pursuit of this goal, analysts employ constraints for a variety of subtle reasons. The reasons generally have a great deal to do with practicality, and they may differ one from the other only in matters of degree or interpretation. They generally have little to do with any philosophical conviction about the virtues of the constrained versus the unconstrained approach. The following illustrations will help you to establish a perspective for the use and relevance of constrained models in real life.

3.8.1 *Immutable Technology and Laws of Nature*

In short-term planning situations, technological constraints may be inevitable. Consider an equilibrium-pricing model that attempts to forecast average regional prices of wheat during a given crop year along with total net imports of wheat in that same period for a number of countries. The total global supply of wheat is fixed. In the real world, there is no way it can be changed until the next crop is harvested. Agricultural technology and botanical laws cannot be altered, no matter what price the planner would pay to do so. The same type of technological restrictions can occur in the steel industry. When a particular furnace or process has been shut down, say by a strike, a fixed amount of time is required to start it up again for physical and chemical reasons. There may be no way to eliminate such a constraint, even for a price. Can you imagine other short-term models for which similar constraints cannot realistically be eliminated?

3.8.2   *The Cost of Search*

An important practical factor in problem solving involves the cost of finding the solution. Constraints are often used to reduce this cost. Consider the parent whose child asks for help in using a book of state topography maps to locate the highest point in the United States. The problem could be tackled by an unconstrained search through the entire book. But with no more than an average knowledge of geography, the parent confidently ignores the maps of Ohio, Michigan, Indiana, Wisconsin, Iowa, Nebraska, and a host of others.

As another example, consider the U.S. distributor of a new French perfume. In making the product available to the public, the distributor wants to select an advertising campaign that maximizes the ratio

$$\frac{\text{Total sales}}{\text{Total advertising expenditure}}$$

The advertising options are numerous:

1   Advertising on buses in major cities
2   Advertising on radio in major cities
3   Advertising on network T.V.
4   Advertising in selected magazines
5   Passing out handbills

The distributor decides on the basis of intuition to eliminate the first, second, and fifth possibilities and then sponsors a study to determine the best way to allocate dollars to specific advertisements within the remaining two categories. The funds for such a study are limited. By imposing constraints, the distributor is able to specialize the study and, hopefully, obtain better results.

As another example, a fellow faculty member recently decided to buy a new house. He applied the following constraints:

1   The house should be within easy walking distance of a station for the Illinois Central commuter line.
2   The house should be located in a good school district.
3   It should be within a modest walk's distance of the high school.

He realized the possiblility that the house he would like most might in fact violate one of these constraints. However, he had neither the time nor energy to conduct an exhaustive search of the entire city. These constraints limited his search to two or three neighborhoods, and he felt that he could do a good job of considering the alternatives in these neighborhoods. Based on experience and intuition, he also felt he would be reasonably satisfied with the results of his search in the chosen neighborhoods.

In all these examples, the constraints make the search easier and less costly. In the first two examples, the searchers feel sure that the constraints do not eliminate the true optimum. In the third example, our colleague would not swear that his constraints had this property. It was entirely conceivable that there would be a house on the market somewhere in Chicago that did not satisfy all of his constraints and yet in which he would like most to live. He simply could not afford the time for the most thorough search.

This third example takes us fairly close to a danger point that you may also have seen lurking in the first two. What if the decision maker's intuition is wrong? What if the tallest point is, in fact, in Michigan? What if advertising on buses is the approach with the largest payoff? What if the best house is not within walking distance of the Illinois Central commuter line? What if it is in a part of town which would force our colleague to drive to the university, but if he saw the house and knew it had been on the market he would have preferred it anyway? After all, there are tradeoffs one is sometimes willing to make, and these cannot always be predicted in advance.

Here is an actual case in point. Years ago, most automobile insurance was sold through individual agents, and most studies on how to optimize sales were constrained by the conventional wisdom that this was the best way to do things. Then, Allstate began over-the-counter sales in Sears stores and dramatically captured a substantial portion of the market.

Thus, we do not suggest that a good way to minimize the search cost is to blindly slap constraints into the model. You should always be aware of the fact that you may be pushing yourself out on a limb. The constraints can end up costing more than the saving.

3.8.3   *Uncertainty, Nonlinearity, and Parametric Analysis*

Next month, capital-budgeting decisions will be made for the box-manufacturing corporation (Section 3.7) at the board of directors' winter meeting. The decisions will affect the maximum amount of printing time available for the following 24 months. The construction of a new printing department is under consideration. During the past 4 months, our manager has been supervising a study to determine the optimal capacity and whether or not the capital investment in the new department should be undertaken. Cost estimates for the new construction, which would begin in late spring, have been disturbingly vague. Much will depend on the new labor contract to be negotiated in April. In addition, material costs have been fluctuating widely. The economic recovery has been so strong that some predictors are calling for a return to high rates of inflation by next spring. Our manager has been burned before by taking bad cost estimates too literally. How does she deal with such uncertainty? Can she make any meaningful recommendations to the directors? Various approaches to dealing with uncertainty are presented in Part 2 of this text. Special models for treating uncertainty are called *stochastic* or *probabilistic* models. However, uncertainty is not always treated with special stochastic models. In fact, in real-world problem solving it is not unusual to incorporate uncertainty within the deterministic framework.

In this manager's situation, for example, a typical approach is to plug the capacity constraint

$$g_4(x_1, ..., x_n) \le b_4$$

into the model. Recall that $g_4(x_1, x_2, ..., x_n)$ is the printing time required if we produce x_1 units of product 1, and so on, and b_4 is the total capacity of the printing department. We then perform what is called a *dual-pricing*, or *parametric, analysis* on the constraining parameter b_4. This technique will be studied in detail in Chapter 8, and in Chapter 12 we discuss a specific application. The approach involves the generation of a so-called *optimal value function* by assigning different values to b_4 and successively re-solving the problem. As a result of her analysis, the manager will be able to say that if the costs are so and so, then the optimal capacity is such and such. Because of the uncertainty about market costs, her conclusions are *conditional,* and she probably will not be able to make a flat recommendation to the directors. But she will be able to show the extent to which the optimal capacity is sensitive to different assumptions about future costs. This means that she can provide a good deal of important information (data) for the directors to examine, but they will have to make the final decision. There is no way the model can do it for them.

This approach is common and successful. It is common because so many real problems are loaded with elements of uncertainty. These elements may be associated with parameters in either the right-hand side, or the objective function, or the constraint functions. Such parameters may be technological as well as economic.

Consider the following technological example. The maximum range of a proposed infra-red sensor is not known with certainty. The model is therefore constructed with a constraint that says

Range $\le R$

A parametric analysis on R will provide results that indicate the extent to which the optimal solution is sensitive to the range. The analysis will enable us to say, "If the maximum range is so and so, then these are the results we can expect."

As another important application for parametric analysis, we again consider the example of the box manufacturer. The manager may understand that there is no such thing as fixed capacity, for unlimited amounts of printing time can be purchased in Taiwan for the right price. In this case, suppose there is little uncertainty about the cost of increasing capacity, but unfortunately these costs are nonlinear. In particular, suppose that the function $g_4(x_1, ..., x_n)$, which denotes the amount of printing time required by the decisions $x_1, ..., x_n$ is linear, but the cost function C_4 is nonlinear. Suppose everything else in the model is linear. In such a case, including $C_4\,[g_4\,(x_1,\,\ldots,\,x_n)\,]$ in the objective function will complicate the mathematics and could make it difficult—perhaps impossible—to solve the model. In any case, the solution procedure would be costly for, in the first place, the manager would have to hire someone who knows something about nonlinear models.

An easy and powerful way to deal with this situation is to ignore the cost function C_4 temporarily and solve the model with the linear constraint

$$g_4(x_1,\,\ldots,\,x_n) \le b_4$$

Parametric analysis is then performed on the constraining parameter, just as in the uncertainty case. The optimal capacity is then found (with certainty) by a simple comparison of the cost function C_4 with the optimal value function obtained from the parametric analysis. This approach keeps the entire model linear, making it easy to solve. Even though the model will have to be solved a number of times in succession, this approach is often more efficient than nonlinear optimization. Moreover, it will be seen that when you solve a linear model you obtain an enormous amount of additional useful information. Thus, in this latter illustration a constraint is imposed and a parametric analysis is performed, not in order to deal with uncertainty as in the previous illustrations, but rather to handle a nonlinear problem with tools of linear analysis. This approach is further illustrated in Chapter 12.

3.8.4   *Surrogate Objectives and Pushing the Solution*

Excuse me, but what's a nice function like you doing in a place like this?

The police department personnel office has just sent over the latest optimal solution. The captain is dismayed for he sees that the new candidate walks with a limp. One leg is shorter than the other. By now, the captain has learned how to massage his model. He slaps on another constraint in order to improve the solution even further. A week later he receives this reply from personnel: "No one on the force satisfies all the constraints you imposed." He is despondent. He knows that many people on the force could effectively impersonate a University of Chicago hurdler and help him smash the dope ring. All he did was employ a fancy model from management science and a little bit of intuition about constraints to find the best impersonator, and he has hit a dead end. What went wrong?

There are two problems with the captain's approach. One involves his choice for an objective function. The other concerns his intuition about the constraints. His *real problem* and *ideal objective* are to find the best impersonator. If it were possible, he should have a function in the model that numerically measures the quality of impersonation. He wants to maximize such a function. Regrettably, he does not know how to measure "ability to impersonate" numerically, and as a substitute he chose the *model objective* to be height. The model objective is a stand-in, or a **surrogate**, for the true objective. Since height alone is not a very good surrogate, the captain had to keep imposing additional constraints, dictated by his intuition, in order to **push** the solution in the right direction. Obviously, he does not know exactly how to set these constraints. Each one taken by itself does not seem overly stringent, but when taken together they rule out everyone on the force.

Here is another situation in which the objective is unclear. A study was recently undertaken for a client involved in several projects of interest to the Department of Health, Education, and Welfare. The client wanted to determine the optimal locations for 16 proposed health care clinics. The clinics were to have a modular design and were architecturally rather innovative. But what does it mean to "optimize locations"? What is the appropriate measure? Some suggestions are:

1   To minimize the distance between locations and dense, low-income-population areas
2   To maximize the geographic coverage without regard to population density or income distribution
3   To minimize the level of government subsidy required
4   To maximize the aesthetic exposure (the visibility of the architect)

The alternatives are numerous. The problem in a study like this is not just how to quantify the objective. Actually, it is not even clear what HEW is looking for. Unless an appropriate objective function can be defined, at least verbally, it seems hopeless to embark on a quantitative study.

Assuming that this obstacle can be overcome, a modeler is faced with the task of quantifying the true objective in order to get it into the model. In many problems, the ideal objective and the model objective will be the same (for example, to maximize profit). In other instances, the ideal objective may not be directly quantifiable. An *indirect* surrogate measure may be chosen. The Hyde Park police captain chose height as an indirect measure for the ideal objective. As it turned out, his approach was disastrous.

In cases where the true objective is either unclear or unquantifiable, the decision maker may be able to justify imposing constraints in order to push the solution in the right direction. Even though the true objective cannot be quantified, the decision maker may feel that he or she understands some of the properties that a true optimal solution to the problem will have. The use of constraints provides assurance that the solution to the model (with the surrogate objective function) will also satisfy these same properties. This use of constraints can thus be viewed as a kind of insurance, or hedging, against an inability to quantify the ideal objective function. It is worth noting that this approach is sometimes employed when the true objective is so vague that even a surrogate cannot be employed. In such a case, the decision maker may be operating without any quantified objective function so that formal optimization is obviously out of the question. Still, the decision maker may impose constraints to select policies he or she feels are in the right direction.

Consider another example of the surrogate approach. Recommendations have to be made to the president and then to Congress for the next year's military budget. These recommendations typically evolve through a complex organizational process. In a highly simplified version of the process, each of the services generates separate proposals and recommendations for procurements and sends these forth to the secretary for that service. Within any given service, there are competitive weapon systems. In the air force, missiles compete with bombers; in the navy, submarines compete with carriers, and so on. The competition is keen for procurement and research and development dollars. This intra-service competition is thrashed out at the secretaries' level, and each secretary then sends the agreed-upon recommendations to the secretary of defense. At this point, for example, missiles and submarines are compared, and competition between the services is a key factor. Finally, some resolution is obtained and recommendations are sent from the secretary of defense to the president. But the president also receives inputs on the defense budget from numerous other advisory sources including the intelligence community, his economic advisors, the National Security Council, the Joint Chiefs of Staff, his personal staff, and so on. During this entire process, many quantitative studies are performed to shed light on one aspect or another of military policy and effectiveness.

In one such study, the client was preparing a case for a submarine-launched ballistic missile system. His job was to show that procurement of this system would significantly enhance our military posture. An optimization model was formulated to determine a combination of weapon systems that would produce "a maximum level of military effectiveness." That phrase verbalizes the ideal objective function for this problem, but no one really knows exactly what it means, in quantitative terms, to maximize military effectiveness. As an indirect surrogate objective, it was decided to seek a combination of weapon systems that would maximize the urban and industrial damage suffered by an adversary in an all-out nuclear war.

The model produced an answer the client did not like. It said that the new system should not be procured. The client was sophisticated and highly experienced in military planning. He felt that the new system was excellent and the model was producing the wrong answer. Thus, it was decided that modifications were in order. Two significant changes were made. Some complicated defense strategies were put into the model, and the objective function was modified. Instead of measuring only urban and industrial damage, the objective became a weighted combination of this and damage to the adversary's military system. The model was solved with these changes, and the client was somewhat more satisfied with the output. The constraints had forced the solution to move in what he thought was the right direction, but not far enough. The new weapon system was now a part of the optimal solution, but the client felt its role should be even more pronounced. The objective function was then changed to measure only military damage. Moreover, the adversary was now constrained to be a first-striker with his first-strike weapons directed at all of our forces and only a few major urban industrial centers. In addition, some assumptions were made about the United States' early-warning capability and response time. With these new constraints, the client's preferred system showed up clearly as a very important part of the optimal solution. The client was pleased.

You may be wondering, "What good is the model if you know the answer all along?" Some people criticize modeling activites for this very reason. In our opinion, such criticism is often based on a complete lack of understanding of the overall process. After all, the client did not *know* the solution with certainty. He had some intuitive ideas, but intuition is a kind of model in itself. It is internal, less formal, and at times more or less complicated than the formal models we construct with symbols and solve on computers. Nevertheless, intuition is a model. What our client really wanted was a good symbolic representation for his internal intuitive model. That is what he eventually ended up with, and the modeling effort proved very useful in at least two respects.

1   The model sharpened his intuition. He learned a great deal about the set of circumstances under which his intuition seemed to be most correct. It seemed to him, after the fact, that those circumstances were quite consistent with the assumptions on which his intuitive model was probably founded. In fact, he learned a good deal about circumstances in which his intuition was probably wrong. Furthermore, by analyzing interactions revealed by the formal model, he learned about some important factors that had not been built into his internal (intuitive) model.

2   The model provided him with a more effective way of demonstrating support for his proposal. He felt that the final assumptions and constraints of the model were quite realistic. He also felt that he could justify the model's objective as a reasonable surrogate for the true objective. His original reasons for supporting the new weapon system had been intuitive and qualitative. That is fine for your own point of view, but it is not the best way to argue a case. He could now back up his intuition with presumably more persuasive quantitative arguments.

In this example, you can see that the use of constraints was motivated by the sponsor's intuition. The true objective could not be easily quantified. The constraints helped him feel his way toward a good surrogate objective (from his point of view) and a good solution.

The foregoing examples, which range from the militarist's "success" to the police captain's "failure," point out the benefits and the dangers of the surrogate-objective/added-constraints approach. These are the key ideas:

In many problems, the real objective is not easily quantifiable. The objective in the model is a surrogate for the real objective.

Constraints are then added to push the solution in the right direction.

Remember that the success of this approach depends on two factors: (1) the appropriateness of the surrogate objective; and (2) the accuracy of the decision maker's intuition. In effect, a model can be manipulated to produce any results, but those results are valid only if the model truly represents the real-world situation.

3.8.5   The Underling Problem

A short course in feathering your own nest

Our examples in Section 3.8.4 illustrate constructive reasons for the use of constraints. True, we pointed out some potential dangers, but these were "honest" mistakes that arose from fuzzy thinking. On the other side of the coin, it

Figure 3.7 *Feathering your own nest*

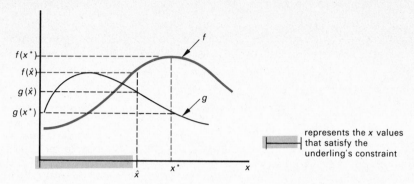

is important to note that constraints have been known to be used deliberately to further individual aims and even compromise the objective. Here's a case in point.

On September 13, 1976, the editorial page of the *Wall Street Journal* featured a story on the new political power of a New York City councilman. The gist of the story was that the councilman used the federal antipoverty programs to build a powerful political machine for his own purposes. Whether funds were illegally used or not is unimportant to us. This item reports on a situation in which a subordinate achieves his own ends in spite of his boss. This situation is called the *underling problem.*

The underling's aspiration is that like everyone else in life he wants to maximize his own well being. As a result, he has a personal objective function that differs from that of the organization (that is, his boss). The underling's solution strategy is to disguise his own objective in a constraint and then argue for the constraint. The constraint looks innocuous to the boss—neither good nor bad. The underling's contrived justification seems plausible; so the boss innocently accepts the constraint, unaware of the full implications. The results of the constraint will be costly to the boss and will benefit the underling, for the solution will be pushed in the underling's direction. A one-dimensional illustration of the basic idea is presented in Figure 3.7.

In this diagram f represents management's objective function and g the underling's objective function. When there are no constraints, the optimal solution is x^* since this value of x maximizes management's objective. If, however, the underling persuades his boss to add a constraint and thus restrict the decision variable to the set shown in the figure, the optimal solution becomes $\hat{x}$. This fact follows from the observation that, of all the allowable values of x, $\hat{x}$ produces the largest value of management's objective function. Note that the net result of moving the solution from x^* to $\hat{x}$ is

Gain to underling $g(\hat{x}) - g(x^*)$

Loss to boss $f(x^*) - f(\hat{x})$

In many cases, the constraints impose a kind of prescreening in order to limit the alternatives that reach the final stage of the decision-making process.

A prominent charitable foundation developed a program of fellowships to give management training in the U.S. to promising young civil servants from a developing African country. Dossiers were assembled for each candidate, and then a committee of representatives from the participating American universities selected the individuals to receive the fellowships. Ten winners were selected annually from a field of over 200 applicants, and everyone thought the program was a great success. A review of the program after several years revealed that all fellowship winners (and, indeed, all applicants) had been members of the same tribe (and political party). This tribe had traditionally held the important administrative positions in the colonial government and thus controlled the application process. The group was in an ideal position to feather its own nest.

Or, for example, imagine how easy it is for a department head to draw up a job description that calls for a recent university graduate who majored in hieroglyphics, minored in engineering, and had work experience as a canoeing instructor. Would you be surprised to learn that her second cousin's son, with exactly those qualifications, was looking for a job?

The 1976 tax reform bill has been described as having at least 60 special-interest provisions. According to Senator Edward Kennedy ("Time," August 16, 1976), some of these provisions were so finely drawn that they resembled legislation for a "one-eyed bearded man with a limp." You are invited to speculate on the motivation for the inclusion of so many special provisions.

As a final and less specific example, notice that in large firms, major capital-investment decisions are typically made by the board of directors. They consider a group of alternatives that have reached them after passing a large number of reviews (departmental, divisional, regional, and so on). There are thus numerous opportunities for subordinates to influence the set of alternatives from which the final decision will be made.

As you can see, the underling phenomenon provides a powerful motivation for the appearance of constraints in a model. The important point to remember is that its general effect can be deleterious to the overall objectives of management.

3.8.6   Hierarchal Structure and the Delegation of Authority

Constraints seem to be an inherent part of organizational structure. The necessity to delegate authority and responsibility for certain activities while maintaining overall responsibility for an entire operation almost always dictates the use of constraints and, consequently, the constrained optimization approach.

A good example is provided by the purchasing activity in multinational firms. When a firm has plants in several nearby countries, a question arises as to who should do the buying for each plant. In some multinational corporations, a centralized purchasing department buys for all plants. Many firms, however, use a decentralized system with a buying group for each plant. In this case, central management usually constrains the activities by insisting that all purchases be from centrally approved suppliers and that certain standard receiving and testing procedures be followed. The buyer at an individual plant then tries to minimize costs subject to constraints on delivery time, the quality of the material, and on the set of possible suppliers.

The process of passing down constraints occurs at all levels in organizational hierarchies. The government constrains the corporation, which constrains its divisions, which constrains their plants, which constrains their departments, and so on. The net result is that most decision makers in organizations find themselves facing problems in constrained optimization. The constraints may change as firms reorganize to meet competition, and the variables may change for an individual as he or she progresses through an organization. But it is difficult to imagine a world in which the delegation of limited responsibility and authority is not a critical part of the management process. This scenario appears to be consistent with the constrained optimization approach.

3.9 Intuitive versus Formal Modeling

In concluding this chapter, let us compare the type of models we've been discussing with what we have referred to as *intuitive* models. We believe that most decisions in life are made in accord with some internal and intuitive optimization model of the problem at hand. Such models, though less formal than the ones we've considered, also try to capture certain tradeoffs and interactions. They are also composed of objectives and constraints—the same fabric as formal models—but in mental rather than external symbolic form.

Within their structure, these internal models tend to incorporate diffuse, hard-to-quantify considerations that pertain to individual tastes and dispositions. To a degree, you are observing a person's outlook on life by seeing the reflection of his model in the way he searches for solutions and in the quality of the solutions he actually finds. The constraints in a formal model serve to define the environment within which we will seek to maximize our objective. The same is true of intuitive internal models.

As an illustration of the kinds of unquantifiable conditions or perceptions that are incorporated in intuitive models, consider the following quotations. Each statement suggests a way to constrain the search for wealth and success.

No man ever lost money underestimating the intelligence of the American people.   H. L. Mencken

There's a sucker born every minute.   P. T. Barnum

These statements reflect a major difficulty with intuitive modeling. Intuitive models generally are not explicit. They are difficult to challenge, or criticize, or subscribe to because what such models say is ambiguous. Are the quotes assertions of fact? If so, how would you go about verifying either one beyond dispute?

By contrast, the formal model at least aspires to "laying it all out" and then, hopefully, "putting it all together." The objective can be disputed or accepted. It may not be the ideal, but it is what it is, and, as we have seen, it may be manipulated and modified. The constraints are a matter of record. They can be challenged, modified, augmented, or eliminated. Because of their explicit and unambiguous nature, formal models provide individuals and groups with a tool for eliminating inconsistency. In this way, the use of formal models is an arm of rational behavior in the quest for good decisions.

3.10   Summary of Key Concepts

What is optimal in the model may not be optimal in reality. (Section 3.1)

The symbolic general form of the constrained optimization model is

Objective function
$$\begin{cases} Maximize \quad f(x_1, ..., x_n) \\ subject\ to \end{cases}$$

Constraints
$$\begin{cases} g_1(x_1, ..., x_n) \begin{array}{c} \leq \\ = \\ \geq \end{array} b_1 \\ \quad . \qquad\qquad\qquad . \\ \quad . \qquad\qquad\qquad . \\ \quad . \qquad\qquad\qquad . \\ g_m(x_1, ..., x_n) \begin{array}{c} \leq \\ = \\ \geq \end{array} b_m \end{cases}$$

(Section 3.2)

The elements of a constrained optimization model are decision variables and data. The decision variables implicitly stand for numbers. The data consist of constants and parameters. (Section 3.4)

The constrained optimizer imposes conditions that irrevocably rule out some decisions and then he optimizes. The unconstrained optimizer allows the potential for any decision to occur at an appropriate cost. (Section 3.7)

In terms of the model's objective, adding a constraint cannot help and may hurt. But in the sense that the model's objective may be a surrogate, the addition of constraints may improve the decision maker's true objective. (Section 3.8)

In real-world problem solving, constraints are imposed when the unconstrained model is either invalid or impractical. For example, constraints are typically imposed

1 because short-term technology cannot be changed
2 to reduce the cost of finding a solution
3 to make conditional recommendations (if . . . then . . .) in the face of uncertainty
4 to "push the solution" in order to make a model with a surrogate objective closer to reality
5 to serve self-interest
6 along with the delegation of limited authority
(Section 3.8)

3.11   Problems

1 What is a constraint? How is it expressed in mathematical terms? Distinguish between a constraint, a right-hand side, and a constraint function.

2 In Section 3.6, we discussed several problems with multiple objectives. Can you think of other examples in the business world?

3 Profit maximization is commonly taken as the objective function for the firm. Is this a surrogate objective or a real objective? For example, consider a firm such as ITT. Can you think of other objectives that might be appropriate? Do not worry about whether or not they are quantifiable.

4 Write out the general form of a constrained optimization model with n decision variables and m constraints. Write out the same model for the case where all functions are linear.

5 What is the difference between a real objective function and a surrogate objective function?

6 We have said that there are no optimal decisions for the complex problems of business. And yet optimization models produce "optimal decisions." In what sense, then, are such decisions optimal?

7 Consider the following statement: "Our production policy should be to achieve maximum output at minimum cost." Comment on this misunderstanding.

8 Discuss the meaning of the following
a A successful application
b A large versus a small problem
c An important constraint versus an unimportant constraint
d Solving a model

9 "An optimization problem has been solved but some of the constraints are violated." Discuss this assertion.

10 What is the meaning of a mathematical constraint when the data (parameter values) are not known with precision? What kinds of assumptions would tend to justify the use of models in such situations?

11 Consider an optimization model involving something called *units of effectiveness*, (E), and suppose that this cannot be realistically translated into dollars. However, greater effectiveness results from expending more dollars, (C). It is desired to obtain high effectiveness, but at not too great a cost. Discuss the pitfalls in
a Maximizing $E - C$
b Maximizing E/C
How might you analyze such a problem?

12 What is meant by the assertion that one model is more structured than another?

13 Can you think of any resource that cannot be obtained at *some* price?

14 Compare constrained and unconstrained optimization models. Try to give some real-life illustrations of each model.

15 List as many motives as you can for the appearance of constraints. For each motive, discuss whether the use of a constraint is constructive or deleterious.

16 Consider the management scientist's model

Max $f(x_1, ..., x_n)$

subject to $\qquad\qquad\qquad\qquad\qquad\qquad$ (1)

$g_i(x_1, ..., x_n \leq b_i \qquad i = 1, ..., m$

where the parameters b_i are specified limits on resource availability. Now consider the economist's model

$$\text{Max} \left\{ f(x_1, ..., x_n) - \sum_{i=1}^{m} \lambda_i g_i(x_1, ..., x_n) \right\} \qquad (2)$$

where the parameters λ_i are specified *positive* numbers that represent resource costs. Show that the economist's model is equivalent to

$$\text{Max} \quad f(x_1, ..., x_n) - \sum_{i=1}^{m} \lambda_i b_i$$

subject to   (3)

$$g_i(x_1, ..., x_n) \leq b_i \qquad i = 1, ..., m$$

where the x_is and b_is are variables and the λ_is are the specified parameters. In what circumstances is there justification for using (1) rather than (2) or (3)?

4 Formulation of Constrained Optimization Models

This chapter provides experience in the art of model formulation. Numerous examples are presented. These include linear and nonlinear programming problems. Applications included in the examples involve models drawn from the areas of finance, marketing, inventory, and operations planning.

4.1 Introduction

Specific rules that tell you exactly how to formulate an optimization model are doomed to fail, for the technique is largely an art that is developed with practice. However, we can offer loose guidelines. The diagram in Figure 4.1 provides a useful schema for our discussion. For the purpose of this discussion, we can think of the real-world transition from problem detection through solution and analysis as a four-stage process. (Note that Figure 4.1 also shows chapters in this text relevant to each stage.) In Step I, the first signal of a problem evolves into a carefully worded description of the problem and the appropriate environment. Relevant data are provided. These data may consist of numbers, parameters, and functions. Step II is purely a translation from words into mathematical symbols. A quantitative model is the result. In step III, the model is solved. In step IV, numerous "sensitivity" properties of the solution are analyzed.

The initial problem detection may be simple observations like "profits should be larger," "resource use appears to be inefficient," or "our inventories are too high." The first big step in model building is the evolution from this signal into a careful description of the problem and the environment. Clearly, in many realistic situations only select parts of the environment can be included in the description. This process is the first step in creating a selective representation of reality. In step II, further selection may occur in choosing the form of the mathematical approximation. The transition via steps I and II results in a quantitative model that *approximates* reality. This model will hopefully be a useful aid in management's efforts to surmount the problem initially detected. It is worth bearing in mind that in a complex real-world situation, two different individuals starting at the beginning and working independently will almost surely construct different models. The reason is that the specific transitions that occur during steps I and II are, to a large extent, determined by the background, training, perceptions, preferences, and special interests of the modeler. The question of whether one model turns out to be better than

Figure 4.1   *The modeling process*

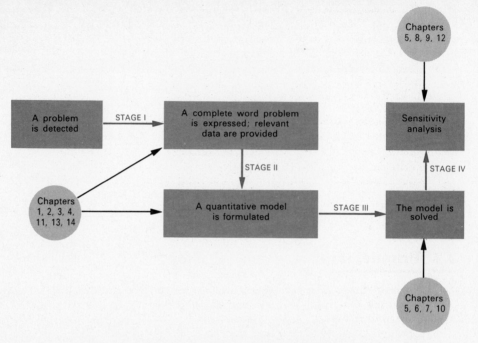

the other is answered by purely pragmatic considerations. The better model is the more useful model (that is, the one that yields the greatest net return to the user). You should keep that goal in mind from the start.

This chapter focuses on step II of the transition. We will present a number of word problems along with the relevant data and then transform them into constrained optimization models.

"Why," we hear you cry, "is this worth doing? As a manager, won't I be able to hire a specialist to do this sort of thing?" To some extent this may be true. However, the modern manager may be required to translate vague verbal descriptions of objectives or constraints into meaningful quantitative formulations. The ability to do so helps to create a basis for communication with the specialist. In addition, on a more pedagogical level, every model is an abstraction, and we believe that a good way to begin learning about models is to actually participate in the creation of this abstraction. To do so will force you to think logically about tradeoffs and interactions and to give a formal symbolic expression to your thoughts. At the outset this may not be easy, but the experience of working through a number of formulations will help to develop your skill in formulation.

The illustrations that follow will be highly simplified for expository purposes, but this is done to enhance their value as a learning tool. In particular, we have attempted to choose the word problems in such a way that, within the described context, the correct formulation should be unambiguous. Later, we will encounter problems where the latitude for interpretation and formulation is broader.

Now, here are some loose guidelines on what to do with a word problem.

---

1 If possible, get into the context by diagramming some of the important interactions in the problem. Use this diagram to associate parameters with the appropriate component of the model (the objective function or a certain constraint).

2 Create a verbal model.
  a Express the objective function in words.
  b Express each constraint.
    (1) Express the constraint function in words.
    (2) Determine the right direction for the inequality.
    (3) Use the appropriate numerical value of the right-hand side.

3 Identify and invent symbolic notation for the decision variables.

4 Write out the complete mathematical model.

Let's apply these guidelines to some examples. First, try to create the model yourself. Then read the solution.

4.2 Product-Mix Examples

In problems of this type, a collection of products can be sold and the set of resources from which these products are made is limited. Each product contributes to profit and utilizes resources. The objective is to find a mix of products to produce (that is, the amount of each product to produce) so as to maximize profit subject to the constraints that resource availabilities are not exceeded.

Example 1

PROTRAC produces the largest member of its earthmoving equipment line (the E–9) and the largest member of its forestry equipment line (the F–9) with essentially the same equipment. Demand for these items is very high at this time, and management believes it is possible to sell as many of both as the firm can produce. The profit is $5,000 for an E–9 and $4,000 for an F–9. In planning production for the next two weeks, management knows it is necessary to produce a total of at least five E–9s and F–9s in order to meet previous commitments. Each of these products requires processing in department A and department B. Over the next two weeks, these departments have 150 and 160 hours of available time respectively. Each E–9 requires 10 hours in department A and 20 hours in department B, whereas each F–9 requires 15 hours in department A and 10 hours in department B. In order to honor the labor contract, the total labor hours used in testing finished products cannot fall more than 10 percent below the agreed goal of 150 hours. (This is independent of the processing requirements in departments A and B.) Each E–9 requires 30 hours of testing and each F–9 requires 10. Finally, in order to maintain the current market position, management feels that it is necessary to build at least one F–9 for every three E–9s produced. How much of each product should PROTRAC produce in the next two weeks to maximize profit? Formulate this problem as a constrained optimization model. Remember, you are entitled to make no assumptions other than those explicitly stated in the preceding description. Also, you must proceed on the principle that *all* relevant data and assumptions are included in this description.

Solution to Example 1

DIAGRAM

Figure 4.2

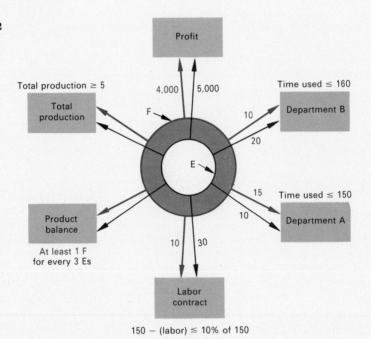

VERBAL MODEL

Maximize   Profit

subject to

Total production	≥	5	(1)
Time used in department A	≤	150	(2)
Time used in department B	≤	160	(3)
150 − (labor used testing)	≤ 10% of 150		(4)
At least 1 F-9 for every 3 E-9s			(5)

Although we have created a verbal model, the fifth constraint is not yet in a form easily convertible to an inequality. To see how to convert such a verbal statement into a mathematical inequality, it is often useful to think through some example cases with numbers plugged in. Suppose we made 3 E-9s. Then we would need *at least* 1 F-9. Now suppose we made 21 E-9s. We would need at least 1 F-9 for every 3 E-9s, or at least 7 F-9s. In general, you can see that

$$\text{Number of F-9s} \geq \frac{\text{number of E-9s}}{3}$$

or

$$3(\text{number of F-9s}) \geq (\text{number of E-9s})$$

DECISION VARIABLES

E = number of E-9s produced in the next 2 weeks

F = number of F-9s produced in the next 2 weeks

THE MODEL

Max $5,000E + 4,000F$

s.t.

$$
\begin{aligned}
E + F &\geq 5 & (1) \\
10E + 15F &\leq 150 & (2) \\
20E + 10F &\leq 160 & (3) \\
-30E - 10F &\leq -135 & (4) \\
E - 3F &\leq 0 & (5) \\
E, F &\geq 0 &
\end{aligned}
$$

Rather arbitrarily, the nonnegativity conditions, $E, F \geq 0$, are usually thought of as being separate from the constraints. Thus, the constrained optimization model has an objective function, constraints, and, when appropriate, nonnegativity conditions.

At this point, we should note the fact that unless we put in a specific constraint forcing the decision variables to be integers, we must in general be prepared to accept fractional answers. Your first reaction is apt to be to add constraints forcing E and F to be integers since in all likelihood a solution that sets E equal to 3.41, (that is, to produce 3.41 E-9s in the next two weeks) would not be physically meaningful. When such so-called *integrality constraints* are added, the problem becomes an *integer program.* Unfortunately, integer programming problems are much more difficult to solve. We shall frequently formulate models such as the one above without paying attention to the integrality constraints. This assumes that either fractional solutions are meaningful or else (for the purpose of implementation) they will be rounded to integers. In Chapter 14, we will take a careful look at this assumption and at types of problems where such a simplification is not justified and hence where integrality constraints simply cannot be ignored.

Example 2

A plant can manufacture five different products (A, B, C, D, E) in any combination. Each product requires time on each of three machines as shown in Figure 4.3.

Figure 4.3 *Machine time (minutes per pound of product)*

| | Machine | | |
Product	1	2	3
A	12	8	5
B	7	9	10
C	8	4	7
D	10	0	3
E	7	11	2

Each machine is available 128 hours per week. Products A, B, C, D, and E are purely competitive, and any amounts made may be sold at respective per-pound prices of $5, $4, $5, $4, and $4. Variable labor costs are $4 per hour for machines 1 and 2, and $3 per hour for machine 3. Material costs for each pound of products A and C are $2. The material costs are $1 for each pound of products B, D, and E. You wish to maximize profit to the firm. Formulate this problem as a constrained optimization model, using as few variables as possible.

Solution to Example 2

DIAGRAM

Figure 4.4

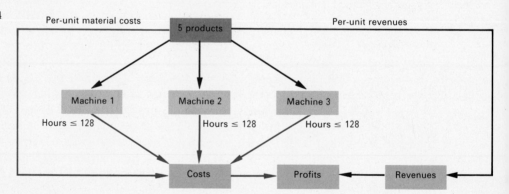

VERBAL MODEL

Maximize   Profit = revenue − cost

subject to

Hours used on machine 1 ≤ 128   (1)

Hours used on machine 2 ≤ 128   (2)

Hours used on machine 3 ≤ 128   (3)

DECISION VARIABLES

A = pounds of product A produced per week

B = pounds of product B produced per week

C = pounds of product C produced per week

D = pounds of product D produced per week

E = pounds of product E produced per week

THE MODEL

First, in order to cost machine usage, we must determine the time used on each machine.

$$\text{Total hours used on machine 1} = \frac{12A + 7B + 8C + 10D + 7E}{60}$$

$$\text{Total hours used on machine 2} = \frac{8A + 9B + 4C + 11E}{60}$$

$$\text{Total hours used on machine 3} = \frac{5A + 10B + 7C + 3D + 2E}{60}$$

We divide by 60 to convert minutes used on each machine into hours. We do this because the processing times were given in minutes but the cost parameters are in dollars per hour. Hence, the model is

$$\text{Max} \quad 3(A + B + C + D + E) - 4\left(\frac{12A + 7B + 8C + 10D + 7E}{60}\right)$$
$$- 4\left(\frac{8A + 9B + 4C + 11E}{60}\right)$$
$$- 3\left(\frac{5A + 10B + 7C + 3D + 2E}{60}\right)$$

s.t.

Capacity on machine 1
$$\frac{12A + 7B + 8C + 10D + 7E}{60} \leq 128$$

Capacity on machine 2
$$\frac{8A + 9B + 4C + 11E}{60} \leq 128$$

Capacity on machine 3
$$\frac{5A + 10B + 7C + 3D + 2E}{60} \leq 128$$

$$A, B, C, D, E \geq 0$$

The objective function in this example could be simplified by collecting terms. However, this translation into a more finished form is purely mechanical algebra.

Our object was just to obtain a logically correct formulation and so it suffices to leave the model in this raw form. We should point out, however, that the formulation of this problem is parsimonious in the sense that we employ the fewest possible number of variables. For an equivalent but less parsimonious approach, see problem 14 in this chapter.

Example 3

A firm operates four farms of comparable productivity. Each farm has a certain amount of usable acreage and a supply of manpower to plant and tend the crops. The data for the upcoming season are shown in Figure 4.5.

Figure 4.5   *Acreage and labor data by farm*

Farm	Usable Acreage	Manhours Available per Month
1	500	1,700
2	900	3,000
3	300	900
4	700	2,200

The organization is considering three crops for planting. These crops differ primarily in their expected profit per acre and in the amount of manpower they require, as shown in Figure 4.6. Furthermore, the total acreage that can be devoted to any particular crop is limited by the associated requirements for harvesting equipment.

Figure 4.6   *Acreage, labor, and profit data by crop*

Crop	Maximum Acreage	Monthly Manhours Required per Acre	Expected Profit per Acre
A	700	2	$500
B	800	4	$200
C	300	3	$300

In order to maintain a roughly uniform workload among the farms, management's policy is that the percentage of usable acreage planted must be the same at each farm. However, any combination of the crops may be grown at any of the farms as long as all constraints are satisfied (including the uniform workload requirement). Management wishes to know how many acres of each crop should be planted at the respective farms in order to maximize expected profit. Formulate this as a constrained optimization model.

Solution to Example 3

DIAGRAM

Figure 4.7

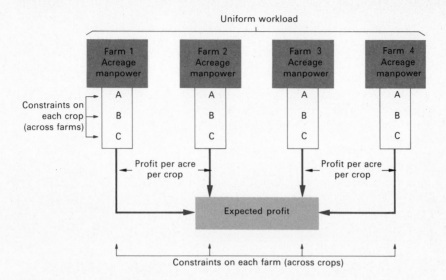

VERBAL MODEL

Maximize   Expected profit

subject to

Acres of crops planted on farm 1	$\leq$ 500	(1)
Acres of crops planted on farm 2	$\leq$ 900	(2)
Acres of crops planted on farm 3	$\leq$ 300	(3)
Acres of crops planted on farm 4	$\leq$ 700	(4)
Manhours per month required on farm 1	$\leq$ 1,700	(5)
Manhours per month required on farm 2	$\leq$ 3,000	(6)
Manhours per month required on farm 3	$\leq$ 900	(7)
Manhours per month required on farm 4	$\leq$ 2,200	(8)
Acres planted with crop A	$\leq$ 700	(9)
Acres planted with crop B	$\leq$ 800	(10)
Acres planted with crop C	$\leq$ 300	(11)

$$\frac{\text{Acres planted on farm 1}}{500} - \frac{\text{acres planted on farm 2}}{900} = 0 \qquad (12)$$

$$\frac{\text{Acres planted on farm 1}}{500} - \frac{\text{acres planted on farm 3}}{300} = 0 \qquad (13)$$

$$\frac{\text{Acres planted on farm 1}}{500} - \frac{\text{acres planted on farm 4}}{700} = 0 \tag{14}$$

DECISION VARIABLES

A_i = acres devoted to crop A at farm i $i = 1, 2, 3, 4$

B_i = acres devoted to crop B at farm i $i = 1, 2, 3, 4$

C_i = acres devoted to crop C at farm i $i = 1, 2, 3, 4$

THE MODEL

$$\text{Max} \quad 500 \sum_{i=1}^{4} A_i + 200 \sum_{i=1}^{4} B_i + 300 \sum_{i=1}^{4} C_i$$

s.t.

$$A_1 + B_1 + C_1 \qquad\qquad \leq \quad 500 \tag{1}$$

$$A_2 + B_2 + C_2 \qquad\qquad \leq \quad 900 \tag{2}$$

$$A_3 + B_3 + C_3 \qquad\qquad \leq \quad 300 \tag{3}$$

$$A_4 + B_4 + C_4 \qquad\qquad \leq \quad 700 \tag{4}$$

$$2A_1 + 4B_1 + 3C_1 \qquad \leq \quad 1{,}700 \tag{5}$$

$$2A_2 + 4B_2 + 3C_2 \qquad \leq \quad 3{,}000 \tag{6}$$

$$2A_3 + 4B_3 + 3C_3 \qquad \leq \quad 900 \tag{7}$$

$$2A_4 + 4B_4 + 3C_4 \qquad \leq \quad 2{,}200 \tag{8}$$

$$\sum_{i=1}^{4} A_i \qquad\qquad\qquad \leq \quad 700 \tag{9}$$

$$\sum_{i=1}^{4} B_i \qquad\qquad\qquad \leq \quad 800 \tag{10}$$

$$\sum_{i=1}^{4} C_i \qquad\qquad\qquad \leq \quad 300 \tag{11}$$

$$\frac{A_1 + B_1 + C_1}{500} - \frac{A_2 + B_2 + C_2}{900} = 0 \tag{12}$$

$$\frac{A_1 + B_1 + C_1}{500} - \frac{A_3 + B_3 + C_3}{300} = 0 \tag{13}$$

$$\frac{A_1 + B_1 + C_1}{500} - \frac{A_4 + B_4 + C_4}{700} = 0 \tag{14}$$

$$\text{All variables} \geq 0$$

Note that constraints (1), (12), (13), and (14) taken together imply that constraints (2), (3), and (4) must be satisfied. For this reason, constraints (2), (3), and (4) are termed *redundant*, and they could just as well be omitted from this particular model. Such redundant constraints are not usually easy to identify, and there is no harm in including them in the model.

4.3 A Blending Example

In this type of problem, it is necessary to mix or blend a collection of raw materials into a finished product, such as cereal grains into dog food, phosphates into fertilizer, or several metals into a high-strength alloy. The objective is to minimize the cost of the finished product subject to minimum requirement constraints (for example, percent protein in the blend $\geq$ 15). These problems usually have a constraint stating that the sum of the parts equals the whole. In other words, the proportions of all components must add up to 1. Care must often be exercised in keeping the units consistent throughout the problem. That is, variables may be either percentages or quantities, and the constraints and the objective must be formulated accordingly. Moreover, if the variables are in quantities, the quantity units must be consistent within all the constraints and the objective. For example, if the variable x is in units of pounds in the objective function, it must also be in units of pounds in every constraint in which it appears.

Example 4

The iron ore from four different locations is blended to make crawler tractor treads. Analysis has shown that there are minimum requirements on three basic elements in order to produce a suitable blend. The ore from each location possesses each of these three elements in different amounts and has a different cost for PROTRAC.

Figure 4.8 gives the number of pounds of each basic element per ton of ore from each location, the minimum requirements of each element per ton of final blend, and the cost per ton of ore from each location. Assume that the quantities of the basic elements are additive; that is, if one ton of ore from location 1 includes 10 pounds of element A and one ton of ore from location 2 includes 3 pounds of element A, then an equal parts blend of these two ores would have 13 pounds of element A for each two tons of blend, or 6.5 pounds per ton. PROTRAC wants to know what blend will satisfy the constraints at minimum cost.

Present a constrained optimization model that will answer this question.

Figure 4.8   *Data for ore-blending example*

Basic Elements	Locations				Minimum Requirements per Ton
	1	2	3	4	
A	10	3	8	2	5
B	90	150	75	175	100
C	45	25	20	37	30
Cost per Ton	$800	$400	$600	$500	

Solution to Example 4

DIAGRAM

Figure 4.9

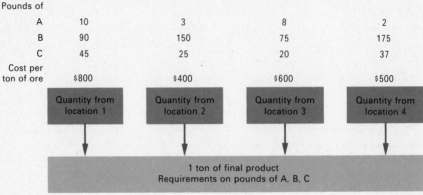

Pounds of				
A	10	3	8	2
B	90	150	75	175
C	45	25	20	37
Cost per ton of ore	$800	$400	$600	$500

Quantity from location 1   Quantity from location 2   Quantity from location 3   Quantity from location 4

1 ton of final product
Requirements on pounds of A, B, C

5, 100, 30

VERBAL MODEL

Minimize   Cost per ton of final blend

subject to

Pounds of A	$\geq$	5	(1)
Pounds of B	$\geq$	100	(2)
Pounds of C	$\geq$	30	(3)
Total tons of ore from all locations per ton of final blend	$=$	1	(4)

DECISION VARIABLES

T_i = the fraction of a ton of ore from location i in one ton of the final blend

THE MODEL

Min $800T_1 + 400T_2 + 600T_3 + 500T_4$

s.t.

$$10T_1 + \ \ 3T_2 + 8T_3 + \ \ 2T_4 \geq \ \ 5 \qquad (1)$$
$$90T_1 + 150T_2 + 75T_3 + 175T_4 \geq 100 \qquad (2)$$
$$45T_1 + \ 25T_2 + 20T_3 + \ 37T_4 \geq \ 30 \qquad (3)$$
$$\ \ T_1 + \ \ \ T_2 + \ \ T_3 + \ \ \ \ T_4 = \ \ 1 \qquad (4)$$
$$T_i \geq \ \ 0 \qquad i = 1, 2, 3, 4$$

4.4 Multiperiod Inventory Examples

This important class of models applies to inventories of materials, cash, and employees carried from one period to the next. Multiperiod models are sometimes referred to as *dynamic* problems. They reflect the fact that the decisions made this period affect not only this period's returns (or costs) but the allowable decisions and returns in future periods as well. For this reason, multiperiod problems cannot be treated as if they were merely a collection of single-period problems. The topic of inventory management is considered in some detail in Chapters 13 and 20.

Example 5

This is a classical, so-called deterministic, single-product inventory problem. It is called *deterministic* because we assume that the demand (that is, the number of orders to be satisfied) in each future period is known at the beginning of period 1. For example, a producer of polyurethane has a stock of orders for the next six weeks. Let d_i be a parameter that denotes this known demand (say, in terms of number of gallons that must be delivered to customers during week i), and assume $d_i > 0$ for all i. Let C_i denote the cost of producing a gallon during week i, and let K_i denote the maximum amount that can be produced (because of capacity limitations) in week i. Finally, let h_i denote the per-unit cost of inventory in stock at the end of week i. (Thus, the inventory is measured as the number of gallons carried from week i into week $i + 1$.) Suppose the initial inventory (at the beginning of period 1 and for which no carrying charge is assessed) is known to be I_0 gallons. Find a production and inventory-holding plan that satisfies the known delivery schedule over the next six weeks at minimum total cost.

Before formulating the constrained optimization model, it will be useful to develop an expression for the inventory on hand at the end of each period. Since there is an inventory carrying charge, this quantity will clearly play a role in the objective function.

Let I_i be the inventory on hand at the end of week i. Define the decision variable x_i to be the gallons of polyurethane produced in week i. We note that

$$I_1 = I_0 + x_1 - d_1$$

That is, the inventory on hand at the end of week 1 is equal to the inventory on hand at the end of week 0 (the beginning of week 1) plus the production in week 1 minus the deliveries in week 1. (We are assuming that all demand must be satisfied. Hence, the known demand in week i, d_i, is by definition the amount delivered in week i.)

Similarly,

$$I_2 = I_1 + x_2 - d_2$$

and, in general, the same reasoning yields, for any period t,

$$I_t = I_{t-1} + x_t - d_t$$

This important inventory equation says that

Inventory at end of t = inventory at beginning of t + production in t − demand in t

Note that if we substitute the known expression for I_1 into the equation for I_2, we obtain

$$I_2 = \underbrace{I_0 + x_1 - d_1}_{I_1} + x_2 - d_2 = I_0 + \sum_{i=1}^{2} x_i - \sum_{i=1}^{2} d_i$$

We could then substitute the above expression for I_2 into the equation for I_3 to obtain

$$I_3 = I_0 + \sum_{i=1}^{3} x_i - \sum_{i=1}^{3} d_i$$

Repeating this procedure leads to an equivalent inventory equation

$$I_t = I_0 + \sum_{i=1}^{t} (x_i - d_i)$$

for any period t.

Note that this last expression relates the inventory at the end of period t to all previous production (the x values). The equation simply says that the inventory at the end of period t is equal to the initial inventory, plus the total production through period t, minus the total deliveries through period t. The variable I_t is sometimes referred to as a *definitional variable* because it is defined in terms of other decision variables (the x_is) in the problem. The use of definitional variables sometimes makes it easier to see the proper formulation. Before writing the verbal model for this problem, we must figure out a way of saying that production in each period must be *at least* great enough so that demand (that is, the delivery schedule) can be satisfied. In period 1 this means $I_0 + x_1 \geq d_1$, or $I_0 + x_1 - d_1 \geq 0$. Since $I_0 + x_1 - d_1$ is the same as I_1, this is the same as saying that the inventory at the end of period 1 is nonnegative. Satisfying period 2 demand means that inventory at the beginning of period 2 (the end of period 1) plus period 2 production $\geq d_2$. That is,

$$I_1 + x_2 \geq d_2 \quad \text{or} \quad I_1 + x_2 - d_2 \geq 0$$

which is the same as saying that the inventory at the end of period 2 is nonnegative. It should now be possible to see the pattern. The condition that demand in period t must be satisfied is equivalent to the condition that inventory I_t at the end of period t must be nonnegative.

Solution to Example 5

DIAGRAM

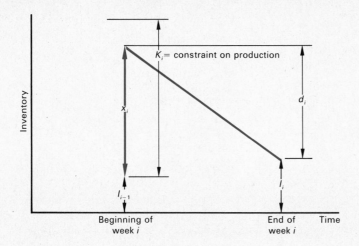

VERBAL MODEL

Minimize   Production cost + inventory cost

subject to

Inventory at the end of week t	≥ 0	$t = 1, 2, ..., 6$	(1)
Production in week t	$\leq K_t$	$t = 1, 2, ..., 6$	(2)

DECISION VARIABLES

x_t = production in week t

THE MODEL

$$\text{Min} \quad \sum_{t=1}^{6} C_t x_t + \sum_{t=1}^{6} h_t I_t$$

s.t.

$$I_t = I_{t-1} + x_t - d_t \quad t = 1, 2, ..., 6 \tag{1}$$

$$\left.\begin{array}{l} x_t \leq K_t \\ x_t \geq 0 \\ I_t \geq 0 \end{array}\right\} \qquad t = 1, 2, ..., 6 \tag{2}$$

In general, the structure of such models is fairly complex. That is, interactions are occurring between large numbers of variables. For example, inventory at the end of a given period t is determined by all production decisions in periods 1 through t. This is seen from the inventory equation

$$I_t = I_0 + \sum_{i=1}^{t} (x_i - d_i)$$

Therefore, the cost in period t is also determined by all production decisions in periods 1 through t. In models such as this, simplified versions can often provide considerable insight into the interactions. This will be illustrated in problem 21 of this chapter. Finally, it is noted that the above formulation can be written in an equivalent form without the I_t variables appearing. Try to do this on your own.

Example 6

In a calculated financial maneuver, PROTRAC has acquired a new blast furnace facility for producing foundry iron. The management science group at PROTRAC has been assigned the task of providing support for the quantitative planning of foundry activities. The first directive is to provide an answer to the following question: How many new slag-pit personnel should be hired and trained over the next six months?

The requirements for trained employees in the pits are 8,000 manhours in January; 9,000 in February; 7,000 in March; 10,000 in April; 9,000 in May; and 11,000 in June. Trainees are hired at the beginning of each month. One consideration we wish to take into account is the union rule that it takes one month of classroom instruction before a man can be considered well enough trained to work in the pits. Therefore, it is mandatory that a trainee be hired at least a month before he is actually needed. Each classroom student uses 100 hours of the time of a trained slag-pit employee, so that 100 less hours of his time are available for work in the pit. We are also informed that, by contractual agreement, each trained employee can work up to 150 hours a month (total time, instructing plus in the pit). If the maximum total time available from trained employees exceeds a month's requirements, each man works fewer than 150 hours, and none are laid off. From historical data, we have learned that by the end of each month approximately 10 percent of the trained men at the beginning of the month have quit their jobs. A trained employee costs the company $800 a month (that is, he is paid for a full 150 hours per month, whether or not he actually works the full amount) and a trainee costs $400 a month in salary and other benefits. There are 60 trained employees available at the beginning of January. Formulate the hiring-and-training problem as a constrained optimization model.

Solution to Example 6

VERBAL MODEL

Minimize   Total salaries paid

subject to

Hours available from trained employees for work in each month $\geq$ number required in each month (1)–(6)

DIAGRAM

Figure 4.11

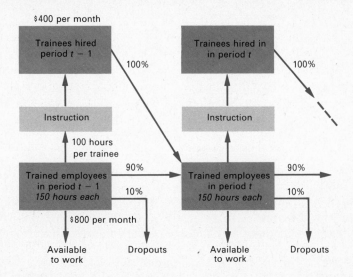

$400 per month

Trainees hired period $t-1$

100%

Trainees hired in in period t

100%

Instruction

Instruction

100 hours per trainee

Trained employees in period $t-1$ *150 hours each*

90%

10%

Trained employees in period t *150 hours each*

90%

10%

$800 per month

Available to work

Dropouts

Available to work

Dropouts

DECISION VARIABLES

y_t = number of trainees hired in period t

It is also convenient to have a definitional variable,

x_t = number of trained employees on hand at the beginning of month t

By definition, this also equals the number of trained employees on hand at the end of month $t-1$.

Relating these definitional variables x_t to the decision variables y_t will require six constraints, which we label (7)–(12).

THE MODEL

$$\text{Min} \sum_{t=1}^{6} (800x_t + 400y_t)$$

s.t.

$$150x_1 - 100y_1 \geq 8{,}000 \tag{1}$$

$$150x_2 - 100y_2 \geq 9{,}000 \tag{2}$$

$$150x_3 - 100y_3 \geq 7{,}000 \tag{3}$$

$$150x_4 - 100y_4 \geq 10{,}000 \tag{4}$$

$$150x_5 - 100y_5 \geq 9{,}000 \tag{5}$$

$$150x_6 - 100y_6 \geq 11{,}000 \tag{6}$$

$$x_1 = 60 \tag{7}$$

$$x_t = x_{t-1} + y_{t-1} - .1x_{t-1} \qquad t = 2, ..., 6 \tag{8-12}$$

$$x_t, y_t \geq 0 \qquad\qquad\qquad\qquad t = 1, ..., 6$$

Example 7

Suppose we add to the above problem new contract provisions proposed by the union:

1   In each month, all trained employees should work the same number of hours. This number can differ from month to month but, as before, cannot exceed 150 hours.
2   Each trained employee should be paid only for the hours he works instead of for 150 hours.
3   The hourly rate for trained employees will be r dollars (where r is a fixed number given by the union).
4   As before, the per-unit cost per month for each trainee is $400.

Assuming the same dropout rate as before, management wants to know whether to accept this new contract or whether it would be preferable to renew the previous contract. How can such a determination be made? Suppose management would be willing to accept the proposed new contract if it were possible to negotiate the value of r. How might a *maximum* acceptable value of r be determined?

Solution to Example 7

Reformulate the model of Example 6 so that employees receive pay only for hours worked subject to constraints that the hours actually worked by trained employees do not exceed the maximum available amount in any given month. Thus

Hours actually worked by trained employees in period $1 = 8,000 + 100y_1$

and so on.

Maximum hours available in period $1 = 150x_1$

and so on. The total cost becomes

$$(8,000 + 100y_1)r + (9,000 + 100y_2)r + (7,000 + 100y_3)r + (10,000 + 100y_4)r$$

$$+ (9,000 + 100y_5)r + (11,000 + 100y_6)r + \sum_{t=1}^{6} 400y_t$$

$$= 54,000r + \sum_{t=1}^{6} (400 + 100r)y_t$$

THE MODEL

$$\text{Min} \sum_{t=1}^{6} (400 + 100r)y_t + 54,000r$$

s.t.

$$150x_1 - 100y_1 \geq 8,000 \qquad (1)$$
$$150x_2 - 100y_2 \geq 9,000 \qquad (2)$$
$$150x_3 - 100y_3 \geq 7,000 \qquad (3)$$
$$150x_4 - 100y_4 \geq 10,000 \qquad (4)$$
$$150x_5 - 100y_5 \geq 9,000 \qquad (5)$$
$$150x_6 - 100y_6 \geq 11,000 \qquad (6)$$
$$x_1 = 60 \qquad (7)$$
$$x_t = x_{t-1} + y_{t-1} - .1x_{t-1} \qquad t = 2, ..., 6 \qquad (8)-(12)$$
$$x_t, y_t \geq 0 \qquad t = 1, ..., 6$$

If the optimal objective value for the reformulated problem is less than the original optimal objective value (in Example 6) then management should accept the new contract.

A *maximum* acceptable value of r is determined by solving the foregoing model, treating r as a nonnegative *variable* rather than a parameter, and adding the constraint

$$\sum_{t=1}^{6} (400 + 100r)y_t + 54,000r \geq V$$

where the number V is the optimal value of the objective function in the model formulated in Example 6. Note that the $\geq$ symbol in this last constraint can just as well be replaced with $=$. However, students often feel that the inequality should be $\leq$. Can you see that this would make the optimal value of r equal to zero, and this is certainly not the *maximum* acceptable value!

It is noteworthy that the above reformulation, treating r as a variable, has a nonlinear objective function because of the term ry_t. Similarly, the new constraint is nonlinear. In other words, the reformulation produces a nonlinear programming (NLP) model. All the previous examples have been linear programs (or LP problems), which means that all functions in the models (objectives and constraints) have been linear.

4.5 Capital-Budgeting Problems

Deciding how to allocate funds to alternative projects that require capital is a major management decision in most firms. One aspect of this process is assigning funds in order to maximize the total present value of the investment while not exceeding a limit on the total amount of investment. The next four examples provide a mathematical programming approach to increasingly more realistic problems in the area of capital budgeting.

Example 8

This example considers a simple, one-period problem. Suppose there are N projects 1, 2, 3, ..., N, and that each project may be undertaken in any fractional amount between zero and one. Let R_i be the present value of the return if project i is selected at a 100-percent level of investment, and assume that the returns on each project are directly proportional to the level of investment. Thus, if project i is undertaken at the 50-percent level, then the present value of the return will be $.5R_i$, and so on. Also let C_i be the cost of selecting project i at the 100-percent level, and let the costs be proportional to the levels, just as for returns. Finally, let C be the limit on the total investment in projects 1, 2, ..., N. Formulate the problem of maximizing total present value as a linear program.

Solution to Example 8

DIAGRAM

Figure 4.12

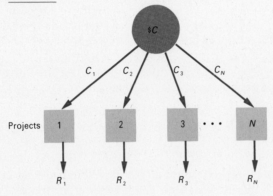

VERBAL MODEL

Maximize   Total present value

subject to

Total capital investment $\le C$

DECISION VARIABLES

x_i = the fraction of project i selected

THE MODEL

Max $\displaystyle\sum_{i=1}^{N} R_i x_i$

s.t.

$\displaystyle\sum_{i=1}^{N} C_i x_i \le C$

$\qquad x_i \le 1 \qquad i = 1, ..., N$

$\qquad x_i \ge 0$

This model deserves several comments. First, it is clear that in many cases fractional values of x_i are meaningless. The decision maker may be constrained either to accept project i completely ($x_i = 1$) or to reject it ($x_i = 0$). It may simply be unrealistic or impossible to accept half the project ($x_i = 1/2$). For example, assume that project i is building a bridge. Introducing constraints that x_i must equal either zero or one (*instead* of $x_i \leq 1$, $x_i \geq 0$) makes this an integer programming problem (Chapter 14).

In particular, the foregoing problem, with the added constraints that each x_i must be either zero or one, is called a ***knapsack model,*** or a ***knapsack problem***[1] (also discussed in Chapter 14). Although the slight difference in formulation (that is, requiring x_i to be either zero or one) may appear to be little more than cosmetic, the mathematical implications turn out to be very significant, and it is generally true that integer programming problems are much more difficult to solve than ordinary linear programs. Incidentally, in *Mathematical Programming and the Analysis of Capital Budgeting Problems,* Martin Weingartner argues that there are advantages to the linear programming (LP) formulation (that is, without requiring x_i to be either zero or one) of more complicated and realistic versions of the foregoing problem. Such arguments lie outside our immediate sphere of interest, but if you have a special interest in financial models, you may want to pursue these topics in more detail.

As a final comment, we note that if the integer constraints are ignored so as to make the problem continuous, there is a simple algorithm to solve the foregoing problem. To find the optimal solution, you first calculate the return per dollar of investment for each project (that is, compute each ratio R_i/C_i). The projects are ranked according to the decreasing order of these ratios. Then the highest-ranked project is undertaken at the 100-percent level, if its cost does not exceed the budget constraint; similarly for the next ranked project, and so on. Eventually, a project is encountered for which a 100-percent undertaking would violate the budget constraint. (Otherwise, all projects can be selected at the 100-percent level and the problem is uninteresting.) At this point, the last-contemplated project is undertaken at the fractional level that would bring total cost exactly up to the budget limit, and the algorithm terminates. All remaining projects are discarded because the limit on capital expenditures has been reached. This procedure for obtaining the *continuous solution* may not yield an optimal solution when the integer constraints are imposed. Can you create a simple example to illustrate this fact?

Example 9

Consider a multiperiod version (say T periods) of the problem presented in Example 8. In this case, each project yields a return in each period. In addition, each project also requires a capital expenditure in each period, and

---

1 Management scientists have created an enigmatic, if not amusing, taxonomy of phyla and genera. These so-called canonical problems include the knapsack problem, the traveling-salesman problem, the streetwalker's dilemma, the cutting-stock problem, the newsboy problem, the capacitated transportation problem, minimal spanning trees, and a host of others. A few of these will be mentioned at appropriate points in the text.

there is an upper limit on the total allowable capital expenditure in each period. Let r_{it} and c_{it} be the return and the capital investment, respectively, associated with maximal commitment ($x_i = 1$) to project i in period t, and assume that α is the interest rate, independent of time. Assume that the cash flows r_{it} (that is, the returns) occur at the *end* of period t and that the investments c_{it} occur at the *beginning* of period t. Finally, let C_t be the upper bound on capital investment in period t. For a given project, it is assumed that the fractional commitment in each period is the same (for instance, we cannot make a 50-percent commitment to project 1 in period 1 and a 25-percent commitment to project 1 in period 2). Formulate as a linear program the problem of maximizing the total present value of the returns.

Solution to Example 9

DIAGRAM

Figure 4.13

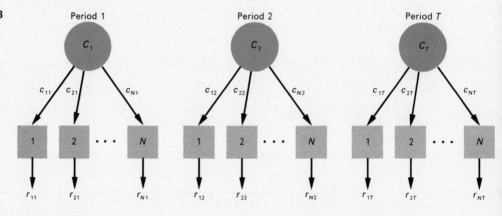

VERBAL MODEL

Maximize   Total present value

subject to

Capital expenditure in period $t \le C_t$ $t = 1, ..., T$

DECISION VARIABLES

x_i = fraction of project i selected

THE MODEL

Note that the objective is to maximize total present value. By definition, the present value of project i (if fully undertaken) is

$$\sum_{t=1}^{T} \frac{r_{it}}{(1 + \alpha)^t}$$

For notational convenience, let us introduce the variable R_i defined by

$$R_i = \sum_{t=1}^{T} \frac{r_{it}}{(1 + \alpha)^t}$$

Thus R_i is the present value of project i when fully undertaken. Then the model is

Max $\quad \sum_{i=1}^{N} R_i x_i$

s.t.

$$\sum_{i=1}^{N} c_{it} x_i \leq C_t \quad t = 1, 2, ..., T$$

$$x_i \leq 1 \quad i = 1, 2, ..., N$$

$$x_i \geq 0 \quad i = 1, 2, ..., N$$

We note that the concern about noninteger solutions continues to exist in this problem, and we may need to complicate the model further (depending on the application) by substituting the constraints $x_i = 0$ or $x_i = 1$ for the last $2N$ inequalities. We also note that the simple technique we used to find an optimal solution to the *continuous* version of the single-period problem in Example 8 does not work for this multiperiod problem. With T c_{it}s for each project and T constraints on capital expenditures, there is no straightforward analogue of the ratio-ranking technique suggested in Example 8.

Example 10

Consider the problem presented in Example 9 with the additional complication that there are contingency relationships among some of the projects. Let us assume we are considering models where the integrality conditions $x_i = 0$ or 1 must be imposed. Now, as an example of contingency relationships, let us assume that project 3 cannot be selected unless project 4 is also selected and that project 5 cannot be selected unless projects 6 and 7 are both selected.

Solution to Example 10

The only difference between the new model and the one in Example 9 is that constraints have to be added to insure that the contingency relationships are enforced. The first contingency requirement states that project 3 cannot be selected unless project 4 is also selected. If project 3 is selected, then $x_3 = 1$. Thus, to force project 4 to be selected whenever 3 is selected, we can use the inequality

$$x_3 \leq x_4$$

Similarly, the second contingency requirement can be enforced by adding the constraint

$$2x_5 \leq x_6 + x_7$$

● **Example 11**

Here is an excellent example of an LP financial model in which the integrality conditions need not be imposed. Winston-Salem Development Management (WSDM) is trying to complete its investment plans for the next three years. Currently, WSDM has $2 million available for investment. At six-month intervals over the next three years, WSDM expects the following income stream from previous investments: $500,000 (six months from now), $400,000; $380,000; $360,000; $340,000; and $300,000 (at end of third year).

There are three development projects in which WSDM is considering participating. The Foster City Development would, if WSDM participated fully, have the following projected cash-flow stream at six-month intervals over the next three years (negative numbers represent investments, positive numbers represent income): −$3,000,000 (beginning of period 1); −$1,000,000; −$1,800,000; $400,000; $1,800,000; $1,800,000; $5,500,000. The last figure is its estimated value at the end of three years.

A second project involves taking over the operation of some old lower-middle-income housing on the condition that certain initial repairs be made and that the housing be demolished at the end of three years. The cash-flow stream for this project, if participated in fully, would be: −$2,000,000 (beginning of period 1); −$500,000; $1,500,000; $1,500,000; $1,500,000; $200,000; −$1,000,000.

The third project, the Disney-Universe Hotel, would have the following cash-flow stream at six-month intervals if WSDM participated fully (again, the last figure is the estimated value at the end of the three years): −$2,000,000 (beginning of period 1); −$2,000,000; −$1,800,000; $1,000,000; $1,000,000; $1,000,000; $6,000,000. WSDM can borrow money for half-year intervals at 3.5-percent interest per half-year. At most, $2 million can be borrowed at one time; that is, the total outstanding principal can never exceed $2 million. WSDM can invest surplus funds at 3 percent per half-year. If WSDM participates in a project at less than 100 percent, all the cash flows of that project are reduced appropriately. Formulate as an LP model the problem of maximizing the net worth of these investments to WSDM after six periods.

Solution to Example 11

We have the following LP formulation of the problem of maximizing WSDM's net worth at the end of three years.

DECISION VARIABLES

F = fractional participation in the Foster City project

M = fractional participation in lower-middle-income housing

D = fractional participation in Disney-Universe Hotel

B_i = amount borrowed in period i, $i = 1, ..., 6$

L_i = amount lent in period i, $i = 1, ..., 6$

Z = net worth after the six periods

THE MODEL

With all numbers measured in units of 1,000, the model is

$$\text{Max} \quad Z \tag{1}$$

s.t.

$$-3{,}000F - 2{,}000M - 2{,}000D + B1 - L1 \qquad\qquad \geq -2{,}000 \tag{2}$$

$$-1{,}000F - 500M - 2{,}000D + B2 - L2 + 1.03L1 - 1.035\,B1 \quad \geq -500 \tag{3}$$

$$-1{,}800F + 1{,}500M - 1{,}800D + B3 - L3 + 1.03L2 - 1.035\,B2 \quad \geq -400 \tag{4}$$

$$400F + 1{,}500M + 1{,}000D + B4 - L4 + 1.03L3 - 1.035\,B3 \quad \geq -380 \tag{5}$$

$$1{,}800F + 1{,}500M + 1{,}000D + B5 - L5 + 1.03L4 - 1.035\,B4 \quad \geq -360 \tag{6}$$

$$1{,}800F + 200M + 1{,}000D + B6 - L6 + 1.03L5 - 1.035\,B5 \quad \geq -340 \tag{7}$$

$$5{,}500F - 1{,}000M + 6{,}000D + 1.03L6 - 1.035\,B6 - Z \geq -300 \tag{8}$$

$$B1, B2, B3, B4, B5, B6 \leq 2{,}000 \tag{9)--(14}$$

$$F, M, D \leq 1 \tag{15)--(17}$$

$$\text{All decision variables} \geq 0 \tag{18}$$

Note that in this example the objective function has been given the label (1). The constraints (2) through (7) state that the amount of money spent must not exceed the amount on hand at the beginning of periods (1) through (6) respectively. The constraint labeled (8) is used to define Z, the net worth at the end of period 6 (year 3). The remaining constraints are self-explanatory.

4.6 A Media-Planning Example

Example 12

A radio network wants to establish revenue-maximizing prices for advertising time. This example presents a simplified version of its pricing problem. Assume that there are three classifications of network advertising time: prime-evening, weekday, and Saturday/Sunday afternoon (before 6 P.M.). Let P_1, P_2, and P_3 be the respective prices per minute for each of these time-slots.

The network sells large blocks of time to K major advertisers, who have a significant effect on the determination of prices. The network knows that major advertiser k wants to purchase a package consisting of a_{1k}, a_{2k}, and a_{3k} minutes in the three time-slots and is willing to pay up to A_k dollars for this package. Each term a_{ik} is assumed to be a function of price, as follows:

$$a_{ik} = \frac{c_{ik}}{(P_i + d_{ik})}$$

where c_{ik} and d_{ik} are specified parameters. Finally, H_i is the total number of hours that can be sold in time-slot i. Formulate the network's problem as a constrained optimization model.

Solution to Example 12

DIAGRAM

Figure 4.14

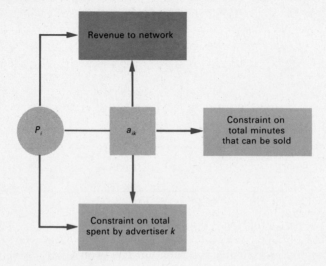

VERBAL PROBLEM

Maximize   Total revenue

subject to

Total spent by advertiser k $\leq A_k$ $k = 1, ..., K$

Total minutes sold in time slot i $\leq 60H_i$ $i = 1, 2, 3$

DECISION VARIABLES

P_i = price per minute in time slot i

THE MODEL

$$\text{Max } P_1 \sum_{k=1}^{K} \frac{c_{1k}}{(P_1 + d_{1k})} + P_2 \sum_{k=1}^{K} \frac{c_{2k}}{(P_2 + d_{2k})} + P_3 \sum_{k=1}^{K} \frac{c_{3k}}{(P_3 + d_{3k})}$$

s.t.

$$\sum_{i=1}^{3} P_i \frac{c_{ik}}{(P_i + d_{ik})} \leq A_k \qquad k = 1, ..., K$$

$$\sum_{k=1}^{K} \frac{c_{ik}}{(P_i + d_{ik})} \leq 60H_i \qquad i = 1, 2, 3$$

$$P_i \geq 0 \qquad i = 1, 2, 3$$

Note that this is a nonlinear programming model. The objective function and all constraints are nonlinear.

4.7 Additional Examples and Solutions

The rationale for the previous examples was to teach you model formulation by enabling you to read the example and then immediately read a detailed discussion of the solution. By now, you should have acquired enough facility to operate more effectively on your own. In this section, then, examples are presented for you to solve, both to check your progress and to further develop your formulation skills. We also provide the solutions to the examples in this section, but with minimal discussion. We strongly recommend that you devote considerable effort to deriving the model on your own before looking at the solution. Agreeing that a model proposed by someone else is correct and creating the model yourself are quite different processes.

Example 1: Diablo-Red Baron

McNaughton Inc. produces two steak sauces, spicy Diablo and mild Red Baron. These sauces are both made by blending two ingredients, A and B. A certain level of flexibility is permitted in the formulas for these products. Indeed, the restrictions are that (1) Red Baron must contain no more than 75 percent of A and (2) Diablo must contain no less than 25 percent of A and no less than 50 percent of B. Up to 40 quarts of A and 30 quarts of B could be purchased. McNaughton can sell as much of these sauces as it produces at a price per quart of $3.35 for Diablo and $2.85 for Red Baron. A and B cost $1.60 and $2.05 per quart, respectively. McNaughton wishes to maximize its net revenue from the sale of these sauces. Formulate their problem as an LP problem.

Solution to Diablo-Red Baron Example

D = quarts of Diablo to be produced

R = quarts of Red Baron to be produced

A_1 = quarts of A used to make Diablo

A_2 = quarts of A used to make Red Baron

B_1 = quarts of B used to make Diablo

B_2 = quarts of B used to make Red Baron

Max $3.35D + 2.85R - 1.60(A_1 + A_2) - 2.05(B_1 + B_2)$

s.t.

$$A_1 + B_1 - D = 0$$
$$A_2 + B_2 - R = 0$$
$$A_1 + A_2 \leq 40$$
$$B_1 + B_2 \leq 30$$
$$A_1 - .25D \geq 0$$
$$B_1 - .50D \geq 0$$
$$A_2 - .75R \leq 0$$
$$A_1, A_2, B_1, B_2, D, R \geq 0$$

As an alternative but equivalent formulation, we can use the relationships

$D = A_1 + B_1$
$R = A_2 + B_2$

to eliminate the variables D and R from the objective function and to reduce the number of constraints. This yields

Max $1.75A_1 + 1.30B_1 + 1.25A_2 + .80B_2$
s.t.

$A_1 + A_2 \qquad \leq 40$
$B_1 + B_2 \qquad \leq 30$
$.75A_1 - .25B_1 \geq 0$
$.50B_1 - .50A_1 \geq 0$
$.25A_2 - .75B_2 \leq 0$
$A_1, B_1, A_2, B_2 \geq 0$

The next scenario gives an example of a so-called transportation model. The particular form of this problem is even more "special" than linear. For example, if your formulation is correct, you will note that all coefficients in the constraints are 1. Other examples of transportation models will appear later in the text. In fact, a transportation model is an example of an entire special class of linear programs called *network problems.* These are discussed in Chapter 14.

Example 2: Transportation Model

A company has two plants and three warehouses. The first plant can supply at most 100 units and the second at most 200 units. The sales potential at the first warehouse is 150, at the second warehouse 200, and at the third 350. The sales revenues per unit at the three warehouses are 12 at the first, 14 at the second, and 15 at the third. The cost of manufacturing one unit at plant i and shipping it to warehouse j is given in Figure 4.15.

Figure 4.15   *Manufacturing and shipping data*

	Warehouse		
Plant	1	2	3
1	8	10	12
2	7	9	11

The company wishes to determine how many units should be shipped from each plant to each warehouse so as to maximize profit. Formulate an LP model for this problem.

Solution to Transportation Model Example

x_{ij} = units sent from plant i to warehouse j

Max $\quad 4x_{11} + 5x_{21} + 4x_{12} + 5x_{22} + 3x_{13} + 4x_{23}$

s.t.

$$x_{11} + x_{12} + x_{13} \leq 100$$
$$x_{21} + x_{22} + x_{23} \leq 200$$
$$x_{11} + x_{21} \quad\quad \leq 150$$
$$x_{12} + x_{22} \quad\quad \leq 200$$
$$x_{13} + x_{23} \quad\quad \leq 350$$
$$\quad\quad\quad\quad 0 \quad \text{all } i, j$$

Example 3: Tape Recorders

A tape recorder company manufactures Models A, B, and C, which have profit contributions of 15, 40, and 60, respectively. The weekly minimum production requirements are 25 for Model A, 130 for Model B, and 55 for Model C. Each type of recorder requires a certain amount of time for the manufacturing of component parts, for assembling, and for packaging. Specifically, a *dozen* units of Model A require four hours for manufacturing, three hours for assembling, and one hour for packaging. The corresponding figures for a dozen units of Model B are 2.5, 4, and 2, and for a dozen units of Model C are 6, 9, and 4. During the forthcoming week, the company has available 130 hours of manufacturing, 170 hours of assembling, and 52 hours of packaging time. Formulate as an LP model the problem of scheduling production so as to maximize profit.

Solution to Tape Recorder Example

A = units of A produced per week

B = units of B produced per week

C = units of C produced per week

Max $\quad 15A + 40B + 60C$

s.t.

$$A \quad\quad\quad\quad\quad \geq \ 25$$
$$B \quad\quad\quad \geq 130$$
$$C \ \geq \ 55$$
$$4\frac{A}{12} + 2.5\frac{B}{12} + 6\frac{C}{12} \leq 130$$
$$3\frac{A}{12} + \ 4\frac{B}{12} + 9\frac{C}{12} \leq 170$$
$$1\frac{A}{12} + \ 2\frac{B}{12} + 4\frac{C}{12} \leq \ 52$$
$$A, B, C \geq \quad 0$$

Example 4: Fertilizer Mix

The University of Chicago is planning to put fertilizer on the grass in the quadrangle area early in the spring. The grass needs nitrogen, phosphorus, and potash in at least the amounts given in Figure 4.16. Three kinds of commercial fertilizer are available; analysis and price are given in Figure 4.17.

Figure 4.16   *Total grass requirements*

Mineral	Minimum Weight (lb)
Nitrogen	10
Phosphorus	7
Potash	5

Figure 4.17   *Fertilizer characteristics (per 1,000 lb)*

Fertilizer	Nitrogen Content (lb)	Phosphorous Content (lb)	Potash Content (lb)	Price ($)
I	25	10	5	10
II	10	5	10	8
III	5	10	5	7

The university can buy as much of each of these fertilizers as it wishes and mix them together before applying them to the grass. Formulate an LP model to determine how much of each fertilizer to buy to satisfy the requirements at minimum cost.

Solution to Fertilizer Mix Example

F_1 = pounds of fertilizer I to purchase

F_2 = pounds of fertilizer II to purchase

F_3 = pounds of fertilizer III to purchase

$$\text{Min} \quad \frac{10}{1,000} F_1 + \frac{8}{1,000} F_2 + \frac{7}{1,000} F_3$$

s.t.

$$25 \frac{F_1}{1,000} + 10 \frac{F_2}{1,000} + 5 \frac{F_3}{1,000} \geq 10$$

$$10 \frac{F_1}{1,000} + 5 \frac{F_2}{1,000} + 10 \frac{F_3}{1,000} \geq 7$$

$$5 \frac{F_1}{1,000} + 10 \frac{F_2}{1,000} + 5 \frac{F_3}{1,000} \geq 5$$

$$F_1, F_2, F_3 \geq 0$$

Example 5: Security Force

The security and traffic force at PROTRAC's Moline plant must satisfy the staffing requirements shown in Figure 4.18. Officers work eight-hour shifts starting at each of the four-hour intervals shown, that is, midnight, 4:00 A.M., 8:00 A.M., and so on. How many officers should report for work at the beginning of each time period in order to minimize the total number of officers required to satisfy the staffing requirements? Formulate this as an LP problem.

Figure 4.18 *Security staff data*

Time	Number of Officers Required
0:01– 4:00	5
4:01– 8:00	7
8:01–12:00	15
12:01–16:00	7
16:01–20:00	12
20:01–24:00	9

Solution to Security Force Example

The secret to solving this example is to choose the decision variables in an appropriate manner. Let

x_i = number of officers who start in shift i

Note that officers who start in one shift are also available to satisfy demand in the next shift. The stated goal is to minimize the number of officers required. The problem then becomes

Min $x_1 + x_2 + x_3 + x_4 + x_5 + x_6$

s.t.

$x_1 + x_2 \geq 7$

$x_2 + x_3 \geq 15$

$x_3 + x_4 \geq 7$

$x_4 + x_5 \geq 12$

$x_5 + x_6 \geq 9$

$x_6 + x_1 \geq 5$

$\qquad x_i \geq 0 \qquad i = 1, ..., 6$

● ## Example 6: Marketing at PROTRAC

This problem is instructive in a special sense. It shows how LP can be applied to a *piecewise linear,* as opposed to linear, objective function.

Figure 4.19

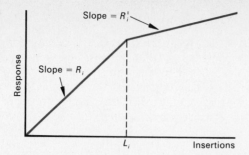

The marketing department at PROTRAC is deciding how to allocate an advertising budget among N different media. In particular, management wishes to determine how many times to use each medium. In marketing jargon, each use of a medium is called an *insertion*. For each medium, say i, there is an assumed response R_i for each insertion until a specified number of insertions, say L_i, is reached. After this, the response rate per insertion becomes R_i', where $R_i' < R_i$. The general shape of a typical response curve is shown in Figure 4.19. The objective of the advertising campaign is to maximize total response.

If C_i is the cost per insertion in medium i and the total advertising budget is B, create an LP model that determines the optimal number of insertions per medium (optimal in the sense of response maximizing) without violating the advertising budget.

Solution to Marketing Problem Example

x_i = number of insertions in medium i with a response of R_i

y_i = number of insertions in medium i with a response of R_i'

$$\text{Max} \quad \sum_{i=1}^{N} (R_i x_i + R_i' y_i)$$

s.t.

$$\sum_{i=1}^{N} C_i(x_i + y_i) \leq B$$

$$x_i \leq L_i \qquad i = 1, ..., N$$

$$x_i, y_i \geq 0$$

Try to convince yourself that the variable y_i will never be positive until x_i has hit its upper bound of L_i. This is because $R_i > R_i'$. A piecewise linear objective function with the above shape (decreasing slopes) is called *concave*. Had the curve been *convex* (that is, increasing slopes), then the foregoing formulation would not work. The general rule is this:

A piecewise linear objective function with decreasing marginal returns (a concave function) can be treated in a maximization LP context. A piecewise linear objective function with increasing marginal returns (a convex function) can be treated in a minimization LP context.

● Example 7: Paint Finishes

In ordering a product from PROTRAC, customers may choose among three finishes, hard, luster, and regular. These finishes are blended from four raw paints purchased by PROTRAC. Since each raw paint has different characteristics, there are constraints on the amounts of each that can be used in making a finish. The paint department at PROTRAC receives transfer price revenues for the various finishes it produces. Paint data are given in Figure 4.20, finish data in Figure 4.21.

Figure 4.20 *Paint data*

Raw Paint	Barrels Available	Cost per Barrel ($)
1	6,000	9
2	8,000	6
3	12,000	8
4	9,000	4

Figure 4.21 *Finish data*

Finish	Composition Constraints	Transfer Price Revenue per Barrel Produced ($)
Hard	Not more than 20% of 1 Not less than 30% of 2 Not less than 15% of 3	15
Luster	Not more than 50% of 4 Not less than 18% of 2 Not more than 25% of 3	12
Regular	Not more than 40% of 2 Not more than 30% of 1	13

Let the net revenue be the transfer price revenue minus the expense for the raw paints used. Create a linear program that determines the amount and blend of each finish that should be made from the supply of raw paints available in order for the paint department to maximize net revenue.

Solution to Paint Finish Example

Let b_{ij} be the number of barrels of raw paint i used in the total production of finish j. Note that $b_{1H} + b_{2H} + b_{3H} + b_{4H}$ is the total amount of hard finish (H) paint produced, whereas $b_{1H} + b_{1L} + b_{1R}$ is the total amount of raw paint 1 used, and $b_{1H}/(b_{1H} + b_{2H} + b_{3H} + b_{4H})$ is the proportion of raw paint 1 used in finish H.

These observations lead to the following LP model.

$$\text{Max}\quad 15(b_{1H} + b_{2H} + b_{3H} + b_{4H}) + 12(b_{1L} + b_{2L} + b_{3L} + b_{4L}) + 13(b_{1R} + b_{2R} + b_{3R} + b_{4R})$$
$$- 9(b_{1H} + b_{1L} + b_{1R}) - 6(b_{2H} + b_{2L} + b_{2R}) - 8(b_{3H} + b_{3L} + b_{3R}) - 4(b_{4H} + b_{4L} + b_{4R})$$

s.t.

These constraints insure using no more raw paint than is available

$$\begin{cases} b_{1H} + b_{1L} + b_{1R} \le 6{,}000 \\ b_{2H} + b_{2L} + b_{2R} \le 8{,}000 \\ b_{3H} + b_{3L} + b_{3R} \le 12{,}000 \\ b_{4H} + b_{4L} + b_{4R} \le 9{,}000 \end{cases}$$

These constraints insure that the blend for hard finish satisfies the percentage requirements

$$\begin{cases} \dfrac{b_{1H}}{b_{1H} + b_{2H} + b_{3H} + b_{4H}} \le .20 \\[2mm] \dfrac{b_{2H}}{b_{1H} + b_{2H} + b_{3H} + b_{4H}} \ge .30 \\[2mm] \dfrac{b_{3H}}{b_{1H} + b_{2H} + b_{3H} + b_{4H}} \ge .15 \end{cases}$$

These constraints insure that the blend for luster finish satisfies the percentage requirements

$$\begin{cases} \dfrac{b_{4L}}{b_{1L} + b_{2L} + b_{3L} + b_{4L}} \le .50 \\[2mm] \dfrac{b_{2L}}{b_{1L} + b_{2L} + b_{3L} + b_{4L}} \ge .18 \\[2mm] \dfrac{b_{3L}}{b_{1L} + b_{2L} + b_{3L} + b_{4L}} \le .25 \end{cases}$$

These constraints insure that the blend for regular finish satisfies the percentage requirements

$$\begin{cases} \dfrac{b_{2R}}{b_{1R} + b_{2R} + b_{3R} + b_{4R}} \le .40 \\[2mm] \dfrac{b_{1R}}{b_{1R} + b_{2R} + b_{3R} + b_{4R}} \le .30 \end{cases}$$

$$\text{All } b_{ij} \ge 0$$

The problem is now formulated. Note that the constraints appear to be nonlinear. However, by using simple arithmetic we obtain the following linear format. Note that terms in the objective function have also been collected.

$$\text{Max}\quad 6b_{1H} + 9b_{2H} + 7b_{3H} + 11b_{4H} + 3b_{1L} + 6b_{2L} + 4b_{3L} + 8b_{4L} + 4b_{1R} + 7b_{2R}$$
$$+ 5b_{3R} + 9b_{4R}$$

s.t.

$$b_{1H} + b_{1L} + b_{1R} \le 6{,}000$$
$$b_{2H} + b_{2L} + b_{2R} \le 8{,}000$$
$$b_{3H} + b_{3L} + b_{3R} \le 12{,}000$$
$$b_{4H} + b_{4L} + b_{4R} \le 9{,}000$$
$$.8b_{1H} - .2b_{2H} - .2b_{3H} - .2b_{4H} \le 0$$
$$-.3b_{1H} + .7b_{2H} - .3b_{3H} - .3b_{4H} \ge 0$$

$$-.15b_{1H} - .15b_{2H} + .85b_{3H} - .15b_{4H} \geq 0$$

$$-.5b_{1L} - .5b_{2L} - .5b_{3L} + .5b_{4L} \leq 0$$

$$-.18b_{1L} + .82b_{2L} - .18b_{3L} - .18b_{4L} \geq 0$$

$$-.25b_{1L} - .25b_{2L} + .75b_{3L} - .25b_{4L} \leq 0$$

$$-.4b_{1R} + .6b_{2R} - .4b_{3R} - .4b_{4R} \leq 0$$

$$.7b_{1R} - .3b_{2R} - .3b_{3R} - .3b_{4R} \leq 0$$

$$\text{All } b_{ij} \geq 0$$

● Example 8: Crankshafts at PROTRAC

Crankshafts for earth-moving equipment are produced in only three of PROTRAC's factories because of the high capital investment necessary to produce these parts economically. The crankshafts, however, are assembled into the engines in six different plant locations. The assembly schedule for the coming month is given in Figure 4.22.

Figure 4.22 *Assembly schedule*

Assembly Plant	Number of Crankshafts Required
1	20
2	60
3	90
4	30
5	50
6	70
Total	320

Figure 4.23 gives the characteristics of the crankshaft department of each of the three producing factories. The overhead costs are independent of the quantity produced; however, if no production is scheduled in a particular plant for the month, the overhead cost falls to zero.

Figure 4.23 *Production data*

Factory	Monthly Production Capacity	Fixed (Overhead) Production Costs per Month ($)	Production Cost per Unit ($)
A	180	900	18
B	130	600	20
C	90	400	22

Figure 4.24 gives the per-unit transportation costs for crankshafts from each factory to each assembly plant.

Figure 4.24   *Transportation costs (in dollars)*

From Factory	To plant					
	1	2	3	4	5	6
A	1.50	1.75	2.00	2.25	2.50	2.75
B	2.60	2.40	2.10	1.90	2.90	3.20
C	1.45	1.25	1.95	2.15	1.60	1.80

The vice-president of production has currently scheduled 160 units of production for factory A, 120 units for factory B, and 40 units for factory C. The manager of factory C calculates his per-unit cost to be [400 + $22(40)] /40 = $32. He feels that this is uneconomical. If the vice-president would transfer 20 units from factory B to him, his per-unit cost would become [400 + $22(60)] /60 = $28.67, a decrease of $3.33. The increase in per-unit cost at plant B due to this transfer of 20 units would be $1, from $25 to $26. The net saving per unit from the transfer would be $3.33 − $1.00 = $2.33. Thus, for the 20 units transferred, a reduction of $46.40 would occur in the costs.

1   Define the appropriate variables and set the allocation problem up as a cost-minimizing LP problem.
2   Comment on the logic of the plant manager's argument.

Solution to the Crankshaft Example

At first glance, it may appear that this is not an LP problem because of the presence of fixed overhead costs. Since these overhead costs in a particular factory depend on the existence of any production in that factory, we must consider the possibility of satisfying the demands most economically by producing in just two or perhaps just one of the factories. We note, however, that monthly demand is 320 units and that no combination of less than three factories is able to satisfy demand. We, therefore, must assume that all three factories will be operating and attempt to find the best allocation of production among them.

Let

x_{ij} = number of crankshafts produced in factory i and sent to assembly plant j

$i = A, B, C$

$j = 1, 2, 3, 4, 5, 6$

The problem then is to minimize production and shipment costs while satisfying demand and not exceeding production capacities.

Min $(18 + 1.50) x_{A1} + (20 + 2.60) x_{B1} + (22 + 1.45) x_{C1}$

$+ (18 + 1.75) x_{A2} + (20 + 2.40) x_{B2} + (22 + 1.25) x_{C2}$

$+ (18 + 2.00) x_{A3} + (20 + 2.10) x_{B3} + (22 + 1.95) x_{C3}$

$+ (18 + 2.25) x_{A4} + (20 + 1.90) x_{B4} + (22 + 2.15) x_{C4}$

$$+ (18 + 2.50)\, x_{A5} + (20 + 2.90)\, x_{B5} + (22 + 1.60)\, x_{C5}$$
$$+ (18 + 2.75)\, x_{A6} + (20 + 3.20)\, x_{B6} + (22 + 1.80)\, x_{C6}$$

s.t.

These constraints insure that capacity is not exceeded

$$\begin{cases} x_{A1} + x_{A2} + x_{A3} + x_{A4} + x_{A5} + x_{A6} & \le\ 180 \\ x_{B1} + x_{B2} + x_{B3} + x_{B4} + x_{B5} + x_{B6} & \le\ 130 \\ x_{C1} + x_{C2} + x_{C3} + x_{C4} + x_{C5} + x_{C6} & \le\ 90 \end{cases}$$

These constraints insure that demand is satisfied

$$\begin{cases} x_{A1} + x_{B1} + x_{C1} & =\ 20 \\ x_{A2} + x_{B2} + x_{C2} & =\ 60 \\ x_{A3} + x_{B3} + x_{C3} & =\ 90 \\ x_{A4} + x_{B4} + x_{C4} & =\ 30 \\ x_{A5} + x_{B5} + x_{C5} & =\ 50 \\ x_{A6} + x_{B6} + x_{C6} & =\ 70 \end{cases}$$

$$\text{All } x_{ij}\ \ge\ 0$$

The plant manager presents an erroneous argument. First, his analysis depends basically on the overhead costs. Since we have seen that any feasible solution must involve operating all three plants, any reasonable solution cannot be centered on these costs.

Furthermore, his solution considers only production costs and ignores transportation costs. Clearly, these latter costs should be considered in the solution. Note that the decision variables in this model are more disaggregated than "what to produce in each plant." They are "what to produce in each plant and where to ship it."

4.8 Problems

WARM-UP EXERCISES

1 (This problem is very similar to Example 3 in Section 4.7.) A TV company produces two types of TV sets, the Astro and the Cosmo. There are two production lines, one for each set. The capacity of the Astro production line is 70 sets per day; the capacity of the Cosmo line is 50 sets per day. The Astro set requires one manhour of labor; the Cosmo set requires two manhours. Presently, a maximum of 120 manhours of labor per day can be assigned to production of the two types of sets. If the profit contributions are $20 and $30, respectively, for each Astro and Cosmo set, what should be the daily production? Formulate this problem as a profit maximizing LP model. Identify the decision variables and state the meaning of each constraint.

2 (This problem is similar to Example 3, Section 4.7, and Example 1, Section 4.2.) Suppose forestry equipment produces a net revenue of $802 per unit and requires 700 pounds of iron, 50 hours of labor, 1 transmission, and 30 hours of heat treatment per unit. Earthmoving equipment yields a net revenue of $660 per unit and requires 4,200 pounds of iron, 110 hours of labor, 1 transmission, and 12 hours of heat treatment per unit. The company's capacity during this period is 680,000 pounds of iron, 21,000 hours of labor, 290 transmissions, and 6,000 hours of heat treatment. Define the decision variables, state the meaning of each constraint, and formulate this as a revenue-maximizing linear program.

3 (This problem is similar to Example 2, Section 4.2.) Two products are manufactured on each of three machines. A pound of each product requires a specified number of hours on each machine, as presented in Figure 4.25. Total hours available on machines 1, 2, and 3 are 10, 16, and 12, respectively. The profit contributions per pound of products 1 and 2 are 4 and 3, respectively. Define the decision variables and formulate this problem as a profit-maximizing linear program.

Figure 4.25 *Machine-time data*

Machine	Product 1	Product 2
1	3	2
2	1	4
3	5	3

4 (This problem is similar to Example 4, Section 4.3.) A 16-ounce can of dog food must contain protein, carbohydrate, and fat in at least the following amounts: protein, 3 ounces; carbohydrate, 5 ounces; fat, 4 ounces. Four types of gruel are to be blended together in various proportions to produce a least-cost can of dog food satisfying these requirements. The contents and prices for 16 ounces of each gruel are given in Figure 4.26.

Figure 4.26 *Dogfood data*

Gruel	Protein content (oz)	Carbohydrate content (oz)	Fat content (oz)	Price
1	3	7	5	4
2	5	4	6	6
3	2	2	6	3
4	3	8	2	2

Define the decision variables and formulate an LP model for the problem.

5 (This problem is similar to Example 5, Section 4.7.) A certain restaurant operates seven days a week. Waitresses are hired to work six effective hours per day. The union contract specifies that each waitress must work five consecutive days and then have two consecutive days off. Each waitress receives the same weekly salary. The restaurant requires the following number of waitress hours: Monday, 150; Tuesday, 200; Wednesday, 400; Thursday, 300; Friday, 700; Saturday, 800; Sunday, 300. Assume that this cycle of requirements repeats forever and ignore the fact that the number of waitresses hired must be an integer. The manager wishes to find an employment schedule that satisfies these requirements at minimum cost. Formulate this problem as a linear program.

6 Consider the restaurant discussed in problem 5. A new union rule will allow management to hire up to one-half the waitresses who have the day off on an overtime basis. Overtime pay is 1.5 times the usual pay, and any waitress who works overtime must be paid for the entire day. How should the LP problem be modified to take this new rule into account?

7 (This problem is similar to Example 2, Section 4.7.) Identify the decision variables and formulate the following model as a cost-minimizing linear program. A corporation has decided to produce two new products. Three branch plants now have excess production capacity. The unit manufacturing costs of each product in each plant are shown in Figure 4.27.

Figure 4.27 *Manufacturing data*

	Product	
Plant	1	2
1	$26	a
2	$28	$33
3	$24	$28

ᵃPlant 1 cannot produce product 2.

Sales forecasts indicate that 100 units of product 1 and 150 units of product 2 can be sold and therefore should be produced each day. Plants 1, 2, and 3 have the respective capacities to produce 100, 200, and 200 units daily, regardless of the product or combination of products (except that plant 1 cannot produce product 2). The corporation wishes to determine how much of each product should be produced at each plant in order to minimize total manufacturing cost.

MORE CHALLENGING PROBLEMS

8 An investor has two money-making activities, coded Alpha and Beta, available at the beginning of each of the next four years. Each dollar invested in Alpha at the beginning of a year returns $1.40 two years later (in time for immediate reinvestment). Each dollar invested in Beta at the beginning of a year returns $1.80 three years later. A third investment possibility, construction projects, will become available at the beginning of the second year. Each dollar invested in construction returns $1.20 one year later. (Construction will be available at the beginning of the third and fourth years also.) The investor starts with $10,000 at the beginning of the first year and wants to maximize the total amount of money he has available at the end of the fourth year.

   a Identify the decision variables and formulate an LP model. (Hint: Let M_i be the money available at the beginning of year i and maximize M_5 subject to the appropriate constraints.)

   b Can you determine the solution by direct analysis?

9 A manufacturer has four jobs, A, B, C, and D, that must be produced this month. Each job may be handled in any of three shops. The time required for each job in each shop, the cost per hour in each shop, and the number of hours available this month in each shop are given in Figure 4.28. It is also possible to split each job among the shops in any proportion. For example, one-fourth of job A can be done in 8 hours in shop 1, and one-third of job C can be done in 19 hours in shop 3. The manufacturer wishes to determine how many hours of each job should be handled by each shop in order to minimize the total cost of completing all four jobs. Identify the decision variables and formulate an LP model for this problem.

Figure 4.28 *Job-shop data*

	Hours required per job				Cost per Hour of Shop Time ($)	Shop Time Available (hr)
Shop	A	B	C	D		
1	32	151	72	118	89	160
2	39	147	61	126	81	160
3	46	155	57	121	84	160

10 Identify the decision variables and formulate an LP model for the following problem. A vineyard wishes to blend wine of five different years ($i = 1, 2, . . ., 5$) to make three types of blended wine. The available supply (in gallons) of wine from year i is S_i, $i = 1$, $2, . . ., 5$. Blend 1 is considered a premium blend and, therefore, no more than 100 gallons are to be made. Restrictions on each of the blends are given in Figure 4.29.

Figure 4.29 *Wine-blend data*

Blend	Restriction	Profit per Gallon
1	At least 60% must be from years 1 and 2, no more than 10% from years 4 and 5	c_1
2	At least 50% must be from years 1, 2, and 3	c_2
3	No more than 50% from year 5	c_3

11 A company manufactures two products and must supply a known demand for each product in each of the next 10 months. The demand for product 1 in month t is D_t^1 $t = 1, . . ., 10$ and for product 2, D_t^2 $t = 1, . . ., 10$. The cost of manufacturing the products varies from month to month. In month t the unit cost (in dollars) of manufacturing product 1 is C_t^1, and the cost of manufacturing product 2 is C_t^2. For each unit of product 1 in inventory at the end of each month, a cost of \$4 per month is incurred, and for each unit of product 2 stored a cost of \$5 per month is incurred. Storage space is limited to 1,000 cubic feet; each unit of product 1 occupies 10 cubic feet, and each unit of product 2 occupies 12 cubic feet. In creating this constraint, assume that all the new product manufactured in period t is made at the beginning of the period and the amount demanded is delivered just prior to the end of the period. Currently, the company is holding no inventory of either product. The company manager wants to minimize manufacturing and storage costs for the next 10 months. Identify the decision variables and formulate an LP model for this problem.

12 A speculator operates a silo with a capacity of 5,000 bushels for storing corn. At the beginning of month 1, the silo contains 2,000 bushels. Estimates of the selling and purchase prices of corn during the next four months are given in Figure 4.30.

Figure 4.30 *Selling and purchase price data*

Month	Purchase Price per 1,000 Bushels (\$)	Selling Price per 1,000 Bushels (\$)
1	40	35
2	50	50
3	70	60
4	70	70

Corn sold during any given month is removed from the silo at the beginning of that month. Thus, 2,000 bushels are available for sale in month 1. Corn bought during any given month is put into the silo during the middle of that month, but it cannot be sold until the following month. Given the above sales and purchase prices, and the assumptions on storage costs presented in parts *a* and *b* below, the speculator wishes to know how much corn to buy and sell each month so as to maximize total profits shortly after the beginning of the fourth month (which means after any sale that may occur in that month).

To aid in defining the assumptions on storage cost let

A_t = bushels in the silo immediately after the quantity sold in period t is removed (t = 1, 2, 3, 4)

B_t = bushels in the silo immediately after the quantity purchased in period t is put into the silo (t = 1, 2, 3)

a Assume that the storage cost in period t (t = 1, 2, 3) is

$$\$.005 \left(\frac{A_t + B_t}{2} \right)$$

Define the decision variables and formulate an LP model for this problem.
b Assume that no storage cost is incurred for corn removed at the beginning of the month immediately following the month of its acquisition, so that corn sold in month t is taken out of purchases in month $t - 1$, to the greatest extent possible. That is, the storage cost in period t (t = 1, 2, 3) is

$$\$.005 \quad \text{Max}(A_t, A_{t+1})$$

Demonstrate that this mathematical expression represents the verbal description of the storage cost. Then define the decision variables and formulate a *mathematical* programming model for this problem. Can you convert this to an LP model?

13 As one phase of its spare parts operation, PROTRAC produces two parts (1 and 2) that are sold as part of three separate components (A, B, and C) and also as individual units. Figure 4.31 indicates the number of parts required by each component.

Figure 4.31 *Part/component data*

	Parts	
Components	1	2
A	2	0
B	0	1
C	1	3

Each part and each component is processed in each of three departments and requires time (in minutes) as shown in Figure 4.32. Note that the processing time for a component does *not* include the processing times for the parts that will later be included in the component. The components also require time in the assembly department.

Figure 4.32 *Processing-time data*

		Time (min) Required in Departments			
Parts	Components	1	2	3	Assembly
1		16	20	24	
2		25	21	18	
	A	27	30	25	15
	B	12	18	21	24
	C	17	22	28	19

In one period there are 8,000, 9,000, 10,000 and 12,000 minutes available in departments 1, 2, 3, and assembly, respectively. To satisfy current commitments, PROTRAC must produce at least five of component A, 7 of component B, and 8 of component C, as well as 20 of part 1 and 60 of part 2. The net profit from selling the components and individual parts is: component A, $30; component B, $38; component C, $45; part 1, $10; part 2, $15.

a Assuming that PROTRAC can sell as much of each of these items as it produces, create an LP problem that yields the optimal production plan.

b Each unit of part 1 and each unit of part 2 requires a single aluminum bearing purchased from outside PROTRAC. How many bearings in total must be ordered to implement the optimal production plan obtained from part *a* of this question?

14 Consider the problem presented in Example 2, Section 4.2. Define three additional variables $M1$, $M2$, and $M3$ as follows:

$M1$ = total hours used on machine 1

$M2$ = total hours used on machine 2

$M3$ = total hours used on machine 3

a Reformulate the model from Example 2 in Section 4.2 with these variables included. The relations between these new variables and the former ones must appear in the reformulation.

b A variable whose values are directly determined by the values of other variables is sometimes referred to as a "definitional variable." Show that this is the case for $M1$, $M2$, and $M3$.

c In what sense is the reformulated model equivalent to the formulation in the text?

d For what reasons might definitional variables be employed?

e Suppose the revenue parameters in Example 2, Section 4.2 in the text are modified as follows. "Products A, B, and C are purely competitive and any amounts made may be sold at respective per-pound prices of $5, $4, and $5. The first 20 pounds of products D and E produced per week can be sold at $4 each, but all made in excess of 20 can only be sold at $3 each." Reformulate the model as modified, using the variables $M1$, $M2$ and $M3$.

15 The Party Nut Company has on hand 550 pounds of peanuts, 150 pounds of cashews, 90 pounds of brazil nuts, and 70 pounds of hazelnuts. It packages and sells four varieties of mixed nuts in standard 8-ounce (half-pound) cans. The mix requirements and net wholesale prices are shown in Figure 4.33. The firm can sell all that it can produce at these prices. How many pounds of each type of nut should be used in each mix? Formulate this problem as a profit-maximizing LP model.

Figure 4.33 *Nut mix data*

Mix	Contents	Price per Can ($)
1 (Peanuts)	Peanuts only	.26
2 (Party Mix)	No more than 50% peanuts; at least 15% cashews; at least 10% brazil nuts	.40
3 (Cashews)	Cashews only	.51
4 (Luxury Mix)	At least 30% cashews; at least 20% brazil nuts; at least 30% hazelnuts	.52

16 A small firm has two processes for blending each of two products, charcoal starter fluid and lighter fluid for cigarette lighters. The firm is attempting to decide how many hours to run each process. For one hour of process 1, an input of 3 units of kerosene and 9 units of benzene produces an output of 15 units of starter fluid and 6 units of lighter fluid. For an hour of process 2, an input of 12 units of kerosene and 6 units of benzene produces an output of 9 units of starter fluid and 24 units of lighter fluid. Let x_1 and x_2 be the number of hours the company decides to use of process 1 and process 2, respectively. Because of a federal allocation program, the maximum amount of kerosene and benzene available is 300 units and 450 units, respectively. Sales commitments require that at least 600 units of starter fluid and 225 units of lighter fluid be produced. The per-hour profits that accrue from process 1 and process 2 are p_1 and p_2, respectively. Formulate this as a profit-maximizing constrained optimization model.

17 In the human diet, 16 essential nutrients have been identified. Suppose there are 116 foods. A pound of food j contains a_{ij} pounds of nutrient i. Suppose a human must have N_i pounds of each nutrient i in the daily diet and that a pound of food j costs c_j cents. What is the least-cost daily diet satisfying all nutritional requirements? Use summation notation in the formulation of this problem. Aside from the question of palatability, can you think of an important constraint that this problem omits?

18 The Pittsburgh Steel (PS) Company has contracted to produce a new type of steel that has the tight quality requirements shown in Figure 4.34.

Figure 4.34 *Steel content requirements*

Mineral Content	At Least (%)	Not More Than (%)
Carbon	3.0	3.5
Chrome	0.3	0.45
Manganese	1.35	1.65
Silicon	2.7	3.0

PS has materials available for mixing a batch as shown in Figure 4.35.

Figure 4.35 *Data on available materials for steel blend*

Available Materials	Cost per Pound ($)	Carbon (%)	Chrome (%)	Manganese (%)	Silicon (%)	Available Amount (lb)
Pig iron 1	.03	4.0	0	0.9	2.25	Unlimited
Pig iron 2	.0645	0	10.0	4.5	15.0	Unlimited
Ferrosilicon 1	.065	0	0	0	45.0	Unlimited
Ferrosilicon 2	.061	0	0	0	42.0	Unlimited
Alloy 1	.10	0	0	60.0	18.0	Unlimited
Alloy 2	.13	0	20.0	9.0	30.0	Unlimited
Alloy 3	.119	0	8.00	33.0	25.0	Unlimited
Carbide (silicon)	.08	15.0	0	0	30.0	20
Steel 1	.021	0.4	0	0.9	0	200
Steel 2	.02	0.1	0	0.3	0	200
Steel 3	.0195	0.1	0	0.3	0	200

How much of each of the 11 materials should be blended in a one-ton batch so as to satisfy all the foregoing requirements at minimum cost? Formulate this as a constrained optimization model.

19 An airline must decide on the amounts of jet fuel to purchase from three oil companies. The airline refuels its aircraft regularly at the four airports it serves. The oil companies have said that they can furnish up to the following amounts of fuel during the coming month: oil company 1, 250,000 gallons; oil company 2, 500,000 gallons; oil company 3, 600,000 gallons. The minimal required amounts of jet fuel are: 100,000 gallons at airport 1; 200,000 gallons at airport 2; 300,000 gallons at airport 3; 400,000 gallons at airport 4.

When transportation costs are added to the price per-gallon supplied, the combined cost per gallon is as shown in Figure 4.36.

Figure 4.36   *Oil cost-per-gallon data (in dollars)*

	Airport				Supply
Oil Company	1	2	3	4	
1	12	11	11	11	250,000
2	9	10	8	13	500,000
3	15	12	12	14	600,000
min. req.	100,000	200,000	300,000	400,000	

a Formulate this problem as a cost-minimizing constrained optimization model. (This is another example of a transportation model.)
b Note that the total supply from all companies will not be used. Is it possible to tell by inspecting the data which companies will sell all their fuel?
c Suppose company 3 wishes to become more competitive. One way would be to reduce transport costs. Instead, management decides to offer a bulk discount of the following form: if the airline purchases at least 400,000 gallons then the company will reduce its price per gallon by $2. How can the airline determine whether or not to accept the discount?

20 A firm wants a production plan that will minimize costs for the next three periods. Let

d_i = quantity demanded in period i

c_i = cost of producing a unit in period i

h_i = cost per unit of inventory on hand at the end of each period i

There is a 10-percent spoilage. That is, 10 percent of the inventory available at the end of period i must be discarded. It is not available to satisfy demand in period $i + 1$. Let

P_i = production in period i

I_i = inventory on hand at the end of period i

a Assume that I_0 is known and formulate an LP problem that yields the optimal production plan.
b Management feels that the model derived in part *a* is inadequate because it does not incorporate the cost of adjusting labor and production facilities from one rate of production to another. An operations analyst thus proposes introducing this adjustment cost into the model by utilizing a factor K_i, where K_i is the cost per-unit-change in the production from period $i - 1$ to period i. For example, if production in period 1 is 300 units and in period 2 it is 100 units, a cost of $200K_2$ is incurred. Similarly, if production in period 1 is 100 units and production in period 2

is 200 units a cost of $100K_2$ is incurred. Assume that I_0, P_0, and P_4 are known. The analyst suggests that the solution to the new problem can be found by replacing the objective function of the problem in part a by the expression:

$$\text{Min} \quad c_1P_1 + c_2P_2 + c_3P_3 + h_1I_1 + h_2I_2 + h_3I_3 + K_1(P_0 - P_1)$$
$$+ K_2(P_1 - P_2) + K_3(P_2 - P_3) + K_4(P_3 - P_4)$$

Will the solution to this LP problem provide the correct answer to the question posed by management? If not, state why.

21 Consider Example 5, Section 4.4. Let $I_0 = 0$, $K_t = \infty$, and $h_t = 0$ for all t. That is, assume no initial inventory, no holding costs, and infinite capacities. Also assume demand in each period is positive.

  a Suppose per-unit production costs are the same in each period. That is, $C_t = C$ for all t. Can you, by inspection, discover an optimal production schedule? What is the total cost of this schedule? Is this schedule unique? (That is, can you discover more than one optimal schedule?)

  b Suppose the per-unit production costs are increasing ($0 < C_1 < C_2, \ldots, < C_6$). Can you discover an optimal policy in this case? Can you discover more than one?

  c Suppose that in part b the holding cost h_1 is increased from zero by a very slight amount. Would you think that the optimal policy will change? Suppose that h_1 is now continuously increased further. Try to discuss the tradeoffs that will occur. What happens as the capacity in period 1 is continuously reduced from ∞?

  d Suppose the per-unit production costs are decreasing ($C_1 > C_2, \ldots, > C_6 > 0$). Answer the questions in part b above.

  e For the case $C_1 > C_2, \ldots, > C_n > 0$, answer the questions in part c above.

  f Suppose the initial inventory is 12 and the remaining parameters for the problem are as specified in Figure 4.37. Can you discover an optimal production plan?

Figure 4.37 *Parameter data*

t	1	2	3	4	5	6
d_t	100	100	100	100	100	100
C_t	15	13	14	9	10	8
h_t	0	0	0	0	0	0
K_t	500	500	500	500	500	500

22 Consider Example 6, Section 4.4. Show how to eliminate the x_t variables from the model given in this example (for $t = 2, \ldots, 6$).

23 Consider Example 7, Section 4.4. The objective function in the model developed in the first part of Example 7 can be replaced with

$$\sum_{t=1}^{6} (400 + 100r) y_t$$

In other words, the term $54,000r$ can be ignored. Why is this so? (How do the optimal decision variables compare in each formulation? What about the optimal objective values?) Can this same term be ignored in the second model given in Example 7?

● 24   Each year, the parts department of PROTRAC takes a physical count of its parts inventory in each of its main warehouses. This work is done during the second shift (4:00 P.M. to midnight) by trained members of the clerical staff, called counters. However, it is possible to train additional members of the staff to be counters. Training is done in classes of size 20 by one of the already trained staff who serves as an instructor. The staff is unionized, and the following work rules are strictly enforced:

1 Only trained personnel can count.
2 A job as a counter is taken for a one-week interval.
3 A person who serves as a counter in a given week can serve as neither an instructor nor a counter in the following week.
4 Any trained person can serve as an instructor.
5 An instructor always handles a class of exactly 20 persons.
6 A training class lasts one week.
7 Once a person has served as an instructor, he cannot serve as either an instructor or a counter again that year.

It is estimated that 900 person-weeks of counting must be done during the next four weeks. There are 400 trained personnel on hand who can act as counters or instructors during the first week. Counters are paid $320 per week. Instructors are paid $600 per week. All trained persons are paid $40 per week if they are not used as either counters or instructors. Express as a linear program the problem of minimizing the total cost of supplying the 900 person-weeks.

25   PROTRAC is considering three capital-investment projects. The initial investment and present value of the return for each project are shown in Figure 4.38. PROTRAC has set a limit of 30 for the total allowable investment.

Figure 4.38   *Data for capital investment projects*

Project	Initial Investment	Present Value of Return
1	20	40
2	15	24
3	12	18

Assume that fractional parts of each project can be initiated; that is, ignore integer constraints on the decision variables.
a Formulate this problem as an LP model.
b Find the optimal solution to this problem.
c Now assume that each project must either be accepted in toto or rejected (that is, the integer constraints must hold). Find the optimal solution.

26   A major retailing chain is considering bidding for space in a new suburban shopping mall that is being designed. This chain has both food and drug outlets and often has both activities in the same building. The chain has a number of alternatives at the proposed mall. Basically, decisions must be made whether to invest in a food outlet and whether to invest in a drug outlet. The food outlet requires a capital investment of $800,000 and yields a return with a present value of $1,000,000. The drug store requires capital of $600,000 and yields a return with a present value of $720,000.

If the food outlet is built, the retailer could include a specialty-shop group (cheese shop, delicatessen, and fish shop), which requires $300,000 and yields a return with a present value of $345,000, and/or a garden and patio center, which requires a capital investment of $400,000 and yields a return of $472,000. If the drug outlet is built, it could include a toyland for a capital investment of $500,000 and a return with a present value of $637,500. Finally, if both the food outlet and the drug outlet are accepted with or without any of their options, the retailer could include a dining facility. This facility requires a capital investment of $200,000 and yields a return with a present value of $260,000.

Because of its current capital structure, the retailing chain has set an upper limit of $1,700,000 on its capital investment. Assume that fractional parts of each project cannot be accepted and formulate this problem as an integer programming problem.

27 Consider three plants, and let b_i be a decision variable denoting the budget allocated to plant i ($i = 1, 2, 3$). Let $f_i(b_i)$ be a function denoting the revenue obtained by plant i, given budget b_i. Consider the following two models:

Profit maximization model
$$\left\{ \begin{array}{l} \text{Max} \quad \sum_{i=1}^{3} (f_i(b_i) - b_i) \\[2mm] \text{s.t.} \\[1mm] \sum_{i=1}^{3} b_i = 5.5 \\[2mm] \quad b_i \geq 0 \qquad i = 1, 2, 3 \end{array} \right.$$

Revenue maximization model
$$\left\{ \begin{array}{l} \text{Max} \quad \sum_{i=1}^{3} f_i(b_i) \\[2mm] \text{s.t.} \\[1mm] \sum_{i=1}^{3} b_i = 5.5 \\[2mm] \quad b_i \geq 0 \qquad i = 1, 2, 3 \end{array} \right.$$

a Are these two models the same or different? That is, will they produce the same or different decisions?

b What is wrong with the following procedure? In the profit maximization model, since the constraint says

$$\sum_{i=1}^{3} b_i = 5.5$$

substitute this into the objective function and then solve

$$\text{Max} \quad \sum_{i=1}^{3} f_i(b_i) - 5.5$$

s.t.

$$b_i \geq 0 \qquad i = 1, 2, 3$$

c Suppose the equality constraints in each of the models are changed to $\leq$. What effect, if any, could such a change have?

5 LP Models and Computer Analysis

In this chapter, the computer analysis of LP problems is introduced. The topics include slack and surplus variables, the standard equality-constraint form, the dual price, and the reduced cost. A sample problem is solved and the output is analyzed.

5.1 Introduction

Now that you have acquired some experience in problem formulation, we could proceed in any of several different directions. We might, for example, move on to a discussion of conceptual and theoretical material designed to create a better understanding of the properties of the models under consideration. This would help lead you to a good grasp of possible applications and a better appreciation for the appropriate use of models. The other tack is to solve some problems immediately on a computer and to discuss the solution and the output produced. We adopt the latter course for two reasons. First, it is a pragmatic approach, and experience tells us that many students prefer to use new tools as quickly as possible. Second, a preliminary look at the entire process from formulation through solution provides motivation for some of the later geometric and conceptual discussions, and the latter, in turn, make a more detailed problem analysis meaningful. In other words, this chapter completes the entire process, but in a once-over-lightly style. We then move into geometry and concepts (Chapter 6) and then return to problem analysis and output interpretation in considerably more depth (Chapters 8 and 9) and in a fairly realistic setting (Chapters 11 and 12).

An important thing to keep clear is that we shall discuss the computer solution of linear programs. This means that the objective function and all the constraints are linear. The reasons for discussing linear programs are simple and practical. First, LP is a tool that has found practical application in almost all phases of business, from advertising and marketing through cash-flow management and production planning. Second, there is a very efficient algorithm (solution method) for dealing with these problems. This algorithm is perhaps the work-horse in the field of management science. The algorithm is called the *simplex method* and was developed by G. Dantzig, A. Charnes, and others. Since that time, Dantzig and others have modified the algorithm so that different forms exist that are particularly efficient for very special types of LP problems such as the transportation model, which we encountered in the previous chapter.

The simplex algorithm is so efficient and so commonly used that almost every computer installation has at least one LP routine in its assortment of software. In many installations the user has two choices. The **conversational** or **interactive** mode features a dialogue between user and computer. From a console the analyst inputs data in compliance with the computer's instructions. Then, usually after a few seconds, the solution is printed. The model can then be modified and rerun if so desired. This capability is useful as an LP instructional aid as well as for solving small problems. The other option is called **batch processing.** Here, the data are read from cards or from magnetic tape. By the time the problem has been submitted and run, several hours will usually have lapsed. The batch mode is particularly appropriate for large problems and situations in which the importance of interaction with the computer is minimal.

In summary, then, we will discuss the computer analysis of linear programs because the models are typical and useful in applications and the solution procedure is highly accessible in several forms. Computer codes also exist for solving constrained optimization problems that are more complicated than linear programs (for example, quadratic programming codes and general nonlinear programming codes), but these codes are not nearly as widely available as LP codes. Ironically, the output for such codes is usually easier to read than LP output. Since the mathematics of LP is not particularly arcane, the simplex method produces a great deal of information about the problem in addition to the solution, and this makes the computer output somewhat detailed. With nonlinear programs, we are lucky just to get a solution.

In the foregoing discussion we have loosely used the terms *small problems* and *large problems.* The main operational distinction between these terms is that small problems are easier (take less time) to solve than large problems. In the early days of LP, a large problem was one with 200 constraints. Today, a large problem is one with 2,000 constraints. Such problems are frequently solved in batch processing on a high-speed computer. A *very* large problem is one with four or five thousand constraints and, today, such problems are also solved, though less routinely. You may wonder why anyone would want to solve a problem with so many constraints, but in fact many important applications are of this size. Indeed, transportation models with 50,000 constraints and 60 million variables have been solved, and much current research in LP is devoted to extending these capabilities.

In linear programming, problem size and hence difficulty is measured more by the number of constraints than by the number of variables. The reasons for this will become clear in our later geometric studies. The point to remember for now is that it is the number of constraints that counts. The number of variables may be essentially unlimited, at least in the large-scale batch-type code.

We strongly urge you, if it is possible, to work through the example in this chapter on your own computer facility. LP is a practical and useful tool employed in a wide variety of scenarios and used on the computer often by individuals who know little more than you already know about the subject. The point is that all these applications are conducted on a computer. Nobody, in practice, solves a linear program with pencil and paper. That is why, throughout this text, we stress computer analysis and why we urge you to take the "hands-on" approach.

We do provide numerous displays of actual computer output for particular problems under discussion in this book. Consequently, it is not essential to your comprehension to use your own computer. However, doing so is instructive and it makes the overall analysis more meaningful and interesting. By the way, there is no need to worry that your computer may not be the same as ours. The form of LP output is more or less standard, and the variation in format in the LP software on different computers is trivial. If you follow the discussion in the text, you will be able to read any LP output you may encounter.

5.2 Setting Up the Problem for Computer Solution

The *general form* of a linear program with, say, n variables and m constraints can be expressed as follows:

Max (or min) $c_1 x_1 \;+\; c_2 x_2 \;+\; \ldots \;+\; c_n x_n$

s.t.

$$a_{11}x_1 + a_{12}x_2 \;+\; \ldots \;+\; a_{1n}x_n \;\begin{matrix}\geq\\=\\\leq\end{matrix}\; b_1$$

$$\vdots \qquad\qquad\qquad \vdots$$

$$a_{m1}x_1 + a_{m2}x_2 \;+\; \ldots \;+\; a_{mn}x_n \;\begin{matrix}\geq\\=\\\leq\end{matrix}\; b_m$$

$$x_1, x_2, \ldots, x_n \;\geq\; 0$$

The symbols x_j denote the decision variables. Each constraint is allowed to be of the form $\geq$, $=$, or $\leq$. Observe that in this general form all variables in the constraints appear on the left. The constant terms are to the right. Of course, the model is the same whether or not all variables are on the left and all constants on the right, and in many of the formulations in the previous chapter we did not observe this formality. But in order to satisfy the computer, the problem must be submitted in this form, and that is our present goal—to solve the problem on the computer.

To approach an LP problem in general and to prepare it for the computer in particular, you must:

---

1 Specify the following three types of data.
   a The c_js, or coefficients in the objective function.
   b The a_{ij}s, or coefficients in the constraint functions (a_{ij} is the coefficient of the variable x_j in the ith constraint).
   c The b_is, or right-hand side.
2 Know whether the problem is a maximization or a minimization.
3 Know the sense of each constraint; that is, whether it is $\geq$, $=$, or $\leq$.

Now, the first important consideration in the computer analysis of linear programs is the following fact:

The simplex algorithm always solves a problem that is in the standard equality-constraint form.

This means that the problem must be expressed in this form prior to being solved. Fortunately, this is not a limitation, for any linear program, regardless of the sense of the constraints, can be transformed into the standard equality-constraint form. This step is accomplished with the use of *slack* and *surplus variables.*

5.3 Slack and Surplus Variables

Let us begin with an illustration. Consider the linear inequality constraint

$$x_1 + 3x_2 \leq 12 \qquad (1)$$

This can be transformed into a linear equality constraint as follows. We add a new nonnegative variable, say s, and write the two conditions

$$\left. \begin{array}{r} x_1 + 3x_2 + s = 12 \\ s \geq 0 \end{array} \right\} \qquad (2)$$

Then the pair of numbers x_1, x_2 satisfies the inequality constraint in (1) if and only if the triple of numbers x_1, x_2, s satisfies the conditions in (2), where we choose s as follows:

$$s = 12 - x_1 - 3x_2$$

For example, $x_1 = 1$, $x_2 = 2$ satisfy (1), for in this case

$$x_1 + 3x_2 = 7$$

and $7 \leq 12$ is certainly true. Also, choosing s to be

$$12 - x_1 - 3x_2 = 12 - 7 = 5$$

we see that $x_1 = 1$, $x_2 = 2$, and $s = 5$ satisfy the conditions in (2). Clearly, for any numbers x_1, x_2 that satisfy (1) we can let $s = 12 - x_1 - 3x_2$. This value of s will be nonnegative, and the values x_1, x_2, and s will then satisfy (2).

On the other hand, suppose x_1, x_2, and s are any three numbers satisfying the pair of conditions (2). For example,

$$x_1 = 2, \quad x_2 = 2, \quad s = 4$$

Then clearly x_1 and x_2 must satisfy (1) because of the stipulation in (2) that s is nonnegative. These arguments show the sense in which (1) and (2) are really equivalent conditions.

This new nonnegative variable s is called a *slack variable*. Note that it is merely the difference between the right-hand side and the left-hand side of a $\leq$ constraint. It is the "slack," or extra amount, that would have to be added in to the left-hand side to turn the $\leq$ into $=$. In summary:

Any $\leq$ constraint can be converted to $=$ by adding a new nonnegative slack variable to the left-hand side.

As another illustration, consider the three inequality constraints

$$4x_1 - x_2 \leq 12$$
$$2x_1 + 6x_2 \leq -21$$
$$-3x_1 + 2x_2 \leq 6.5$$

In this case, converting to equalities requires the introduction of *three* new nonnegative slack variables, say x_3, x_4, x_5 (the three slacks could just as well be labeled as s_1, s_2, and s_3). We then obtain the following equivalent system of equalities

$$4x_1 - x_2 + x_3 \qquad\qquad = 12$$
$$2x_1 + 6x_2 \qquad + x_4 \qquad = -21$$
$$-3x_1 + 2x_2 \qquad\qquad + x_5 = 6.5$$
$$x_3, x_4, x_5 \geq 0$$

Note that there is a *different* slack variable associated with each constraint.

We have now to consider the case of a $\geq$ constraint. As a first step in converting a $\geq$ constraint to equality, we can multiply both sides by -1. This produces a $\leq$ constraint, and then we can take the foregoing approach. Equivalently, we can employ the device of subtracting a new nonnegative variable from the left-hand side and changing the $\geq$ to $=$. For example

$$2x_1 + 4x_2 \geq 13 \qquad\qquad (3)$$

can be changed to an equality constraint in either of the following ways.

METHOD 1

Rewrite (3) as the equivalent condition

$$-2x_1 - 4x_2 \leq -13 \qquad\qquad (4)$$

and add a nonnegative slack to obtain the *two* conditions

$$-2x_1 - 4x_2 + s = -13 \qquad\qquad (5)$$
$$s \geq 0 \qquad\qquad (6)$$

METHOD 2

Subtract a nonnegative variable from the left-hand side of (3) and change the inequality to equality. This produces

$$2x_1 + 4x_2 - s = 13 \qquad\qquad (7)$$
$$s \geq 0 \qquad\qquad (8)$$

Note that Method 2 is equivalent to Method 1 since multiplying both sides of (5) by -1 gives (7). When a nonnegative variable is subtracted from a $\geq$ constraint, it is often termed a *surplus variable* (as opposed to a slack variable, which is added to a $\leq$ constraint).

The foregoing discussion shows how any $\leq$ constraint can be converted to an equality by adding a new nonnegative slack variable. Any $\geq$ constraint can be converted to an equality by subtracting a new nonnegative surplus variable.

When converting an LP problem into standard equality-constraint form, the slack and surplus variables are never added to the objective function. Equivalently, you may think of them as being included in the objective function, but with zero coefficients.

Now let us apply this discussion to a complete model. Consider the following LP problem:

$$\text{Max} \quad 2x_1 + 3x_2 - 14x_3 \qquad\qquad (9)$$

s.t.

$$
\begin{aligned}
x_1 \quad\qquad - 2x_3 &\geq -4 \\
12x_1 + 2x_2 + x_3 &\geq 15 \\
x_1 - 3x_2 \quad\qquad &= 4 \\
-2x_1 + x_2 + 4x_3 &\leq 26 \\
x_1, x_2, x_3 &\geq 0
\end{aligned}
$$

This LP problem has three variables and four constraints, two of them $\geq$, one $=$, and one $\leq$. In order to convert this problem into an equivalent problem in standard equality-constraint form, we must introduce slack and surplus variables to change the first, second, and fourth constraints into equivalent equalities. Letting x_4, x_5, and x_6 denote the three new variables, we obtain:

$$\text{Max} \quad 2x_1 + 3x_2 - 14x_3 \qquad\qquad (10)$$

s.t.

$$
\begin{aligned}
x_1 \quad\qquad - 2x_3 - x_4 \quad\qquad\qquad &= -4 \\
12x_1 + 2x_2 + x_3 \quad\qquad - x_5 \quad\qquad &= 15 \\
x_1 - 3x_2 \quad\qquad\qquad\qquad\qquad &= 4 \\
-2x_1 + x_2 + 4x_3 \quad\qquad\qquad + x_6 &= 26 \\
x_1, x_2, x_3, x_4, x_5, x_6 &\geq 0
\end{aligned}
$$

Note that the objective function in the problem is unchanged. The variables x_4 and x_5 are surplus, x_6 is a slack. The new problem still has four constraints, but now it has six variables instead of three. We emphasize that this standard equality-constraint form has all the terms with variables on the left and the constant terms on the right. The computer will accept this format.

You can see that the process of converting a problem to standard equality-constraint form is purely mechanical. For this reason, most LP computer codes will change the inequalities to equalities for you. For example, most interactive software will allow you to input the problem as stated in (9) directly, from a desk console, without worrying about slack or surplus variables. Knowing the sense of each constraint ($\leq$, $=$, or $\geq$), the computer can automatically convert the model to (10) before solving. Incidentally, the nonnegativity conditions are not explicitly entered into the computer. The simplex algorithm for solving linear programs automatically assumes that all variables are nonnegative. It would therefore be extraneous to input these conditions explicitly.

You may wonder what to do in the case when, for logical reasons, some of the variables in your model are *not* required to be nonnegative. This is easily treated. Suppose that in the particular model you have formulated there is a variable z that can meaningfully be positive, negative, or zero. In order to transform your model into the standard form (in which *all* variables must be nonnegative), introduce two new *nonnegative* variables, say z_1 and z_2, and let $z = z_1 - z_2$. Everywhere a z appears in your original model, simply replace it by $z_1 - z_2$ and rewrite the model. It can be shown that the new problem is equivalent to the old. By the way, this is a manipulation that most LP codes will not do for you; so, when not all variables are nonnegative, you must transform the model so that they are. We hasten to add that in most business or economics models, the variables in your formulation will be quantities such as price, amount of a product to be manufactured, and so on, which means that by definition these variables will satisfy the nonnegativity conditions. As a result, the difficulties associated with variables unconstrained in sign are mainly academic.

Summarizing the material of this section, we can say the following:

1   The original model may have all sorts of constraints: $\leq$, $=$, and $\geq$. Prior to solution, the computer converts the original model to an equivalent one, all of whose constraints are equalities. This is called the standard equality-constraint form. The models are equivalent in the sense that if the original model can be solved, so can the new one, and any solution to the new one provides a solution to the original.

2   In the process of transforming the original model, slack and surplus variables are introduced as appropriate. Thus, the equality-constraint model will have more variables than the original (unless all the original constraints were equalities, in which case no conversion is required). The number of constraints in the original and transformed models is the same.

3   A $\leq$ constraint is converted to $=$ by adding a slack variable to the left-hand side. A $\geq$ constraint is converted to $=$ by subtracting a surplus variable from the left-hand side. The same slack variable never appears in more than one constraint. The same surplus variable never appears in more than one constraint. Slack and surplus variables are always nonnegative.

4   Slack and surplus variables are never seen in the objective function (that is, they are included with zero coefficient).

5   The constraints of a problem that is ready for solution must have all terms with variables on the left and the constant term on the right. (Note that the number zero may be the only constant term; for example, $4x_1 - 3x_2 + x_3 = 0$.)

6   Nonnegativity conditions are not explicitly input to the computer.

5.4 Reading the Output

Now that you are familiar with the form of an LP problem that the computer solves, let us work through an example. For this purpose we refer to the iron-ore-blending problem in Example 4, Section 4.3. Recall that in this problem the ore from four different locations is blended to make crawler tractor treads. Each ore contains three essential elements that must appear in the final blend at minimum threshold levels. PROTRAC pays a different price per ton for the ore from each location. The cost-minimizing blend is obtained by the following LP model, where T_i = the fraction of a ton of ore from location i in one ton of the blend.

Min $800T1 + 400T2 + 600T3 + 500T4$ (Total cost)

s.t.

$$10T1 + \quad 3T2 + \quad 8T3 + \quad 2T4 \geq \quad 5 \qquad \text{(Requirement on } A\text{)}$$
$$90T1 + 150T2 + 75T3 + 175T4 \geq 100 \qquad \text{(Requirement on } B\text{)}$$
$$45T1 + \quad 25T2 + 20T3 + \quad 37T4 \geq 30 \qquad \text{(Requirement on } C\text{)}$$
$$T1 + \quad T2 + \quad T3 + \quad T4 = \quad 1 \qquad \text{(Blend condition)}$$
$$T_i \geq \quad 0 \qquad i = 1,2,3,4$$

In order to discuss and analyze the solution to this problem, place yourself in the position of the manager who is responsible for planning future production. A number of questions are on the manager's mind. The modeler responds.

Manager   First of all, what is the solution to our problem?

I have run the problem on the computer, and here's the output [see Figure 5.1]. By "solution" I take it you mean the optimal values of the decision variables. These are printed in the section of output that I've labeled *Variables*. The optimal values of the variables appear under the second column, headed VALUE. You can see that the optimal values are

$T1 = \ .25926$

$T2 = \ .70370$

$T3 = \ .03704$

$T4 = 0.0$

Manager   How much does a ton of this blend cost?

The optimal value of the objective function is the last entry in the same column. You can see that the minimum cost is $511.11.

Manager   I'd like to keep my costs under $500 per ton. Isn't there any way I can do this?

It is impossible to find a lower-cost mixture that satisfies the constraints you have imposed.

Manager   You mean the requirements on essential elements?

Exactly.

Figure 5.1   *Solution to the ore-blending problem*

```
MIN  800T1+400T2+600T3+500T4
SUBJECT TO
   2)    10T1+3T2+8T3+2T4  >=  5
   3)    90T1+150T2+75T3+175T4  >=  100
   4)    45T1+25T2+20T3+37T4  >=  30
   5)    T1+T2+T3+T4= 1
```

VARIABLE	VALUE	REDUCED-COST	
T1	0.25926	0.00000	⎫
T2	0.70370	0.00000	⎬ *Variables*
T3	0.03704	0.00000	⎭
T4	0.00000	91.11107	
OBJ FCTN	511.111		

ROW	SLACK	DUAL-PRICE	
2	0	-44.4444	⎫
3	31.6667	0	⎬ *Constraints*
4	0	-4.44445	
5	0	-155.555	⎭

```
SENSITIVITY ANALYSIS

RANGE IN WHICH BASIS REMAINS THE SAME
    COST SENSITIVITY
```

VARIABLE	INCREASE IN C(J)	DECREASE IN C(J)
T1	223.63632	120.00018
T2	66.84779	300.00036
T3	85.71440	118.26919
T4	INFINITE	91.11107

```
    RIGHT HAND SENSITIVITY
```

ROW	ALLOWABLE INCREASE	ALLOWABLE DECREASE
2	2.37500	0.25000
3	31.6667	INFINITE
4	0.71429	7.00000
5	0.25000	0.04348

Manager   Well, maybe I can modify those requirements. But first, I recall that the requirements were expressed as minimum threshold levels. Is there any way I can tell exactly how much of each essential element gets into the optimal mix?

That information is deduced from the second section of the output which I've identified *Constraints*. The computer labels the four constraints of the problem as rows 2 –5, respectively, since it regards the objective function as row 1. The first three constraints of the problem are the requirements on essential elements. This corresponds to the output labeled as rows 2, 3, and 4.

Manager   I see a column labeled SLACK and one labeled DUAL-PRICE, but where are the amounts of the essential elements?

This has to be deduced. Remember that before the inequality problem was solved, the computer had to transform it to standard equality-constraint form. The column labeled SLACK is the optimal value of the slack variable associated with each constraint in the transformed problem.

Manager   I think I see what you're getting at. The slack in row 2 is zero. But wait a minute. The first constraint is the requirement on A, which was 5 pounds. Since the original constraint is $\geq$, after conversion to equality form it must look like:

$$10T1 + 3T2 + 8T3 + 2T4 - S1 = 5$$

Exactly.

Manager   But the variable $S1$ is surplus, not slack. Where is the surplus on the output?

This particular computer code thinks of both types of variables as slack. It adds slack to a $\leq$ constraint and subtracts slack from a $\geq$ constraint. It's just a matter of terminology.

Manager   Fine. Let's keep the terminology to a minimum. But now something else is bothering me. The last constraint in the original model was an equality constraint. This means that it has neither a slack nor a surplus variable in standard form. Right?

Correct.

Manager   Then why is there a slack value of zero printed on the output for row 5? Doesn't that suggest that there is a slack variable in that row?

You may be right, but the suggestion is unintended. For a constraint that was originally an equality the entry in the slack column is always zero. As you have correctly observed, the actual slack variables in this problem are associated only with the first three constraints of the original model. That is, rows 2, 3, and 4.

Manager   Fine. Now let's return to the slack variable $S1$. I see that its optimal value is zero. What does that have to do with the amount of essential element A in the final mix? I thought I saw the answer before, but now I'm confused.

It's easy. Since the optimal slack value is zero, and since we know the other optimal values, it must be true that if we substitute the optimal values of all of the variables into the equality form of the constraint we will obtain the following result:

$$10(.25926) + 3(.70370) + 8(.03704) + 2(0.0000) - 0 = 5$$

In other words, since the optimal slack value is zero, the optimal mix contains exactly 5 pounds of A.

Manager   I see. And since the slack in row 4 is zero, the optimal mix must contain exactly 30 pounds of C. Is that right?

Precisely, and you can also figure out how much B there is.

Manager   Okay. For B, I have to look at row 3. Since the slack is 31.6667 it must be true that

$$90(.25926) + 150(.70370) + 75(.03704) + 175(0.0000) - 31.6667 = 100$$

But where do I go from here?

Well, your equation means that in the optimal mix the minimal requirement of 100 pounds is actually exceeded by 31.6667. That is, there are 131.6667 pounds of B actually included.

Manager   Isn't that odd? You'd think I could make a cheaper blend by using less B. Why should I use more than 100 pounds if I need only 100?

The combination of ores that satisfies the requirements on A and C at a minimum cost just happens to contain more than 100 pounds of B. Any combination of ores that includes less B will either not have enough of A and/or C, or, if it does have enough, then it will cost more than $511.11 per ton. In other words, forcing yourself to include less of the excess amount of B while still satisfying the requirements on A and C will end up costing you more. You may have to think about that assertion, but it is exactly what the solution to the model is telling us.

Manager   Okay. I guess I can see your point. So how can I get my total cost down to $500 or less?

You will have to relax your constraints. This means relaxing the requirements on A or C.

Manager   Why not on B?

Because, in order to satisfy the requirements on A and C at minimum cost, you're already including over 100 pounds of B, which is more than your minimal threshold. Relaxing this requirement to a smaller number won't get us anywhere. You have to relax one of the tight requirements.

Manager   You mean one where there's zero slack?

Precisely.

Manager   Okay. So I have to relax the requirement on A or C. But which one? And how much?

We can use the information under the DUAL–PRICE heading to analyze these questions.

Manager   I was wondering what that dual-price column meant.

Let's look at the dual price on row 2. It is −44.44. This means that as your requirement for A is relaxed, your minimum cost will go down at the rate of $44.44 per pound.

Manager   Relaxing the requirement for A must mean reducing it from 5 pounds to something less. Right?

Right.

Manager   And the dual price of −44.44 says that for each pound of reduction the cost goes down $44.44?

Right.

Manager Great. This means if I require only 4 pounds per ton of *A*, instead of 5, the cost goes down to about $466.67 and I'm under $500. Right?

Well, not quite. But you're right in spirit. You have the correct rate of change, but this rate applies only to some *interval* of values around the original value of 5. The appropriate interval may not allow you to analyze the decrease of a whole unit—maybe only half a unit, for example.

Manager Even so, if I cut the requirement only to 4.5 pounds then I'd save 1/2(44.44), which is over $22. My final cost would still be under $500!

True enough, but the allowable interval may not even include 4.5.

Manager Obviously, we need to know that interval.

Right. And it appears on the bottom of the output under the section labeled RIGHT HAND SENSITIVITY.

Manager I see. In the allowable decrease column for row 2 we have .25000. That must mean I can analyze a change from 5 down to 4.75. Right?

Right.

Manager So my saving would be .25(44.44), which is $11.11, and this gets me exactly down to $500. But what if I relaxed the requirement a little more, like to 4.50. Wouldn't that reduce the cost further?

Probably, but I can't tell you exactly how much because the rate of change is probably different after a decrease of .25.

Manager In technical language, that must mean the dual price changes.

Exactly.

Manager So there isn't anything I can say about a change to 4.50?

Not quite. You can say that the decrease in cost would be *at least*

$(.25)(44.44) = \$11.11$

and *at most*

$(.50)(44.44) = \$22.22$

The actual change could be anywhere between $11.11 and $22.22.

Manager I see. So even though the dual price changes we at least have some estimates and that could be useful.

Right.

Manager Okay. Now just to see if I have it all straight, let me analyze the potential savings if I relax the requirement on *C*.

Go ahead.

Manager The requirement on C is identified as ROW 4. The original right-hand side is 30. The output shows an allowable decrease of 7, so I can go down to 23. The dual price on row 4 is −4.44. This is my rate of saving as I decrease the right-hand side from 30. Hence, if I decrease the requirement to 23, I save

$$7(4.44) = \$31.08$$

This also gets me well under $500. In fact, if I cut down the requirement only 2.5 pounds I can apply the same rate of change, and consequently I should save

$$(2.5)(4.44) = \$11.10$$

and this gets me just down to a cost of $500. How am I doing?

Very well.

Manager Okay. I see that I can get the cost per ton down to $500 if I relax the requirement on A to 4.75 pounds per ton *or* the requirement on C to 27.5 pounds per ton. But what if I relax both requirements on A and C, perhaps a little less but both at the same time. Then what?

Sorry, but again we don't have precise information on the answer to that. In this case, I could give you an estimate but I'd rather not for now.

Manager So when I use the dual price on one of the right-hand-side values, it's important to keep the others unchanged.

Correct. At least for the time being. We can modify that statement later.

Manager By the way, I've also been noticing the column that says ALLOWABLE INCREASE. I would guess that pertains to increases in the right-hand side.

Right again.

Manager Would you just run through the analysis on the increase side to make sure that I'm with you?

Let's take row 2, the requirement on A. Suppose you want to tighten this requirement.

Manager That means an increase in the required amount of A.

Correct. The allowable increase is 2.375, and the same dual price of −44.44 applies. Since we are tightening the requirement, the constraint will be more difficult to satisfy, and, as you would expect, the cost will go up. Consequently, if we increase the original amount, 5, by any amount up to 2.375, the increase in cost is given by 44.44 times that amount.

Manager In other words, the same dual price pertains to both increases and decreases in the right-hand side. The allowable increase and decrease are provided by the computer, and the dual price is the per-unit change in the objective value over that entire allowable range.

Right. And relaxing a constraint means the objective is improved. Tightening means the objective is impaired.

Manager I even notice that the dual price on B is zero, which means that changes in the value of 100 don't have any effect. In fact, the output indicates that this requirement can be decreased by an infinite amount. I guess that means we don't even need a constraint on B. Why is that?

Because, as I mentioned earlier, if you satisfy the requirements for A and C at a minimum cost, then the requirement for B will automatically be satisfied.

Manager You mean it's redundant?

Well yes, it is redundant in terms of all of the data you provided. If you change that data then it may not be redundant. So I don't really want to say that it is redundant to the model.

Manager Could you be a little more explicit, without getting into a lot of terminology?

Last week, I heard that the cost of ore from location 2 might increase.

Manager That is certainly something I'm concerned about. But I don't see how we can take that kind of uncertainty into account.

This relates to your question about redundancy. The cost of ore from location 2 is the coefficient of $T2$ in the objective function, namely 400. If this value is increased, we would expect the minimum cost of our blend to increase. If the cost of ore from location 2 goes up enough, we might even expect that less of it or maybe even none of it would be used in the optimal blend. This means more of the others must be used because the total amount used has to sum up to 1. This means that the relative importance of the constraints could change. One that had previously been redundant may not now be, and one of the others that had previously been tight may become redundant. A lot of things can happen when you start playing with the data.

Manager Tell me again what you mean by a tight constraint.

It means a constraint with an optimal slack value of zero. Such a constraint is also called *active,* or *binding,* or *effective.*

Manager I'm glad you told me that. What about an equality constraint? Is it considered active or binding or whatever?

Yes. Always.

Manager Fine. But I'm still confused. What does all this have to do with the cost of ore from location 2? Or is the whole thing just too complicated to explain?

Not at all. Let's look at the cost of ore from location 2. We can actually determine the range over which this cost can vary without influencing the optimal blend. In particular, look at the portion of output headed COST SENSITIVITY. In the row corresponding to $T2$ there is something called INCREASE IN C(J) and DECREASE IN C(J). This gives the range in which the cost of $T2$ can vary.

Manager   You mean without changing the optimal mix?

Yes.

Manager   Okay. In other words the cost of $T2$ is now $400 in our model. You mean the output says it could be anywhere between $100 and $466.84 and the optimal mix stays the same?

Exactly.

Manager   I don't see how we can know that.

It's all in the mathematics.

Manager   I'll take your word for that. So if the cost increases from $400 to $450 we have nothing to worry about.

Well, I don't know about that. We know that the optimal mix will stay the same. This means the optimal values of all the variables, including the slacks, stays the same. But our total cost will increase by 50 times the amount of $T2$ being used in the current solution.

Manager   I see. The objective value will go from the old value, $511.11, to the new value

$$511.11 + 50(.70370) = \$546.30$$

Yes. I see what you mean. Everything stays the same except the total cost. Did you say that even the slack values stay the same?

Yes. If the decision variables stay the same then the slacks would have to also.

Manager   That must mean the constraints that are binding also stay the same.

Good for you.

Manager   I see. By the way, what happens if the cost of $T2$ changes by more than the allowable amount?

Then we can no longer be certain about exactly what happens. First of all, the optimal value of $T2$ will change. Second, the optimal values of some of the other variables may also change, but it isn't possible to say exactly which ones or how much. This means that a slack that was positive could become zero, and hence a constraint that was redundant could become binding, if you know what I mean.

Manager   Yes, I think I'm with you.

Good. And it could also mean that a constraint that previously had zero slack could now become redundant in the sense that its slack becomes positive. In other words, once the cost change exceeds the limit of the indicated range, all sorts of things can happen.

Manager   You're talking about a cost change that *exceeds* the allowable limit. What if it actually hits the limit?

Well, then we can say a little more, but it gets a bit complicated.

Manager   Then let's skip it. Anyway, at least we have a limited amount of information about the influence of uncertainty. That strikes me as remarkable.

I agree.

Manager   Okay. Thank you very much. I think I can do pretty well now on my own with the output analysis. We should really call it model analysis, shouldn't we?

I guess so.

Manager   Okay. Thanks again. I'm amazed at how much we can learn about the actual problem, above and beyond the solution.

Right. That is because of the relative simplicity of linear mathematics. By the way, do you mind if I ask you just one question to more or less check you out.

Manager   Okay. Shoot.

You have already noticed on the output that the optimal value of $T4$ is zero.

Manager   True.

I happen to know that ore from location 4 has some desirable tensile properties that haven't really been built into the model.

Manager   That is true.

Also, I understand that it isn't unreasonable to renegotiate the cost of $T4$ periodically.

Manager   Are you referring to the fact that PROTRAC has some family connections in the location 4 enterprise?

Something like that. But my point is this. How much would the cost of $T4$ have to decrease before you're willing to buy some?

Manager   Let's see. The current cost of $T4$ is $500 per ton. I think what you're trying to ask me is this: How much must this cost decrease before we obtain an optimal policy that uses $T4$? Is that your question?

Yes.

Manager   Okay. To find the answer I look at the cost sensitivity portion of the output. If the cost of $T4$ decreases by less than $91.11 per ton then, according to what you just said, the optimal value of this variable remains unchanged. That means it remains at zero. Consequently, in order for $T4$ to become positive its cost would have to be renegotiated down to about $408 a ton, or even less. Right?

Correct. Now can you tell me what happens to the optimal objective value?

Manager   I guess I can figure that out. If the cost decreases as much as $91.11, no change occurs in the optimal values of any of the variables. In the objective function only the cost of T4 is changing. But since the value of T4 stays at zero, the objective value won't change either. I guess it stays at $511.11 as long as the reduction in cost is less than $91.11.

Correct.

Manager But what happens if the reduction exactly equals 91.11? You've told me that in this case the optimal value of T4 will become positive. Is that right?

It *may* become positive at that point. For now let's assume that it does.

Manager Okay, but does this mean that when the cost of T4 is reduced by exactly $91.11 then the total cost suddenly drops down from $511.11?

No. If the cost of T4 decreases by *exactly* the allowable amount per ton, then under normal conditions there will be a solution in which *some* amount of T4 will be used in the optimal mix but other variables also change in value and the total cost will remain at $511.11.

Manager Can we tell how much of T4 will be used?

I'm afraid not. All we know is that there will be some positive value for this variable.

Manager And how do you know all that?

From the mathematics.

Manager And what about these "normal conditions" you've been referring to?

In technical jargon, it's called *nondegeneracy*. We'll get into it later.

Manager Okay. Great. Anyway, under these normal conditions I suppose that if the decrease *exceeds* the allowable amount, the objective value will also begin to decrease.

Very good.

Manager Well then, I think I know what's going on. Do you agree?

Yes. Shall we stop?

Manager Really, since I'm doing so well, I have to ask one final question. What about that column in the first section of the output under the heading REDUCED-COST?

It applies to a variable whose optimal value is zero. It tells how much the per-unit cost of that variable can be reduced before the optimal value of the variable will become positive.

Manager We just answered that question about T4.

I know.

Manager   But we didn't use this column. We used the cost sensitivity part of the output. In fact, I see that exactly the same value, 91.11, appears in both places.

Right.

Manager   So why bother with this reduced-cost column if the same value appears under the cost sensitivity column?

Simply for convenience. The reduced cost pertains to variables whose optimal value is zero. You can easily spot these variables in the top section of the output. In the next column you can immediately read the reduced cost, which is a little easier than going down into the cost sensitivity section.

Manager   Thank you. It's been very instructive!

My pleasure.

5.5 A Summary

When a linear program is solved, the computer output contains the following information.

1   Optimal values are given for the decision variables, the slack variables and the objective function. From the optimal value of the slack variables you can quickly deduce the value of the constraint functions (the amount of resources used, the levels of requirements satisfied, and so on) at an optimal solution. The constraints with zero slack are called *tight, effective, binding,* or *active.* Those with positive slack are called *loose* or *inactive,* and they are redundant in terms of the given data (the given parameters of the problem).

2   The dual price tells you the rate of improvement in the optimal value of the objective function as the right-hand side of a constraint increases. *Improvement* means increase in a max model and decrease in a min model. Right-hand-side sensitivity output gives you an allowable range in right-hand-side (RHS) changes over which the dual price is valid. Remember that the dual price of the ith constraint is the *rate of improvement* in the optimal value of the objective function as the ith RHS is increased with all other right-hand sides held fixed. *Rate of improvement* means improvement in the optimal objective value per unit increase in the ith RHS. For example, if the units of the objective function are dollars and the units of the ith RHS are pounds, then the ith dual price is in units of dollars per pound. If the units of the jth RHS are hours, then the units of the jth dual price are dollars per hour. The dual price is also frequently referred to as a ***dual variable,*** a ***shadow price,*** or an ***imputed price.*** Most computer codes (including the one we use) employ the convention that when an increase in the value of the RHS improves the optimal value of the objective function (increases it for a max problem, decreases it for a min problem), the dual price is positive. This is consistent with our definition in terms of rate of improvement. In the foregoing example, an increase in the value of the minimal requirement for A would make the constraint harder to satisfy and thus impair the optimal objective value, that is, it would make the minimum cost larger. Hence, the rate of improvement is negative, and the dual price is printed as -44.44.

3   Cost sensitivity output tells you the allowable changes that can be made in the objective function coefficients without changing the solution (the optimal values of the variables). If an objective function coefficient is changed by an amount that equals or exceeds an allowable change then under normal conditions (termed *nondegenerate*), there will be an optimal solution with new values for the variables. (This will be clarified in Chapter 9).

4   Reduced cost output applies to variables whose optimal value is zero. It provides the same information as the cost sensitivity output for these variables.

The format used for the solution of LP problems differs somewhat from one software package to another. However, a solid understanding of one system prepares you to deal with any system with a minimum of effort.

The items discussed in items 2, 3, and 4 are in the realm of what is called *sensitivity analysis* or *postoptimality analysis.* These topics, of great importance in applications, will be covered in much more detail in Chapters 8 and 9. For now, the treatment has been introductory, but it should enable you to successfully read and interpret the important information in the output of any LP routine. After some discussion of the geometry of linear programs in the next chapter, these notions will acquire added meaning.

5.6   An Illustration

In Section 5.4, we said that a change in the RHS of the first constraint from 5.0 to 4.5 would lead to an improved optimal cost, but we could not say by how much. All we could say was that the change would be between 11.11 and 22.22. In order to find the exact change, we resubmitted the model to the computer with an RHS of 4.5 on the first constraint. The output is shown in Figure 5.2. You can see that the new optimal objective value is 493.269. Thus

Improvement = 511.11 − 493.269 = 17.841

This result is within the estimates provided in the first analysis.

Suppose that in the manager's original model we wish to know the effect of changing the cost of $T3$ from 600 to 480. This is a decrease of 120, which exceeds the allowable decrease for $T3$ (118.26919) specified in the cost sensitivity section of Figure 5.1. This means we may expect the optimal values of some of the variables to change. Also, the optimal objective value will be improved by at least 120(.03704) = 4.44. That is the most we can say specifically. To get an exact analysis, we resubmitted the problem with a modified objective to the computer. The output is shown in Figure 5.3. Note the changes in the optimal values of the variables. Also note that for the optimal objective value

Change = 511.11 − 505.978 = 5.132

Figure 5.2 *Solution to the ore-blending problem with a new RHS*

```
MIN  800T1+400T2+600T3+500T4
SUBJECT TO
   2)    10T1+3T2+8T3+2T4 >= 4.5
   3)    90T1+150T2+75T3+175T4 >= 100
   4)    45T1+25T2+20T3+37T4 >= 30
   5)    T1+T2+T3+T4= 1
```

VARIABLE	VALUE	REDUCED-COST
T1	0.22115	0.00000
T2	0.73077	0.00000
T3	0.00000	118.26919
T4	0.04808	0.00000
OBJ FCTN	493.269	

ROW	SLACK	DUAL-PRICE
2	0	-26.9231
3	37.9327	0
4	0	-10.5769
5	0	-54.8075

SENSITIVITY ANALYSIS

RANGE IN WHICH BASIS REMAINS THE SAME
    COST SENSITIVITY

VARIABLE	INCREASE IN C(J)	DECREASE IN C(J)
T1	223.63629	233.33328
T2	66.84779	350.00006
T3	INFINITE	118.26919
T4	140.00000	91.11107

RIGHT HAND SENSITIVITY

ROW	ALLOWABLE INCREASE	ALLOWABLE DECREASE
2	0.25000	1.91667
3	37.9327	INFINITE
4	9.50000	0.71428
5	0.04348	0.24077

5.7 Examples and Solutions

Example 1

Use slack and surplus variables as required to convert the following LP problem to standard equality-constraint form.

Min $\quad 7x_1 + 5x_2 - 9x_3 + x_6$

s.t.

$$12x_1 - 2x_4 \geq 13x_3 - 29$$
$$-4x_2 + 5x_3 + 7x_5 \leq 6x_2 + 3x_4 + 15$$
$$x_1 + x_2 + x_3 = x_4 + x_5 - x_6$$
$$x_4 + 7x_6 \leq 92$$
$$x_i \geq 0 \qquad i = 1, 2, 3, 4, 5, 6$$

Figure 5.3   *Solution to the ore-blending problem with a new coefficient for T3*

```
MIN  800T1+400T2+480T3+500T4
SUBJECT TO
    2)    10T1+3T2+8T3+2T4 >= 5
    3)    90T1+150T2+75T3+175T4 >= 100
    4)    45T1+25T2+20T3+37T4 >= 30
    5)    T1+T2+T3+T4= 1


VARIABLE          VALUE
    T1           0.04891         REDUCED-COST
    T2           0.00000         0.00000
    T3           0.43478         0.97825
    T4           0.51630         0.00000
 OBJ FCTN        505.978         0.00000


ROW               SLACK           DUAL-PRICE
    2              0               -26.8478
    3              27.3641          0
    4              0               -10.6522
    5              0               -52.1738

SENSITIVITY ANALYSIS

RANGE IN WHICH BASIS REMAINS THE SAME
    COST SENSITIVITY


VARIABLE        INCREASE        DECREASE
                IN C(J)         IN C(J)


    T1          INFINITE         3.27270
    T2          INFINITE         0.97825
    T3          1.73075         617.50036
    T4          1.33332         980.00024



    RIGHT HAND SENSITIVITY


ROW     ALLOWABLE INCREASE       ALLOWABLE DECREASE


    2          2.24276                 0.52941
    3          27.3641              INFINITE
    4          10.00000                1.50000
    5          0.03516                 0.19395
```

Solution to Example 1

Min $7x_1 + 5x_2 - 9x_3 + x_6$

s.t.

$$12x_1 \qquad\qquad - 13x_3 \; - 2x_4 \qquad\qquad\qquad - s_1 \qquad\qquad = -29$$

$$- 10x_2 \; + \; 5x_3 \; - 3x_4 \; + 7x_5 \; + s_2 \qquad\qquad = \;\;\; 15$$

$$x_1 \; + \; x_2 \; + \; x_3 \; - \; x_4 \; - \; x_5 \; + x_6 \qquad\qquad = \qquad 0$$

$$x_4 \qquad\qquad + 7x_6 \qquad\qquad + s_3 \; = \;\; 92$$

$$x_i \; \geq \quad 0 \qquad i = 1, ..., 6$$

$$s_i \; \geq \quad 0 \qquad i = 1, 2, 3,$$

Example 2

Consider a profit-maximizing LP problem with 100 variables, 50 constraints of the $\leq$ form, and 20 constraints of the $\geq$ form. Use slack and surplus variables as required to convert the problem to standard equality-constraint form and express the result with summation notation. Let c_j denote the objective function coefficients, b_i denote the right-hand sides, and a_{ij} the coefficients of the variables x_j in the constraints.

Solution to Example 2

$$\text{Max} \sum_{j=1}^{100} c_j x_j$$

s.t.

$$\sum_{j=1}^{100} a_{ij} x_j + s_i = b_i \qquad i = 1, 2, ..., 50$$

$$\sum_{j=1}^{100} a_{ij} x_j - s_i = b_i \qquad i = 51, ..., 70$$

$$x_j \geq 0 \qquad j = 1, ..., 100$$
$$s_i \geq 0 \qquad i = 1, ..., 70$$

An alternative but equivalent formulation is

$$\text{Max} \sum_{j=1}^{100} c_j x_j$$

s.t.

$$\sum_{j=1}^{100} a_{ij} x_j + x_{100+i} = b_i \qquad i = 1, ..., 50$$

$$\sum_{j=1}^{100} a_{ij} x_j - x_{100+i} = b_i \qquad i = 51, ..., 70$$

$$x_j \geq 0 \qquad j = 1, ..., 170$$

Example 3

Recall problem 1, Chapter 4, concerning the production of Astros and Cosmos. The solution to this problem is presented in Figure 5.4.
a What are the optimal values of the decision variables?
b What profit will be attained from the optimal solution?
c Does the firm have any excess capacity? If so, how much excess capacity exists, and where?
d How much will the optimal value of the objective function change if the capacity of the Astro line is increased from 70 to 72? Will the value of the objective function increase or decrease?

Figure 5.4 *Solution to Astro-Cosmo production problem*

```
MAX 20A +30C
SUBJECT TO
   2)   A   <= 70
   3)   C   <= 50
   4)   A +2C  <= 120

VARIABLE        VALUE         REDUCED-COST
   A          70.00000         0.00000
   C          25.00000         0.00000
 OBJ FCTN       2150

ROW            SLACK          DUAL-PRICE
   2             0                5
   3             25               0
   4             0                15

SENSITIVITY ANALYSIS

   RANGE IN WHICH BASIS REMAINS THE SAME
       COST SENSITIVITY

VARIABLE        INCREASE       DECREASE
                IN C(J)        IN C(J)

   A            INFINITE       5.00000
   C            10.00000       30.00000


       RIGHT HAND SENSITIVITY

   ROW    ALLOWABLE INCREASE      ALLOWABLE DECREASE


    2           50.00000             50.00000
    3           INFINITE             25.0000
    4           50.00000             50.00000
```

e How much will the value of the objective function change if the capacity of the Cosmo line is decreased from 50 to 40? Will the value of the objective function increase or decrease?

f If labor capacity could be expanded by 10 manhours per day for a cost of $10 per manhour *or* the capacity of the Astro line could be expanded by 16 sets per day at a cost of $2 per set, which alternative would you choose?

g What is the current rate of change in the optimal value of the objective function as the capacity of the Astro line changes? Over what set of values for the capacity of the Astro line does this rate hold?

h What happens to the optimal production plan if the profitability of a Cosmo set increases from $30 to $35? What happens to the optimal value of the objective function?

i What happens to the optimal production plan and the optimal value of the objective function if the profitability of an Astro set decreases by $2?

j What can you say about the optimal value of the objective function if the profitability of a Cosmo set increases from $30 to $45?

Solution to Example 3

a The optimal values of *A* and *C* are 70 and 25, respectively.
b Profit equals $2,150.
c Yes. The firm has excess capacity of 25 sets on the Cosmo line.

d The optimal value of the objective function will increase by 2($5) = $10.
e The optimal value of the objective function will not change because the dual price on row 3 is zero, and this value holds for a decrease of up to 25 units.
f The increase in the optimal value of the objective function from expanding labor capacity by 10 manhours per day would be 10($15) = $150. The cost would be $10(10) = $100 and thus a net increase of $50 would result from this change. A net increase of 16($5) − 16($2) = $48 results from expanding the capacity of the Astro line by 16 sets per day. Thus the correct choice is to expand labor capacity.
g The current rate of change is $5 per Astro set. This rate holds for an increase or a decrease of 50 sets; thus it holds for a line capacity of anywhere between 20 and 120 sets.
h The optimal production plan remains the same, but the optimal value of the objective function increases by $125.
i The optimal production plan remains the same but the optimal value of the objective function decreases by 70($2) = $140.
j The optimal value of the objective function will increase by *at least* 25($15) = $375.

Example 4

A farmer who has specialized in chickens and eggs adjusts the size of her flock on a monthly basis. Let $h_t I_t$ be the *profit* of having I_t chickens on hand at the end of month t. Shortly before the end of month t, she may either buy or sell chickens for c_t dollars each. During month t she cannot sell more chickens than she had on hand at the end of the previous month. She cannot have more than 2,000 chickens on hand at the end of any month. Let I_o be a constant denoting the number of chickens on hand initially (that is, at the end of month 0). The farmer would like to know how many chickens to buy (or sell) in each month in order to maximize her profit over the next T periods.

a Let z_t be the number of chickens bought just before the end of month t. A negative value of z_t will indicate that chickens are sold. Formulate the farmer's problem as an LP model with the variable z_t unconstrained in sign.
b Transform the problem in part a into an LP problem with all variables nonnegative. How does the farmer obtain the optimal values of z_t from the solution to this transformed model?

Solution to Example 4

a

$$\text{Max } \sum_{t=1}^{T} (h_t I_t - c_t z_t)$$

s.t.

$$I_t = I_{t-1} + z_t \qquad t = 1, ..., T$$
$$I_t \leq 2,000 \qquad t = 1, ..., T$$
$$I_t \geq 0 \qquad t = 1, ..., T$$

b Let $z_t = x_t - y_t$

$$\text{Max} \sum_{t=1}^{T} (h_t I_t - c_t x_t + c_t y_t)$$

s.t.

$$I_t = I_{t-1} + x_t - y_t \quad t = 1, ..., T$$
$$I_t \le \quad\quad 2{,}000 \quad\quad t = 1, ..., T$$
$$I_t, x_t, y_t \ge 0$$

The optimal values of z_t, say z_t^*, are obtained by computing $z_t^* = x_t^* - y_t^*$, where x_t^* and y_t^* are optimal values of x_t and y_t in the above model.

Example 5

The E and F production problem presented in Example 1, Section 4.2 was formulated as the following LP problem:

Max $5{,}000E + 4{,}000F$

s.t.

$$E + F \ge 5 \tag{1}$$
$$10E + 15F \le 150 \tag{2}$$
$$20E + 10F \le 160 \tag{3}$$
$$-30E - 10F \le -135 \tag{4}$$
$$E - 3F \le 0 \tag{5}$$
$$E, F \ge 0$$

a Assuming the sign convention stated in the text, what can you say about the dual prices associated with constraints (1) and (2)? Will they be ≥ 0 or ≤ 0?

b Suppose that, rather than maximizing profit, this problem was formulated as a cost-minimization problem. Specifically, assume that the objective is to min $2{,}000E + 3{,}000F$ subject to the same constraints. Now what is the answer to the questions posed in part a?

c Does "impairing" the optimal value of the objective function mean that it becomes larger or smaller?

Solution to Example 5

a The dual price for constraint (1) will be negative since *increasing* the right-hand side will impair the optimal value of the objective function. The dual price for constraint (2) will be positive since *increasing* the right-hand side will enhance the optimal value of the objective function.

b The answers remain the same. The sign of the dual prices is not influenced by the fact that the model is a maximization or a minimization problem.

c The answer to this question depends upon whether or not the problem is max or min. If the objective is max, then impairing means making it smaller. If the objective is min, then impairing means making it larger.

● **Example 6**

What is the interpretation of the dual price on row 5 in Figure 5.1?

Solution to Example 6

Ignoring, for the moment, the allowable increase of .25, the dual price on row 5 indicates the *additional* cost required to make *two* tons of a blend with one-half the original requirements on contents per ton. Thus, $\frac{1}{2}$ (511.111 + 155.55) would be the *total* cost of blending one ton of ore with one-half the original content requirements. In order to see this, suppose we change the RHS value on row 5 from 1 to 2. The constraint then becomes

$$T1 + T2 + T3 + T4 = 2$$

If we divide both sides by 2, we obtain

$$\frac{T1}{2} + \frac{T2}{2} + \frac{T3}{2} + \frac{T4}{2} = 1$$

Let's introduce new variables

$$U1 = \frac{T1}{2}, U2 = \frac{T2}{2}, U3 = \frac{T3}{2}, U4 = \frac{T4}{2}$$

and rewrite the problem using these new variables (replacing $T1$ with $2U1$, and so on), and using the new version of row 5. The objective function becomes

Min $800(2U1) + 400(2U2) + 600(2U3) + 500(2U4)$

Let's consider the first constraint. It becomes

$$10(2U1) + 3(2U2) + 8(2U3) + 2(2U4) \geq 5$$

or

$$10U1 + 3U2 + 8U3 + 2U4 \geq 2.5$$

Continuing this way, we see that replacing the RHS value of 1 in row 5 with the value 2 gives the following equivalent model.

Min $1,600U1 + 800U2 + 1,200U3 + 1,000U4$

s.t.

$$10U1 + 3U2 + 8U3 + 2U4 \geq 2.5$$
$$90U1 + 150U2 + 75U3 + 175U4 \geq 50$$
$$45U1 + 25U2 + 20U3 + 37U4 \geq 15$$
$$U1 + U2 + U3 + U4 = 1$$
$$U1, U2, U3, U4 \geq 0$$

The objective value for this problem is the minimum total cost of blending one ton of ore with half the previous requirements and twice the previous costs.

Equivalently, the objective value is the minimum total cost of blending two tons of ore with half the previous requirements and the same previous costs. The dual price on row 5 is -155.555. The negative sign means the increase from 1 to 2 in the RHS will hurt the objective value. Hence, $511.111 + 155.555$ is the total cost of making two tons of ore with half the previous requirements. Therefore, one-half $(511.111 + 155.555)$ is the total cost of blending one ton of ore with half the previous requirements.

The allowable increase of .25 can now be taken into account. Suppose the value of 1 for the RHS on Row 5 is changed to $1 + c$ where $c \leq .25$. Then the foregoing argument can be followed, replacing the RHS value of 2 with the value $1 + c$. The conclusion is that $(1/1 + c)(511.111 + 155.555c)$ is the total cost of blending one ton of ore with $(1/1 + c)$ times the previous requirements.

5.8 Problems

1 Use slack and surplus variables as required to convert the following LP problem to standard equality-constraint form.

Max $2x_1 - x_3 + 14x_6$

s.t.

$$3x_1 - 2.4x_2 + 12x_3 - 10 \leq \qquad -29x_4$$
$$-x_1 + x_5 + 41x_6 \geq \qquad 22 + 6x_5$$
$$-12 + x_2 + 33x_4 + 16x_5 = 8 - 13x_3 - x_6$$
$$3x_2 - 24x_6 \leq \qquad 18$$
$$x_i \geq \qquad 0 \qquad i = 1, 2, 3, 4, 5, 6$$

2 Consider a linear program with m inequality constraints and n variables, where $m > n$. Show that when this problem is transformed to standard equality-constraint form, the number of variables will exceed the number of constraints; that is, there will be more than m variables.

3 Use summation notation to write a cost-minimizing LP problem with 200 variables, 160 constraints of the form $\leq$, and 60 constraints of the form $\geq$. Let c_j denote the objective function coefficients, b_i denote the right-hand sides, and a_{ij} the coefficients of the variables x_j in the constraints. Use slack and surplus variables as required to convert to standard equality-constraint form and express the result with summation notation.

4 Consider the following problem:

Max $4x_1 + x_2$

s.t.

$$3x_1 + 2x_2 - x_3 \leq 0$$
$$x_1 - 3x_2 \qquad \geq 14$$
$$x_1, x_3 \geq 0$$

Thus, the variable x_2 is unconstrained in sign. Replace x_2 with $y_1 - y_2, y_1 \geq 0, y_2 \geq 0$ to convert this problem to an equivalent form in which all variables are nonnegative. Then convert the latter model to a problem in standard equality-constraint form, with all variables denoted by the symbol z_j (replace xs, ys, and so on, with zs).

5 Consider the Buster Sod problem: Buster Sod operates a 1,200 acre irrigated farm in the Red River Valley of Arizona. Sod's principal activities are raising wheat, alfalfa, and beef. The Red Valley Water Authority has just given its water allotments for next year (Sod was alloted 2,000 acre feet) and Sod is busy preparing his production plan for next year. He figures that beef prices will hold at around $600 per ton and wheat will sell at $1.60 per bushel. Best guesses are that he'll be able to sell alfalfa at $34 per ton, but if he needs more alfalfa to feed his beef than he can raise, he will have to pay $36 per ton to get the alfalfa to his feedlot.

Some technological features of Sod's operation are as follows: wheat yield, 50 bushels per acre; alfalfa yield, 3 tons per acre. Other features are given in Figure 5.5.

Figure 5.5 *Data for Buster Sod problem*

Activity	Labor, Machinery, and Other Costs($)	Water Requirements (acre ft)	Land Requirements (acres)	Alfalfa Requirements (tons)
1 acre wheat	8	1.5	1	
1 acre alfalfa	30	2.5	1	
1 ton of beef	40	.1	.05	4

Define the variables:

W = wheat raised and sold (acres)

A = alfalfa raised (tons)

B = beef raised and sold (tons)

$A3$ = alfalfa bought (tons)

$A5$ = alfalfa sold (tons)

An LP formulation and solution to Buster Sod's problem are shown in Figure 5.6.

a Show calculations that explain the values of the coefficient of W in the objective function and the coefficients of A in the first and second constraints.

b How much water is being used?

c How much beef is being produced?

d Does Sod buy or sell alfalfa?

e How much should Sod pay to acquire another acre of land?

f Interpret the dual price on row 3.

g What happens to the optimal planting policy if the price of wheat triples?

h How much profit will Sod receive from the optimal operation of his farm?

i What happens to the optimal value of the objective function if the cost of alfalfa purchased increases from $36 to $37? (Note: The coefficient of $A3$ is currently—$36 and it will become —$37. Thus the coefficient has *decreased* by $1.)

j How much can the cost of buying alfalfa decrease before the current optimal planting policy will change?

6 Recall the nut-blending scenario in problem 15, Section 4.8. The Party Nut Company has on hand 550 pounds of peanuts, 150 pounds of cashews, 90 pounds of brazil nuts, and 70 pounds of hazelnuts. It packages and sells four varieties of mixed nuts in standard 8-ounce (half-pound) cans. The mix requirements and net wholesale prices are shown in Figure 5.7. The firm can sell all that it can produce at these prices. What mixes of products should it produce?

Figure 5.6   *LP formulation for Buster Sod problem*

```
OBJECTIVE FUNCTION

MAX 72W -10A +560B -36A3+34A5
SUBJECT TO
    2)   W +.33333A +.05B  <= 1200     (Land in acres)
    3)   1.5W +.833330A +.1B  <= 2000  (Water in acre feet)
    4)   -A +4B -A3+A5= 0              (Alfalfa in tons)

VARIABLE        VALUE           REDUCED-COST
    W          0.00000        6168.00092
    A          0.00000        3440.65329
    B      19999.99980           0.00000
    A3     79999.99922           0.00000
    A5         0.00000           2.00000
OBJ FCTN        8.32000E+06

ROW            SLACK          DUAL-PRICE
    2           200              0
    3             0           4160.
    4             0             36.

SENSITIVITY ANALYSIS

RANGE IN WHICH BASIS REMAINS THE SAME
    COST SENSITIVITY

VARIABLE      INCREASE        DECREASE
              IN C(J)         IN C(J)

    W       6168.00092        INFINITE
    A       3440.65329        INFINITE
    B         INFINITE      411.19995
    A3         2.00000      100.21358
    A5         2.00000        INFINITE


        RIGHT HAND SENSITIVITY

    ROW    ALLOWABLE INCREASE        ALLOWABLE DECREASE


    2          INFINITE              200.0000
    3          399.99988            1999.99950
    4        79999.9992              INFINITE
```

Figure 5.7   *Nut mix data*

Mix	Contents	Price per Can ($)
1 (Peanuts)	Peanuts only	.26
2 (Party Mix)	No more than 50% peanuts; at least 15% cashews; at least 10% brazil nuts	.40
3 (Cashews)	Cashews only	.51
4 (Luxury Mix)	At least 30% cashews; at least 20% brazil nuts; at least 30% hazelnuts	.52

The problem can be formulated as the following linear program. Let

Pi = pounds of peanuts used in mix i

Ci = pounds of cashews used in mix i

Bi = pounds of brazil nuts used in mix i

Hi = pounds of hazelnuts used in mix i

Note that in the model given in Figure 5.8:
(1) The coefficient of $P1$ in the objective function is 52 rather than 26 because there are two 8-ounce cans for each pound of peanuts sold as peanuts only.
(2) Row 6 is a rewritten version of the constraint $P2/(P2 + C2 + B2 + H2) \leq .5$. A similar comment applies to each of the rows 7 through 11.

The output in Figure 5.8 is obtained from solving the problem. (We have purposely omitted several of the dual prices.) Use this output to answer the questions. If it is impossible to answer the question, state why.

a What can you say about the dual price associated with row 2? In other words, will it be ≥ 0, or ≤ 0?

Figure 5.8 *Solution for the Party Nut problem*

```
MAX  52P1+80P2+80C2+80B2+80H2+102C3+104P4+104C4+104B4+104H4
SUBJECT TO
   2)    P1+P2+P4 <= 550
   3)    C2+C3+C4 <= 150
   4)    B2+B4 <= 90
   5)    H2+H4 <= 70
   6)    .5P2-.5C2-.5B2-.5H2 <= 0
   7)    -.15P2+.85C2-.15B2-.15H2 >= 0
   8)    -.1P2-.1C2+.9B2-.1H2 >= 0
   9)    -.3P4+.7C4-.3B4-.3H4 >= 0
  10)    -.2P4-.2C4+.8B4-.2H4 >= 0
  11)    -.3P4-.3C4-.3B4+.7H4 >= 0


AFTER ITERATION 12
VARIABLE        VALUE        REDUCED-COST
  P1          380.00000       0.00000
  P2          123.33337       0.00000
  C2           80.00000       0.00000
  B2           43.33333       0.00000
  H2            0.00000      23.99997
  C3            0.00000       6.00002
  P4           46.66667       0.00000
  C4           70.00000       0.00000
  B4           46.66667       0.00000
  H4           70.00000       0.00000
OBJ FCTN      63760.


ROW             SLACK        DUAL-PRICE
  2               0
  3               0
  4               0              108
  5               0              132
  6               0               56
  7              43.               0
  8              18.6667
  9               0              -56.
 10               0              -56
 11               0              -80.
```

Figure 5.8   *Solution for the Party Nut problem* (cont.)

```
SENSITIVITY ANALYSIS

RANGE IN WHICH BASIS REMAINS THE SAME
      COST SENSITIVITY

VARIABLE      INCREASE        DECREASE
              IN C(J)         IN C(J)

   P1         6.00001        11.99998
   P2         8.99999         6.00001
   C2        23.99997         6.00002
   B2        35.99995        56.00000
   H2        23.99997        INFINITE
   C3         6.00002        INFINITE
   P4        INFINITE        35.99995
   C4        55.99998        23.99997
   B4        56.00000        35.99995
   H4        INFINITE        23.99997

       RIGHT HAND SENSITIVITY

  ROW    ALLOWABLE INCREASE        ALLOWABLE DECREASE

    2         INFINITE              380.0000
    3          93.33365              61.42858
    4         143.33334              23.33337
    5          56.00001              70.00000
    6          93.33337              61.66669
    7          43.0000               INFINITE
    8          18.6667               INFINITE
    9          46.66669              70.00000
   10          23.33337              46.66667
   11          28.00000              56.00001
```

b Noting the economic meaning of row 2, can you give a lower bound (not zero) for the dual variable associated with row 2?

c How many 8-ounce cans of Party Mix (mix 2) will be produced at optimality?

d Analyze the effect of changing the price of mix 1 to $.27 per can; $.30 per can.

7 Recall Example 2, Section 4.2. A plant can manufacture five different products in any combination. Each product requires time on each of three machines, as shown in Figure 5.9. All figures are in minutes per pound of product. Each machine is available 128 hours per week. Products *A, B, C, D,* and *E* are purely competitive, and any

Figure 5.9   *Machine-time data (min)*

Product	Machine 1	Machine 2	Machine 3
A	12	8	5
B	7	9	10
C	8	4	7
D	10	0	3
E	7	11	2

amounts made may be sold at respective per-pound prices of $5, $4, $5, $4, and $4. Variable labor costs are $4 per hour for machines 1 and 2, and $3 per hour for machine 3. Material costs for each pound of products *A* and *C* are $2, and $1 for each pound of products *B, D,* and *E.* You wish to maximize profit to the firm. The *LP* formulation and solution are shown in Figure 5.10.

Figure 5.10 *Solution for 5-product, 3-machine problem*

```
MAX 1.41667A +1.43333B +1.85C +2.18333D +1.7E
SUBJECT TO
   2)   12A +7B +8C +10D +7E   <= 7680
   3)    8A +9B +4C +11E       <= 7680
   4)    5A +10B +7C +3D +2E   <= 7680
```

VARIABLE	VALUE	REDUCED-COST
A	0.00000	1.38000
B	0.00000	0.24500
C	512.00000	0.00000
D	0.00000	0.07500
E	511.99994	0.00000
OBJ FCTN	1817.6	

ROW	SLACK	DUAL-PRICE
2	0	.225833
3	0	1.08334E-02
4	3072	0

SENSITIVITY ANALYSIS

RANGE IN WHICH BASIS REMAINS THE SAME
    COST SENSITIVITY

VARIABLE	INCREASE IN C(J)	DECREASE IN C(J)
A	1.38000	INFINITE
B	0.24500	INFINITE
C	0.09286	0.04091
D	0.07500	INFINITE
E	0.11250	0.08125

    RIGHT HAND SENSITIVITY

ROW	ALLOWABLE INCREASE	ALLOWABLE DECREASE
2	2671.30418	2792.72703
3	4388.57125	3839.99899
4	INFINITE	3072.0000

a How many hours are used on each of the three machines?

b What are the units of the dual prices on the constraints that control machine capacity?

c How much should the firm be willing to spend to obtain another hour of time on machine 2?

d How much can the sales price of product *A* increase before the optimal production plan changes? State your answer in the proper units.

8 Problem 7 can be reformulated with definitional variables as suggested in problem 14, Chapter 4. This formulation and solution are shown in Figure 5.11. Use this new solution and reanswer parts *a* through *d* of problem 7 above. In addition, answer parts *a* and *b*, which follow.

  a How much can the variable labor cost of machine 2 increase before the optimal production plan changes?

● b Why is it impossible to find the answer to part *a*, problem 8, with the techniques currently at your disposal if you use the formulation in problem 7? (Looking at the formulation in Example 2, Section 4.2, may be helpful in answering this question.)

9 Use your own computer to find the solution to the first formulation of the Diablo/Red Baron problem given in Example 1, Section 4.7. Then answer the following questions.

Figure 5.11   *Reformulation with definitional variables*

```
MAX 3A +3B +3C +3D +3E -4M1-4M2-3M3
SUBJECT TO
  2)    12A +7B +8C +10D +7E -60M1= 0
  3)     8A +9B +4C +11E -60M2= 0
  4)     5A +10B +7C +3D +2E -60M3= 0
  5)    M1 <= 128
  6)    M2 <= 128
  7)    M3 <= 128
```

VARIABLE	VALUE	REDUCED-COST
A	0.00000	1.38000
B	0.00000	0.24500
C	511.99975	0.00000
D	0.00000	0.07500
E	512.00024	0.00000
M1	128.00000	0.00000
M2	128.00000	0.00000
M3	76.79997	0.00000
OBJ FCTN	1817.6	

ROW	SLACK	DUAL-PRICE
2	0	.2925
3	0	.0775
4	0	.05
5	0	13.55
6	0	.65
7	51.2	0

SENSITIVITY ANALYSIS

RANGE IN WHICH BASIS REMAINS THE SAME
    COST SENSITIVITY

VARIABLE	INCREASE IN C(J)	DECREASE IN C(J)
A	1.38000	INFINITE
B	0.24500	INFINITE
C	0.09286	0.04091
D	0.07500	INFINITE
E	0.11250	0.08125
M1	INFINITE	13.55000
M2	INFINITE	0.65000
M3	1.18182	0.52941

RIGHT HAND SENSITIVITY

ROW	ALLOWABLE INCREASE	ALLOWABLE DECREASE
2	2671.30564	2792.72654
3	4388.56930	3840.00192
4	4607.99898	3072.00192
5	44.52176	46.54544
6	73.14281	64.00001
7	INFINITE	51.2000

a How many quarts of Diablo are produced?

b How much profit does the firm make on these two products?

c Will the dual price on row 4 be ≥ 0, or ≤ 0? Why? Answer the same question about row 6.

d How much should the firm be willing to pay to have another quart of ingredient B available? For how many additional quarts would the firm be willing to pay this price?

e How much can the price of Diablo increase before the composition of the current optimal blend changes?

f How would you explain to your nonmathematical boss the purpose of row 6 and how well the current solution satisfies the condition imposed in this constraint?

10 Solve Example 3, Section 4.7 on your own computer, and then answer the following questions.

a How many units of model B are produced?

b What is the total profit obtained from the optimal plan?

c Will the sign of the dual price associated with row 3 be ≥ 0 or ≤ 0? Explain your answer.

d How much per unit does the firm pay for its decision to satisfy the minimum weekly production requirement for model C? Over how large a decrease would this cost hold?

e How much can the profitability of model B decrease before the optimal production plan would change?

f What are the units of the dual price on row 5?

6 Geometric Representation of the Complete Model

In this chapter, a review of plotting equalities and inequalities is presented. Then, an LP problem is represented in the plane. Slack and surplus variables are introduced. The important facts concerning corner solutions and positive variables are explained and interpreted with the geometric representation.

6.1 Introduction

Geometry can be used as a "picture" to illustrate many of the concepts of constrained optimization. This chapter develops the geometric tools that will enable us to illustrate some important aspects of the LP model. We restrict this geometric presentation to only two decision variables. As you already know, real-world problems are always in higher dimensions, but the general concepts we want you to understand can be clearly represented in two-dimensional space. Our purpose here is not to solve LP problems with geometry—indeed, real-world problems are solved algebraically by computers. The purpose of this approach is to provide you with an understanding of the interrelationships of the model, an understanding that will enable you to use a computer-generated solution more intelligently and to answer conceptual questions about the problem that the computer does not answer.

Although two-dimensional geometry is obviously a very special case, many general concepts can be nicely represented with two-dimensional pictures. For example, a picture will intuitively answer the question, Why is the number of positive variables in an LP solution equal at most to the number of constraints? As another side of the same coin, a picture will show why a linear profit-maximization problem with n products (n variables) and $m > n$ inputs (m resource constraints) will normally have at least $m - n$ resources in excess. In more general models (not necessarily linear), geometric tools can be used to show what can happen if a constraint is added to a problem or if a constraint is tightened or relaxed by changing the right-hand side or if a constraint is unintentionally left out of the model, or included, but in the wrong way.

When you have acquired facility in transforming these and related conceptual questions to a pictorial representation, you will have a good tool for problem analysis. The geometric approach developed and used in this chapter will help you to rely with greater confidence on your own reasoning to answer questions the computer will not answer for you.

6.2 Plotting Equalities and Inequalities

First, let us briefly recall the technique for plotting equalities and inequalities. Begin with the relations

$$2y - x = -2$$
$$2y - x \leq -2$$

In Figure 6.1, the pairs (x,y) satisfying each relation are plotted. Note that the inequality

$$2y - x \leq -2$$

is plotted by first plotting the equality and then determining the appropriate side. Any trial point not on the line can be used to distinguish the sides. For example, let us use the point $(0,0)$, which we note is *above* the line. Evaluate $2y - x$ at the pair $(0,0)$ to obtain $2(0) - 0 = 0$. Since 0 is > -2, and since $(0,0)$ is above the line, all points above the line must satisfy the condition

$$2y - x > -2$$

This is because it is always true that the points on one side of a linear equality plot satisfy $>$, and the points on the other side satisfy $<$. Consequently, the points satisfying the original condition

$$2y - x \leq -2$$

are all points on the line and below it. Students often have an incorrect feeling that the $<$ side of an equality plot is always below the line. Hence, to plot the points satisfying a $\leq$ relation, they change the $\leq$ to $=$, plot the equality, and then hastily include all points below the equality. This is false, since the $<$ side can be above and not below.

For example, consider the relations

Figure 6.1 *Plots of = and ≤ (linear)*

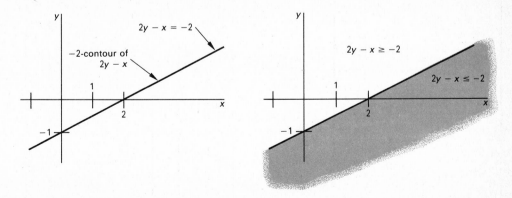

$$2x - y = 2$$
$$2x - y \leq 2$$

The geometric representation (of the pairs (x, y) satisfying each condition) is shown in Figure 6.2. In order to plot

$$2x - y \leq 2$$

we first plot

$$2x - y = 2$$

and then identify the $<$ side. Picking the point $(0,0)$, which is *above* the line, we see that $2(0) - 0 = 0$. Since $0 < 2$, the point $(0,0)$ is on the $<$ side. Hence, the $<$ side in this case is *above* the line. Thus you can see that there is no relationship between the sense of the inequality (that is, $\leq$ or $\geq$) and the "above" or the "below" side of the equality plot. The appropriate side can always be found by using a trial point, as we have demonstrated.

The technique for plotting a $\geq$ inequality or for plotting a nonlinear condition is analogous. Consider, for example, the *nonlinear conditions*

$$x^2 - y = 1$$
$$x^2 - y \geq 1$$

The geometric interpretations are shown in Figure 6.3.

As before, in order to plot the inequality, we first plot the equality and then identify the appropriate side. This can be accomplished by using a trial point, as we did in the linear case. We can use the trial point $(0,0)$ once again, since it does not lie on the equality plot. The value of $x^2 - y$ at $(0,0)$ is 0. Since $0 < 1$ and $(0,0)$ is *above* the equality, the $<$ side is above the curve and the $>$ side is below.

Figure 6.2 *Plots of = and ≤ (linear)*

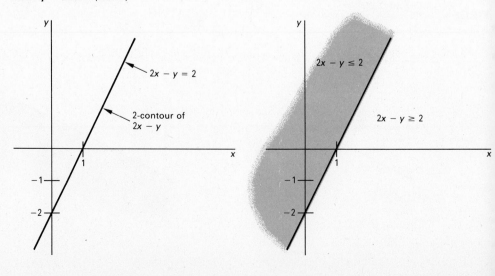

Figure 6.3 *Plots of = and ≥ (nonlinear)*

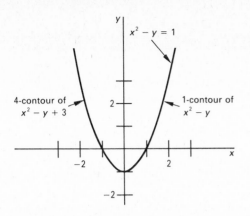 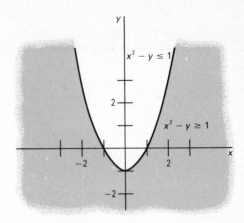

In concluding this review, recall that a *contour* of a function f of two variables is the set of all pairs (x,y) for which $f(x,y)$ is some specified value. When f is a profit function, the contours are often referred to as *isoprofit lines*. When f is a cost function, the contours represent *isocost lines*.

As an example of a contour, suppose f is defined by

$$f(x,y) = 2x - y$$

Then f is a function of the two variables x and y, and the 2-contour of f is the set of all pairs (x,y) for which $f(x,y) = 2$. That is, the 2-contour is the set of all pairs (x,y) for which

$$2x - y = 2$$

The plot of the 2-contour of f is shown in Figure 6.2.

As other examples, Figure 6.1 shows the -2-contour of the function $q(x,y)$ defined by

$$q(x,y) = 2y - x$$

and Figure 6.3 shows the 1-contour of the nonlinear function g defined by

$$g(x,y) = x^2 - y$$

For our final example, consider the nonlinear function h defined by

$$h(x,y) = x^2 - y + 3$$

Suppose we wish to represent the 4-contour of h. Notice that

$$h(x,y) = x^2 - y + 3 = 4 \quad \text{if and only if} \quad x^2 - y = 1$$

Hence, the 4-contour of h coincides with the 1-contour of g. This is also illustrated in Figure 6.3.

In summary:

Plotting contours reduces to plotting equalities. Plotting inequalities also reduces to plotting equalities, or contours, and then identifying the correct side.

6.3   A Linear Model with Inequality Constraints

Let us return to the PROTRAC E and F problem (Example 1, Section 4.2). This problem was formulated as the following linear program:

Max $5{,}000E + 4{,}000F$ (Max profit)

s.t.

$$
\begin{aligned}
E + F &\geq 5 && \text{(Minimal production requirement)}\\
E &\leq 3F && \text{(Market position balance)}\\
10E + 15F &\leq 150 && \text{(Capacity in Department } A)\\
20E + 10F &\leq 160 && \text{(Capacity in Department } B)\\
-30E - 10F &\leq -135 && \text{(Contractual labor agreement)}\\
E, F &\geq 0
\end{aligned}
$$

Recall that E and F denote, respectively, the quantities of earth-moving and forestry equipment to be produced in the next two weeks. Since there are only two decision variables (E and F) in the model, we can provide a geometric interpretation. First of all, consider the constraints:

The set of all nonnegative values of the decision variables that satisfies all the constraints is termed the constraint set, or the feasible set.

In keeping with this definition, any pair of nonnegative values for E, F that satisfies all the constraints is said to be *feasible*. These are the *allowable values* of (E,F) according to our model. Note that it is incorrect to speak of a feasible value of E separately, or a feasible value of F separately. The term *feasible* (in this two-dimensional illustration) applies to a pair of numbers, not to a single number. Thus, in this case, we speak of feasible pairs of values (E,F), not of feasible values for E (or F) separately. In order to illustrate these feasible pairs geometrically, you merely plot the constraint set, which is done by plotting one constraint at a time in the same picture. To accomplish this, for each constraint:

1 Change the inequality to equality.
2 Plot the equality.
3 Identify the correct side for the original inequality.

Let us start by observing that since we are only interested in nonnegative values of the decision variables, we need only plot the constraints in the first (northeast) quadrant of the plane. Now consider the first constraint

$E + F \geq 5$

Letting E denote the horizontal axis and F the vertical, the points (E,F) that satisfy the first constraint are shown in Figure 6.4. Notice our convention of denoting the relevant side of the equality line with an arrow and $\leq$ or $\geq$ as appropriate. In this case, since the first constraint is $\geq$, and since the $\geq$ side is above the line, we show an arrow labeled with $\geq$ pointing above the line.

Now consider the second constraint

$$E \leq 3F \quad \text{or} \quad E - 3F \leq 0$$

In Figure 6.5, the plot of this condition appears along with the first condition $E + F \geq 5$. The points (E,F) that simultaneously satisfy both constraints lie in the shaded region. Note that adding the second constraint to the picture has imposed more stringent conditions on the decision variables, and, as shown in Figure 6.5, has "trimmed down" the constraint set.

It will always be the case that adding more constraints either trims down the constraint set, or, possibly, leaves the set unaffected. Adding additional constraints can never enlarge the constraint set.

Adding constraints amounts to imposing tighter conditions on the decision variables, and it is clear that this can never increase the number of allowable decisions. This is easily seen geometrically in Figures 6.6, 6.7, and 6.8, which show consecutive additions of the third, fourth, and fifth constraints. Figure 6.8, with all five constraints plotted, illustrates the entire *feasible set,* also called the *constraint set.* In two dimensions, a problem with only linear constraints will always have a set of feasible points that is a convex, flat-sided figure called a *polygon.* A generalization of this fact also holds for problems with only linear constraints in any dimension, and the resulting figure is called

Figure 6.4 *PROTRAC E and F problem: the first constraint*

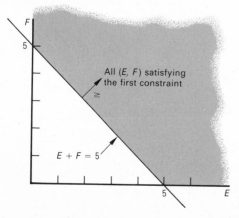

Figure 6.5 *PROTRAC E and F problem: the second constraint added*

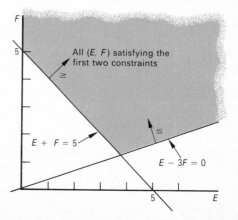

Figure 6.6   *PROTRAC E and F problem: the third*
constraint added

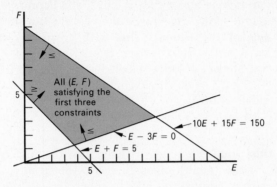

Figure 6.7   *PROTRAC E and F problem: the fourth*
constraint added

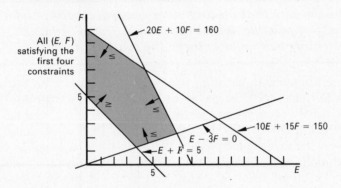

Figure 6.8   *PROTRAC E and F problem: the entire*
constraint set

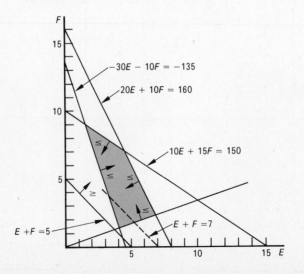

Figure 6.9 *Possible LP constraint sets*

a *convex polytope.* Figure 6.9 suggests the latitude of the possible shapes for these constraint sets in two dimensions. Figure 6.10 shows what LP constraint sets cannot look like. With pencil and paper and a few examples, you will be able to convince yourself that none of the shapes in Figure 6.10 can be produced by a system of linear inequalities. The shape of an LP constraint set is important, and later we shall investigate how it endows the model with many of its exceptional properties.

Returning to Figure 6.8, notice that although the problem has five constraints, only four of them are required to define the feasible set. This is because, as the picture clearly indicates, any point that satisfies constraints 2 through 5 will also, automatically, satisfy the first constraint, $E + F \geq 5$, as well. In the sense that the first constraint is superfluous for the given set of data, it could be (and often is) termed *redundant*. This redundant constraint helps to illustrate the significance of a geometric representation. The algebraic representation of the model does not reveal the presence of the redundant constraint, but simply translating the model into geometry (algebra in pictures) reveals the phenomenon immediately. The geometric representation is distinctly more revealing than just "saying the same thing as the algebra says but in a slightly different language." Moreover, the geometric representation shows you in a picture the precise meaning of the term *redundant*. We have defined *redundant* in words, but the picture has a more effective intuitive appeal.

Now, having said that the first constraint is redundant, we quickly add that this terminology can be misleading. Given the parameter values (the data) we are using, it is true that the first constraint adds nothing to the model; that is, it does not help to define the constraint set. However, suppose that management insists that at least seven units of E and F be produced in total in the next two weeks. Then the RHS of the first constraint changes to 7 instead of 5. Using geometry again and plotting the modified first constraint, you will see that it is no longer redundant. In other words, *tightening* the requirement from 5 to 7 forces us to cut off some previously allowable decisions. (This is shown with the dotted line in Figure 6.8.) It is generally true that a constraint that is redundant for a given set of data may no longer be redundant

Figure 6.10 *Sets that cannot be LP constraint sets*

when some of the data are changed. That is why the constraint is in the model—because the planner believes that there may be conditions under which it may become important. In short, we must be careful when terming a constraint *redundant*, and we must appreciate the specificity of this designation.

Now that a clear representation of the allowable decisions has been obtained, we can state the essence of a constrained optimization model as follows:

Find a feasible point that, relative to all other feasible points, produces an optimum value of the objective function.

The optimum value will be a maximum or minimum value, depending on the particular model. It is important to understand the displayed key concept completely. It does *not* say, "Find a point that, first of all, optimizes the objective function, and, second, also lies in the feasible set." It says, "Find a point that, first of all, lies in the feasible set, and second, find such a point that yields an optimal value for the objective function when compared *only* to all other points in the feasible set."

To clarify this, suppose that we are working in a max context and that f is the objective function. Let f be a function of two variables, which we shall denote as (x_1, x_2) instead of (x, y). Thus, we are considering the function $f(x_1, x_2)$. The maximum value of this function may occur at some point, say $(\hat{x}_1, \hat{x}_2)$, situated far from the constraint set. Or, possibly, the function f may not even have a maximum value. There may, for example, be points in the domain of f that produce larger and larger values for the function, with no bound. However, neither of these possibilities concerns us. We care *only* about the values $f(x_1, x_2)$ produced by points (x_1, x_2) in the constraint set. We are restricting the domain of f, if you like, to this set. Our vision is extremely myopic, for it is over only these restricted values that we seek to maximize the objective. Such a feasible point, say (x_1^*, x_2^*), that maximizes the objective over the constraint set, is called a *solution* to the problem. The values $x_1 = x_1^*$, $x_2 = x_2^*$ are called the *optimal values of the decision variables.* More precisely, (x_1^*, x_2^*) is often called an *optimal solution*, but we shall frequently use the simpler term *solution* to mean the same thing. If f is the objective function, and if (x_1^*, x_2^*) is a solution, then $f(x_1^*, x_2^*)$ is called the *optimal objective value*, or, sometimes, merely the *optimal value*. The important point to keep straight is that the term *solution* refers to optimal values of the decision variables. The term *optimal value* (singular) refers to the objective function evaluated at a solution.

You will ultimately learn that a given problem may or may not have a solution and, if it does, there may be more than one. If there is a single (one and only one) solution, the solution is said to be *unique*. Otherwise, we sometimes say that the problem has *multiple*, or *alternative, optima*.

Now let us analyze geometrically whether the above PROTRAC E and F model has a solution. Thus far we have seen how to illustrate the entire constraint set. In order to illustrate the complete model, we need to get the objective function values into the picture. One way to do this would be to attempt to plot the graph of the objective function over the constraint set.

Unfortunately, to do so requires a two-dimensional rendering of a three-dimensional phenomenon; in other words, we would have to represent E, F, and $f(E, F)$ with a picture on a two-dimensional sheet of paper. Such drawings are usually meaningful only to those who already understand the subject. A much simpler and more direct approach is to use the contours of the objective function. Here's how that is done.

For the above model, the objective function $f(E, F)$ is defined by

$$f(E, F) = 5,000E + 4,000F$$

Contours of this function are points (E, F) for which $f(E, F)$ has some fixed, preassigned value. It is easy to plot such sets of points. For example, three contours are shown in Figure 6.11. We obtained these contours by plotting the three straight lines

$$5,000E + 4,000F = 8,000$$
$$5,000E + 4,000F = 20,000$$
$$5,000E + 4,000F = 32,000$$

You see from the illustration that the contours are parallel lines. Of course, we have plotted only three. There are, in fact, an infinite number of contours. Each one has the equation

$$5,000E + 4,000F = C$$

We can assign any value whatsoever to the constant C and we obtain a contour. There are as many contours of this function as there are possible values for

re 6.11 *Three contours of f where f(E, F) = 5,000E +*
4,000F

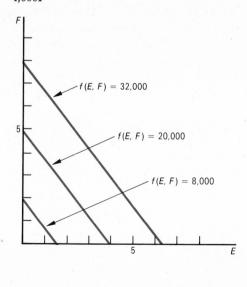

Figure 6.12 *The complete model*
(inequality-constraint representation)

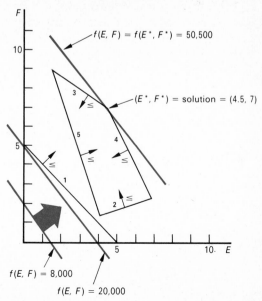

C. We cannot plot very many, but we don't need to. If we plot only two contours we gain most of the important information we need: namely, the shape of the contours and the uphill direction. One contour of *f* shows the shape (in this case, a straight line with a particular tilt). Two contours of *f* are enough to indicate that the contour values increase as the line moves to the northeast, which is thus the "uphill" direction. Now we can illustrate the complete model by placing the objective function contours in the same picture with the constraint set. This is done in Figure 6.12.

Here is what Figure 6.12 reveals. First, the numbers in boldface type label the constraints. Thus, the line labeled **1** is the first constraint, **2** is the second constraint, and so on. The colored lines represent three contours of the objective function $f(E, F) = 5{,}000E + 4{,}000F$. Since we are considering a max problem, we want to identify the position of the highest-valued contour that touches the constraint set in at least one point. To help locate this contour, you can plot one contour, such as $f(E, F) = 8{,}000$. Then you identify the uphill direction. You can do this with a trial point, just as we did when plotting inequalities. For example, since $f(0, 0) = 0 < 8{,}000$, it is clear that the uphill direction is to the northeast. Identify this direction with an arrow, as in Figure 6.12. Then, in your mind's eye, imagine sliding the plotted contour uphill, always parallel to itself, into the constraint set, and finally stopping at the point just before you leave the constraint set behind. In this way you can see that the highest-valued contour is the one that touches the constraint set at the point labeled (E^*, F^*). The value of the objective function at (E^*, F^*) is the number $f(E^*, F^*)$. Consequently, the contour that passes through the point (E^*, F^*) represents the set of all points (E, F) for which $f(E, F) = f(E^*, F^*)$. This contour is identified in Figure 6.12 as $f(E, F) = f(E^*, F^*)$. The distinguished point (E^*, F^*) is the solution to the problem. You can see that the solution in this case is unique. Reading from the graph, it looks like E^* is about 4.5 and F^* is about 7. You can find the exact solution as follows. The point (E^*, F^*) lies on the intersection of line **3** and line **4**. This means that (E^*, F^*) satisfies the third and fourth constraints as equalities. That is, it must be true that:

$$10E^* + 15F^* = 150$$

$$20E^* + 10F^* = 160$$

If you solve this system of equations, you will find that

$$E^* = 4.5$$

$$F^* = 7$$

Thus the optimal objective value is

$$f(E^*, F^*) = 5{,}000E^* + 4{,}000F^* = 5{,}000(4.5) + 4{,}000(7) = 50{,}500$$

Thus, with the help of the picture we can conclude that the solution to the problem (the optimal production levels) is the point (4.5,7), and the optimal objective value (the maximum profit) is 50,500.[1]

---

1   For now, we are ignoring the fact that fractional quanties such as 4.5 may be meaningless in the *E* and *F* context. This complication will be treated in some detail in Chapter 14.

Figure 6.13 *You always get a corner solution*

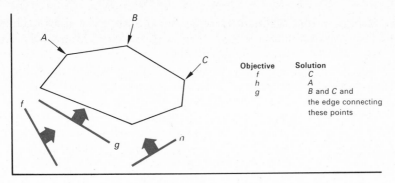

We shall now use this geometric solution to motivate and explain some important properties of the solutions of LP problems. Note that the above solution occurs at a corner of the constraint set. In LP jargon such corners are called *extreme points*. Now imagine taking a different linear objective function, with the same constraint set, and solving the problem again. All that happens is that the contours of the objective function will assume a new tilt and, again you will find a corner solution. This will happen no matter how much you change the objective, as long as it remains linear. You can even change the constraint set, and the same result is obtained, as long as everything is kept linear.

In Figure 6.13, you see a six-sided constraint set and contours of three *different* objective functions, denoted *f, g,* and *h.* In each case, the arrow on the contour indicates the direction in which we are sliding the plotted contour (uphill for a max problem, downhill for a min problem). We see that in each case there is an optimal solution at a corner. We also note that when the objective contours are parallel to the far side, as are the contours of *g,* the optimal contour is coincident with that side. In this case, there are many solutions (two corners and all points between the two). But, still, it is true that there is a corner solution. Thus, the geometry illustrates an important fact about LP problems:

In an LP problem, if there is a solution, there is always a corner solution. (There may be noncorner solutions as well.)

In the next section, you will see that this fact explains why the computer solution to a linear program never has more positive variables than the number of constraints.

6.4 A Linear Model with Equality Constraints

In Chapter 5, you studied the standard equality-constraint form of an LP model. Recall that this means slack and surplus variables are employed to convert all inequality constraints to equality form. You may wish to review the discussion of slack and surplus variables in Section 5.3 at this point, for our next goal is to convert the E and F model of Section 6.3 into standard equality-constraint form. This means one surplus variable and four slack variables must be used. The result is

Max $5,000E + 4,000F$

s.t.

$$
\begin{aligned}
E + F - x_1 &= 5 \\
E - 3F + x_2 &= 0 \\
10E + 15F + x_3 &= 150 \\
20E + 10F + x_4 &= 160 \\
-30E - 10F + x_5 &= -135 \\
E, F, x_i &\geq 0 \qquad i = 1, 2, 3, 4, 5
\end{aligned}
$$

This is a problem with a total of seven variables: two decision variables, four slacks, and one surplus. This is the problem the computer would solve. Since there are seven variables in this problem, you may think that we cannot represent it geometrically. However, in determining whether or not you can picture a model with geometry, the important factor is the number of *decision variables*. If there are more than two decision variables the model cannot be pictured, but if there are only two decision variables then indeed we can obtain a useful geometric representation. The basic idea is this. Plot the complete model as in Figure 6.12, but now replace the numerical label on each constraint (that is, on the line corresponding to the equation for each constraint) with the corresponding slack or surplus variable. This labeling is exhibited in Figure

Figure 6.14   *The complete model (equality-constraint representation)*

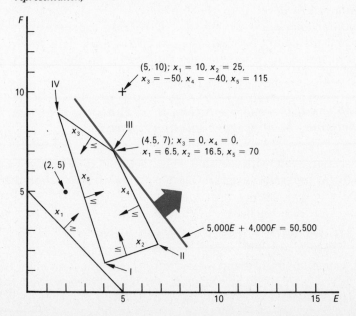

6.14, where you will see x_1 written on the first constraint, x_2 written on the second, and so on.

Here is how you interpret this figure. Take a given constraint, say the third. It is labeled with its slack variable x_3. You know that x_3 is a slack (not a surplus) because you see the constraint is also labeled with the $\leq$ sign, and we have learned that this means a slack variable must be added to the left-hand side in order to form an equality. Associated with each point (E, F) in the plane there will be a value for this slack variable x_3. This value will depend on the particular point (E, F) being considered. At any particular set of values (E, F) the value of x_3 will always be given by

$$x_3 = 150 - 10E - 15F$$

This equality shows that as the values of E and F change the value of x_3 will also change. At each pair of values (E, F) that lies *on* the third constraint line, the slack variable x_3 has a value of zero. This is because for any pair of values (E, F) on this line we know that, by the definition of the line,

$$10E + 15F = 150$$

Hence, for such values of E and F it must be true that

$$x_3 = 150 - 10E - 15F = 0$$

For example, consider the point (4.5,7), which lies on the line. The value of x_3 is given by

$$x_3 = 150 - 10E \quad - 15F$$
$$= 150 - 10(4.5) - 15(7)$$
$$= 150 - 150$$
$$= 0$$

Note that for completely analogous reasons, the value of x_4 associated with the point (4.5,7) is also zero.

Now consider any point (E, F) *not* on the third constraint line. If it is in the direction of the arrow, the value of x_3 is positive. Otherwise, in the opposite direction, the value of x_3 is negative. Thus, the arrow on the third constraint points in the direction of *increasing* values of x_3.

For example, consider the point (2,5). The associated value of x_3 is given by

$$x_3 = 150 - 10E - 15F = 150 - 10(2) - 15(5) = 55$$

We know that in order for an inequality constraint to be satisfied the associated slack (or surplus) variable must be nonnegative in the converted equality constraint. Thus we can conclude that this point (2,5) is on the "correct" side of the third constraint (that is, in the direction of the arrow). Indeed, you can verify in Figure 6.14 that the point (2,5) does lie on the $\leq$ side of the third constraint. But at the point (5,10) you can compute

$$x_3 = 150 - 10E - 15F = 150 - 10(5) - 15(10) = -50$$

Since the slack value is negative, it must be the case that this point is on the "wrong" side of the constraint. This means that (5,10) does not satisfy

$$10E + 15F \leq 150$$

Another way of saying the same thing is that the equivalent conditions

$$10E + 15F + x_3 = 150$$
$$x_3 \geq 0$$

are not satisfied by the pair of values $E = 5$, $F = 10$.

Thus, you can see that there is a particular value for x_3 associated with each possible pair of values (E,F). In the same way, at each possible pair (E,F) there are also particular values for the other slack and surplus variables x_1, x_2, x_4, and x_5. All these values are shown in Figure 6.14 for the two points (4.5,7) and (5,10). At (4.5,7), we have

$$x_1 = E + F - 5 = 4.5 + 7 - 5 = 6.5$$
$$x_2 = 3F - E = 3(7) - 4.5 = 16.5$$
$$x_5 = -135 + 30E + 10F = -135 + 30(4.5) + 10(7) = 70$$

Thus, at (4.5,7), since this is a feasible point, all slack and surplus values are nonnegative. Or, we could reverse this sentence and say that since all slack and surplus values are nonnegative, as are the values of E and F, the point is feasible.

At the pair of values (5,10), we have

$$x_1 = E + F - 5 = 5 + 10 - 5 = 10$$
$$x_2 = 3F - E = 3(10) - 5 = 25$$
$$x_3 = 150 - 10E - 15F = 150 - 10(5) - 15(10) = -50$$
$$x_4 = 160 - 20E - 10F = 160 - 100 - 100 = -40$$
$$x_5 = -135 + 30E + 10F = -135 + 150 + 100 = 115$$

You can see in Figure 6.14 that the point (5,10) is on the correct side of the first, second, and fifth constraints but on the wrong side of the third and fourth constraints. This is why the associated values of x_3 and x_4 are negative in the above equations.

Now let us consider any *feasible* pair of values (E,F) in Figure 6.14. You have seen that with this point (E,F) are associated particular slack and surplus values x_1, x_2, x_3, x_4, x_5. Since (E,F) is feasible, we know that all of these slack and surplus values are nonnegative. However, some of these values may be zero. The values that are zero identify the constraints which are called *active* (or, sometimes, called *effective*, or *binding*, or *tight*) at the pair of values (E,F). For example, if (E,F) is *well inside* the constraint set, as is, for example, the point (5,5) in Figure 6.14, then all x_i associated with this point are positive and no constraints are active. At such a point, all of the constraints are termed *inactive*. Note that since the slack variable x_1 is *positive* for every feasible point (because the first constraint does not touch the constraint set), it is true that the first constraint is inactive at all feasible points.

For any pair of values lying *on* a constraint, the associated slack or surplus variable is always zero. For example, for any point lying on the second constraint, we know that x_2 must be zero and hence the second constraint is active at such a point. Note that whether or not a constraint is active depends on the particular point being considered. That is, the concept of *active* or *inactive* is a concept relative to a particular point. We also observe that at each corner in Figure 6.14, two of the x_i variables will be zero, and hence there are two active constraints at each corner.

In summary:

Given any feasible point, the slack and surplus variables that are zero at that point identify the active constraints at that point. In other words, the active constraints at a point are those constraints on which the point lies.

The slack and surplus variables that are positive identify the inactive constraints at that point.

6.5 Positive Variables and Corner Solutions

There are five constraints in the model picture in Figure 6.14. In this figure, you can see that there are four corners to the constraint set, marked I, II, III, and IV. At each corner, it is clear that two and only two of the x_is will be zero. Since there are seven variables in total in this problem (in standard equality-constraint form), this means that exactly five variables must be positive at each corner. Thus, in this picture, the number of positive variables at each corner exactly equals the number of constraints. The geometric interpretation in Figure 6.14 enables you to read off the positive and zero variables at each corner. The easiest way to do this is to identify the zero variables first, since they are determined by the lines that intersect at the corner. The remaining variables must always be positive, since each corner is feasible and in our standard equality-constraint form all variables are nonnegative at a feasible point. You can verify the facts in Figure 6.15 for the corners in Figure 6.14.

Figure 6.15 *Variables data for geometric representation in Figure 6.14*

Corner	Zero Variables	Positive Variables
I	x_2, x_5	E, F, x_1, x_3, x_4
II	x_2, x_4	E, F, x_1, x_3, x_5
III	x_3, x_4	E, F, x_1, x_2, x_5
IV	x_3, x_5	E, F, x_1, x_2, x_4

You may have noted that in Figure 6.14 the decision variables E and F are always positive. In general this certainly need not be the case. (Be sure you make the distinction between positive (> 0) and nonnegative (≥ 0) at

Figure 6.16   *An LP constraint set with decision variables*
at some corners = 0

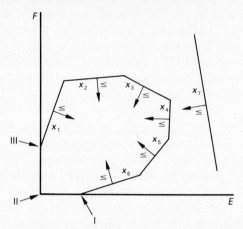

this point.) For example, consider the hypothetical constraint set illustrated in Figure 6.16.

As before, each constraint is labeled with its slack variable and three corners are identified with roman numerals. For these three corners in Figure 6.16 we have variables as noted in Figure 6.17.

Figure 6.17   *Variables data for geometric representation in*
Figure 6.16

Corner	Zero Variables	Positive Variables
I	F, x_6	$E, x_1, x_2, x_3, x_4, x_5, x_7$
II	E, F	$x_1, x_2, x_3, x_4, x_5, x_6, x_7$
III	E, x_1	$F, x_2, x_3, x_4, x_5, x_6, x_7$

Thus there are some corners at which one or more of the decision variables are zero.

There is another point to be made about Figure 6.16, one that reemphasizes our earlier statement about the analytic power of geometric interpretations of LP problems. To demonstrate that it is possible to have a corner at which one or more decision variables take the value zero, we simply drew a feasible set that used an axis to form at least one of the corners. The constraint set we drew corresponds to an actual problem with seven inequality constraints. Indeed, it would be a matter of simple arithmetic to find the algebraic representation of the inequalities we drew, if we wanted to. There is no advantage to doing so, however. The point is that it is often possible to reach conclusions about LP problems with an appropriately chosen diagram in two-dimensional space.

We now note that there are seven positive variables at corners I, II, and III in Figure 6.16, and again we see that this is *exactly* equal to the number of constraints. You can easily see from Figure 6.16 that this will also be the case at the remaining five corners. At each such corner, two slack variables are zero and the remaining seven variables (two decision and five slack) must be positive.

The natural question to ask is whether the number of positive variables is always equal to the number of constraints. The answer is no, and we can illustrate the case with a picture of another constraint set. In Figure 6.18, at the corner identified as D, we have zero variables x_1, x_2, and x_3, and positive variables E, F, x_4, and x_5. Thus, at this corner there are only four positive variables but the problem has five constraints. Here the number of positive variables is less than the number of constraints. You can see in this figure that at every other corner the number of positive variables is exactly equal to the number of constraints (five).

The problem with the corner D is that it is "overdetermined." Normally, in two dimensions, a point will be determined by the intersection of two lines. As you can see in Figure 6.18, three lines go through corner D. When we say that this corner is overdetermined we mean that there are too many lines going through this point, and for this reason the number of positive variables is less than the number of constraints. This is a situation that in technical LP jargon is called *degeneracy*. The corner D is said to be *degenerate*.

In summary, then, our geometric interpretations have illustrated the following important fact:

For any LP problem in standard equality-constraint form, the number of positive variables at any corner is less than or equal to the number of constraints. If it is less than the number of constraints, the corner is degenerate.

At this point it is time to introduce some additional LP jargon. At a nondegenerate corner, the positive variables are called *basic variables*, and the set of positive variables is called the *basis*. The zero variables at a nondegenerate corner are called *nonbasic variables*. At a degenerate corner these definitions break down, but any further elaboration would not suit our present purposes.

Figure 6.18 *A degenerate corner: five constraints but only four positive variables at D*

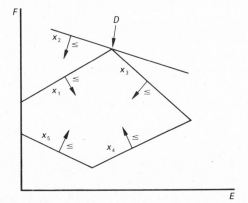

We are now led to a very important result. We have stated in Section 6.3 that in an LP problem, if there is a solution, then there is always a corner solution (though there may be others as well). In this section, we have stated that for a problem in standard equality-constraint form, at *any* corner the number of positive variables is less than or equal to the number of constraints. We have also stated previously that the computer always solves a problem in standard equality-constraint form. These assertions are all tied together with a single additional fact. When the computer produces a solution, it is always a corner solution. That is because the simplex algorithm, which is employed in computer codes, works by moving from one corner of the constraint set to another until it reaches an optimal corner solution. Thus, we have developed the following key concept:

The computer solution to an LP problem always has at most m positive variables, where m is the number of constraints.

The number m can be determined by looking either at the original problem or at the problem in standard equality-constraint form, since the conversion from one to the other affects only the number of variables, not the number of constraints. If the computer solution has less than m positive variables it is called a *degenerate solution* because it corresponds to a degenerate corner.

To illustrate this important fact, let us return to the PROTRAC E and F model. We can now prove that under normal conditions there will always be a solution to this problem in which *at least* three of the constraints will be inactive or ineffective. By the phrase "under normal conditions," we mean "in a nondegenerate situation." In such a case, there will be exactly five positive variables in any computer solution because the problem has five constraints. Two of the five positive variables could be E and F. Thus, *at least* three of them must be x_is. This means at least three constraints are inactive. For any given set of data (parameter values) at least three of the constraints can, in theory, be ignored. They do not have any effect on the problem. Unfortunately, it is not possible to tell which particular constraints will be inactive before obtaining a solution. We only know there will be at least three. Consequently, in practice, all constraints must be included in the model. Referring back to the graphic solution in Figure 6.12, you can see that the third and fourth constraints are active at the solution (4.5,7). The remaining three constraints (first, second, and fifth) are inactive.

As another more general illustration, consider an LP problem with m stockpile constraints of the $\leq$ form. Each stockpile represents the limited availability of a particular resource. Suppose that these are the only constraints, and suppose there are two decision variables in the problem, and $m > 2$. Then, under normal conditions at least $m - 2$ of the stockpiles will *not* be completely consumed at optimality. By now, you should be able to illustrate this fact for yourself with a picture. The generalization to n decision variables is straightforward. If $m > n$, then under normal conditions at least $m - n$ of the stockpiles will not be completely consumed at optimality.

As a final illustration, recall the diet model specified in problem 17, Chapter

4. The problem is to select the quantities of each of 116 foods so as to satisfy the requirements for 16 essential nutrients at a minimum cost. There are 16 inequality constraints ($\geq$) representing nutrient requirements. Hence, in the standard equality-constraint form there are a total of 132 variables (116 decision variables and 16 surplus variables). Since there are only 16 constraints, at most 16 of these 132 variables will be positive in an optimal computer solution. This means we know ahead of time that in such a solution the minimum-cost diet can include *at most* 16 foods. For each nutrient requirement that is inactive, there will be one less food in the optimal diet.

6.6 Examples and Solutions

Example 1

Plot the set of values for x_1 and x_2 that satisfy the inequality

$$7x_1 + 6x_2 \leq 42$$

Solution to Example 1

The solution is shown in Figure 6.19.

 igure 6.19

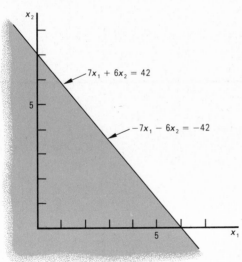

$7x_1 + 6x_2 = 42$

$-7x_1 - 6x_2 = -42$

Example 2

Suppose you have a constraint of the form $a_1x_1 + a_2x_2 \geq b$. Would you expect the set of points satisfying the constraint to be above or below the line $a_1x_1 + a_2x_2 = b$?

Now, plot the set of values for x_1 and x_2 that satisfy the inequality

$$-7x_1 - 6x_2 \geq -42$$

Solution to Example 2

The set of points (x_1, x_2) that satisfy

$7x_1 + 6x_2 \leq 42$

also satisfy the inequality

$-7x_1 - 6x_2 \geq -42$

Thus, the required plot is the same as the one shown in Figure 6.19.

Note that although the constraint is of $\geq$ form, the points satisfying the constraint lie below, not above, the equality line. From Example 1 you can see that the points satisfying $7x_1 + 6x_2 \geq 42$ lie above the line. Thus, in general you cannot say whether the $\geq$ side of a constraint is above or below the line. The appropriate side must be determined by using a trial point and the actual data that define the constraint.

Example 3

Plot the feasible set for the following problem:

Min $5x_1 + 2x_2$

s.t.

$3x_1 + 6x_2 \geq 18$

$5x_1 + 4x_2 \geq 20$

$8x_1 + 2x_2 \geq 16$

$7x_1 + 6x_2 \leq 42$

$x_1, x_2 \geq 0$

Solution to Example 3

The solution is shown in Figure 6.20.

Figure 6.20

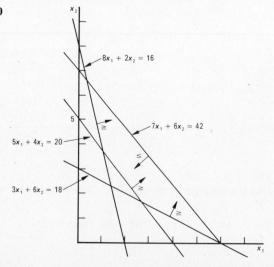

Example 4

Plot the 10- and 20-contours for the objective function in the problem given in Example 3. Indicate the downhill side of the 10-contour and the uphill side of the 20-contour.

Solution to Example 4

The solution is shown in Figure 6.21.

Figure 6.21

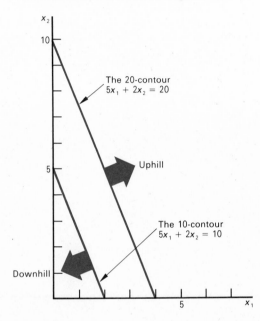

Example 5

On a plot, indicate the location of the optimal solution for the problem in Example 3. Which constraints are active? Which are inactive? Having identified the active constraints, use algebra to find the exact numerical value of the optimal solution and the optimal value of the objective function.

Solution to Example 5

The optimal solution lies on the intersection of the second and third constraints. This means that the second and third constraints are active and the first and fourth constraints are inactive. The optimal numerical value of the decision variables can be found by solving the equations for the second and third constraints simultaneously:

$$5x_1 + 4x_2 = 20$$
$$8x_1 + 2x_2 = 16$$

The solution is

$$x_1^* = 1\frac{1}{11} \quad \text{and} \quad x_2^* = 3\frac{7}{11}$$

and the optimal value of the objective function is therefore

$$5\left(1\frac{1}{11}\right) + 2\left(3\frac{7}{11}\right) = \frac{140}{11} = 12\frac{8}{11}$$

The solution is shown in Figure 6.22.

Figure 6.22

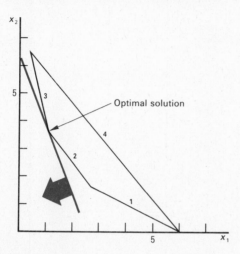

Optimal solution

Example 6

Assume that the objective function in the problem is $15x_1 + c_2x_2$ rather than $5x_1 + 2x_2$. First, verify that if $c_2 = 6$ the optimal solution is $x_1 = 1\frac{1}{11}$, $x_2 = 3\frac{7}{11}$ and that the optimal value of the objective function is $\frac{420}{11}$, or $38\frac{2}{11}$. Then, determine the smallest value of $c_2 \geq 6$ for which there are alternative optimal solutions to this problem.

Solution to Example 6

Note that $15x_1 + 6x_2 = 3(5x_1 + 2x_2)$. Thus, whatever values of x_1 and x_2 maximize $5x_1 + 2x_2$, these same values must also maximize $15x_1 + 6x_2$. This implies that the optimal solution must be the same as the values found in Example 5 and the optimal value of the objective function is multiplied by 3. This result can be seen geometrically by noting that the contours of $15x_1 + 6x_2$ and $5x_1 + 2x_2$ are parallel.

If $c_2 > 6$, the contours of the objective function will have less tilt than the contours of the current objective function. To illustrate this, compare the 45-contour of the function $15x_1 + 9x_2$ with the 30-contour of the function $15x_1 + 6x_2$, as shown in Figure 6.23. The effect of making $c_2 > 6$ can be thought of as rotating the contour of the objective function around the current optimal solution in a counterclockwise direction. Alternative optima occur when the contour of the objective function coincides with the side of the constraint set formed by the second constraint as you can see in Figure 6.24.

The problem thus reduces to finding a value for c_2 so that the contours for the objective function $15x_1 + c_2x_2$ are parallel to the constraint line $5x_1 + 4x_2 = 20$. Letting k denote an arbitrary constant, the contours for $15x_1 + c_2x_2$ are given by $15x_1 + c_2x_2 = k$, or, equivalently

Figure 6.23

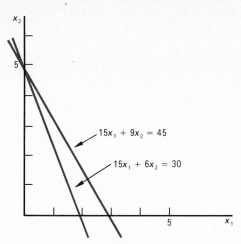

Figure 6.24

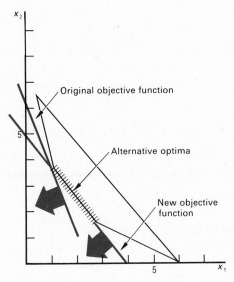

$$x_2 = -\frac{15}{c_2} x_1 + \frac{k}{c_2}$$

Hence, the slope is $-15/c_2$. The constraint line $5x_1 + 4x_2 = 20$ is equivalently written as $x_2 = -5x_1/4 + 5$. Thus its slope is $-5/4$. The objective function contours will be parallel to this constraint when c_2 has a value that makes the slopes equal. Hence $-15/c_2 = -5/4$, or $c_2 = 12$.

Example 7

Change the above problem into standard equality form. Plot the feasible set and indicate which variables are nonzero at each corner.

Solution to Example 7

Min $5x_1 + 2x_2$

s.t.

$$3x_1 + 6x_2 - s_1 \qquad\qquad = 18$$
$$5x_1 + 4x_2 \quad - s_2 \qquad\qquad = 20$$
$$8x_1 + 2x_2 \qquad\quad - s_3 \qquad = 16$$
$$7x_1 + 6x_2 \qquad\qquad\quad + s_4 = 42$$
$$x_1, x_2 \geq 0$$

The feasible set is shown in Figure 6.25.

Figure 6.25

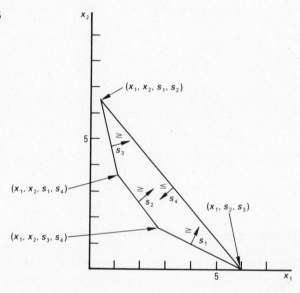

Example 8

Is the solution to the problem in Example 7 degenerate? Which variables are basic in the solution to the problem? Which slacks are zero?

Solution to Example 8

Recall from Example 5 that the optimal solution is the corner determined by the second and third constraints. Hence, the solution is *not* degenerate since there are as many positive variables in the solution (four) as there are constraints in the model. The basic variables are the positive variables x_1, x_2, s_1, and s_4. Note that both decision variables are basic and two of the slack variables are basic. The zero slacks correspond to the active constraints. Hence, they are s_2 and s_3.

Example 9

Change the min to a max in Example 3, and answer the questions posed in Example 8.

Solution to Example 9

When the objective is to maximize $5x_1 + 2x_2$, the solution is $x_1 = 6$ and $x_2 = 0$. This can be seen by sliding the contour for the objective function in the solution to Example 5 as far in the uphill direction as possible while continuing to intersect the constraint set. At this point there are only 3 positive variables in the solution, x_1, s_2, and s_3. Since there are four constraints and only three positive variables, the solution is degenerate. We have provided no definition for basic variables at a degenerate corner and thus you cannot answer this part of the question. The zero slacks in this case are s_1 and s_4.

6.7 Summary of Key Concepts

Plotting contours reduces to plotting equalities. Plotting inequalities also reduces to plotting equalities, or contours, and then identifying the correct side. (Section 6.2)

It will always be the case that adding more constraints either trims down the constraint set or, possibly, leaves the set unaffected. Adding additional constraints can never enlarge the constraint set. (Section 6.3)

A constrained optimization model seeks a feasible point that, relative to all other feasible points, produces an optimum value of the objective function. (Section 6.3)

In an LP problem, if there is a solution, there is always a corner solution. There may be noncorner solutions as well, but the computer can produce only a corner solution. (Section 6.3)

For any LP problem in standard equality-constraint form, the number of positive variables at any corner is less than or equal to the number of constraints. If it is less than the number of constraints, the corner is degenerate. (Section 6.5)

The computer solution to an LP problem always has at most m positive variables, where m is the number of constraints. (Section 6.5)

6.8 Problems

1 Plot the following inequalities.
   a $3x + 2y \le 12$
   b $4y - 2x \ge 8$
2 Plot the following inequalities.

    a $3y - x^2 \leq 9$
    b $x^2 + y \leq 4$

3 Plot the 3-contour of $4x + 2y - 7$.
4 Plot the 5-contour of $3x - y - 1$.
5 Plot the 2-contour and the 4-contour of $(xy/3) + 1$.
6 Consider the following LP model:

Max $600E + 1{,}000F$

s.t.

$$100E + 60F \leq 21{,}000$$
$$4{,}000E + 800F \leq 680{,}000$$
$$E + F \leq 290$$
$$12E + 30F \leq 6{,}000$$
$$E, F \geq 0$$

    a Let E be the horizontal axis, F the vertical axis, and use graphical means to find the optimal solution to this problem. Now use algebra to determine the optimal values of E and F and the optimal value of the objective function. Label the corners of the constraint set as I, II, III, IV, V, where I is on the vertical axis above the origin and you continue clockwise, ending with V at the origin.
    b One of the constraints is redundant in the sense that it plays no role in determining the constraint set. Which one is it?
    c What is the minimum change in the RHS of this constraint that would cause the constraint to become active?
    d The coefficient of E in the third constraint is currently 1. What is the minimum increase in this coefficient that would cause the constraint to become active? Don't be concerned that this answer may not make sense physically.
    e Suppose that the net revenue per unit of earth-moving equipment (r_E) increased, whereas the net revenue per unit of forestry equipment (r_F) remained fixed. At what value of r_E would there be more than a single optimal production plan?
    f Use the labels put on the corners of the constraint set in part a. Consider all possible nonnegative values for r_F and r_E, and on a graph with r_F as the horizontal axis and r_E as the vertical axis, show the regions of the plane in which each of the corners is optimal.
7 Consider the following problem:

Min $300E + 600F$

s.t.

$$E + F \geq 5$$
$$E \leq 3F$$
$$10E + 15F \leq 150$$
$$20E + 10F \leq 160$$
$$150 - (30E + 10F) \leq 15$$
$$E, F \geq 0$$

    a Use graphical means to find a solution to the problem (that is, to locate its position in the picture).
    b Use algebraic means to find the exact solution.
    c Create an objective function for a min problem with the constraints given in part a so that the optimal solution lies at the intersection of the lines $20E + 10F =$

160 and $E - 3F = 0$. Find the exact value of the objective function at the solution.

d Create an objective function for a max problem with the constraints given in part *a* so that the optimal solution lies at the intersection of the lines $10E + 15F = 150$ and $-30E - 10F = -135$. Find the optimal value of the objective function.

8 Consider the following problem:

Min $\quad 3y + 4x$

s.t.

$$2x + 6y \geq 12$$

$$5x + 2y \leq 25$$

$$7x + 7y \leq 49$$

$$21x + 3y \geq 42$$

$$x, y \geq 0$$

a Let s_i be the slack or surplus variable in constraint i and write the problem in standard equality-constraint form.

b Plot the equality constraint representation of the model.

c Starting with the corner that has the largest value of y and moving in a clockwise direction, label the corners with roman numerals.

d Identify the variables that are zero and those that are positive at each corner.

e Is there a degenerate corner in the problem? Why?

f Find the values for *all variables* (including slacks) in the optimal solution.

g Use the geometric representation (not algebra) obtained in part *b* to specify the appropriate sign for the variables s_1, s_2, s_3 and s_4 if $x = y = 5$.

h Find the value for s_1 if $x = 3$ and $y = 1$. Explain why s_1 assumes this particular value.

9 Add the constraint

$$3x + 2y \leq 17\frac{2}{3}$$

to the model in problem 8. Verify that it passes through corner II.

a Where is the new optimal solution?

b How many variables and slacks will be positive at the optimal solution?

c Indicate which variables will be zero and which will be positive at the optimal solution.

d List the variables in the basis.

e Is there a degenerate corner in this problem?

f Is the optimal solution degenerate?

g Is there a redundant constraint? If so, which one?

10 Consider adding the constraint $x + y \geq 3.2$ to the model in problem 8.

a How many variables and slacks will be positive at the optimal solution?

b Indicate which variables will be zero and which will be positive.

c Is there a degenerate corner in this problem?

d Are there alternative optima?

11 Give a geometric example of an LP problem where the RHS of an active constraint can be changed, in a degenerate setting, and the optimal solution will not change.

12 Give a geometric example of an LP problem where the RHS of an active constraint can be changed, in an alternative optima setting, and the optimal objective value will not change.

13 Assume $(\hat{x}_1, \hat{x}_2)$ and (x_1^*, x_2^*) are alternative optimal solutions for an LP problem. Consider a new solution

$$\alpha(\hat{x}_1, \hat{x}_2) + (1 - \alpha)(x_1^*, x_2^*)$$

where α is some specified number with the property that $0 < \alpha < 1$. Geometrically, this new solution happens to lie on the straight line connecting the two points $(\hat{x}_1, \hat{x}_2)$ and (x_1^*, x_2^*). Use algebra to show that the new point is an alternative optimal solution. That is, show that the new point is feasible (satisfies each constraint) and that the objective value at the new point is the same as at the previous solutions.

7

The Dual Problem and the Simplex Algorithm

This chapter provides an elementary introduction to the duality theory of linear programs and to the simplex algorithm for solving an LP problem. Major theoretical relationships between the primal and dual, including the dual theorem and complementary slackness, are presented but not proved. The computational and economic significance of the dual are stressed. In the final section, the simplex method is explained for a simple illustrative problem.

7.1 Introduction

We wrote this chapter especially for those of you who want to dig deeper into some of the theoretical and technical specifics of LP. Chapter 7 is not a prerequisite for any of the succeeding material in the book, but its coverage, especially of duality theory and its ramifications, will give you valuable insight toward becoming more expert in the *use* of LP.

The material in the last part of the chapter deals in an elementary way with the mathematics of the simplex algorithm, which we do by exploring a relatively simple example. We leave proofs of the mathematical results to the standard reference literature.

7.2 The Dual Problem: A Special Case

Given any set of data for an LP model, we can use the same data to form another *different* LP model. The resulting problem is called the *dual* of the original problem. The dual has theoretic, computational, and economic importance, all of which we discuss in Sections 7.4–7.6.

First, let us see exactly how the dual problem is formed. Consider the problem

Max $3x_1 + 4x_2$

s.t.

$$-2x_1 + 3x_2 \leq 6$$
$$5x_1 - x_2 \leq 40 \qquad \text{(E1)}$$
$$x_1 + x_2 \leq 7$$
$$x_1, x_2 \geq 0$$

This problem consists of three inequality constraints and two variables. In total, such a problem requires 11 elements of data, 6 a_{ij} parameters, 2 c_j parameters, and 3 b_i parameters. This is a special instance of a general linear program with m constraints and n variables that requires $mn + m + n$ elements of data.

The dual to this problem is the following LP problem:

Min $6y_1 + 40y_2 + 7y_3$

s.t.

$$-2y_1 + 5y_2 + y_3 \geq 3 \qquad\qquad \text{(E2)}$$
$$3y_1 - y_2 + y_3 \geq 4$$
$$y_1, y_2, y_3 \geq 0$$

Now we shall note that a *precise pattern* is to be followed in constructing (E2) from the data in (E1). First, there is an interchange of the number of constraints and variables in forming the dual problem. There were three constraints and two variables in the original problem. The dual problem has two constraints and three variables. A moment's thought will convince you that 11 elements of data are still required for this new problem. We note that the old b_i values are employed for the new c_j values, the old c_j values for the new b_i values, and the same coefficients are used in the constraints, turning the old rows into the new columns. We have chosen to use the symbols y_1, y_2, and y_3 as the decision variables in the dual problem. As is the case with almost all mathematical notation, the choice of y_1, y_2, y_3 is entirely arbitrary. The symbols w_1, w_2, and w_3, or any other set of three symbols, could have been used equally well.

7.3 The Dual Problem in General

We now define a problem that is dual to an LP model written in a completely general form. Consider a maximization problem in n variables, where p of the variables are required to be *nonnegative,* q of the variables are required to be *nonpositive,* and the remaining $n - p - q$ variables are *unconstrained* in sign. Suppose there are m constraints, where r of the constraints are of $\leq$ form, s of the constraints are of $\geq$ form, and the remaining $m - r - s$ constraints are of equality form.

In this formulation, do not be concerned that some of the variables are constrained to be nonpositive and others are unconstrained in sign. This problem can easily be converted into the standard equality-constraint form as is required to obtain a solution with the simplex method on the computer. In Section 5.3, we have already explained how to deal with the variables that are unconstrained in sign. A nonpositive variable, say x_3, is treated by replacing x_3 with $-z_3$ where z_3 is *nonnegative.* In considering dual problems, it is necessary to treat linear programs in the general form described above.

In symbolic notation, this generalized version of a maximization model takes the form

Max $\quad c_1 x_1 + c_2 x_2 + \cdots + c_n x_n$

s.t.

$$
\begin{aligned}
a_{11} x_1 + \quad & a_{12} x_2 + \cdots + \quad && a_{1n} x_n \le b_1 \\
& \vdots && \vdots \\
a_{r1} x_1 + \quad & a_{r2} x_2 + \cdots + \quad && a_{rn} x_n \le b_r \\
a_{r+1,1} x_1 + \quad & a_{r+1,2} x_2 + \cdots + \quad && a_{r+1,n} x_n \ge b_{r+1} \\
& \vdots && \vdots \\
a_{r+s,1} x_1 + \quad & a_{r+s,2} x_2 + \cdots + \quad && a_{r+s,n} x_n \ge b_{r+s} \\
a_{r+s+1,1} x_1 + \quad & a_{r+s+1,2} x_2 + \cdots + \quad && a_{r+s+1,n} x_n = b_{r+s+1} \\
& \vdots && \vdots \\
a_{m1} x_1 + \quad & a_{m2} x_2 + \cdots + \quad && a_{mn} x_n = b_m
\end{aligned}
$$

(I)

$x_1, \ldots, x_p \ge 0,\ x_{p+1}, \ldots, x_{p+q} \le 0,\ x_{p+q+1}, \ldots, x_n$ unconstrained in sign

From the data in (I), we now form a new problem, (II), called the *dual* of (I).

Min $\quad y_1 b_1 + y_2 b_2 + \ldots + y_m b_m$

s.t.

$$
\begin{aligned}
a_{11} y_1 + \quad & a_{21} y_2 + \cdots + \quad && a_{m1} y_m \ge c_1 \\
& \vdots && \vdots \\
a_{1p} y_1 + \quad & a_{2p} y_2 + \cdots + \quad && a_{mp} y_m \ge c_p \\
a_{1,p+1} y_1 + \quad & a_{2,p+1} y_2 + \cdots + \quad && a_{m,p+1} y_m \le c_{p+1} \\
& \vdots && \vdots \\
a_{1,p+q} y_1 + \quad & a_{2,p+q} y_2 + \cdots + \quad && a_{m,p+q} y_m \le c_{p+q} \\
a_{1,p+q+1} y_1 + \quad & a_{2,p+q+1} y_2 + \cdots + \quad && a_{m,p+q+1} y_m = c_{p+q+1} \\
& \vdots && \vdots \\
a_{1n} y_1 + \quad & a_{2n} y_2 + \cdots + \quad && a_{mn} y_m = c_n
\end{aligned}
$$

(II)

$y_1, \ldots, y_r \ge 0,\ y_{r+1}, \ldots, y_{r+s} \le 0,\ y_{r+s+1}, \ldots, y_m$ unconstrained in sign

Problems (E1) and (E2) of Section 7.2 provide a special case of the pair (I) and (II). In problem (E1), $r = m$ and $p = n$. Making these identifications in (II), it is seen that problem (E2) is obtained.

The pair of problems (I) and (II) are called *dual linear programs*. Though problem (II) is called the *dual* of problem (I), it is also correct to say that (I) is the dual of (II). Thus, duality is termed a *symmetric* relationship. The y variables are the decision variables for problem (II). When thinking of (II) as the dual of (I), we also refer to the y variables as *dual variables*. The x variables are the decision variables for problem (I). When we think of (I) as the dual of (II), the x variables also may be termed *dual variables*.

For a pair of linear programs to be dual problems they must be related to one another precisely in the way in which (I) and (II) are. This means

1 One problem is *max* and the other problem is *min*.

2 Number of variables in either problem = number of constraints in the other.

3 The objective function coefficients in either problem are identical with the right-hand side of the other problem.

4 To a constraint of ≤ (≥, or =) form in the max problem corresponds a nonnegative (nonpositive, or unconstrained in sign) dual variable in the min problem.

5 To a constraint of ≤ (≥, or =) form in the min problem corresponds a nonpositive (nonnegative, or unconstrained in sign) dual variable in the max problem.

6 The coefficient of the jth variable in the ith row of either problem equals the coefficient of the ith variable in the jth row of the other problem.

As an illustration, suppose we wish to construct the dual to

Min $3x_1 + 4x_2$

s.t.

$$-2x_1 + 3x_2 \leq 6$$
$$5x_1 - x_2 \geq 40$$
$$x_1 + x_2 = 7$$

(E3)

$x_1 \geq 0$, x_2 unconstrained in sign

According to the above six rules, we obtain the dual

Max $6y_1 + 40y_2 + 7y_3$

s.t.

$$-2y_1 + 5y_2 + y_3 \leq 3$$
$$3y_1 - y_2 + y_3 = 4$$

(E4)

$y_1 \leq 0, y_2 \geq 0, y_3$ unconstrained in sign

The above six rules show how to form the dual of any linear program. An additional illustration is given in Example 2, Section 7.8.

7.4 The Relations between Primal and Dual Problems

In referring to the pair of problems (I) and (II), it is often said that one of them (usually the original model) is the *primal* problem and the other is the *dual* problem. We shall conform to this usage, though we wish to stress that duality is what is called a *symmetric* and *reflexive* relationship. This means that either problem should be considered to be the dual of the other, and whichever of the problems (I) and (II) is designated as the primal,

The dual of the dual problem is again the primal problem.

For convenience, in this section let us adopt the convention that problem (I), the max model with, in general, m constraints and n variables, is the *primal,* and problem (II), the min model with n constraints and m variables, is the *dual.*

The theoretic relationships between the primal and the dual are very simply stated, and yet these relations have considerable importance in the theory of linear problems.

Let us say that a set of decision variable values is *feasible* for a given model if the set of values satisfies the constraints and sign requirements which are specified by the model. Moreover, we shall say that a specific set of decision variable values $(x_1, ..., x_n)$ is *primal feasible* if these values are feasible in (I), and similarly that a specific set of values $(y_1, ..., y_m)$ is *dual feasible* if these values are feasible in (II). The following result is important.

If $(x_1, ..., x_n)$ is any set of primal feasible values and $(y_1, ..., y_m)$ is any set of dual feasible values, the primal objective function evaluated at x cannot exceed the dual objective function evaluated at y.

As an example of this fact, let us again refer to problems (E1) and (E2) in Section 7.2. Verify that the values (3, 2) are primal feasible (that is, $x_1 = 3$, $x_2 = 2$) since they satisfy all the primal constraints and nonnegativity conditions. The associated primal objective value is 17. The values (0, 1, 6) are dual feasible (that is, $y_1 = 0$, $y_2 = 1$, $y_3 = 6$) since they satisfy all the constraints and nonnegativity conditions of (E2). The associated objective value is 82, which exceeds the primal value. You may wish to select other sets of primal feasible values and other dual feasible values. No matter what values are selected, as long as they are primal and dual feasible, the primal objective value will not exceed the dual value.

Since the primal is a max problem and the dual a min problem, the foregoing result implies that if primal and dual feasible values are found that produce equal objective function values, then those decision variable values are optimal in their respective problems. In fact, an even stronger result links the primal and dual problems. Namely,

---

Either of the two problems has a solution if and only if the other does.

When there is a solution, the optimal value of the objective function in the primal is the same as the optimal value of the objective function in the dual.

This elegant result says that solving either problem yields the same optimal objective value. It does *not* say that the *optimal solution* to each problem is the same. Such a result would not be reasonable since the two problems are in spaces of different dimension. That is, there are n of the x variables (the primal variables) and m of the y variables (the dual variables).

In order to explain the relations between the primal and dual problems more fully, it is useful to use the technical terms *infeasible* (or *inconsistent*) and *unbounded*. An LP problem is said to be *infeasible,* or *inconsistent* if the constraints (including the nonnegativity conditions) cannot all be (simultaneously) satisfied. This means that the set of points described by the constraints is an empty set. An LP problem is said to be *unbounded* if the objective contour can be slid arbitrarily far in the desired direction without leaving the constraint set behind. This means that in a max problem there are allowable decision variable values that make the value of the objective function arbitrarily large. The reverse interpretation holds for a min problem.

It turns out that any linear program falls into one of the following three categories:

1　The problem has an optimal solution. (This implies a finite optimal objective value.)

2　The problem is unbounded. (This implies consistent constraints but, if you like, an infinite—or negatively infinite, for a min model—optimal objective value.)

3　The problem is infeasible. (This implies that there is no allowable choice for the decision variables.)

Although perfectly respectable as mathematical possibilities, the second and third phenomena are, in terms of applied problems, abnormal. Infinite profits do not exist, and a real-world problem, correctly formulated, cannot lead to an inconsistent model. Such phenomena usually occur because of human error, either in model formulation or in the process of entering the model and its data into the computer. Too many constraints, or the wrong sense for a constraint (= instead of ≤, for example) can produce infeasibility. Too few constraints, or the wrong sense (≤ instead of =, for example) can produce an unbounded problem, and almost any type of input error can lead to either abnormality. The point to remember, as far as applications are concerned, is that a properly formulated LP model will always have an optimal solution. If the model is correctly input to the computer, then the simplex algorithm will find this solution. Otherwise, if the submitted problem is either unbounded or infeasible, the simplex algorithm will inform the user as to which of these conditions exists.

Using the foregoing terminology, we can now more completely characterize the relations between any pair of dual linear programs. These relations are known as the *dual theorem of linear programming*.

In any pair of dual linear programs, both may have optimal solutions, in which case the optimal objective values will be the same.

In any pair of dual linear programs, both may be inconsistent.

In any pair of dual linear programs, one may be unbounded and the other inconsistent.

The dual theorem states that these combinations are mutually exclusive and exhaustive. For example, the possibility that both the primal and dual are unbounded is ruled out. The possibility is also ruled out that one problem can be unbounded while the other has an optimal solution. Thus, the dual theorem implies that if either problem is unbounded then the other *must* be inconsistent.

There is a final theoretic relationship between the primal and dual problem of considerable importance in applications. This is called the *principle of complementary slackness,* which can be stated as follows:

Consider an inequality constraint in any LP problem. If that constraint is inactive for any optimal solution to the problem, then the corresponding dual variable will be zero in any optimal solution to the dual of that problem.

This principle is used in some of the analyses in Chapters 8, 11, and 12.

We have now presented essentially all the important theoretic relationships between pairs of dual linear programs. This theory is of considerable mathematical interest in its own right. In addition, the theory of duality has computational and economic significance. This will become apparent in the following sections.

7.5 Computational Importance of the Dual Problem

When the simplex algorithm is used to solve an LP problem, it turns out that optimal solutions to both the original problem (which may be either a max or min model) and its dual are obtained, as we will illustrate in Section 7.7. Thus, if you want to solve a particular problem you can, of course, go about it by solving the problem directly. Alternatively, you can take the dual of the original problem and then solve the dual problem on the computer. This will also provide a solution to the dual of the dual, which is the original problem. Since each of these possible routes leads to the same result, it is of interest, from the computational point of view, to inquire as to which procedure is more efficient.

In order to shed light on this question, we take note of the empirical fact that the amount of time required to solve a linear program depends more critically on the number of constraints than on the number of variables. If the original problem has m constraints and n variables, then the dual problem has n constraints and m variables. It is then apparent that, *all other things being equal,* you should choose to solve the problem with fewer constraints.

Although the foregoing rule of thumb is a reasonably good general prescription, when you get into fairly large and structured models it may well break down, for in such cases, all other things may not be equal. Possible reasons for departure from this rule of thumb tend to become quite technical in nature. In some cases, irrespective of the number of constraints, one of the two problems, because of its form, may be solvable with a very special code, such as what we call a *network code,* as opposed to a general purpose LP code. The other problem, however, may not have the required special structure and hence may have to be solved with the general purpose code. Since special structure codes tend to be computationally more efficient than a general purpose code, this is an important consideration. One important special type of linear program, a transportation model, has already been encountered in Chapter

4. The important special class called *network models* will be discussed in Chapter 14.

Other technical considerations have to do with the fact that even with a general LP code it may be easier to "get started" with one problem rather than the other. We will explain this start-up procedure, sometimes called *phase I of the simplex method,* briefly in Section 7.7.

Finally, general purpose codes provide sensitivity data as well as the optimal solution for the original problem while providing only the optimal solution for the dual. The importance of sensitivity data might well play a decisive role in determining which version of the problem to solve.

The choice between solving the original problem or its dual does not have much computational significance for small problems, say when either model has no more than several hundred constraints, since such problems can be handled with great speed on modern computing equipment. As the problems grow larger, into the ballpark of several thousand constraints, then the choice between the original problem and its dual can become very important. On such occasions, technical consultation with a professional linear programmer may well be worthwhile.

7.6 Economic Significance of the Dual Problem

From the point of view of applied analysis, the most important aspect of the dual problem is probably the associated economic interpretation. The values of the optimal dual variables are frequently called *dual prices,* or *shadow prices.* Recall that associated with each primal constraint is a dual variable, and these dual variables are used in constructing the dual problem. In terms of economic considerations, the interpretation of the dual variables is facilitated by assuming that the primal (that is, the original) problem has a *nondegenerate solution* (as defined in Section 6.5). In such a case, the optimal dual variable, y_i^*, associated with the ith primal constraint, represents the *marginal value* of the resource whose availability is b_i, the RHS on the ith constraint. In other words, suppose b_i is slightly increased. Then,

---

The optimal value of the ith dual variable is the amount by which the primal optimal objective value will change per unit increase in b_i, assuming that all other data are unchanged.

If an increase in the RHS increases (decreases) the optimal value, then the dual variable is positive (negative), regardless of whether the primal is a max or a min problem.

We have previously discussed the economic interpretation of dual variables in Chapter 5, where an important caveat was stated. The above interpretation is valid only over some specified range of allowable increases or decreases in the b_i values, namely, the range over which the basis does not change. We have seen in Chapter 5 that this specified range of validity appears in the computer output under the *Sensitivity Analysis* section. At this point, another word of caution is in order. This concerns our computer output convention on dual prices. Suppose we solve a min model on the computer. If a particular dual price on the computer output is positive, our computer output convention tells us that increasing the RHS of the corresponding primal constraint will improve, and hence decrease, the optimal objective value. Hence, by the statement displayed above, the dual variable is negative. Similarly, a negative dual price on the computer output signifies that increasing the RHS will impair, and hence increase, the optimal value. In this case, the above-displayed statement implies that the dual variable is positive.

On the other hand, this sign reversal does not occur when a max model is solved directly on the computer. In this case, it is easy to see that the dual prices that appear in the output will all have the same sign as the optimal dual variables. This inconsistency may seem confusing, but unfortunately, it is well-imbedded in tradition. You should have little difficulty if you simply keep in mind the output convention that the dual price on the printout is the rate of improvement, whereas the optimal dual variable reflects the rate of increase. This means that

---

In a max problem,
Dual price on printout = dual variable

In a min problem,
Dual price on printout = −dual variable

In order to illustrate the shadow price interpretation of the dual variables, let us imagine ourselves in a profit-maximization production context with constraints on the input resources. Suppose that aluminum is one of our resources and that the first constraint of our model is of $\leq$ form and represents a limitation on the availability of aluminum. Imagine that 8,000 pounds of aluminum are currently in our stockpile, and so we solve the model using the value 8,000 for the first RHS, b_1. Let us suppose that in reading the computer output we find that the first dual price is \$16.50, which is the optimal value of y_1 in the dual problem. This means that the *marginal* contribution of aluminum (the value of the last, or the next, unit consumed) to the total profit, is \$16.50. Suppose the sensitivity information shows that this value of \$16.50 holds for b_1 values between 7,500 and 9,000, and suppose the market price of aluminum is \$20 per pound. We can infer that our last 500 pounds of aluminum are yielding us less than the market value. We could presumably sell 500 pounds on the market for a return of $(20)(500) = \$10,000$, whereas the cost, in terms of the output profit, would be $(16.50)(500) = \$8,250$. This transaction would net us an additional \$1,750 above current profits. You may ask, "Why not continue to sell the aluminum on the market?" This may be a good suggestion, but with the information at our disposal we cannot be sure. The computer output indicates only that the value of 16.50 is valid for b_1 values between 7,500 and 9,000. It will be demonstrated in Chapter 8 that when b_1 falls below 7,500, the dual price can be expected to increase. It should be intuitively plausible that the shadow price of a resource increases as the availability becomes more limited. In any case, the information at our disposal does not provide the amount by which the dual will increase. It may rise to a value beyond 20, in which case it would be disadvantageous to continue the sale of aluminum.

On the other hand, suppose the market value of aluminum is only $14 per pound. In this case, the dual price of 16.50 indicates that we should purchase an additional 1,000 pounds of aluminum, for this would net us 16.50 − 14.00 = $2.50 per pound, or $2,500 above and beyond the current profit. In this case, as we increase b_1, and consequently relax the aluminum constraint, it is shown in Chapter 8 that the dual price may be expected to decrease, but again we cannot tell how much. Thus, we are again in the situation of not knowing whether or not to continue the purchase beyond 1,000 additional pounds.

The above discussion illustrates how the dual variables enable the planner to compare the relative worth of his inputs and to compare the market values of resources with the value obtained from the consumption of those resources in his own operations. It seems intuitive that, at least within the context described by the model, a maximum return will be obtained when *resource levels* (RHS values) are such that market prices and shadow prices are identical. Otherwise, greater profit can be realized by buying or selling the resource, as above.

Let us suppose that this intuitive argument is correct. Now consider two different enterprises, each highly complicated and each employing many resources. Suppose one particular resource is used by each enterprise. Our intuitive arguments suggest that if each enterprise is using the "correct amount" of this resource, then at optimality its dual price will be the same for each enterprise. Why, then, in real life is it extremely unlikely that different enterprises will have the same dual price on the same resource? Are entrepreneurs so naive as to not use the correct resource levels? This is certainly not believable. Thus, we have what appears to be a paradox. The difficulty here is that we have ignored the meaning of a constraint. Constraints occur precisely because there is not a market price at which the resource is available at those quantity levels in which the planner, at least conceivably, may be interested. Suppose, for example, that in planning for next month's production we need to have aluminum knuckles on hand. We cannot get them "on demand" because of lead times to delivery. Thus, practically speaking, next month's quantity must be ordered in advance. We then have a valid constraint on the availability of knuckles. Of course, the dual price will tell us a great deal about the importance of bottlenecks created by such scarce resources.

In concluding this section, it should be mentioned that in special types of LP models the dual variables may have a special economic significance. For example, in a transportation model there is a dual variable associated with each origin and with each destination. These dual variables can be interpreted as either the F.O.B. (free-on-board) value of the product at its origin, or the value of the product after delivery to the destination. As another example, in the minimum-cost diet problem, the dual variable is interpreted as the imputed value of a unit of nutrient i.

Dual variables also play an important role in decentralized planning and management. In large corporations, decision making is often decentralized into component departments. Each department can be thought of as an independent "suboptimizing unit." From a solution, for example, of a large-scale linear program for the entire corporation, the optimal activities of each subunit are known. However, top management wants to create a set of incentives, or operating rules, which will guarantee that departmental managers, in optimizing their own departmental interests, will also be optimizing overall corporate objectives. It has been shown theoretically that the correct incentives can be created by using shadow prices (as opposed to market prices) as the costs that departments must pay for resources. Using these costs, the individual departments are then encouraged to maximize profits, and this procedure will lead to overall optimality.

Now that you have some feeling for the economic interpretation of the individual dual variables, we may inquire further as to the economic meaning of the dual problem as a whole. This is explored in the following scenario. Additional information on the properties of dual prices and economic applications will appear in Chapters 8, 11, and 12. Our emphasis on this topic reflects its importance in managerial decision making.

7.6.1 A PROTRAC Illustration

We have now completed our formal development of the dual problem. The following specific scenario illustrates a way in which the dual problem arises naturally. Understanding this scenario gives some students a better appreciation for the economic meaning of the dual problem and its relationship to the primal.

The PROTRAC New Zealand plant produces two types of forestry equipment from three raw materials. The market prices on the two types of equipment are r_1 and r_2, respectively. Figure 7.1 shows the quantities of raw materials used in the production of a unit of each of the two types of equipment. The inventories of the three raw materials are b_1, b_2, and b_3, respectively, and the decision variables x_1 and x_2 denote the quantities of type 1 and type 2 equipment to be produced. The following LP model determines revenue-maximizing values of x_1 and x_2 subject to the constraints on current inventory.

Max $r_1 x_1 + r_2 x_2$

s.t.

$$a_{11} x_1 + a_{12} x_2 \leq b_1$$
$$a_{21} x_1 + a_{22} x_2 \leq b_2 \qquad\qquad (P)$$
$$a_{31} x_1 + a_{32} x_2 \leq b_3$$
$$x_1, x_2 \geq 0$$

PROTRAC also has a plant in Australia that produces several kinds of farm equipment from the same three raw materials. It has just been learned that the Australian government is about to introduce a farm subsidy program

Figure 7.1 *Raw material use in equipment production*

Quantity of Raw Material	Equipment Type	
	1	2
1	a_{11}	a_{12}
2	a_{21}	a_{22}
3	a_{31}	a_{32}

that is expected to greatly increase the demand for farm machinery beyond the levels previously estimated. PROTRAC management wishes to increase the capacity of its Australian plant as quickly as possible to meet this new demand but faces long lead times in ordering additional raw materials. Since the revenue associated with the Australian farm equipment is significantly greater than that of the forestry equipment produced in New Zealand, management decides that the Australian plant should purchase the entire inventory of the New Zealand plant.

As a result of this decision, management seeks to determine a set of per-unit prices for the three raw materials (irrespective of their market prices) that will minimize the total cost to the Australian plant of the inventory and yet provide the New Zealand plant manager with an incentive to sell. That is, speaking loosely, the price PROTRAC sets on a given raw material must be at least as great as the revenue the New Zealand plant could realize by using that material in production. (Before continuing, you should attempt to formalize the meaning of this assertion.)

In order to construct a model for this problem, let y_1, y_2, and y_3 be decision variables representing the per-unit prices for the raw materials. The following linear program minimizes the cost to the Australian plant of the entire inventory subject to constraints that assure that the New Zealand plant manager is willing to liquidate. That is, he no longer has a financial incentive to use his resources for production.

Min $y_1 b_1 + y_2 b_2 + y_3 b_3$

s.t.

$$a_{11}y_1 + a_{21}y_2 + a_{31}y_3 \geq r_1 \qquad\qquad\qquad\qquad\qquad\qquad (D)$$
$$a_{12}y_1 + a_{22}y_2 + a_{32}y_3 \geq r_2$$
$$y_1, y_2, y_3 \geq 0$$

The constraints in this model guarantee that the manager of the New Zealand plant will have no financial incentive to produce. This is accomplished by paying him at least as much for the raw materials consumed in the production of a unit of *each product* as the revenue he would gain from the production of that unit. This gives formal content to the previous assertion that the prices on the raw materials must be at least as great as the revenues obtained from their employment.

We now note that the price-determining model (D) is precisely the dual of the New Zealand production model (P). The three variables y_i are the shadow prices on the three resource constraints in the primal problem, (P). Let us denote the optimal solutions to the primal and dual problems as (x_1^*, x_2^*) and (y_1^*, y_2^*, y_3^*), respectively. Then, according to the dual theorem, it will be the case that the minimum acceptable payment for the New Zealand plant's resources, namely $y_1^* b_1 + y_2^* b_2 + y_3^* b_3$, will be equal to the maximum possible revenue in that plant, which is $r_1 x_1^* + r_2 x_2^*$.

This scenario illustrates the economic interpretation that the optimal dual variables represent prices we would be willing to accept to "liquidate" all our resources, and the optimal value of the dual objective function represents the minimum acceptable liquidation payment. Intuitively, it is plausible that this minimum acceptable payment should be the same as the maximum obtainable return from the employment of those resources.

7.7 The Simplex Algorithm

G. Dantzig and A. Charnes created the simplex method in the early 1950s. Many have advanced its development. It is a systematic way of examining the corners (also called *vertices*, or *extreme points*) of an LP constraint set in search of an optimal solution. In particular, the algorithm first seeks an initial corner. This is called *phase I*. If the problem is *inconsistent*, phase I will discover this fact. Otherwise, an initial corner is found and phase I is complete. Then the algorithm proceeds to generate a sequence of *adjacent* corners with the property that the objective function will not decrease and will generally increase at each successive corner. If the problem is unbounded, the algorithm will discover this during its execution. The mathematics of the uphill move from one corner to an adjacent corner requires a so-called *pivoting operation* on a tableau of data. When an optimal corner has been reached the algorithm terminates. Optimal solutions to both the primal and dual problems are provided.

We shall illustrate the algorithm on the following problem:

Max $x_1 + 2x_2$

s.t.

$$
\begin{aligned}
x_1 - 2x_2 &\le 2 \\
2x_1 - x_2 &\le 7 \\
4x_1 + x_2 &\le 29 \\
-2x_1 + 3x_2 &\le 17 \\
-3x_1 + 2x_2 &\le 8 \\
x_1, x_2 &\ge 0
\end{aligned}
$$

The constraint set corresponding to this problem is shown in Figure 7.2. The objective contour is also shown. Note that the solution is at corner *D*.

In order to apply the simplex algorithm, this problem must first be converted to standard equality-constraint form. Normally, a computer would make this conversion for you. However, since in this example we will not use the computer, it is necessary for us to perform the transformation explicitly. This will be accomplished by adding a nonnegative slack variable to each constraint and converting the $\le$ to $=$. In this way we obtain the problem

Max $x_1 + 2x_2$

s.t.

$$
\begin{aligned}
x_1 - 2x_2 + x_3 \qquad\qquad\qquad &= 2 \\
2x_1 - x_2 \qquad + x_4 \qquad\qquad &= 7 \\
4x_1 + x_2 \qquad\qquad + x_5 \qquad &= 29 \\
-2x_1 + 3x_2 \qquad\qquad\qquad + x_6 \quad &= 17 \\
-3x_1 + 2x_2 \qquad\qquad\qquad\qquad + x_7 &= 8 \\
x_j \ge 0 \qquad j = 1, \ldots, 7
\end{aligned}
$$

(1)

Figure 7.2   *The constraint set and objective contour*

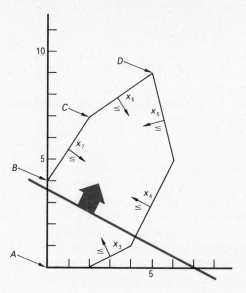

In mathematical terms, the set of points described by linear equations in nonnegative variables, such as system (1), is called a ***convex polytope.*** Before describing the simplex algorithm, we state several important facts about m linear equations in n nonnegative variables:

1   At each corner of the convex polytope described by these equations there are at most m positive variables. Under a nondegeneracy assumption there will, at each corner, be a *unique* set of exactly m positive variables. These variables are called *basic*. The remaining variables (which are zero in value) are *nonbasic*.

2   Given any set of linear equations and any set of basic variables, the equations can be solved explicitly for the basic variables in terms of the nonbasic variables.

We will employ these facts in illustrating the simplex algorithm in the above problem. Let us note that there is a one-to-one correspondence between the corners of the convex polytope described by system (1) (a polytope that resides in seven-dimensional space) and the corners in Figure 7.2. This correspondence will be useful in showing the geometric analogue of the simplex calculations. For convenience, we shall circumvent phase I by arbitrarily selecting the corner denoted A as the initial corner, and noting that in Figure 7.2 the basic variables at the origin are x_3, x_4, x_5, x_6, x_7. It is particularly easy to solve the equations of system (1) for these basic variables in terms of the nonbasic variables. In fact, the purpose of phase I is to obtain an explicit representation of *some* set of basic variables (corresponding to some corner) in terms of nonbasic variables. We must have such a representation in order to construct our first tableau. The representation for the basic variables at corner A is

Row 1 $\quad x_3 = \quad 2 - \quad x_1 + 2x_2$

Row 2 $\quad x_4 = \quad 7 - 2x_1 + \quad x_2$

Row 3 $\quad x_5 = 29 - 4x_1 - \quad x_2$

Row 4 $\quad x_6 = 17 + 2x_1 - 3x_2$

Row 5 $\quad x_7 = \quad 8 + 3x_1 - 2x_2$

Clearly, any nonnegative set of x values satisfies the constraints (1) if and only if they satisfy the above equivalent system.

Let us now use the symbol Z to denote the objective function. Given any representation of basic variables in terms of nonbasic, we can substitute into the objective function so that it is expressed exclusively in terms of nonbasic variables. That is, suppose

$$Z = \sum_{j=1}^{n} c_j x_j$$

is our objective function. Suppose we have identified a particular corner at which the set of basic variables is $x_j, j \in B$, and the set of nonbasic variables is $x_j, j \in N$. Suppose each basic x_j is explicitly solved for in terms of the nonbasic variables. Then there are numbers z_0 and $\hat{c}_j, j \in N$, for which

$$Z = z_0 + \sum_{j \in N} \hat{c}_j x_j$$

In other words, at *any* feasible point the same objective value is produced by either of the expressions

$$\sum_{j=1}^{n} c_j x_j \quad \text{or} \quad z_0 + \sum_{j \in N} \hat{c}_j x_j$$

For our particular example, the nonbasic variables corresponding to corner A are x_1 and x_2. Thus the objective function as initially given is in terms of only nonbasic variables, and we have

$$Z = x_1 + 2x_2$$

At the corner corresponding to $x_1 = x_2 = 0$, the value of Z, the objective function, is zero. Increasing either x_1 or x_2 will increase the objective function. Since a per-unit increase in x_2 yields two units of return, as opposed to one unit return per unit increase in x_1, let us increase x_2 and continue to keep x_1 at the value zero. In Figure 7.2 this corresponds to moving vertically from the origin. We shall call x_2 the *enter* variable since it is becoming positive and hence is coming into the basis. It is seen from the geometry that x_2 can be increased until reaching corner B, at which x_1 and x_7 are nonbasic. That is, we have moved to a new corner at which x_2 and x_7 have exchanged roles. The previously nonbasic variable x_2 has become basic and x_7, which was previously basic, has become nonbasic. The other basic and nonbasic variables at corner B are the same as at corner A.[1] In looking at the above five equations

---

[1] This does not mean that these variables remain the same in *value*. For example, Figure 7.2 indicates that x_6 is basic at each of the corners A and B, but it has a larger value at A than at B.

for the basic variables, it is seen that as x_2 gradually becomes positive, x_3 and x_4 will increase but x_5, x_6, and x_7 will decrease from their values at the first corner (where $x_5 = 29$, $x_6 = 17$, $x_7 = 8$). It turns out that x_7 is the first of these variables to hit zero. That is,

$$x_5 = 29 - x_2 = 0 \Rightarrow x_2 = 29$$
$$x_6 = 17 - 3x_2 = 0 \Rightarrow x_2 = \tfrac{17}{3}$$
$$x_7 = 8 - 2x_2 = 0 \Rightarrow x_2 = \tfrac{8}{2}$$

Consequently, when x_2 increases to the value 4, the variable x_7 becomes zero, and this is the variable that becomes nonbasic at the new corner. Let us call this the *exit* variable since it is the one chosen to leave the basis. The formal rules for obtaining the enter and exit variables can be easily stated if we first rewrite the above data in the *tableau* format shown in Figure 7.3

Figure 7.3   *The basis at corner A*

		x_1	x_2	x_3	x_4	x_5	x_6	x_7	
x_3	2	1	-2	1	0	0	0	0	
x_4	7	2	-1	0	1	0	0	0	
x_5	29	④	①	0	0	1	0	0	
x_6	17	-2	3	0	0	0	1	0	
x_7	8	⊝③	☐2	0	0	0	0	1	→
Z	0	-1	-2	0	0	0	0	0	
			↑						

The first row of the tableau, for example, is read "$2 = x_1 - 2x_2 + x_3$," which is equivalent to row 1 above. The last row is read "$0 = Z - x_1 - 2x_2$." It is to be noted that the last row is read differently than the other rows. This situation could be redressed by adding a Z column with all zeros except for a one in the Z row. However, our approach is traditional. You may wish to "imagine" the existence of such a column when reading the last row. We now state the following rules:

Enter rule: The variable to enter the basis is the one that has the most negative entry in the last row.

Exit rule: Consider the ratio of each number in the first column to the corresponding number in the enter column, for which the enter column number is positive. The variable corresponding to the row with a minimum ratio is the exit variable.

In accordance with the exit rule above, we consider the ratios $\tfrac{29}{1}$, $\tfrac{17}{3}$, $\tfrac{8}{2}$. The minimum ratio is $\tfrac{8}{2}$, which identifies the exit variable as x_7.

The next step in the simplex algorithm is to obtain an updated tableau corresponding to corner B. Since x_2, x_3, x_4, x_5, and x_6 are basic at corner

B, we want to solve the initial system of equations for these basic variables in terms of the nonbasic variables x_1 and x_7. The arithmetic for doing this is called *Gaussian elimination.* It turns out that the new set of equations can be obtained by a sequence of mechanical operations on the tableau in Figure 7.3 as follows:

1 The entry in the enter column and the exit row is called the *pivot element.* Divide each entry in the exit row by this element and replace the exit variable in the row labels with the entering variable. We now have the row of the new tableau corresponding to the entering variable. That is, the row label x_7 is replaced with x_2 and the entries in that row become $4, -\frac{3}{2}, 1, 0, 0, 0, 0, \frac{1}{2}$. (See the x_2 row of Figure 7.4.)

2 The *columns* under each former basic variable other than the exit variable remain the same. Hence the columns labeled x_3, x_4, x_5, x_6 remain the same. (See the x_3, x_4, x_5, x_6 columns of Figure 7.4.)

3 By virtue of the first step above, the new enter column already contains a 1. Make the remaining entries zero. (See the x_2 column of Figure 7.4.)

Using steps 1, 2, and 3, we now have obtained the partial tableau in Figure 7.4.

Figure 7.4 *A partial update of Figure 7.3. Former basic variables were x_3, x_4, x_5, x_6, x_7; x_2 and x_7 have exchanged roles.*

	x_1	x_2	x_3	x_4	x_5	x_6	x_7
x_3		0	1	0	0	0	
x_4		0	0	1	0	0	
x_5		0	0	0	1	0	
x_6		0	0	0	0	1	
x_2	4	$-\frac{3}{2}$	1	0	0	0	0	$\frac{1}{2}$
z		0	0	0	0	0	

The remaining entries are obtained by the so-called *pivot rule,* which works as follows. Suppose we want the new entry in the x_5 row and the x_1 column. In Figure 7.3, it is seen that the former entry is a 4. This number, along with the pivot element (in the x_7 row, the x_2 column), can be used to define a rectangle whose corners are distinguished in Figure 7.3. The *pivoting operation* consists of the following opposite corner rule:

$$\text{New entry} = \text{old entry} - \frac{product\ of\ opposite\ corners}{pivot\ element}$$

Thus, we have

$$\text{New entry} = 4 - \frac{(1)(-3)}{2} = 5\frac{1}{2}$$

We use the same rule to obtain the new entry in, for example, the x_3 row, x_7 column. This gives

$$\text{New entry} = 0 - \frac{(1)(-2)}{2} = 1$$

The new entry in the Z row, the first column, is given by

$$\text{New entry} = 0 - \frac{(-2)(8)}{2} = 8$$

The entire tableau is completed in this fashion as shown in Figure 7.5.

Figure 7.5 *The basis at corner B*

		x_1	x_2	x_3	x_4	x_5	x_6	x_7	
x_3	10	-2	0	1	0	0	0	1	
x_4	11	$\frac{1}{2}$	0	0	1	0	0	$\frac{1}{2}$	
x_5	25	$5\frac{1}{2}$	0	0	0	1	0	$-\frac{1}{2}$	
x_6	5	$\boxed{2\frac{1}{2}}$	0	0	0	0	1	$-\frac{3}{2}$	→
x_2	4	$-\frac{3}{2}$	1	0	0	0	0	$\frac{1}{2}$	
Z	8	-4	0	0	0	0	0	1	
		↑							

The first five equations represented by Figure 7.5 are read as follows:

$$10 = -2x_1 + x_3 + x_7 \quad \text{or} \quad x_3 = 10 + 2x_1 - x_7$$
$$11 = \tfrac{1}{2}x_1 + x_4 + \tfrac{1}{2}x_7 \quad \text{or} \quad x_4 = 11 - \tfrac{1}{2}x_1 - \tfrac{1}{2}x_7$$
$$\vdots \qquad\qquad \vdots$$
$$4 = -\tfrac{3}{2}x_1 + x_2 + \tfrac{1}{2}x_7 \quad \text{or} \quad x_2 = 4 + \tfrac{3}{2}x_1 - \tfrac{1}{2}x_7$$

These equations are equivalent to those in system (1) and to the first five equations in Figure 7.3. We have simply obtained a new representation of the same conditions. This new representation corresponds to corner B because x_1 and x_7 are the nonbasic variables, both in the equations and at corner B. The equations express the basic variables at corner B explicitly in terms of x_1 and x_7. For example, the first equation says that at corner B, where $x_1 = x_7 = 0$, the slack variable x_3 has the value 10. But the equation also says much more. In particular, at *any* feasible point in Figure 7.2, if we determine the x_1 value and the value of the slack variable x_7, then the first equation says that the value of x_3 at that point will be given by $10 + 2x_1 - x_7$. The remaining equations have analogous interpretations.

The last row of Figure 7.5 is read "$8 = Z - 4x_1 + x_7$," which says that the objective function is given by

$$Z = 8 + 4x_1 - x_7$$

This means that the value of the original objective function at any point on the feasible set can be expressed by $x_1 + 2x_2$ or by $8 + 4x_1 - x_7$. This is because, at any feasible point, Figure 7.5 says that

$$x_2 = 4 + \tfrac{3}{2}x_1 - \tfrac{1}{2}x_7$$

Hence, $2x_2 = 8 + 3x_1 - x_7$, and $x_1 + 2x_2 = 8 + 4x_1 - x_7$.

The above expression for Z indicates that the objective function can be increased by increasing x_1 as much as possible while keeping x_7 at the value zero. This corresponds to a motion from corner B to corner C in Figure 7.2. Note that at corner C the variable x_6 becomes nonbasic. Any additional increase in x_1, while keeping x_7 fixed at zero, would force x_6 to become negative, which means we would be leaving the feasible region. Hence we see that x_1 should enter and x_6 should exit. Let us now apply the enter and exit rules to Figure 7.5 to obtain this same result. The most negative entry in the Z row is -4, and hence the rule says that x_1 enters. To find the exit variable we must check the ratios

$$11/.5, \quad 25/5.5, \quad 5/2.5$$

The minimum ratio is $5/2.5 = 2$. Accordingly, the rule says that x_6 leaves the basis, and $2\tfrac{1}{2}$ is the pivot element.

Using the above steps 1, 2, 3, and the opposite corner rule, we obtain Figure 7.6. This tableau indicates that x_7 should enter the basis because $-\tfrac{7}{5}$ is the most negative entry in the Z row. The ratios

$$14/(14/5), 10/(4/5)$$

indicate that x_5 should exit, and $\tfrac{14}{5}$ is the pivot element. The tableau is now updated to obtain Figure 7.7. This last tableau is said to be optimal because all the entries in the last row are nonnegative. In this case, the last row tells us that $Z = 23 - \tfrac{1}{2}x_5 - \tfrac{1}{2}x_6$. Remember that this equation indicates the value of the objective function at *any* feasible point. Hence, the value is a maximum when $x_5 = x_6 = 0$, and this maximum value is 23. The tableau also gives the

Figure 7.6   *The basis at corner C. Former basic variables were x_2, x_3, x_4, x_5, x_6; x_1 and x_6 have exchanged roles.*

		x_1	x_2	x_3	x_4	x_5	x_6	x_7	
x_3	14	0	0	1	0	0	$\tfrac{4}{5}$	$-\tfrac{1}{5}$	
x_4	10	0	0	0	1	0	$-\tfrac{1}{5}$	$\tfrac{4}{5}$	
x_5	14	0	0	0	0	1	$-\tfrac{11}{5}$	$\boxed{\tfrac{14}{5}}$	$\rightarrow$
x_1	2	1	0	0	0	0	$\tfrac{2}{5}$	$-\tfrac{3}{5}$	
x_2	7	0	1	0	0	0	$\tfrac{3}{5}$	$-\tfrac{2}{5}$	
Z	16	0	0	0	0	0	$\tfrac{8}{5}$	$-\tfrac{7}{5}$	

$\uparrow$

Figure 7.7   *The optimal solution at corner D. Former basic variables were x_1, x_2, x_3, x_4, x_5; x_7 and x_5 have exchanged roles.*

		x_1	x_2	x_3	x_4	x_5	x_6	x_7
x_3	15	0	0	1	0	$\frac{1}{14}$	$\frac{9}{14}$	0
x_4	6	0	0	0	1	$-\frac{2}{7}$	$\frac{3}{7}$	0
x_7	5	0	0	0	0	$\frac{5}{14}$	$-\frac{11}{14}$	1
x_1	5	1	0	0	0	$\frac{3}{14}$	$-\frac{1}{14}$	0
x_2	9	0	1	0	0	$\frac{1}{7}$	$\frac{2}{7}$	0
z	23	0	0	0	0	$\frac{1}{2}$	$\frac{1}{2}$	0

optimal values of the basic variables, namely

$$x_1^* = 5,\ x_2^* = 9,\ x_3^* = 15,\ x_4^* = 6,\ x_7^* = 5$$

We now state a number of additional facts about the simplex algorithm:

1   An optimal set of dual variables (an optimal solution to the dual problem) appears in the last row under the slack variable columns. In this case the slack variables are x_3, x_4, x_5, x_6, x_7, corresponding to constraints 1 through 5 of the problem we have solved. Letting $y_1, y_2, …, y_5$ be the dual variables, we read from Figure 7.6 that

$$y_1^* = 0,\ y_2^* = 0,\ y_3^* = \tfrac{1}{2},\ y_4^* = \tfrac{1}{2},\ y_5^* = 0$$

You can verify that these values are dual feasible and provide a value of 23 for the dual objective function, which is the same as the optimal primal objective value. It follows then from the dual theorem (Section 7.4) that the y_i^* values are optimal.

2   If a degenerate corner is reached there will not be a unique minimum ratio in seeking the exit vector. A number of formal tie-breaking rules exist, the simplest of which is to remove the variable with the smallest subscript.

3   The rule for bringing variables into the basis assures that the objective function will not decrease (and in the absence of degeneracy will increase) as it moves from corner to corner. In fact, this will be true if we bring in *any* variable whose entry in the last row is negative, as opposed to the *most* negative. It may happen that a column occurs with the following property: the bottom entry is negative and all other entries are nonpositive. This indicates that the problem is unbounded. Moreover, any unbounded problem will produce such a signal.

4   In order to solve a min problem, multiply the objective function by -1 and solve as a max problem. The solution so obtained will also solve the min model. The optimal objective value for the min problem will be the negative of the value obtained for the max problem.

5   Alternative optima are revealed by discovering, in the optimal tableau, a nonbasic variable with a zero entry in the bottom row. Such a variable can be entered into the basis without changing the objective value.

6   When the constraints are all of the form

$$\sum_{j=1}^{n} a_{ij} x_j \le b_i \qquad b_i \ge 0$$

then the slack variables will provide an initial basis, as illustrated for the above problem. The following phase I technique will find an initial basis under more general conditions, such as the presence of equality constraints, or $\leq$ constraints with a negative RHS. For the ith such constraint, convert it to standard equality form, in the usual way, and then express it in such a way that the RHS is ≥ 0. Then add an *artificial variable*, z_i. Include each artificial variable in the objective function with a large negative coefficient.

For example, consider the problem

Max $x_1 + 6x_2 - 3x_3 + 4x_4$

s.t.

$$
\begin{aligned}
2x_1 - 3x_2 + x_3 &\leq -3 \\
3x_1 + x_2 + 4x_3 + x_4 &= 6 \\
-8x_1 + 6x_3 &= 7 \\
3x_1 + 4x_2 &\geq 3 \\
8x_2 - 12x_3 &\leq 6
\end{aligned}
$$

x_1, x_2, x_3, x_4 all nonnegative

In order to apply the simplex method, we first convert to standard equality-constraint form. This gives

Max $x_1 + 6x_2 - 3x_3 + 4x_4$

s.t.

$$
\begin{aligned}
2x_1 - 3x_2 + x_3 + x_5 &= -3 \\
3x_1 + x_2 + 4x_3 + x_4 &= 6 \\
-8x_1 + 6x_3 &= 7 \\
3x_1 + 4x_2 - x_6 &= 3 \\
8x_2 - 12x_3 + x_7 &= 6
\end{aligned}
$$

$x_j \geq 0$ all j

We next restate this in such a way that all right-hand sides are nonnegative. We obtain

Max $x_1 + 6x_2 - 3x_3 + 4x_4$

s.t.

$$
\begin{aligned}
-2x_1 + 3x_2 - x_3 - x_5 &= 3 \\
3x_1 + x_2 + 4x_3 + x_4 &= 6 \\
-8x_1 + 6x_3 &= 7 \\
3x_1 + 4x_2 - x_6 &= 3 \\
8x_2 - 12x_3 + x_7 &= 6
\end{aligned}
$$

$x_j \geq 0$ all j

Certainly it is true that any LP problem can be expressed in such a form. Any variable that appears only in a single constraint and that has a coefficient of +1 in that constraint can be used as part of an initial basis. Thus, x_4 and

x_7 qualify (and note that x_4 is not a slack variable since it appears in the objective function). To obtain a complete initial basis we add artificial variables to the first, third, and fourth equations, respectively. These variables are included in the objective function with a large negative coefficient, say -10^6. Hence, we obtain

Max $x_1 + 6x_2 - 3x_3 + 4x_4 - 10^6 z_1 - 10^6 z_2 - 10^6 z_3$

s.t.

$$-2x_1 + 3x_2 - x_3 \qquad - x_5 \qquad\qquad + z_1 \qquad\qquad = 3$$
$$3x_1 + x_2 + 4x_3 + x_4 \qquad\qquad\qquad\qquad\qquad = 6$$
$$-8x_1 \qquad + 6x_3 \qquad\qquad\qquad\qquad + z_2 \qquad = 7$$
$$3x_1 + 4x_2 \qquad\qquad\qquad - x_6 \qquad\qquad + z_3 = 3$$
$$8x_2 - 12x_3 \qquad\qquad + x_7 \qquad\qquad\qquad = 6$$

$x_i \geq 0$, $i = 1, ..., 7$; $z_i \geq 0$, $i = 1, 2, 3$

The variables x_4, x_7, z_1, z_2, z_3 provide an initial basis. However, before writing the first tableau we must replace each basic variable in the objective function with nonbasic variables, as follows. Since, from the above equations,

$$z_1 = 3 + 2x_1 - 3x_2 + x_3 + x_5$$
$$z_2 = 7 + 8x_1 - 6x_3$$
$$z_3 = 3 - 3x_1 - 4x_2 + x_6$$
$$x_4 = 6 - 3x_1 - x_2 - 4x_3$$

the objective function becomes

$$Z = x_1 + 6x_2 - 3x_3 + 4(6 - 3x_1 - x_2 - 4x_3) - 10^6(3 + 2x_1 - 3x_2 + x_3 + x_5)$$
$$\quad - 10^6(7 + 8x_1 - 6x_3) - 10^6(3 - 3x_1 - 4x_2 + x_6)$$
$$= [-11 - 7(10^6)]x_1 + [2 + 7(10^6)]x_2 + [-19 + 5(10^6)]x_3 - 10^6 x_5 - 10^6 x_6$$
$$\quad - 13(10^6) + 24$$
$$= -13(10^6) + 24 - [11 + 7(10^6)]x_1 - [-2 - 7(10^6)]x_2 - [19 - 5(10^6)]x_3$$
$$\quad - 10^6 x_5 - 10^6 x_6$$

Now we obtain the first tableau as shown in Figure 7.8. This tableau is then transformed by a series of updates in exactly the way we described above. For example, x_2 is the first variable to enter, and either z_3 or x_7 can be chosen to exit. Each time an artificial variable is removed from the basis, the corresponding column can thereafter be ignored. When all artificial variables are driven out of the basis, phase I is complete and the pivoting algorithm is continued until either an optimality signal or an unbounded signal occurs. If an optimality signal occurs before all artificial variables have been removed, then the initial problem is infeasible. The use of artificial variables is illustrated in Example 4, Section 7.8.

In concluding our discussion of the simplex algorithm, we wish to stress

Figure 7.8 *The first tableau with artificial variables*

		x_1	x_2	x_3	x_4	x_5	x_6	x_7	z_1	z_2	z_3
z_1	3	−2	3	−1	0	−1	0	0	1	0	0
x_4	6	3	1	4	1	0	0	0	0	0	0
z_2	7	−8	0	6	0	0	0	0	0	1	0
z_3	3	3	4	0	0	0	−1	0	0	0	1
x_7	6	0	8	−12	0	0	0	1	0	0	0
Z	24	11	−2	19	0	0	0	0	0	0	0
$x10^6$	−13	7	−7	−5	0	1	1	0	0	0	0

that the LP software carried by the large computers employs much more sophisticated computations than those outlined above. The phase I procedure often allows the user to preselect a set of variables to be included in the initial basis. Product inverse computation methods are usually employed in the pivoting procedure, and the codes are often of an in-core-out-of-core variety. Nevertheless, at the heart of the simplex method is the above-described concept of pivoting, in order to update one basic system to another, thereby moving uphill from extreme point to adjacent extreme point on the underlying convex polytope. However, the efficient computational implementation of the algorithm becomes quite complicated and is a topic worthy of study in its own right.

7.8 Examples and Solutions

Example 1

Use summation notation to write the primal problem as a max model with n nonnegative variables and m inequality ($\leq$) constraints. Let c_j, a_{ij}, and b_i denote the parameters for the objective function, the constraint functions, and the RHS, respectively. Then write out the dual of this problem.

Solution to Example 1

PRIMAL

$$\text{Max} \sum_{j=1}^{n} c_j x_j$$

s.t.

$$\sum_{j=1}^{n} a_{ij} x_j \leq b_i \qquad i = 1, \ldots, m$$

$$x_j \geq 0 \qquad j = 1, \ldots, n$$

DUAL

$$\text{Min} \ \sum_{i=1}^{m} b_i y_i$$

s.t.

$$\sum_{i=1}^{m} a_{ij} y_i \geq c_j \qquad j = 1, \ldots, n$$

$$y_i \geq 0 \qquad i = 1, \ldots, m$$

Example 2

Find the dual to the following problem:

$$\text{Min} \ \sum_{j=1}^{n} c_j x_j$$

s.t.

$$\sum_{j=1}^{n} a_{ij} x_j \leq b_i \qquad i = 1, \ldots, m$$

$$x_j \geq 0 \qquad j = 1, \ldots, n$$

Solution to Example 2

The dual of this problem is

$$\text{Max} \ \sum_{i=1}^{m} b_i y_i$$

s.t.

$$\sum_{i=1}^{m} a_{ij} y_i \leq c_j \qquad j = 1, \ldots, n$$

$$y_i \leq 0 \qquad i = 1, \ldots, m$$

The dual variables for the original problem are negative since, in this case, a per-unit increase in each RHS value b_i will help and, hence, decrease the optimal objective value. This negative sign is consistent with the explanation given in Section 7.6 that the dual variable is the rate of *change* in the optimal objective value as the RHS increases. Note that in this instance the dual prices that appear on the computer printout will be positive.

Example 3

Suppose that the primal problem

$$\text{Max} \ \sum_{j=1}^{n} c_j x_j$$

s.t.

$$\sum_{j=1}^{n} a_{ij} x_j \le b_i \qquad i = 1, ..., m \tag{P}$$

$$x_j \ge 0 \qquad j = 1, ..., n$$

is unbounded for some set of RHS parameters b_i, $i = 1, ..., m$. Use the dual theorem to show that this implies (P) is either unbounded or inconsistent for every choice of b_is.

Solution to Example 3

If (P) is unbounded for some choice of b_is, say $b_i = \hat{b}_i$, $i = 1, ..., m$, then by the dual theorem the following dual problem must be inconsistent:

$$\text{Min} \quad \sum_{i=1}^{m} \hat{b}_i y_i$$

s.t.

$$\sum_{i=1}^{m} a_{ij} y_i \ge c_j \qquad j = 1, ..., n \tag{D}$$

$$y_i \ge 0 \qquad i = 1, ..., m$$

The fact that (D) is inconsistent depends only on the constraints of (D), not on the objective function. Changing the b_i values in (P) will not affect the constraints in (D). Consequently, (D) will remain inconsistent for all choices of the parameters b_i. It follows then from the dual theorem that, for any set of right-hand sides, (P) will be either unbounded or inconsistent.

Example 4

Use the simplex method to solve the following linear program.

Max $\quad -3x_1 + 4x_2 + 6x_3$

s.t.

$$-3x_1 - x_2 + 3x_3 = -20$$
$$6x_1 - x_2 \qquad \ge \quad 12$$
$$x_1, x_2, x_3 \ge \quad 0$$

Solution to Example 4

First, convert to the form

Max $\quad -3x_1 + 4x_2 + 6x_3$

s.t.

$$3x_1 + x_2 - 3x_3 \qquad = 20$$
$$6x_1 - x_2 \qquad - x_4 = 12$$
$$x_j \ge 0 \qquad \text{all } j$$

To obtain an initial basis, we employ artificial variables z_1, z_2 with very negative coefficients in the objective function, say -10^6. This gives

Max $-3x_1 + 4x_2 + 6x_3 - 10^6 z_1 - 10^6 z_2$

s.t.

$3x_1 + x_2 - 3x_3 \qquad + z_1 \qquad = 20$

$6x_1 - x_2 \qquad - x_4 \qquad + z_2 = 12$

$\qquad\qquad x_1, x_2, x_3, x_4, z_1, z_2 \geq 0$

In the first tableau, the basis will be z_1, z_2 and the nonbasic variables are x_1, x_2, x_3, and x_4. The equations are used to substitute for z_1 and z_2 in the objective function to obtain

$$Z = -3x_1 + 4x_2 + 6x_3 - 10^6(20 - 3x_1 - x_2 + 3x_3) - 10^6(12 - 6x_1 + x_2 + x_4)$$
$$= -32(10^6) - [3 - 9(10^6)]x_1 - (-4)x_2 - [-6 + 3(10^6)]x_3 - 10^6 x_4$$

The first tableau is given in Figure 7.9. The variable x_1 enters, z_2 leaves, and 6 is the pivot element.

The second tableau is shown in Figure 7.10, where we have omitted the z_2 column since z_2, an artificial variable, is no longer basic. Now x_2 enters, z_1 leaves, and $\frac{3}{2}$ is the pivot element. The new tableau is shown in Figure 7.11.

Now phase I is complete, for the artificial variables are completely eliminated. The new entry variable is x_3 (because of the -13 in the Z row), but the x_3 column consists of all negative entries, and hence the original problem is unbounded. It can be seen from the final tableau that if the variable x_4 is

Figure 7.9   *The first tableau for Example 4*

		x_1	x_2	x_3	x_4	z_1	z_2	
z_1	20	3	1	-3	0	1	0	
z_2	12	[6]	-1	0	-1	0	1	→
Z	0	3	-4	-6	0	0	0	
$\times 10^6$	-32	-9	0	3	1	0	0	
		↑						

Figure 7.10   *The second tableau for Example 4*

		x_1	x_2	x_3	x_4	z_1	
z_1	14	0	$\left[\frac{3}{2}\right]$	-3	$\frac{1}{2}$	1	→
x_1	2	1	$-\frac{1}{6}$	0	$-\frac{1}{6}$	0	
Z	-6	0	$-3\frac{1}{2}$	-6	$\frac{1}{2}$	0	
$\times 10^6$	-14	0	$-\frac{3}{2}$	3	$-\frac{1}{2}$	0	
			↑				

Figure 7.11   *The third tableau for Example 4*

		x_1	x_2	x_3	x_4
x_2	$\frac{28}{3}$	0	1	-2	$\frac{1}{3}$
x_1	$3\frac{5}{9}$	1	0	$-\frac{1}{3}$	$-\frac{1}{9}$
Z	$\frac{80}{3}$	0	0	-13	$\frac{5}{3}$
$\times 10^6$	0	0	0	0	0
				↑	

fixed at zero, with x_3 increased arbitrarily, the variables x_2 and x_1 will remain nonnegative, that is,

$$x_2 = \tfrac{28}{3} + 2x_3, \; x_1 = 3\tfrac{5}{9} + \tfrac{1}{3}x_3$$

and the objective function

$$Z = \tfrac{80}{3} + 13x_3$$

will grow arbitrarily large.

7.9   Summary of Key Concepts

Given any linear program, there is a corresponding dual problem. **(Section 7.2)**

The dual of the dual is the original problem. **(Section 7.4)**

The value of the objective function in the max problem can never exceed the value of the objective in the min problem, where each function is understood to be evaluated only at feasible points.

The dual theorem of LP states that the following mutually exclusive relations are the only ones that can prevail between a pair of dual problems:

1 Both may have optimal solutions, in which case the optimal objective values are equal.
2 Both may be inconsistent.
3 One may be unbounded and the other inconsistent.
(Section 7.4)

The principle of complementary slackness says that whenever a primal constraint is inactive, the corresponding dual variable must be zero (in any optimal solution to the dual problem). Equivalently, if the optimal value of a dual variable is nonzero, then the corresponding primal constraint must be active (in any optimal solution to the primal). **(Section 7.4)**

If we assume that the primal problem has a nondegenerate solution, then the optimal value of the ith dual variable is the rate of change in the value of the primal objective function as the RHS b_i is increased. **(Section 7.6)**

> *Shadow prices and market prices differ because of the existence of constraints or, equivalently, because of the nonexistence of a perfect market for the constrained resources. (Section 7.6)*

7.10   Problems

1   Find the dual of the following linear program:

$$\text{Min} \quad \sum_{j=1}^{n} c_j x_j$$

s.t.

$$\sum_{j=1}^{n} a_{ij} x_j = b_i \qquad i = 1, \ldots, m$$

$$x_j \geq 0 \qquad j = 1, \ldots, n$$

2   Consider the PROTRAC illustration in Section 7.6.1. Let x_1, x_2 be any feasible values in (P), and y_1, y_2, y_3 be any feasible values in (D). Prove that
$r_1 x_1 + r_2 x_2 \leq b_1 y_1 + b_2 y_2 + b_3 y_3$.

3   Use the simplex algorithm to solve

Max $5x_1 + 3x_2$

s.t.

$3x_1 + 5x_2 \leq 15$

$5x_1 + 2x_2 \leq 10$

$x_1, x_2 \geq 0$

4   Use the simplex algorithm to solve

Min $-2x_1 - x_2 - 4x_3 - 5x_4$

s.t.

$x_1 + 3x_2 + 2x_3 + 5x_4 \leq 20$

$2x_1 + 16x_2 + x_3 + x_4 \geq 4$

$3x_1 - x_2 - 5x_3 + 10x_4 \leq -10$

$x_1, x_2, x_3, x_4 \geq 0$

8 Dual Pricing and the Optimal Value Function

This chapter provides a complete conceptual development of dual price analysis. At the outset, a geometric interpretation is presented for the dual-price output found on the computer solution to LP problems. Then, the optimal value function is defined and is generated by a parametric analysis on the RHS for a particular problem. The relationship between the optimal value function and the dual price is examined. It is shown how the optimal value function can be used to obtain exact and estimated effects of RHS perturbations.

8.1 Introduction

This chapter is the first of two consecutive chapters devoted to topics that are variously referred to as *sensitivity, postoptimality,* or *parametric analysis* in mathematical programming problems. In the context of mathematical programming (linear or nonlinear), the terms *sensitivity analysis* and *parametric analysis* refer to the analysis of changes in the optimal solution and the optimal value of the objective function (to be denoted as OV) as changes are made in the numerical value assigned to a parameter. This type of analysis occurs after one has already found an optimal solution to an initial problem, and that is why the term *postoptimality analysis* is also employed.

The sensitivity topic is one where the art and some of the technicalities of modeling come together. It is based upon theory, but it has great practical importance. In order to appreciate this importance, let us suppose that a constrained optimization model (linear or nonlinear) has been formulated and solved. The manager now has a solution to the problem, and this obviously provides him with information not previously at his disposal. However, he knows that his model is only an approximation of his real decision problem. In order to construct a usable model, some logical considerations and interactions have not been included. This is one sense in which the model is an approximation. But there is another quite different and equally important sense in which the model is an approximation. Obviously, every model has parameters, and the values assigned to the parameters constitute the data of the model for a given execution. These data appear in both the objective function and the constraints. For example, in the PROTRAC *E* and *F* model, the RHS of the fifth constraint is -135. You will recall that this value comes from a formula based upon an existing contractual agreement with the union. But this value is renegotiated every six months with the union. Management believes that a value of -135 will be agreed upon for the next six-month period, but this is far from certain. A look at historical data reveals that the figure has changed a number of times during the last ten years. Even though the manager feels that -135 is the current best estimate, he cannot help wondering, "What if it turns out to be -130 or -140 instead?" When he solves the problem he uses the value -135, but he wonders, "How valid is this solution if the true parameter value turns out to differ from my estimate?" This is a *sensitivity question.* In the face of uncertainty, the manager wants to know how sensitive his solution is to the data he has provided. If a sensitivity analysis reveals that the optimal policies are rather insensitive to the particular parameter values employed and if the decision maker "believes in" the model, then he will have more confidence in the results in spite of the uncertainty in the data. If small changes in parameter values can lead to large changes in the results (a high degree of sensitivity), then the manager must exercise more caution in obtaining good data and in transforming model output into real-world decisions.

In general, the term *sensitivity analysis* can apply to any of the data in a problem. One possible way to answer sensitivity questions is simply to solve the model again and again, using different parameter values. In fact, for nonlinear problems this is usually the only way to address such questions. As you might imagine, this can be expensive.

Because of the special structure of LP problems, a good deal of useful sensitivity information is easily produced along with a solution to the problem. Thus, although the topic is of importance for all constrained optimization models, because of both practical and theoretic obstacles one rarely sees a sensitivity study outside the realm of LP. For this reason, our discussion in this and the following chapter will focus exclusively upon sensitivity analysis in the LP environment.

In this particular chapter, the emphasis is upon the RHS parameters. In Chapter 3, we discussed in general terms some of the reasons for management's interest in this type of analysis. In summary, the reasons are twofold:

---

1 The desire to perform a sequence of conditional analyses because of uncertainty about the true value of the parameter
2 The desire to find the proper or *optimal value* for a parameter in circumstances when the parameter itself cannot be included as a variable in the LP model

---

Such circumstances could arise when, for example, there is a nonlinear cost associated with changing the parameter value. A specific analysis of this sort is performed in Chapter 12.

In Chapter 5, the topic of sensitivity analysis on the RHS was introduced. It was seen that when a particular RHS value was perturbed within a given allowable range, precise statements about the resulting optimal objective value can be made. In this chapter, we focus on the way in which dual prices change as the RHS is perturbed by more than these allowable amounts. Moreover, the topic of dual pricing is given a geometric interpretation, and the geometry is presented hand in hand with relevant computer printout. The combination of these two tools, geometry and the computer, makes it possible to obtain a deep understanding of the structure of LP problems and to perform revealing and useful postoptimality analysis with elementary college level algebra.

8.2 Illustrating Dual-price Output

Consider the PROTRAC E and F problem. The computer output, which includes the problem statement, is shown in Figure 8.1.

It will be useful to compare this output with the geometric interpretation in Figure 6.14. In order to facilitate this comparison, we suggest that you make a rough sketch of this figure with your own pencil and paper. Review the interpretation of Figure 6.14 and then verify the following observations:

Figure 8.1   *Computer output for the E and F model*

```
MAX 5000E +4000F
SUBJECT TO
   2)    E +F   >= 5
   3)    E -3F   <= 0
   4)   10E +15F  <= 150
   5)   20E +10F  <= 160
   6)  -30E -10F  <=-135
```

VARIABLE	VALUE	REDUCED-COST
E	4.50000	0.00000
F	7.00000	0.00000
OBJ FCTN	50500.	

ROW	SLACK	DUAL-PRICE
2	6.5	0
3	16.5	0
4	0	150
5	0	175
6	70	0

SENSITIVITY ANALYSIS

RANGE IN WHICH BASIS REMAINS THE SAME
    COST SENSITIVITY

VARIABLE	INCREASE IN C(J)	DECREASE IN C(J)
E	2999.99998	2333.33299
F	3499.99997	1499.99999

RIGHT HAND SENSITIVITY

ROW	ALLOWABLE INCREASE	ALLOWABLE DECREASE
2	6.5000	INFINITE
3	INFINITE	16.5000
4	90.00003	47.14286
5	73.33333	40.00000
6	INFINITE	70.0000

1 The optimal values of E and F are

$E^* = 4.5$

$F^* = 7.0$

2 The third and fourth constraints are active (alternatively called *tight, binding, effective*).
   a In the picture (Figure 6.14), the lines defining these constraints define the optimal corner.
   b On the output, the slack values in rows 4 and 5 are zero. Note that in this particular code, the computer treats the objective function as row 1, and thus the third and fourth constraints are designated on the output as rows 4 and 5.
3 The first, second, and fifth constraints are inactive.
   a In the picture, the lines defining these constraints do not intersect the optimal corner.
   b On the output, the optimal slack values associated with these constraints are positive. They assume the values 6.5, 16.5, and 70, respectively.
4 The solution is nondegenerate.
   a In the picture, only two lines intersect at the optimal corner.
   b On the output, there are five constraints, and this equals the number of positive variables (including slacks) in the optimal solution.

Now suppose you want a sensitivity analysis on the availability of labor hours in department B, which is the RHS of the fourth constraint (row 5). We shall let b_4 denote possible values for this parameter. Observe that on row 5 there is a dual price of 175 and that under the section of output labeled RIGHT HAND SENSITIVITY there is an allowable increase of 73.33 and an allowable decrease of 40. In Chapter 5, it was stated that the following interpretation is correct. As b_4 (whose current value is 160) is allowed to change to any new value between $160 - 40 = 120$ and $160 + 73.33 = 233.33$, the change in the optimal objective value per unit change in the RHS (that is, per unit change from the value 160) will be equal in magnitude to the dual price, which is 175. Thus, for any fixed RHS value between 120 and 233.33, the dual price of 175 remains constant, and it tells us the rate of change in the optimal objective value as that RHS is allowed to change. Concerning the sign of the dual price, the following common computer output convention, which we shall employ, is also recalled from Chapter 5. The dual price is interpreted as the *rate of improvement in the OV.* This means that

The dual price is positive if increasing the RHS helps (improves) the optimal objective value (OV).

The dual price is negative if increasing the RHS hurts (impairs) the optimal objective value (OV).

For a max model, help means "increase" and hurt means "decrease."

For a min model, help means "decrease" and hurt means "increase."

Since in this situation the dual price (175) is positive, a unit *increase* in the RHS will help the OV. This also means that a unit *decrease* in the RHS will hurt the OV. Since the units of the objective function are dollars and the units of b_4 are hours, the units of the dual price are dollars per hour. Specifically, if one additional hour of labor were available in department B and the resulting 161 units were *optimally used*, then the increase in revenue would be $175. (In the language of economics, one would say that in the context of this model the marginal return to labor is 175.) It is important to note that in order to obtain this $175 of incremental return, the 161 units of labor must be used *optimally*. This does not mean the same thing as "the extra unit of labor must be used optimally." What it does mean is this. If you were to change b_4 to 161, leaving all other data unchanged, and again solve the problem, the computer output for the new problem would indicate the new optimal values for the decision variables, and producing these quantities would *optimally* employ the 161 units of labor. The resulting OV would be 175 units larger than before.

New OV = 50,500 + 175 = 50,675

In general, the new optimal production policy will *not* be obtained by taking the former optimal production policy and "adding to it" the "optimal employment of another hour of labor."

The same dual price of 175 applies over the entire interval from 120 hours to 233.33 hours. The rate of increase of revenue as b_4 increases is the same as the rate of decrease in revenue as b_4 decreases. For example, a 10-hour *decrease* in labor hours available would, *at optimality*, decrease the revenue at the rate of $175 per hour. That is,

New OV = 50,500 − 10(175)

$\qquad$ = 48,750

For the geometric interpretation of dual prices let us return to Figure 6.14 and suppose the RHS value of 160 is replaced by a somewhat larger number (that is, the value of b_4 is slightly increased). You now have a new fourth constraint which replaces the old one. You could plot this new constraint to see that it is a line parallel to the old and displaced somewhat to the right. That is, the increase in b_4 does not change the slope of the line; it increases the intercept. However, without bothering to plot the new line you could conclude that the implied motion must be to the right. An increase in the RHS of

$20E + 10F \le b_4$

must relax or loosen the constraint, making it easier to satisfy. That is, every feasible pair (E,F) that satisfies the old condition with RHS 160 will surely satisfy the new condition with an increase in the RHS value. This means the new constraint cannot prohibit or rule out any previously allowable (E,F) pairs. Hence, in the figure (6.14), the new line must be to the right, thereby expanding the constraint set. Similarly, a decrease in b_4 means the constraint is being tightened. The line will move to the left, thereby contracting the constraint set and prohibiting some previously allowed values for (E,F).

Figure 8.2 *Changing the value of b_4*

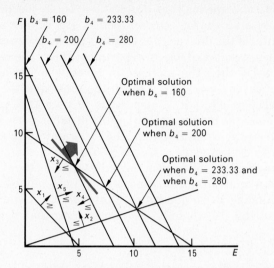

Figure 8.2 will help us to elaborate upon these interactions by showing the solution to the PROTRAC E and F problem with several possible changes in b_4. Referring to this figure, let us consider the following cases.

CASE 1: $b_4 = 160$

This is the original problem. As shown in Figure 8.1, $E^* = 4.5$ and $F^* = 7.0$. The optimal objective value is 50,500, and constraints 3 and 4 are active.

CASE 2: $b_4 = 200$

The increase in b_4 of 40 hours $(200 - 160)$ is well within the allowable increase of 73.333. Thus

New OV $= 50,500 + 40(175) = 57,500$

This value is achieved at the point $(7.5,5)$, which is the new optimal solution. This point lies on the intersection of the lines

$$10E + 15F = 150$$
$$20E + 10F = 200$$

Thus constraints 3 and 4 are still active, and the optimal objective value has increased at the rate of \$175-per-hour increase in b_4. This situation with $b_4 = 200$ is typical of any increase in b_4 of h hours, where h is any number between 0 and 73.33. Your intuition probably tells you that as b_4 is slightly increased, the new optimal policy should be to make a little more E and a little more F in some appropriate amounts. But quite to the contrary, Figure 8.2 shows that as b_4 increases, the optimal solution moves to the southeast down the line $10E + 15F = 150$, and the optimal solution says to make more E and less F. This illustrates the earlier remarks that as b_4 is increased one hour, the new optimal production levels cannot be described as "the same as before plus the addition of another hour's optimal utilization."

CASE 3: $b_4 = 233.33$

As Figure 8.2 shows, at this value for b_4, the fourth constraint passes through the intersection of the second and third constraints. This intersection point is the optimal solution. Thus constraints 2, 3, and 4 are all active and, as a result, the solution is now degenerate. The optimal objective value now equals

New OV = 50,500 + 73.33(175)

$\quad$ = 63,333.33

The optimal solution is (10,3.33).

CASE 4: $b_4 = 280$

As soon as b_4 becomes larger than 233.33, the fourth constraint becomes redundant. The optimal solution remains at the same corner as when $b_4 = 233.33$. However, this corner is no longer degenerate since the second and third constraints are the only ones active at the solution.

Before summarizing the phenomena illustrated by these four cases, it is useful to recall the following definitions:

The basic variables are the positive variables at a nondegenerate corner.

The basis is the set of basic variables at a nondegenerate corner.

In summary, then, Cases 1–4 have helped to demonstrate the following facts:

1 For changes in the RHS *less than* the allowable increase, the basis at the new solution is the same as at the old, and so is the dual price. The change in the OV between the new solution and the old is obtained by multiplying the dual price at the old solution by the change in the RHS.

2 For a change in the RHS *exactly equal to* the allowable increase, the new solution is degenerate. The change in the OV between the new solution and the old is obtained by multiplying the dual price at the old solution by the change in the RHS.

3 For a change in the RHS *greater than* the allowable increase, the basis at the new solution differs from that at the old. The dual price can also be expected to differ.[1] The change in the OV between the new solution and the old can *not*, in general, be obtained by multiplying the dual price at the old solution by the change in the RHS.

Although all of the discussion and the illustrations have been for increases in the RHS, the same type of analysis holds for decreases as well.

---

1 Under unusual circumstances, the dual price before and after the allowable increase could be the same. This phenomenon is illustrated in Example 4 of Section 8.8.

8.3 The OV Function

In Figure 8.2 we saw that for changes in b_4 between the allowable increase and the allowable decrease, the optimal values of E and F are determined by the point of intersection of the third and fourth constraints. Thus, if b_4 is a specific value between 120 and 233.33 then the optimal values, say E^* and F^*, must satisfy the algebraic conditions

$10E^* + 15F^* = 150$ (third constraint line)

$20E^* + 10F^* = b_4$ (fourth constraint line)

Solving this system of simultaneous equations for E^* and F^*, in terms of b_4, it must be true that

$$E^* = \left(\frac{3}{40}\right)b_4 - 7\frac{1}{2}$$

$$F^* = 15 - \frac{b_4}{20}$$

The corresponding optimal objective value is

$$OV = 5{,}000E^* + 4{,}000F^*$$
$$= 5{,}000\left(\frac{3b_4}{40} - 7.5\right) + 4{,}000\left(15 - \frac{b_4}{20}\right)$$
$$= 175b_4 + 22{,}500$$

This equation tells us that as b_4 moves from 120 to 233.33, the OV is produced by a new linear function. Let us use the symbol V_4 to denote this function. Its values are $V_4(b_4)$, and for $120 < b_4 < 233.33$ the above equation shows that

$$V_4(b_4) = 175b_4 + 22{,}500$$

The slope of the graph of this function is 175. Thus, we have demonstrated algebraically that for $120 < b_4 < 233.33$ the slope of the graph of V_4, which is by definition the rate of change in the optimal objective value, is the same as the dual price that has appeared in the computer printout (Figure 8.1). Since the active constraints change at 120 and 233.33, the above simultaneous equations that determine E^* and F^* will change, and hence the equation for the values $V_4(b_4)$ will generally be expected to change. That is why the dual price of 175 can be expected to change as b_4 falls below 120 or rises above 233.33.

The above analysis has led to the notion of a new and important function, V_4, whose values are the optimal values of the LP objective function as the RHS b_4 changes, with all other data remaining the same. This new function is called the *optimal value function*, which we often refer to as simply the OV function. It is a function of a single variable, and you can associate such a function with the RHS of each constraint in any LP problem. Thus, if an LP problem has m constraints, with some given values for the RHS parameters,

Figure 8.3 *Geometric interpretation as b_4 varies*

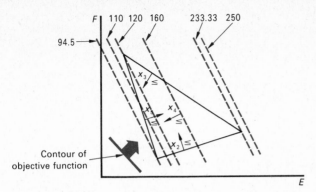

say $\bar{b}_1$, $\bar{b}_2$, . . ., $\bar{b}_m$, then associated with this problem are m different OV functions, V_i, one for each constraint. This means you think of the ith RHS as a variable b_i and keep the other parameters fixed at the assigned values $\bar{b}_j$, $j \neq i$. The number $V_i(\bar{b}_i)$ is the OV of the original linear program, and $V_i(b_i)$ is the OV of a new linear program, with $\bar{b}_i$ replaced by some other value b_i and all other data unchanged. The domain of the function V_i is all values of b_i for which the constraint set is nonempty. In the E and F model, the domain of the function V_4 is all values of $b_4 \geq 94.50$, because when b_4 is less than 94.50 there is no point (E,F) satisfying *all* the inequalities. (This is easily seen from Figure 8.3.) In general, when all of the constraints cannot be satisfied, the problem is termed *inconsistent* or *infeasible*. This pathological condition can occur by making a constraint *too tight* (such as choosing $b_4 < 94.50$), or by including too many constraints in the model, or simply by making an error in submitting the model to the computer, such as entering incorrect data, inadvertently entering $\leq$ instead of $\geq$, and so on.

Figures 8.3 and 8.4 show the relation between the OV function and the geometry of the underlying model. These figures should be carefully compared. Note that the graph of V_4 is piecewise linear; that is, it consists of pieces

Figure 8.4 *The graph of the optimal value function V_4*

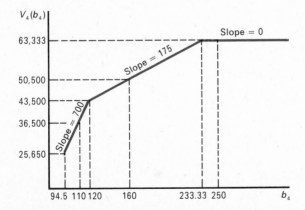

that are linear between points at which the slope changes. The slopes change at the following two values for b_4:

$b_4 = 120$

$b_4 = 233.33$

These values correspond to two of the points of degeneracy shown in Figure 8.3. The third point of degeneracy ($b_4 = 94.50$) is the point where the domain of V_4 ends (or, if you like, begins). Suppose $(\bar{b}_4, V_4(\bar{b}_4))$ is any point where the graph of V_4 is smooth (that is, is not a point where the slope changes). Then the slope at $(\bar{b}_4, V_4(\bar{b}_4))$ is unambiguously defined. It is by definition the rate of change in the optimal objective value at $b_4 = \bar{b}_4$, which for a max model is the same as the dual price corresponding to the RHS b_4.

At RHS values that produce a degenerate solution ($b_4 = 94.5, 120, 233.33$), it will generally, though not always, be the case that the slope of the OV graph will differ to the right and to the left of that RHS value. (Or it may not be defined in one direction, as at $b_4 = 94.5$.) This typically means that the dual price is not unambiguously defined at such a point. There are two values. The computer will print out only one value, and this value will represent either a slope to the left or a slope to the right, but there is no simple way of describing, in advance, which of these will be chosen. However, in any given case the computer printout will provide this information in the following way. Either the allowable increase or the allowable decrease will be zero. If the increase is zero, the dual price printed out is the slope to the left, and if the decrease is zero it is the slope to the right.

Several computer runs have been made in order to compare the above assertions with the output produced.

1　In Figure 8.5, the output for $b_4 = 94.5$ is reproduced. Note that the optimal solution is degenerate. Since the allowable decrease is printed out as 0, the dual price of 700 must be the rate of change to the right. More precisely, since the allowable increase is 25.5, this dual price is the slope of that portion of the graph of V_4 corresponding to values of b_4 between 94.5 and 120. This slope of 700 is entered on the appropriate segment of Figure 8.4. Note that the computer gives no indication that the problem is actually infeasible for values of $b_4 < 94.5$. The allowable decrease of zero simply means that the indicated dual price applies to values of $b_4 \geq 94.5$.

2　In Figure 8.6, the output for $b_4 = 110$ is reproduced. Note that the solution is nondegenerate and, as expected from the discussion in item 1 above, the dual price is 700. Note that the allowable increase (10) and decrease (15.5) in b_4 are also as expected.

3　In Figure 8.7, the output for $b_4 = 120$ is reproduced. Note that the optimal solution is degenerate. Since the allowable decrease is printed out as 0, the dual price of 175 must be the rate of change to the right. This will be the slope of that portion of the graph of V_4 for values of b_4 between 120 and 233.33, because the allowable increase is 113.33. The slope of 175 is entered on the appropriate segment of Figure 8.4.

4　The output for $b_4 = 160$ has already appeared in Figure 8.1. The solution is nondegenerate, and, as expected from the discussion in item 3 above, the dual price is 175. Note that the allowable increase (73.33) and decrease (40) are also as expected.

5　In Figure 8.8, the output for $b_4 = 233.33$ is reproduced. The optimal solution is

Figure 8.5 *A degenerate solution, $b_4 = 94.5$*

```
MAX 5000E +4000F
SUBJECT TO
   2)    E +F   >= 5
   3)    E -3F   <= 0
   4)   10E +15F  <= 3²0
   5)   20E +10F  <= 94.5
   6)  -30E -10F  <=-135
```

VARIABLE	VALUE	REDUCED-COST
E	4.05000	0.00000
F	1.35000	0.00000
OBJ FCTN	25650	

ROW	SLACK	DUAL-PRICE
2	.4	0
3	0	0
4	89.25	0
5	0	700
6	0	300.

```
SENSITIVITY ANALYSIS

RANGE IN WHICH BASIS REMAINS THE SAME
      COST SENSITIVITY
```

VARIABLE	INCREASE IN C(J)	DECREASE IN C(J)
E	2999.99949	INFINITE
F	INFINITE	1499.99974

```
     RIGHT HAND SENSITIVITY
```

ROW	ALLOWABLE INCREASE	ALLOWABLE DECREASE
2	0.4000	INFINITE
3	INFINITE	0.0000
4	INFINITE	89.2500
5	25.50000	0.00000
6	40.50001	0.00000

degenerate. The optimal value of the slack on row 3 (the variable x_2) is printed as .000755. This should be interpreted as zero. It does not appear as exactly zero because of the small errors inherent in computer arithmetic (called *roundoff error*). The allowable increase of .00336 should also be interpreted as zero. Thus, the dual price of 175 must be a rate of change to the left. Note that the allowable decrease of 113.33 takes the RHS b_4 back to the last degenerate point. Also note that the two previous degenerate solutions each produced slopes to the right. This solution unpredictably produces a slope to the left.

6 In Figure 8.9, the output for $b_4 = 250$ is reproduced. The optimal solution is nondegenerate. The dual price of 0 is the slope of the graph of V_4 corresponding to all values of b_4 greater than 233.33. Note the allowable increase reads "INFINITE." This is because the fourth constraint has become redundant and will remain redundant as b_4 increases indefinitely. Such increases will lead to no further changes in the optimal objective value. The allowable decrease (16.66) would take the constraint line back to the former degenerate corner at $b_4 = 233.33$.

Figure 8.6 *A nondegenerate solution, $b_4 = 110$*

```
MAX 5000E +4000F
SUBJECT TO
   2)    E +F   >= 5
   3)    E -3F   <= 0
   4)   10E +15F  <= 150
   5)   20E +10F  <= 110
   6)  -30E -10F  <=-135
VARIABLE        VALUE         REDUCED-COST
   E           2.50000        0.00000
   F           6.00000        0.00000
OBJ FCTN       36500.

ROW            SLACK         DUAL-PRICE
   2            3.5              0
   3           15.5              0
   4           35                0
   5            0              700
   6            0              300.

SENSITIVITY ANALYSIS

RANGE IN WHICH BASIS REMAINS THE SAME
       COST SENSITIVITY

VARIABLE       INCREASE       DECREASE
               IN C(J)        IN C(J)

   E         2999.99949       INFINITE
   F          INFINITE       1499.99974


    RIGHT HAND SENSITIVITY

  ROW    ALLOWABLE INCREASE      ALLOWABLE DECREASE


   2            3.5000              INFINITE
   3           INFINITE            15.5000
   4           INFINITE            35.0000
   5           10.00000            15.50000
   6           17.50000            22.14286
```

8.4   The Dual Price and the OV Function: An Example

Let us determine the effect on the value of labor in Department B as the available amount increases. That is, let us analyze the way in which the dual price changes as the RHS, b_4, increases. Figure 8.4 illustrates the fact that in this particular example the dual prices are decreasing with increases in the value of the parameter b_4. More precisely, they are nonincreasing, but for simplicity let's use the term *decreasing*, with the understanding that this allows for the possibility of no change in particular intervals. The fact that the dual prices are decreasing means that as additional increments of labor are added, they tend to help less and less. Eventually, as the number of labor hours exceeds 233.33, additional increments do not help at all. In economic terms, the above description says that additional increments of the RHS are most profitable when a $\leq$ constraint is *tightest*. This is a direct manifestation

Figure 8.7   *A degenerate solution, $b_4 = 120$*

```
MAX 5000E +4000F
SUBJECT TO
  2)    E +F  >= 5
  3)    E -3F  <= 0
  4)   10E +15F  <= 150
  5)   20E +10F  <= 120
  6)  -30E -10F  <=-135
```

VARIABLE	VALUE	REDUCED-COST
E	1.50000	0.00000
F	9.00000	0.00000
OBJ FCTN	43500.	

ROW	SLACK	DUAL-PRICE
2	5.5	0
3	25.5	0
4	0	150
5	0	175
6	0	0

SENSITIVITY ANALYSIS

RANGE IN WHICH BASIS REMAINS THE SAME
    COST SENSITIVITY

VARIABLE	INCREASE IN C(J)	DECREASE IN C(J)
E	2999.99998	2333.33299
F	3499.99997	1499.99999

RIGHT HAND SENSITIVITY

ROW	ALLOWABLE INCREASE	ALLOWABLE DECREASE
2	5.5000	INFINITE
3	INFINITE	25.5000
4	0.00000	72.85715
5	113.33333	0.00000
6	INFINITE	0.0000

of diminishing marginal returns, which means that additional increments of investment (or effort) yield increasingly smaller *incremental* returns.

To sharpen this picture of RHS analysis and the role of dual pricing in the management context, let us analyze the above situation somewhat further. Refer back to the graph of V_4 shown in Figure 8.4. You understand that in any single run of the LP model, the parameter b_4 is fixed at some assigned value. The OV graph shows how the revenue would vary over *all* values of b_4 for which the constraint set is not empty. Now let us suppose that the manager has this graph of the OV function before him and that he is no longer compelled by his higher management to set b_4 at the previous value of 160. He is now free to select at will a value for b_4, provided he pays the "going" price for what he uses. Figure 8.4 shows that if labor hours in department B are a free good (the going price is zero), then the manager should make

Figure 8.8   *A degenerate solution, $b_4 = 233.33$*

```
MAX 5000E +4000F
SUBJECT TO
   2)    E +F   >= 5
   3)    E -3F   <= 0
   4)   10E +15F  <= 150
   5)   20E +10F  <= 233.33
   6)  -30E -10F  <=-135

VARIABLE       VALUE        REDUCED-COST
    E         9.99975       0.00000
    F         3.33350       0.00000
  OBJ FCTN    63332.7


ROW            SLACK        DUAL-PRICE
  2           8.33325          0
  3           7.55310E-04      0
  4           0              150
  5           0              175
  6           198.327          0


SENSITIVITY ANALYSIS

RANGE IN WHICH BASIS REMAINS THE SAME
     COST SENSITIVITY

VARIABLE       INCREASE      DECREASE
               IN C(J)       IN C(J)

    E         2999.99998    2333.33299
    F         3499.99997    1499.99999


      RIGHT HAND SENSITIVITY

 ROW    ALLOWABLE INCREASE      ALLOWABLE DECREASE


   2          8.3333              INFINITE
   3          INFINITE            0.0008
   4          199.99496           0.00216
   5          0.00336             113.32999
   6          INFINITE            198.3275
```

at least 233.33 hours available, for clearly this would maximize his maximum revenue. However, let us suppose that this resource is not a free good to our planner.

Suppose that the manager can purchase in the marketplace as much labor as he wants—at the rate of $600 per hour. (We might justify this high wage rate by imagining that in this model, labor is really an aggregate measure of many resources, and hence the value of an hour of labor in department B is really an index that measures not only the worker's wage rate but also the market value of the resources used by a worker in one productive hour.) Then, at a wage rate of $600 per hour, the graph of V_4 (Figure 8.4) indicates that the manager should employ only 120 hours of labor. If he employs 121 hours, the last hour will give him a return of only 175, whereas the cost to him would have been 600. If he employs less than 120 hours, an additional hour will give him a return of 700 at a cost of only 600. Thus, 120 is the optimal parameter value. What we have indirectly done in the above analysis,

Figure 8.9 *A nondegenerate solution, $b_4 = 250$*

```
MAX 5000E +4000F
SUBJECT TO
   2)    E +F   >= 5
   3)    E -3F   <= 0
   4)   10E +15F   <= 150
   5)   20E +10F   <= 250
   6)  -30E -10F   <=-135
```

VARIABLE	VALUE	REDUCED-COST
E	10.00000	0.00000
F	3.33333	0.00000
OBJ FCTN	63333.3	

ROW	SLACK	DUAL-PRICE
2	8.33333	0
3	0	777.778
4	0	422.222
5	16.6667	0
6	198.333	0

SENSITIVITY ANALYSIS

RANGE IN WHICH BASIS REMAINS THE SAME
    COST SENSITIVITY

VARIABLE	INCREASE IN C(J)	DECREASE IN C(J)
E	INFINITE	2333.33299
F	3499.99997	18999.99981

RIGHT HAND SENSITIVITY

ROW	ALLOWABLE INCREASE	ALLOWABLE DECREASE
2	8.3333	INFINITE
3	3.75000	25.50000
4	10.71429	89.25000
5	INFINITE	16.6667
6	INFINITE	198.3333

conceptually, is expand the model by making b_4 a decision variable rather than a fixed parameter. This expanded model could be directly formulated as follows:

Max $5,000E + 4,000F - 600b_4$

s.t.

$$E + \quad F \quad\quad \geq \quad 5$$
$$E - \quad 3F \quad\quad \leq \quad 0$$
$$10E + 15F \quad\quad \leq \quad 150$$
$$20E + 10F - b_4 \leq \quad 0$$
$$-30E - 10F \quad\quad \leq -135$$

E, F, b_4 all nonnegative

You can see that b_4 is now explicitly treated as a decision variable with a

Figure 8.10 *The expanded model with price of $b_4 = 600$*

```
MAX 5000E +4000F -600B4
SUBJECT TO
   2)    E +F   >= 5
   3)    E -3F   <= 0
   4)   10E +15F   <= 150
   5)   20E +10F -B4 <= 0
   6)   -30E -10F   <=-135
```

VARIABLE	VALUE	REDUCED-COST
E	1.50000	0.00000
F	9.00000	0.00000
B4	120.00000	0.00000
OBJ FCTN	-28500	

ROW	SLACK	DUAL-PRICE
2	5.5	0
3	25.5	0
4	0	28.5714
5	0	600
6	0	242.857

cost of 600 in the objective function. You can also see that this expanded model is still an LP problem. If you were to solve this model on the computer, the optimal value of b_4 would turn out to be 120, just as the analysis of the OV function indicated. This is shown by the output reproduced in Figure 8.10.

Let us now suppose that the price of labor falls below 600, say to 500. Since labor has become cheaper, you might intuitively suspect that an optimal solution to the expanded model should now employ more hours of labor than previously. But this intuition is incorrect. The output reproduced in Figure 8.11 shows that at a price of 500, the optimal level of b_4 remains at 120.

We shall now show that the utilization of labor (that is, the optimal value of b_4) does *not* increase until the price falls *below* 175. To see why, let us again refer to the graph of V_4 (Figure 8.4). Suppose we are currently using 120 hours in department B at a price of $600 per hour. If the price were

Figure 8.11 *The expanded model with price of $b_4 = 500$*

```
MAX 5000E +4000F -500B4
SUBJECT TO
   2)    E +F   >= 5
   3)    E -3F   <= 0
   4)   10E +15F   <= 150
   5)   20E +10F -B4 <= 0
   6)   -30E -10F   <=-135
```

VARIABLE	VALUE	REDUCED-COST
E	1.50000	0.00000
F	9.00000	0.00000
B4	120.00000	0.00000
OBJ FCTN	-16500	

ROW	SLACK	DUAL-PRICE
2	5.5	0
3	25.5	0
4	0	57.1429
5	0	500
6	0	185.714

Figure 8.12   *The expanded model with price of $b_4 = 175$*

```
MAX 5000E +4000F  -175B4
SUBJECT TO
   2)    E +F   >= 5
   3)    E -3F   <= 0
   4)   10E +15F  <= 150
   5)   20E +10F -B4 <= 0
   6)   -30E -10F  <=-135
```

VARIABLE	VALUE	REDUCED-COST
E	1.50000	0.00000
F	9.00000	0.00000
B4	120.00000	0.00000
OBJ FCTN	22500	

ROW	SLACK	DUAL-PRICE
2	5.5	0
3	25.5	0
4	0	150
5	0	175
6	0	0

to fall to 175, the graph of V_4 shows that each additional hour beyond 120 would produce a return of 175 (since the slope to the right of $b_4 = 120$ is 175). But if the cost is also 175 per hour, we are indifferent about using more, for the *net* return is zero. Suppose, however, that the price falls to 174. Then there will be a *net* return of \$1 per additional hour employed, and this will be true up to an employment level of 233.33 hours. Thus, if the price falls *below* 175, the optimal value of b_4 will be 233.33. Figures 8.12 and 8.13 show the computer output for prices of 175 and 174, respectively, and you can see that the above analysis is confirmed.

The above discussion has been limited to a particular constraint in a particular model. In this illustrative context, you saw the technique of parametric analysis at work, and you saw how the OV function can be used when treating a parameter as a variable. Although this example is very simple, it should

Figure 8.13   *The expanded model with price of $b_4 = 174$*

```
MAX 5000E +4000F  -174B4
SUBJECT TO
   2)    E +F   >= 5
   3)    E -3F   <= 0
   4)   10E +15F  <= 150
   5)   20E +10F -B4 <= 0
   6)   -30E -10F  <=-135
```

VARIABLE	VALUE	REDUCED-COST
E	10.00000	0.00000
F	3.33333	0.00000
B4	233.33334	0.00000
OBJ FCTN	22733.3	

ROW	SLACK	DUAL-PRICE
2	8.33333	0
3	0	4.44443
4	0	151.556
5	0	174
6	198.333	0

give you a feeling for the quantity of useful economic information that resides in the dual prices and the OV function, and a feeling for some of the potential applications. A more realistic illustration of RHS analysis and the OV function is presented in Chapter 12.

8.5 The Dual Price and the OV Function in General

We shall now present the general facts about the OV function corresponding to any type of constraint ($\leq$, $\geq$, $=$) in any type of LP problem (max or min). In order to deduce these general facts, one must keep in mind the following important concepts about inequality constraints in the LP context:

Loosening an inequality constraint can't hurt, and when it helps it helps less and less.

Tightening an inequality constraint can't help, and when it hurts it hurts more and more.

In any given situation, one must also deduce whether the terms *help* or *hurt* imply *increases* or *decreases* in the OV. With these simple concepts, the OV shape can be easily determined, as follows.

Max Problem, $\leq$ Constraint   In this case, increasing the RHS means to loosen. This can't hurt and may help. Since we are maximizing, *help* means "increase." But since loosening helps less and less, the rates of increase become smaller and smaller. Hence, the OV shape as shown in Figure 8.14 is the same as the one presented earlier in Figure 8.4.

Max Problem, $\geq$ Constraint   In this case, increasing the RHS means to tighten. This can't help and may hurt. Since we are maximizing, *hurt* means "decrease." But since tightening hurts more and more, the rates of decrease become more severe. This implies the shape shown in Figure 8.15.

Figure 8.14   *OV function for a $\leq$ constraint in a max LP problem*

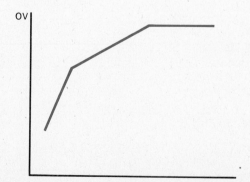

Figure 8.15   *OV function for a $\geq$ constraint in a max LP problem*

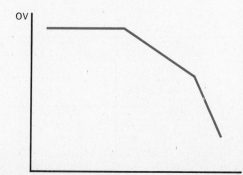

Min Problem, ≤ Constraint   In this case, increasing the RHS means to loosen. This can't hurt and may help. Since we are minimizing, *help* means "decrease." But since loosening helps less and less, the rates of decrease become less severe. This implies the shape shown in Figure 8.16.

Figure 8.16   *OV function for a ≤ constraint in a min LP problem*

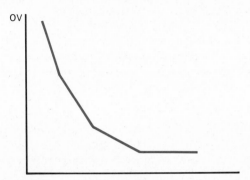

Min Problem, ≥ Constraint   In this case, increasing the RHS means to tighten. This can't help and may hurt. Since we are minimizing, *hurt* means "increase." But since tightening hurts more and more, the rates of increase will become larger and larger. This implies the shape shown in Figure 8.17.

Figure 8.17   *OV function for a ≥ constraint in a min LP problem*

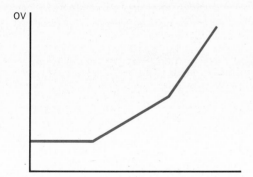

Thus, whether we have a max model or a min model, we know that a ≤ constraint can be tightened (decrease the RHS) or loosened (increase the RHS). A ≥ constraint can be tightened (increase the RHS) or loosened (decrease the RHS). With either type of constraint, regardless of whether the model is max or min, we have witnessed the following phenomena:

Tightening hurts more and more.

Loosening helps less and less.

This is a mathematical fact about inequality constraints and is independent of whether you are maximizing or minimizing your objective.

There is, however, a difference between the max and min models relative to the OV that is worth noting. This has to do with the relationship between the slopes of the OV function and the dual prices that appear in the computer printout. The slope of the OV graph, by definition, is the rate of increase. The dual price has been previously interpreted as the rate of improvement in the OV as the RHS increases. In a max model, *improvement* means "increase." Rate of improvement and rate of increase are the same. Hence,

---

In a max model, for a given RHS value, the dual price is the slope of the OV graph.

For a min model the situation reverses. In this case, *improvement* means "decrease." Hence, when the dual price (the rate of improvement in the OV) is positive (negative), the OV will decrease (increase). Consequently,

---

In a min model, for a given RHS value, the dual price is the negative of the slope of the OV graph.

One additional observation about tightening and loosening can be made. It was noted in Section 8.4 that "loosening helps less and less" is a manifestation of the law of diminishing returns. The fact that tightening hurts more and more is a manifestation of increasing marginal cost. That is, as the numerical value of the RHS increases, stronger requirements are being imposed. As this occurs, a greater and greater price must be paid to satisfy *incremental* increases in these requirements.

In concluding this section, we will consider the OV function associated with a constraint that, in original form, is an *equality* as opposed to an *inequality*. The cases for max and min must be treated separately. Figure 8.18 shows the geometric representation of a hypothetical max model that, in standard equality format, has the following form:

Max $c_1 x_1 + c_2 x_2$

s.t.

$$
\begin{aligned}
a_{11}x_1 + a_{12}x_2 + y_1 &= b_1 \\
a_{21}x_1 + a_{22}x_2 \quad\quad + y_2 &= b_2 \\
a_{31}x_1 + a_{32}x_2 \quad\quad\quad\quad + y_3 &= b_3 \\
a_{41}x_1 + a_{42}x_2 &= b_4 \\
a_{51}x_1 + a_{52}x_2 \quad\quad\quad\quad\quad\quad + y_5 &= b_5 \\
x_1, x_2, y_1, y_2, y_3, y_5 &\geq 0
\end{aligned}
$$

Since the fourth constraint in original form is an equality, there is no slack

Figure 8.18   *A hypothetical max LP model with an equality constraint*

Figure 8.19   *The graph of V_4 (an OV function for an equality constraint in a max LP model)*

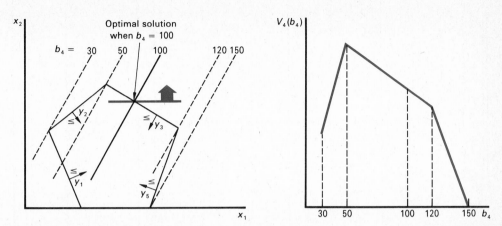

variable associated with it (or, if you prefer, the associated slack must always be zero), and the constraint set consists of the points *on* the fourth constraint line that also satisfy the other four inequalities. In Figure 8.18, the optimal objective contour is also drawn, and the solution is shown when $b_4 = 100$. The dotted lines represent alternative positions of the fourth constraint for other values of b_4. The graph of the corresponding OV function V_4 is shown in Figure 8.19. It should be clear to you that the positive and negative slopes of the graph are a direct consequence of the geometry shown in Figure 8.18. Note that the problem is infeasible if either $b_4 < 30$ or $b_4 > 150$.

Since this is a max problem, a positive slope on the graph in Figure 8.19 means that the objective is being improved, which also means that the dual price is positive and hence the same as the slope of the graph. The fact that the slopes of the graph of V_4 are both positive and negative shows that the dual price associated with an equality constraint can be positive or negative. (It could also be zero.) It is also possible that the OV graph for an equality constraint in a max problem could have the shape displayed either in Figure 8.14 or 8.15. You may wish to verify this by constructing an appropriate geometric rationale (for example, analogous to Figure 8.18).

Now consider a min problem with an equality constraint. We shall simply state that in this case the OV function corresponding to the equality constraint can have any of the shapes shown in Figures 8.16, 8.17, or 8.20. Since we are considering a min problem, a negative slope on the OV graph means the objective is being improved. Hence, at such a point the dual price would be positive. Reverse statements hold for positive slopes on the OV graph. Thus, for the min problem, we see that for an equality constraint as well as for an inequality constraint, it is true that the dual price is the negative of the slope of the OV function.

In summary, for an equality constraint, changing the RHS in a given direction may hurt or help, and

Figure 8.20   *An OV function for an equality constraint in a min LP problem*

Moving the RHS in a direction of hurt hurts more and more.

Moving the RHS in a direction of help helps less and less and may eventually even hurt.

The observations in this section concerning the general shape of the OV function can be presented more concisely by resorting to more mathematical language. For a max problem the OV functions are always concave, and for a min problem the OV functions are always convex. It is convenient to employ these facts without proof, and we have implicitly done so in the diagrams used in the previous development. These facts are a mathematical statement of the economic concepts of diminishing marginal returns and increasing marginal costs, respectively.

8.6   Dual Pricing and Estimation

Knowing the shape of the OV function and the current value of the dual price makes it possible to find bounds on the value of the objective function when the change in the RHS exceeds the allowable limit, as the following examples will show.

For the first situation, suppose we start with the PROTRAC E and F problem with the value 110 assigned to the parameter b_4. The solution, shown in Figure 8.6, has the following characteristics:

OV	=	36,500
Value of the dual price on the fourth constraint =		700
Allowable increase	=	10.0
Allowable decrease	=	15.5

Suppose that without re-solving the problem you are interested in knowing as much as possible about the OV when $b_4 = 150$. Since the increase $(150 - 110 = 40 > 10)$ is out of the allowable range, you cannot determine the exact value. It is possible, however, to find both an upper and a lower bound on what the exact value must be.

LOWER BOUND

If b_4 is increased by 10 hours to 120 hours, the OV would increase by $700(10) = 7,000$. Since the fourth constraint is a $\leq$ constraint, increasing b_4 can never hurt (decrease) the OV. Thus, when $b_4 = 150$, the OV must be at least $36,500 + 7,000 = 43,500$.

UPPER BOUND

The rate of increase in the OV as a function of b_4 is 700 when b_4 equals 110. Since we know that loosening helps less and less, as we increase b_4 the dual price will never exceed 700. Thus, the increase in the OV can be no greater than $(150 - 110)(700) = 28,000$ and the OV can be no greater than $36,500 + 28,000 = 64,500$.

This bounding procedure is illustrated in Figure 8.21. In this figure, the segment of the graph with slope 700 over the interval $b_4 = 110$ to $b_4 = 120$ is a known part of the graph of the OV function. The slope of the adjoining segment to the right of $b_4 = 120$ is *not* known. It is only known that this slope is not less than zero and not more than 700, and hence this portion of the graph must lie in the shaded region in Figure 8.21. This means that when $b_4 = 150$, the OV graph is, in Figure 8.21, above point P and below point Q. This is all that is needed to obtain the bounds.

Figure 8.21 *Obtaining a two-sided bound for $V_4(150)$ using the solution for $b_4 = 110$*

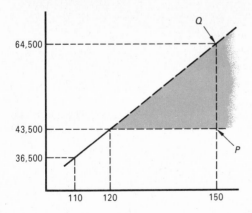

To take another example, suppose we start with the PROTRAC E and F problem with the value 160 assigned to the parameter b_4. The solution, shown in Figure 8.1 has the following characteristics:

OV	=	50,500
Value of the dual price on the fourth constraint =		175
Allowable increase	=	73.33
Allowable decrease	=	40.00

Suppose that without re-solving the problem you are interested in as much information as you can obtain about the OV when $b_4 = 100$. Since this decrease is outside the allowable range (values of b_4 between 120 and 233.33), you can only *estimate* the desired value. Since we are tightening a constraint beyond the allowable range, we must also worry about the possibility of making the problem infeasible, as pointed out in Section 8.3. In general, when we tighten a constraint more than the allowable amount, the computer output gives no indication of whether or not this will create infeasibility. However, in the present example we saw in Figure 8.3 that b_4 can in fact be reduced to the value 94.5 without making the constraints inconsistent, and so the decrease to 100 will cause no problem.

In this instance, as opposed to the previous example, we are able to obtain only an upper bound for the OV. We, of course, do have a "very loose" lower bound for the OV. That is, since the objective function is $5,000E + 4,000F$, the nonnegativity constraints on E and F guarantee that the OV will be at least as great as zero. The statement that we are only able to find an upper bound implies that knowing the solution with $b_4 = 160$ does not provide any new information that enables us to find a larger lower bound than zero.

UPPER BOUND

Since tightening hurts more and more, we know that the slope of the V_4 graph when b_4 is less than 120 must be at least as great as the slope to the right of 120. Thus, V_4 must decrease by at least $(160 - 100)(175) = 10,500$, and the OV must be no greater than $(50,500 - 10,500) = 40,000$.

The bounding procedure in this case is illustrated in Figure 8.22. The portion of the OV graph to the left of 120 must lie in the shaded region. This means that when $b_4 = 100$, the OV graph is, in Figure 8.22, below point Q. Thus it is clear from the picture that only an upper bound is available.

Figure 8.22   *Obtaining a one-sided bound for $V_4(100)$ using the solution for $b_4 = 160$*

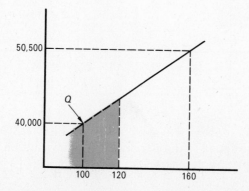

The above two examples show that in some cases two-sided bounds may be obtained, whereas in other cases the analysis is limited to a one-sided bound. It will not always be true that a two-sided bound goes with an increase in the RHS, as in the above example. A differently shaped OV graph may produce a two-sided bound for a decrease in the RHS and a one-sided bound for an increase. Figure 8.23 recalls the six possible shapes for the OV graphs for max and min problems and each type of constraint. Each of these curves has its "own" cases for estimating bounds that could be considered and that should be understood. For example, the graph in Figure 8.23e provides a two-sided bound for RHS decreases and a one-sided bound for increases.

After a casual glance at this material, you may conclude that there are too many combinations and too many details to learn in this area. It may seem like a topic where you have to get out the book and review the process before you can use it. This is not true. In order to estimate the bounds in any given instance, one need only reproduce the appropriate shape for the OV graph and then extrapolate from the graph, as shown in Figures 8.21 and 8.22. "Big deal," you say, "I still must memorize the shape of the graph for each possible case." This is not true either. The possible shapes of the OV graph for each case can be constructed by memorizing only *two* facts about the change induced in the OV when a change in the RHS exceeds the allowable limit. These facts, which have already been seen in various forms, are:

Figure 8.23 *Possible shapes for the OV graph for max and min problems and all types of constraints*

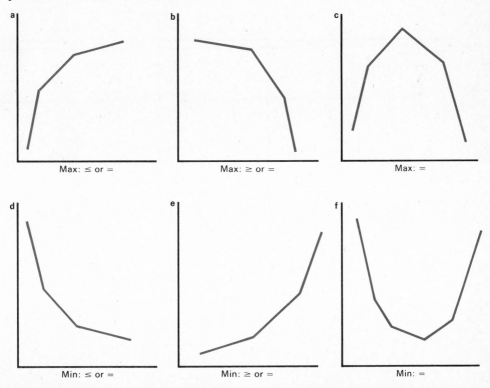

a

Max: ≤ or =

b

Max: ≥ or =

c

Max: =

d

Min: ≤ or =

e

Min: ≥ or =

f

Min: =

Tightening, or hurting, hurts more and more.

Loosening, or helping, helps less and less.

To use these facts to estimate changes in the OV, you employ the following procedure.

Estimating Changes in the OV for An Inequality Constraint

1   First, observe the sense of the inequality and whether the problem is max or min. This is all the information needed to tell whether the segment of the OV graph that includes the current solution is increasing or decreasing. For example, if the inequality is ≥, then increasing the RHS will obviously hurt. Hurting means that if the problem is min the OV will increase, and if the problem is max the OV will decrease. The dual price from the current solution gives the exact slope of this current segment. The convention on signs (a positive dual means increasing the RHS helps) gives you a check on your reasoning. You can now use the dual price along with the allowable increase and allowable decrease to plot the segment of the OV function that includes the current solution.

2   The key concepts about tightening and loosening allow you to determine whether the adjoining segments (immediately to the right and immediately to the left of the segment plotted in item 1) must have larger or smaller slopes than the current segment. Plot each adjoining segment with an assumed slope that satisfies the appropriate property.

3   The three line segments created in items 1 and 2 are all that is required to find estimates for a change in OV corresponding to either an increase or decrease in the RHS. (See Figures 8.21 and 8.22.)

4   When a constraint is tightened by more than the allowable amount, the possibility of creating infeasibility must be recognized.

Estimating Changes in the OV for an Equality Constraint

1   First, obtain the dual price from the current solution and then observe whether the problem is max or min. This, along with the sign of the dual price and the allowable increase and decrease, is all that is needed to plot the segment of the OV graph that includes the current solution. For example, suppose the dual is negative, which means that increasing the RHS will hurt. This means that if the problem is max, then the segment is decreasing and the slope is the dual price. If the problem is min, then the segment is increasing and the slope is the negative of the dual price.

2   *For an equality constraint, it must be recognized that an infeasible problem could be created in changing the RHS by more than the allowable amount.* Moreover, as for an inequality, if changing the RHS in one direction will hurt the OV, then successive changes in the same direction will hurt more and more. For an inequality, successive changes in a direction of help will continue to help, but less and less. For an equality, the situation is different. Although successive changes in a direction of help will help less and less, the slope of the OV graph may change in sign, at which point further RHS changes begin to hurt. In other words, changing the RHS of an equality can help and then hurt. In estimating bounds for OV changes, it is not possible to know whether or not the adjoining segment of the graph, in a direction of help, does in fact change in sign. For this reason, it turns out that one can obtain only a one-sided bound for the OV for a change in either direction in the RHS of an equality constraint (assuming infeasibility is not created). This one-sided bound always turns out to be an upper

bound for a max problem and a lower bound for a min problem. It is obtained by extrapolating the OV segment obtained in item 1.

An example of equality-constraint estimation is illustrated in Figure 8.24 for a min problem with a positive dual price at the current RHS value $\bar{b}$. Suppose our goal is to obtain a bound on the OV at $\hat{b}$, and assume the problem remains feasible when $b = \hat{b}$. Since the dual price at $\bar{b}$ is assumed positive,

Figure 8.24 *Obtaining a one-sided bound for $V_4(\hat{b})$ using the solution for $b_4 = \bar{b}$*

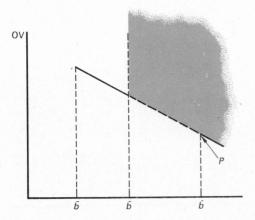

increasing the RHS beyond $\bar{b}$ will help. In accord with the above remarks in item 2, the slope of the OV graph could change in sign after the allowable increase (at $\bar{b}$), or, alternatively, the slope could retain the same sign. This implies that the OV graph either goes through point P or is above P, and hence it can be anywhere in the shaded region. It follows that we have no estimate for an upper bound, and the linear extrapolation to $\hat{b}$ provides a lower bound.

8.7 Multiple Parameter Changes

In all of the sensitivity discussion thus far, we have focused upon the effects of changing a single parameter, with all other data unchanged. In this section, we consider the possibilities for analyzing optimal value changes induced by varying several RHS values simultaneously.

Suppose that the given model has m constraints and that a computer solution has been obtained. Now suppose that two of the RHS parameters, say b_1 and b_2, are to be simultaneously perturbed. Accordingly, we can think of the OV as now being a function of two variables, say $V(b_1, b_2)$. Even more generally, suppose that all m of the RHS parameters may be perturbed. Extending the above interpretation, we should think of the OV as a function of m variables, $V(b_1, ..., b_m)$. Given any fixed set of values for the parameters, say $\bar{b}_1, ..., \bar{b}_m$, the value $V(\bar{b}_1, ..., \bar{b}_m)$ is the OV for the linear program with that RHS.

Since we are now dealing with a function of more than one variable, the previous geometric analysis is no longer at our disposal. Nevertheless, there remains a direct and analogous relationship between the OV changes and the dual prices, as follows. Suppose $c_1 x_1 + \ldots + c_n x_n$ is the objective function for the problem at hand and $\bar{b} = (\bar{b}_1, \ldots, \bar{b}_m)$ is the RHS. Suppose we have just obtained a *nondegenerate* computer solution $x^* = (x_1^*, \ldots, x_n^*)$. Thus $V(\bar{b}_1, \ldots, \bar{b}_m)$ is the OV; that is,

$$V(\bar{b}_1, \ldots, \bar{b}_m) = c_1 x_1^* + \ldots + c_n x_n^*$$

Suppose that $d_1, \ldots, d_m$ are the dual prices with signs according to our adopted convention. Suppose the RHS is now changed to $\hat{b} = (\hat{b}_1, \ldots, \hat{b}_m)$ and that this new problem has a new optimal solution, say $\hat{x} = (\hat{x}_1, \ldots, \hat{x}_n)$. Suppose the new solution is also nondegenerate. The following rules apply if the basis at x^* is the same as at $\hat{x}$:

Rule 1: For a max problem
$$V(\hat{b}_1, \ldots, \hat{b}_m) = V(\bar{b}_1, \ldots, \bar{b}_m) + (\hat{b}_1 - \bar{b}_1) d_1 + (\hat{b}_2 - \bar{b}_2) d_2 + \ldots + (\hat{b}_m - \bar{b}_m) d_m$$

Rule 2: For a min problem
$$V(\hat{b}_1, \ldots, \hat{b}_m) = V(\bar{b}_1, \ldots, \bar{b}_m) - (\hat{b}_1 - \bar{b}_1) d_1 - (\hat{b}_2 - \bar{b}_2) d_2 - \ldots - (\hat{b}_m - \bar{b}_m) d_m$$

These rules simply say that when the basis does not change, the total OV change is obtained additively. For a change in a single RHS parameter, the rules above reduce to our previous procedures.

As an example, suppose we begin with the solution in Figure 8.1 for the E and F model. The OV in Figure 8.1 is 50,500. Let us examine the effect on this value of simultaneously changing the capacity in departments A and B to 165 and 150, respectively. The relevant data are given in Figure 8.25.

Figure 8.25 *Data for capacity change in E and F problem*

Department	Current Capacity	New Capacity	Current Dual Price
A	150	165	150
B	160	150	175

The current basis is $\{E, F, y_1, y_2, y_5\}$ where the ys are the slacks on constraints 1, 2, and 5. According to the above prescription, if the basis does not change in a solution corresponding to the new capacities, then the new OV is given by

New OV = old OV + (165 − 150)(150) + (150 − 160)(175)

$\qquad$ = 50,500 + 15(150) − 10(175)

$\qquad$ = 50,500 + 2,250 − 1,750 = 51,000

The difficulty with the above rules is that in order to use the formulas, one needs to know whether or not the considered RHS changes will force a basis change. In general, one doesn't know whether or not this is the case. The allowable limits for increases and decreases in the RHS, which appear in the computer printout, do not apply. They are valid only as previously interpreted, namely, for changes in a single parameter, with all other data unchanged.

In general, then, when we in fact do not know whether or not the basis will change, we cannot predict the exact value for the OV. However, we can obtain a one-sided estimate. If the equality sign in rule 1 is replaced by $\leq$, the resulting condition is always true. The same conclusion applies to rule 2, with the equality replaced by $\geq$. Thus, for the above specific example, in the absence of any knowledge about a basis change, it is true that

New OV $\leq$ old OV $+ (165 - 150)(150) + (150 - 160)(175)$

or

New OV $\leq 51,000$

Concerning the most general form of the OV function, $V(b_1, ..., b_m)$, there is one additional theoretic fact which is worth noting. As above, let $(\bar{b}_1, ..., \bar{b}_m)$ denote the RHS for a problem just solved. Suppose the solution is nondegenerate, and let $d_1, ..., d_m$ be the dual prices with signs according to the adopted convention. Let $(b_1, ..., b_m)$ denote either $(\bar{b}_1, ..., \bar{b}_m)$ or any other RHS that does not force a basis change. Then, for any such value of $(b_1, ..., b_m)$, the optimal objective value $V(b_1, ..., b_m)$ is given by

---

Rule 3: For a max problem
$$V(b_1, ..., b_m) = d_1 b_1 + ... + d_m b_m$$

Rule 4: For a min problem
$$V(b_1, ..., b_m) = -d_1 b_1 - ... - d_m b_m$$

For example, in the output shown in Figure 8.1 you can see that, using rule 3,

$$V(5, 0, 150, 160, -135) = 0(5) + 0(0) + (150)(150) + 175(160) + 0(-135)$$
$$= 50,500$$

Also, in Figure 8.1, it can be seen that

OV $= 5,000E^* + 4,000F^* = 5,000(4.5) + 4,000(7.0) = 50,500$

The fact that the OV of 50,500 can be obtained with either the original E, F variables or with the dual prices $d_1, ..., d_5$ is a consequence of the dual theorem given in Chapter 7.

We also recall from Section 8.3 that, for the output in Figure 8.1, we directly derived the expression

$$V_4(b_4) = 175b_4 + 22,500$$

as long as $120 < b_4 < 233.33$ and the other RHS values remain fixed at $b_1 = 5$, $b_2 = 0$, $b_3 = 150$, $b_5 = -135$. For b_4 in the above range, the basis does not change (assuming b_1, b_2, b_3, and b_5 remain fixed) and, again using rule 3,

$$V_4(b_4) = d_1 b_1 + d_2 b_2 + d_3 b_3 + d_4 b_4 + d_5 b_5$$
$$= 0(5) + 0(0) + (150)(150) + 175b_4 + 0(-135)$$
$$= 175b_4 + 22{,}500$$

which is the same as the expression derived in Section 8.3. Thus, rules 3 and 4 show the way in which different sections of the OV function have different linear representations.

8.8 Examples and Solutions

Example 1

Recall the Astro and Cosmo TV production problem presented in problem 1, Chapter 4. This problem can be formulated as the following LP model:

Max $20A + 30C$

s.t.

$$A \quad\quad\leq \quad 70$$
$$C \leq \quad 50$$
$$A + 2C \leq 120$$
$$A, C \geq \quad 0$$

Assume that the RHS of the third constraint is b_3 rather than 120. Use a combination of geometric and algebraic techniques to find the V_3 function. Find the coordinates of any corners in this function and the slope of any linear segments.

Solution to Example 1

Figure 8.26 shows four values for b_3 and the associated location of the optimal solution. As b_3 increases, the location of the optimal solution moves from the origin along the A axis to the corner $(70,0)$ and then along the line $A = 70$. It follows the path indicated by the roman numerals I, II, III, IV. We observe that since corner II is given by $A = 70$, $C = 0$, it clearly lies on the line $A + 2C = 70$. Similarly, corner IV with coordinates $(70,50)$ lies on the line $A + 2C = 170$.

For $0 \leq b_3 \leq 70$, the location of the optimal solution is determined by the intersection of the lines

$$C = 0$$
$$A + 2C = b_3$$

Figure 8.26

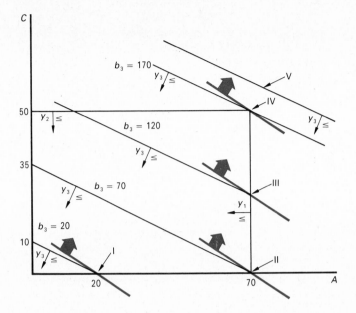

The solution is $A = b_3$, $C = 0$. Thus, the OV function is

$$20A + 30C = 20(b_3) + 30(0) = 20b_3$$

For $70 \leq b_3 \leq 170$, the location of the optimal solution is determined by the intersection of the lines

$$A = 70$$
$$A + 2C = b_3$$

The solution is $A = 70$, $C = (b_3 - 70)/2$. Thus, the OV function is

$$20A + 30C = 20(70) + 30\left(\frac{b_3 - 70}{2}\right) = 350 + 15b_3$$

For $b_3 > 170$, the third constraint becomes redundant, as indicated by roman numeral V. The optimal solution remains at the point (70,50). Thus, for $b_3 > 170$ the OV function is

$$20(70) + 30(50) = 2,900$$

Figure 8.27 shows the plot of the V_3 function.

Example 2

Recall the ore-blending problem from Example 4, Section 4.2 and from Chapter 5. The output for this problem (including the formulation) is shown in Figure 8.28.

Figure 8.27

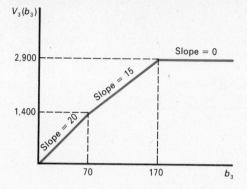

Figure 8.28

```
MIN 800T1+400T2+600T3+500T4
SUBJECT TO
   2)    10T1+3T2+8T3+2T4 >= 5
   3)    90T1+150T2+75T3+175T4 >= 100
   4)    45T1+25T2+20T3+37T4 >= 30
   5)    T1+T2+T3+T4= 1
```

VARIABLE	VALUE	REDUCED-COST
T1	0.25926	0.00000
T2	0.70370	0.00000
T3	0.03704	0.00000
T4	0.00000	91.11107
OBJ FCTN	511.111	

ROW	SLACK	DUAL-PRICE
2	0	-44.4444
3	31.6667	0
4	0	-4.44445
5	0	-155.555

SENSITIVITY ANALYSIS

RANGE IN WHICH BASIS REMAINS THE SAME
   COST SENSITIVITY

VARIABLE	INCREASE IN C(J)	DECREASE IN C(J)
T1	223.63632	120.00018
T2	66.84779	300.00036
T3	85.71440	118.26919
T4	INFINITE	91.11107

RIGHT HAND SENSITIVITY

ROW	ALLOWABLE INCREASE	ALLOWABLE DECREASE
2	2.37500	0.25000
3	31.6667	INFINITE
4	0.71429	7.00000
5	0.25000	0.04348

Specify the tightest bounds possible for the OV function if

a The RHS of the first constraint (row 2) becomes 4 and all other parameters remain as shown.

b The RHS of the third constraint (row 4) becomes 32 and all other parameters remain as shown. (Assume that the constraint set is not empty when $b_3 = 32$.)

Solution to Example 2

a The allowable decrease for the first constraint is 0.25. The change under consideration is 1. Therefore, an exact answer is not available. We shall obtain bounds using the procedure presented in Section 8.6.

(1) The constraint is of the $\geq$ type. Therefore, decreasing the RHS will loosen the constraint, thereby helping the objective function. Since this is a min problem, helping means that the OV function will decrease. The segment of the OV function that includes the current solution (with $b_1 = 5$) is plotted in Figure 8.29.

(2) Since loosening helps less and less, the graph of the OV function to the left of 4.75 must be in the shaded region. That is, $V_1(4)$ is above point P, whose coordinates are $(4, V_L)$, and below point Q, whose coordinates are $(4, V_U)$. Combining this knowledge with the value of the OV slope when $b_1 = 5$ (which is seen from the output to be 44.44) and with the formula for the slope of a line, we are able to easily compute the values of V_L and and V_U, and this provides the bounds of interest.

In particular, we have

$$\text{Slope} = 44.44 = \frac{511.11 - V_U}{5 - 4.75}$$

or

$$V_U = 511.11 - (.25)(44.44) = 500$$

Similarly,

$$\text{Slope} = 44.44 = \frac{511.11 - V_L}{5 - 4}$$

or

$$V_L = 511.11 - 44.44 = 466.67$$

We have thus obtained the bounds

$$466.67 \leq V_1(4) \leq 500$$

b The suggested increase of two units exceeds the allowable increase (.71429), and thus the same approach as followed in part *a* is required. The segment of the OV graph that includes the current solution (with $b_3 = 30$) is shown in Figure 8.30.

To the right of 30.71 the OV graph can be anywhere in the shaded region. Hence for $b_3 = 32$, the graph must lie above the point P, whose coordinates

Figure 8.29

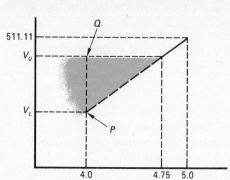

Figure 8.30

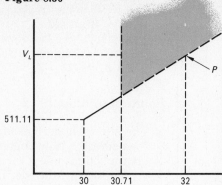

are $(32, V_L)$ with V_L to be determined. Using the formula for slope and obtaining the value of the slope from Figure 8.28, we have

$$4.44 = \frac{V_L - 511.11}{32 - 30}$$

and hence

$$V_L = 8.88 + 511.11 = 519.99$$

This shows that $V_3(32) \geq 519.99$. Since for $b = 32$ the OV graph can lie anywhere above P, an upper bound cannot be obtained.

Example 3

Use a hypothetical constraint set diagram to illustrate that in a max problem the slope of the graph of the OV function *need not always* become zero as the constraint continues to loosen.

Solution to Example 3

An illustrative constraint set diagram is shown in Figure 8.31. Assume that constraint 3 is a $\leq$ inequality. As b_3 increases, constraint 3 continues to

Figure 8.31

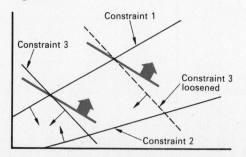

loosen, and the plot of constraint 3 will move to the northeast, parallel to its initial position. The optimal solution will move along constraint 1 indefinitely, and the increase in the OV per unit increase in b_3 remains constant and is not zero.

Example 4

Construct a hypothetical example that illustrates the fact that the slope of the $V(b)$ function does not always change when the basis changes. Note that in such a situation there are alternative optimal solutions.

Solution to Example 4

The secret to success in this example is to make the contours of the objective function parallel to the constraint whose RHS is being manipulated. Such a situation is shown in Figure 8.32.

Suppose that you are constructing the $V(b_1)$ function. Note that when $b_1 = \bar{b}_1$, the solution at corner I is degenerate and, with reference to the solution at corner I, the basis changes as b_1 passes through the value $\bar{b}_1$. For b_1 slightly smaller than $\bar{b}_1$, at point A, s_2 is in the basis and s_3 is not, whereas for b_1 slightly greater than $\bar{b}_1$, at point B, s_3 is in the basis and s_2 is not. "Normally," one would expect a change in the slope of the $V(b_1)$ function at an RHS value such as $\bar{b}_1$ for which there is a degenerate optimal solution. From Figure 8.32, however, it is clear that corner II is also an optimal solution. However, the basis does not change at corner II (it is a nondegenerate corner) and so, with reference to this solution, there will be an interval around $\bar{b}_1$ in which the dual price will not change. It follows that the slope of the OV does not change at $\bar{b}_1$, and this function will have the shape shown in Figure 8.33.

Figure 8.32

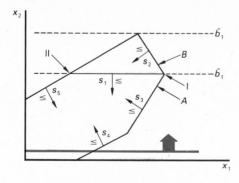

Figure 8.33

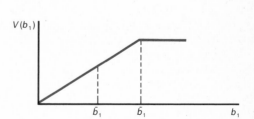

We remark that in general linear programs, regardless of the number of decision variables, if there is a degenerate solution at which the slope of the graph of the OV function does not change, there must also be alternative optimal solutions.

8.9   Summary of Key Concepts

Because of both practical and theoretic obstacles one rarely sees a sensitivity study outside the realm of LP. (Section 8.1)

The following three cases describe the effect on the OV of changing the RHS of a constraint:

1 For changes in the RHS less than the allowable increase, the basis at the new solution is the same as at the old, and so is the dual price. The change in the OV between the new solution and the old is obtained by multiplying the dual price at the old solution by the change in the RHS.

2 For a change in the RHS exactly equal to the allowable increase, the new solution is degenerate. The change in the OV between the new solution and the old is obtained by multiplying the dual price at the old solution by the change in the RHS.

3 For a change in the RHS greater than the allowable increase, the basis at the new solution differs from that at the old. The dual price can also be expected to differ. The change in the OV between the new solution and the old cannot, in general, be obtained by multiplying the dual price at the old solution by the change in the RHS.
(Section 8.2)

For any type of LP problem (max or min) it is true that loosening an inequality constraint can't hurt, and when it helps it helps less and less. Tightening an inequality constraint can't help, and when it hurts it hurts more and more. (Section 8.5)

When an inequality constraint is tightened by more than the allowable amount, the possibility of creating infeasibility must be recognized. (Section 8.6)

For an equality constraint, changing the RHS in a given direction may hurt or help, and moving in a direction of hurt hurts more and more. Moving in a direction of help helps less and less and may eventually even hurt. (Section 8.6)

According to our computer output convention, the dual price in a max (min) problem is the slope (negative of the slope) of the OV function. (Section 8.5)

The OV function for a max model is always concave, reflecting diminishing marginal returns. For a min model, the shape is always convex, reflecting increasing marginal costs. (Section 8.5)

The shape of the OV function can be used to provide bounds on the optimal objective value when the RHS change exceeds the allowable amount. (Section 8.5)

8.10   Problems

1   Consider the linear program

Max x_1

s.t.

$$5x_1 + 3x_2 \geq 15$$
$$-x_1 + x_2 \leq 3$$
$$-x_1 + 3x_2 \geq 0$$
$$4x_1 + x_2 \leq b_4$$
$$-3x_1 + 2x_2 \geq -15$$
$$x_1, x_2 \geq 0$$

where b_4 is a parameter.

a Plot the constraint set and the OV function, V_4.

b Does the slope of the graph of V_4 eventually become zero (for b_4 sufficiently large)? Explain the value of the eventual slope.

c Use algebraic means to find an expression for the first segment of V_4.

2 Picture a hypothetical situation with a zero dual price on an equality constraint.

3 Picture a hypothetical inequality-constraint problem with a nondegenerate solution and a constraint with both a zero slack and a zero dual price.

4 Consider the output reproduced in Figure 8.1. The dual price on labor hours in department B is 175.

a Does this mean that if we (1) use the original 160 hours in the optimal way (namely, make 4.5 E–9s and 7.0 F–9s) and then (2) use an additional hour to make some small additional amounts of E or F or both in some appropriate mix that then $175 of additional revenue would be obtained? Use the geometric interpretation of this model (Figure 8.2) for guidance.

b Use Figure 8.2 and the appropriate algebra to determine *exactly* what the optimal values of E and F would be if $b_4 = 161$. Verify that the change from the previous optimal policy ($E = 4.5$, $F = 7.0$) does in fact generate $175 of additional revenue.

5 Consider the output reproduced in Figure 8.1.

For parts *a–c*, specify either the exact value or the best possible bounds on the OV given the stated changes.

a Management decides to cut back the labor supply in department A (row 4) by 40 hours.

b Management decides to cut back the labor supply in department A by 60 hours. (Assume that the problem remains feasible.)

c Management decides to increase the labor supply in department A by 100 hours.

d What would happen to the OV if the RHS of the first constraint is changed from 5 to 12? (Hint: use Figure 8.2.)

e The current labor contract specifies that at least 135 hours must be used in testing finished product. This is expressed by the fifth constraint. The union wishes to renegotiate this contract in such a way as to increase the testing time. How much would management be able to increase the 135 figure before it would begin to cut into current revenues?

6 Consider the expanded E and F model:

Max $5,000E + 4,000F - 175b_4$

s.t.

$$E + F \geq 5$$
$$E - 3F \leq 0$$
$$10E + 15F \leq 150$$
$$20E + 10F - b_4 \leq 0$$
$$-30E - 10F \leq -135$$

E, F, b_4 all nonnegative

a Suppose that for some reason you prefer a policy that employs more labor than less as long as it costs you no more. Use Figure 8.4 to determine the optimal value of b_4 under this assumption.

b Suppose now that the price of labor in department B falls to zero. Under normal conditions, what would be the optimal value of b_4? What about under the preference stated in part a?

c Suppose that in this model the price of b_4 were increased to 800. Use Figure 8.4 to deduce the optimal value of b_4. Why is it *not* zero?

● **d** In Figure 8.1, we have a solution to the E and F model. In this solution, 160 hours of labor are being used in department B. The dual price on labor is 175. In Figure 8.12, we use only 120 hours of labor in department B. We have saved 40(175) on labor cost but lost 40(175) on potential profit, for no net change. In other words, if we deduct the department B labor cost of 175 per hour from the objective value in Figure 8.1, we obtain

$$50,500 - (175)(160) = 50,500 - 28,000 = 22,500$$

and this is the optimal objective value in Figure 8.12. Thus,

$$E = 4.5$$
$$F = 7.00$$
$$B4 = 160$$

is an alternative optimal solution to the problem solved in Figure 8.12. Could the computer ever produce the above alternative solution?

7 The principal of complementary slackness (Section 7.4) says that if an inequality constraint is inactive (that is, if the optimal value of the slack variable is positive) then the dual price for that constraint must be zero. In this instance the allowable increase and decrease will both be positive.

a Provide an economic rationale for this principle.

b Use arguments that rely on an understanding of the relation between dual prices and the OV function to justify this principle.

8 Consider the solution to the ore-blending problem shown in Example 2, Section 8.8. Specify the tightest bounds possible for the OV if the RHS of the third constraint becomes 20 and all other parameters remain as shown.

9 Consider the tape recorder production problem originally presented in Example 3, Section 4.7. The solution (including the formulation) is shown in Figure 8.34. Specify the best possible bounds on the OV in the following cases:

a The RHS of the first constraint increases by 125. (Although this may destroy feasibility, assume that it does not.)

b The RHS of the first constraint decreases by 30.

10 Recall the transportation problem presented in problem 19 of Chapter 4. Let Ai (or Bi or Ci), $i = 1, 2, 3, 4$ be the number of gallons of jet fuel sent from oil company A (or B or C) to airport i. The LP solution to this problem (including the formulation) is shown in Figure 8.35. Specify the tightest bounds possible for the OV in the following cases:

a The RHS of the sixth constraint increases by 140,000 gallons, and all other parameters remain as shown.

b The RHS of the sixth constraint decreases by 150,000 gallons, and all other parameters remain as shown. (Assume that this decrease does not destroy feasibility.)

● **11** In general, the dual price measures the rate of change in the optimal objective function as a function of the RHS, assuming that the basis does not change as the RHS changes (refer to Section 8.7).

a Use geometry to illustrate changes in two constraints for which the total change in the optimal objective value would be given by the calculation

(Change in the RHS of constraint 1)(dual of 1)

+ (change in the RHS of constraint 2)(dual of 2)

b Use geometry to show a situation in which the calculation in part *a* will not work.

12 PROTRAC research has developed plans for a new product combining some of the capabilities of *E* and *F*. Management has decided that in the upcoming one-month production period, an expensive prototype will be built at either plant 1 or plant 2. Since both plants are presently scheduled to capacity, and since the prototype will employ resources, it will reduce the projected revenue at the plant at which it is produced.

Management must now decide which plant will suffer the smallest loss in revenue from the production of the prototype. Before this management decision (to build a

Figure 8.34

```
MAX 15A +40B +60C
SUBJECT TO
    2)    A   >= 25
    3)    B   >= 130
    4)    C   >= 55
    5)   4A +2.5B +6C   <= 1560
    6)   3A +4B +9C   <= 2040
    7)    A +2B +4C   <= 624


VARIABLE        VALUE         REDUCED-COST
    A         25.00000         0.00000
    B        189.50000         0.00000
    C         55.00000         0.00000
  OBJ FCTN      11255


ROW             SLACK         DUAL-PRICE
    2            0               -5
    3           59.5             0
    4            0              -20
    5          656.25            0
    6          712               0
    7            0               20


SENSITIVITY ANALYSIS

RANGE IN WHICH BASIS REMAINS THE SAME
    COST SENSITIVITY


VARIABLE        INCREASE       DECREASE
                IN C(J)        IN C(J)


    A           5.00000        INFINITE
    B           INFINITE       10.00000
    C           20.00000       INFINITE


        RIGHT HAND SENSITIVITY


  ROW    ALLOWABLE INCREASE      ALLOWABLE DECREASE


    2          119.00000              25.00000
    3           59.5000              INFINITE
    4           29.7500              55.00000
    5          INFINITE             656.2500
    6          INFINITE             712.0000
    7          356.00000            119.00000
```

Figure 8.35

```
MIN 12A1+11A2+11A3+11A4+9B1+10B2+8B3+13B4+15C1+12C2+12C3+14C4
SUBJECT TO
 2)     A1+B1+C1 >= 100000.
 3)     A2+B2+C2 >= 200000.
 4)     A3+B3+C3 >= 300000.
 5)     A4+B4+C4 >= 400000.
 6)     A1+A2+A3+A4 <= 250000.
 7)     B1+B2+B3+B4 <= 500000.
 8)     C1+C2+C3+C4 <= 600000.
```

VARIABLE	VALUE	REDUCED-COST
A1	0.00000	4.00000
A2	0.00000	2.00000
A3	0.00000	4.00000
A4	249999.99721	0.00000
B1	99999.99925	0.00000
B2	99999.99925	0.00000
B3	299999.99605	0.00000
B4	0.00000	1.00000
C1	0.00000	4.00000
C2	99999.99925	0.00000
C3	0.00000	2.00000
C4	149999.99803	0.00000
OBJ FCTN	1.03500E+07	

ROW	SLACK	DUAL-PRICE
2	0	-11
3	0	-12
4	0	-10
5	0	-14
6	0	3
7	.0	2
8	350000.	0

SENSITIVITY ANALYSIS

RANGE IN WHICH BASIS REMAINS THE SAME
      COST SENSITIVITY

VARIABLE	INCREASE IN C(J)	DECREASE IN C(J)
A1	INFINITE	4.00000
A2	INFINITE	2.00000
A3	INFINITE	4.00000
A4	2.00000	INFINITE
B1	4.00000	11.00000
B2	1.00000	2.00000
B3	2.00000	10.00000
B4	INFINITE	1.00000
C1	INFINITE	4.00000
C2	2.00000	1.00000
C3	INFINITE	2.00000
C4	1.00000	2.00000

RIGHT HAND SENSITIVITY

ROW	ALLOWABLE INCREASE	ALLOWABLE DECREASE
2	99999.99925	99999.99925
3	349999.99627	99999.99925
4	99999.99925	99999.99925
5	349999.99627	149999.99803
6	149999.99803	249999.99721
7	99999.99925	99999.99925
8	INFINITE	349999.9963

Figure 8.36

	Dual Prices ($)		
Resource	Plant 1	Plant 2	Resource Requirements of Prototype
Labor (hr)	1,500	1,200	2
Iron (lb)	200	100	10
Transmissions	900	1,700	1
Axles	0	200	0

prototype in the upcoming month) was made, each plant had already performed an extensive and costly LP analysis to arrive at an optimal production plan. Management plans to repeat this procedure for each plant (it is known how much of each resource the prototype will use) with forced production of the prototype included in the LP formulation. The plant whose revenue is least reduced will be chosen to build the prototype.

a Assuming that both plants have the resources on hand to build the prototype, suggest a better method for determining how its production will influence the revenues of the two plants. Assume that production of the prototype does not force a basis change (refer to Section 8.7).

b In its present production plan, plant 1 has a dual price of $10 per hour for labor. What does this mean?

c A prototype requires 60 hours of labor. What does this mean in relation to part *b*? Again, assume that production of the prototype does not force a basis change.

d In Figure 8.36 are listed the dual prices from the present LP optimization for both plants, as well as the resource requirements of the prototype. Given the assumption of no basis change, which plant should build the prototype?

e Suppose someone actually wanted to buy the prototype. What selling price would give PROTRAC a revenue 10 percent greater than the loss in revenue incurred from building the prototype?

13 This problem illustrates alternative optima and dual-price invariance.
Example 4 in Section 8.8 illustrates the fact that under certain conditions the dual price may not change when the basis changes. For example, consider the geometry in Figure 8.37. The objective function contour is parallel to the second constraint line. Let b_2 denote the RHS on the second constraint in the illustration. Suppose b_2 is now increased. Show geometrically where the next basis change (point of degeneracy) will occur, and argue that in the above case the dual price does *not* change at this point; that is, it is the same before and after the basis change.

Figure 8.37

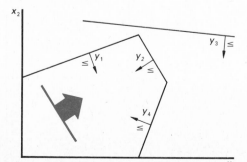

9 Profitability and Sensitivity Analysis on the Objective Function

This chapter provides a complete conceptual development of sensitivity analysis on the objective function. At the outset, a geometric interpretation is presented for the cost sensitivity output found on the computer solution to LP problems. Exact and estimated effects both on the solution and the OV are determined as an objective function coefficient is perturbed. The related topic of reduced cost is given two equivalent interpretations, and the underlying geometry is illustrated. The topic of alternative optima is also discussed, and alternative optima signals on the computer output are linked to the geometric representation.

9.1 Introduction

This chapter pursues the topic of sensitivity analysis in LP problems. It is thus concerned with analyzing the changes in the optimal solution and the optimal value of the objective function (OV) as a function of changes in the numerical value assigned to a parameter. In Chapter 9, we look at changes in the coefficient of a term in the objective function. For example, consider the purchasing problem in Figure 9.1. Suppose that PROTRAC is purchasing P different products from M different suppliers and having the products delivered to N destinations. Let

x_{ijk} = amount of product i sent from supplier j to destination k

c_{ijk} = cost of purchasing and sending one unit of product i from supplier j to destination k

S_{ij} = supply of product i at supplier j

D_{ik} = demand for product i at destination k

The LP formulation of the purchasing problem is thus

$$\text{Min} \sum_{i=1}^{P} \sum_{j=1}^{M} \sum_{k=1}^{N} c_{ijk} x_{ijk}$$

s.t.

$$\sum_{j=1}^{M} x_{ijk} \geq D_{ik} \qquad i = 1, ..., P; k = 1, ..., N$$

$$\sum_{k=1}^{N} x_{ijk} \leq S_{ij} \qquad i = 1, ..., P; j = 1, ..., M$$

$$x_{ijk} \geq 0$$

Figure 9.1 *Purchasing problem with three products, four suppliers, and four destinations*

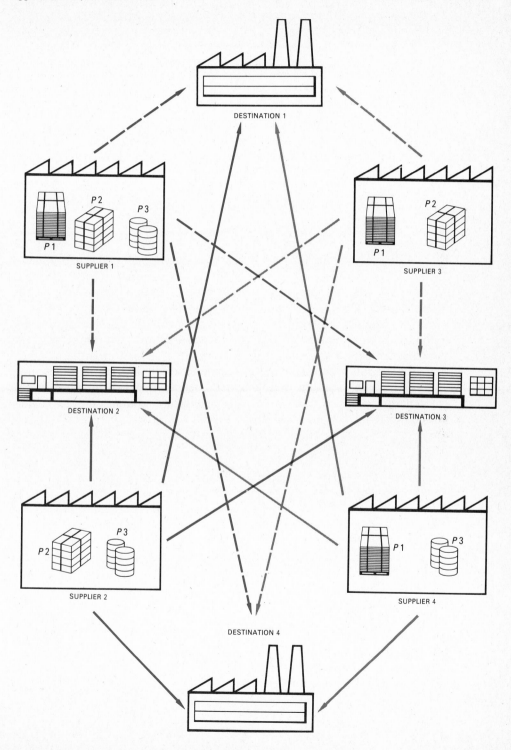

Having obtained an optimal solution to this problem, there are several questions of managerial interest that naturally arise among which we shall be particularly concerned with the following:

1   The most straightforward question involves a price change. Suppose that in the current optimal solution PROTRAC purchases some amount of product 2 from supplier 3 and has it delivered to destination 1; that is, the optimal value of x_{231} is positive. Supplier 3 announces a 10-percent price increase. Should management change its purchasing plans? The answer to this question is obtained by a sensitivity analysis on c_{231}.

2   Management believes it should follow various rules of thumb in its purchasing activity. One such rule is to always have more than one supplier for any product. Suppose that in the optimal solution produced by the LP problem, all of product 1 is purchased from supplier 3. If management wants to stick to the above rule of thumb, a decision must be made on who the new supplier should be. Management also wants to know how much it will cost to follow this rule. Again, such questions involve sensitivity analysis on the objective function coefficients.

Rules of thumb like "at least two suppliers for every product" and "at least two suppliers for every destination" could, in principle, be incorporated in a mathematical programming model directly. Unfortunately, the logical formulation of such constraints requires the use of integer-valued variables, which means that the problem is no longer an LP model, and finding an optimal solution then becomes a much more difficult process. This topic is pursued in Chapter 14.

In the following discussion, the geometric interpretation and the computer output for the same LP problem are used to motivate and explain the topic of sensitivity (or parametric, or postoptimality) analysis on the coefficients in the objective function.

9.2   Interpreting the Computer Output

Consider the PROTRAC E and F problem again. The computer output (which includes the problem statement) for this problem is shown in Figure 9.2 (which is a reproduction of Figure 8.1). Information for performing sensitivity analysis on the coefficients in the objective function is presented in the section identified as COST SENSITIVITY. To illustrate the use of the information in this section, let us focus on the per-unit revenue for E-9s. This is one of the input parameters for the problem. For the current computer run (Figure 9.2) we have used a value of 5,000 for this parameter. Now consider the question, What happens to the number of E-9s in the optimal solution as the per-unit revenue of E-9s is increased? In providing a partial answer to this question, it might first be observed that if the per-unit revenue of E-9s were to increase, with all other data unchanged, we would then expect to produce more, rather than less, E-9s. In the current solution (Figure 9.2), the optimal level of E-9 production is 4.5. The per-unit revenue is $5,000. If we were to increase the per-unit revenue, say to 5,010 or to 6,000, and then resubmit the problem for solution, it would

Figure 9.2 *Computer output for the E and F model*

```
MAX 5000E +4000F
SUBJECT TO
   2)    E +F   >= 5
   3)    E -3F   <= 0
   4)   10E +15F  <= 150
   5)   20E +10F  <= 160
   6)  -30E -10F  <=-135
```

VARIABLE	VALUE	REDUCED-COST
E	4.50000	0.00000
F	7.00000	0.00000
OBJ FCTN	50500.	

ROW	SLACK	DUAL-PRICE
2	6.5	0
3	16.5	0
4	0	150
5	0	179
6	70	0

```
SENSITIVITY ANALYSIS

RANGE IN WHICH BASIS REMAINS THE SAME
     COST SENSITIVITY
```

VARIABLE	INCREASE IN C(J)	DECREASE IN C(J)
E	2999.99998	2333.33299
F	3499.99997	1499.99999

```
        RIGHT HAND SENSITIVITY
```

ROW	ALLOWABLE INCREASE	ALLOWABLE DECREASE
2	6.5000	INFINITE
3	INFINITE	16.5000
4	90.00003	47.14286
5	73.33333	40.00000
6	INFINITE	70.0000

surely defy intuition if the resulting solution were to specify a production level of *less* than 4.5 E–9s. Recall that all other data have remained the same. The only change has been to make E–9s more profitable. How could this ever persuade us to make a smaller number of E–9s? It cannot, and this illustrates a first important principle in the realm of sensitivity analysis on objective function coefficients:

In a max model, increasing the profitability of an activity, keeping all other data unchanged, cannot reduce the optimal level of that activity.

Alternatively, suppose you are working in a min context. You would expect that increasing the per-unit cost of an activity, keeping all other data unchanged, could certainly *not* lead to an increase in its level at optimality. On the other hand, as the cost contribution becomes smaller, that activity becomes more attractive. Thus, we have the following counterpart to the preceding key concept:

In a min model, lowering the cost of an activity, keeping all other data unchanged, cannot reduce the optimal level of that activity.

Now then, let us return to the question raised above. Suppose the per-unit revenue of E–9s is only *slightly* increased. Does this mean there will be more E–9s produced at optimality? Your intuition may say yes, or you may think that the above discussion implies that the answer is yes, but the correct answer is no. In optimization models, it is important to pay careful attention to the logical difference between phrases such as "cannot reduce" and "must increase." It turns out that as the per-unit revenue is gradually and continuously increased from 5,000, the optimal production remains *unchanged* at the value 4.5—until the profitability increase is sufficiently large. With this in mind, let us refine the earlier question to, *How much* would the per-unit revenue of E–9s have to increase before the number of E–9s in the optimal solution would increase?

The discussion in Chapter 5 suggests the following analysis. The entry in the INCREASE IN $C(J)$ column is 3,000 (2999.99998). This tells us the amount that the coefficient of E in the objective function could be increased *without* changing the optimal solution, where it is understood that all other data in the problem remain unchanged. In this problem, if the change is more than 3,000 the optimal solution *will* change. The objective function for the E and F model is

$$5,000E + 4,000F$$

The optimal solution is $E = 4.5$, $F = 7$, and the optimal objective value is 50,500. We have just stated that if the objective function is changed to

$$cE + 4,000F$$

where c is any specific number between 5,000 and 8,000, and if the problem is then solved, the optimal solution will still be $E = 4.5$, $F = 7$. Of course, you can see that the new optimal objective value will be

$$\text{New OV} = c(4.5) + 4,000(7) = 4.5c + 28,000$$

That is, as our choice for the number c varies between 5,000 and 8,000, the OV is given by a linear function of c. Letting $V(c)$ denote the values of this function,[1] we see that

$$V(c) = 4.5c + 28,000 \qquad \text{for } 5,000 \le c \le 8,000$$

Thus, if the coefficient of E is increased the maximum amount, by 3,000, c will be 8,000, and we have

$$V(8,000) = 64,000$$

It is quite simple to represent the above facts geometrically. Let us refer

---

1   Do not confuse this $V(c)$ function with the $V(b)$ function of Chapter 8. The latter is a function of an RHS value. The former is a function of an objective function coefficient. Since the argument explicitly appears, there should be no confusion in using the same symbol, V.

Figure 9.3 *Effects of increasing c in the equation*
cE + 4,000F = K

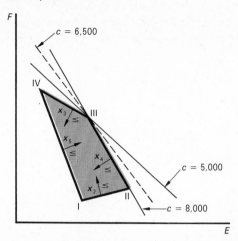

to the interpretation in Figure 9.3. We suggest that you rough out a sketch of this figure to facilitate future reference. Having done this, note that a change in the coefficient of a variable in the objective function has the effect of changing the tilt in the objective function contours. Considering our new objective function (that is, letting c denote the per-unit revenue for E–9s), the general isorevenue contour is given by

$$cE + 4,000F = K$$

or

$$F = -\left(\frac{c}{4,000}\right)E + \frac{K}{4,000}$$

where K is a constant representing the revenue at each point on the K-contour. (Recall that K is fixed on a given contour, and K differs on different contours.)

As c, the coefficient of E, is increased, the slope of the contour becomes more negative (that is, the contour tilts downward more steeply). When the coefficient of E is 8,000, the slope of the contour is

$$-\frac{8,000}{4,000} = -2$$

But, referring again to Figure 9.3, you can see that -2 is also the slope of the fourth constraint line, whose equation is

$$20E + 10F = 160 \qquad \text{or } F = -\frac{20}{10}E + \frac{160}{10} = -2E + 16$$

Now you can see in Figure 9.3 exactly what is happening. As the coefficient (c) of E increases, the tilt of the objective contour changes, becoming more steep. The optimal solution, however, remains at the same corner, although the optimal objective value $V(c)$ changes. As the coefficient of E continues to increase, this same state of affairs persists until the coefficient hits the value 8,000. When this occurs, the objective function contours are parallel to the fourth constraint line, and both of the corners II and III are optimal solutions. In this case the problem has *alternative, or multiple, optima.* Thus, at a per-unit revenue of 8,000 for E, the model is indifferent between using the production policy prescribed by corner II or the one associated with corner III. At corner II, the optimal value of E is larger. Thus, at the point when the per-unit revenue for E is 8,000, you would be willing to produce more than 4.5 E–9s, and this is the answer to the question posed above. Of course, you don't know exactly *how many* more without obtaining the values of the variables at the newly introduced optimal corner.

Note in Figure 9.3 that as the coefficient of E increases slightly beyond 8,000, then corner II becomes the unique solution. Further increases in the coefficient of E will have no effect on the solution since the objective contour will merely become increasingly steep approaching, but never reaching, a vertical line (that is, the slope approaches $-\infty$). It follows from this discussion and the interpretation shown in Figure 9.3 that the range of coefficient values between 5,000 and 8,000 is the range of increase over which the basis does not change. (Recall that the basis at a nondegenerate corner is the *set* of variables that are positive at optimality.) Since the set of variables that are positive does not change (in the 5,000 to 8,000 range for c), the same must be true for the set of variables that are zero. But the zero variables determine the corner of the constraint set at which the optimal solution is located. Hence, the range of increase (in c values) over which the basis does not change is the same as the range of increase over which the optimal corner does not change.

By similar reasoning, a *decrease* in the coefficient of E will give the objective contours a less negative tilt. Verify that when the coefficient is decreased by 2,333.33, the slope of the contour is $-.67$, which is the same as the slope of the third constraint line

$$10E + 15F = 150$$

When this occurs, the corners III and IV are optimal, and you should be willing to produce fewer E–9s and more F–9s. As the price decreases by more than 2,333.33, corner IV becomes the unique solution. This is true even when $c = 0$. Note, however, that at corner IV the value of E is still positive. Does it surprise you that the optimal value of E is positive even when the per-unit revenue is zero?

Let us now turn from the analysis of the PROTRAC E and F model to the general case. It will be seen that, with one exception concerning degeneracy, the analysis is entirely analogous. Suppose x_j is one of the decision variables in a max LP model. Let x^* denote an optimal solution to the current problem. Thus, x^* is the vector $(x_1^*, x_2^*, ..., x_n^*)$, and x_j^* is the optimal value of x_j in this solution. Suppose c_j denotes the coefficient of x_j in the objective function and that $c_j = \bar{c}_j$ in the problem that has just been solved. Unfortunately, in order to discuss the general case it is necessary to use this more general and more abstract notation. If the abstraction seems to interfere with your understanding, you should substitute specific numbers for the symbols. For example, you might let $n = 2, j = 1$, and let x_1^* have the value of E^* in the above E and F discussion. That is, we could let $\bar{c}_1 = 5,000$, and then, following the E and F context, x_1^* would be 4.5. Substituting specific values in this way should help you to understand the abstraction.

We shall now describe the information provided on the computer output for sensitivity analysis on *increases* in c_j. Let I be the number in the column INCREASE IN $C(J)$. (In the above E and F discussion, I had the value 3,000.)

---

1 If the coefficient c_j increases by an amount less than I (which can only be true if $I > 0$), then x^* remains a solution to the problem. (Of course, the OV will change.) This does not imply that x^* is a unique solution for $\bar{c}_j \le c_j < \bar{c}_j + I$. It is possible to have alternative optima. (To see this, one must consider a problem with more than two decision variables.) However, if alternative optima do exist, then in any such solution the optimal value of x_j is x_j^*.

2 If c_j increases by an amount equal to I or by an amount greater than I, there are two cases to consider:

 a Suppose x^* is a *nondegenerate* solution. In this case, if I is zero, then there are multiple optimal corner solutions and in one of these it will be true that $x_j > x_j^*$. For an increase in c_j beyond $\bar{c}_j$, any optimal solution will have $x_j > x_j^*$. If I is positive rather than zero, then we are assured that when c_j is increased by *exactly* this amount (from $\bar{c}_j$, to $\bar{c}_j + I$) there will be multiple optimal corner solutions. One of these will be the previous solution, x^*, and another of these will have an optimal value of x_j larger than x_j^*. Thus, we would be willing to increase the optimal level of x_j when the profitability is increased to $\bar{c}_j + I$. At this value of c_j ($\bar{c}_j + I$) the basis changes. For values of c_j greater than $\bar{c}_j + I$ (keeping all other data fixed), any optimal solution will have $x_j > x_j^*$.

 b Suppose x^* is a *degenerate* solution. In this case we *cannot* be assured that there will be a solution with an increased level of x_j when c_j is given the value $\bar{c}_j + I$ (regardless of whether I is positive or zero). In addition, it could be possible that, even when c_j is greater than $\bar{c}_j + I$, the former solution x^* remains optimal.

The two cases in items a and b cover the interactions for an increase in c_j in a max model. Analogous statements can be made for decreases in c_j in a max model or for increases and decreases in c_j in a min model. All of the above considerations can be graphically illustrated and amplified by further emphasis on the $V(c)$ function. This is accomplished in the next section.

9.3 The $V(c)$ Function

In Chapter 8, extensive use was made of $V(b)$, the OV function, whose argument is the RHS of a particular constraint. We have suggested in the previous section that it is possible to define a similar function whose argument is the coefficient of a particular variable in the objective function. For example, we saw that for the PROTRAC E and F model displayed in the computer output (Figure 9.2) it was possible to express the OV as a function

$$V(c) = 4.5c + 28,000$$

for values of c between 2,666.67 and 8,000. When $c = 8,000$, we saw that there were two alternative optimal solutions, namely corners II and III in Figure

9.3. Moreover, as the coefficient c takes on values larger than 8,000, corner II becomes the unique solution. This corner is determined by the intersection of the second and fourth constraint lines, namely the equalities corresponding to rows 3 and 5 in the model. Solving these equations

(Row 3) $E - 3F = 0$

(Row 5) $20E + 10F = 160$

simultaneously, one obtains the optimal values of the decision variables

$E^* = 6\frac{6}{7}$

$F^* = 2\frac{2}{7}$

Consequently, for values of $c \geq 8,000$ one can obtain the OV from the expression

$V(c) = cE^* + 4,000F^*$

$= c(6\frac{6}{7}) + 4,000(2\frac{2}{7})$

$= (6\frac{6}{7})c + 9142.86$

Also, for a value of c equal to $5,000 - 2,333.33 = 2,666.67$ we saw that corners III and IV are optimal, and for $0 \leq c < 2,666.67$ corner IV becomes the unique solution. (Since c denotes a revenue, we assume that its value must remain nonnegative.) Corner IV is determined by the intersection of the third and fifth constraint lines, namely the equalities corresponding to rows 4 and 6 in the model. Solving these equations

(Row 4) $10E + 15F = 150$

(Row 6) $-30E - 10F = -135$

simultaneously, one obtains the optimal decision variable values

$E^* = 1.5$

$F^* = 9$

Consequently, for $0 \leq c \leq 2666.67$ one obtains the OV from the expression

$V(c) = cE^* + 4,000F^*$

$= c(1.5) + 4,000(9)$

$= (1.5)c + 36,000$

We can now put this together by plotting the graph of the $V(c)$ function for *all* values of $c \geq 0$. This is done in Figure 9.4. This function $V(c)$ gives the OV corresponding to all nonnegative values of c, with all other data in the original model unchanged.

It is important to note the following fact:

The slope of the V(c) graph, for a given value of c is precisely the optimal value of E when the per-unit revenue is c.

Figure 9.4 *The* OV *as a function of c, the per-unit revenue of E*

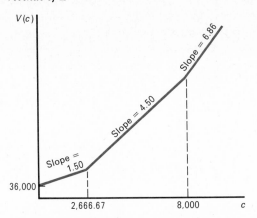

Also note that the slopes of the graph in Figure 9.4 are increasing. Since these slopes are the optimal values of E, the shape reflects the fact that increasing the profitability of E–9s cannot reduce the optimal level of production of E–9s. In this case, the profitability is the per-unit revenue, c. As c increases from 0 to 2,666.67, the optimal level of production (of E–9s) remains at 1.5, as shown by the slope of the $V(c)$ graph between 0 and 2,666.67. When $c = 2,666.67$ there are two optimal corner solutions. In one of these solutions, the optimal level of production is the old value, 1.5 (the slope to the left of 2,666.67). In the other corner solution, the optimal level of production has increased to 4.5, which is the slope to the right of 2,666.67. (Of course, the optimal values of F and of some of the slack variables also differ in each solution. The graph of $V(c)$ shows only the relationship among the value of c, the optimal value of E, and the OV.) As c increases above 2,666.67 to 8,000, the optimal level of E remains at 4.5, as shown by the slope of the graph between 2,666.67 and 8,000. When $c = 8,000$ there are again two optimal corner solutions. In one of these solutions, the optimal level of production is the old value, 4.5 (the slope to the left of 8,000). In the other, it has increased to $6\frac{6}{7}$ (the slope to the right of 8,000). As c increases beyond 8,000, the optimal value of E remains at $6\frac{6}{7}$. You can see from this analysis that the following statement is true:

Each corner on the V(c) graph corresponds to a c value for which there is more than one optimal corner solution, and the values of E differ at these solutions.

Throughout the following exposition, when we wish to distinguish between the OV as a function of an RHS, b_i, and the OV as a function of an objective coefficient, c_j, we shall loosely refer to the former as $V(b)$ and the latter as $V(c)$. Of course, these are not the same functions V, but the explicit reference to the argument of the function should eliminate any confusion.

It is of interest to contrast the facts that the corners on the $V(b)$ graph correspond to values of b for which there is a degenerate optimal solution, whereas the corners on the $V(c)$ graph correspond to values of c for which there are multiple optima. Recall from Chapter 7 that changing coefficients in the objective function of an LP problem corresponds to changing the RHS for the dual of that problem This observation suggests that if an LP problem has alternative optimal solutions, the solution to the dual of that problem will be degenerate. This suggestion is indeed correct and can be rigorously established by other means. This is explored further in Example 6, Section 9.7.

The above discussion has been couched in terms of a max problem and the development referred to the specific E and F model. However, the convex shape of the $V(c)$ graph revealed in Figure 9.4 is representative of *any* max model, since for any such problem increasing the profitability of an activity cannot reduce the optimal level of that activity and hence cannot reduce the slope; that is, the slope must remain the same or increase as the profitability increases.

In the general max model, consider the current solution (for, say $c_j = \bar{c}_j$) and let I be the number on the output under INCREASE IN $C(J)$ and let D denote the number under DECREASE IN $C(J)$. Then, as discussed under items 1 and 2 at the end of section 9.2, several observations can be made:

1 In all cases, the slope of $V(c)$ surely will not change for values of c_j greater than $\bar{c}_j - D$ and less than $\bar{c}_j + I$.

2 If the solution is *nondegenerate*, then corners in $V(c_j)$ will occur when c_j equals $\bar{c}_j - D$ and $\bar{c}_j + I$. (This case is illustrated in Figure 9.4.)

3 If the solution is *degenerate*, the nearest corners in each direction may be at (one or the other or both of) the end points of the above interval, or they may lie beyond the interval in either direction.

For a min problem, the general shape of the $V(c)$ graph can be easily inferred. In this case, increasing the cost (c) of an activity can only hurt the OV. For a min problem, hurting the objective value means that it must increase. Consequently, $V(c)$ is again an increasing function. However, it is intuitively clear that increasing the cost of an activity while everything else remains

Figure 9.5   *The V(c) function for a min problem*

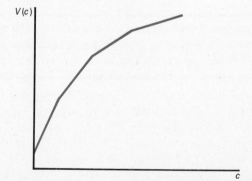

constant *cannot* increase the level of that activity in an optimal solution. Thus, just as for a max problem, since the optimal level of the activity in any optimal solution is the slope of $V(c)$, the slopes cannot increase for a min problem. They must either decrease or remain the same. (Of course the slopes will always be nonnegative, because the optimal values of the decision variables are always nonnegative.) Figure 9.5 shows the general concave shape of the $V(c)$ graph for a min problem. Again, the corners to the left and to the right of a current solution are given by the output values under DECREASE IN $C(J)$ and INCREASE IN $C(J)$, respectively, provided that the current solution is nondegenerate.

9.4 Estimating Changes in OV

Consider a linear program in which

$$\sum_{j=1}^{n} \bar{c}_j x_j$$

is the objective function and

$$x^* = (x_1^*, x_2^*, ..., x_n^*)$$

is an optimal solution. Let us focus on the effects of perturbations in a particular coefficient c_j, with all other data in the model held fixed. In the previous discussion, we have defined $V(c_j)$ as the OV as a function of c_j. Thus, $V(\bar{c}_j)$ is the OV for the initial problem. That is,

$$V(\bar{c}_j) = \sum_{j=1}^{n} \bar{c}_j x_j^*$$

In order to plot the general shape of the $V(c_j)$ graph for a max model, one need only remember that increasing c_j (the profitability) cannot hurt and cannot reduce the optimal level of x_j, which is the slope. Thus, the graph must have the shape shown in Figure 9.6. The shaded regions show where the $V(c_j)$ graph must lie to the right of $\bar{c}_j + I$ and to the left of $\bar{c}_j - D$.

In order to plot the general shape of the $V(c_j)$ graph for a min model, one need only remember that increasing c_j (the cost) cannot help and cannot increase the optimal level of x_j, which is the slope. Thus, the graph must have the shape shown in Figure 9.7, where the shaded regions are interpreted as in Figure 9.6. The distances D and I in Figures 9.6 and 9.7 are the decrease in $C(J)$ and increase in $C(J)$, respectively, that appear on the computer printout. The corners on the $V(c_j)$ graphs correspond to values of c_j at which there are alternative optimal corner solutions with different values for x_j. The basis "before and after" each such corner (on the $V(c_j)$ graph) differs, and hence these corners correspond to c_j values at which the basis changes.

Using Figures 9.6 and 9.7, you can easily see how to determine the change in OV when c_j is perturbed from $\bar{c}_j$ to some new value $\hat{c}_j$ for which $\bar{c}_j - D \le \hat{c}_j \le \bar{c}_j + I$. In this case, the change in OV is given by

$$V(\hat{c}_j) - V(\bar{c}_j) = (\hat{c}_j - \bar{c}_j)x_j^*$$

Figure 9.6 *V(c_j) for a general max model*   **Figure 9.7** *V(c_j) for a general min model*

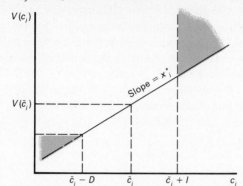   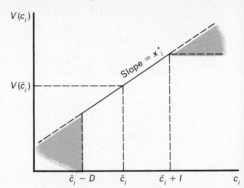

In Chapter 8, we saw that the $V(b)$ graphs could be used to estimate OV changes when an RHS is perturbed to a value outside the allowable range. The same methodology can be used on the $V(c)$ graphs for estimating OV changes when c is perturbed to a value larger than $\bar{c}_j + I$ or smaller than $\bar{c}_j - D$. In particular, the following facts can be deduced from Figures 9.6 and 9.7:

---

1 For a max problem, two-sided estimates can be obtained for decreases in c_j, and one-sided estimates can be obtained for increases.

2 For a min problem, two-sided estimates can be obtained for increases in c_j, and one-sided estimates can be obtained for decreases.

Let us illustrate these ideas with a particular example. Consider the output in Figure 9.2. We shall estimate the change in the OV if the per-unit price of E is decreased from 5,000 to 2,500. (Of course, the exact value $V(2,500)$ could be obtained from Figure 9.4, but we are assuming here that the entire $V(c)$ function has not been generated. We are acting as if we have at our disposal only the output from the single computer run shown in Figure 9.2.) Since the allowable decrease is only 2,333.33, the desired decrease of 2,500 takes us outside the range for making exact inferences. The estimation is illustrated in Figure 9.8.

Figure 9.8 *Using V(c) to estimate OV changes*

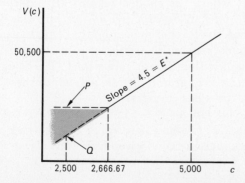

When $c = 2,500$ the $V(c)$ graph lies between the points P and Q. Thus the OV would decrease by at least $(2,333.33)(4.5) = 10,500$ to the value $50,500 - 10,500 = 40,000$. Similarly, the decrease would be at most $(2,500)(4.5) = 11,250$ to the value $50,500 - 11,250 = 39,250$. In this way the $V(c)$ graph makes it quite simple to estimate changes in the OV when c_j is assigned a value outside the allowable range. The procedure involved is entirely analogous to the technique discussed in Chapter 8 for the $V(b)$ function.

As a final point, we note that this entire discussion on use of the $V(c)$ graph for the estimation of OV changes is applicable whether or not the current solution is degenerate.

9.5 Reduced Costs

All the output in Figure 9.2 except that in the column labeled REDUCED-COST has now been given a geometric interpretation. The reduced-cost numbers apply to the decision variables, x_j.[2] Let c_j denote the coefficient of x_j in the objective function, and suppose we have a current *nondegenerate* optimal solution.

In a nondegenerate solution, the reduced cost of the decision variable, x_j, is the amount c_j would have to change before the optimal value of x_j would be positive.

According to this definition, the reduced cost will be zero if the optimal value of x_j is already positive. Consequently, the reduced cost of a positive variable is of no interest. Now suppose that the optimal value of x_j is zero. Then it follows directly from the definition that if the problem is a max problem, the reduced cost is precisely the number in the INCREASE IN $C(J)$ column. That is because the solution will not change and x_j will not become positive until c_j is *increased* by this amount (that is, this increases the profitability of x_j). If the problem is a min problem then the reduced cost is precisely the number in the DECREASE IN $C(J)$ column. In this case, a *decrease* in c_j by this amount reduces the cost per unit of x_j to the point that it becomes economical for its optimal value to be positive.

All we know from this analysis is that when the optimal value of x_j is zero in a nondegenerate solution, and when c_j is changed (increased in a max problem, decreased in a min problem) by the reduced cost, then there will be alternative optimal corner solutions with the following properties: The optimal value of x_j will be zero in one of these solutions and positive in the other. We do *not* know how positive this latter value will be. But since these corner solutions are alternative optima, we do know that the optimal objective value at the corner with x_j positive will be the same as at the corner with $x_j = 0$.

---

2 This statement is true of the particular computer code we have employed. In other codes, there may also be reduced-cost numbers corresponding to the slack variables. Such a reduced cost, however, will be the same number as the dual price associated with the constraint in which that slack variable is employed, and in that case the interpretation of the reduced cost and the dual price will be the same.

Figure 9.9 *The reduced cost, I, of x_j in a max model*

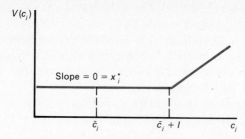

Thus with c_j changed by an amount equal to the reduced cost, we are indifferent to the "use" of x_j. The interpretation of the reduced cost in terms of the $V(c)$ function for a max problem is shown in Figure 9.9. In this figure the quantity I is the reduced cost of x_j.

It is also possible to use Figure 9.9 to deduce the meaning of the reduced cost on the variable x_j in a *degenerate* solution (with $x_j^* = 0$). In this case (for a max model), the reduced cost will again be the value I, the increase in $C(J)$, but as discussed in the previous section the corner "to the right" of $\bar{c}_j$ may correspond to a value of c_j greater than $\bar{c}_j + I$. Thus,

---

For a degenerate solution, c_j must be increased by at least (possibly more than) the reduced cost before x_j will become positive in an optimal solution.

The reduced cost for a nondegenerate solution to a min problem is shown in Figure 9.10. For a nondegenerate solution in either a max or a min problem, the reduced cost is sometimes given the following alternative interpretation:

In a nondegenerate solution, the reduced cost of the decision variable x_j is the per-unit amount the optimal objective value is hurt as x_j is forced into an optimal solution.

Figure 9.10 *The reduced cost, D, of x_j in a min model*

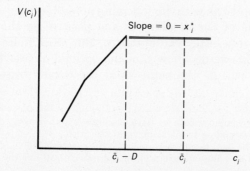

It is possible to formally justify the fact that this interpretation is implied by the one initially given. However, the proof amounts to an exercise in mathematical reasoning we choose to omit.

There are, however, several points to be stressed concerning the second interpretation. First of all, it applies only to a nondegenerate solution. Secondly, when the decision variable x_j is forced into an optimal solution, the values of the remaining variables must adjust to maintain feasibility. This adjustment is made in an optimal fashion. Thirdly, requiring "too much" of x_j to be forced into the solution may make the problem unsolvable; that is, doing so may create an empty constraint set. Even if this infeasibility does not occur and the problem is solvable, the current value of the reduced cost may not be valid for "too large" an increase in x_j. These facts will be illustrated in Example 3, Section 9.7. Unfortunately, it is not possible to find in the computer output the range for which the value of the reduced cost is valid. All we know is that there exists *some* value, say k, for which (1) for any positive $\varepsilon \leq k$ the constraint $x_j = \varepsilon$ can be added to the original problem and the new problem has a solution, and (2) ε(reduced cost) is the change in the OV. (See problem 13 in this chapter.) As a final comment, we note that the units of reduced cost are units of the objective function per unit x_j.

The economic meaning of the above two interpretations of reduced cost is indicated by referring once again to the ore-blending problem first introduced as Example 4 in Section 4.3. The output, including the formulation, is reproduced in Example 1 of Section 9.7 in this chapter. We first note that the optimal value of the decision variable $T4$ is zero and the solution is nondegenerate. The reduced cost of $T4$ is 91.11.

INTERPRETATION 1

Suppose the PROTRAC purchasing manager is approached by the salesman at location 4, who asks, "How much would we have to reduce our current price ($500 per ton) before you are willing to begin using ore from location 4 in your blend?" The answer is provided by the reduced cost of $T4$. That is, the price would have to be reduced by at least $91.11 per ton. We cannot say how much will be used, but at least we know the price change required before we are willing (in an optimal policy) to begin purchasing.

INTERPRETATION 2

Suppose the PROTRAC vice-president tells his purchasing manager he wants to begin giving some business to location 4 at their current price of $500 per ton. Although he will incur an added cost of $500 per ton from location 4, his change in policy will enable him to use less ore from the other locations in his blending process, and he will thereby save those costs. For example, if he modifies the current optimal plan by blending in 0.1 ton from location 4, then he will need, on net, 0.1 ton less from the other three locations. (This does not mean the new optimal strategy is to take less from each location—it could mean less from some and more from others, with a *net* decrease of 0.1). The vice-president now asks the following question: "If I begin purchasing from location 4, and *optimally* readjust my other purchases, what will be the net *additional* cost?" The answer is provided by the reduced cost of T4. That is, his costs will go up, *initially*, at the *rate* of $91.11 per ton of ore purchased from location 4. We cannot say how many tons can be purchased from location 4 at this rate of change in the OV. All we know is that this is the initial rate, and that as he purchases more and more from location 4, under normal circumstances, the rate will increase.

The truth of this last statement may not be apparent. Here is the justification. It can be proven that for some small enough positive number, say ε, if the vice-president adds the following constraint to the original model

$$T4 \geq \varepsilon$$

then the optimal value $T4^*$ will turn out to be ε, and the OV will be increased by $(91.11)\varepsilon$. This is consistent with our earlier assertion that the OV is increasing *initially* at the *rate* of $91.11 per ton of ore purchased from location 4. It turns out then that the reduced cost of T4 in the original model is the same as the dual price (ignoring the sign) on the constraint $T4 \geq \varepsilon$ in the new model (since that dual price is also the rate of change in OV per additional unit of ore purchased from location 4). Now, as the RHS ε is increased, the constraint is tightened, and we have seen that this cannot help and will generally hurt more and more. Thus, the magnitude of the dual price would generally increase, which means that as more and more ore is purchased from location 4 the rate of OV impairment would normally also increase.

9.6 Alternative Optima

This section links the geometric interpretation of alternative optimal corner solutions with the signals that indicate alternative optima on the computer printout. Suppose you are reading the computer output corresponding to a nondegenerate solution.

In a nondegenerate solution, the basic signal for alternative optima is the presence in the output of a zero allowable increase or zero allowable decrease in one of the objective function coefficients.

This fact should be clear from the geometric interpretations presented in the above discussions. In particular, if there is a unique nondegenerate optimal corner solution, it must be possible to change each coefficient in the objective function at least a small amount in either the positive or negative direction without changing the current basis. Therefore, if there is no allowable change for some coefficient in either direction, there must be multiple solutions. It should also be clear from the geometry that whenever there are alternative optimal corners, it must be the case that every feasible point on the line segment between the two corners is also optimal. However, since such solutions are not corner solutions, they would never be produced by the computer.

It is worth pointing out that there are two special cases of the above

Figure 9.11 *Alternative optima signals*

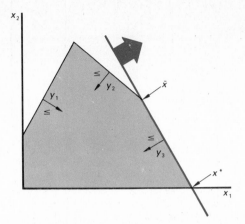

displayed signal for alternative optima. First of all, consider the max model with the geometry shown in Figure 9.11. There are two decision variables x_1, x_2 and three inequality constraints with slacks y_1, y_2, and y_3. The alternative optimal solutions are x^* and $\bar{x}$. Each solution is nondegenerate. Suppose the computer has produced x^*. You can see that x_2^* is zero and the reduced cost of x_2 is also zero. That is, the per-unit cost of forcing x_2 into the optimal solution is zero. Thus,

In a nondegenerate solution, a zero decision variable with zero reduced cost signals alternative optima.

In the above case, the zero reduced cost on a decision variable with zero optimal value shows that you are already at the point of indifference between a positive and a zero optimal value for that variable. This can only be true if there are alternative optima.

The second special case is seen by supposing that for Figure 9.11 the computer has produced the solution $\bar{x}$ rather than x^*. (There is no way in general to tell which one would actually be obtained.) You can see that the optimal slack value on the second constraint is zero, namely $\bar{y}_2 = 0$. You can also see that the dual price associated with this constraint must be zero. That is because an increase in b_2 will slide the second constraint line to the northeast and the new solution will have the same optimal objective value as before. Thus,

In a nondegenerate solution, the appearance of a zero slack on an inequality constraint with a zero dual price signals alternative optima.

You may be wondering whether this applies to an equality constraint. That is, if you discover an equality constraint with a zero dual price, does this signal alternative optima? A negative answer can be quickly obtained

Figure 9.12   *An equality constraint with zero dual price*

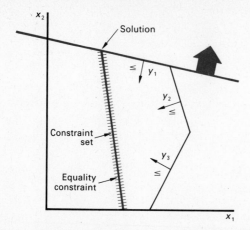

Figure 9.13   *Computer output for E and F model with price*
of E = 8,000; alternative optima signals

```
MAX 8000E +4000F
SUBJECT TO
   2)    E +F    >= 5
   3)    E -3F    <= 0
   4)   10E +15F  <= 150
   5)   20E +10F  <= 160
   6)  -30E -10F  <=-135
```

VARIABLE	VALUE	REDUCED-COST
E	6.85714	0.00000
F	2.28571	0.00000
OBJ FCTN	64000.	

ROW	SLACK	DUAL-PRICE
2	4.14286	0
3	0	4.35965E-05
4	47.1429	0
5	0	400
6	93.5714	0

SENSITIVITY ANALYSIS

RANGE IN WHICH BASIS REMAINS THE SAME
    COST SENSITIVITY

VARIABLE	INCREASE IN C(J)	DECREASE IN C(J)
E	INFINITE	0.00031
F	0.00015	27999.99969

    RIGHT HAND SENSITIVITY

ROW	ALLOWABLE INCREASE	ALLOWABLE DECREASE
2	4.1429	INFINITE
3	8.00000	16.50000
4	INFINITE	47.1429
5	73.33333	65.50000
6	INFINITE	93.5714

with a geometric analysis. Consider Figure 9.12, in which there are three inequality constraints and one equality constraint. The constraint set is the hatched line, and there is a unique solution. It is nondegenerate. The objective function contours are parallel to the first constraint line. As the RHS on the equality constraint is perturbed, the solution will slide along the first constraint line. Hence, the optimal objective value will not change. This means the dual price on the equality constraint is zero. But there are *not* alternative optima.

In Figure 9.13, computer output for a modified version of the E and F problem is reproduced. The per-unit revenue for E has been changed to 8,000, and the solution produced corresponds to corner II in Figure 9.3. Recall from the earlier discussion that a per-unit revenue on E of 8,000 produces alternative optima. In the output in Figure 9.13, this is signaled by the zero slack and zero dual on the second constraint. (The dual value 4.35×10^{-5} is a computer zero.) It is also signaled by the zeros (.00031 and .00015) under DECREASE IN $C(J)$ and INCREASE IN $C(J)$, respectively, of the cost sensitivity section.

Note in Figure 9.13 the following geometric interpretations, which should be compared with Figure 9.3:

---

1 The increase in the coefficient of E can be infinite. Such an increase will make the slope of the objective contours increasingly negative and will not change the solution.
2 A decrease in the coefficient of E from 8,000 will transfer the solution to corner III.
3 An increase in the coefficient of F will transfer the solution to corner III.
4 A decrease of 28,000 in the coefficient of F will give the objective function contours a slope of .33. Alternative optima will occur at corners I and II. Of course, this would create a negative per-unit revenue for F and hence would not make economic sense.

9.7 Examples and Solutions

Example 1

Recall the ore-blending problem originally presented as Example 4, Section 4.3. The output (including the formulation) is presented in Figure 9.14.
a For each of the changes suggested below, first, specify the exact value of the OV or the tightest possible bounds. Then, state as precisely as possible what happens to the optimal solution.
(1) The price of ore from location 1 increases by $100.
(2) The price of ore from location 2 increases by $100.
(3) The price of ore from location 1 decreases by $150.

b At what rate and in what direction does the optimal value of the objective function change if the ore from location 4 is introduced into the solution?

Solution to Example 1

a (1) The allowable increase in the coefficient $T1$ is 223.6. The suggested increase is 100. Therefore, the optimal solution remains the same. The OV will increase by 100(0.25926) = 25.926 to 537.037.

Figure 9.14

```
MIN 800T1+400T2+600T3+500T4
SUBJECT TO
    2)    10T1+3T2+8T3+2T4 >= 5
    3)    90T1+150T2+75T3+175T4 >= 100
    4)    45T1+25T2+20T3+37T4 >= 30
    5)    T1+T2+T3+T4= 1

VARIABLE        VALUE         REDUCED-COST
   T1          0.25926         0.00000
   T2          0.70370         0.00000
   T3          0.03704         0.00000
   T4          0.00000        91.11107
 OBJ FCTN      511.111


ROW            SLACK          DUAL-PRICE
   2             0             -44.4444
   3           31.6667           0
   4             0             -4.44445
   5             0            -155.555


SENSITIVITY ANALYSIS

RANGE IN WHICH BASIS REMAINS THE SAME
     COST SENSITIVITY

VARIABLE        INCREASE       DECREASE
                IN C(J)        IN C(J)

   T1          223.63632      120.00018
   T2           66.84779      300.00036
   T3           85.71440      118.26919
   T4          INFINITE        91.11107


        RIGHT HAND SENSITIVITY

   ROW   ALLOWABLE INCREASE     ALLOWABLE DECREASE


    2          2.37500              0.25000
    3         31.6667              INFINITE
    4          0.71429              7.00000
    5          0.25000              0.04348
```

(2) The allowable increase in the coefficient of $T2$ is 66.85. The suggested increase is 100. Since the current solution is nondegenerate, we know for sure that the increase of 100 will produce a new optimal solution. Moreover, in this new solution the optimal value of $T2$ will be smaller. Bounds on the new value of the OV function can be found by using Figure 9.15.

(Lower bound) $511.11 + 66.8(.7037) = 558.118$

(Upper bound) $511.11 + 100(.7037) = 581.48$

(3) The allowable decrease is 120. The suggested decrease is 150. Again, since the current solution is nondegenerate, we know for sure that a change beyond the allowable amount will produce a new optimal solution with a new value for $T1$. In this case, since the price is decreasing, the new

Figure 9.15

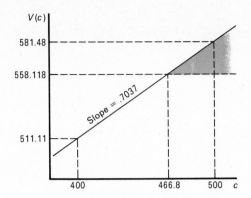

optimal value of $T1$ will be larger. Bounds on the value of the OV function can be found by using Figure 9.16

(Upper bound) $511.11 - 150(.25926) = 472.22.$

It is impossible to specify a lower bound other than zero.
b The OV function will *increase* at the rate of $91.11 per ton.

Example 2

Recall the TV production model, which first appeared as problem 1 in Chapter 4. The LP formulation of this problem is:

Max $20A + 30C$

s.t.

$$A \qquad \leq \quad 70$$
$$C \leq \quad 50$$
$$A + 2C \leq 120$$
$$A, C \geq \quad 0$$

Figure 9.16

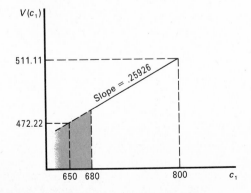

Use geometry and algebra to plot the graph of the $V(C_A)$ function for all values of $C_A \geq 0$, where C_A is the coefficient of A in the objective function. Specify the value of C_A and $V(C_A)$ for all corners on the graph and indicate the slope of the graph on each linear segment.

Solution to Example 2

The constraint set is plotted as shown in Figure 9.17. We then determine the values of A and C at the corners of the feasible set. Corners I, II, and V can be read directly from the constraints. Corner III occurs at the intersection of the two lines

$$A + 2C = 120$$
$$C = 50$$

or $A = 20$, $C = 50$. Corner IV occurs at the intersection of the two lines

$$A + 2C = 120$$
$$A = 70$$

or $A = 70$, $C = 25$.

Now we determine the $V(C_A)$ function. When $C_A = 0$, the objective function is simply $30C$ and the contours of the objective function are parallel to the A axis. Thus, the optimal solutions lie on the line between corners II and III. The value of the objective function is $30(50) = 1,500$. We can thus plot the point (0, 1,500) on the $V(C_A)$ graph.

As C_A increases, the optimal solution remains at point III, with $A^* = 20$, until the contour of the objective function becomes parallel to the line $A + 2C = 120$. Rewriting the equation of this line as $C = 60 - .5A$ shows that the slope of the line is $-.5$. The slope of the contours of the objective function equals $-.5$ when $C_A = 15$. At this point the value of the objective function is $15(20) + 30(50) = 1,800 = 15(70) + 30(25)$. We can thus plot the point (15, 1,800) on the $V(C_A)$ graph.

For values of $C_A > 15$, the optimal solution will remain at corner IV with

Figure 9.17

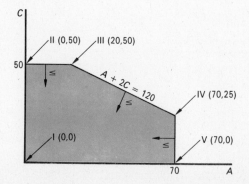

Figure 9.18

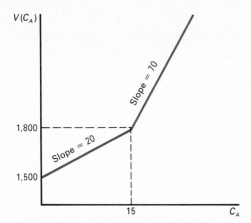

$A^* = 70$. The slope of the contour of the objective function will become arbitrarily close to $-\infty$.

The previous information has given us the graph for the $V(C_A)$ function shown in Figure 9.18.

Example 3

Picture geometrically a hypothetical linear program in two dimensions, illustrating the following:

a The optimal value of x_2, x_2^*, is zero in a unique nondegenerate optimal solution.

b The range of x_2 values for which the reduced cost is valid.

c The cost of forcing x_2 into the optimal solution by an amount exceeding the above range becomes even greater; that is, the per-unit "hurt" in the OV will increase.

d If x_2 is forced in at too high a level, the problem becomes infeasible.

Solution to Example 3

Consider the geometry shown in Figure 9.19.

a The optimal solution is at point A. Clearly, $x_2^* = 0$. The solution is nondegenerate since the problem has three constraints and three positive variables at A.

b If x_2 is forced into the optimal solution to any level up to $x_2^{(1)}$, the change in OV per unit change in x_2 will equal the reduced cost. Thus, the reduced cost is valid for x_2 values between 0 and $x_2^{(1)}$. It is to be noted that the validity holds for an increase in x_2 up to the amount for which a new basis (at corner C) is obtained.

c If x_2 is forced in at the level $x_2^{(0)}$, you can see that the optimal solution moves from point A to point B. The per-unit "hurt" in the objective function (the reduced cost) is not very large. If x_2 is changed by the same amount, but from the value $x_2^{(1)}$ to $x_2^{(2)}$, then the optimal solution moves from C to D and you can see that the per-unit "hurt" will be much more.

Figure 9.19

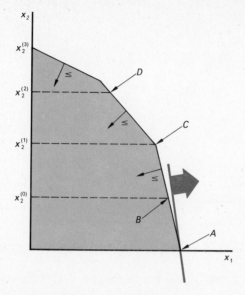

d If an attempt is made to force x_2 in at any level greater than $x_2^{(3)}$, the problem is infeasible.

Example 4

Picture geometrically a hypothetical linear program in two dimensions, with three inequality constraints, where the variable $x_1^* = 0$ and the reduced cost of $x_1 = 0$.

Solution to Example 4

Consider the geometry shown in Figure 9.20. The objective function is parallel to the constraint joining points A and B. The point A is an optimal corner solution with $x_1^* = 0$, and the reduced cost of x_1 is also zero. This means, as you can see from the picture, there are alternative optimal solutions where x_1^* is positive.

Example 5

In Section 8.7 we discussed the possibilities for analyzing $V(b)$ changes induced by varying several RHS values simultaneously. The same type of analysis can be performed on the $V(c)$ function. In particular, let $\bar{x}$ be a current nondegenerate optimal corner solution corresponding to objective function coefficients $(\bar{c}_1, \ldots, \bar{c}_n)$. Let $\hat{x}$ be a nondegenerate optimal corner solution corresponding to objective function coefficients $(\hat{c}_1, \ldots, \hat{c}_n)$. If the basis at $\bar{x}$ and $\hat{x}$ is the same (which means $\bar{x} = \hat{x}$) then rule 1

(Rule 1) $V(\hat{c}) = V(\bar{c}) + \sum_{j=1}^{n} (\hat{c}_j - \bar{c}_j)\bar{x}_j = \sum_{j=1}^{n} \hat{c}_j \bar{x}_j$

Figure 9.20

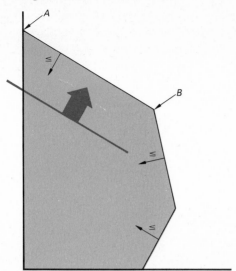

holds for a max problem, and rule 2

$$(\text{Rule 2}) \qquad V(\hat{c}) = V(\bar{c}) + \sum_{j=1}^{n} (\hat{c}_j - \bar{c}_j)\bar{x}_j = \sum_{j=1}^{n} \hat{c}_j \bar{x}_j$$

holds for a min problem.

If the bases at $\bar{x}$ and $\hat{x}$ are different (or if it is simply not known whether or not the two bases are the same), then since $\bar{x}$ is feasible the first equality sign in rule 1 must be replaced by $\geq$ and the first equality in rule 2 must be replaced by $\leq$.

For example, consider the PROTRAC E and F model in Figure 9.2. Estimate the new OV when the per-unit revenue of E is 6,000 and the per-unit revenue of F is 3,000.

Solution to Example 5

Basing our analysis only on the computer output shown in Figure 9.2 (that is, without further geometric analysis), it is not possible to tell whether the indicated *simultaneous* changes in the coefficients will induce a change in basis at the new solution. Since we are dealing with a max problem, the above discussion indicates that

$$V(6{,}000, 3{,}000) \geq V(5{,}000, 4{,}000) + (1{,}000)4.5 - (1{,}000)7 = 50{,}500 + 4{,}500 - 7{,}000$$

or

$$V(6{,}000, 7{,}000) \geq 48{,}000$$

In this instance, we are able to obtain only a lower bound on the new OV.

● **Example 6**

In Chapter 7, the following *dual problems* were discussed:

Max $\displaystyle\sum_{j=1}^{n} c_j x_j$

s.t.

$$\sum_{j=1}^{n} a_{ij}x_j \leq b_i \qquad i = 1, \ldots, m \tag{I}$$

$$x_j \geq 0 \qquad j = 1, \ldots, n$$

Min $\displaystyle\sum_{i=1}^{m} b_i y_i$

s.t.

$$\sum_{i=1}^{m} a_{ij}y_i \geq c_j \qquad j = 1, \ldots, n \tag{II}$$

$$y_i \geq 0 \qquad i = 1, \ldots, m$$

Let $V(c_k)$ denote the OV for model (I) as a function of the objective function coefficient c_k, for some fixed index k. Let $\hat{V}(c_k)$ denote the OV for model (II) as a function of the RHS parameter c_k. Important relations between (I) and (II) include the following fact: if either of the problems has a solution, then so does the other, and the respective optimal objective values are equal. In this case then,

$$V(c_k) = \hat{V}(c_k)$$

In other words, the $V(c_k)$ function for (I) is equal to the $\hat{V}(c_k)$ function for (II). The shape of the graph of $\hat{V}$ in (II) was discussed in Chapter 8.

a Use this information concerning $\hat{V}(c_k)$ and the above-stated relationship between (I) and (II) to confirm the shape and slopes of the $V(c_k)$ graph for (I).

b Consider the OV function corresponding to an objective coefficient b_k in (II). Use the above relationship between (I) and (II) to deduce the shape of this graph.

c If (I) has alternative optimal solutions, then argue that the dual must have a degenerate solution.

Solution to Example 6

a For (II) we know from Chapter 8 that the graph of $\hat{V}(c_k)$ is increasing, piecewise linear, and has increasing slopes, since tightening the RHS in (II) hurts more and more. Since $V(c_k) = \hat{V}(c_k)$, the graph of $V(c_k)$ must have the same properties.

b Increasing an objective function coefficient in (II) is equivalent to loosening the RHS of a $\leq$ constraint in (I). This produces a piecewise linear increasing function with decreasing slopes.

c Suppose (I) has alternative optimal solutions when $c_k = \bar{c}_k$, in which the x_k^* values differ. Then the $V(c_k)$ graph must have a corner when $c_k = \bar{c}_k$. Since the $V(c_k)$ graph is the same as the $\hat{V}(c_k)$ graph, it follows that $\hat{V}(c_k)$, the RHS OV function, also has a corner at $\bar{c}_k$. This means that the dual problem must have a degenerate solution corresponding to the RHS value $\bar{c}_k$.

9.8 Summary of Key Concepts

In a max model, increasing the profitability of an activity, keeping all other data unchanged, cannot reduce the optimal level of that activity. (Section 9.2)

In a min model, lowering the cost of an activity, keeping all other data unchanged, cannot reduce the optimal level of that activity. (Section 9.2)

The slope of the $V(c_j)$ graph for a given value of c_j is precisely the corresponding optimal value of x_j. (Section 9.3)

Each corner on the $V(c)$ graph corresponds to a c value for which there is more than one optimal corner solution. (Section 9.3)

The $V(c)$ function can be used to estimate OV changes when c is assigned a value outside the allowable range. (Section 9.4)

In a nondegenerate solution, the reduced cost has the following two interpretations:
1 The reduced cost of the decision variable x_j is the amount c_j would have to change before the optimal value of x_j would be positive.
2 The reduced cost of the decision variable x_j is the per-unit amount the OV is hurt as x_j is forced into an optimal solution.
(Section 9.5)

In a degenerate solution, c_j must be increased by at least (possibly more than) the reduced cost before x_j will become positive in an optimal solution. (Section 9.5)

In a nondegenerate solution, there are three indications of alternative optima. The basic signal for alternative optima is the presence in the output of a zero allowable increase or zero allowable decrease in one of the objective function coefficients. This basic sign will be accompanied by one or the other of the following two signs: (1) a zero decision variable with zero reduced cost; or (2) the appearance of a zero slack on an inequality constraint with a zero dual price. (Section 9.6)

9.9 Problems

1 Consider the output in Figure 9.2. Assume the coefficient of F in the objective function decreases from 4,000 to 2,800. What is the optimal solution? What is the OV?

2 Consider the E, F model displayed at the top of Figure 9.2. Suppose the per-unit revenue of E–9s is changed to zero. Will the optimal production of E–9s go to zero? Explain the reason for your answer. (Hint: refer to Figure 9.3.)

3 Consider a special case of the general purchasing problem presented in the introduction to this chapter. In general terms, the problem is

$$\text{Min} \sum_{i=1}^{P} \sum_{j=1}^{M} \sum_{k=1}^{N} c_{ijk} x_{ijk}$$

s.t.

$$\sum_{j} x_{ijk} \geq D_{ik} \qquad i = 1, \ldots, P; \, k = 1, \ldots, N$$

$$\sum_{k} x_{ijk} \leq S_{ij} \qquad i = 1, \ldots, P; \, j = 1, \ldots, M$$

$$x_{ijk} \geq 0$$

where

x_{ijk} = quantity of product i sent from supplier j to destination k

c_{ijk} = the per-unit cost of purchasing and sending product i from supplier j to destinatio

S_{ij} = quantity of product i at supplier j

D_{ik} = demand for product i at destination k

The model and solution for a particular version of this problem with three products, four suppliers, and four destinations is shown in Figure 9.21.

Figure 9.21

```
MIN    50 X111 + 30 X112 + 60 X113 + 70 X114 + 60 X121 + 50 X122
      + 80 X123 + 90 X124 + 80 X131 + 90 X132 + 70 X133 + 80 X134
      + 70 X141 + 100 X142 + 110 X143 + 90 X144 + 150 X211 + 10 X212
      + 30 X213 + 80 X214 + 50 X221 + 50 X222 + 90 X223 + 80 X224
      + 90 X231 + 60 X232 + 60 X233 + 40 X234 + 60 X241 + 80 X242
      + 120 X243 + 80 X244 + 40 X311 + 20 X312 + 50 X313 + 90 X314
      + 55 X321 + 80 X322 + 100 X323 + 70 X324 + 100 X331 + 40 X332
      + 50 X333 + 60 X334 + 40 X341 + 70 X342 + 120 X343 + 85 X344
SUBJECT TO
  2)     X111 +  X121 +  X131 +  X141  >=    700
  3)     X112 +  X122 +  X132 +  X142  >=    500
  4)     X113 +  X123 +  X133 +  X143  >=    400
  5)     X114 +  X124 +  X134 +  X144  >=    600
  6)     X211 +  X221 +  X231 +  X241  >=   1000
  7)     X212 +  X222 +  X232 +  X242  >=    750
  8)     X213 +  X223 +  X233 +  X243  >=   1250
  9)     X214 +  X224 +  X234 +  X244  >=   1500
 10)     X311 +  X321 +  X331 +  X341  >=    200
 11)     X312 +  X322 +  X332 +  X342  >=    500
 12)     X313 +  X323 +  X333 +  X343  >=    300
 13)     X314 +  X324 +  X334 +  X344  >=    400
 14)     X111 +  X112 +  X113 +  X114  <=   2500
 15)     X121 +  X122 +  X123 +  X124  <=   1000
 16)     X131 +  X132 +  X133 +  X134  <=   1500
 17)     X141 +  X142 +  X143 +  X144  <=   1750
 18)     X211 +  X212 +  X213 +  X214  <=   1000
 19)     X221 +  X222 +  X223 +  X224  <=    800
 20)     X231 +  X232 +  X233 +  X234  <=   1500
 21)     X241 +  X242 +  X243 +  X244  <=   1400
 22)     X311 +  X312 +  X313 +  X314  <=    700
 23)     X321 +  X322 +  X323 +  X324  <=    300
 24)     X331 +  X332 +  X333 +  X334  <=    400
 25)     X341 .+  X342 +  X343 +  X344  <=    100
```

a Suppose that because of an increase in costs by a particular carrier, the cost of supplying product 2 from supplier 2 to destination 4 were to increase by $10. Would the optimal solution change? Can you specify or give bounds for the new optimal objective value?

b Suppose that the cost of supplying product 3 from supplier 3 to destination 2 were to decrease by $20. Would the optimal solution change? Can you specify or give bounds for the new optimal value?

ure 9.21   *(Continued)*

OBJECTIVE FUNCTION VALUE

1)   387000.0

VARIABLE	VALUE	REDUCED COST
X111	700.000000	0.000000
X112	500.000000	0.000000
X113	400.000000	0.000000
X114	600.000000	0.000000
X121	0.000000	10.000000
X122	0.000000	20.000000
X123	0.000000	20.000000
X124	0.000000	20.000000
X131	0.000000	30.000000
X132	0.000000	60.000000
X133	0.000000	10.000000
X134	0.000000	10.000000
X141	0.000000	20.000000
X142	0.000000	70.000000
X143	0.000000	50.000000
X144	0.000000	20.000000
X211	0.000000	160.000000
X212	0.000000	20.000000
X213	1000.000000	0.000000
X214	0.000000	70.000000
X221	50.000000	0.000000
X222	750.000000	0.000000
X223	0.000000	0.000000
X224	0.000000	10.000000
X231	0.000000	70.000000
X232	0.000000	40.000000
X233	250.000000	0.000000
X234	1250.000000	0.000000
X241	950.000000	0.000000
X242	0.000000	20.000000
X243	0.000000	20.000000
X244	250.000000	0.000000
X311	100.000000	0.000000
X312	500.000000	0.000000
X313	100.000000	0.000000
X314	0.000000	30.000000
X321	0.000000	5.000000
X322	0.000000	50.000000
X323	0.000000	40.000000
X324	200.000000	0.000000
X331	0.000000	60.000000
X332	0.000000	20.000000
X333	200.000000	0.000000
X334	200.000000	0.000000
X341	100.000000	0.000000
X342	0.000000	50.000000
X343	0.000000	70.000000
X344	0.000000	25.000000

Figure 9.21   *(Continued)*

ROW	SLACK	DUAL PRICES
2)	0.000000	-50.000000
3)	0.000000	-30.000000
4)	0.000000	-60.000000
5)	0.000000	-70.000000
6)	0.000000	-60.000000
7)	0.000000	-60.000000
8)	0.000000	-100.000000
9)	0.000000	-80.000000
10)	0.000000	-50.000000
11)	0.000000	-30.000000
12)	0.000000	-60.000000
13)	0.000000	-70.000000
14)	300.000000	0.000000
15)	1000.000000	0.000000
16)	1500.000000	0.000000
17)	1750.000000	0.000000
18)	0.000000	70.000000
19)	0.000000	10.000000
20)	0.000000	40.000000
21)	200.000000	0.000000
22)	0.000000	10.000000
23)	100.000000	0.000000
24)	0.000000	10.000000
25)	0.000000	10.000000

c Suppose that the cost of supplying destination 3 with product 1 from supplier 1 were to become $30. Using the data from Figure 9.21, provide the best answer you can as to whether the optimal solution would change. Can you specify or give bounds on the optimal objective value? What other additional data would you wish to have available to answer these questions?

d Management has a rule of thumb that no product should be purchased from a single supplier. Is this rule satisfied by the optimal solution? If not, can you determine from the output what change you would introduce? That is, what new supplier would you use? What would be the best way to describe the cost of following the rule of thumb? Would additional output be useful?

e Management has a rule of thumb that each destination should be supplied by at least three suppliers. The manager of purchasing claims that the current solution does *not* satisfy this rule. He feels that he would be happy if even three out of the four destinations were to satisfy this condition. However, he has given up attempting to accomplish this because he believes it will be too expensive. Comment on his reasoning.

4   Consider the Buster Sod problem (problem 5, Chapter 5). The formulation and output are reproduced in Figure 9.22 for the case of 1,200 acres available. Let

W = wheat raised and sold (acres)

A = alfalfa raised (tons)

B = beef raised and sold (tons)

$A3$ = alfalfa bought (tons)

$A5$ = alfalfa sold (tons)

a Suppose the cost of buying alfalfa and having it delivered to Sod's farm were to increase by $3 per ton. Would the solution change? What can you say about the OV? By changing the crop rotation scheme, Buster Sod suddenly has 1,000 acres

Figure 9.22

```
MAX 72W -10A +560B -36A3+34A5
SUBJECT TO
    2)    W +.33333A +.05B  <= 1200      (Land, in acres)
    3)    1.5W +.833330A +.1B  <= 2000   (Water, in acre-feet)
    4)    -A +4B -A3+A5= 0               (Alfalfa, in tons)

VARIABLE          VALUE          REDUCED-COST
    W            0.00000         6168.00092
    A            0.00000         3440.65329
    B        19999.99980            0.00000
    A3       79999.99922            0.00000
    A5           0.00000            2.00000
OBJ FCTN          8.32000E+06

ROW              SLACK          DUAL-PRICE
    2             200                0
    3               0             4160.
    4               0               36.


SENSITIVITY ANALYSIS

RANGE IN WHICH BASIS REMAINS THE SAME
    COST SENSITIVITY

VARIABLE        INCREASE        DECREASE
                 IN C(J)         IN C(J)

    W          6168.00092       INFINITE
    A          3440.65329       INFINITE
    B          INFINITE         411.19995
    A3            2.00000       100.21358
    A5            2.00000       INFINITE


        RIGHT HAND SENSITIVITY

    ROW    ALLOWABLE INCREASE      ALLOWABLE DECREASE


     2          INFINITE            200.0000
     3          399.99988           1999.99950
     4        79999.9992            INFINITE
```

available. The formulation is changed appropriately. The new solution is shown in Figure 9.23.

b Is the following statement true or false? Since the solution is now degenerate, we are unable to interpret the reduced costs.

5 Recall the LP formulation of the TV production model discussed in Example 2 of this chapter.

Max $20A + 30C$

s.t.

$$A \quad\ \le\ 70$$

$$C \le 50$$

$$A + 2C \le 120$$

$$A, C \ge \quad 0$$

Figure 9.23

```
VARIABLE        VALUE         REDUCED-COST
   W           0.00000       6168.00092
   A           0.00000       3440.65329
   B        19999.99980         0.00000
   A3       79999.99922         0.00000
   A5          0.00000          2.00000
OBJ FCTN       8.32000E+06
```

```
ROW              SLACK        DUAL-PRICE
  2                0               0
  3                0             4160.
  4                0               36.
```

```
SENSITIVITY ANALYSIS

RANGE IN WHICH BASIS REMAINS THE SAME
    COST SENSITIVITY

VARIABLE        INCREASE        DECREASE
                IN C(J)         IN C(J)

   W          6168.00092       INFINITE
   A          3440.65329       INFINITE
   B           INFINITE       411.19995
   A3            2.00000      100.21358
   A5            2.00000       INFINITE
```

```
        RIGHT HAND SENSITIVITY

  ROW    ALLOWABLE INCREASE      ALLOWABLE DECREASE


   2         INFINITE                0.0000
   3         0.00000              1999.99950
   4       79999.9992              INFINITE
```

Use geometry and algebra to plot the graph of the $V(c_C)$ function for all values of $c_C > 0$, where c_C is the coefficient of C in the objective function. Specify the values of c_C and $V(c_C)$ for all corners on the graph and indicate the slope of the graph on each linear segment.

6   Consider the output in Figure 9.2. For each of the changes suggested below, either specify the exact value or provide the best possible bounds for the new OV.
   a Suppose the per-unit price of E is increased to 9,000 and all other parameters remain the same.
   b Suppose the per-unit price of F is decreased to 2,000 and all other parameters remain the same.

7   Consider problem 4 above, part a. Suppose that due to a preharvest blight the price of alfalfa bought increases to 140 per ton and all other parameters remain the same. Specify the exact value or provide the best possible bounds for the new OV.

8   Let $cE + 4,000F$ be the objective function in the PROTRAC E and F problem.
   a Try to provide a rigorous logical argument to support the fact that the values $V(c)$ are increasing.
   b What is the slope of the $V(c)$ graph when $c = 5,000$?

9   Refer to part c of problem 21, Section 4.8. Answer the first part of this question (concerning h_1) in light of your knowledge of sensitivity analysis.

10   Create a diagram of a hypothetical LP problem in two variables x_1 and x_2, with a solution in which there is an alternative optimum signal based on reduced cost.

11 Suppose an LP problem has originally had a nondegenerate corner solution x^*, and that several of the c_j coefficients are simultaneously changed. Let $\hat{c}_j$ be the new value of c_j.

a Specify the new OV if the basis does not change.

b Assume that the problem is a max problem. If the basis changes, what is the relationship between the new OV and the value specified in part a? (Hint: Note that x^* is still feasible.)

c Assume that the problem is a min problem. If the basis changes, what is the relationship between the new OV and the value specified in part a?

12 In Chapter 7, it was stated that if one of the following pair of dual problems has a solution then so does the other, and the OVs are equal.

$$\text{Max} \ \sum_{j=1}^{n} c_j x_j$$

s.t.

$$\sum_{j=1}^{n} a_{ij} x_j \le b_i \quad i = 1, \dots, m \tag{I}$$
$$x_j \ge 0 \quad j = 1, \dots, n$$

$$\text{Min} \ \sum_{i=1}^{m} b_i y_i$$

s.t.

$$\sum_{i=1}^{m} a_{ij} y_i \ge c_j \quad j = 1, \dots, n \tag{II}$$
$$y_i \ge 0 \quad i = 1, \dots, m$$

The following PROTRAC E and F model was originally presented as Example 1 in Section 4.2.

Max $5{,}000E + 4{,}000F$

s.t.

$$
\begin{aligned}
-E - \ F &\le \ -5 \\
E - \ 3F &\le \ 0 \\
10E + 15F &\le \ 150 \\
20E + 10F &\le \ 160 \\
-30E - 10F &\le -135 \\
E, F &\ge \ 0
\end{aligned}
\tag{I}
$$

The dual of this problem is

Min $\ -5y_1 + 150y_3 + 160y_4 - 135y_5$

s.t.

$$
\begin{aligned}
-y_1 + \ y_2 + 10y_3 + 20y_4 - 30y_5 &\ge 5{,}000 \\
-y_1 - 3y_2 + 15y_3 + 10y_4 - 10y_5 &\ge 4{,}000 \\
y_i &\ge \ 0 \quad i = 1, \dots, 5
\end{aligned}
\tag{II}
$$

Note that the RHS of the fourth constraint in problem (I) (call it b_4) is the coefficient in the objective function of y_4 (call it $\bar{c}_4$) in problem (II).

Use this fact and the $V(b_4)$ function for the PROTRAC E and F model that is presented in Figure 8.4 to find the graph of the $V(\bar{c}_4)$ function for problem (II).

13 Suppose a point x^* is a current nondegenerate optimal corner solution to a max LP problem, with $x_j^* = 0$. Let the number I be the reduced cost of x_j. If c_j is increased to $c_j + I$ with all other data unchanged, then there is an alternative optimal corner solution, say $\bar{x}$, with $\bar{x}_j > 0$. Now suppose the original problem is modified by adding the constraint $x_j = \varepsilon$, where ε is any positive number $\leq \bar{x}_j$.

a Show that $\hat{x}$ is a solution to the modified problem, where

$$\hat{x} = \left(1 - \frac{\varepsilon}{\bar{x}_j}\right) x^* + \frac{\varepsilon}{\bar{x}_j} \bar{x}$$

b Show that the change in the OV $= \varepsilon I$.

14 Suppose the problem

$$\text{Max} \quad \sum_{j=1}^{n} c_j x_j$$

s.t.

$$\sum_{j=1}^{n} a_{ij} x_j = b_i \qquad i = 1, \ldots, m$$

$$x_j \geq 0, \text{all } j$$

(I)

is solved to obtain a nondegenerate solution x^*. Suppose $x_k^* = 0$. Let $R_k > 0$ be the corresponding reduced cost. Now solve the problem

$$\text{Max} \quad \sum_{j=1}^{n} c_j x_j$$

s.t.

$$\sum_{j=1}^{n} a_{ij} x_j = b_i \qquad i = 1, \ldots, m$$

$$x_k = F$$

$$x_j \geq 0, \text{all } j$$

(II)

Suppose $\hat{x}$ is a nondegenerate solution. Let D_k be the dual price on the computer printout for the constraint $x_k = F$. Suppose that F is small enough that the basis for (II) consists of adjoining x_k to the basis for (I). What is the relationship between R_k and D_k?

10 Nonlinearity, Computational Considerations, and Suboptimization

In this chapter, it is shown that the general nonlinear model can be interpreted with the geometric approach already introduced. Linear and nonlinear models are compared both conceptually and computationally. Unbounded and infeasible problems are discussed and constraint manipulation is again considered. In concluding, the topic of suboptimization and decentralized planning is given considerable attention.

10.1 An Overview of Chapters 4–9

By now, you have covered a great deal of material on linear optimization models. By working just with geometry and with computer output, you should have become somewhat of an expert. Your command of linear programming as a tool should be quite complete. You should be able to formulate the model, solve it on a computer, and understand the wealth of information available in the output. Of course, we have not gone into mathematical derivations and so there are undoubtedly loose ends to our discussion. But the mathematical route would require a substantial use of linear algebra, and this type of development amounts to more than a brief excursion. For the amount of time that is available, it seems to us that the geometric approach is preferable since it provides considerable insight and certainly demands less in the way of preparation.

But at this time it is appropriate for you to wonder about the context of what we have done. How does LP fit into the general picture?

The answers to this question are "very well" and "not at all well," for we have a tool that is at the same time quite general and highly specialized. Here is what this equivocation means. Linear programming has won a highly respected position in the applied world. It has demonstrated relevance and usefulness in numerous contexts. *To that extent,* what we've been doing has general utility. On the other hand, it must be clear that the LP model is very specialized. In order to use this model, the linear assumptions must be reasonable approximations to the situation of interest—otherwise, the model can be a gross distortion of the relevant interactions. Certainly there are many situations where the assumptions of linearity are wholly unwarranted and, this being the case, it would be equally correct to say that linear programming is quite specialized and does not fit very well into the general picture.

It is true that we have general theories for nonlinear models that include LP models as a special case. But these general theories are often very difficult to apply, and therein lies the crux, for the tools we have available for solving nonlinear models are effective only in quite specialized cases. Usually, because of computational considerations, the size of the model (as measured by the number of decision variables and the number of constraints) cannot be large. Also, in nonlinear models, it is desirable that the nonlinearities are not "too severe" (as measured, for example, by departures from concavity and convexity). Usually, it is also true that you must have access to a very large scientific computer library in order to obtain effective and up-to-date nonlinear programming codes. Therefore, in actual fact, we can solve many more kinds of linear problems than nonlinear problems, and in this sense also the LP model has general applicability.

Perhaps an accurate summary would be that linear programming is, in theory, a highly specialized body of mathematics that turns out, in practice, to be quite a useful tool. To put these ideas in solid perspective you should have a better understanding of more general models, at least in the conceptual and geometric sense. For this reason, we shall discuss the ways in which linear and nonlinear models differ and the ways in which they are similar.

10.2 Illustrating the General Nonlinear Model

The general (not necessarily linear) mathematical programming or constrained optimization model can be written as

---

Max $f(x_1, ..., x_n)$

s.t.

$g_i(x_1, ..., x_n) \leq b_i \qquad i = 1, ..., k$

$g_i(x_1, ..., x_n) = b_i \qquad i = k + 1, ..., m$

This is a problem in n variables and m constraints. The constraints may be either equalities or inequalities.

For the case of two decision variables ($n = 2$), this model can be geometrically illustrated using exactly the approach we took with LP problems. A model becomes nonlinear as soon as one of the constraint functions, or the objective function, or both, become nonlinear.

The first big difference between linear and nonlinear models is that constraint sets need no longer be polytopes (flat-sided figures), and even if they are this need not imply that an optimal solution will lie on a corner. Figure 10.1 illustrates the following nonlinear model:

Max $x - y$

s.t.

$-x^2 + y \geq 1$

$x + y \leq 3$

$-x + y \leq 2$

$x, y \geq 0$

Figure 10.1   *A nonlinear model*

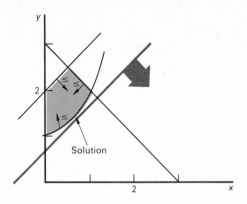

Figure 10.2   *A noncorner solution*

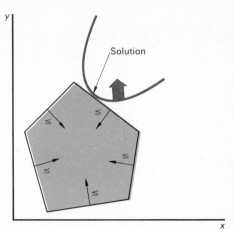

You can see in the figure that the nonlinear constraint puts curvature into the boundary of the constraint set. The feasible set is no longer a polytope, and the optimal solution does not lie on a corner. Figure 10.2 shows a *hypothetical* nonlinear constrained maximization model. The constraints are all linear, and hence the constraint set is a polytope. The objective function, however, is nonlinear and again it is seen that the solution does not occur at a corner. Of course, a solution *could* appear at a corner, but the important point is that this property is not guaranteed, as it is in the linear model.

This fact has significant algorithmic implications. It means that in the nonlinear case, we cannot use a "corner-searching" method like the simplex algorithm for finding a solution. This enormously complicates the solution procedure. Aside from this single devastating difference, many of the concepts are the same. For example:

Increasing (decreasing) the RHS on a ≤ (≥) constraint loosens the constraint. This cannot contract and may expand the constraint set.

Increasing (decreasing) the RHS on a ≥ (≤) constraint tightens the constraint. This cannot expand and may contract the constraint set.

Loosening a constraint cannot hurt and may help the optimal objective value.

Tightening a constraint cannot help and may hurt the optimal objective value.

Another similar concept is the right-hand-side OV(optimal value) *function* $V(b_i)$, discussed in Chapter 8. For nonlinear problems, this function has the same meaning as in the linear case. The rate of change of the values $V(b_i)$ at the currently specified value of b_i, say $\bar{b}_i$, is called, as in the linear case, the *dual price* of the ith constraint. Often in the nonlinear model the term *Lagrange multiplier* is used instead of *dual price*. In the nonlinear case,

Figure 10.3   *A hypothetical nonlinear maximization model*   **Figure 10.4**   *The OV function $V(b_1)$*

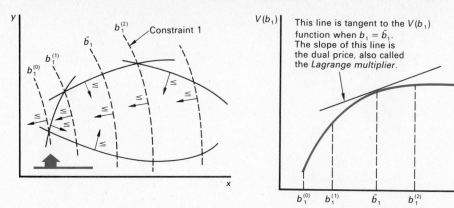

the graphs of the optimal value functions are not generally piecewise linear. They are thus much more difficult (in fact, usually impossible) to construct. The dual price (or Lagrange multiplier) corresponding to the RHS $\bar{b}_i$ is represented geometrically as the slope of the tangent to the graph of $V(b_i)$ at the point on the graph with coordinates $(\bar{b}_i, V(\bar{b}_i))$. Some nonlinear programming codes do print out dual prices along with the solution, but additional sensitivity analysis is generally not available. Consequently, the output is generally much easier to read and understand but of more limited use than LP output. Figures 10.3 and 10.4 depict a hypothetical nonlinear model and the associated OV function $V(b_1)$ and the geometric interpretation of the dual price.

This pair of figures illustrates several typical phenomena for nonlinear models. First of all, the graph of the OV function in Figure 10.4 consists of *curves*, rather than linear segments, that connect at "corners" (the points where b_1 takes the values $b_1^{(1)}$ and $b_1^{(2)}$ in this example). These "corners" are the values of b_1 for which there is a change in the constraints that are *active* at optimality.

It is also worth noting that in the nonlinear case, some of the sensitivity concepts from the linear model do not directly carry over. For example, suppose the right-hand-side parameter b_1 is assigned the value $\bar{b}_1$ and we obtain an optimal solution. The concept of allowable increase in b_1 might now be meaningfully interpreted as the amount b_1 can be increased before the set of active constraints changes. Thus, in Figure 10.4, the "allowable increase" would take b_1 from $\bar{b}_1$ up to $b_1^{(2)}$. Similarly, according to this interpretation the allowable decrease would be given by $\bar{b}_1 - b_1^{(1)}$. However, note that in contrast to the linear case, the dual price does not remain constant over this range. Just as in the linear case, however, the slope is not unambiguously defined at $b_1^{(0)}$, $b_1^{(1)}$, and $b_1^{(2)}$, and hence at these points the dual price makes sense only if a direction of change in b is specified.

Another important difference for the nonlinear case should be mentioned. It may no longer be true that loosening a constraint helps less and less, or that tightening hurts more and more. You can verify this by constructing the $V(b_1)$ function for the problem

Max x^2

s.t.

$x \leq 5$

$x \geq 0$

However, if the problem is a so-called concave or convex programming problem, then the tightening and loosening rules will continue to hold. These classes of problems (concave and convex programs) are defined in Section 10.5.2.

As a final note, we observe that for general nonlinear programs, since the objective function need not be linear, the $V(c)$ function, discussed in Chapter 9, is not generally defined. Of course, in special cases with a linear objective (nonlinear constraints), it may also be of interest.

10.3   Unbounded and Infeasible Problems

Recall the PROTRAC E and F model, but in this case suppose the third and fourth constraints (rows 4 and 5) had been inadvertently omitted from the model. Then, as shown in Figure 10.5, the constraint set would extend indefinitely to the northeast and it would be possible to slide the objective contour arbitrarily far in this direction. Since this is the uphill direction, the objective function would achieve arbitrarily large values on the constraint set. Such a problem is termed *unbounded*. A min model in which the objective function can be

Figure 10.5   *The PROTRAC E and F model with the third and fourth constraints missing*

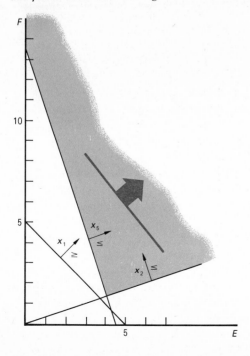

Figure 10.6   *An unbounded constraint set but a finite solution*

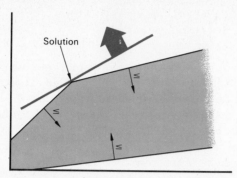

made arbitrarily small (large in magnitude and negative in sign) is also termed *unbounded*.

Unbounded problems, in applications, occur because either an important constraint has been left out of the model or some critically erroneous data have been supplied to the computer. In real life, no one has yet discovered an infinite profit or an infinite value for a decision variable. Thus, the relevant constraints will always assure that unbounded problems cannot occur.

Students often confuse the term *unbounded problem* with the concept "unbounded constraint set." An ***unbounded constraint set*** is a constraint set (feasible region) in which at least one decision variable can be made arbitrarily large in value. Figure 10.6 shows a model with an unbounded constraint set but with a finite optimal objective value. It turns out that if the problem is unbounded, the constraint set must also be unbounded, but the converse is not true.

It is clear that for an unbounded problem, there are no optimal values for the decision variables. Such a problem has *no solution*. More generally, a problem can fail to have a solution for three pathological reasons. The problem may be

1   Unbounded
2   Asymptotic
3   Infeasible

Asymptotic behavior is exhibited in Figure 10.7, where the problem is to maximize a function f of one variable, x, subject to the constraint $x \geq a$. The numerical values of f on the constraint set increase arbitrarily close to the value c but never equal c. Asymptotic behavior is considered bizarre. As indicated in Figure 10.7, this phenomenon appears to require an unbounded constraint set, and indeed under normal conditions this is the case. Thus, asymptotic behavior does not occur in properly formulated real models. In Figure 10.7, for example, an additional constraint such as $x \leq b$ would transform the problem into one with a solution, in this case at the value $x = b$.

The third possible pathology is called *infeasibility*. This has been previously

Figure 10.7 *Asymptotic behavior*

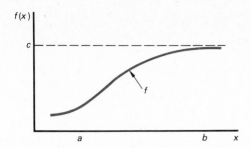

discussed in Chapter 8. Alternatively, an infeasible problem might be called *inconsistent.* This means the constraint set is empty; that is, there is no point satisfying *all* the constraints. Any problem is either *feasible* or *infeasible.* A *feasible* problem could possibly be unbounded or asymptotic. An infeasible problem cannot be either unbounded or asymptotic.

Infeasibility depends solely on the constraints and has nothing to do with the objective function. In real problems, infeasibility always means that the model has been incorrectly specified. Either too many constraints or wrong constraints have been included, or perhaps the model formulator has been too demanding in his assignment of values to parameters. For example, you can verify in the PROTRAC E and F problem shown in Figure 10.8 that if the first constraint were erroneously entered as

$$E + F \le 5$$

instead of

$$E + F \ge 5$$

Figure 10.8 *PROTRAC E and F is now infeasible*

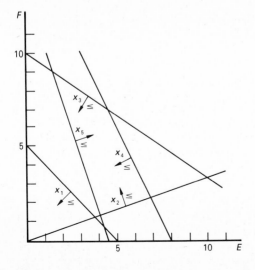

then the problem would be infeasible. The problem would also be infeasible if the constraint were entered as

$E + F \geq 12$

In LP models, asymptotic behavior cannot occur. (You can see that curvature in the objective function is needed.) Consequently, every linear program is in one of the following states:

---

1 There is a solution; that is, the problem is solvable.
2 There is no solution because the problem is unbounded.
3 There is no solution because the problem is infeasible.

The simplex algorithm considerately informs the user as to which state the problem is in. That is, if there is a solution, a corner solution is presented. If there is no solution, the output will indicate the cause, namely, whether the problem is unbounded or infeasible. If there is no solution, the logic of the model should be checked. If the logic underlying the construction is correct, then there must be an error in the input data. For example, an inequality may have been entered in the wrong direction or a parameter value may be entered incorrectly.

Students sometimes wonder why constraints are never formulated as < or >. We have always insisted that the inequalities be ≤ or ≥. The reason for this is to assure that a well-formulated problem will have a solution. The importance of allowing the possibility of equality (< and > conditions prohibit equality) is easily demonstrated for a function of one variable. Compare the two problems:

Max $f(x)$

s.t.
                              (I)
$x \leq 10$

$x \geq 0$

Max $f(x)$

s.t.
                              (II)
$x < 10$

$x \geq 0$

Figures 10.9 and 10.10 illustrate these two problems for a linear function f. In Figure 10.9, with the ≤ constraint there is a solution at $x = 10$. In Figure 10.10, with the < constraint there is no solution, for the values $f(x)$ increase but there is no maximum value. The problem here is that the value $x = 10$ is not feasible (it does not satisfy the constraint $x < 10$), and as you may know there happens to be no number "just to the left" of the number 10.

In summary, then, suffice it to say that we formulate problems with ≤ or ≥ inequalities because of the mathematical fact that under reasonable assumptions such a problem will have a solution.

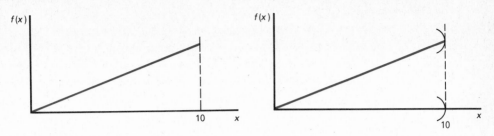

Figure 10.9 *x ≤ 10, with solution x* = 10*   **Figure 10.10** *x < 10, with no solution*

10.4 Adding Constraints and Perturbing the Right-Hand Side

Suppose you have an optimal solution to some problem of interest. Let us call this the *current* solution. You have already seen that the effect of changing the right-hand side of an *inequality* can be analyzed by determining whether the change tightens or loosens the constraint. This is true whether or not the problem is linear. If the constraint under consideration is *inactive*, then in the linear case, and in reasonable nonlinear cases (cases that obey reasonable mathematical assumptions), small changes in the right-hand side will have no effect on the solution. If the constraint is *active*, then small changes in the right-hand side will usually change both the solution and the optimal objective value. The term *usually* is employed because even in the linear case there are some exceptional situations (see Chapter 6, problems 11 and 12). When perturbing the right-hand side of an active *inequality* constraint does lead to a change in the objective value, we know with certainty the direction of the change. This knowledge is a simple consequence of whether the constraint in question is being tightened or loosened and, in turn, whether the constraint set is being expanded or contracted.

The analysis for adding a constraint to the problem is quite analogous. If the current solution satisfies the new constraint, then it is still an optimal solution, even with the new constraint. This is illustrated in Figure 10.11.

If, however, the current solution violates the new constraint (the new constraint "cuts off" the current solution), then the solution will obviously change and the objective value will usually also change. Clearly, such a change will not help and usually hurts. Formerly attractive alternatives may be eliminated by adding a new constraint. This is illustrated in Figure 10.12.

Deleting a constraint can be similarly analyzed. For example, if the deleted constraint was active, the solution will usually change along with the objective value. In this case, the deletion will usually help.

By now, you should have the facility to analyze specific cases geometrically in order to determine exactly what can and cannot happen. To test this ability, you should justify or illustrate the following points which are valid for general models:

1 Adding a new constraint or tightening an existing constraint may make a feasible problem infeasible. It can never make an infeasible problem feasible.

Figure 10.11   *Adding a constraint*   **Figure 10.12**   *Adding a constraint*

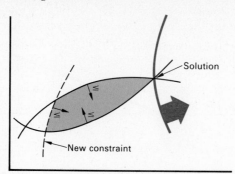
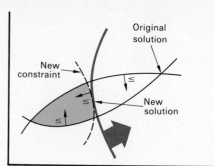

2 Adding a new constraint or tightening an existing constraint may make an unbounded problem solvable. It can never make a solvable problem unbounded.

3 Deleting or loosening a constraint may make an infeasible problem feasible. It can never make a feasible problem infeasible.

4 Deleting or loosening a constraint may make a solvable problem unbounded. It can never make an unbounded problem solvable.

We note that in the linear case it is a consequence of duality theory that loosening a constraint (or changing the RHS of an equality constraint) can never make a solvable problem unbounded (see Example 3, Chapter 7).

The fact that loosening a constraint in a nonlinear problem can cause a solvable problem to become unbounded is illustrated in Figure 10.13. This figure shows an optimization problem in a single variable. The problem is

Max $f(x)$

s.t.

$g(x) \leq \bar{b}$

and the solution is at x^*. However, if $\bar{b}$ is replaced by *any* larger value, say

Figure 10.13   *Loosening a constraint can make a problem unbounded*

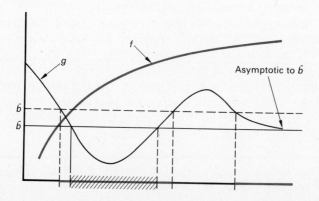

$\bar{b}$, the constraint set becomes unbounded because the values of g are asymptotic to $\bar{b}$, and the objective value becomes infinitely large.

The above remarks about tightening and loosening refer, of course, to *inequality* constraints. In the case of an equality constraint, almost anything can happen. Changing the right-hand side may make a feasible problem infeasible, or it may make an infeasible problem feasible. In the nonlinear case, it may make a solvable problem unbounded, or it may make an unbounded problem solvable. You should be able to illustrate these phenomena with pictures similar to Figure 10.13, that is, with hypothetical examples with one decision variable.

10.5 Problem Complexity and Computational Considerations

10.5.1 *Linear Programs and the Simplex Method*

As mentioned earlier in the text, LP problems are solved by computers with an algorithm known as the simplex method. The mathematics of the simplex algorithm was summarized in Chapter 7. Since in this section we are concerned with computational considerations, it seems fitting to present a brief review of the simplex algorithm. The method contains two main parts that are described below. The algorithm is also illustrated in Figure 10.14 for the PROTRAC E and F model, and you may wish to follow the steps on this diagram.

First, an initial corner of the constraint set (this is called a *basic feasible solution*) is located. Various procedures are used to locate this corner depending on the form of the problem, and it is impossible to say in general what corner will be chosen. All we can say is that if the problem is feasible, then some initial corner will be determined. Otherwise, if the problem is infeasible, a signal to that effect is produced.

Starting with the initial corner, the algorithm moves along an *edge* of the constraint set (never "through" the set) to an *adjacent* corner at which

Figure 10.14   *The simplex algorithm*

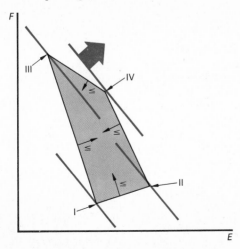

1 Find an initial corner, say I.
2 Move to an adjacent corner with a larger value for the objective function. Could be II or III; suppose II.
3 Move to adjacent corner IV with a larger value for the objective function.
4 Corner IV is optimal solution because no adjacent corner has a larger objective value.

the value of the objective function is improved. Continuing in this way, the algorithm moves from corner to corner, always improving the value of the objective function, until it reaches a corner for which no adjacent corner yields a better value for the objective function. This is the optimum. At any given corner in a space of three or more dimensions, there will often be more than one adjacent corner at which the objective is improved. The one the algorithm selects is mainly a computer-coding convention.

The algorithm is complete in the sense of "covering all possibilities." If the problem is infeasible, the algorithm will detect this fact and so inform the user. If the problem is unbounded, a signal to that effect is produced. If the problem has at least one solution, then the simplex algorithm will find a solution without fail.

Each step or move from one corner to another is called a *pivot* or an *iteration.* It is performed by mathematically manipulating a system of linear equations, as discussed in Chapter 7. The difficulty encountered in solving a linear program will depend upon the number of iterations required, because the larger the number of iterations, the more computing time required. It should be clear from the geometry that the number of corners in an LP constraint set depends more directly on the number of constraints than on the number of variables. Thus the "complexity" or "size" of a linear program is usually measured by the number of constraints. More constraints, in general, imply more corners. More corners, in turn, usually imply more iterations, and more iterations imply more computing time.

A practical rule of thumb based on years of experience with a variety of models is that the number of iterations is between m and $3m$, where m is the number of constraints. On latest-generation computers, with up-to-date software, problems with 1,000–2,000 constraints can typically be solved with little difficulty (in a matter of minutes). General problems with 4,000–5,000 constraints are near the limit of the state of the art and may require many hours to solve. However, even larger problems with special structure, such as the network models discussed in Chapter 14, can be successfully handled.

An LP problem that is "too large" presents two obstacles to the person hoping to solve the problem. First, a great deal of computer time may be consumed in executing the iterations. The solution process thus becomes long and expensive. In a situation where the model has to be solved on a regular basis, such costs can be prohibitive. The second difficulty with large problems and lengthy computing is that so-called round-off errors accumulate in the machine. After a large number of iterations, the computer is no longer solving the original problem. It is looking at a distortion of that problem. This has undesirable numerical consequences that could lead to a significant increase in computation time. It turns out that very large problems do appear in applications, and much of the current research in management science is devoted to extending the capabilities for solving very large problems with special structures. It is generally true that, the more specialized the mathematical form of the model, the more possible it is to develop more efficient algorithms for solving the model.

It is notable that at the time the simplex algorithm was originally developed in the early 1950s, there was little hope that it would be as computationally efficient as it has turned out to be in practice. The best formal theoretic estimates for the number of corners of a constraint set for a linear program were frighteningly high (much higher than $3m$), and as a result it was felt that, "on the average," convergence would be slow. Only after considerable computing experience did it become clear that the typical efficiency is much better than that indicated by theory. There is still not much solid theoretical justification for the m-to-$3m$ rule and for this surprising efficiency of the method in practice.

10.5.2 *Nonlinear Programs*

A detailed analysis of the procedures for solving nonlinear programs is beyond the scope of this book in terms of the mathematical prerequisites such a development would demand, and it is inconsistent with our stated purposes. However, even without learning details of specific algorithms, it is possible and useful to have a broad understanding of the current state of the art in this area, and this section is devoted to presenting such an overview.

Nonlinear models are divided into two classes: (1) those that can be solved, and (2) those that one can try to solve. The models that can be solved must typically conform to certain qualifications of structure and size. The hierarchy of increasing computational difficulty is shown in Figure 10.15. It is assumed in this figure and in the ensuing discussion that all variables in the problem are continuous. In Chapter 14, we consider the computational difficulties and other nuances associated with problems in which all or some of the variables are required to take on integer values.

In Figure 10.15, the increasing roman numerals reflect increasing computational difficulty. In terms of applications, the increasing roman numerals reflect *decreasing* importance. In the programming field, it appears as though "computability" has been the stimulus for demand in the marketplace. We now consider the several classes of nonlinear programs in somewhat more detail.

Figure 10.15 *Increasing computational difficulty*

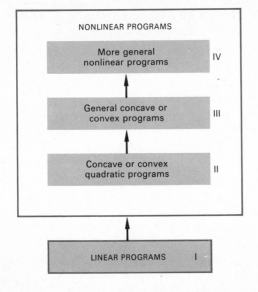

Nonlinear Programs that can be Solved   These problems are called *concave* or *convex programs.* In order to describe what this means, it is necessary to introduce a new technical term, a *convex set of points.* Loosely speaking, this is a set of points without any "holes." More formally, a convex set is any set that has the following property:

Consider the straight-line segment joining any two points in the set. That line segment must lie entirely within the set.

Figure 10.16 shows two-dimensional sets of points that do not satisfy this property and hence are *not* convex sets, along with sets that are convex. The polygon in the second of these two figures may remind you of the constraint sets that occur in LP problems. This is appropriate since any constraint set for a linear program is a convex set. The nonlinear programs that we can be reasonably sure of solving must also have convex constraint sets.

The next question to be asked then is, What kinds of nonlinear programs have convex constraint sets? It is useful to be able to use the notion of concave and convex functions in answering this question. If the function has two variables, a *concave function* is shaped like an umbrella. The shape of such a function reflects diminishing marginal returns. Any line connecting two points on the graph of the function has the property that it lies under the graph. Similarly, if the function has two variables, a *convex function* is shaped like an upside-down umbrella. The shape of such a function reflects increasing marginal returns. Any line connecting two points on the graph of the function lies above the graph. The same ideas hold for functions that have a single variable, or more than two variables. For example, the OV function for any constraint in a maximization LP problem is concave, and the OV function for any constraint in a minimization LP problem is convex. It should also be noted that a linear function is considered to be both concave and convex.

Now suppose we have a nonlinear program with only inequality constraints. If the constraint function associated with each ≤ constraint is convex and the constraint function associated with each ≥ constraint is concave, then the constraint set will be a convex set.

Figure 10.16   *Convex and nonconvex sets of points*

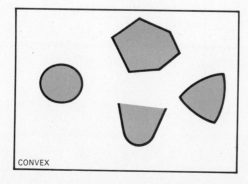

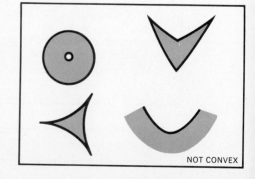

Figure 10.17   *The constraint sets $g(x) \leq 2$ and $g(x) \geq 2$*

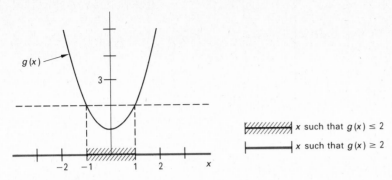

These facts are illustrated in Figure 10.17, which shows a convex function g of a single variable, given by

$$g(x) = x^2 + 1$$

You can see that the set of x values for which

$$g(x) \leq 2$$

is convex, while the set of x values for which

$$g(x) \geq 2$$

is not convex. Since the negative of a convex function is concave, and vice versa, and since the constraint

$$g(x) \leq 2$$

is the same as the constraint

$$-g(x) \geq -2$$

you can see why the convexity rule requires that the sense of the inequality is $\leq$ for convex functions and $\geq$ for concave functions. In the case of problems involving one or more *nonlinear equality* constraints, there is great difficulty in characterizing whether or not the constraint set is convex. Consequently, this issue will not be explored.

Now that you understand the meaning of a convex set, it is easy, at least formally, to define a concave or convex program:

A concave program is a max model with a concave objective function and a convex constraint set.

A convex program is a min model with a convex objective function and a convex constraint set.

The rationale for the above characterization has to do with the fact that in the maximization context, concave objective functions are very convenient to work with in terms of the mathematical properties associated with the umbrella shape. Convex objective functions are convenient in the minimization context. Finally, the convexity of the constraint set endows the problem with other attractive mathematical properties that can be exploited both theoretically and computationally.

Unfortunately, there is no simple way to motivate an understanding of these facts. If, however, you have a background in introductory calculus, the results are easy to remember. Recall that for problems without constraints, it is convenient to use the rules of calculus to find a maximum for a concave function. The key result is that for a concave function, any point at which the derivative is zero (that is, the tangent is horizontal) is a point that maximizes the function (for example, the point x^* in Figure 10.18).

Similarly, for unconstrained problems it is convenient to use the rules of calculus to find the minimum of a convex function. Thus, we see a certain degree of consistency in the fact that, for both constrained and unconstrained problems, finding a maximum is convenient with a concave function and finding a minimum is convenient with a convex function.

Let us now turn to computational considerations. Figure 10.15 indicates that the easiest type of nonlinear program is a concave or convex quadratic program. These problems, by definition, have linear constraints. The objective function is quadratic and concave if it is a max model and quadratic and convex if it is a min model. It turns out that a variation of the simplex method can be used to solve such problems, and in practice this is reasonably efficient. It is not uncommon to solve quadratic programs with hundreds of constraints and several thousand variables. Financial models such as those used in portfolio analysis are often quadratic programs, and so this class of models is of considerable applied importance.

In Figure 10.15, the next level of difficulty involves the general (nonquadratic) concave or convex program. There are numerous mathematical approaches and corresponding algorithms for solving such problems. For example, suppose the problem to be solved is a max model. One typical approach proceeds as follows:

---

1 Find an initial feasible point "inside" the constraint set (not on the edge).
2 Move in an uphill direction until hitting some edge of the constraint set.
3 Modify the direction of motion so as to continue uphill while remaining in the feasible region.

Figure 10.18 *The maximum of a concave function*

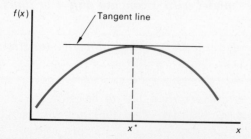

In this type of algorithm, as well as most others that apply to nonlinear programs that are not quadratic, there is considerable use of advanced calculus, and hence it is not possible in this development to get into much detail. Suffice it to say that for general concave or convex programs, as opposed to linear programs, the number of variables seems to be more significant than the number of constraints as an indicator of problem difficulty. Without making use of additional special structure, it would be fairly unusual to solve a general concave or convex program with more than 100 variables.

Nonlinear Programs that We Try to Solve   Finally, we consider problems in the next and highest level of difficulty. These problems are often called *highly nonlinear*, which usually means that the convexity and concavity properties discussed above are absent. To attack such problems, it is common practice to use the same algorithm one would use for general concave and convex programs. The results are different, however. When it is applied to concave and convex problems, the algorithm terminates with a solution to the problem. For general nonlinear programs (not concave or convex), the algorithm may terminate at feasible points that are *not* solutions. This is illustrated for a problem in one variable in Figure 10.19. The objective function f, which is to be maximized, is neither concave nor convex. The solution to the problem is given by x^*, but the algorithm may terminate at any of the points x_1, x_2, x_3, or x^*, and, in general, the analyst has no way to determine which of these cases he has actually obtained. To date, no one has been smart enough to invent algorithms that overcome this possibility.

Thus, it appears that our capabilities in this realm are woefully inadequate, and you may well wonder, Since we seem to have no assurance that what we're getting is really a solution, why do we even attempt to solve these general highly nonlinear problems? The answer and justification is surprisingly unpedantic and empirical. The firm may be currently employing the policy designated as C in Figure 10.19, with an associated profit of P. If our algorithm can produce a *better* solution, whether it be x_1, x_3, or x^*, then the use of the algorithm is justified. This is consistent with the overall theme that in practice there is nothing so pure as a truly optimal solution. The goal in quantitative modeling is always to assist in the search for *better* decisions.

In concluding this section, let us address one additional practical aspect.

Figure 10.19   *A nonconcave constrained max problem*

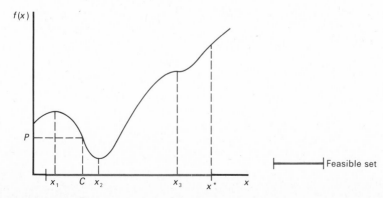

How can we tell whether a nonlinear program in many variables is concave, convex, or neither? In other words, how do we know whether the objective function and the constraints have the right mathematical form? There are several answers to this question:

1 Sometimes, there are mathematical tests that can be applied to the problem functions in order to determine whether they are concave, convex, or neither.

2 Sometimes, economic intuition is used to assert that such and such a phenomenon reflects diminishing marginal returns or increasing marginal costs, and hence the associated function is concave or convex.

3 In many real problems nothing is done to address the question. One simply attempts to solve the problem and then inquires as to the practical usefulness of the terminal point (the purported "solution" produced by the algorithm). For a problem that is thought or known to be nonconvex or nonconcave, one frequently restarts the algorithm from a different initial point with the hope of producing a better terminal point. Nonlinear optimization theory can be as much an art as a science.

10.6 Suboptimization and Decentralized Planning

The topic of *suboptimization* has intrigued management theorists for a long time, perhaps because it has considerable importance in applied work. *Suboptimization* is a term often used and often confused, both in support of, and in opposition to, the work of quantitative modelers. In either case, the topic is worthy of consideration.

Suboptimization is the process of optimizing a subcomponent or subproblem of an overall system.

In Chapter 3, we described the flow of constraints as an inherent aspect of organizational structure. Constraints naturally arise in the delegation of limited responsibility. In part, suboptimization is a natural consequence of this phenomenon. But there are at least two potential dangers that should be explicitly recognized.

1 Some of the quantities that are taken as given in a suboptimization model might be more appropriately treated as decision variables in a larger, more comprehensive model.

2 Suboptimization models frequently ignore linkages with other components of the overall system.

In real-world applications, the formal models that tend to be developed and used are generally of the suboptimization variety, as opposed to models that are concerned with overall system optimization. Because of such factors as limited time, limited data, computational difficulties, or any other constraints on the modeler, it may simply be the case that suboptimization is the best way to attack a given problem.

It might be noted that the critics of formal models will sometimes argue that no model at all is better than a model that only suboptimizes. Such criticism is based on the incorrect assumption that the primary purpose of a model is to provide the complete solution to a given problem. As we have repeatedly stated, a model is only one component of the decision-making process. Of course, it may be true that a suboptimizing model ignores too much, and that it is misleading and perhaps can be improved by including more of the total system. But, as stated above, there may be valid reasons for suboptimizing, and in numerous instances such models can play a useful role in the overall decision process.

10.6.1   Suboptimization in Practice

Some of the aspects of suboptimization may be more clearly illustrated by exploring examples in the following specific contexts: (1) scheduling given requirements; (2) decentralized profit maximization; (3) decentralized purchasing; (4) inventory policies that are not coordinated with financial planning.

Scheduling Given Requirements   Production planning problems often require consideration of two issues: (1) *how much* to produce, and (2) *when* to produce. Although, in practice, these issues are often considered separately in a two-step process, they are intimately related; separate consideration, at least ideally, is inappropriate. In many instances, detailed production operations (for example, assigning a particular job to a particular machine) are scheduled on a daily or perhaps weekly basis. A number of costs in the plant clearly depend on the particular schedule that is selected. Examples of such costs include in-process inventory costs, down-time due to setups, and materials handling costs. On the other hand, overall production decisions are typically made on a monthly, quarterly, or even yearly basis. Because of the aggregated nature of such a decision, the detailed scheduling costs are typically either ignored in the decision-making process or averaged in some way. The quantities to be produced are then passed down to the scheduler. He takes these quantities as given and proceeds to schedule this level of production in such a way as to minimize costs. This is an example of suboptimization, and it also illustrates the first danger listed in Section 10.6. To the extent that schedule-dependent costs are important (in the sense that different schedules lead to significantly different costs), the scheduling should, at least in theory, be built into an overall, comprehensive production planning model. This implies that the latter model must be disaggregated to the daily or weekly level, depending on the scheduling time frame. The solution to the overall model then provides the solution to the scheduling problem and also determines the appropriate production quantities. Unfortunately, for anything except the most automated processes, such as oil refineries, such a comprehensive model would typically have to contain too many contingencies and variables. It is probably true that in reality, for practical reasons, overall production decisions are made without much regard for scheduling considerations and indeed without even a formal aggregated model. The model is often implicit and intuitive, based mainly on previous experience. The major decisions are made, and *then* a formal optimization model would be used to obtain the optimal schedule. In such a scenario, it is well worth pondering the meaning of an "optimal" schedule.

Decentralized Profit Maximization

Consider a case where two of the PROTRAC plants produce P-9 tractors and where, because of the evaluation scheme employed by corporate management, each plant manager adopts a profit-maximization objective. For simplicity, assume that the marketing department has estimated that the demand for P-9s in the approaching sales period will be 1,100 units and that these two plants are the only sources of P-9s. They then must share the market of 1,100 units. Before each plant manager can decide how much to produce, he must attempt to guess what the other will do. (Neither can really tell the other what he will do until he himself knows what the other will do.) Moreover, each plant manager may even resort to competition with the other in terms of price cutting, and so on. In this example, where each plant attempts a decentralized optimization, we have a clear case of the second danger listed in Section 10.6, for each plant manager is excluding from his model the profit linkage with the other plant. It is clear that the effect of this is to diminish overall PROTRAC profits. The suboptimization is not working very well.

Given these assumptions, it would be more appropriate for the operation of the two plants to be combined in a single model. But who must take the responsibility for developing such a model? Will the plant managers? Probably not, because the optimal policy given by the model will inevitably make one plant look more profitable than the other, at least as measured by total plant profits, and the compromised plant manager will quickly lose enthusiasm for such a policy. Consequently, the responsibility for centralized optimization modeling must be at the top. The solution of a centralized model at the top then produces requirements that are sent down to the individual plants. If the centralized model at the top is a credible optimization model with decision variables that are disaggregated according to plant, then not only requirements are sent down to the plants, but many operating decisions on producing these requirements can also be passed down, since these would also have been determined by the model.[1] What is more likely, however, is that the decisions that are passed down are determined not from a disaggregated optimization model but from qualitative or, at best, semiquantitative reasoning, from past experience, and from good executive judgment. In this case, after the requirements are passed down, it is likely that the goal of each plant manager would be to produce these requirements on a cost-minimization basis, and hence their competition is transferred from profit max to cost min. If the requirements passed down are not optimal (in the sense of what would be dictated by a disaggregated centralized optimization model), then each plant's cost-min model produces results that are less than optimal by the overall criterion. However, given the requirements, the suboptimization model gives a policy that is the best the plant can do. The more judicious the requirements passed down, the closer the suboptimization comes to overall optimality. If, by chance, the requirements passed down were actually optimal, then the cost-min model would also produce an optimal policy. This assertion is subject to mild assumptions and will be illustrated in problem 14 at the end of this chapter.

1　In a related context, see the discussion in Section 7.6 on the use of dual prices in decentralized decision making.

It should be noted that the above type of centralized planning would naturally lead to centralized marketing as well. That is, since requirements on production are passed down to the plant, it would seem unlikely that the plants should have the responsibility for independently marketing the requirements. One reason for this is that marketing considerations and potentials were probably a part of the overall centralized model that produced the requirements sent down to the plants. Hence, the marketing strategy and the requirements are probably linked in the model, and this linkage should be preserved.

As a final point on this illustration, we note one way in which decentralized production and marketing might be a reasonable practice in the sense that suboptimization might produce results about as close to optimal (in an overall sense) as one could hope for. Suppose it is known from experience that various plants by and large tend to operate in separate marketing districts. Then one might exclusively assign districts to plants with no overlap, so that the potential sales of one plant are decoupled from the potential sales of the other. In reality, this sort of practice occurs not only with plants in a private firm, but also with members of a cartel in a given industry.

The previous discussion illustrates why a more comprehensive centralized model is preferable, from a certain point of view. Except in the case of totally separate plants, decentralization implies suboptimization, and consequently, decentralized decision making emerges as an evil forced on management by the complexity of the problems. If this is true, one must wonder why one of the most successful detergent manufacturers chooses an almost completely decentralized organization in which its various brands of detergents compete against each other as vigorously as against brands produced by other firms. From a modeling point of view, the answer seems to be that they choose a different comprehensive model. They do not assume that the market is a pie of fixed size to be divided among their plants but, rather, that by making the individual managers responsible for marketing and production, they will get more aggressive and innovative behavior from their employees. Hopefully, this will lead to an expanded market for their products and improved production performance so that, overall, the firm will be better off.

It is clear then that questions of organizational design and suboptimization are complicated. Basic assumptions about how individuals perform in organizations and how an organization fits into society strongly affect one's views on this subject. The variety of organizational designs to be found in practice, and even the difference in government policies toward cartels and antitrust legislation, indicates that there is far-from-uniform agreement in specific cases.

The remaining examples provide other specific instances of situations in which the question of suboptimization arises.

Decentralized Purchasing   The following example of decentralized purchasing again illustrates the danger of ignoring linkages. A particular raw material is used in all the European plants of a multinational manufacturer. The total usage is 2,200 tons per year. With decentralized purchasing, the overall need of 2,200 tons was supplied by nine suppliers at an average price of $6,400 per ton. A new centralized purchasing program based on a coordinated planning model was introduced. Common specifications were determined for all plants, and suppliers were forced to submit bids for a major part of the total need. Only five of the nine original sources were large enough even to be considered as potential companywide suppliers. After the bids were in, it turned out that the overall need of 2,200 tons could be supplied by three suppliers at an average price of $4,800 per ton. Concomitant advantages included the facts that supplier reliability and service increased and purchasing administration costs within the firm declined.

Thus, it is seen that the possibility of lower per-unit prices for raw materials purchased in bulk provides arguments against suboptimization of individual plants. In other cases, however, individual firms are able to provide glowing examples of success due to individual plant initiative, or dismal examples of failure due to the constraints imposed by corporate headquarters. These scenarios are, of course, supportive arguments for suboptimization.

Inventory Policies   As a final example of a suboptimization ignoring a linkage, we note that most "optimal" inventory policies have been determined without considering the overall financial-planning policy of the firm. Since holding inventories is equivalent to holding capital, it could be that the policy of the inventory control department is inconsistent with the financial policies of the comptroller's department.

The above examples are intended to provide a brief insight into the difficult question of suboptimization and how it relates to organizational design and the sequence in which decisions are made. The next section considers a specific idealized decision process to illustrate more formally the concept of suboptimization.

10.6.2 Suboptimization in Concept

Let us consider three levels in the PROTRAC hierarchy: The president, the vice-president in charge of production, and the Moline plant manager. Each of these employees faces his own problem.

The President's Problem   The board of directors has given the president a budget of B dollars to allocate to each of the following activities: production, marketing, research, and investment in new plant and equipment. The president's problem is to make a decision on how much of his budget to allocate to each activity.

The Vice-president's Problem   Once the president makes his decision, the vice-president will have a production budget to control. For simplicity, assume there are only two plants under his control. Then the vice-president's problem is to decide how much of his budget to allocate to each plant.

The Plant Manager's Problem   As soon as the vice-president makes his decision, the plant manager will have an operating budget to control. For simplicity, assume that his problem reduces to deciding how much of each of two products to produce.

The process of suboptimization could be described by the following sequence of events:

EVENT 1

The president makes his decision (based on judgment, advice, intuition, or divine guidance). He allocates B_p dollars to the vice-president.

EVENT 2

Given his budget of B_p dollars, the vice-president makes his decision (based on judgment, advice, and so on). He allocates b_1 dollars to plant 1 and b_2 dollars to plant 2.

EVENT 3

Given his allocation of b_i dollars, the manager of plant i determines his optimal production plan by solving the following model, where i is fixed at either $i = 1$ or $i = 2$:

Max $R_i(E_i, F_i)$

s.t.

$$\sum_{k=1}^{K} C_k [I_k^i (E_i, F_i)] \leq b_i$$

$$E_i, F_i \geq 0$$

where

E_i = quantity of product 1 produced in plant i

F_i = quantity of product 2 produced in plant i

$R_i(E_i, F_i)$ = revenue obtained from the production plan (E_i, F_i) in plant i

$I_k^i(E_i, F_i)$ = quantity of input k consumed in plant i by the production plan (E_i, F_i), where there are K inputs; that is, $k = 1, ..., K$

$C_k(I_k^i)$ = cost of consuming the quantity I_k^i of input k

Thus, the manager of each plant faces a similar problem. Given his value of b_i, either plant manager is doing the best he can do by using the above model. However, in terms of the overall potential of the system, it is clear that the production decisions, say $(\hat{E}_i, \hat{F}_i)$, produced by that model can only be termed *suboptimal*.

Let us now illustrate a different conceptual approach—one that will determine optimal values for E_i and F_i in the overall context. The question we are facing is the following: Given that the president allocates B_p dollars to total production, how much of each product should be made in each plant? Whether or not the value B_p is the "best" allocation to total production is, in this context, a "meta-question" that we are not considering. We take B_p as given and seek the implied overall optimal values (E_i^*, F_i^*) for each plant i.

Conceptually, the answer is obtained as follows. The vice-president solves the following comprehensive model, where the decision variables include b_1 and b_2 as well as E_1, F_1, E_2, F_2.

Max　$R_1(E_1, F_1) + R_2(E_2, F_2)$

s.t.

$$\sum_{k=1}^{K} C_k [I_k^1(E_1, F_1)] \leq b_1$$

$$\sum_{k=1}^{K} C_k [I_k^2(E_2, F_2)] \leq b_2$$

$b_1 + b_2 \qquad\qquad = B_p$

E_i, F_i, b_i nonnegative　　$i = 1, 2$

In this model, the optimal values of b_1 and b_2, say b_1^* and b_2^*, are determined, as well as the optimal production levels (E_i^*, F_i^*) for each plant. Thus, the overall optimization model solves the problem of the vice-president, as well as the problem of each plant manager. If, in event 2 above, the vice-president had correctly divined the optimal values b_1^* and b_2^* for his allocations, then the suboptimization model solved in event 3 would, in fact, also have produced the overall optimal values (E_i^*, F_i^*).

The discussion in this section provides a conceptual view of the distinction between optimization and suboptimization. Whether or not a policy is "suboptimal" depends upon (1) the frame of reference and (2) the *level* at which optimization occurs within that frame of reference. Thus, there is a notion of relativity implicit in the term *suboptimization*. The solution to the plant manager's model provides production levels that are optimal within his own frame of reference (given the value of b_i) but only suboptimal within the scope of the vice-president's frame of reference. The "given the value of B_p" solution to the vice-president's problem provides production levels that are optimal within his own frame of reference; that is, they are optimal for his problem and for all "lower-level" problems in the hierarchy. But it could be true that this solution is only suboptimal within an even larger context, that of the president.

10.7　Summary of Key Concepts

For any constrained optimization model, linear or nonlinear, you cannot reduce and may increase the set of feasible alternatives if you do either or both of the following:
1 Loosen a constraint, which means increasing (decreasing) the RHS on a $\leq$ ($\geq$) constraint.
2 Remove a constraint.
This cannot hurt and may help the optimal objective value. **(Section 10.1)**

For any constrained optimization model, linear or nonlinear, you cannot increase and may reduce the set of feasible alternatives if you do either or both of the following:
1 Tighten a constraint, which means decreasing (increasing) the RHS on a $\leq$ ($\geq$) constraint.
2 Add a constraint.
This cannot help and may hurt the optimal objective value. **(Section 10.1)**

For a nonlinear programming problem, in contrast to an LP problem, it may not be true that loosening a constraint helps less and less or that tightening hurts more and more. It is true for concave and convex programs. (Section 10.2)

Infeasibility depends solely on the constraints and has nothing to do with the objective function. (Section 10.3)

Suboptimization is the process of optimizing a subcomponent or subproblem of an overall system. (Section 10.6)

Suboptimization models frequently ignore linkages with other components of the overall system. (Section 10.6)

Quantities that are taken as given in a suboptimization model often can be interpreted as decision variables in a larger, more comprehensive model. (Section 10.6)

Decentralized decision making often involves suboptimization modeling. (Section 10.6.1)

10.8 Problems

1 The shaded region in Figure 10.20 represents feasible values of E and F in one of the PROTRAC plants.

 a Plot two contours of the function $R(E, F) = 3E + 3F$. Show which contour has higher value.

 b Show the rough shape of two contours of the function $R(E, F) = EF$. Show which contour has higher value.

 c In your diagram, label by A, B, and so on, a feasible point described by each of the following statements:

 (1) A point maximizing $3E + 3F$.

 (2) A point minimizing $3E + 3F$.

 (3) A point maximizing EF.

 (4) A point minimizing $-13E$.

Problems 2 through 5 refer to the following scenario. An auto agency feels that sales revenue is a function of advertising expenditures (x) and promotional expenditures (y). In particular, it is felt that the revenue function, $f(x, y)$, takes the following form:

$$f(x, y) = 4x^2 + 3xy + 2y^2$$

Figure 10.20

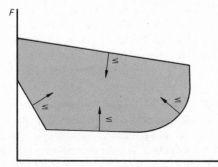

In deciding on a plan for expenditures, the agency does not want to move too far from the current plan ($x_o = 2$, $y_0 = 2$). Thus, there is a constraint

$$(x - x_0)^2 + (y - y_0)^2 \leq 4$$

There is also a constraint on total expenditures, namely

$$x + y \leq 6$$

Organizationally, it is impossible to spend more than three units effectively on promotion. Thus,

$$y \leq 3$$

Experience has shown that for a campaign to be effective,

$$3y \geq 5x - 10$$

This description yields the following mathematical programming problem:

Max $4x^2 + 3xy + 2y^2$

s.t.

$$
\begin{align}
(x - 2)^2 + (y - 2)^2 &\leq 4 \tag{1} \\
x \qquad + y \quad &\leq 6 \tag{2} \\
y \quad &\leq 3 \tag{3} \\
3y \quad &\geq 5x - 10 \tag{4} \\
x, y &\geq 0
\end{align}
$$

The optimal solution occurs at the point $x^* = 3.5$, $y^* = 2.5$ where the value of the objective function is 87.75.

2   The advertising director feels that the fourth constraint is not correct and that it should be $3y \geq 5x - 11$. In general terms, what effect will this change have on the optimal value of the objective function?

3   The comptroller feels that in order to insure the success of the program, the constraint $5xy \leq 45$ must be added to the problem. What effect will this change have on the optimal value of the objective function?

4   If total expenditures are restricted to be no more than 5, what effect, in general terms, will this have on the optimal value of the objective function?

5   The maintenance manager feels that the constraint $5x + 5y = 20$ must be added to the problem. In general terms, what effect will this have on the optimal value of the objective function?

6   After some negotiation, the constraint suggested in problem 5 is changed to $5x + 5y = 19$. In general terms, what will be the relationship between the optimal value of the objective function in problem 5 and the optimal value with this new constraint?

7   Consider the general mathematical programming problem

Min $f(x_1, x_2)$

s.t.

$$g_1(x_1, x_2) \leq b_1$$

$$g_2(x_1, x_2) \leq b_2$$

$$g_3(x_1, x_2) \leq b_3$$

$$g_4(x_1, x_2) \leq b_4$$

$$x_1, x_2 \geq 0$$

Assume that $g_1(x_1, x_2)$, $g_2(x_1, x_2)$, $g_3(x_1, x_2)$, and $g_4(x_1, x_2)$ are all linear functions and that the contours for $f(x_1, x_2)$ are concentric circles with their center at the point $x_1 = 10$, $x_2 = 10$. Sample contours for $f(x_1, x_2)$ are shown in Figure 10.21. Indicate whether the following statement is true or false, and provide a rationale for your reason (the use of diagrams may be helpful): There are two decision and four slack variables in the formulation of this problem. Ignoring the problem of degeneracy, there is *always* an optimal solution in which exactly four of these variables are positive and the other two are equal to zero. That is, there is always an optimal basic solution.

8 Construct a hypothetical case where, for a given set of constraints and a given objective function, the solution is unbounded whether or not you wish to minimize or maximize the objective function.

In problems 9 through 11, indicate whether the statement in quotation marks is true or false. If it is false, comment on the true state of affairs.

9 Consider an LP in which all the coefficients in the *objective function* are positive and it is a min problem. "Adding a $\leq$ constraint, for example,

$$\sum_{j=1}^{n} a_{ij} x_j \leq b_i$$

will have no effect on the optimal value of the objective function since we wish to make the x_js small anyway."

10 "In a mathematical programming problem, it is impossible to make a universal statement about what effect changing the right-hand side of an equality constraint will have on the optimal value of the objective function."

11 Consider an LP min problem with a $\geq$ constraint whose right-hand side is a negative number. "If the right-hand side is made more negative, the optimal objective value can increase."

Figure 10.21

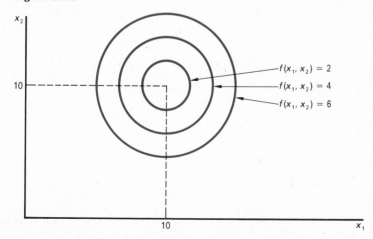

12 The marketing department has created an LP model to find an optimal advertising media mix. There are three constraints. Unfortunately, when the problem was submitted to the computer for solving, it was found to be infeasible. When the marketing manager asked the analyst from systems about the problem, the analyst said, "The second constraint was inadvertently entered as ≤ (less than or equal to), rather than ≥ (greater than or equal to). Ignoring the details of this particular application, I know from the theory of LP that when this error is corrected, we will *inevitably* obtain a solution." Comment on this answer. Be sure your comment is complete in the sense of covering all possibilities. If the analyst is correct, argue or use a diagram to show why. If he is incorrect, show all the possible implications of the change he suggests.

13 The marketing department is using an LP model to optimally select its advertising media mix. It is a max problem. Unfortunately, when the problem was submitted to the computer for solving, the problem was unbounded. When the marketing manager asked the systems analyst about this, the analyst said, "There was a keypunch error when this problem was entered. The computer solved a min problem. We can correct this error, but unfortunately, something else must be wrong. I know this because, ignoring the details of this particular application, I learned from the theory of LP that if a min problem is unbounded, then changing the objective to max will lead to an infeasible problem."

a Comment on the analyst's statement. Give a *theoretic* answer as to whether the analyst's statement is correct or not.

b If it is incorrect, illustrate in two-dimensional space all the possible situations that can arise from the change the analyst suggests. Would the answers to parts *a* and *b* be the same if the constraint set is nonlinear? Illustrate.

14 In the example of decentralized profit maximization in Section 10.6.1, it was stated that if the requirements in the cost-min suboptimization model are optimal, then the policy produced for that specific plant is the same as the policy that would be obtained from the overall disaggregated centralized profit-max model. To simply illustrate the ideas, consider the problem

Max $R(x)$

s.t.   (I)

$C(x) \leq \bar{C}$

and let x^* be a solution. Now consider the problem

Min $C(x)$

s.t.   (II)

$R(x) \geq R(x^*)$

These problems are simple conceptual representations of the models of interest.

a Show that any optimal solution to (II) is optimal for (I).

b Show that any optimal solution to (I) is feasible in (II).

c Show that x^* is optimal in (II) if and only if every solution to (I) is in the set $\{x : C(x) \geq C(x^*)\}$.

d Show that every optimal solution to (I) is optimal in (II) if and only if every solution to (I) is in the set $\{x : C(x) = C(x^*)\}$.

15 This problem concerns optimization and suboptimization.

a Suppose that the firm's sole objective is to maximize profit over the next 12 time periods. Let the index t denote these time periods, where t will be allowed to vary from 1 to 12. Suppose the overall operation of the firm is analyzed in terms of a collection of highly disaggregated and well-defined tasks performed in each time period. For example, a task might be the operation of a specified furnace or a specified milling machine in a specified plant. In mathematical notation, let

x_i^t = hours allotted to task i in period t, $i = 1, ..., q_t$, $t = 1, ..., 12$

Thus, in each time period, t, there are q_t possible tasks throughout the entire firm, and in the 12 time periods there are

$$\sum_{t=1}^{12} q_t$$

tasks. Use the symbol $\sim$ to denote tuples. That is, let $\underset{\sim}{x}^t$ denote the tuple $(x_1^t, ..., x_{qt}^t)$ of q_t tasks in period t. Assuming there are n products that can be produced in each period, let the product mix in period t be denoted by $\underset{\sim}{p}^t = (p_1^t, ..., p_n^t)$, where p_i^t = amount of product i produced in period t. Suppose that production in period t is given as a function of the hours allotted to tasks. That is,

$$\underset{\sim}{p}^t = \underset{\sim}{p}^t(\underset{\sim}{x}^t) = (p_1^t(\underset{\sim}{x}^t), ..., p_n^t(\underset{\sim}{x}^t))$$

In each time period t let there be m_t constraints on the tasks

$k_i^t(\underset{\sim}{x}^t) \le K_i^t$ $i = 1, ..., m_t$, $t = 1, ..., 12$

These constraints may include capacity limitations, satisfaction of demand, sequencing considerations, union contractual arrangements, and so on. The constraints describe a feasible, or allowable, set of hours devoted to tasks. Finally, let $R[p^1(\underset{\sim}{x}^1), p^2(\underset{\sim}{x}^2), ..., p^{12}(\underset{\sim}{x}^{12})]$ and $C(\underset{\sim}{x}^1, \underset{\sim}{x}^2, ..., \underset{\sim}{x}^{12})$ denote revenue and cost functions, respectively. Using this notation, write the firm's overall disaggregated profit-max problem. Suppose $\bar{x}^t$, $t = 1, ..., 12$ is an optimal solution. Let $\bar{P} = C(\bar{x}^1, ..., \bar{x}^{12})$. Now put a budget constraint of P dollars in the model. If $P \ne \bar{P}$, then, in terms of profit maximization over the next 12 months, the model, because of the budget constraint, is a suboptimization model. What if $P = \bar{P}$? In the case of $P \ne \bar{P}$, could the model with a budget constraint, though suboptimal by the above criterion, actually be part of an overall optimal policy by some other criterion? Give an illustration to support your answer.

b Consider the manager of a given plant. Let $\underset{\sim}{y}^t$ denote the subset of tasks that is relevant to his plant in periods $t = 1, 2, ..., 12$, and let $\hat{C}(\underset{\sim}{y}^1, ..., \underset{\sim}{y}^{12})$ denote his cost function. Suppose production requirements of $\hat{P}^t$, $t = 1, ..., 12$ are sent down to his plant. Let the model

Min $\hat{C}(\underset{\sim}{y}^1, ..., \underset{\sim}{y}^{12})$

s.t.

Production in period $t \ge$ requirements $t = 1, ..., 12$

Other feasibility constraints on tasks

$\underset{\sim}{y}^t \ge 0$ $t = 1, ..., 12$

be called the plant manager's cost-min model. Discuss why this is a suboptimization model by the criterion of profit maximization over the next 12 months. Under what conditions might you expect the model to lead to optimal results, that is, to results the same as those that would be obtained from the firm's overall disaggregated profit-max model in part a.

c Is the function $\hat{C}$ in part b the same as the function C in part a? If not, how are they related? Devise appropriate mathematical notation for the constraints of the model in part b.

11

A Case Study in Constrained Optimization: The PROTRAC Model

A specific LP production and marketing model is used to analyze a realistic application in which the logical interactions are dynamic and nontrivial. The purpose of the chapter is to formulate and then explore and study the interactions in the specific model prior to computer analysis. The exercises at the end of the chapter will stress model manipulation and interpretations of the logical structure. Some of the problems involve the incorporation of alternative interactions. Other problems involve applications of the previous development of sensitivity analysis to analyze potential uses of the model above and beyond merely "finding a solution." In Chapter 12, the computer analysis of this problem will be studied and interpreted from several points of view.

11.1 Introduction

The following verbal description gives a fairly structured but not overly detailed portrayal of some of the important interactions involved in production and marketing at PROTRAC. Our goal is to construct a formal constrained optimization model as an aid for decision making in this environment.

The problem centers around the production and marketing of the large E–9 crawler tractor. The planning of production and marketing for this particular product is centralized at corporate headquarters.

ASSUMPTIONS BEHIND THE MODEL

Facilities   Seven of the plants in the midwest tractor division are geographically located in two clusters. In regard to the production of E–9s, each cluster of plants has similar operating characteristics. As a result, the seven plants have been aggregated into two groups, identified as plant 1 and plant 2. The *individual* plants within each group have no separate identity in the model.

Time   The questions to be answered concern the next *two* planning periods.

Inputs   The thousands of individual items and processes that go into the production of an E–9 are aggregated into three major categories. Iron (I), which includes all the iron castings used in an E–9, transmissions (T), which includes all the material associated with the power train except the engine, and, finally,

298

labor hours (L), which is an aggregated measure of human and machine hours. This measure combines the inputs of both the work-force and the machinery in the manufacturing and assembly-line facilities.

Production Processes A unit of *finished product* consists of a *tractor body* and a *transmission.* The components of the transmissions are fabricated in a different division and are then shipped to the midwest tractor division where they are assembled in the two PROTRAC plants. The tractor bodies are entirely produced and assembled in the two plants. Units of *finished* product and units of *transmissions* can be carried in inventory from period 1 into period 2. Because of the assembly-line design and established union procedures, as soon as a complete body is assembled, the transmission is immediately installed. This means that a tractor body without a transmission cannot be carried in inventory. In computing costs, a specified charge is assessed at each plant for each unit of finished product in inventory at the end of each period and for each transmission in inventory at the end of each period. The per-unit carrying costs will differ for finished product and transmissions.

Cross-Shipment of Transmissions The plants can cross-ship the assembled transmissions from one plant to another at a specified cost per unit. Transmissions cross-shipped from either plant 1 or 2 in either period are assumed to leave the plant during the period and arrive at the other plant at the beginning of the next period. Transmissions that are eligible for installation in the tractor bodies produced in a specific plant in a specific period come from one of three sources: those that arrive at the beginning of the period via cross-shipment from the other plant; those that are assembled in the specific plant in the specific period; and those that are carried in inventory in the specific plant into the specific period.

Labor-Hour Utilization The *assembly* of transmissions and the production and assembly of tractor bodies requires the utilization of labor hours. The labor required for *installing* a transmission is negligible and therefore is not directly measured.

The Supply of Iron The firm owns a foundry, which produces a limited amount of iron available for purchase by the individual plants. The firm uses a transfer-pricing scheme under which the manufacturing plants are charged for iron purchased from the foundry. In calculating each plant's costs, these transfer prices are treated the same as the prices paid for other items purchased by the plant. Additional iron can be purchased from outside sources (in any quantity) on the open market at the market price. Currently, the exogenously purchased iron has a higher price than the transfer price. Iron cannot be stored in inventory at either plant. That is, iron taken from the company's foundry or purchased from outside sources must be used in the same period in which it is purchased. Obviously, this requirement is not dictated by the physical properties of the materials being purchased. It results from the fact that management has discovered that it can, in this way, force the supplying firms to absorb part of the inventory carrying cost. However, since this policy might imply underutilization of the PROTRAC foundry, it may not be optimal in an overall sense. It provides a good example of suboptimization. Iron is used only in producing the tractor bodies. Iron is not used for transmissions since they are prefabricated elsewhere.

Marketing   The two plants serve dealers in the midwest regional marketing district. There is a known demand (called *existing demand*) for the finished product that, according to the firm's goodwill policy, must be satisfied. The marketing department can expend dollars to cultivate additional demand (called *new demand*). Finished product can be shipped to the marketing district in the period in which it is produced. Finished product that is shipped to the marketing district in any period will satisfy demand in that same period.

Transportation Costs   There is an "average" transportation cost associated with the shipment of each unit of finished product from each plant to the marketing district. The cost depends on the plant of origin. Only the amount that can be sold is shipped to the district; in other words, no finished product can be stored at the district.

Cost and Price Assumptions   Linearity is assumed throughout. There are revenues from the sale of finished product. Costs are associated with the use of iron, the transportation of finished product, the holding of inventories, the cross-shipping of transmissions, and the creation of new demand. The size of the labor force is assumed *not* to be a decision variable, and its cost is part of the fixed overhead. This assumption is reasonable if the planning periods are not too long. Union agreements and lack of experience in working with alternative sources of capacity make it economically impossible for PROTRAC to expand capacity in the short run. It is not unusual for management to consider short-run capacity and labor costs as fixed. As a result of this assumption, labor costs are not included in the model.

A schematic diagram of these interactions is shown in Figure 11.1. Centralized management intends to use the previous assumptions in developing a planning model to use as an input to their deliberations to determine a production plan, a distribution plan, and a marketing plan that will *maximize total profit*.

A production plan specifies:

1   The number of bodies that should be produced in each plant in each period
2   The number of transmissions to be assembled in each plant in each period
3   The number of transmissions to be cross-shipped from each plant to the other in each period
4   The number of tons of iron purchased by each plant in each period from the company owned foundry
5   The number of tons of iron purchased by each plant in each period from outside sources
6   The amount of finished product and the number of transmissions to be carried in inventory in each plant

A distribution plan specifies the amount of finished product to be sent from each plant to the marketing district in each period.

The marketing plan specifies how many dollars to invest in creating new demand in each period.

Figure 11.1 *Schematic diagram of the PROTRAC interactions*

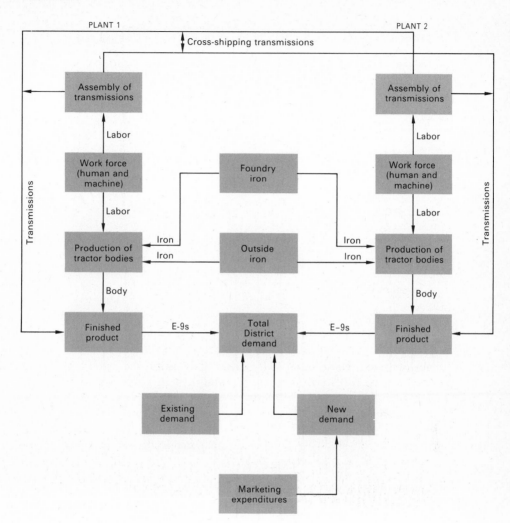

11.2 The Formal Model

The decision variables used in creating a formal model for this problem are defined in Figure 11.2. It is seen that there are 34 variables in the model. The following mnemonic abbreviations are employed: FP for finished product, TR for transmissions, FI for foundry iron, OI for outside iron, ND for new demand, BOD for bodies, and INFP, INTR for inventories of finished product and transmissions, respectively.

THE CONSTRAINTS

There are six sets of constraints in the model.

Figure 11.2   *Decision variables for PROTRAC production and marketing model*

Decision Variables	Plant	Notation	
		Time Period 1	Time Period 2
Number of BOD produced in	1	$BODP1T1$	$BODP1T2$
	2	$BODP2T1$	$BODP2T2$
Amount of FP shipped from	1	$FPP1T1$	$FPP1T2$
	2	$FPP2T1$	$FPP2T2$
TR assembled in	1	$TRP1T1$	$TRP1T2$
	2	$TRP2T1$	$TRP2T2$
TR cross-shipped	1→2	$CSTRP1T1$	$CSTRP1T2$
	2→1	$CSTRP2T1$	$CSTRP2T2$
Tons of FI purchased in	1	$FIP1T1$	$FIP1T2$
	2	$FIP2T1$	$FIP2T2$
Tons of OI purchased in	1	$OIP1T1$	$OIP1T2$
	2	$OIP2T1$	$OIP2T2$
Amount of ND created		$NDT1$	$NDT2$
FP inventory in	1	$INFPP1T1$	$INFPP1T2$
	2	$INFPP2T1$	$INFPP2T2$
T inventory in	1	$INTRP1T1$	$INTRP1T2$
	2	$INTRP2T1$	$INTRP2T2$

Demand   The goodwill policy requires that all demand (existing demand plus new demand) be satisfied. The existing demand (the orders on hand for finished product) is 130 in time period 1 and 190 in time period 2. Thus, a demand constraint for period t will say

$$\left.\begin{array}{c} FP \text{ shipped from plant 1 in time } t \\ + \\ FP \text{ shipped from plant 2 in time } t \end{array}\right\} = \text{total demand (existing + new) in time } t$$

The symbolic formulation is

$$FPP1T1 + FPP2T1 - NDT1 = 130 \qquad \text{(Time 1)}$$
$$FPP1T2 + FPP2T2 - NDT2 = 190 \qquad \text{(Time 2)}$$

Note that $NDT1$ and $NDT2$ have been moved to the left-hand side of the equations since they are variables and, in the standard LP format, the right-hand side must be a specified number.

Labor Capacity   In plant 1, there are 80,000 hours of labor available in each time period. It requires 90 hours of labor to assemble each transmission and 900 hours to produce and assemble each tractor body. Thus, in plant 1 a total of 990 labor hours goes into each unit of finished product. In plant 2, there are only 70,000 hours of labor available in each time period. It takes 60 hours to assemble each transmission and 600 hours to produce and assemble each tractor body. Thus, in plant 2 a total of 660 hours goes into each unit of finished product. The symbolic formulation of the labor constraints is

$$900BODP1T1 + 90TRP1T1 \leq 80,000$$

$$900BODP1T2 + 90TRP1T2 \leq 80,000$$

(Plant 1)

$$600BODP2T1 + 60TRP2T1 \leq 70,000$$

$$600BODP2T2 + 60TRP2T2 \leq 70,000$$

(Plant 2)

Foundry Capacity   In each time period, the foundry capacity is 1,000 tons. The symbolic form of the relevant constraints is

$$FIP1T1 + FIP2T1 \leq 1,000 \qquad \text{(Time 1)}$$
$$FIP1T2 + FIP2T2 \leq 1,000 \qquad \text{(Time 2)}$$

Iron Consumption   In each plant and each time period, the production of a single tractor body requires six tons of iron. Since iron cannot be stored in inventory, we can say that in each plant and each time period

Total iron purchased = total iron used

Thus, the symbolic formulation of the iron consumption constraints is

$$6BODP1T1 - FIP1T1 - OIP1T1 = 0 \qquad \text{(Plant 1, time 1)}$$
$$6BODP2T1 - FIP2T1 - OIP2T1 = 0 \qquad \text{(Plant 2, time 1)}$$
$$6BODP1T2 - FIP1T2 - OIP1T2 = 0 \qquad \text{(Plant 1, time 2)}$$
$$6BODP2T2 - FIP2T2 - OIP2T2 = 0 \qquad \text{(Plant 2, time 2)}$$

Finished-product Inventory   In plant 1, the initial inventory of finished product is five units. The amount of finished product held in inventory in plant 1 at the end of time period 1 is determined as follows

$$FP \text{ inventory at end of time 1} = \begin{cases} FP \text{ inventory at beginning of time 1} \\ + \\ FP \text{ produced in time 1} \\ - \\ FP \text{ delivered in time 1} \end{cases}$$

To obtain the appropriate symbolic expression, we must use the fact that after each tractor body is produced, a transmission is immediately installed. This means that the number of units of finished product produced in each time period is synonymous with the number of bodies produced in that period. Hence the symbolic representation of the above condition is

$$INFPP1T1 - BODP1T1 + FPP1T1 = 5 \qquad \text{(Plant 1, end of time 1)}$$

Similarly for plant 1, at the end of time 2

$$FP \text{ inventory at end of time 2 } = \begin{cases} FP \text{ inventory at beginning of time 2} \\ + \\ FP \text{ produced in time 2} \\ - \\ FP \text{ delivered in time 2} \end{cases}$$

The symbolic formulation is

$$INFPP1T2 - INFPP1T1 - BODP1T2 + FPP1T2 = 0 \quad \text{(Plant 1, end of time 2)}$$

In plant 2, the initial inventory of finished product is two units. The relevant constraints are

$$INFPP2T1 - BODP2T1 + FPP2T1 \qquad\qquad = 2 \quad \text{(Plant 2, end of time 1)}$$

$$INFPP2T2 - INFPP2T1 - BODP2T2 + FPP2T2 = 0 \quad \text{(Plant 2, end of time 2)}$$

Transmissions Inventory   In plant 1, the initial inventory of transmissions is six units. The number of transmissions held in inventory in plant 1 at the end of time period 1 is determined as follows:

$$TR \text{ inventory at end of time 1 } = \begin{cases} TR \text{ inventory at beginning of time 1} \\ + \\ TR \text{ assembled in time 1} \\ - \\ \text{number of } TR \text{ installed in time 1} \\ - \\ \text{number of } TR \text{ cross-shipped out in time 1} \end{cases}$$

We now use the fact that the number of transmissions installed in plant 1, time 1, is equal to the number of bodies produced in plant 1, time 1. Hence, the symbolic representation of the above constraint is

$$INTRP1T1 - TRP1T1 + BODP1T1 + CSTRP1T1 = 6 \quad \text{(Plant 1, end of time 1)}$$

In order to determine the transmissions inventory at the end of time 2 in plant 1, it is necessary to add in the transmissions *received* at the beginning of time period 2 via cross-shipment from plant 2. Recall that these transmissions are sent out from plant 2 during time period 1, and they arrive at plant 1 at the beginning of time period 2. Thus, the relevant constraint is

$$INTRP1T2 - INTRP1T1 - TRP1T2 + BODP1T2$$

$$+ CSTRP1T2 - CSTRP2T1 = 0 \quad \text{(Plant 1, end of time 2)}$$

In an analogous way, the transmission inventory constraints in plant 2 are as follows. (Note that the initial inventory is 4 transmissions.)

$$INTRP2T1 - TRP2T1 + BODP2T1 + CSTRP2T \quad = 4 \quad \text{(Plant 2, end of time 1)}$$

$$\begin{aligned} INTRP2T2 - INTRP2T1 - TRP2T2 + BODP2T2 \\ + CSTRP2T2 - CSTRP1T1 \quad = 0 \quad \text{(Plant 2, end of time 2)} \end{aligned}$$

Thus, there are a total of 20 constraints in the model.

THE OBJECTIVE FUNCTION

The revenue for finished product is 30,000 per unit in each period. The costs are

Shipping finished product from plant 1	=	30 per unit
Shipping finished product from plant 2	=	90 per unit
Foundry iron	=	1,000 per ton
Outside iron	=	1,200 per ton
Cross-shipping transmissions	=	20 per unit
Transmission inventories	=	20 per unit
Finished-product inventories	=	300 per unit
Marketing cost of creating new demand	=	3,000 per unit

The objective function is

$$\text{Revenue} - \text{cost} = \begin{cases} 30,000(FPP1T1 + FPP1T2 + FPP2T1 + FPP2T2) \\ \quad -30(FPP1T1 + FPP1T2) - 90(FPP2T1 + FPP2T2) \\ -1,000(FIP1T1 + FIP1T2 + FIP2T1 + FIP2T2) \\ -1,200(OIP1T1 + OIP1T2 + OIP2T1 + OIP2T2) \\ \quad -20(CSTRP1T1 + CSTRP1T2 + CSTRP2T1 + CSTRP2T2) \\ \quad -20(INTRP1T1 + INTRP1T2 + INTRP2T1 + INTRP2T2) \\ \quad -300(INFPP1T1 + INFPP1T2 + INFPP2T1 + INFPP2T2) \\ -3,000(NDT1 + NDT2) \end{cases}$$

THE COMPLETE MODEL

Maximize the above objective function subject to the above 20 constraints (sets 1, 2, 3, 4, 5, 6) and nonnegativity of all 34 variables.

11.3 Examples and Solutions

In Chapter 12, the complete computer solution for this problem will be presented and several policy issues of concern to management will be studied. As a prelude, however, it is useful to analyze the formulated but unsolved model. A thorough understanding of the assumptions in the model and their implications is a prerequisite for proper interpretation of the solution. In practice, it is often the case that each of a number of assumptions and constraints seems reasonable in its own right. However, the joint effect of these considerations in the complete model can produce a substantially less-than-satisfactory result. The manager who will have the opportunity to use the output from a model in determining his course of action should do his best in advance to analyze the complete model. This exercise may well persuade him that certain aspects of the model require modification. The following examples and solutions illustrate questions that might be raised in a preliminary analysis of the PROTRAC *E* and *F* model.

Example 1

Is this model solvable? Could it be unbounded or infeasible?

Solution to Example 1

The capacity constraints on labor eliminate the possibility of having an unbounded solution. To see this, we note that all quantities in the model are determined or bounded by the quantity of bodies and transmissions produced. Since each of these requires labor, and that quantity is also bounded, the solution must be bounded. On the other hand, the problem could be infeasible. If existing demand were very large and labor capacity too small, it would simply be impossible to produce enough to meet demand. It is interesting to note that the relation between existing demand and labor capacity is the only phenomenon in the model which could cause infeasibility. Even when costs are relatively higher than revenues, so that losses will be incurred, the model forces the firm to produce. This characteristic is due to the goodwill policy (namely, all existing and new demand must be satisfied) as captured in the demand constraints.

Example 2

Does PROTRAC have sufficient capacity to satisfy existing demand in each of the two time periods considered separately? If not, does this imply that the problem is infeasible?

Solution to Example 2

The following computation shows that the combined labor capacity of both plants *in time period 2* is insufficient to satisfy the existing demand in time period 2.

PLANT 1

Labor available	=	80,000 hours
Required labor per unit of finished product	=	990 hours

$$\text{Maximum possible production of finished product} = \frac{80,000}{990} = 80.808 \text{ units}$$

PLANT 2

Labor available	=	70,000 hours
Required labor per unit of finished product	=	660 hours

$$\text{Maximum possible production of finished product} = \frac{70,000}{660} = 106.06 \text{ units}$$

DEMAND AND COMBINED PRODUCTION

Existing demand in time period 2	=	190 units

Maximum total production in time period 2 $= 80.808 + 106.06 = 186.868$ units

The total production potential is 3.132 units *short* of the required amount. This does not cause infeasibility because there is considerably more than enough labor capacity to satisfy the 130 units of existing demand in time period 1. Thus, the necessary 3.132 units of finished product could be produced in time 1 and carried over in inventory into time 2. We note, however, that if existing demand were to exceed capacity in time 1, then the problem would be infeasible.

Example 3

What is the meaning of the dual price on a demand constraint? Consider, for example, the equation from the first time period:

$$FPP1T1 + FPP2T1 - NDT1 = 130$$

Solution to Example 3

Note that the RHS represents units of *existing demand.* Hence, the dual price would be interpreted as the improvement in the optimal objective value per unit increase in existing demand. It is the maximum amount the manager should be willing to pay for the creation of one additional unit of demand, assuming the allowable increase in this RHS is not less than 1.

Example 4

What is the meaning of the dual price on an inventory constraint? Consider, for example, the equations for finished product in plant 1 in each time period:

$$INFPP1T1 - BODP1T1 + FPP1T1 \qquad\qquad = 5 \quad \text{(Time 1)}$$
$$INFPP1T2 - INFPP1T1 - BODP1T2 + FPP1T2 = 0 \quad \text{(Time 2)}$$

Solution to Example 4

Clearly, increasing the RHS of the equation for time period 1 can be interpreted as increasing the inventory on hand at the beginning of time 1. Similarly, increasing the RHS of the equation for time period 2 by a unit is, alternatively, equivalent to decreasing the left-hand side by the same unit. This, then, can be thought of as increasing the value of *INFPP*1*T*1, the inventory on hand at the beginning of time 2, by a unit. The dual price then can be interpreted as the maximum amount a manager would be willing to pay to have an additional unit on hand in the appropriate plant at the beginning of that time period.

Example 5

The actual decision variables (the number of bodies to be produced, transmissions to be assembled, and so on), are, in reality, integral quantities, but our LP formulation may well yield fractional answers. Does this seriously impair the usefulness of the model?

Solution to Example 5

Forcing the variables to satisfy "integrality conditions" would take the model out of the LP framework and would consequently make it considerably more difficult to solve. There is, therefore, a substantial advantage to following the common approach of allowing fractional optimal values for the variables and then rounding the solutions to integers before implementation. This approach is usually justified by the fact that there is almost always a good deal of noise and error both in the model logic and in the data. In this case, that is certainly true. Seven plants are coalesced into two aggregates, transportation costs to the district are "averages," and "labor hours" is a composite measure of man and machine time. In such an instance, it seems clear that the process of rounding will not detract from the overall role of the model as only one of possibly many inputs to the decision-making process.

11.4 Problems

1 In Section 11.2, in the paragraph discussing iron consumption, the text states that since iron cannot be stored in inventory, we can say that in each plant and in each time period, total iron purchased equals total iron used. Provide an economic rationale for this statement. In this context, discuss whether or not the fourth group of constraints could be ≤ instead of =.

2 Could the first group of constraints be written as ≥ instead of = ?

3 What, in general, would be the effect on the feasible set and the optimal value of the objective function if the second group of constraints were changed to =?

4 Is it assumed that the firm can sell as much as it produces? If not, how much can it sell?

5 Suppose it is known in advance that it is simply too expensive to create new demand in either time period. How might the model be rewritten? Is this new formulation preferable?

6 Suppose it is known in advance that it never pays to buy outside iron. How might this be incorporated in the original model?

7 Suppose it is known in advance that it pays to create new demand, but only until all foundry iron is consumed. What type of investment should be considered in order to increase overall profits?

8 Is it possible to have an optimal solution with slack in the foundry in both time periods and slack in labor in both time periods in both plants? Under what conditions? For example, could this phenomenon occur in an optimal solution that also calls for positive new demand? Could this phenomenon occur in an optimal solution that yields a positive optimal objective value (that is, a positive profit)?

9 Suppose it pays to create as much new demand as possible and to buy on the market as much outside iron as needed. What prevents the occurrence of infinite policies?

10 What, if anything, could make the model infeasible?

11 Suppose existing demand can be satisfied with slack in all labor constraints and in the foundry constraint in both periods. Set up a model for determining how to satisfy this demand most economically (that is, at minimum cost).

12 What in the model specifies that finished product can be produced only if enough transmissions are available?

13 What specifies that the number of transmissions cross-shipped from a given plant cannot exceed the number available?

14 What in the model specifies that the amount of finished product shipped to the marketing district cannot exceed the amount of finished product actually produced?

15 Suppose the cost of outside iron is so expensive, and all other costs sufficiently reasonable, that an optimal solution consists of producing and selling as much as possible in each time period (and creating new demand as required) until the foundry capacity is exhausted. Suppose it turns out that an optimal policy has the property that it also completely exhausts the labor supply in both plants in time period 1. In reality, how likely would it be that the foundry capacity in a given time period is exhausted by exactly the same amount of production that completely exhausts the labor capacity? What term would be used to describe this situation?

16 What is the economic interpretation of the dual variable of an iron-consumption constraint? For example, consider the constraint for plant 1, time period 1:

$$6BODP1T1 - FIP1T1 - OIP1T1 = 0$$

17 Suppose the dual price corresponding to one of the labor constraints is 21 and the cost of labor is \$4 per hour. Is this enough information to know whether all available labor hours are being used? Discuss the logic of the following statement: "Since each additional hour of labor will gain me 21 additional dollars, and each hour costs only \$4, there is a net gain of \$17, and consequently I should hire an unlimited amount of labor. That is, I should get all that I can."

18 Suppose that in a given optimal solution all of the labor force in plant 1, time period 1 is used. However, the union contract is about to expire. This introduces speculation in management about the effects of inadvertently establishing potentially dangerous precedents on utilization of work force. For political reasons, management is contemplating underutilization of labor by 10,000 hours in plant 1, time period 1. What would this do to profits? Discuss how the dual prices might be used to estimate the *minimum* change in profit that would be incurred. Graph the optimal objective value as a function of the RHS of the appropriate constraint, and show why the actual profit change could be more than the estimate.

19 a Reformulate the constraints of the model so that bodies (without transmissions), transmissions, and finished product can all be separately carried in inventory. Only finished product can be shipped to the marketing district. Assume zero initial

inventory of bodies and initial inventories of transmissions and finished product as stated in the text. Define any new decision variables that are required in your reformulation. Discuss the appropriate modifications to the objective function. Show how your reformulation assures that (1) the amount of finished product assembled in a given plant in a given time period will not exceed either the number of available bodies or the number of available transmissions; and (2) the amount of finished product shipped from a given plant in a given time period will not exceed the amount on hand.

b Reformulate the constraints of the model so that only bodies and transmissions can be carried in inventory, not finished product. Take initial inventories of transmissions and bodies as in part *a*. Assume that only finished product can be shipped to the marketing district. Discuss the appropriate modifications to the objective function.

c Reformulate the model so that only finished product can be carried in inventory, though it is still possible to cross-ship transmissions.

20 Consider the demand constraint for time period 1 and the corresponding dual price.

a Suppose the dual price is negative in a nondegenerate optimal solution. Could the optimal value of the "new demand" variable be positive? What is the interpretation of the dual price in this case? What can you conclude about the profitability of the goodwill policy?

b Suppose at optimality the "new demand" variable is positive. What can you say about the dual price?

c Suppose the dual price is positive. What can you say about the optimal value of the new demand variable? Discuss whether or not it would be possible to have, at optimality, a positive dual price and a zero value for new demand.

d Graph the possible shapes of the maximum profit curve (the optimal objective value) as a function of the existing demand RHS. Give possible interpretations to the points at which the slope changes.

12 Constrained Optimization in Action: Computer Analysis of the PROTRAC Model

The computer output of the PROTRAC model is studied. Several operational changes are contemplated, and it is shown how the analyst can use the output to learn far more than the "optimal solution" and to gain a better understanding of the way in which various operating policies affect the cost of operation. In addition, a capacity expansion problem with nonlinear costs is analyzed. A parametric analysis is employed to construct the optimal value functions for capacities in plants 1 and 2, and the optimal investment is then determined.

12.1 Introduction

This chapter provides fairly realistic illustrations of an important theme in this text. Often, the solution to a problem is only a starting point and is, in itself, the least interesting part of the analysis to follow. In particular, this chapter provides illustrations of two important motives for modeling.

The first motive is to learn as much as possible about the real-world problem at hand. Of course, the solution provides optimal decisions, but looking at the solution alone provides about as much insight into the logical interactions in a complex problem as the hands on a fine Swiss watch reveal about the underlying mechanism.

Let us be more specific. One of the great advantages of LP is that one is able to solve problems with many constraints and an even greater number of variables. In such problems, it is typically impossible for a person to trace through the many interactions between the decision variables to get a measure of the effect of changing this or that decision or to determine the effect on the operating policies of changing a parameter. For example, in a manufacturing and distribution system that involves a number of products, more than one manufacturing location, several marketing districts, and alternative means of transportation, it is extremely difficult to "cost-out" the effect of increasing the production of a given product in a specific plant. Analysis of such problems might progress somewhat as follows: "If I expand production of product A in plant 1, then I must reduce the amount of B, C and/or D that I make in plant 1. This implies that I'll have less of at least one of these products to distribute unless I change my production plans in some other location. In a way, I'd like to decrease the amount of B I make in plant 1 because it takes the most time per unit in the heat-treat department, where we're really short of capacity. But our largest demand for B is in the district closest to plant

1, so that would have a negative effect on our transportation costs. Maybe we should decrease C instead, since . . ."

The number of possible alternatives, each with its own advantages and disadvantages, is, for practical purposes, endless. Without the help of a model, management must often settle for a feasible (as opposed to optimal) solution, justified on the basis of some qualitative or intuitive arguments that, though plausible, may be far from optimal.

In previous chapters, we have seen that formulating a problem as a linear program and solving it on a computer provides not only an optimal set of decisions but also a wealth of sensitivity information. This type of information reveals the effect on the objective of changing various parameters, like an RHS or a coefficient in the objective function, or of introducing a new variable into the solution. Although this is extremely useful, it still leaves many questions unanswered. For example, suppose that the dual variable associated with a particular constraint equals $2,000. What changes in the decision variables must one make to achieve this increase? Or, suppose the reduced cost of a particular variable not in the basis is $72. What adjustments in the other decision variables must one make in order to introduce the new variable into the solution at the cost of $72 per unit?

It is, of course, always possible to answer these questions by appropriately modifying the LP problem (changing a parameter value or adding a constraint) and solving it again. This limits the analyst's involvement, but it also limits the amount of thinking he has to do about his real-world problem and hence the amount he can learn about important interactions and relations between activities. In the first part of this chapter, we shall see that the analyst or manager can obtain a deeper understanding by using the information provided in the computer output and then "working backward" with marginal cost and marginal revenue arguments. This is a process that we call *activity analysis,* which involves determining the sequence of actions or activities that produce a particular dual price or reduced cost.

An unstructured process, activity analysis can be frustrating. But it is potentially rewarding, for it provides a method for determining how the model is operating at optimality and what costs are associated with particular activities. In more technical jargon, this is called looking at the optimal technology for the problem at hand. The insight as to how the model is operating at optimality gives the analyst or manager a deeper understanding of the logical structure and the important tradeoffs in the decision-making environment. An activity analysis will show that certain interactions and cost assumptions are essential to the fact that the current optimal solution is in fact optimal. A constraint or coefficient that was initially easy to agree to as 1 of 1,000 or 1 of 10,000 may seem to merit change, or at least further consideration, when one understands the way in which the optimal decisions would change if that particular constraint or coefficient were to be changed. What all of this means is that activity analysis is really applied economics at work. The implications that are uncovered by activity analysis may clash with a manager's intuition or prior judgments. This presents another situation where the manager must either adjust her concept of reality or modify the logic of the model. It is a successful way to force a manager or analyst to think critically about the model she is using.

In the second part of this chapter, we illustrate an application of the PROTRAC model to a specific planning problem. This desire to answer *specific questions,* as opposed to learning as much as possible about the general interactions for the problem at hand, provides our second important motive for modeling.

12.2 Activity Analysis

The manager for centralized planning in the midwest tractor division has been recently transferred to this job from marketing and sales. This move is intended to give him manufacturing experience as a step toward broader responsibilities. He has set aside several hours to discuss some operational policies with one of the articulate members of the operations analysis group. The modeler arrives, lugging a printout that shows the current operating plan for the two-plant, two-period PROTRAC problem discussed in the previous chapter, and some schematic diagrams concerning the model. The decision variables used in the model are shown in Figure 12.1. The printout and a diagram of the model are displayed in Figures 12.2 and 12.3, respectively.

igure 12.1 *Decision variables for the PROTRAC production and marketing model*

Decision Variables	Plant	Notation	
		Time Period 1	**Time Period 2**
Number of BOD produced in	1	$BODP1T1$	$BODP1T2$
	2	$BODP2T1$	$BODP2T2$
Amount of FP shipped from	1	$FPP1T1$	$FPP1T2$
	2	$FPP2T1$	$FPP2T2$
TR assembled in	1	$TRP1T1$	$TRP1T2$
	2	$TRP2T1$	$TRP2T2$
TR cross-shipped	1→2	$CSTRP1T1$	$CSTRP1T2$
	2→1	$CSTRP2T1$	$CSTRP2T2$
Tons of FI purchased in	1	$FIP1T1$	$FIP1T2$
	2	$FIP2T1$	$FIP2T2$
Tons of OI purchased in	1	$OIP1T1$	$OIP1T2$
	2	$OIP2T1$	$OIP2T2$
Amount of ND created		$NDT1$	$NDT2$
FP inventory in	1	$INFPP1T1$	$INFPP1T2$
	2	$INFPP2T1$	$INFPP2T2$
T inventory in	1	$INTRP1T1$	$INTRP1T2$
	2	$INTRP2T1$	$INTRP2T2$

Manager I assume you have the optimal two-period operating plan with you.

Yes, I have the printout, and it includes both the solution and the sensitivity analysis. Do you want to look it over?

Manager No, not yet. Let me first explain what I need. There are two pressing

Figure 12.2 PROTRAC computer analysis; the model and solution are shown in black, and the sensitivity analysis is in color.

```
MAX  - 29970 FPP1T1 + 29970 FPP1T2 + 29970 FPP2T1 + 29910 FPP2T2
     - 1000 FIP1T1 - 1000 FIP1T2 - 1000 FIP2T1 - 1000 FIP2T2
     - 1200 OIP1T1 - 1200 OIP1T2 - 1200 OIP2T1 - 1200 OIP2T2
     - 20 CSTRP1T2 - 20 CSTRP2T1 - 20 CSTRP2T2
     - 3000 NDT1 - 3000 NDT2 - 20 INTRP1T1 - 20 INTRP1T2 - 20 INTRP2T1
     - 20 INTRP2T2 - 300 INFPP1T1 - 300 INFPP1T2 - 300 INFPP2T1
     - 300 INFPP2T2

SUBJECT TO
 2)  FPP1T1 + FPP2T1 - NDT1 = 130
 3)  FPP1T2 + FPP2T2 - NDT2 = 190
 4)  900 BODP1T1 + 90 TRP1T1 <=  80000
 5)  900 BODP1T2 + 90 TRP1T2 <=  80000
 6)  600 BODP2T1 + 60 TRP2T1 <=  70000
 7)  600 BODP2T2 + 60 TRP2T2 <=  70000
 8)  FIP1T1 + FIP2T1 <=  1000
 9)  FIP1T2 + FIP2T2 <=  1000
10)  - FIP1T1 - OIP1T1 + 6 BODP1T1 =  0
11)  - FIP2T1 - OIP2T1 + 6 BODP2T1 =  0
12)  - FIP1T2 - OIP1T2 + 6 BODP1T2 =  0
13)  - FIP2T2 - OIP2T2 + 6 BODP2T2 =  0
14)  FPP1T1 - BODP1T1 + INFPP1T1 =  5
15)  FPP1T2 - BODP1T2 + INFPP1T1 + INFPP1T2 =  0
16)  FPP2T1 - BODP2T1 + INFPP2T1 =  2
17)  FPP2T2 - BODP2T2 + INFPP2T1 + INFPP2T2 =  6
18)  CSTRP1T1 + INTRP1T1 - BODP1T1 - TRP1T1 =  0
19)  CSTRP1T2 - CSTRP1T1 - INTRP1T1 + INTRP1T2 + BODP1T2 - TRP1T2 =  0
     - TRP1T2 =  0
20)  CSTRP2T1 + INTRP2T1 + BODP2T1 - TRP2T1 =  4
21)  - CSTRP2T1 + CSTRP2T2 - INTRP2T1 + INTRP2T2 + BODP2T2 + PODP2T2
     - TRP2T2 =  0
```

OBJECTIVE FUNCTION VALUE

1) 8942181.

VARIABLE	VALUE	REDUCED COST
FPP1T1	86.353537	0.000000
FPP1T2	83.939392	0.000000
FPP2T1	105.292932	0.000000
FPP2T2	106.060608	0.000000
FIP1T1	0.000000	-0.000031
FIP1T2	380.242416	0.000000
FIP2T1	0.000000	-0.000031
FIP2T2	619.757591	0.000000
OIP1T1	363.636360	0.000000
OIP1T2	636.363640	0.000000
OIP2T1	107.878805	0.000000
OIP2T2	140.000000	0.000000
CSTRP1T1	0.000000	10.909225
CSTRP1T2	0.000000	1831.818220
CSTRP2T1	1826.363660	0.000000
CSTRP2T2	0.000000	0.000000
NDT1	61.646467	0.000000
NDT2	0.000000	160.000000
INTRP1T1	0.000000	1831.818220
INTRP1T2	0.000000	5.454666
INTRP2T1	0.000000	1826.363660
INTRP2T2	0.000000	0.000000
BODP1T1	81.353537	0.000000
BODP1T2	75.353537	-0.000122
BODP2T1	83.939392	0.000000
BODP2T2	49.494958	0.000000
TRP1T1	103.292932	0.000000
TRP1T2	133.737366	-0.000015
TRP2T1	106.060608	0.000000
TRP2T2	106.060608	0.000381
INFPP1T1	0.000000	140.000000
INFPP1T2	0.000000	27430.000000

ROW	SLACK	DUAL PRICES
2)	0.000000	3000.000000
3)	0.000000	2840.000000
4)	0.000000	19.969697
5)	0.000000	20.131314
6)	0.000000	29.863637
7)	0.000000	30.106061
8)	0.000000	199.999970
9)	0.000000	200.000000
10)	0.000000	1200.000000
11)	0.000000	1200.000000
12)	0.000000	1200.000000
13)	0.000000	1200.000000
14)	0.000000	26970.000000
15)	0.000000	27130.000000
16)	0.000000	26910.000000
17)	0.000000	27000.000000
18)	0.000000	1797.272890
19)	0.000000	1811.818220

SENSITIVITY ANALYSIS

RANGES IN WHICH THE BASIS IS UNCHANGED

COST COEFFICIENT RANGES

VARIABLE	CURRENT COEFF	ALLOWABLE INCREASE	ALLOWABLE DECREASE
FPP1T1	29970.000000	INFINITY	60.001326
FPP1T2	29970.000000	159.99999R	60.000152
FPP2T1	29910.000000	60.001327	159.999998
FPP2T2	29910.000000	60.000152	19870.000500
FIP1T1	-1000.000000	0.000000	10.000221
FIP1T2	-1000.000000	0.000000	9.999999
FIP2T1	-1000.000000	10.000221	9.999999
FIP2T2	-1000.000000	9.999999	0.000000
OIP1T1	-1200.000000	23.333333	0.000000
OIP1T2	-1200.000000	26.668400	INFINITY
OIP2T1	-1200.000000	0.000000	INFINITY
OIP2T2	-1200.000000	0.000000	INFINITY
CSTRP1T1	-20.000000	10.909225	INFINITY
CSTRP1T2	-20.000000	1831.818220	INFINITY
CSTRP2T1	-20.000000	14.545454	5.454559
CSTRP2T2	-20.000000	1826.363660	INFINITY
NDT1	-3000.000000	INFINITY	160.000000
NDT2	-3000.000000	160.000000	INFINITY
INTRP1T1	-20.000000	1831.818220	INFINITY
INTRP1T2	-20.000000	5.454666	INFINITY
INTRP2T1	-20.000000	5.454559	INFINITY
INTRP2T2	-20.000000	1826.363660	INFINITY
BODP1T1	0.000000	INFINITY	60.001326
BODP1T2	0.000000	159.999998	60.000152
BODP2T1	0.000000	0.000015	16.000000
BODP2T2	0.000000	60.001327	159.99999R
TRP1T1	0.000000	16.000000	6.000133
TRP1T2	0.000000	60.000152	6.000015
TRP2T1	0.000000	140.000000	INFINITY
TRP2T2	0.000000	27430.000000	INFINITY
INFPP1T1	-300.000000	140.000000	INFINITY
INFPP1T2	-300.000000	27430.000000	INFINITY
INFPP2T1	-300.000000	140.000000	INFINITY
INFPP2T2	-300.000000	27370.000000	INFINITY

RIGHTHAND SIDE RANGES

ROW	CURRENT RHS	ALLOWABLE INCREASE	ALLOWABLE DECREASE
2	130.000000	61.646467	INFINITY
3	190.000000	4.949496	3.131312
4	80000.000000	INFINITY	17800.002700
5	80000.000000	3099.998990	4454.546200
6	70000.000000	41826.665500	11866.668500
7	70000.000000	2066.665990	3266.667240
8	1000.000000	107.878805	380.242416
9	1000.000000	139.999996	363.636360
10	0.000000	107.878805	INFINITY
11	0.000000	107.878805	380.242416
12	0.000000	139.999996	INFINITY
13	0.000000	139.999996	363.636360
14	5.000000	INFINITY	61.646467
15	0.000000	3.131312	4.949496
16	2.000000	INFINITY	1.646467
17	6.000000	3.131312	4.949496
18		34.444433	197.777803
19		82.888890	197.777805

Figure 12.3 *Schematic diagram of the PROTRAC model*

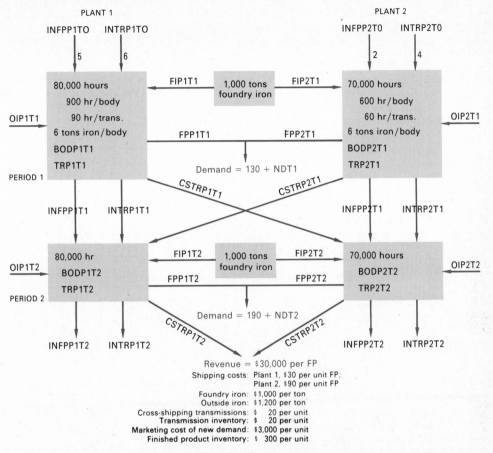

matters at the moment. Let's begin with the first. As you may know, we've received orders from upstairs to improve our methods for inventory handling.

What do you mean by "improve our methods?"

Manager I can't go into all that detail right now. But what I basically mean is that we've got to have lower per-unit carrying charges. This means that the industrial engineers are going to step in and analyze how things are currently being done and then make recommendations to reduce costs. One of my difficulties is that I'm in a new position and I am already in the middle of a dispute. I want your help in providing a solid quantitative basis for settling this thing.

I see. Can you give me any details?

Manager The supervisors at the plant 1 complex are telling me that I should worry about plant 2 because that's where the inefficiencies are. But the plant 2 people are telling me that their operations are optimal and I should be looking at plant 1. So that's where I am. Do you have an opinion from what your model tells you?

If I understand you correctly, you want to know where an improvement in inventory handling would give the most return. Is that correct?

Manager   Yes, and I'd like you to give me some quantitative support for taking one side or the other in this dispute.

To be honest with you, it looks to me like a toss-up.

Manager   Why is that?

Because neither side is right. Or, maybe I should say both sides are right.

Manager   That's what your output tells you?

Yes.

Manager   Well, I'm not really sure what you mean. Let's have a look at it.

Okay. I'll show it to you in a minute. But first, I want to mention something relevant. You may recall that the combined labor capacity of both plants in period 2 is insufficient to satisfy the current figure of 190 units of existing demand in period 2.

Manager   Hmmm . . . would you take a second to review your thinking on that?

We have 80,000 hours of labor in the plant 1 complex. Using the estimated requirement of 990 hours of labor per unit of finished product, we can obtain an estimated maximum total production of 80.808 units of finished product from plant 1. In the plant 2 complex, we have 70,000 hours of labor. At 660 hours of labor per unit of finished product, we get a maximum output of 106.06 units. Thus, maximum total production is about 3.13 units short, and we must somehow carry inventories into period 2. There are three options for doing that, right?

Manager   Right. We can carry forward finished product in inventory, or carry forward transmissions in inventory, or we can cross-ship transmissions. Of course, any combination of these activities could be employed and I would guess that we're probably doing some of each.

If you don't mind my saying so, that is where you're wrong.

Manager   Really?

Let's look at the computer output. The inventory variables are denoted by *INFPPiTj* and *INTRPiTj* where *i* and *j* indicate the appropriate plant and period, respectively. You can see that they're all zero, but that *CRTRP2T1*, which represents the transmissions cross-shipped from plant 2 to plant 1 in period 1, is positive. Remember, these transmissions leave plant 2 in period 1 and cannot be used in plant 1 until period 2.

Manager   I see. So the model claims that we cross-ship and do nothing else. But I thought we usually carry inventories also. I'm not sure the model's policy seems right.

Perhaps I can explain the reason.

Manager   You mean you can tell me why the solution turns out this way?

I think so.

Manager Well, okay. But I don't see how you can do that. Do you solve the whole model in your head?

No. I can't duplicate what the computer does, but I can use the computer results as a starting point to figure out some of the tradeoffs the computer analysis must be taking into account. Can I show you what I mean?

Manager Go ahead.

Well, you've already observed that we have to get 3.13 additional units of finished product into period 2. One way to do this would be to carry forward finished product inventory at a cost of $300 per unit.

Manager Right. So in that case it would cost $939 to make up the 3.13-unit deficit. That seems to be the obvious way to do it. In fact, I'm not sure that I clearly understand how to do it any other way.

Let me explain another possibility. Suppose that in one of the plants we carry 11 transmissions in inventory into period 2. That means that in this plant we could assemble 10 fewer transmissions in period 2 than we did previously.

Manager Wait a minute. Why are you carrying 11 transmissions into period 2? I don't get it.

You'll see in a minute. For now, assume that we are using all labor in both plants in period 2 and still we cannot make enough finished product to satisfy the period 2 demand. Now suppose that I have excess labor in period 1 relative to the existing demand. Certainly I can decide to carry forward 11 transmissions into period 2. You'll grant that I can do that?

Manager Yes, I don't see why not. But I still don't see the point.

And you'll also grant that I can assemble 10 fewer transmissions in period 2 and replace those with 10 of the 11 that are carried in?

Manager Yes. But since you're carrying 11 in, why don't you assemble 11 fewer?

It is also true that I could assemble 11 fewer. In fact, there are many different adjustments we could pursue, but I've done my homework and I want to show you what I've learned. So let's say that we assemble exactly 10 fewer in period 2 and replace these with 10 of the 11 that are carried forward.

Manager Okay. Then what?

Since we now assemble 10 fewer in period 2, we have released enough labor to make an additional body, because in either plant the amount of labor required to make a body is the same as the amount required to assemble 10 transmissions.

Manager Okay. Go on.

Now we're sitting here with an extra body and an eleventh transmission. We slap the eleventh transmission into the body, and we have an additional unit of finished product. So the 11 transmissions that are carried forward allow us to create an additional unit of finished product.

Manager I see. Pretty neat! What you are really saying is that the transmissions release enough labor to make another finished product, and that is true in either plant. And for each 11 carried into period 2, only 10 fewer will be assembled in period 2. Since an extra body is made with the released labor, the new policy continues to use all labor in period 2 but now we have an additional unit of output.

Right. Now let's see what these adjustments would cost in additional inventory charges.

Manager Since the inventory charge on a transmission is $20, it must cost 20(11), or $220. So that would be (3.13)(220), or $686.60 to make up our total shortage of finished product. That's clearly better than the $939-cost of carrying finished product forward. So holding transmissions is preferred to holding finished product?

Right. One way to look at it is like this. The tight resource in period 2 is labor. So what we would like to do is carry labor in inventory from period 1 into period 2. But we cannot do that. So what we do instead is carry forward something that consumes labor, and that is an implicit way of carrying forward labor.

Manager Sure. The labor is already in the transmission. That's clear enough. But let's get back to the optimal solution in your printout. We just figured out that carrying forward transmissions is preferable to carrying finished product. But the optimal solution says to cross-ship transmissions. Since the per-unit charge for cross-shipping is $20, and that is the same as the carrying charge for transmissions, I can't see why cross-shipping would be preferred to holding transmissions in inventory. I would guess that it's probably a situation involving—oh heck, what is that phrase?—optimal alternatives. You know what I mean.

Are you referring to the existence of alternative optima?

Manager Yes, that's it. Since it costs $20 both to cross-ship and to carry forward in either plant, we must clearly be indifferent. Right?

No. There is a good reason for the fact that cross-shipping is preferred. Recall that cross-shipping involves a transfer from one plant to the other. Now the important fact that you've overlooked is that the charge for shipping finished product is $60 less in plant 1 than in plant 2. When we cross-ship 11 transmissions from plant 2 to plant 1, the net final effect over the two periods is to ship one less unit of finished product from plant 2 in period 1 and one additional unit of finished product from plant 1 in period 2. The net saving on shipping charges is $60. This means that the cross-shipment policy has a net cost of 220 − 60 or $160 for each 11 transmissions.

Manager I'm sorry, but you lost me on that one. I understand the $220-cross-shipping charge, and I see that it costs $90 to ship finished product from plant 2 and only $30 from plant 1. But it seems to me that the total cost of the cross-shipping policy should be 220 + 30, or $250, and this is the same as what it would cost to carry forward 11 transmissions in plant 1 and then send out the finished product. Again, it looks to me like we should be indifferent between the two policies.

Okay, I can explain it very clearly. The idea is this. Suppose that we're producing at full capacity in both plants in each period, and everything produced is being sold. Now we want to produce and sell one less in period 1 and one more in period 2 in the cheapest possible way, right?

Manager Absolutely. No problem so far.

Figure 12.4 *Comparing the cost of alternative policies*

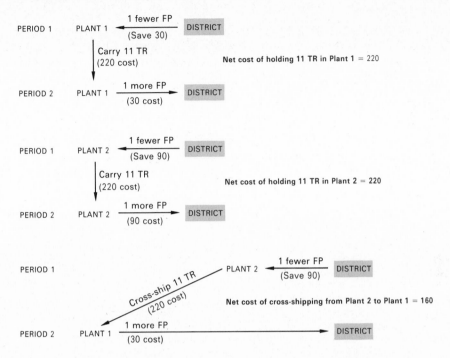

Good. Now look at this diagram [see Figure 12.4]. The top two sections show what happens costwise if we carry transmissions forward in plant 1 or plant 2, respectively. In each case, the net cost is 220. But in the lower section, you can see the effects of cross-shipping from plant 2 to plant 1. Can you now see that the net cost is only 160?

Manager Yes, I can. How long does it take you to figure all that out?

It isn't bad once you've done it a few times.

Manager I see. So in this case it looks like the total cost of the cross-shipping policy is (3.13)160, or $500.80. I agree that this is the cheapest way to do things. So I assume this is our current recommended operating policy.

Correct. By the way, you can also see why the optimal value of $CSTRP2T1$ is 34.44.

Manager I can? Let's see, that is the number of transmissions cross-shipped, so 34.44 must equal (3.13)11, and indeed that is true. So now let's figure out what this has to do with our dispute. I can see why you said it's a toss-up. Since neither plant should currently be planning to carry inventories, there doesn't seem to be much room for improvement in that respect. Since neither of the plants' management knows what the other is doing, it is clear why each one thinks I should look at the other.

That seems to be what's happening.

Manager Even though this is an interesting analysis, I am not very sure how helpful it is. After all, the upstairs wants to improve inventory handling, and they have their own reasons for wanting to do so. So suppose I just say, the heck with optimality. I want to make the old man upstairs happy, so I'm going to adjust our current activities and start carrying inventories even though we'll pay a price to do so. How much would it cost?

> Look at the reduced costs of *INTRP*1*T*1 and *INTRP*2*T*1. The value is 5.45. That is the initial per-unit cost of forcing yourself to carry an inventory of transmissions. As you can see, it's independent of the plant in this case.

Manager Yes, and I see that the reduced cost of finished product inventory is 140. That seems much too costly, so let's concentrate on the transmissions. Now suppose we tell one of the plant managers to start holding transmissions in inventory. How do I know that he'll adjust in an optimal way so that the cost doesn't go up by more than the 5.45 per unit?

> We could tell him not only what to do but also how to do it.

Manager You mean we have to rerun the problem, or what?

> No. We can see what's going on from the output we already have, but it requires some coordination of activities. Suppose that you decide to carry forward 11 transmissions in plant 1. This means that in period 1 the manager of plant 1 will produce 1 less body and instead he will assemble 10 additional transmissions. He will ship one less unit of finished product to the district. In period 1, the plant 2 manager must cross-ship 11 less transmissions over to plant 1. He will assemble 10 fewer transmissions and 1 additional body. An additional unit of finished product goes to the district to replace the one withdrawn by plant 1. The policies in period 2 will all be the same as they are now planned.

Manager How do you know that's the optimal adjustment?

> Let's figure out the cost. If it turns out to be 5.45 per transmission it will be optimal. Do you agree?

Manager Of course.

> In plant 1 there will be a holding cost of 220 and a period 1 shipping saving of 30. In plant 2 there will be a cross-shipping saving of 220 and an added period 1 shipping cost of 90. The net added cost is 60. There will also be six tons of iron that had been purchased in plant 1 and must now be purchased in plant 2. So that cost nets out to 0. In summary, the added cost is $60 for carrying the 11 transmissions forward in plant 1. That figures to be 60/11, or $5.45 per transmission. Since that is the value of the reduced cost, the adjustment must be optimal.

Manager Very good. Now suppose that instead I decide to carry the transmissions in plant 2. Let's see if I can figure out how to do it optimally. All I have to do is find some adjustments that lead to the number 5.45, right?

> Right you are.

Manager Okay, here we go. If I carry forward 11 transmissions in plant 2, I will cross-ship 11 less. The saving in cross-shipment costs will equal the added holding costs. In period 2, plant 2 will make 1 additional body and plant 1 will make 1 less body. The adjustments in iron charges cancel. In period 2, plant 1 assembles 10 more transmissions and plant 2 assembles 10 less. Plant 1 satisfies one less unit of demand in period 2, and plant 2 satisfies one more. Thus there is an added cost for shipping of (90-30)/11, or 60/11, which again gives $5.45. It looks like I've got it. Do you agree?

Absolutely. Of course, you remember that we can't be sure how long that figure of 5.45 will remain valid.

Manager   I understand. The incremental cost will probably change as we force more and more of these transmissions to be carried forward.

In fact, it will increase.

Manager   How can you tell?

Look at it this way. When you force F transmissions in plant 2 to be carried forward, you are implicitly imposing a constraint

$$INTRP2T1 \geq F$$

As you increase F, you are tightening the constraint, and we know that tightening a constraint hurts more and more.

Manager   I see. So the penalty of satisfying the upstairs is incrementally increasing—or, more correctly, nondecreasing. Right?

Yes.

Manager   By the way, I recall that we can reinterpret this current reduced cost of 5.45 somewhat differently. Isn't it correct to say that this is the amount the carrying charge would have to be reduced before the activity of carrying transmissions will actually be as good as cross-shipping?

Exactly.

Manager   Very interesting. That means about a 25-percent reduction would be required, which seems an unlikely possibility in either plant.

Perhaps you could persuade the upstairs to focus on the cross-shipping charges, since any reduction there will result in immediate added profits.

Manager   I see what you mean. We could reduce carrying costs 10 or 15 percent and still obtain no payoff. Even a 1-percent reduction in cross-shipping charges will give some added profits. Well, I can now see much more clearly into some of these interactions, but I still have the feeling that some of our past optimal policies have involved carrying inventories.

You mean historically?

Manager   Yes.

That could well have been the case at different levels of demand.

Manager   I see. Maybe we should analyze some of those interactions.

Which ones?

Manager The interactions related to increases in the level of demand. I haven't told you this, but that seems to be the underlying motive for the upstairs interest in reducing our inventory costs. I guess there is some reason to believe that there may be a windfall of demand in period 2. It has something to do with an anticipated change in the farm subsidy program.

When would this become apparent?

Manager I'm not sure. Maybe by the middle of period 1.

How do they know that?

Manager Because the old man has a son-in-law on one of the congressional committees. Anyway, if they can give us the right signals by the middle of period 1, I would assume that we could react appropriately. But what I am wondering is this: how much additional demand would there have to be before the optimal activities change?

I think what you're asking me is this: if existing demand increases enough, will the optimal inventory activities change?

Manager Right, but not just inventory. Let's look at all of the activities.

Fine, let's first take a look at the allowable increase in existing demand in period 1. That is 61.45 units, which is the optimal value of the new demand variable for period 1.

Manager I can see how to interpret that. For each additional unit of existing demand in period 1, we simply create one less unit of new demand in that same period. This would save $3,000 of marketing expense. All other decision variables remain unchanged in value. After 61.64 additional units of existing demand, there will be 0 new demand. At that point, I can see that any additional existing demand would make the problem infeasible.

Very good. And you've also explained why the dual price on row 2 is $3,000.

Manager You mean because the only change in cost would be the $3,000-saving in the marketing cost.

Yes.

Manager All right. That much is clear. But I see on your printout that the allowable change in period 2 existing demand is only 4.94. Frankly, that puzzles me.

In what particular way?

Manager For each additional unit of existing demand in period 2, we should create one less unit of new demand in period 1 and cross-ship 11 transmissions from plant 2 to plant 1. This should save 3,000 and cost 160, giving a net saving of $2,840. The dual price on row 3 is indeed 2,840, which shows that my analysis is correct. I don't see why we can't continue doing this until 61.45 units of existing demand have been added in period 2, with a new demand of 0 in period 1, just as we did in the other case.

Because the cost structure will change after you've increased existing demand by only 4.94.

Manager   I understand that's what the output means. But I don't see the reason. Do you?

Yes, I believe so. Here is what happens. Your analysis begins correctly, but you've overlooked an important fact. At optimality, plant 1 currently assembles 49.49 transmissions in period 2. This is the optimal value of $TRP1T2$. If we continue to use the optimal cross-shipping scheme, plant 1 will be producing only bodies and assembling no transmissions after 4.949 additional units of existing demand are satisfied in period 2. This is because the assembly of transmissions is reduced by 10 for each additional unit of demand, and 10(4.949) = 49.49. At this point, sending additional transmissions into plant 1 does nothing for you. Worse than that, it's wasteful because they cannot be used. The cost structure will therefore change at this point because a new optimal inventory activity will go into effect. In fact, the new activity will be to begin carrying forward transmissions in inventory in plant 2.

Manager   I see. Since plant 2 is still assembling transmissions, 106.06 of them, in fact, it is possible for them to cut back on transmission assembly in period 2 and make more bodies. Well, it looks to me like we've arrived at some interesting ideas.

Yes, but we haven't really settled your dispute.

Manager   Nevertheless, if I understand you correctly, we have good support for the following two recommendations. First of all, we should continue to operate optimally if possible, and that means we should have the industrial engineers examine the cross-shipping activity. Any increased efficiency in that area will be realized in immediate returns. Secondly, if it is true that we may have a significant increase in existing demand in period 2, then we should look at the inventory handling in plant 2. Of course, I am assuming that what you said is correct.

In particular?

Manager   That after an increase of 4.94 units of demand in period 2, we will see inventories of transmissions in plant 2.

By the way, if you are really expecting a surge in period 2 demand, why not increase the labor supply?

Manager   I'm glad you asked, because that leads me to the second thing I wanted to discuss, and this is a more detailed study. It involves capacity expansion.

I thought so.

Manager   I'd like you to take notes on this and prepare an analysis. No, better yet, I'll send you a memo. You can do the study and send me your analysis. I don't think you will need my help.

12.3 An Investment Analysis

12.3.1 The Cost Functions and the Plan of Analysis

The board of directors has approved a recommendation to modernize and expand the company foundry. The new capacity will be 1,400 tons in each period. A revised transfer-pricing policy will set the cost of foundry iron at $900 per ton. It is clear to management that the availability of labor hours is going to be the single binding constraint in future operations. Therefore, in order to make the most of the new foundry, the capacity of *one* (and only one) of the plants, as indirectly measured in the model by available labor hours, is going to be expanded. The management science department has been asked for recommendations on the following questions:

1 Which plant should be expanded?
2 What is the optimal capacity in the chosen plant?

In order to answer these questions, a study has been performed using the PROTRAC model discussed above as a starting point. Management has requested that the recommendations be based on a two-period problem with estimated existing demands as follows:

160 units (Period 1)

210 units (Period 2)

Because of union agreements and lead-time requirements, the plant capacity expansion will not be effective until period 2. In other words, the study should assume that the period 1 availability of labor is the same as it is currently (80,000 hours in plant 1, 70,000 hours in plant 2). However, it should be assumed that the new foundry and the new costs of iron will be operative and effective in both periods. Moreover, all initial inventories should be taken as in the foregoing model (refer to Figure 12.2).

Unfortunately, the cost of capacity expansion is not linear. As the scale of the effort increases, the basic construction plans become more elaborate. Increasing amounts of architectural and design time are required, and material specifications become more rigid and more costly. Management has solicited bids for potential expansion in each plant, and cost curves have been constructed. These are shown in Figures 12.5 and 12.6. For plant i, the function $C_i(b_i)$ denotes the cost of expanding capacity from the current level (80,000 in plant 1, 70,000 in plant 2) up to the level b_i. All costs are expressed in equivalent value at the end of period 2; that is, appropriate discounting has been performed.

Figure 12.5 *Cost of expansion to b_1 hours in plant 1*

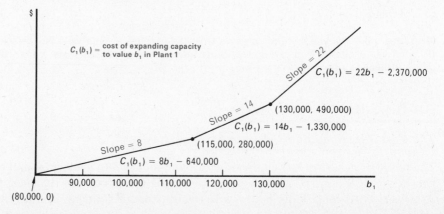

Figure 12.6 *Cost of expansion to b_2 hours in plant 2*

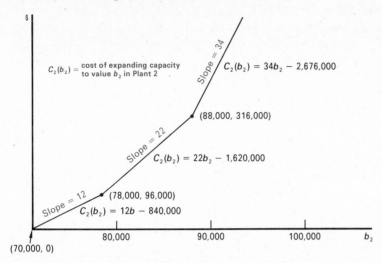

As you can see, each function is increasing, and the functions are *convex* (the rates of change are increasing). You will recall that the plant 2 facilities are more advanced and more efficient than plant 1. They require only 660 hours to produce a unit of finished product, as opposed to 990. As a result, the facilities and equipment in plant 2 are also more expensive, and that is reflected in the C_2 function.

Since the costs of expansion are nonlinear, they cannot be incorporated per se in the existing model. One approach for handling this problem, and the one we shall pursue, is now described. Another useful approach is shown in problem 14 at the end of this chapter.

First of all, each plant is considered separately. Let us use plant 1 as an illustration. We have learned that the optimal value function for labor hours in period 2 is an increasing concave function (the rate of change is decreasing). This is true because we are considering a max problem and a $\leq$ constraint, and relaxing a constraint helps less and less. As already noted, the cost-of-expansion curve is convex. For the moment, assume that each of these curves is smooth, as shown in Figure 12.7. This figure reveals that the number b_1^* is the optimal capacity. To demonstrate this, suppose the capacity is at a value of b_1 to the left of b_1^*, such as $\hat{b}_1$ in Figure 12.7. Now consider a small increase in b_1, to $\hat{b}_1 + \Delta$. The associated increase in the OV function is $V_1(\hat{b}_1 + \Delta) - V_1(\hat{b}_1)$. The associated increase in the expansion cost is $C_1(\hat{b}_1 + \Delta) - C_1(\hat{b}_1)$. Clearly, the increase in OV exceeds the increase in expansion cost, and hence the net increase in profit is positive. This means that $\hat{b}_1$ cannot be optimal. The same argument applies to all values of the capacity that are smaller than b_1^*. You can also convince yourself that if b_1 is larger than b_1^*, a small decrease will cut the expansion cost by more than the cut in the optimal objective value. Consequently, the optimal capacity must be b_1^*; that is, current capacity should be expanded to b_1^*. As shown in Figure 12.7, b_1^* is the point at which the tangent to each of the graphs has the same slope.

Figure 12.7 *Hypothetical smooth functions for the OV and the cost of expansion*

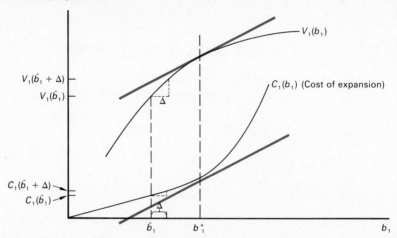

Assuming that the curves for plant 2 are also smooth, the same method can be followed to obtain an optimal capacity b_2^*. The plant to be chosen is obtained as follows. Recall that the current capacities are 80,000 and 70,000 in plants 1 and 2, respectively. The number $V_1(b_1^*) - V_1(80,000) - C_1(b_1^*)$ denotes the net gain associated with the optimal expansion in plant 1, since $V_1(b_1^*) - V_1(80,000)$ is the increase in profits, and $C_1(b_1^*)$ is the cost of obtaining this increase. Similarly, $V_2(b_2^*) - V_2(70,000) - C_2(b_2^*)$ is the net gain for the optimal plant 2 expansion. The plant with the largest net gain will be selected, since this is the one that yields the greatest net return from the proposed investment.

Basically, this is the approach to be employed. The optimal value functions for each plant, as a function of labor hours in period 2, will be generated. Each OV function will be compared with the cost of expansion function to determine the optimal capacity for each plant. The only departure from the above analysis involves the fact that the OV functions and the cost functions

Figure 12.8 *Hypothetical functions for the OV and the cost of expansion*

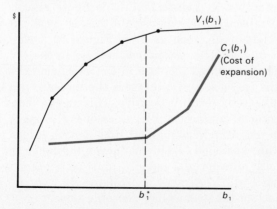

are not everywhere smooth. Each curve is piecewise linear and has corners at several points. However, this is only a minor complication. Figure 12.8 shows an illustration for this hypothetical situation at plant 1 with the optimal value b_1^*.

The point b_1^* is the unique capacity with the property that a change in either direction will diminish the net profit. This point b_1^* is characterized by the fact that the slope of the graph of C_1 to the right of b_1^* is greater than the slope of the graph of V_1, whereas to the left of b_1^* the situation is reversed.

Following the above approach, we shall now

1 Present the OV function for each plant
2 Determine the optimal investment

12.3.2 The OV Function for Each Plant and the Optimal Investment

The model is shown in Figure 12.9. Row 5 represents the capacity constraint on labor in plant 1, period 2. The right-hand side of 80,000 was increased in successive steps to generate the OV function for plant 1. This is called a *parametric analysis* on b_1. Specifically, the following calculations were performed:

1 The model in Figure 12.9 is run.
  a The optimal objective value $V_1(80,000)$, is recorded, and we thus have obtained the point $(80,000, V_1(80,000))$, which lies on the graph of V_1.

Figure 12.9 *The PROTRAC model*

```
MAX      29970 FPP1T1 + 29970 FPP1T2 + 29910 FPP2T1 + 29910 FPP2T2
         - 900 FIP1T1 - 900 FIP1T2 - 900 FIP2T1 - 900 FIP2T2 - 1200 OIP1T1
         - 1200 OIP1T2 - 1200 OIP2T1 - 1200 OIP2T2 - 20 CSTRP1T1
         - 20 CSTRP1T2 - 20 CSTRP2T1 - 20 CSTRP2T2 - 3000 NDT1 - 3000 NDT2
         - 20 INTRP1T1 - 20 INTRP1T2 - 20 INTRP2T1 - 20 INTRP2T2
         - 300 INFPP1T1 - 300 INFPP1T2 - 300 INFPP2T1 - 300 INFPP2T2
SUBJECT TO
  2)       FPP1T1 +  FPP2T1 -  NDT1 =       160
  3)       FPP1T2 +  FPP2T2 -  NDT2 =       210
  4)     900 BODP1T1 + 90 TRP1T1 <=     80000
  5)     900 BODP1T2 + 90 TRP1T2 <=     80000    (Labor in plant 1, period 2)
  6)     600 BODP2T1 + 60 TRP2T1 <=     70000
  7)     600 BODP2T2 + 60 TRP2T2 <=     70000    (Labor in plant 2, period 2)
  8)       FIP1T1 +  FIP2T1 <=    1400
  9)       FIP1T2 +  FIP2T2 <=    1400
 10)       FIP1T1 +  OIP1T1 - 6 BODP1T1 =      0
 11)       FIP2T1 +  OIP2T1 - 6 BODP2T1 =      0
 12)       FIP1T2 +  OIP1T2 - 6 BODP1T2 =      0
 13)       FIP2T2 +  OIP2T2 - 6 BODP2T2 =      0
 14)       FPP1T1 -  BODP1T1 +  INFPP1T1 =      5
 15)       FPP1T2 -  BODP1T2 -  INFPP1T1 +  INFPP1T2 =      0
 16)       FPP2T1 -  BODP2T1 +  INFPP2T1 =      2
 17)       FPP2T2 -  BODP2T2 -  INFPP2T1 +  INFPP2T2 =      0
 18)       CSTRP1T1 +  INTRP1T1 +  BODP1T1 -  TRP1T1 =      6
 19)       CSTRP1T2 -  CSTRP2T1 -  INTRP1T1 +  INTRP1T2 +  BODP1T2
         -  TRP1T2 =      0
 20)       CSTRP2T1 +  INTRP2T1 +  BODP2T1 -  TRP2T1 =      4
 21)     -  CSTRP1T1 +  CSTRP2T2 -  INTRP2T1 +  INTRP2T2 +  BODP2T2
         -  TRP2T2 =      0
```

b The allowable increase is 4,000.01. From this, we know that the first corner on V_1 will occur when $b_1 = 80,000 + 4,000.01 = 84,000.01$.

c The dual price is 22.105. Using this value, we can calculate that

$$V_1(84,000.01) = V_1(80,000) + [4,000.01(22.105)] = V_1(80,000) + 88,420$$

2 The model in Figure 12.9 is modified so that b_1 takes on a value slightly larger than 84,000.01 (in this case 84,005), and the model is run again. The same procedure as in item 1 above is followed to find the value of b_1 at the next corner and the optimal objective value at that point.

3 The process in item 2 is repeated until the allowable increase becomes infinite. At this point, we have the entire OV function for values of $b_1 \geq 80,000$.

The table in Figure 12.10 shows the successive right-hand sides with the associated data and summarizes the important changes in the optimal activities and the cost structure that occur at each corner of the OV graph (that is, at each degenerate solution). The notation used in this table is FP = finished product; TR = transmissions; CSTR = cross-ship transmissions; FI = foundry iron; OI = outside iron; ND = new demand; and the plants are referred to as 1 and 2. For our investment analysis, the differences $V_1(b_1) - V_1(80,000)$ are of more interest than $V_1(b_1)$, because these are the added returns, and so it is these differences that are recorded.

The sequence of computer runs revealed that, for each value of b_1, all labor is used in each period. There is always slack in the foundry in period 1 since the labor constraint is binding before the foundry capacity is exhausted, and iron cannot be carried in inventory. Initially, there is also foundry slack in period 2. The *initial* labor supply in period 2 is insufficient to satisfy all 210 units of existing demand. In order to make up the deficit (in the initial solution), transmissions are cross-shipped from plant 2 to plant 1, transmissions

Figure 12.10   *Analysis for capacity expansion in plant 1, period 2*

b_1	$V_1(b_1) -$ $V_1(80,000)$	Dual	Allowable Increase	Degenerate Solution?	Changes in Activities and Cost Structure
80,000	0	22.105	4,000.01	No	
84,000.01	88,420			Yes	Holding of FP in 1 goes to zero
84,005		22.0162	9,540.45	No	
93,545.45	298,574			Yes	Holding of TR in 2 goes to zero
93,565		21.9495	9,335.01	No	
102,900.01	503,902			Yes	CSTR goes to zero and begin to create ND in period 2
103,000		21.7879	23,000.019	No	
126,000.019	1,007,202			Yes	Foundry slack goes to zero in period 2, hence begin to buy OI
127,000		19.97	104,000	No	
231,000				Yes	
232,000		19.97	Infinite	No	

are carried forward in inventory in plant 2, and finished product is carried forward in inventory in plant 1.

You can see from the changes in the activities that as the labor supply in plant 1, period 2 increases (that is, as the constraint is loosened), the possibilities for greater economy are increased. In earlier chapters, we saw that loosening a $\leq$ constraint in a max problem leads to improvement in the optimal objective value and that the improvement occurs at a decreasing rate. In this problem, we have a specific demonstration of the interactions that yield this result. We note in Figure 12.10 that as the labor supply in period 2 (b_1) increases, PROTRAC first stops holding finished goods inventory, since this is the most costly way of using capacity in period 1 to satisfy demand in period 2. As b_1 is further increased, the carrying of transmissions inventory is eliminated, since this is the next most expensive way to satisfy period 2 demand. Finally, when b_1 becomes large enough, the cross-shipping of transmissions is terminated, since this is the least expensive way of satisfying period 2 demand. At this point, there is enough labor in period 2 to satisfy all 210 units of demand. PROTRAC then begins creating new demand in period 2. At the point the firm begins to buy outside iron in period 2 (that is, as soon as the foundry capacity is completely exhausted), the optimal activities and the cost structure stabilize, and the dual price on the labor constraint remains at 19.97 from that point. It is interesting to note that there is another basis change ("corner") after this point, but the slope does not change at this "corner." (This phenomenon is discussed in Example 4 in Section 8.8. It is taken up again in problem 13 at the end of this chapter.)

In Figure 12.11, the graph of $V_1(b_1) - V_1(80,000)$ appears, with the graph of $C_1(b_1)$. It is apparent from the graphic representation that the optimal capacity is given by $b_1^* = 130,000$. This is the value of b_1 that maximizes $V_1(b_1) - V_1(80,000) - C_1(b_1)$. If the capacity is, in fact, expanded from 80,000 to 130,000, the net return will be

$$V_1(130,000) - V_1(80,000) - C_1(130,000) = 1,087,080 - 490,000 = 597,080$$

The analysis for plant 2 parallels that for plant 1. The graph of $V_2(b_2) - V_2(70,000)$ appears with the graph of $C_2(b_2)$ in Figure 12.12. The parametric analysis for generating $V_2(b_2)$ is left as an exercise for the student (see problem 9). The graphic representation shows that the optimal capacity is given by $b_2^* = 88,000$. This is the value of b_2 that maximizes $V_2(b_2) - V_2(70,000) - C_2(b_2)$. The associated net return will be

$$V_2(88,000) - V_2(70,000) - C_2(88,000) = 591,611 - 316,000 = 275,611$$

Comparing the results from the two plants, the analysis indicates that the optimal investment is to expand the capacity in plant 1 to 130, 000.

This example provides a good illustration of how the parametric dual-pricing analysis can be used to deal with nonlinear conditions. The process of plotting the graphs of the OV function and the cost function on the same axis allows management to see what the return would be for any particular decision. Such data could be of considerable help in the decision-making process. As we have pointed out, any real decision problem is likely to involve factors not included

Figure 12.11 *The functions $V_1(b_1) - V_1(80,000)$ and $C_1(b_1)$*

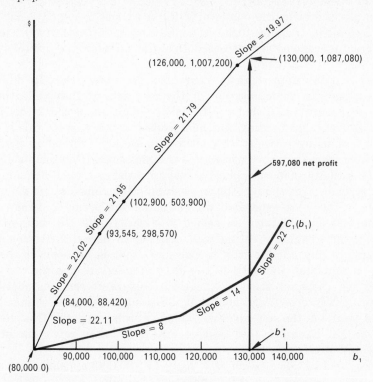

in the model, and thus the question of optimality is often less important than giving management an opportunity to accurately assess at least some of the quantitative effects of the chosen decision.

12.4 Examples and Solutions

Example 1

This example involves activity analysis in the PROTRAC scenario. Consider the computer output shown in Figure 12.2. Suppose another unit of labor is available in plant 2 in period 2. How would this extra unit affect the optimal levels of all activities?

Solution to Example 1

A preliminary analysis of the relevant production and shipping changes is indicated by Figure 12.13. Note that the extra hour of labor in period 2 leads to the shipping of additional finished product in period 1, not in period 2. The interactions work as follows. The extra hour of labor in plant 2 (period 2) permits production of $\frac{1}{660}$ more finished product, and hence $\frac{1}{660}$ less finished

gure 12.12   *The functions $V_2(b_2) - V_2(70,000)$ and $C_2(b_2)$*

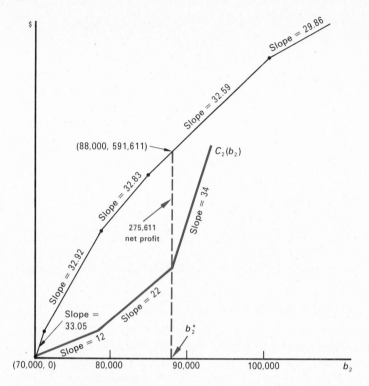

product will be required from plant 1 in satisfying the period 2 existing demand. This means that, in period 2, plant 1 produces $\frac{1}{660}$ fewer bodies. With the released labor $\frac{10}{660}$ transmissions are assembled. Thus fewer transmissions need to be cross-shipped from plant 2 to plant 1, and this in turn releases the

igure 12.13   *The relevant production and shipping changes*

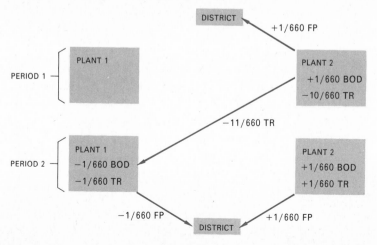

resources in plant 2 (period 1) to create the additional finished product. Using Figure 12.13, it is not difficult to verify the optimality of these proposed changes. To do this, however, it will be useful to more completely specify all of the activity changes. These are enumerated in the table in Figure 12.14.

Figure 12.14 *Activity changes*

Period	Plant	FP Shipped	BOD	TR	INTR	CSTR	ND	OI	FI	INFP
1	1							$+\frac{6}{660}$	$-\frac{6}{660}$	
1	2	$+\frac{1}{660}$	$+\frac{1}{660}$	$-\frac{10}{660}$		$-\frac{11}{660}$	$+\frac{1}{660}$		$+\frac{6}{660}$	
2	1	$-\frac{1}{660}$	$-\frac{1}{660}$	$+\frac{10}{660}$					$-\frac{6}{660}$	
2	2	$+\frac{1}{660}$	$+\frac{1}{660}$	$+\frac{1}{660}$					$+\frac{6}{660}$	

In order to demonstrate the optimality of these changes, we first observe that they are feasible and then must show that the associated net return is equal to the dual price on the relevant labor constraint (row 7). The net return is computed as follows:

Additional revenue		**Additional cost**	
Sales	$\dfrac{30,000}{660}$	New demand	$\dfrac{3,000}{660}$
Savings on cross-shipping	$\dfrac{220}{660}$	Shipping	$\dfrac{180}{660}$
Savings on shipping	$\dfrac{30}{660}$	Outside iron	$\dfrac{7,200}{660}$
Total	$\dfrac{30,250}{660}$	Total	$\dfrac{10,380}{660}$

$$\text{Net} = \frac{30,250 - 10,380}{660} = \frac{19,870}{660} = 30.106$$

Since the dual price on row 7 is also 30.106, the proposed changes are optimal. We note in passing that we have not claimed uniqueness for these optimal changes. In some situations, there may be more than one way to adjust optimally.

Example 2

The Party Nut problem was originally presented as problem 15 in Chapter 4. The Party Nut Company has on hand 550 pounds of peanuts, 150 pounds of cashews, 90 pounds of brazil nuts, and 70 pounds of hazelnuts. It packages and sells four varieties of mixed nuts in 8-ounce (half-pound) cans. The mix requirements and net wholesale prices are indicated in Figure 12.15. The firm can sell all that it can produce at these prices. When addressing the issue of what quantities of the various mixes should be produced, a consulting firm formulated the problem as follows: Let

P_i = pounds of peanuts used in mix i

C_i = pounds of cashews used in mix i

B_i = pounds of brazil nuts used in mix i

H_i = pounds of hazelnuts used in mix i

The computer solution is shown in Figure 12.16.

Figure 12.15 *Product Data for Party Nut Company*

Mix	Contents	Price per Can ($)
1 (Peanuts)	Peanuts only	.26
2 (Party Mix)	No more than 50% peanuts; at least 15% cashews; at least 10% brazil nuts	.40
3 (Cashews)	Cashews only	.51
4 (Luxury Mix)	At least 30% cashews; at least 20% brazil nuts; at least 30% hazelnuts	.52

Figure 12.16 *Computer solution to the Party Nut Company problem*

```
MAX 52P1+80P2+80C2+80B2+80H2+102C3+104P4+104C4+104B4+104H4
SUBJECT TO
   2)    P1+P2+P4 <= 550
   3)    C2+C3+C4 <= 150
   4)    B2+B4 <= 90
   5)    H2+H4 <= 70
   6)    .5P2-.5C2-.5B2-.5H2 <= 0
   7)    -.15P2+.85C2-.15B2-.15H2 >= 0
   8)    -.1P2-.1C2+.9B2-.1H2 >= 0
   9)    -.3P4+.7C4-.3B4-.3H4 >= 0
  10)    -.2P4-.2C4+.8B4-.2H4 >= 0
  11)    -.3P4-.3C4-.3B4+.7H4 >= 0

VARIABLE        VALUE        REDUCED-COST
   P1         380.00000        0.00000
   P2         123.33337        0.00000
   C2          80.00000        0.00000
   B2          43.33333        0.00000
   H2           0.00000       23.99997
   C3           0.00000        6.00002
   P4          46.66667        0.00000
   C4          70.00000        0.00000
   B4          46.66667        0.00000
   H4          70.00000        0.00000
 OBJ FCTN       63760.
```

Figure 12.16 *(Continued)*

ROW	SLACK	DUAL-PRICE
2	0	52
3	0	108.
4	0	108
5	0	132
6	0	56
7	43.	0
8	18.6667	0
9	0	-56.
10	0	-56
11	0	-80.

SENSITIVITY ANALYSIS

RANGE IN WHICH BASIS REMAINS THE SAME
      COST SENSITIVITY

VARIABLE	INCREASE IN C(J)	DECREASE IN C(J)
P1	6.00001	11.99998
P2	8.99999	6.00001
C2	23.99997	6.00002
B2	35.99995	56.00000
H2	23.99997	INFINITE
C3	6.00002	INFINITE
P4	INFINITE	35.99995
C4	55.99998	23.99997
B4	56.00000	35.99995
H4	INFINITE	23.99997

RIGHT HAND SENSITIVITY

ROW	ALLOWABLE INCREASE	ALLOWABLE DECREASE
2	INFINITE	380.0000
3	93.33365	61.42858
4	143.33334	23.33337
5	56.00001	70.00000
6	93.33337	61.66669
7	43.0000	INFINITE
8	18.6667	INFINITE
9	46.66669	70.00000
10	23.33337	46.66667
11	28.00000	56.00001

a What is the meaning of the dual price for the second row (availability of peanuts)? Suppose an additional pound of peanuts is available. What changes in the optimal solution would occur?

b Answer part *a* for the third row.

Solution to Example 2

a The dual price for the second row implies that the optimal value of the objective function would increase at the rate of 52¢ per additional pound of peanuts available. Since mix 1, peanuts (only), sells for 52¢ per pound (26¢ per 8-ounce can), it seems clear that each additional pound of peanuts that becomes available would be sold as mix 1. This solution is consistent with the facts that: (1) in the current optimal solution peanuts are being sold in their least profitable employment (as mix 1), and (2) the allowable increase in the RHS of the second row is infinite. Under the assumptions of the model, Party Nut can use as many peanuts as are available and sell them as mix 1 for 52¢ per pound.

b The dual price for the third row states that the optimal value of the objective function will increase at the rate of 108¢ per pound of additional cashews available. Since mix 3, cashews (only), sells for 102¢ per pound, it is clear that one cannot obtain an additional return of 108¢ by selling an additional pound of cashews as mix 3. The cashews must be mixed to obtain a higher return. The clue that suggests how to best use an additional pound of cashews is provided by the coefficients in the objective function. Note that if the additional pound of cashews was added to mix 2 and one pound of peanuts currently sold as mix 1 was also added to mix 2, the increase in revenue would be 108¢. Two additional pounds of mix 2 yield an increase of 160¢, but one less pound of mix 1 yields a decrease of 52¢ for a net increase of 108¢. Although this change provides the proper increase in the objective function, we cannot be sure that this is the correct answer until we verify its feasibility. That is, we must verify that the proposed change satisfies the constraints.

If a pound of cashews and a pound of peanuts are added to mix 2, its composition would be 124.33 pounds of peanuts, 81 pounds of cashews, and 43.33 pounds of brazil nuts. The percentage of each nut in the mix is as follows:

Peanuts   = 124.33/248.66 = 50%

Cashews   =   81/248.66 = 33%

Brazil nuts =   43.33/248.66 = 17%

Since this blend satisfies the constraints, the suggested answer is correct.

It should be noted that the profitability of the most profitable mix is 104¢ per pound, and yet the value of another pound of cashews exceeds this figure. This says that to obtain an additional unit of a resource, we are willing to pay more than the per-unit profitability of the most profitable use of that resource!

Example 3

The Winston-Salem Development Planning problem was originally presented as Example 11 in Chapter Four. The problem is restated here. Winston-Salem Development Management (WSDM) is trying to complete its investment plans for the next three years. Currently, WSDM has $2 million available for investment. At six-month intervals over the next three years, WSDM expects the following income stream from previous investments: $500,000 (six months from now); $400,000; $380,000; $360,000; $340,000; and $300,000 (at end of third year). There are three development projects in which WSDM is considering participating. The Foster City Development would, if WSDM participated fully, have the following projected cash-flow stream at six-month intervals over the next three years (negative numbers represent investments, positive numbers represent income): −\$3,000,000 (beginning of period 1); −\$1,000,000; −\$1,800,000; \$400,000; \$1,800,000; \$1,800,000; \$5,500,000. The last figure is its estimated value at the end of three years. A second project involves taking over the operation of some old, lower-middle-income housing on the condition that certain initial repairs to it be made and that it be demolished at the end of three years. The cash-flow stream for this project, if participated in fully, would be: −\$2,000,000 (beginning of period 1); −\$500,000; \$1,500,000; \$1,500,000; \$1,500,000; \$200,000; −\$1,000,000.

The third project, the Disney-Universe Hotel, would have the following cash-flow stream (six-month intervals) if WSDM participated fully. Again, the last figure is the estimated value at the end of the three years: −\$2,000,000 (beginning of period 1); −\$2,000,000; −\$1,800,000; \$1,000,000; \$1,000,000; \$1,000,000; \$6,000,000. WSDM can borrow money for half-year intervals at 3.5 percent interest per half-year. At most, \$2 million can be borrowed at one time; that is, the total outstanding principal can never exceed \$2 million. WSDM can invest surplus funds at 3 percent per half-year.

Consider the problem of maximizing WSDM's net worth at the end of three years. Disregard taxes, and assume that if WSDM participates in a project at less than 100 percent, all the cash flows of that project are reduced proportionately. Then this problem can be formulated as an LP model. In order to do this, let

F = fractional participation in Foster City

M = fractional participation in Lower-Middle

D = participation in Disney

B_i = amount borrowed in period i, $i = 1, ..., 6$

L_i = amount lent in period i, $i = 1, ..., 6$

Z = net worth *after* the six periods

The formulation and computer solution are shown in Figure 12.17. (Note: All numbers are measured in units of 1,000.) Row 2 imposes the condition that at the beginning of period 1, WSDM can spend only the money that is available at that time. Rows 3–7 impose a similar condition on periods 2–6, respectively. Row 8 defines the profit variable, Z. Rows 9–14 are borrowing constraints. Rows 15–17 limit the participation in each of the projects to no more than 100 percent.

a Is the solution degenerate?

b Can there ever be slack in rows 2–8 (if, for example, the RHS is changed)?

c What is the meaning of the dual price associated with row 6 (the beginning of period 5)? Assuming the allowable increase in the RHS of row 6 is at least 1, what changes in the optimal solution would occur from such an increase?

d Perform activity analysis for an *extra* dollar of availability at the beginning of periods 6, 4, and 3.

Solution to Example 3

a The problem has 16 constraints. The solution shows that nine variables are positive. In order to demonstrate that the solution is nondegenerate, we must be able to conclude that seven slack variables are positive. Note that

Figure 12.17   *The WSDM problem*

```
MAX Z
SUBJECT TO
   2)    -3000F -2000M -2000D +B1-L1 >=-2000
   3)    -1000F -500M -2000D -1.035B1+1.03L1+B2-L2 >=-500
   4)    -1800F +1500M -1800D -1.035B2+1.03L2-L3+B3 >=-400
   5)     400F +1500M +1000D +B4-L4+1.03L3-1.035B3 >=-380
   6)    1800F +1500M +1000D -1.035B4+1.03L4+B5-L5 >=-360
   7)    1800F +200M +1000D -1.035B5+1.03L5+B6-L6 >=-340
   8)    -Z +5500F -1000M +6000D -1.035B6+1.03L6 >=-300
   9)    B1 <= 2000
  10)    B2 <= 2000
  11)    B3 <= 2000
  12)    B4 <= 2000
  13)    B5 <= 2000
  14)    B6 <= 2000
  15)    F  <= 1
  16)    M  <= 1
  17)    D  <= 1
```

VARIABLE	VALUE	REDUCED-COST
Z	7665.17866	0.00000
F	0.71533	0.00000
M	0.63840	0.00000
D	0.00000	452.37945
B1	1417.44335	0.00000
L1	0.00000	0.00879
B2	1999.99999	0.00000
L2	0.00000	0.33317
B4	448.44958	0.00000
L4	0.00000	0.00530
L3	0.00000	0.25052
B3	2000.00047	0.00000
B5	0.00000	0.00515
L5	2137.48338	0.00000
B6	0.00000	0.00500
L6	3954.86375	0.00000
OBJ FCTN	7665.18	

ROW	SLACK	DUAL-PRICE
2	0	-1.81922
3	0	-1.7577
4	0	-1.38193
5	0	-1.09803
6	0	-1.0609
7	0	-1.03
8	0	-1
9	582.557	0
10	0	.327403
11	0	.245466
12	1551.55	0
13	2000	0
14	2000	0
15	.284669	0
16	.361603	0
17	1.	0

$B1$, $B4$, $B5$ and $B6$ are all less than 2,000. This implies that there must be a positive slack in each of rows 9, 12, 13, and 14. Also F, M, and D are less than 1. This implies that there must be a positive slack in each of rows 15, 16, and 17. Since this yields a total of seven positive slacks, the solution is nondegenerate.

b There cannot be slack in rows 2–8. If there were, lending could always be increased, or borrowing decreased, to the benefit of the company. Therefore, rows 2–8 will always be satisfied with equality.

c The dual price for row 6 is -1.0609. This implies that the optimal value of the objective function would *decrease* $1.0609 if the RHS of the fifth constraint is increased by a unit. Note that a unit increase in the RHS of the fifth constraint, from -360 to -359, implies that Winston-Salem has $1,000 less income at the beginning of year 3, and so the fact that the net worth, Z, decreases is intuitively appealing. To see what changes in the current optimal solution will yield a decrease of $1.0609, we note that Winston-Salem is currently lending money in period 5; that is, $L_5 = 2137.48$. Since the company now has one less dollar at its disposal, it seems reasonable that one less dollar will be lent. The loss of $1 lent at 3 percent per period for two periods yields a total loss of $(1.03)^2$, or $1.0609. In terms of the variables, let $\wedge$ (for example, $\hat{L}_5$) indicate the changed variables. All variables remain the same except those shown below.

$$\hat{L}_5 = L_5 - 1$$
$$\hat{L}_6 = L_6 - 1.03$$
$$\hat{Z} = Z - 1.0609$$

It is intuitive and easily checked that this new policy is feasible. We merely note that if the right-hand side of row 6 is -359, then the above new values for the variables will maintain equality in rows 6–8.

d For row 7 (beginning of period 6), the dual is -1.03. Thus, an extra dollar available should produce an additional 1.03 return. This is obtained by lending one more dollar in period 6, to produce 1.03 at the end of period 6. Variables are redefined in the obvious way.

For row 5 (beginning of period 4), the dual is -1.09803. An additional return of 1.09803 is obtained from an extra dollar available in period 4 by borrowing one less dollar at the beginning of period 4. We will then have 1.035 extra on hand at the beginning of period 5. Lend this amount and lend the accrued amount at the beginning of period 6 to obtain

$$(1.035)(1.03)(1.03) = 1.09803$$

Variables are redefined in the obvious way.

For row 4 (beginning of period 3), the analysis is more difficult. The dual is -1.38193. Suppose one unit extra income is available at the beginning of period 3. Since $B3 = 2,000$, it must be optimal to invest as much as possible in period 3. Thus, since rows 2–8 will always, at optimality, be satisfied with equality, F, M, and $B1$ change by ΔF, ΔM, and $\Delta B1$, in such a way that

$$\left. \begin{array}{r} -1800\Delta F + 1500\Delta M = -1(\text{From row 4}) \\ 3000\Delta F + 2000\Delta M = \Delta B1(\text{From row 2}) \\ -1000\Delta F - 500\Delta M - (1.035)\Delta B1 = 0(\text{From row 3}) \end{array} \right\} \Rightarrow \begin{array}{l} \Delta F = .00023833 \\ \Delta M = -.00038067 \\ \Delta B1 = -.04635 \end{array}$$

The changes ΔF and ΔM create a surplus of dollars at the start of period 4, 5, 6, 7. This leads to borrowing less at the beginning of period 4 and lending more at the beginning of periods 5 and 6.

The additional profit will be

$$(1.09803) \quad \underbrace{[400\Delta F + 1,500\Delta M]}_{\substack{\text{Extra units at} \\ \text{beginning of} \\ \text{period 4; treat as} \\ \text{discussed above.}}} + (1.0609) \quad \underbrace{[1,800\Delta F + 1,500\Delta M]}_{\substack{\text{Extra at beginning} \\ \text{of period 5; treat} \\ \text{as discussed above.}}}$$

$$+ (1.03) \quad \underbrace{[1,800\Delta F + 200\Delta M]}_{\substack{\text{Extra at beginning} \\ \text{of period 6; treat} \\ \text{as discussed above}}} + \quad \underbrace{5,500\Delta F - 1,000\Delta M}_{\substack{\text{Extra at end of} \\ \text{period 6 from } \Delta F \\ \text{and } \Delta M}}$$

$$= 1.38193 = \text{added net worth}$$

12.5 Problems

1 Refer to Figure 12.2.

 a Due to forecasting errors, PROTRAC's Australian plant has some excess units of final product in inventory. What is the maximum amount that the midwest tractor division manager should pay to obtain a unit from Australia? Where and when should it be delivered, that is, to which plant and at the beginning of which period?

 b Rather than using conventional methods for creating new demand, PROTRAC is considering hiring a consultant who will accept payment on the basis of the number of units of new demand that he generates. What is the maximum amount PROTRAC should be willing to pay him for the first unit of new demand that he generates in period 2?

 c How many units would management be willing to have him create at this price? Assume that, all other things equal, we prefer more production to less.

 d How much should management be willing to pay to have demand increased by an additional unit if it had already been increased by the amount specified in part c? Give an exact answer. (See problem 15.)

 e A private contractor feels that he can help increase the existing demand by using his contacts in the construction industry. What is the most you would be willing to pay him to obtain another unit of demand in period 1?

 f Explain any difference between this figure and the answer to part b.

 g What is the maximum number of units you would have this contractor increase the existing demand at the price specified in part e? (Again, assume that, all other things equal, you prefer more production to less.)

 h How much would you be willing to pay to have existing demand increased beyond the answer you found in part g? Why?

 i Suppose that a competitor offers to supply you with iron at less than the foundry price of $1,000 per ton because he has excess capacity. How many tons should you purchase from him in each period?

2 Note that the reduced cost on transmission inventory in plant 1 at the end of period 2 (*INTRP*1*T*2) is 1,831.82. The dual price on labor in plant 1, period 2 is 20.1313. It takes 90 hours of labor to assemble a single transmission in plant 1. Carrying a single transmission in inventory at the end of period 2, in plant 1, might thus be interpreted as being equivalent to "throwing away" 90 hours of the labor supply. But 90(20.1313) = 1,811.82 < 1,831.82. How do you explain this discrepancy of $20?

3 The dual price on an iron consumption constraint can be interpreted as the maximum amount a manager should be willing to pay to have a ton of iron on hand in the appropriate plant at the beginning of the period. The computer output shows that outside iron is purchased in plant 1 in each period. The dual price on the iron consumption constraints for plant 1 would therefore be expected to equal the price of outside iron, which is 1,200. Indeed, this is the case. For plant 2 there is no purchase of outside iron in either period. Why then is the dual price on the plant 2 iron consumption constraints also 1,200?

4 *The Parsimony of Corner Solutions.* Figure 12.2 reveals that outside iron is purchased only in plant 1. Why couldn't a little less be purchased in plant 1 and have this amount purchased in plant 2, with a corresponding change in the levels of foundry iron purchased? (That is, let plant 1 purchase Δ fewer units of OI in period 1, and Δ more units of FI. Let plant 2 purchase Δ fewer units of FI and Δ more units of OI.) Would such a policy be optimal? Could it be produced by the computer? Comment on what this reveals about the "parsimony" of optimal basic solutions.

5 Refer to Figure 12.2. Is there any way a solution could be produced with outside iron purchased in plant 2 in period 1? Support your answer.

6 Refer to Figure 12.2. In period 2, all labor is used and no new demand is created. Thus, it appears that existing demand is satisfied at just the point that all labor is used. Is this improbable phenomenon a correct interpretation?

7 Refer to the Party Nut problem presented in Example 2.
  a The dual price on row 4 (brazil nuts available) is 108. Suppose an extra pound of brazil nuts is available. What changes in the optimal solution would occur that would cause the optimal value to increase by 108?
  b The dual price on row 5 (hazelnuts available) is 132. Suppose an additional pound of hazelnuts is available. What changes in the optimal solution would occur that would cause the optimal value to increase by 132? Hint: Be guided by the fact that any changes you make should preserve the current basis. No currently active (inactive) constraint should become inactive (active). No currently positive (zero) variable should become zero (positive).

8 Refer to the Winston-Salem Development Management problem presented in Example 3. A summary of the solution is presented in Figure 12.18.

Figure 12.18 *The WSDM solution summarized*

Variable	Value	Row	Dual Price
Z	7,665.18	2	−1.81922
F	.71533	3	−1.7577
M	.6384	4	−1.38193
D	0	5	−1.09803
B1	1,417.44	6	−1.0609
B2	2,000	7	−1.03
B3	2,000	8	−1
B4	448.45	9	0
B5	0	10	.327403
B6	0	11	.245466
L1	0	12	0
L2	0	13	0
L3	0	14	0
L4	0	15	0
L5	2,137.48	16	0
L6	3,954.86375	17	0

  a Explain the algebraic relation between the dual prices on rows 2 and 3.
  b The dual price on borrowing at the beginning of period 2 is .327404; that is, the ability to borrow an additional unit at the beginning of period 2 would increase the net worth at the end by .327404 units. Explain the relation

$$.327404 = (1.7577 - 1.035)(1.38193)$$

  What is the maximum interest rate we would be willing to pay to borrow an additional unit at the beginning of period 2?

9 Use your own computer to generate the OV function for plant 2. Produce (for plant 2) the analogue of Figure 12.10.

10 Refer to Figure 12.2. Consider the values and allowable increases for the dual prices on labor capacity in plants 1 and 2, period 1. Use this information to analyze the optimal change in activities and costs that would result from an additional hour of labor in each plant (separately) in period 1. Explain why the allowable increase has the indicated value.

11 Refer to Figure 12.2. Suppose the labor supply in plant 2, period 1, is increased by the allowable amount, 41,826.66 hours. The associated activity changes were analyzed in problem 10. Based on this analysis, do you expect the dual price to change at this point? Present a rationale to defend your answer.

12 Consider Figure 12.2. Explain the costs and the activities associated with the following deviations from optimality. Pay attention to all adjustments in both plants in both periods on: the purchases of iron (both from the foundry and outside), the assembly of transmissions, the production of bodies, the shipment of finished product, the creation of new demand, the inventory of finished product and transmission, and the cross-shipment of transmissions.
a Holding a unit of finished product in inventory at the end of period 1 in plant 1.
b Holding a unit of finished product in inventory at the end of period 1 in plant 2.
c Holding a transmission in inventory at the end of period 2 in plant 1.
d Holding a transmission in inventory at the end of period 1 in plant 1.
e Holding a transmission in inventory at the end of period 2 in plant 2.

13 Refer to Figure 12.10. At $b_1 = 231,000$ the dual price does not change, which means that although the activities change, the cost structure does not. Analyze why. The information in Figure 12.19 on iron activities in period 2 should be used. (The symbol $+FI$ means the optimal solution involves the purchase of foundry iron. Similarly for $+OI$.)

Figure 12.19 *Iron activities in period 2*

For b_1 = 127,000		For b_1 = 231,000		For b_1 = 232,000	
Plant 1	Plant 2	Plant 1	Plant 2	Plant 1	Plant 2
$+FI$	$+FI$	$+FI(1,400)$	$FI = 0$	$+FI(1,400)$	$FI = 0$
$OI = 0$	$+OI$	$OI = 0$	$+OI$	$+OI$	$+OI$

14 *An Alternative Approach to the Investment Problem.* Recall that there are three "pieces" to the cost of expansion function for plant 1. That is, letting $C(b_1)$ denote the cost of expanding the capacity to b_1, we have

$$C(b_1) = \begin{cases} 8b_1 - 640,000 & \text{if } 80,000 \le b_1 \le 115,000 \\ 14b_1 - 1,330,000 & \text{if } 115,000 \le b_1 \le 130,000 \\ 22b_1 - 2,370,000 & \text{if } 130,000 \le b_1 \end{cases}$$

The model in Figure 12.9 is modified by introducing two new variables. Let

B = capacity in plant 1

C = cost of obtaining that capacity

The following changes are then required:
(1) C is subtracted from the current expression for the objective function
(2) Row 5 becomes

$900\,BODP1T2 + 90\,TRP1T2 - B \le 0$

(3) Three new constraints are added:

$$C \geq 8B - 640,000, \text{ i.e., } C - 8B \geq - 640,000$$

$$C \geq 14B - 1,330,000, \text{ i.e., } C - 14B \geq - 1,330,000$$

$$C \geq 22B - 2,370,000, \text{ i.e., } C - 22B \geq - 2,370,000$$

Figure 12.20

```
    MAX   29970 FPP1T1 + 29970 FPP1T2 + 29910 FPP2T1 + 29910 FPP2T2
          - 900 FIP1T1 - 900 FIP1T2 - 900 FIP2T1 - 900 FIP2T2 - 1200 OIP1T1
          - 1200 OIP1T2 - 1200 OIP2T1 - 1200 OIP2T2 - 20 CSTRP1T1
          - 20 CSTRP1T2 - 20 CSTRP2T1 - 20 CSTRP2T2 - 3000 NDT1 - 3000 NDT2
          - 20 INTRP1T1 - 20 INTRP1T2 - 20 INTRP2T1 - 20 INTRP2T2
          - 300 INFPP1T1 - 300 INFPP1T2 - 300 INFPP2T1 - 300 INFPP2T2 - C
    SUBJECT TO
     2)      FPP1T1 + FPP2T1 - NDT1 =      160
     3)      FPP1T2 + FPP2T2 - NDT2 =      210
     4)    900 BODP1T1 + 90 TRP1T1 <=   80000
     5)    900 BODP1T2 + 90 TRP1T2 - B <=    0
     6)    600 BODP2T1 + 60 TRP2T1 <=   70000
     7)    600 BODP2T2 + 60 TRP2T2 <=   70000
     8)      FIP1T1 + FIP2T1 <=   1400
     9)      FIP1T2 + FIP2T2 <=   1400
    10)  -   FIP1T1 - OIP1T1 + 6 BODP1T1 =      0
    11)  -   FIP2T1 - OIP2T1 + 6 BODP2T1 =      0
    12)  -   FIP1T2 - OIP1T2 + 6 BODP1T2 =      0
    13)  -   FIP2T2 - OIP2T2 + 6 BODP2T2 =      0
    14)      FPP1T1 - BODP1T1 + INFPP1T1 =      5
    15)      FPP1T2 - BODP1T2 - INFPP1T1 + INFPP1T2 =      0
    16)      FPP2T1 - BODP2T1 + INFPP2T1 =      2
    17)      FPP2T2 - BODP2T2 - INFPP2T1 + INFPP2T2 =      0
    18)      CSTRP1T1 + INTRP1T1 + BODP1T1 - TRP1T1 =      6
    19)      CSTRP1T2 - CSTRP2T1 - INTRP1T1 + INTRP1T2 + BODP1T2
             - TRP1T2 =      0
    20)      CSTRP2T1 + INTRP2T1 + BODP2T1 - TRP2T1 =      4
    21)  -   CSTRP1T1 + CSTRP2T2 - INTRP2T1 + INTRP2T2 + BODP2T2
             - TRP2T2 =      0
    22)      C - 8 B >= - 640000
    23)      C - 14 B >= - 1330000
    24)      C - 22 B >= - 2370000

    OBJECTIVE FUNCTION VALUE

 1)        9959167.
```

VARIABLE	VALUE	REDUCED COST	ROW	SLACK	DUAL PRICES
FPP1T1	86.353538	0.000000	2)	0.000000	3000.000000
FPP1T2	131.313131	0.000000	3)	0.000000	3000.000000
FPP2T1	108.424244	0.000000	4)	0.000000	21.787880
FPP2T2	106.060607	0.000000	5)	0.000000	19.969698
FIP1T1	488.121216	0.000000	6)	0.000000	32.590909
FIP1T2	763.636375	0.000000	7)	0.000000	29.863637
FIP2T1	638.545479	0.000000	8)	273.333317	0.000000
FIP2T2	636.363640	0.000000	9)	0.000000	300.000000
OIP1T1	0.000000	300.000000	10)	0.000000	900.000000
OIP1T2	24.242417	0.000000	11)	0.000000	900.000000
OIP2T1	0.000000	300.000000	12)	0.000000	1200.000000
OIP2T2	0.000000	0.000000	13)	0.000000	1200.000000
CSTRP1T1	0.000000	189.090988	14)	0.000000	26970.000000
CSTRP1T2	0.000000	1817.272810	15)	0.000000	26970.000000
CSTRP2T1	0.000000	178.181732	16)	0.000000	26910.000000
CSTRP2T2	0.000000	1811.818220	17)	0.000000	26910.000000
NDT1	34.777780	0.000000	18)	0.000000	1960.909210
NDT2	27.373738	0.000000	19)	0.000000	1797.272810
INTRP1T1	0.000000	183.636398	20)	0.000000	1955.454540
INTRP1T2	0.000000	1817.272810	21)	0.000000	1791.818220
INTRP2T1	0.000000	183.636322	22)	89999.996100	0.000000
INTRP2T2	0.000000	1811.818220	23)	0.000000	-0.253788
BODP1T1	81.353537	0.001007	24)	0.000000	-0.746212
TRP1T1	75.353536	-0.000031			
BODP1T2	131.313131	0.000839			
TRP1T2	131.313137	-0.000015			
BODP2T1	106.424244	0.000198			
TRP2T1	102.424245	0.000031			
BODP2T2	106.060607	0.000351			
TRP2T2	106.060608	-0.000015			
INFPP1T1	0.000000	300.000000			
INFPP1T2	0.000000	27270.000000			
INFPP2T1	0.000000	300.000000			
INFPP2T2	0.000000	27210.000000			
C	490000.008000	0.000000			
B	130000.001000	0.000000			

The complete formulation and solution of this problem is shown in Figure 12.20. You can see that the optimal value of B is 130,000, just as obtained from the analysis in the text. Try to analyze why this approach works. Would the approach work for any nonlinear C that is convex? What about the approach in the text?

15 Consider the PROTRAC model shown in Figure 12.2. Use activity analysis arguments (and *not* the computer!) to construct the OV function corresponding to the constraint on existing demand in period 2. Show the *entire* OV function, with all corners and all slopes.

13 Special Topics: Inventory Control and Project Scheduling

The discussion of inventory control and project management is conceptual and devoid of algorithms. Applications and uses of the tools are stressed. In the inventory sections, reasons for holding inventories and conceptual components of mathematical inventory models are discussed. The EOQ model is given as a specific illustration. In the project management section, network representations are given for the precedence relations in PERT and CPM models. The critical path concept is discussed and illustrated in a specific example, and applications are emphasized.

13.1 Introduction

This chapter deals with two particularly important areas in real-world applications, inventory management and project management. Each of these topics is worthy of a book, and indeed books can be found that are exclusively devoted to models in either area. Our purpose is not to present the mathematical details of these models nor the algorithms that exist for their solution. Rather, we wish to give you some insight into the underlying concepts, for this will provide an understanding and appreciation for what the models can do and how they are used in actual managerial problems. Thus, the discussion in this chapter will be informal, but informative, and heavily laced with illustrations.

13.2 Managing the Inventory Function

13.2.1 Introduction

Inventory plays a central role in the production-planning activity of any manufacturing firm. In fact, the ability to produce in anticipation of demand, that is, the ability to hold inventory, is *the* factor that distinguishes manufacturing from service industries. As an obvious example, everyone is aware that it's tough to run off a few dozen haircuts on a slow Tuesday morning in anticipation of the high demand over the weekend. What may not be so obvious, however, is that the ability to hold inventories is of critical importance in determining the types of policies that are "optimal" for the firm as it attempts to meet its demand at minimum cost.

The role of inventory in the production process has been of interest to students of management for a long time. In fact, the Wilson lot-size formula, which is also called the *economic order quantity* (see "The EOQ Model" in Section 13.2.4), may well have been one of the first generally recognized mathematical models for management. Currently, there is a large and continuously growing professional literature concerned with problems of inventory control. Books, academic courses, and indeed the careers of certain academics are devoted to this subject. It should be noted that in its broadest conception, *inventory theory* includes models related to *cash management*, in which the inventory being held is cash; *water resources management*, in which the water behind a dam is the quantity being held in inventory; and other areas of *environmental control*, in which a particular species or pollutant may be the entity in inventory.

This spectrum of applications indicates that the topic of inventory control is not only of academic interest. The question of how to manage the inventory function effectively is of serious importance to many managers, especially those employed in the manufacturing, retailing, or distributing areas. Inventory control is also a topic in which mathematical models and computer technology have had a major impact. Indeed, it is difficult to imagine a major firm that is not using a computer-based inventory control system with a rationale provided by a mathematical model. Such systems may be developed by the individual firm but are often purchased as a package from the systems analysis group of the computer manufacturer with whom the firm deals. In any case, such systems are by now "old hat."

Inventory models, like all other mathematical models, are a selective representation of reality. One model or one class of model does not apply to all situations. In some cases, an inventory model provides a conceptual framework for analyzing tradeoffs and interactions in a given scenario. In other cases, an inventory model is used to provide a specific solution to a specific problem. In general, then, these models should be viewed as a supplement to the management decision-making process. Different models and different levels of managerial input are required for different situations.

Some of these ideas are captured by the so-called ABC classification scheme. The gist of this scheme is that a small percentage of the total number of items that the firm holds in inventory accounts for a large percentage of the total inventory cost. These items thus deserve a larger share of management attention and control. Graphically, the situation is presented in Figure 13.1. In this classification, *A* percent of the items deserve the most detailed analysis and management attention, the next *B* percent deserve less attention, and the next *C* percent less yet. For the last *C* percent of the items, mechanically applied inventory models or rules of thumb are probably appropriate, whereas more sophisticated models are probably worthwhile for the first *A* percent.

A discussion of inventory management that features an analysis of a number of specific models, emphasizing the assumptions specified in each particular model and the algorithm used to solve the model, is, in our opinion, too specialized and technical to be of general value to a wide audience of current or potential managers. In subsequent sections, we will stress the following:

1 The reasons for holding inventories
2 The structural components of inventory models
3 A few specific models as examples to illustrate the general ideas

Figure 13.1 *The ABC classification scheme for items in inventory*

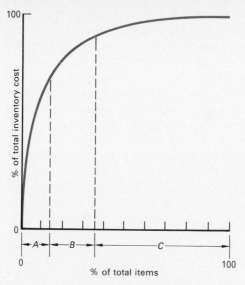

13.2.2 Reasons for Holding Inventories

Inventories may consist of raw materials, goods in process, and finished goods. There are a number of factors that make it attractive for a firm to hold inventories. Several of these factors are discussed below.

Economies of Scale in Production and Procurement   In many circumstances, the average cost (the total cost of production or purchasing divided by the number of units produced) decreases as the number of units produced increases. The fact that it is possible to incur a lower "per-unit cost" by increasing the number of items produced or purchased provides an incentive for a firm to produce more items than are needed in order to satisfy the immediate demand. The phenomenon of decreasing average costs typically results from the fact that the total cost of production has a "lumpy" or *fixed-cost* component. For example, let $C(x)$ be the total cost of producing x items. If

$$
\begin{aligned}
C(x) &= 0 & x &= 0 \\
&= K + c(x) & x &> 0
\end{aligned}
$$

then we see that a fixed cost of K is incurred as soon as any items are produced, no matter how many units are produced. To visualize the rationale for this type of total cost function, think of a production process in which a substantial amount of time must be devoted to setting up the machine before any production can take place. A set-up can easily be a nontrivial event. In highly automated machine tools, for example, a number of jigs and fixtures must be located and attached, tools must be sharpened and adjusted, the sequence of operations must be changed, and a number of sample items must be produced and inspected to make certain that the machine is operating correctly before the batch production actually begins. Special, highly-skilled individuals or crews may be used to perform set-ups, and thus the cost of the set-up crew as well as the opportunity cost of having nonproductive equipment must be included in K, the cost of the set-up. As other related examples, consider the manufacture of chemicals, food products, or photographic film. Here, the set-up consists of cleaning the equipment so that the current ingredients are not contaminated by those used in the previous operation.

Load Leveling   In certain activities, there are substantial costs associated with changing the level of production activity. The process of contracting and expanding a work-force by means of laying off and hiring workers is an expensive proposition in terms of benefits that must be paid, the cost of processing the paper work associated with the changes, and perhaps in terms of a decreased ability to hire quality workers. Similarly, there may be substantial costs associated with starting up and/or shutting down certain manufacturing processes, such as blast furnaces. These costs encourage a firm to diminish fluctuations in the level of production and to use inventory to satisfy variations in demand.

Flexibility in Scheduling Sequential Facilities   A common manufacturing technique is to produce parts in a given lot size or batch size. Each batch of parts is often stored in portable bins and moved from machine to machine by fork truck as the part passes through the manufacturing process. These partially completed parts stored in the bins are referred to as *in-process inventory*, and the ability to hold this inventory makes it possible for a firm to use its manpower and machines more efficiently. For example, suppose a part requires one minute of machining on a mill and then five minutes on a grinder. The ability to carry in-process inventory makes it possible for the mill to complete its work and be used for other activities without waiting for the slower grinder.

Variability in Procurement or Production Costs   The fact that the price of obtaining or processing a certain material varies over time provides a reason for a firm to hold inventory. Obviously, it is advantageous to buy or produce when costs are low. Perhaps the best examples are provided by the variability of prices of raw materials, such as soybeans, and the existence of special "bargain basement" sales by manufacturers and retailers. It is hard to imagine a thrifty homemaker buying sheets other than at a January white sale.

Uncertainty in Supply and Demand   Manufacturers who wish to increase confidence in their ability to satisfy demand and to adhere to predetermined production plans use inventories of raw materials, in-process parts, and finished goods to protect themselves against the uncertainties of their environment. For example, suppose that it normally takes seven days to obtain a certain part from a supplier, but under unusual circumstances it might take as much as ten days. A firm will typically hold an inventory of such a part to protect itself against the possibility of a delay in delivery. This same philosophy applied to breakdowns in the manufacturing process and the variability in demand leads to the maintenance of inventories at various points in the manufacturing process.

Service Requirements   Manufacturers, distributors, and retailers are often obliged to maintain inventories of finished goods or parts in a number of geographic locations in order to provide delivery of ordered material or service within a competitive interval of time. For example, a firm specializing in the distribution of steel products believes that orders have to be satisfied within 24 hours in order to meet the competition successfully. The policy formulated in response to this belief dictates the establishment of a number of regional warehouses throughout the country and an associated accumulation of inventory. Clearly, all demands cannot be satisfied within 24 hours from the firm's headquarters in the midwest.

13.2.3   *Structural Components of Mathematical Inventory Models*

An amazing variety of inventory models have been presented in the professional literature. Most models can be described in terms of three structural components:

---

1   Type of review
2   Type of demand
3   Type of cost

These structural components are discussed more fully below.

Type of Review   The designer of an inventory control system or a mathematical model must designate the points in time at which he will know the current status of the system (the inventory on hand and on order) and the points at which he will be able to make replenishment decisions. Typically, one assumes that either there is continuous or periodic monitoring of the system. In a *continuous review system*, the inventory manager knows the status of the system at all times and is able to order replenishment items at any point in time. In a *periodic review system*, the status of the system and the opportunity to make an ordering decision only occur at discrete points in time (say the beginning of each month). Historically, periodic systems have played an important role in many industries. The continuing development of cheaper and more effective methods of handling and storing data suggests that continuous review models will become increasingly important.

Type of Demand   Inventory models are classified into two categories by the type of demand, deterministic and stochastic (or probabilistic). In *deterministic models*, it is assumed that demand in the future is known with certainty. *Stochastic*, or *probabilistic*, *models* are based on the assumption that demand is a random quantity that is generated by a known *stochastic process*. (We realize that stochastic models have not been discussed yet, and the use of this terminology may be premature. Stochastic models are not considered again until Chapter 15, in which an appropriate foundation is developed.)

Type of Cost   Typically, inventory models contain three elements of cost:

---

1   A cost of replenishment (that is, a cost of ordering)

2 A cost of holding inventory

3 A penalty cost

Each of these costs is discussed briefly below.

COST OF REPLENISHMENT

Let $C(x)$ be the cost of ordering, which means the cost of purchasing or producing x items. In most inventory models, $C(x)$ is assumed to have one of two forms. It is either assumed to be linear

$$C(x) = c(x) \qquad x \geq 0$$

or $C(x)$ is assumed to have a lumpy component and a constant marginal cost

$$C(x) = K + c(x) \qquad x > 0$$
$$\quad\;\; = 0 \qquad\qquad\;\; x = 0$$

If all other parameters of the model are held constant, changing the form of $C(x)$ will typically change the form of the optimal ordering policy.

The function $C(x)$ is, of course, not restricted to the two forms shown above. In certain contexts, particularly mathematical programming problems, $C(x)$ may simply be assumed to be a concave function. In other cases, especially in some work on planning horizons,[1] $C(x)$ is assumed to be a convex function.

COST OF HOLDING INVENTORY

Section 13.2.2 presented a number of reasons for holding inventory. The countervailing force is provided by the fact that it costs money to hold items in inventory. Part of this cost is attributable to the necessity of having a physical facility and a labor force to store items. Another component is provided by the *opportunity cost* of having funds tied up in inventory, which means that if these funds were not invested in inventory they could be invested in other revenue-producing ventures. This loss of potential revenue must also be considered as a cost of holding inventory.

Inventory holding costs are represented in a variety of ways in inventory models. To understand the representation in continuous review systems, it is convenient to plot the inventory on hand as a function of time. If $I(t)$ is the inventory on hand at time t, then Figure 13.2 is a typical plot of inventory on hand. The value of $I(t)$ decreases as items are taken out of inventory to satisfy demand. The increases in $I(t)$ are caused by replenishment (the arrival of an order). In Figure 13.2, the orders arrive all at once at three discrete points in time. The inventory holding cost in a continuous review system is often assumed to be proportional to the area under the graph of inventory on hand, which is shown by the shaded area in Figure 13.2. If inventory is

---

1 *Planning horizons* are an important concept in the areas of production and inventory control. Consider an N-period problem. We regard a planning horizon as any time interval, say periods 1 through $t_1 - 1$, that can be planned optimally with less than complete information on all N periods, but possibly requiring some information beyond t_1.

Figure 13.2 *A typical plot of inventory on hand*

measured in units and time is measured in weeks, then the area under the graph is measured in unit-weeks. If the holding cost is assumed to be proportional to the area under the graph, the constant of proportionality, say h, must be measured in dollars per unit-week.

In periodic models, the inventory holding cost is usually assumed to be proportional to the inventory on hand either at the beginning or the end of a period. In this case, the cost constant is simply measured in dollars per unit. Example 5 in Section 4.4 is an example of a periodic model in which inventory holding costs are assumed to be proportional to the inventory on hand at the end of the week.

In concluding this section, it can be noted that, in the continuous review model, the cost constant should represent the marginal cost of adding a unit-week to the area under the graph. In any real situation, if one ignores the opportunity cost, the marginal cost of adding a unit-week to inventory holding is obviously small, if not zero. Who would ever know if one additional brake shoe was held in inventory for a week? It is equally obvious that the total cost, again ignoring opportunity costs, of holding literally hundreds of thousands of individual items in inventory can be very large. The point is that the true costs are almost certainly not linear in unit-weeks. This implies that our theoretical models are often quite approximate representations of reality, and thus there is a great deal of room for judgment and discretion in assigning values to the cost parameters in an inventory model. This is true of almost all cost parameters in mathematical models.

PENALTY COSTS

Clearly, a firm may incur costs when it does not have a unit of inventory on hand to satisfy a unit of demand when it occurs. If the firm is unable to satisfy demand from a customer, it may well lose the profit that would have been associated with the sale and, in addition, lose future sales by offending the customer. If demand is satisfied, but with delays, the firm may incur special handling costs or be obliged to offer price concessions to its customer. In addition, it still runs the risk of losing future sales by offending the customer. If a firm is unable to satisfy an internal demand for an item, it then incurs the costs associated with disrupting its production plans and, in many cases, increases the probability that it will be unable to satisfy a customer demand at a later date.

In mathematical inventory models, there are two different assumptions that can be made in terms of demand fulfillment, and these assumptions influence the nature of penalty costs. The first assumption, called *backlogging*, means that fulfillment of demand can be delayed. This is illustrated in Figure 13.3, where the negative values of $I(t)$ represent unsatisfied demand. If at time $\hat{t}$ it is understood that q_1 orders arrive, the unsatisfied demand becomes satisfied. Thus, orders were allowed to backlog. On the other hand, if only q_2 orders arrive at time $\hat{t}$, then the unsatisfied demand is lost. In this latter case, penalty costs must include lost revenue. Under the backlogging assumption, a penalty cost would be imposed for late fulfillment, but *not* for lost revenue.

When penalty costs are included in the model, they are represented by means that are analogous to those used for holding costs. In continuous review systems, the penalty cost is typically assumed to be proportional to the number of unit-weeks of unsatisfied demand. As shown in Figure 13.3, this can be represented on the $I(t)$ graph as the area above the plot of $I(t)$ whenever $I(t)$ is negative. In periodic models, the penalty cost is typically assumed to be a function of the quantity of unsatisfied demand at the end of a period.

We have already suggested that obtaining a precise measure for the holding cost is not easy. The same statement applies, perhaps with more force, to the penalty cost. The cost of not satisfying a customer's demand is, in most cases, a great imponderable. However, this does not imply that models that incorporate a penalty cost are useless. The fact that an inventory model forces management to think about this quantity and provides an opportunity to investigate the sensitivity of the inventory policy to various assumptions concerning the value of the penalty cost is, in our opinion, a real strength of the modeling approach.

Some deterministic models do not include an explicit penalty cost but, rather, have a restriction that all demand must be satisfied, without backlogging. (For example, this was the assumption in the PROTRAC model of Chapters 11 and 12.) This restriction is equivalent to assuming that the penalty cost is so large that the firm would always choose to satisfy demand on schedule. Thus, imposing an assumption that all demand must be satisfied without backlogging is equivalent to specifying a range of values, although not a precise value, for the penalty cost.

A large variety of other features are incorporated into the inventory models that appear in the professional literature. A few examples are listed below.

Figure 13.3 *A hypothetical plot illustrating unsatisfied demand*

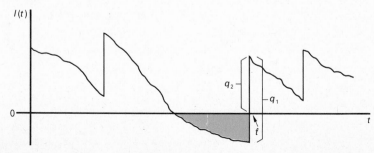

1 It is possible to vary the assumptions concerning the *lead time* (the time that elapses from the moment a replenishment order is placed until the goods arrive).

2 Items stored in inventory may *deteriorate*. Good examples are provided by the whole-blood inventory of hospitals and the milk in your grocer's dairy case.

3 Items may be stored in a hierarchy of warehouses and outlets. Such models are referred to as *multiechelon models*.

Adding to this list of other features or discussing in more detail the features we have listed does not seem consistent with our goal of providing the potential manager with a basic understanding of inventory models.

13.2.4   *Some Specific Inventory Models*

The structural components presented in the previous section will now be combined to yield several specific inventory models. Three basic types of models will be presented. This material will provide you with an exposure to the most commonly used deterministic models as well as with experience in understanding the cost tradeoffs incorporated in these models.

The EOQ Model   By far the best known inventory model is the one that leads to the *Wilson lot-size formula*, or the so-called *economic order quantity (EOQ)*. This model may indeed be the original operations research model, as it appears to have been first derived by Ford Harris of the Westinghouse Corporation in 1915. The model is a continuous review system with deterministic demand. Indeed, demand is assumed to be constant per unit time over an infinite time horizon. The cost of ordering items (that is, of replenishing inventory) includes a lumpy cost for placing the order plus a constant per-unit cost for each item ordered. Inventory holding costs are assumed to be proportional to the number of unit-weeks of inventory that are held. There is no explicit penalty cost, but it is implicit in the sense that all demand must be satisfied without backlogging.

More formally, let

d = demand per unit time

$C(x)$ = cost of ordering x items where $C(x) = K + c(x)$ if $x > 0$ and $C(x) = 0$ when $x = 0$

h = cost per unit-week of holding inventory

Figure 13.4 shows a plot of $I(t)$, the inventory on hand, that illustrates the assumptions underlying this model. Note (1) that the inventory on hand, $I(t)$, decreases linearly as a result of the fact that demand per unit time is constant, and that (2) the rate of decrease is the same as the rate of demand, d units per week. A replenishment of q_1 items arrives at time t_1, and another replenishment of q_2 items arrives at time t_2.

The objective of the model is to find an optimal ordering or replenishment policy, which is a policy that minimizes the cost per unit of time (say per week) of satisfying demand. An optimal ordering policy refers to an optimal quantity, denoted Q^*, and an optimal interval of time between orders, denoted T^*. With some thought, you should be able to convince yourself that an optimal ordering policy for this model will have the following properties:

Figure 13.4 *I(t) if demand is deterministic and constant*

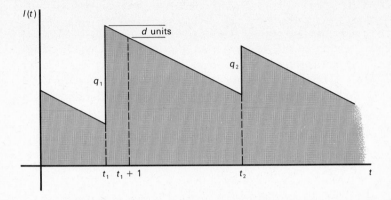

1 A replenishment will occur at the instant $I(t)$ assumes the value zero. If it occurs after this point, then $I(t)$ becomes negative, and this is prohibited by the assumption that demand must be satisfied with no backlogging. If the replenishment occurs before $I(t) = 0$, then the firm would incur additional holding costs. Since demand is deterministic, this additional cost can be avoided. This fact implies that $I(t)$ for the optimal policy will resemble the plot shown in Figure 13.5, where the graph of the inventory on hand is a series of triangles.

2 All of these inventory triangles will be exactly the same size. The size of the inventory triangle gives the optimal policy. The height provides the quantity, the base gives the time between orders. Now consider calculating the cost per unit time (that is, the average cost) for any inventory triangle. If one can isolate the size of the triangle that yields the lowest cost per unit time, the optimal policy must consist of a continuing sequence of these triangles.

From the arguments above, it follows that the problem of finding an optimal ordering policy has been reduced to finding the inventory triangle that has the minimum cost per week. By definition,

$$\text{Cost per week} = \frac{\text{total cost per triangle}}{\text{number of weeks per triangle}}$$

or

Figure 13.5 *The optimal form for I(t)*

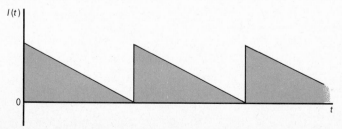

$$\text{Cost per week} = \frac{\text{ordering cost} + \text{holding cost per triangle}}{\text{number of weeks per triangle}}$$

Suppose that an inventory triangle with a base of T weeks is selected. The resulting graph of $I(t)$ is shown in Figure 13.6. The ordering cost is $K + c(d)\,(T)$. The area under the graph of $I(t)$ is given by the familiar formula for the area of a triangle, namely, $dT^2/2$. Thus, the inventory holding cost is $hdT^2/2$. Finally, then, the cost per week is given by the expression

$$\text{Cost per week} = \frac{K + cdT + (hdT^2/2)}{T}$$

$$= \frac{K}{T} + cd + \frac{hdT}{2}$$

Figure 13.6   *An inventory triangle with a base of T weeks*

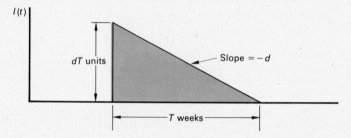

The problem of finding an optimal inventory policy is equivalent to the problem of choosing a value of T that yields a minimum value for this expression. In attempting to choose such a T, note that the term cd is not a function of T and can be ignored. This is easily understood. If demand is d units per week and we must satisfy all demand, then we must certainly incur a minimal cost of cd dollars per week. The functions K/T, $hdT/2$, and their sum are illustrated in Figure 13.7. The optimal base length, T^*, occurs at the point where the cost per week achieves its minimum. The rules of differential calculus can be used to show that the value of T^* is given by the expression

$$T^* = \sqrt{\frac{2K}{hd}}$$

Figure 13.7   *Cost per week as a function of T*

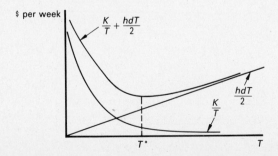

Since the optimal order quantity, Q^*, equals $d(T^*)$, the expression for Q^* is

$$Q^* = \sqrt{\frac{2Kd}{h}}$$

This quantity, Q^*, is called the *economic order quantity*.

Most students find the EOQ formula to be moderately interesting at best, and overwhelmingly artificial. The assumptions are clearly unrealistic. No uncertainty! Uniform demand forever! What product ever had these characteristics? Clearly, the answer is none. It may suprise you to learn that this formula is an integral part of almost all the commercial and privately developed inventory control systems of which we are aware. These systems typically include a simple forecasting package often based on exponential smoothing (see Chapter 17), a safety stock to protect against uncertainty, and an optimal order quantity whose calculation is based on the economic lot-size formula. These inventory systems are typically combined with a computer-based information storage and retrieval system. The message seems to be that these systems are a substantial improvement over the systems previously employed, in spite of the lack of realism in the underlying assumptions. Furthermore, it is *perhaps* the case that systems based on a more realistic representation of reality would require more in the way of additional systems costs than could be justified by the incremental reductions in inventory-related costs.

A former Ph.D. student at Chicago had an interesting, if frustrating, experience concerning the EOQ model while doing some consulting work for a local steel distributor. The firm was developing an inventory control system, and the student, busily involved in classes dealing with inventory theory, was called in as an outside expert. The analysts from the firm decided on a system based on the EOQ model. Moreover, since they had difficulty estimating the "true" values for the fixed cost, K, and the holding cost, h, they chose different combinations for K and h, until one pair yielded an inventory cycle of approximately the length that the firm was currently using for several important items that management followed quite closely. This pair of values for K and h was then selected to be used in the calculation of order quantities. One might conclude that the model was useless, that it simply allowed the analysts to rationalize what the firm was already doing. Another view suggests that the approach was quite rational. The firm probably was doing a good job with the few important products under close management supervision. It is usually a bad idea to assume that management doesn't know what it is doing. The approach used to develop the system was an attempt to extend current management practice to less important items while at the same time using less direct management attention.

There are a variety of permutations on the basic economic lot-size model. One popular change is to assume that items arrive at a constant rate during the replenishment, rather than all at once. This model may be more appropriate when items are produced rather than purchased. Another change is to assume that orders can be backlogged at a specific cost. If you've understood the development of the basic model, you can quickly grasp a model incorporating these or other changes when and if it becomes important.

The economic lot-size model balances the cost of placing orders against the cost of holding inventory. In other models, other tradeoffs are important. For example, the most basic stochastic inventory model deals with the tradeoff between the cost of holding inventory and the penalty cost of not being able to satisfy demand.

Models with Variable Costs   To further illustrate the basic idea of a model that deals with the tradeoff between the cost of holding inventory and the replenishment cost, consider the following particularly simple periodic deterministic inventory model.

A firm requires d_t items in period t. These items generally can be purchased for C dollars each. It costs h dollars to carry an item in inventory from one period to the next. If these are the only costs in the model, then the solution is simple. The firm simply buys d_t items at the beginning of period t. No inventory is carried, and no inventory holding cost is incurred. No saving is available by purchasing at different times. Now, assume that in period 1 the items can be purchased for $\hat{C}$ dollars each, where $\hat{C}$ is less than C (the per-unit cost in periods 2, 3, . . .). Does it now pay for the firm to buy additional items in period 1 and carry them in inventory? Let $\Delta C = C - \hat{C}$; that is, ΔC is the ordering cost savings per unit from buying the item in period 1. If ΔC is greater than h, then it pays to buy items in period 1 to satisfy demand in period 2. Similarly, if ΔC is greater than $2h$, it pays to buy items in period 1 to satisfy demand in period 3. In general, if $[\Delta C/h]$ is the largest integer smaller than $\Delta C/h$, then it pays to buy items in period 1 to satisfy demand in the periods from 1 up to and including period $[\Delta C/h] + 1$. A numerical example may help to clarify this notation. Assume that

$C = \$10$ (the usual ordering price)

$\hat{C} = \$5$ (the special ordering price in period 1)

$h = \$2$ (the inventory holding cost)

Then

$\Delta C \quad = C - \hat{C} = \$5$

$\dfrac{\Delta C}{h} \quad = \dfrac{5}{2} = 2.5$

$\left[\dfrac{\Delta C}{h}\right] = 2$

Thus, the firm should purchase the demand for the first three periods in period 1 and purchase the quantity demanded in each period starting with period 4. If $d_1 = 15$, $d_2 = 12$, $d_3 = 18$, $d_4 = 9$, the firm should purchase 45 items in period 1, and 9 items in period 4.

In this example, it is easy to understand and actually execute the marginal cost calculations that must be performed to determine the optimal policy. However, the situation changes when a number of items are considered, purchase costs and holding costs are allowed to vary with time, and constraints are added to the model. Such constraints could be on the total amount of inventory that can be held or on the quantity that can be purchased at any given time. It is still easy to understand the calculations that would have to be performed to determine the optimal policy, but actually executing them in some ad hoc manner would not be an easy task. Fortunately, for models of this type (in which all costs are strictly proportional to the quantities purchased), LP can be used to determine the optimal purchasing policy. Models of this sort have been considered in some detail in Chapter 4. A review of Section 4.4 should be useful in the context of the current discussion of inventory models.

Periodic Models with Lumpy Ordering Costs   The continuous-time EOQ model included a lumpy ordering cost, that is,

$$C(x) = K + c(x) \qquad x > 0$$
$$= 0 \qquad\qquad x = 0$$

and yielded a nice, clean, analytic solution for the optimal policy. In the above discussion, we mentioned that periodic models with costs proportional to the quantities purchased can be conveniently solved by LP. It might then be reasonable to presume that periodic models with lumpy ordering costs could also be quite easily solved. Unfortunately, this presumption is wrong. Consider the following model. Let

d_t = demand in period t

$C_t(x_t)$ = cost of purchasing (or producing) x_t items where

$$C_t(x_t) = K_t + c_t(x_t) \qquad x_t > 0$$
$$= 0 \qquad\qquad x_t = 0$$

h_t = cost of carrying a unit of inventory from period t into $t + 1$

With these assumptions, it is not easy to find a purchasing (or production) plan that satisfies all demand at minimum cost. For a single item, there is a method (called the *Wagner-Whitin algorithm*) that can be used to find the optimal solution to the problem as it is posed above, and a detailed description of that algorithm is readily available in the technical literature.

The model just presented is called the *dynamic lot-size model.* It balances the cost of ordering against the cost of carrying inventory for the periodic case, just as the EOQ model did for the continuous case. Intuitively, the dynamic lot-size model seems much more useful than the EOQ model. It does, after all, allow demand to vary over time, and that is certainly more realistic than the constant demand assumption of the EOQ model. It is somewhat sobering to realize that currently the EOQ model is extensively used in industry, and the applications of the dynamic lot-size model are few and far between. Apparently, practitioners believe that the selective representation of reality included in the EOQ model captures enough of the essence of the real problem to make the installation of systems based on this model a good investment, whereas, in most cases, the refinements available in the dynamic lot-size model do not justify the additional systems and computation costs.

If the model involves several items, each of which has a lumpy ordering cost, it is computationally even more difficult to find an optimal purchasing (production) plan. Such problems can be described by integer programming models, a topic discussed in Chapter 14.

13.3   Project Management: PERT and CPM

13.3.1   *Introduction*

The task of managing major projects is an ancient and honorable art among management scientists. In about 2600 B.C., the Egyptians built the Great Pyramid for King Khufu. The ancient Greek historian Herodotus claimed that 400,000 men worked each year for 20 years to build this structure. Although these figures are now in doubt, there is no doubt concerning the enormity of the project. The Book of Genesis reports that the Tower of Babel was not completed because God made it impossible for the builders to communicate. This project is especially important, since it establishes a historical precedent for the ever-popular practice of citing divine intervention as a rationale for failure.[2]

Modern projects ranging from building a suburban shopping center to putting a man on the moon are amazingly large, complex, and costly. Completing such projects on time and within the budget is not an easy task. For example, some people are still wondering what happened to the stadium roof for the 1976 Summer Olympics in Montreal.

PERT and CPM, acronyms for program evaluation review technique, and critical path method, respectively, have made and are making a real contribution to the management of large projects. PERT was developed by the Navy Special Projects Office in cooperation with the management consulting firm of Booz, Allen, and Hamilton. The technique received substantial favorable publicity for its use in the engineering and development program for the Polaris missile. Since that time, it has been widely adopted in other branches of the government and in industry. Today, many firms or government agencies require all contractors to use PERT.

CPM was developed in 1957 by J. E. Kelly of Remington Rand and M. R. Walker of DuPont. It differs from PERT primarily in the details of how a project is represented in a diagram and in the way time is estimated. For our purposes, these differences are not important. Both *PERT* and *CPM* are based on a method of representing a project as a network and on the important management concept of the *critical path.* Our goal is to provide the current or potential manager with a basic understanding of these two aspects of the techniques. An examination of other details, such as the intricacies of the various ways of estimating times, is better left, in our opinion, to those occasions when they will be immediately used.

13.3.2   *A Network Representation*

The first step in analyzing a project is to break it down into its component parts. Two definitions are important in this process:

---

2   The *Chicago Tribune* (August 5, 1977) noted the following comment concerning the blackout in New York in July of that year: "Con Ed called the disaster an act of God."

Event: An event is a specific accomplishment that occurs at a recognizable point in time.

Activity: An activity is the work required to achieve a specific event or the work initiated by a specific event.

For example, to develop a new E–9 model, PROTRAC would divide the project into a number of identifiable *activities,* such as

1 Designing a new supercharger with certain specifications
2 Building five prototypes to use in testing the new tread assembly
3 Running endurance tests on each of three prototype engines

Note that each of these *activities* involves performing a number of tasks and will require some time. The *events* associated with these activities are simply mileposts that indicate when each activity begins and ends. Thus, PROTRAC might have

1 Event 5: begin supercharger design; event 6: supercharger design completed
2 Event 17: start production of the prototypes of the tread assembly; event 20: complete production of the prototypes of the tread assembly

An event does not require any time. It is simply a set of circumstances that either has or has not occurred.

There are clearly a number of possible levels of detail that could be used in describing a project. In the E–9 project, for example, the activity of building prototypes of the tread assembly could be broken down into its component parts. The appropriate level of detail depends on the decisions being made and the level of control desired. It's easy to imagine several layers of PERT charts for the same project.

In a *PERT diagram,* or *chart,* events are indicated by numbered circles and activities are arrows (sometimes called *directed arcs*) connecting the events. Continuing the above E–9 example, Figure 13.8 shows activity 5–6, design a new supercharger, connecting events 5 and 6.

Figure 13.8   *Two events and an activity*

This type of representation is useful because it provides a graphic and easily understood presentation of precedence relationships. The basic notion of *precedence relationships* is that during the progress of a project, certain events must occur before other events can occur. If the project is getting dressed, then socks are typically donned before shoes, underwear before pants, and pants in turn precede shoes. (This may not be a good example, since in certain emergencies such a systematic approach is forsaken.) Figure 13.9 provides an illustration of the precedence relationships in a simple PERT network.

In this diagram, it is easy to see that activity 5–6 can begin only after

Figure 13.9 *Precedence relationships in a PERT network*

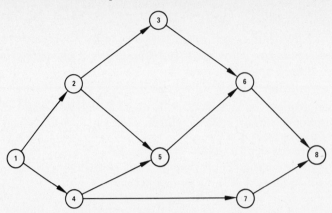

event 5 has occurred, and event 5 cannot occur until activities 2–5 and 4–5 are both completed. Thus, event 2 and event 4 must each precede event 5. Note that precedence relationships exist among the activities as well as the events. For example, Figure 13.9 indicates that activities 2–5 and 4–5 are immediate predecessors of 5–6.

The precedence chart in Figure 13.10 is an alternative means of presenting the activity precedence information contained in Figure 13.9. Note that from the data in this chart, the event precedence can also be determined, and Figure 13.9 could be reconstructed. For human consumption, the graphical representation seems to have rather obvious advantages. The precedence chart, however, is a useful device for communicating with computers.

Figure 13.10 *A Precedence Chart*

Activity	Immediate Predecessors
1–2	None
1–4	None
2–5	1–2
4–5	1–4
2–3	1–2
3–6	2–3
5–6	2–5, 4–5
4–7	1–4
6–8	3–6, 5–6
7–8	4–7

13.3.3 The Critical Path

PERT and CPM perform an important function by isolating sets of activities that are "critical" in attempting to complete a project by a specified time. To accomplish this function, each activity must be assigned a *completion time*. Alternatively, this can be thought of as the time required to get from one event to the next. In terms of the previous PROTRAC example, it is the time that will transpire between event 5, begin supercharger design, and event 6, supercharger design completed. In Figure 13.11, completion times measured

A PERT network with times

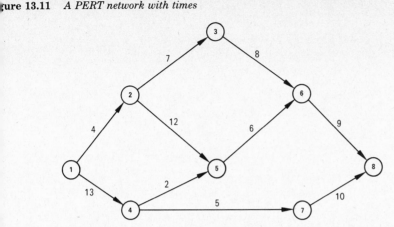

in weeks for each activity have been written beside the arrow that represents that activity.

Assigning a completion time to each activity makes it possible to calculate several quantities that are useful guides to management control of the project. These quantities are described below.

Earliest Start Time, ES   As the name suggests, this is the earliest moment at which an event can occur if all activities take their assigned times. Hence, for a given event, ES is the earliest possible starting time for any of the activities initiated by that event. To calculate the quantity ES for a given event, one must evaluate the time associated with each path leading to that event, and then take the maximum of these times. To illustrate this idea, assume that event 1 in Figure 13.11 occurs at time 0. It is obvious then that the earliest time for event 2 is 4. Since this is also the earliest possible launch time for all activities emanating from event 2, we deduce that neither activity 2–3 nor activity 2–5 can be initiated before time 4.

The calculation for event 5 is slightly more complicated. The sequence of activities 1–4 and 4–5 that requires 15 weeks must be completed before event 5 occurs. Similarly, the sequence 1–2 and 2–5 that requires 16 weeks must be completed before event 5 occurs. Therefore, the earliest start time for event 5 is 16 weeks.

Every PERT network can be constructed with an "artificial" original event signifying the start of the project and another "artificial" terminal event signifying the end of the project. The earliest start time for the terminal event, then, is the minimum time in which the entire project can be completed. A sequence of activities that determines this minimum time is called a *critical path*. (We note that such a path need not be unique—there may be numerous critical paths.) For the above example, the path defined by the events 1–2–5–6–8 is the critical path (which in this case is unique), and since ES for event 8 is 31 weeks, this is the minimum time in which the project can be completed. Note that the critical path could also be defined in terms of the *activity* sequence 1–2, 2–5, 5–6, 6–8.

The *concept* of a critical path is important to management with or without

PERT or CPM networks. The concept, which is now obvious, is that a certain critical subset of activities will determine the time at which a project will be completed. If a manager wishes to influence the completion time of a particular project, his attention and whatever additional resources he wishes to devote to the project should be focused on the critical path.

Latest Start Time, LS This quantity is the latest time at which an event can occur without delaying the completion of the entire project. Clearly then, for each event on the critical path, LS = ES. Let us now consider the PERT network presented in Figure 13.11. We have just observed that the earliest time that the project can be completed is at time 31. (It is convenient to assume that the project begins at time 0.) We also note that activity 7-8 requires 10 weeks. Clearly, if event 7 occurs later than time 21 and it takes 10 weeks to get from event 7 to event 8, the project cannot be completed by time 31. The latest start time for event 7 is thus 21.

The following simple rule shows how to compute LS for any event: find the critical path from that event to the terminal event and then subtract the time needed to travel that critical path from the minimum completion time for the entire project. For example, LS for event 4 is calculated as follows:

1 The critical path from event 4 to event 8 is the sequence 4-5-6-8. This path requires 17 weeks. The alternative path 4-7-8 requires only 15 weeks.

2 LS for event 4 is thus 14 weeks (31-17). If event 4 occurs after time 14, the project cannot be completed by time 31.

Figure 13.12 shows the PERT network from Figure 13.11 with ES and LS for each event.

Slack, S The word *slack* has roughly the same meaning as it had in the LP context. It is the unused amount of a resource, in this case time. It is defined by the equation

Figure 13.12 *A PERT network with ES and LS shown*

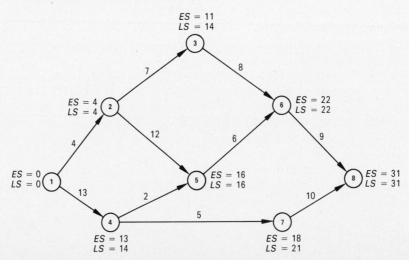

$S = LS - ES$

Slack is thus the amount of time that the starting time for an event can be delayed without delaying the completion time for the entire project.

In the example, we see that the slack for event 7 is 3 weeks and indeed its earliest starting time of 18 weeks could be delayed by 3 weeks until time 21 without delaying the completion of the project. We also note that ES = LS (slack is zero) for all events on the critical path.

To the extent that resources are interchangeable among activities, slack provides an indication of possible sources of resources that could be transferred to activities on the critical path in order to reduce the completion time for the entire project.

13.3.4 *Algorithms, the Computer, and Other War Stories*

There are, of course, algorithms for finding the critical path in a PERT network and we, as usual, do not believe that this is the appropriate place to discuss these algorithms. In practice, small networks can be (and are) easily solved by hand without the use of an algorithm. Large problems are solved on computers with preprogrammed critical path packages. Thus, the manager does not *need* to learn complicated algorithms to solve PERT problems. Moreover, learning the mechanics of how to solve a PERT network with an algorithm provides little insight into most of the important concepts associated with critical path methods or into the use of these tools.

For illustrative purposes, the PERT problem presented in Figure 13.11 was solved using the on-line computer facility at the University of Chicago. In order to use the package available on this particular computer, each activity must be given an identifying number. Numbers were assigned as shown in Figure 13.13. The number in parentheses under the activity arc is the activity number. The number above the activity arc is the time required to complete that activity. The data entry and the output are presented in Figure 13.14.

Data are entered in the following manner. For each activity, the activity number, the time required for that activity and the immediate predecessors must be listed. Thus, in line 1006 we see activity 7 requires 8 weeks and

ure 13.13   *A PERT network with activity numbers*

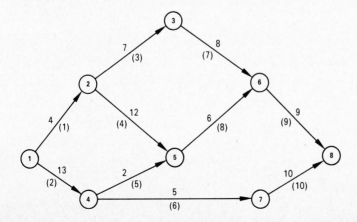

Figure 13.14 *A computer solution to the PERT problem*

```
1000 DATA 1,4,-1
1001 DATA 2,13,-1
1002 DATA 3,7,1,-1
1003 DATA 4,12,1,-1
1004 DATA 5,2,2,-1
1005 DATA 6,5,2,-1
1006 DATA 7,8,3,-1
1007 DATA 8,6,4,5,-1
1008 DATA 9,9,7,8,-1
1009 DATA 10,10,6,-1
RUN
GCPATH

HAVE YOU ENTERED YOUR DATA ALREADY?Y
JOB    TIME   PREDECESSORS
---    ----   ------------
 1      4
 2     13
 3      7     1
 4     12     1
 5      2     2
 6      5     2
 7      8     3
 8      6     4       5
 9      9     7       8
10     10     6

EARLIEST COMPLETION TIME FOR THE ENTIRE PROJECT = 31

            EARLIEST         LATEST
JOB     START  FINISH    START  FINISH
---     -----  ------    -----  ------
 1       0       4         0      4      *** CRITICAL ***
 2       0      13         1     14
 3       4      11         7     14
 4       4      16         4     16      *** CRITICAL ***
 5      13      15        14     16
 6      13      18        16     21
 7      11      19        14     22
 8      16      22        16     22      *** CRITICAL ***
 9      22      31        22     31      *** CRITICAL ***
10      18      28        21     31

DONE
```

is preceded by activity 3. The −1 indicates the end of the entry for an individual activity. The computer repeats the data (illiterately referring to activities as *jobs*), and prints out the solution. It clearly indicates the critical path (of activities) and the earliest completion time for the entire project.

Since this particular computer program is activity- rather than event-oriented, ES and LS are not directly calculated for each event. These quantities are, however, easily available from the output provided. To find ES for any event, simply take the earliest start of any activity emanating from the event.[3] Thus to find ES for event 2, we first note from Figure 13.13 that activities 3 and 4 emanate from event 2. Next, we consult the computer output and see that the earliest start time is 4. Similarly, to find LS for an event, take

---

3 Alternatively, this equals the maximum of the earliest finish times for all the activities that lead into the event.

the latest finish time of any activity that leads into the event.[4] It follows, for example, that LS for event 5 is 16.

A great deal more could be said about PERT and CPM. PERT, in particular, includes a system for estimating activity completion times and for including uncertainty (in terms of these completion times) in the analysis of the problem. CPM includes the option for performing activities on either a normal or a crash basis. In any particular application, it may be helpful to consult an expert who understands how these additional techniques may apply. However, experience has shown that in many cases you can get the benefits of a PERT analysis with the brief amount of information that we have provided. Even if different people were to apply different estimates for activity times, it could well be the case that the same severe bottleneck would be exposed by a PERT analysis. In other words, in a significant set of circumstances uncertainty in the time estimates is not a major problem, for the critical path is often rather insensitive to these estimates. The major problem, and the major achievement of these techniques, is in acquiring an understanding of the precedence relationships and formally analyzing the implications.

We conclude this section with the following example of a typical PERT application. A major manufacturer with headquarters in the midwest decided to move its financial section from the midwest headquarters to a sun belt city. A PERT chart for the entire process from construction through moving to training was created. The firm had planned on an August 1 completion date, but the PERT chart yielded an earliest completion date of November 15. By renting a facility to train new employees, rather than waiting for the new facility to be completed before starting the training, the firm was able to arrive at a satisfactory completion date. Furthermore, the firm assigned two people full time for 15 months to make sure that the project was completed on time. The PERT chart was used as a monitoring and control device. Actual progress was measured against planned performance, and encouragement or additional resources were provided as necessary to keep the project on target.

13.4 Summary of Key Concepts

Inventory models apply to a wide spectrum of problems. The inventory can be anything from piece parts to second lieutenants or from cash to water. (Section 13.2.1)

Motivations for holding inventory include:
1 The possibility of achieving economies of scale in production and procurement
2 The possibility for maintaining a constant level of production
3 The opportunity to permit flexibility in scheduling sequential facilities
4 The necessity to insure against uncertainty in supply, demand, and the production process
5 The necessity of providing a competitive response to demand
(Section 13.2.2)

---

4   Alternatively, this equals the minimum of the latest start times for all activities emanating from the event.

Inventory models consist of three structural components.
1 Type of review: continuous or periodic
2 Type of demand (with or without backlogging): deterministic or stochastic
3 Type of cost: cost of replenishment, cost of holding inventory, and penalty cost
(Section 13.2.3)

PERT and CPM are useful techniques both for planning and controlling projects involving a number of activities with interrelated activities. (Section 13.3.1)

The critical path for a project is that sequence of activities that determines the earliest completion time of the project. Thus, managerial attention should be focused on these activities. (Section 13.3.3)

13.5 Problems

For problems 1 through 4, consider a *continuous time* inventory control system in which inventory is measured in units and time is measured in weeks. Assume that the holding cost and the penalty cost are proportional to the number of unit-weeks of inventory and shortage respectively. Let

$I(t)$ = inventory on hand at time t

h = dollars of holding cost per unit-week

d = demand per unit time (that is, per week)

p = dollars of penalty cost per unit week

$C(x)$ = cost of ordering x items

1 Assume $I(3) = 0$ and that an order for 75 units arrives at time $t = 3$. Also assume that $d = 50$, and the next order of 75 units arrives at time 5. If $h = .05$ and $p = .10$, calculate the holding and penalty costs incurred by the firm between times 3 and 5.

2 The firm decides to adopt the policy that all demand must be satisfied without backlogging. If $h = .04$, $d = 50$, and

$$C(x) = 100 + 3x \quad x > 0$$
$$= \quad 0 \qquad x = 0$$

find the optimal quantity to order and the optimal time between orders. (Hint: Use the EOQ formula.)

3 Assume all demand must be satisfied without backlogging. Let $I(0) = I(10) = 0$, and assume that exactly two orders are placed between times 0 and 10, the first at time 0 and the second at some *integral* time before 10. Show that total holding cost is minimized if the second order is placed at time 5. (Hint: Let t_1 be the time at which the second order is placed, and compute the total holding cost of $t_1 = 1, 2, 3, 4, 5, 6, 7, 8, 9$.)

4 Assume all demand must be satisfied without backlogging. Then, for an inventory triangle with a base of T weeks the average cost per week is given by the expression

$$AC = \frac{K}{T} + cd + \frac{hdT}{2}$$

For the parameters specified in problem 2

a Find the value of the minimum average cost per week.
b Let Q^* be the optimal order quantity. Assume that the firm orders $1.10Q^*$ items. Find the percentage increase in the average cost per week.
c Based on the calculation in part *b*, do you believe that the average cost per week is sensitive or insensitive to changes away from the optimal ordering policy?

For problems 5 through 9, consider a *periodic* inventory control system in which inventory is measured in units, and it is possible to make an ordering decision at the beginning of each month. Assume that holding costs in a month are proportional to the number of units carried from that month into the next and penalty costs in a month are proportional to the number of units of unsatisfied demand in that month. Let

$I(t)$ = inventory carried from month t into month $t + 1$ ($I(0)$ is the initial inventory)

h = cost for carrying a unit of inventory

p = cost per unit of shortage

d_t = demand in period t

x_t = items ordered in period t

$C_t(x)$ = cost of ordering x items in period t

Assume that items ordered in period t arrive at the beginning of period t and hence can be used to satisfy demand in that period. Thus

$$I(t) = I(t - 1) + x_t - d_t$$

5 Let $I(0) = 0$

x_1 = 100, $x_2 = 0$, $x_3 = 40$, $d_1 = 50$, $d_2 = 75$, $d_3 = 15$

$C_t(x)$ = $C(x) = 100 + 3(x)$ $x > 0$ for all t

     = 0 $x = 0$

h = .04

p = .10

a Calculate the total cost incurred by the firm during the first three periods.
b Can you suggest an alternative policy with a lower total cost?

6 Let

d_1 = 100, $d_2 = 75$, $d_3 = 80$, $d_4 = 25$

h = 3

$C_1(x) = 7x$

$C_2(x) = 3x$

$C_3(x) = 9x$

$C_4(x) = 10x$

Assume that all demand must be satisfied without backlogging. Find the optimal ordering policy.

7 Assume the parameter values specified in problem 6. Now assume that demand can be backlogged and that $p = 2$. Find the optimal ordering policy.

8 Let $d_t = 100$ for all t, $h = 3$, and assume that all demand must be satisfied without backlogging. Prices vary in a repeating three-month cycle.

$C_t(x) = 15x$, $C_{t+1}(x) = 20x$, $C_{t+2}(x) = 22x$ $t = 1, 4, 7, 10, 13, \ldots$

Thus

$$C_1(x) = 15x, \; C_2(x) = 20x, \; C_3(x) = 22x, \; C_4(x) = 15x, \; C_5(x) = 20x, \; C_6(x) = 22x$$

and so on. Find the optimal ordering policy.

9 Assume the same parameter values specified in problem 8 except now assume that

$$C_t(x) = 15x, \; C_{t+1}(x) = 20x, \; C_{t+2}(x) = 20x \qquad t = 1, 4, 7, 10, 13, \ldots$$

Find the optimal ordering policy.

10 For the network shown in Figure 13.15
a Find the earliest time to complete the project.
b Specify the critical path of events.
c Find ES and LS for every event.
d Since the time for activity 1–4 is zero, what sequential (precedence) relationship must hold between these events?

Figure 13.15

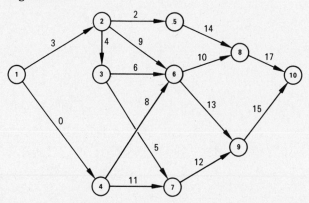

11 a Create a PERT network associated with the data shown in Figure 13.16.
b Find the earliest completion time for the project.

Figure 13.16

Activity	Time	Immediate Predecessors
1	8	None
2	17	None
3	20	None
4	30	1
5	32	1
6	18	1
7	28	2,6
8	10	2,6
9	12	3
10	35	3
11	20	4,10
12	19	5,7
13	24	5,7
14	14	8,9,13

c Find the critical path of activities.

Note that although many "visual" different networks can be created, in terms of labels on events, and the positioning of the event nodes on the paper, the same critical path of activities will be obtained.

Problems on formulation of inventory models can be found in Chapter 4, problems 20, 21, 22, and 23.

14

Special Topics: Integer Programming, Network Mode Multiple Objectives, and Goal Programming

Integer programming models are discussed from a conceptual and applied point of view. No specific algorithms are presented, but there is some discussion of the computational difficulties and the combinatorial nature of the solution techniques. Specific applications of 0/1 variables are considered, and network models are discussed in both general and specific applications. Problems with multiple objective functions are discussed, and the "satisficing" technique of goal programming is summarized.

14.1 Introduction

Previous chapters have dealt exclusively with constrained optimization models in which the variables are *continuous*. This means that the decision variables have been permitted to take on *fractional* values, such as 6.394. In particular, the previous treatment has dealt with *continuous linear models* in considerable detail. All such models are distinguished by two properties:

---

1 The effects of a single variable by itself are *proportional*. For example, doubling the sales of E–9s will double revenue from the sales of E–9s, regardless of the absolute level of sales; doubling the marketing activity will double the marketing expense and the amount of new demand created, regardless of the absolute level of the activity.

2 All interactions among variables must be *additive*. For example, the amount of labor used is the *sum* of the amount used to produce E–9s, F–9s, and so on, while the total dollar revenue is the *sum* of E–9 revenues, F–9 revenues, and so on.

It follows from these properties that in a linear model, all marginal (per unit) costs, returns, utilizations of inputs, and contributions to requirements are constant (independent of the values of any of the variables). The algebraic counterpart of these assertions is that a linear model is one in which all functions (objective and constraint) are linear, and in previous chapters we have looked in detail at the geometric characterization and the computer solution of such models.

A model with continuous variables in which the above mentioned properties do not hold for all variables or, equivalently, in which not all functions are linear, is called *nonlinear*. In a nonlinear model, some marginal quantities are dependent upon levels. For example, consider a revenue-maximization model containing the decision variables

p = price per unit

q = quantity of units to be sold

The interaction between these variables is *multiplicative* rather than *additive,* since in this case

Revenue = pq

It is also clear that the marginal revenue from each additional unit of sales q depends on the level (that is, the value) of the price variable p.

The above two classes of *continuous* models are exhaustive and exclusive in the context of constrained optimization. Any model in continuous variables is either linear or nonlinear. However, it turns out that continuity of the variables is a privileged attribute. In many important problems, the variables cannot be allowed to be continuous. This requires nontrivial changes in the mathematics of the model and in the algorithms that can be used for solving the problem. In this chapter, we wish to consider this new class of models—a class that is very large and important in applications. These models deal with problems in which not all of the variables are allowed to be continuous. Constrained optimization models of this type are called *integer programming (IP) problems,* or *discrete* (as opposed to continuous) *models.* Applications include capital budgeting, equipment utilization and scheduling, sequencing and routing decisions, problems with fixed set-up costs, and critical path scheduling (PERT). In the present chapter, these and other applications will be discussed, along with computational considerations. This topic, IP, constitutes the central theme for the present chapter. In later sections, a special and important class of integer programs are discussed, the so-called network models. In order to help expose you to a spectrum of special topics, especially those that appear in applications, we have chosen to conclude this chapter with discussions of multiple objectives and goal programming.

Let us now move into the area of integer models. Within this topic, it is well to distinguish between two subclasses of problems that fall under this same general heading, for in some senses these two classes are quite different.

The First Type of Integer Program   The first subclass is illustrated by the PROTRAC E and F model, or by the two-period production, inventory, distribution, and marketing application of Chapters 11 and 12. These are problems in which many of the decision variables, in the most ideal sense, should be constrained to integer values, for fractional levels of production do not have much physical meaning in the case of large crawler tractors. The same remark applies to fractional values for the inventory variables. Conceptually, this is a question of units. In the manufacture of pounds of peanut butter or gallons of polyurethane, it is usually physically meaningful to allow continuous quantities, such as 6.394 gallons of production. In the manufacture of E-9s, or 747 aircraft, the quantity 6.394 has little, if any, physical meaning, for how do you define .394 aircraft, and even if you could, who would buy it?

In practice, there are two ways to approach this difficulty. The easiest and most common approach is to ignore the ideal integrality conditions and solve the problem as though it were truly a continuous model. The second approach is to use a more costly algorithm that does not ignore the integer constraints and that is designed to find the true solution to the integer program.

In the first case, for the purpose of implementation, the continuous solution would be rounded to integer values. The usual justification for this approach is that the error introduced by rounding is minor compared to other errors in the model introduced by approximation, averaging, aggregation, and so on. For this first type of IP problem the procedure of rounding the variables is frequently adopted. However, there may be applications when it is not justified, because:

---

1 The rounded solution may violate critical constraints. For example, suppose three of the decision variables, say E, F, G, have optimal values 2.3, 2.4, and 5.3, respectively, in the continuous model, which includes a constraint

$$E + F + G = 10$$

Then feasibility of the current solution is lost in applying any uniform rounding rule to the variables. That is, feasibility of the current solution is destroyed when all three variables are simultaneously rounded to the nearest integer, simultaneously rounded down, or simultaneously rounded up. In the next section, it will become clear that, in fact, there may be no way to round a solution and preserve feasibility (with respect to several constraints), even when some variables are rounded up and others rounded down.

2 The rounding approach may be unjustifiable because even when a rounded solution preserves feasibility, the objective value produced by that solution may be unacceptably far from the true optimal value. That is, the potential error introduced may not be acceptable. Unfortunately, we can never tell exactly how much error is introduced by rounding, because to know this would require advance knowledge of the optimal value for the integer program. The best we can do is place a bound on the maximum error that could occur. For example, consider a max model. One way to measure the potential error is as follows. Let T denote the true integer optimal value, C denote the continuous optimal value, and R denote the objective value produced by rounded variables. Since the integer model is *more constrained* than the continuous problem, we know that its optimal value can be no larger. Hence

$$T \le C$$

If the rounded integer solution is feasible (satisfies all constraints), then we also know that

$$R \le T \le C$$

Consequently, the difference

$$C - R$$

is an upper bound on the absolute error $(C - T)$ that rounding could introduce. Also, since

$$\frac{T - R}{T} \le \frac{C - R}{T} \le \frac{C - R}{R}$$

it must be true that

$$\frac{C - R}{R}$$

is an upper bound on the relative error $(T - R/T)$ that rounding could introduce.

It is often stated that the bound on relative error tends to be small when the optimal continuous variables are large in value.[1] For example, rounding 968.21 down to 968 will typically introduce less error than rounding 6.21 down to 6, or even more drastically, 1.21 down to 1. This is perhaps intuitively plausible, since it may be interpreted as stating that small percentage deviations from optimality in the decision variables should lead to a small percentage deviation in the objective value. In practice, the number $C - R/R$ is a possible and not uncommon criterion for determining whether or not the rounded solution is acceptable. If this bound on relative error is too large, then it may be considered important to have more confidence in the solution and to use a more costly algorithm designed to find the true integer solution. In practice, then, in this first subclass of integer programs, integrality conditions are frequently ignored and solutions are rounded.

The Second Type of Integer Program   There is a second subclass of IP problems in which the integer variables are constrained to take on only the values 0 or 1 (denoted 0/1). In this class of problems, the process of rounding is almost never justifiable because the potential error introduced can be very large. For example, a decision variable x_i may have the following interpretation in the model:

$x_i = 1$ means build a new warehouse in city i

$x_i = 0$ means do not build a new warehouse in city i

As another example, a variable x_{ij} may have the following interpretation in the model:

$x_{ij} = 1$ means assign individual i to task j

$x_{ij} = 0$ means do not assign individual i to task j

---

1   To see the facts more precisely, consider an LP max model in which all variables x_j are rounded from optimal (in the continuous problem) noninteger values x_j^* to $\hat{x}_j$ to obtain a feasible integer solution. Also, let I be the set of subscripts of the positive values x_j^*, and suppose $\sum_I c_j \hat{x}_j > 0$.

$$\frac{C - R}{R} = \frac{\sum_I c_j x_j^* - \sum_I c_j \hat{x}_j}{\sum_I c_j \hat{x}_j} \leq \frac{\sum_I |c_j| \, |x_j^* - \hat{x}_j|}{\sum_I c_j \hat{x}_j} \leq \frac{\sum_I |c_j|}{\sum_I c_j \hat{x}_j}$$

As a special case, suppose that for j in I the c_j values are all positive. Then the right side of the above expression will be $\leq 1/\min_{j \, in \, I} \hat{x}_j$. For example, if $\min_{j \, in \, I} x_j^* \geq 100$, then $C - R/R \leq 1$ percent.

These variables are allowed to take on only the values 0 or 1. In a continuous version of such a model the variable may be constrained to lie between 0 and 1. When the continuous version is solved, a fractional value such as .6 could be produced. If the fractional values are rounded to produce a feasible 0/1 solution, it is clear that the possibility of introducing large errors exists. This is especially true when the coefficients of the variables in the objective function are large (see footnote 1). Thus, it is almost always the case that problems with 0/1 variables must be attacked with algorithms particularly designed to handle these constraints. Such problems, though difficult and costly to solve, are prominent in applications, as will be illustrated in later sections of this chapter.

In concluding this introduction, we remark that numerous special types of models will be formulated in the following pages. It should be kept in mind that our main motive in converting linguistic descriptions into the symbolic model is to give you additional training in problem formulation and additional insight into the real-world applicability of constrained optimization models. In many instances, it will be true that an alternative formulation which is logically equivalent will be computationally more efficient because of the nature of the particular algorithms that exist for solving the model in question. Such considerations may become important when one is solving integer programming problems, but they also become more involved with the theory and mechanics of specific algorithms. Limitations of space and purpose preclude a detailed discussion of such matters.

14.2   The Linear IP Model: Geometry and Computation

In IP, the problems usually considered are linear except for the dramatic corruption of the added *integrality conditions*. These integrality conditions essentially annihilate the applicability of linear algebra to this model, and this helps to explain the difficulty of the problem. If *all* variables are required to be integers, the problem is called a *pure integer program*. If some but not all of the variables are required to be integers, the problem is called a *mixed integer program*. Consider the following example of an integer program:

Max $21x_1 + 11x_2$

s.t.

$7x_1 + 4x_2 \leq 13$

$x_1, x_2 \geq 0$, x_1 and x_2 integers

The geometric representation of this model is shown in Figure 14.1. Note that there are only six feasible points: (0,3), (0,2), (0,1), (0,0), (1,1), and (1,0). The continuous LP solution is $(\frac{13}{7},0)$. Rounding to the nearest point with all integer coordinates gives (2,0) *which is infeasible*. Now note that the solution to the IP problem is (0,3); that is, the objective function value is 33 at (0,3) and 32 at (1,1). This solution (0,3) is about as "far" as we can get, in this case, from the continuous solution. Rounding the continuous solution down to (1,0) gives a feasible integer point, but this point also is far from the optimal point

Figure 14.1 *Geometric representation of an IP model*   **Figure 14.2** *Rounding cannot produce feasibility*

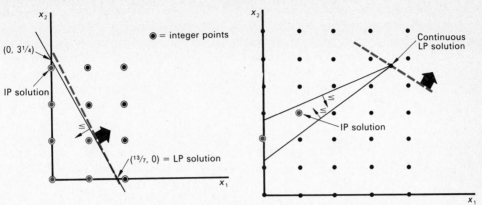

(0,3). This example provides a geometric illustration of some of the potential difficulties associated with rounding a continuous LP solution. Figure 14.2 shows a hypothetical model where the continuous solution cannot be rounded in any way to produce a feasible point.

For certain types of constraints, the process of rounding a feasible solution can be guaranteed to preserve feasibility. For example, suppose all constraints in original form are $\leq$, and the coefficients of all variables in the constraints are nonnegative. Then, it should be clear that any fractional feasible values can be rounded down without destroying feasibility.

The above discussion, along with the geometric representation, suggests and helps to make plausible the fact that IP problems are really drastically different from continuous problems. As another dramatic difference, you can see that under reasonable conditions (a bounded LP constraint set) the IP will have only a *finite* number of feasible points. You may intuitively feel that this should make the problem easier to solve. For example, in Figure 14.1 the solution can be easily found by evaluating the objective function at the six feasible points. You may wonder why this sort of enumeration cannot always be used when the constraint set is bounded. Why should it be any more difficult, in principle, than enumerating the corners of the LP constraint set? Unfortunately, in terms of complete enumeration, the two-dimensional representation in Figure 14.1 is somewhat misleading. If we had an IP with 100 0/1 variables, there could be 2^{100} feasible points. The time required to enumerate these even on the fastest computer would exceed a lifetime. By comparison with LP, it is true that the simplex method can be viewed as a way of visiting corners of the constraint set and evaluating the objective function at the corners visited. However, in this case, recall that the enumeration method is very efficient. In general, it is far from true that *all* corners are visited. The algorithm always proceeds in such a way as to improve the objective function at each successive corner. Thus, we could say that the simplex method *partially enumerates* the constraint set corners.

In fact, some of the most useful algorithms for solving integer programs are also enumeration techniques. These techniques are quite refined and are much more intelligent than total enumeration. In technical jargon, such techniques are formally referred to as *partial enumeration*. They are designed to examine only a "few" of the feasible points but in such a way as to be assured of obtaining an optimal solution. For example, consider a pure 0/1 IP model. In the optimal solution, some *combination* of the decision variables will have the value 1, while the remaining variables have the value 0. The partial enumeration algorithms consist of rules for searching certain combinations and for eliminating numerous other combinations without having to explicitly "look" at them. For example, suppose the algorithm "learns" that the variable x_4 cannot have an optimal value of 1 (the basis for such an insight could be the discovery that there is no feasible point for which $x_4 = 1$). Then we can eliminate from consideration *all* combinations of decision variables in which $x_4 = 1$. Solution techniques based on this type of underlying rationale are also referred to as *combinatorial algorithms*.

The mathematical complexity of integer programs is reflected in the following pathological phenomenon. In Figure 14.1, the objective value at (1,1) is 32. This is larger than the objective value at any of the neighboring feasible points, (0,1), (1,0), (0,0), and (0,2). Thus, the problem has what is called a local optimal solution at one of the feasible points. This local optimal solution is not the global (true) solution. This phenomenon cannot occur with a continuous LP problem, in which case any local optimum is also global.

This type of mathematical complexity, along with the limited power of the available algorithms, makes the state of the art in IP decidedly inferior to that in continuous LP. In terms of the combinatorial algorithms, the complexity of an IP problem is usually measured in terms of the number of variables, as opposed to the number of constraints. In fact, with some of the algorithms, the constraints are actually an asset because they help to eliminate combinations. In any case, one rarely encounters applications with more than several hundred variables, and even in such cases execution times can be long and costly. For these reasons, and because of the importance of the applications, IP is currently an active area of research. As a final comment, it should be noted that much of this research is in the area of *heuristic algorithms*. These are algorithms designed to efficiently produce "good," although not necessarily optimal, solutions. (An example appears in Section 14.3.5.) It should be clear by now that

---

From the viewpoint of the manager, a heuristic procedure may certainly be as acceptable as, and possible even preferable to, a "more exact" algorithm that produces an optimal solution. The dominant considerations should be the amount of insight and guidance the model can provide, and the cost of obtaining these.

14.3   Specific Applications for 0/1 Variables

A large number of real-world problems have constraints that cannot be directly expressed as an equality or an inequality involving a simple and obvious mathematical function. In such cases, a variable that is constrained to take on the value 0 or 1 often provides a mechanism for translating the appropriate logical conditions into a symbolic mathematical representation. For example, consider a continuous security analysis model in which an "optimal" portfolio (collection of securities) is to be selected from a universe of 500 securities. In a typical model of this sort:

---

1 The decision variables x_i denote the proportion of security i in the portfolio; for example, if D dollars are to be invested in the entire portfolio, then $x_i D$ dollars are invested in security i.

2 The objective function measures the "degree of risk" in any given portfolio.

3 The problem is to minimize risk subject to specific constraints on expected return, the allowable percentages of certain types of securities in the portfolio, and so on.

It is often the case, for good theoretic reasons, that the solution to this problem will entail holding a very small amount of each security in the universe; that is, each x_i would be positive but near zero. For compelling reasons, such a solution may be very impractical, and the security analyst may, for example, insist on keeping the size of the portfolio to less than 100 securities. Unfortunately, there is no way to add such a constraint to the model without introducing integer variables. The analyst might, for example, introduce 0/1 variables z_i defined as follows:

$$z_i = \begin{cases} 1 & \text{if security } i \text{ is in the portfolio} \\ 0 & \text{if security } i \text{ is not in the portfolio} \end{cases}$$

If no more than 100 securities are to be held, then the constraint

$$\sum_{i=1}^{500} z_i \leq 100$$

would be included in the model. Of course, there would have to be other constraints that would express the fact that z_i can be 1 if and only if the proportion of security i is positive ($x_i > 0$).

Alternatively, the analyst may wish to specify that the quantity of any security in the portfolio is either zero or is at least as large as some prespecified amount. That is, there are constraints of the form

Either $x_i = 0$ or $x_i \geq p_i$

where p_i is the minimum allowable holding of security i. This type of logical condition is called a *minimal lot-size* constraint. The problem with such a constraint is that, again, there is no way to express such a constraint symbolically with the use of continuous variables. Also, we do not have algorithms or computer codes that allow the analyst to type in an either/or condition directly. We shall soon see that 0/1 variables can again be used to cast such a constraint into a symbolic form that is more acceptable.

In fact, it could be said that the main role of 0/1 variables is to cast a variety of different "noncontinuous" logical conditions into a standard symbolic form. This is a desirable thing to do because then any algorithm designed to solve a problem in that standard form can be applied. This point will become clearer as we now look at a number of specific applications in more detail.

14.3.1 Fixed-Charge Problems

In this type of problem, there is a fixed start-up cost associated with some particular activity. There is an inexhaustible list of specific examples of this phenomenon in the production and inventory control area alone. Consider, for example, the utilization of an open-hearth furnace or an ice-cream machine. If the activity is not being used (there is no production), then there is no associated cost. If the activity is used, even at a minute level, then there is a significant associated start-up cost (for example, to reline and heat the furnace or to clean and cool the ice-cream machine). A fixed cost associated with the variable x_j is shown in Figure 14.3. It is seen that if $x_j = 0$, then the cost is zero, but if $x_j > 0$, then there is a fixed cost F_j as well as a marginal cost c_j. It is the discontinuity of this cost function at $x_j = 0$ that is responsible for the mathematical complexity of this problem. Let us denote the cost function in Figure 14.3 as $C_j(x_j)$. Thus

$$C_j(x_j) = \begin{cases} x_j & \text{if } x_j = 0 \\ c_j x_j + F_j & \text{if } x_j > 0 \end{cases}$$

A typical fixed-charge model can then be formulated as:

$$\text{Min} \sum_{j=1}^{n} C_j(x_j)$$

s.t.   (I)

$$\sum_{j=1}^{n} a_{ij} x_j = b_i \qquad i = 1, \ldots, m$$

$$x_j \geq 0, \text{ all } j$$

The difficulty with this formulation is that there is no algorithm for attacking problems in the above form. (Note that the objective function is not linear; in fact, it is badly nonlinear, because of the behavior at $x_j = 0$.) The problem is cast into a mixed integer program as follows.

Figure 14.3 *A fixed cost associated with x_j*

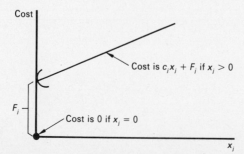

$$\text{Min} \sum_{j=1}^{n} (c_j x_j + z_j F_j)$$

s.t.   (II)

$$\sum_{j=1}^{n} a_{ij} x_j = b_i \qquad i = 1, \dots, m$$

$$x_j - z_j U \le 0 \qquad j = 1, \dots, n$$

$$x_j \ge 0, \text{ all } j; \, z_j = 0 \text{ or } 1, \text{ all } j$$

The symbol U denotes a number that is so large that whenever x is feasible in model (I), it is true that $x_j \le U$ for all j. (We will assume that such a value can be assigned to U; that is, the constraint set in the original model (I) is assumed bounded.) Note that the group of constraints

$$x_j - z_j U \le 0$$

force x_j to be zero if z_j is 0. In the problems, you are asked to prove that if x^* is a solution to (I), then x^*, z^* is a solution to (II), where

$$z_j^* = \begin{cases} 1 & \text{if } x_j^* > 0 \\ 0 & \text{if } x_j^* = 0 \end{cases}$$

and if x^*, z^* is a solution to (II), then x^* is a solution to (I). That is, if (I) has a solution then so does (II), and any solution to (II) provides a solution to (I). The advantage of casting the problem into form (II) is that an algorithm for attacking problems with 0/1 variables can then be applied.

14.3.2 *Plant Location and Capital Budgeting*

In Chapter 4, the following *transportation model* was described. A single product is considered. There are m plants and n marketing districts, with limited supply at each plant and known demand at each district. There is a per-unit cost c_{ij} associated with a shipment from plant i to district j. The problem is to determine how much to ship from each plant to each district, in such a way as to minimize total shipping cost while satisfying all demands and not exceeding available supplies. This model can be formulated as follows. Let x_{ij} be a decision variable denoting the quantity shipped from plant i to district j. The model is

$$\text{Min} \sum_{i=1}^{m} \sum_{j=1}^{n} c_{ij} x_{ij}$$

s.t.

$$\sum_{j=1}^{n} x_{ij} \le S_i \qquad i = 1, \dots, m \tag{I}$$

$$\sum_{i=1}^{m} x_{ij} \ge D_j \qquad j = 1, \dots, n$$

$$x_{ij} \ge 0, \text{ all } i, j$$

Now let us complicate the above model as follows. Suppose a fixed cost of F_i dollars is associated with the use of plant i. That is, if any amount of material is shipped out of plant i, then a fixed charge of F_i dollars is incurred. If nothing is shipped from plant i, then there is no associated cost. This is often called a plant location model, since it can be used to determine which of m possible locations should be selected for the construction of plants. In this case, the charge F_i would be the cost of constructing a plant in location i. To formulate this model, introduce new $0/1$ decision variables y_i, defined as

$$y_i = \begin{cases} 1 & \text{means use location } i \\ 0 & \text{means do not use location } i \end{cases}$$

Now the complete model is

$$\text{Min} \quad \sum_{i=1}^{m} y_i F_i + \sum_{i=1}^{m} \sum_{j=1}^{n} c_{ij} x_{ij}$$

s.t.

$$\sum_{j=1}^{n} x_{ij} - y_i S_i \leq 0 \quad i = 1, \dots, m \tag{II}$$

$$\sum_{i=1}^{m} x_{ij} \geq D_j \quad j = 1, \dots, n$$

$x_{ij} \leq 0$, all i, j; $y_i = 0$ or 1; $i = 1, \dots, m$

The constraints assure that if plant i is not used ($y_i = 0$), then nothing can be sent out of plant i, since in this case

$$\sum_{j=1}^{n} x_{ij} \geq 0$$

Also note that if $y_i = 0$, then the fixed charge F_i in the objective function is not incurred for plant i.

As another complication, suppose there is a fixed overhead cost F_{ij} associated with the maintenance of a shipping route between location i and district j. The problem is now to select the plant locations, routings, and shipping schedule so as to minimize total cost. The new model is formulated by introducing $0/1$ variables z_{ij} defined as

$$z_{ij} = \begin{cases} 1 & \text{means use the route between } i \text{ and } j \\ 0 & \text{if not} \end{cases}$$

The complete model is

$$\text{Min} \sum_{i=1}^{m} y_i F_i + \sum_{i=1}^{m} \sum_{j=1}^{n} c_{ij} x_{ij} + \sum_{i=1}^{m} \sum_{j=1}^{n} F_{ij} z_{ij}$$

s.t.

$$\sum_{j=1}^{n} x_{ij} - y_i S_i \leq 0 \quad i = 1, \dots, m \tag{III}$$

$$\sum_{i=1}^{m} x_{ij} \geq D_j \quad j = 1, \dots, n$$

$x_{ij} - z_{ij} U \leq 0$, all i, j

$x_{ij} \geq 0$, all i, j; $y_i = 0$ or 1, all i; $z_{ij} = 0$ or 1, all i, j

In this model, the number U is chosen so large that any point that is feasible in model (II) has the property that $x_{ij} \leq U$, all i, j. This number U could be taken as the maximum of the supplies $S_1, S_2, \dots, S_m$.

Models of the above type are sometimes also referred to as *capital-budgeting models*. This type of model usually involves 0/1 variables x_j with the interpretation

$$x_j = \begin{cases} 1 & \text{means select project } j \\ 0 & \text{means decline project } j \end{cases}$$

A project may mean build a new factory, open a sales territory, locate a warehouse in a district, acquire another business, sell an asset, construct a new science building in the university. Such decisions are called capital-budgeting decisions, and the solutions to such problems are important because considerable amounts of money tend to be involved in the decisions.

14.3.3 Batch Sizes

Suppose product j can be manufactured in lot sizes $\geq L_j$, or security j in a portfolio can be purchased only in lot sizes $\geq L_j$. Let x_j be the decision variable denoting the quantity of the item in question. Then the constraint

$x_j = 0 \quad \text{or} \quad x_j \geq L_j$

can be reformulated with 0/1 variables as follows. Suppose U is a sufficiently large number that for any feasible point it is always true that $x_j \leq U$. Let y_j be a new 0/1 decision variable. Then the above dichotomy is captured by the *two* constraints

$x_j - U y_j \leq 0$

$x_j - L_j y_j \geq 0$

These conditions together imply that if $y_j = 0$, then x_j must equal zero. If $y_j = 1$, then $x_j \geq L_j$.

14.3.4 k of m Constraints

Suppose we have a model requiring that *at least k* of the following conditions are satisfied:

$g_i(x_1, \dots, x_n) \leq b_i \quad i = 1, \dots, m$

To express this requirement, introduce m new 0/1 variables y_i and let U be chosen so large that for each i, $g_i(x_1, \dots, x_n) \leq U$ for every x satisfying any set of k inequalities taken from the above m. Then the following $m + 1$ constraints express the desired condition:

$$\sum_{i=1}^{m} y_i \geq k$$

$$g_i(x_1, ..., x_n) \leq b_i y_i + (1 - y_i) U \qquad i = 1, ..., m$$

Note that

$$\sum_{i=1}^{m} y_i \geq k$$

forces at least k of the y_i variables to have the value 1. This means that at least k of the last m inequalities are equivalent to $g_i(x_1, ..., x_n) \leq b_i$. The remaining inequalities are equivalent to $g_i(x_1, ..., x_n) \leq U$, and by the above assumption on the choice of U, these conditions are innocuous.

For a particular application, let us recall the purchasing model from Section 9.1:

$$\text{Min} \quad \sum_{i=1}^{P} \sum_{j=1}^{M} \sum_{k=1}^{N} c_{ijk} x_{ijk}$$

s.t.

$$\sum_{j} x_{ijk} \geq D_{ik} \quad i = 1, ..., P; \quad k = 1, ..., N$$

$$\sum_{k} x_{ijk} \leq S_{ij} \quad i = 1, ..., P; \quad j = 1, ..., M$$

$$x_{ijk} \geq 0$$

where x_{ijk} is the amount of product i sent from supplier j to destination k. Let us add to the model the following rules of thumb:

A: at least two suppliers for every product

B: at least two suppliers for every destination

Before these rules can be incorporated into the model, one must specify what it means (in terms of the model) to be a supplier. The first natural reaction is that a firm is a supplier if the amount shipped is > 0. A little thought soon reveals that this constraint neither captures management's goals in a practical way nor can it be handled analytically, because it is a strict inequality. More specifically, management uses rule A to insure that the firm does not become too dependent on a single supplier. It is hard to believe that this dependence is reduced by purchasing some extremely small quantity from a second supplier, and that is all a > 0 would require. From an analytic point of view, we have already observed in Chapter 10 that strict inequalities cannot be included in a mathematical programming problem because the resulting problem may have no solution. Thus, you can see that although the above rules sound plausible, they are in fact not useful as stated. In order to make these rules sensible, let us say

A: For any product i there must be at least two suppliers each of whom provides at least Q_i units (Q_i is a specified number smaller than at least two S_{ij} values)

B: For every destination k there must be at least two suppliers, each of whom provides a total across all products of at least R units

We can now add the first rule to the model by requiring that, for each product i, at least two of the following M conditions are satisfied:

$$\sum_{k=1}^{N} x_{ijk} \geq Q_i \qquad j = 1, ..., M$$

This is accomplished as follows:

$$\sum_{j=1}^{M} z_{ij} \geq 2 \qquad i = 1, ..., P$$

$$\sum_{k=1}^{N} x_{ijk} \geq z_{ij} Q_i \qquad i = 1, ..., P; j = 1, ..., M$$

$z_{ij} = 0$ or 1, all i, j

We can add the second rule to the model by requiring that, for each destination k, at least two of the following M conditions are satisfied:

$$\sum_{i=1}^{P} x_{ijk} \geq R \qquad j = 1, ..., M$$

This is accomplished as follows:

$$\sum_{j=1}^{M} w_{jk} \geq 2 \qquad k = 1, ..., N$$

$$\sum_{i=1}^{P} x_{ijk} \geq w_{jk} R \qquad j = 1, ..., M; k = 1, ..., N$$

$w_{jk} = 0$ or 1, all j, k

14.3.5   The Knapsack Problem

This is an important problem that arises in different contexts, such as loading containers in box cars or aircraft or satisfying the demand for various lengths of cloth which must be cut from fixed-length bolts of fabric that are held in stock. The generic statement is quite simple. Consider a set of indivisible items that differ in weight and value. We are given a knapsack that holds a maximum allowable weight. The problem is to load the knapsack in such a way as to maximize the value it holds.

As an example, suppose a knapsack holds 91 pounds. Assume that there is one unit of each of five items that can be placed in the knapsack. The weight and value of each item is given in Figure 14.4. Suppose the items are divisible, so that less than one unit of each is allowed to be loaded. Then the problem is one in continuous variables and the solution is easy. Simply rerank the items in the order of decreasing value per unit weight, as shown in Figure 14.5. Then place items in the knapsack in the order of decreasing value per unit weight, as shown in Figure 14.6.

Figure 14.4   *Weight/value data for the knapsack problem*

Item Number	Weight	Value
1	36	54
2	24	18
3	30	60
4	32	32
5	26	13

Figure 14.5   *Ranking when items in knapsack are divisible*

Item Number	Weight	Value	Value/weight
3	30	60	2
1	36	54	$1\frac{1}{2}$
4	32	32	1
2	24	18	$\frac{3}{4}$
5	26	13	$\frac{1}{2}$

Figure 14.6   *Solution to the knapsack problem with divisible items*

Load	Weight	Value
All of item 3	30	60
All of item 1	36	54
$\frac{25}{32}$ of item 4	25	25
	91	139

For the discrete (indivisible) case, one might use the ranking approach to conjecture the following solution. Load 3 and 1 to get 66 pounds, then 2 to add 24 pounds, using 90 pounds of total capacity and obtaining a value of 132. Though this, in fact, is a solution to the above example, this technique will not, in general, be valid. Perhaps you can construct an example to illustrate this fact. You are asked to do so in problem 6.

The above intuitive approach (that is, ranking items according to value per unit weight and then selecting from this list from top down) is an example of a heuristic algorithm for solving a combinatorial problem. In many applications, heuristic algorithms work quite well in the sense of efficiently producing solutions that, though not optimal, are good enough to enable management to improve current operations, and, after all, that is the name of the game. Moreover, heuristic algorithms are often able to produce bounds on the "goodness" of a candidate solution so that the manager can, for example, have assurance that he is within such and such a percentage of optimality.

The formal IP formulation of the knapsack problem is extremely simple. Suppose there are n distinct items for potential inclusion. Let

$$x_i = \begin{cases} 1 & \text{if item } i \text{ is to be included in the knapsack} \\ 0 & \text{otherwise} \end{cases}$$

Let

w_i = weight of item i

v_i = value of item i

W = capacity of the knapsack

Then the formulation is

$$\text{Max} \quad \sum_{i=1}^{n} v_i x_i$$

s.t.

$$\sum_{i=1}^{n} w_i x_i \leq W$$

$x_i = 0$ or 1, all i

Any integer program with *one* constraint and *nonnegative data* is called a knapsack problem. If unlimited numbers of each item i can be selected, subject only to the capacity constraint, then the 0/1 condition is replaced by the requirement that each x_i is integer valued.

14.3.6 *Sequencing, Scheduling, and Routing Problems*

These problems tend to be quite large, involving many combinations to be scanned, and consequently they tend to be difficult to solve. In practice, heuristic algorithms are often applied with considerable success. A generic routing problem is the so-called traveling salesman problem. It is a good example of a problem that is easy to state but hard to solve. There are n cities. A *tour* is a route that begins at city 1, visits each city once and only once, and returns to city 1. The problem is to find the shortest tour. The data of the problem consist of the terms c_{ij}, the distance between city i and city j. Some of the c_{ij} could be infinity (you cannot go from i to j), and c_{ij} need not equal c_{ji}. Note that when one starts in city 1, he can choose any of the remaining $(n-1)$ cities to visit first. Having chosen this city, he can now select any of the remaining $(n-2)$ cities, and so on. There are thus a total of $(n-1)(n-2)\ldots(2)(1)$ possible tours. This product is written as $(n-1)!$. You may be surprised that $29! = 8.84 \times 10^{30}$; thus, the notion of solving a 30-city problem by total enumeration is clearly out of the question. To state a formal mathematical model of this problem, let

$$x_{ij} = \begin{cases} 1 & \text{if a tour includes traveling from } i \text{ to } j \\ 0 & \text{otherwise} \end{cases}$$

Then, the model can be written as

Figure 14.7 *A solution with subtours*

Figure 14.8 *Four-city tour costs*

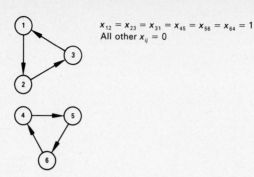

$x_{12} = x_{23} = x_{31} = x_{45} = x_{56} = x_{64} = 1$
All other $x_{ij} = 0$

From	To			
	1	2	3	4
1	∞	6	4	5
2	2	∞	5	4
3	5	30	∞	20
4	7	3	6	∞

Min $\displaystyle\sum_{i=1}^{n} \sum_{j=1}^{n} c_{ij} x_{ij}$

s.t.

$\displaystyle\sum_{j=1}^{n} x_{ij} = 1 \qquad i = 1, ..., n$ (Leave each city exactly once)

$\displaystyle\sum_{i=1}^{n} x_{ij} = 1 \qquad j = 1, ..., n$ (Enter each city exactly once)

$x_{ij} \ge 0$, integer, all i, j (With the above constraints, this insures $x_{ij} = 0$ or 1)

In this formulation, $c_{jj} = \infty; j = 1, ..., n$ because $x_{jj} = 1$ is meaningless.[2] The above formulation is not complete, for a feasible solution to the problem stated above may contain disconnected *subtours,* which are not allowed. A solution with two subtours is presented in Figure 14.7. Since such a solution does not provide an answer to the real problem, subtours must be ruled out. We shall merely state that this can be done formally by introducing additional nonnegative integer variables $u_i, i = 2, 3, ..., n$ with the additional constraints

$u_i - u_j + n x_{ij} \le n - 1$ for $\begin{cases} i = 2, ..., n \\ j = 2, ..., n \end{cases} \quad i \ne j$

One of the most intuitive ways to approach sequential decision problems is to follow a policy that "does the best at each stage." The costs shown in the four-city example in Figure 14.8 can be used to illustrate the fallacy of such an approach. Suppose you select the cheapest alternative at each stage, while maintaining a tour. The tour obtained would be $1 \to 3 \to 4 \to 2 \to 1$, with a cost of 29. The tour $1 \to 4 \to 2 \to 3 \to 1$ is better, with a cost of 18.

The traveling salesman model is actually applicable to numerous diverse problems in real life; it is probably rarely applied to abate the dilemmas of a traveling salesman. A more meaningful application might involve drawing up routes for delivery trucks. As an example of the diversity of the scheduling

---

2 When the model is input to the computer for solution, a very large number is input for the c_{jj} values.

problems that are actually traveling salesman models, consider the problem of scheduling the flavors of ice cream to run through a manufacturer's equipment.

Let

c_{ij} = time spent setting up (cleaning and preparing equipment) for j when flavor j follows i

These c_{ij}s vary considerably, since many flavors are near variants (chocolate ripple and chocolate fudge almond) and others require significant clean-up time (chocolate followed by vanilla). The problem of scheduling production to minimize total set-up time is a traveling salesman problem, where

$$x_{ij} = \begin{cases} 1 & \text{if flavor } j \text{ follows flavor } i \\ 0 & \text{if not} \end{cases}$$

In addition to the traveling salesman model, there are numerous other types of problems that involve sequencing decisions. Many of these are discussed in the standard reference texts on IP.

14.3.7 The Stock-cutting Problem

This is an illustrative application of LP/IP theory to a real-world problem. A stock of standard lengths $L_1, L_2, ..., L_k$ of one material is maintained, from which you are to cut lengths to fill incoming orders. An unlimited number of bolts of material are available in stock for each of the lengths $L_1, ..., L_k$. An order consists of a request for a given number N_i pieces of length r_i of the stocked material, for $i = 1, ..., m$. The allowable lengths $r_1, ..., r_m$ are *fixed*. Orders are taken only for these lengths. Assume max $\{L_j, j = 1, ..., k\} \geq r_i$ for every i. The problem is to satisfy all orders in such a way as to minimize the material wasted. Schematically, the problem is shown in Figure 14.9.

Figure 14.9   *The stock-cutting problem*

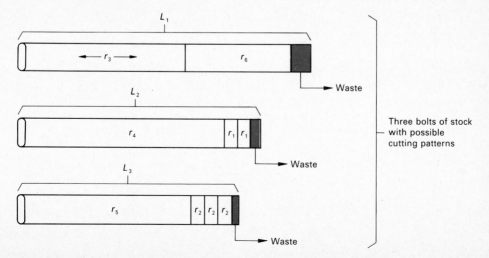

To construct the model, we shall consider the simple case when $k = 1$ (there is only one standard length L_1). Let a_{ij} be the number of pieces of length r_i created by the jth cutting pattern (a cutting pattern is any vector $(a_1, ..., a_m)$ such that $a_i \geq 0$ and integer, $i = 1, ..., m$, and

$$\sum_{i=1}^{m} a_i r_i \leq L$$

Each cutting pattern is assumed to consume a whole roll. Suppose, for example, there are orders for three lengths, r_1, r_2, r_3.

Each column j satisfies the condition $\sum_{i=1}^{3} a_{ij} r_i + w_j = L_1$. Each column of numbers represents a cutting pattern.

$$
\begin{array}{ccccc}
 & x_1 & x_2, & ..., & x_n \\
r_1 & a_{11} & a_{12}, & ..., & a_{1n} & N_1 \\
r_2 & a_{21} & a_{22}, & ..., & a_{2n} & N_2 \\
r_3 & a_{31} & a_{32}, & ..., & a_{3n} & N_3 \\
\text{Waste} & w_1 & w_2, & ..., & w_n
\end{array}
$$

As a concrete example, suppose

$r_1 = 28''$, $r_2 = 6''$, $r_3 = 3''$, $L = 100''$, $N_1 = 4$, $N_2 = 14$, $N_3 = 1$

One possible policy would be

First roll: $2r_1, 7r_2$	waste =	$2''$
Second roll: $2r_1, 7r_2$	waste =	$2''$
Third roll: $1r_3$	waste =	$97''$
	Total waste =	$101''$

A better policy would be

First roll: $1r_1, 12r_2$	waste =	0
Second roll: $3r_1, 2r_2, 1r_3$	waste =	$1''$

This policy is optimal because the total quantity ordered is 199 inches. Since each roll is 100 inches, no fewer than two rolls can be employed.

Now, letting the variable x_j be the number of times cutting pattern j is employed, we have the constraints

$$\sum_{j=1}^{n} a_{ij} x_j \geq N_i \qquad i = 1, 2, 3.$$

Verify that the total inches of waste is given by

$$\sum_{j=1}^{n} x_j w_j + \sum_{i=1}^{3} r_i \quad (\text{number of excess cuts of length } r_i)$$

Hence, the objective function is

$$\text{Min} \quad \sum_{j=1}^{n} x_j w_j + \sum_{i=1}^{3} r_i \left(\sum_{j=1}^{n} a_{ij} x_j - N_i \right)$$

$$= \min \quad \sum_{j=1}^{n} x_j \left(w_j + \sum_{i=1}^{3} r_i a_{ij} \right) - \sum_{i=1}^{3} r_i N_i$$

$$= \min \quad L_1 \sum_{j=1}^{n} x_j - \sum_{i=1}^{3} r_i N_i$$

$$= \min \quad \text{(total material used} - \text{material ordered)}$$

Note that in this case it suffices to minimize

$$\sum_{j=1}^{n} x_j$$

and hence the model can be written

$$\text{Min} \quad \sum_{j=1}^{n} x_j$$

s.t.

$$\sum_{j=1}^{n} a_{ij} x_j \geq N_i \quad i = 1, 2, 3$$

$$x_j \geq 0, \, x_j \quad \text{integer, all } j$$

A major difficulty in solving this problem is created by the number of cutting patterns that might exist. Since there is a decision variable x_j for each cutting pattern (x_j is the number of times cutting pattern j is employed), a large number of cutting patterns implies a large number of variables. For example, a standard roll of 200 inches in length and demands for 40 different lengths ranging from 20–80 inches yields a number of cutting patterns that could easily exceed 10 million, and this size problem is encountered in practice. Thus, we are faced with an integer program in 10 million variables. What to do? A first approximation step is to drop the integer restrictions. If we solve the continuous linear program to obtain values x_j^*, and then round up, the solution will stay feasible because each $a_{ij} \geq 0$. If there are 40 different lengths, r_i, then there are only 40 constraints. This means the LP problem will have at most 40 positive optimal values to be rounded. According to the discussion in Section 14.1 (see footnote 1 and note that in the present case each $c_j = 1$), if the number 40 is small compared to the rounded objective value, then the relative objective value error caused by rounding up will usually be acceptably small. However, how does one solve a linear program with 10 million variables? The solution technique is called a *column-generating* method. It is a typical approach to solving large-scale problems. Rather than having to store in the computer the amount of data required to solve a 10 million variable problem, the necessary data are "generated" as needed by solving certain subproblems. The mechanics of column generation would lead us too far afield into the area of technique and the actual mathematics of the simplex algorithm. We shall merely state that in this instance, columns are generated by solving an appropriate knapsack problem. Thus, the latter arises directly (for example, loading a boxcar) and indirectly, as a subproblem in finding solutions to stock-cutting problems.

14.4 Network Models

Network problems constitute a large and special class of LP models. These problems have a special mathematical form, called a *special structure*, that endows the model with two powerful properties:

Property 1: Very efficient solution algorithms have been developed.

Property 2: There is always an optimal solution for which the decision variables have integer values. Moreover, such a solution (as opposed to an alternative optimal fractional solution) is always produced by the existing algorithms.

Property 2 is of great interest since, as we've seen, integrality conditions may be important. Models *requiring* fractional (as opposed to integer) solutions simply do not exist. Thus it is entirely advantageous that an integer solution is always produced. A general symbolic form of a network model with the above properties can be stated as follows. Suppose the subscripts i and j run from 1 to n:

$$\text{Min} \quad \sum_i \sum_{j \neq i} c_{ij} x_{ij}$$

s.t.   (I)

$$\sum_{k \neq j} x_{jk} - \sum_{k \neq j} x_{kj} = L_j \qquad j = 1, ..., n$$

$$0 \leq x_{ij} \leq b_{ij}, \text{ all } i, j \neq i$$

---

where all L_j and b_{ij} are integer values. For simplicity, we also want to assume that all $c_{ij} \geq 0$ and

$$\sum_{j=1}^{n} L_j = 0$$

A schematic representation of the above model is obtained as follows. For each $j = 1, ..., n$, construct a **node**. Interpret the variable x_{ij} as denoting a quantity of "flow" from node i to node j. The term c_{ij} is the cost of each unit of flow from node i to node j. Some of the c_{ij}s could be infinite, which is merely a formal way of specifying that there can be no flow from i to j. Alternatively, the corresponding variables x_{ij} could be omitted from the model. For each ordered pair (i,j) with a finite value for c_{ij}, draw an **arc** from node i to node j. The parameter L_j denotes the *net* flow *leaving* node j. The term

$$\sum_{k \neq j} x_{jk}$$

represents the total flow leaving node j. The term

$$\sum_{k \neq j} x_{kj}$$

represents the total flow entering node j. Thus if L_j is positive, more units of flow must leave the node than enter it, in which case node j is called a *source* or *origin*. If L_j is negative, then more units of flow must enter the node than leave it, in which case node j is called a *sink* or *destination*. If L_j is zero, then all flow entering the node must also leave it. The constraints

$$\sum_{k \neq j} x_{jk} - \sum_{k \neq j} x_{kj} = L_j \qquad j = 1, \ldots, n$$

are called the *flow balance equations*. The term b_{ij} denotes a capacity on the total flow from i to j. If b_{ij} is zero, there can be no flow and the corresponding variable and arc could be merely eliminated from the model. If b_{ij} is infinite, there is no limitation on capacity.

To illustrate the correspondence between a network diagram and the symbolic model, let us begin with an example of the former and derive the latter. Figure 14.10 shows a network problem involving inventory redistribution among eight district outlets. The corresponding model, in algebraic symbols, can be simplified by noting that since there are only ten arcs, only 10 of the 56 possible x_{ij} variables need to explicitly appear. Thus we obtain

ure 14.10 *Inventory redistribution among eight outlets*

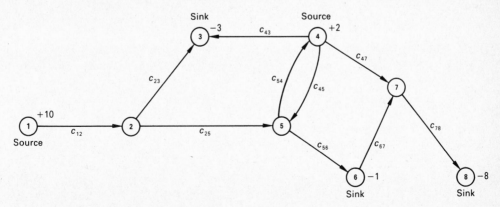

$$\text{Min} \quad c_{12}x_{12} + c_{23}x_{23} + c_{25}x_{25} + c_{43}x_{43} + c_{45}x_{45}$$
$$+ c_{47}x_{47} + c_{54}x_{54} + c_{56}x_{56} + c_{67}x_{67} + c_{78}x_{78}$$

s.t.

$$
\begin{aligned}
x_{12} &= 10 \\
-x_{12} + x_{23} + x_{25} &= 0 \\
- x_{23} - x_{43} &= -3 \\
x_{43} + x_{45} + x_{47} - x_{54} &= 2 \\
- x_{25} - x_{45} + x_{54} + x_{56} &= 0 \\
- x_{56} + x_{67} &= -1 \\
- x_{47} - x_{67} + x_{78} &= 0 \\
- x_{78} &= -8
\end{aligned}
$$

All variables nonnegative

A convenient way to look at the structure of a network problem such as the above is to construct a table of the coefficients in the flow balance equations. Such a table, for the above model, appears in Figure 14.11. This is called a **node-arc incidence matrix.** There is a row corresponding to each node, and the row reflects the flow balance at that node. There is a column, and hence a variable, for each arc. Each column has two and only two entries, +1 and −1. The row in which the +1 appears designates the node at the beginning of the arc. The row in which −1 appears designates the node at the end of the arc.

The above discussion indicates that any model of the form (I) can be schematically represented with a network diagram and, conversely, a network diagram as in Figure 14.10 can be formally represented as an LP model of form (I). Such models can, of course, be solved with the ordinary simplex method, but other special algorithms, including variants of the simplex method, have proved to be more efficient for this class of models. (To give you some idea of the power of such algorithms, network models with 50,000 constraints and 60 million variables have been solved in an hour of computing time on high-speed

Figure 14.11 *Node-arc incidence matrix*

Nodes	(1,2)	(2,3)	(2,5)	(4,3)	(4,5)	(4,7)	(5,4)	(5,6)	(6,7)	(7,8)	Supplies
				Arcs (i,j)							
1	1										10
2	−1	1	1								0
3		−1		−1							−3
4				1	1	1	−1				2
5			−1		−1		1	1			0
6								−1	1		−1
7						−1			−1	1	0
8										−1	−8

equipment. Solving such a problem turns out to be much faster than reading the output.) All network algorithms exploit the special mathematical structure of the model, as characterized by the node-arc incidence matrix. Also, as mentioned above, all such algorithms produce optimal solutions that turn out to be integer-valued. In the following pages, we shall discuss special cases of the general network model (I).

14.4.1 The Transportation and Assignment Models

We encountered the transportation model in Section 14.3.2. There are m origins or supply points (plants, for example), and n destinations (warehouses, marketing areas, and so on) for a single product. Each destination has a demand, D_j, and each origin has a supply, S_i. It costs c_{ij} to ship a unit from origin i to destination j. The problem is to find a shipping schedule that does not violate the supply constraints and satisfies the demand constraints at a minimum cost.

We have previously presented this model with inequality constraints. However, it can always be written with equality constraints instead, by making the following observations. The demand constraints will always be active. Hence, they can be written as either $\geq$ or $=$. If total supply is equal to total demand, then since all supply must be used, the $\leq$ constraints may be written as $=$. If total supply exceeds total demand, then each $\leq$ supply constraint can be converted to an equality by introducing a slack variable. (Each such slack, say $x_{i,n+1}$, can be interpreted as the amount shipped from origin i to some artificial destination called $n + 1$, to which the shipping cost is zero.) Hence, without loss of generality, the formal model can be stated in equality form as

$$\text{Min} \quad \sum_{i=1}^{m} \sum_{j=1}^{n} c_{ij} x_{ij}$$

s.t.

$$\sum_{j=1}^{n} x_{ij} = S_i \qquad i = 1, ..., m$$

$$\sum_{i=1}^{m} x_{ij} = D_j \qquad j = 1, ..., n$$

$$x_{ij} \geq 0, \text{ all } i, j$$

We now note that this is a special case of the network model, model (I) in Section 14.4. In particular, it is a problem with m sources, n sinks, and mn possible arcs. It follows that if the S_i and D_j are positive integers, then at least one optimal corner solution will be integer-valued, and the simplex method will lead to such a solution. We also note that the c_{ij}s can incorporate per-unit production costs as well as the cost for shipping.

As a special case of the transportation problem, let each $S_i = 1$, each $D_j = 1$, and $m = n$. Then we obtain

$$\text{Min} \quad \sum_{i=1}^{n} \sum_{j=1}^{n} c_{ij} x_{ij}$$

s.t.

$$\sum_{j=1}^{n} x_{ij} = 1 \quad i = 1, ..., n$$

$$\sum_{i=1}^{n} x_{ij} = 1 \quad j = 1, ..., n$$

$$x_{ij} \geq 0$$

This special form of the transportation model is called the *assignment problem.* Note that since there is always an integer solution, the constraints imply there is always a solution in which each x_{ij} is zero or one. The variables are often interpreted as follows:

$$x_{ij} = \begin{cases} 1 & \text{means assign agent } i \text{ to task } j \\ 0 & \text{means do not assign agent } i \text{ to task } j \end{cases}$$

In accordance with these definitions, the assignment model can be given the following meaning. There are n agents and n tasks. Each agent must be assigned to a single task, and each task must have a single agent assigned to it. The cost of assigning agent i to task j is c_{ij}. Find a minimum-cost assignment that satisfies all of the constraints. Of course, the literal problem underlying such a model may have nothing to do with the assignment of people to tasks. The same model can arise in allocating weapons to targets, in predicting high-risk applicants for commercial loans, or in analyzing n^{th}-order wave patterns in a model tub basin.

14.4.2 *The Shortest-route Problem*

As an illustration, consider the network in Figure 14.12. With each arc (i,j) is associated a number c_{ij} that is the distance, time, or cost from i to j. The problem is to find the route from node 1 to node 8 of minimum distance, time, or cost. One might imagine that there is a unit of supply at the source and

Figure 14.12 *Alternative routes from node 1 to node 8*

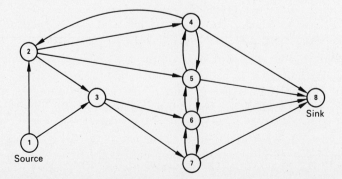

gure 14.13   *A network diagram for the replacement problem*

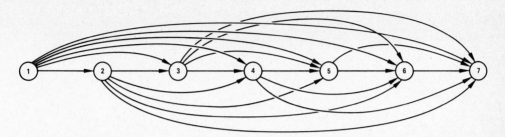

a unit of demand at the sink. The objective could then be interpreted as minimizing the cost of sending a unit from node 1 to node 8. According to this interpretation, the formal statement of the model is

$$\text{Min} \quad \sum_{i} \sum_{j \neq i} c_{ij} x_{ij}$$

s.t.

$$\sum_{k \neq j} x_{jk} - \sum_{k \neq j} x_{kj} \;=\; \begin{cases} 1 & \text{if } j = \text{source} \\[2mm] 0 & \text{if } j \neq \text{source, sink} \\[2mm] -1 & \text{if } j = \text{sink} \end{cases}$$

$$x_{ij} \geq 0$$

The solution to this problem will reveal the optimal (the shortest) route.

As an application of this model, consider the following equipment replacement problem. There are six time periods during which a piece of equipment must be used. The term c_{ij} is the cost of renting a new item at the beginning of period i, maintaining it until the beginning of period j, and then trading it in for another new item. For example, c_{17} would involve a cost of minimum rental but maximum maintenance and operating costs; that is, the cost c_{17} corresponds to a policy of renting the same piece of equipment for all six periods, with no replacement. The policy of renting at the beginning of each period would cost $c_{12} + c_{23} + c_{34} + c_{45} + c_{56} + c_{67}$. This would undoubtedly be a policy of minimum maintenance and operating cost but maximum payments for rental. The optimal policy is apt to be somewhere between the two extremes. A network representation of this problem is shown in Figure 14.13. The objective is to find the shortest route from node 1 to node 7. Each node entered on this route represents a replacement.

14.4.3   *The Min-Cost-Flow Problem*

This is a generalization of the shortest-route model. Consider a network with n nodes and m arcs. Associated with every arc there is an arc capacity b_{ij} that indicates the maximum amount of flow that is allowed to traverse the arc from node i to node j. If x_{ij} is the arc flow, then $0 \leq x_{ij} \leq b_{ij}$. As before, c_{ij} is the cost of shipping one unit of flow along (i, j). The objective is to find the min-cost path of sending v units of flow from source to sink. Note that if for all (i, j) on the shortest path from source to sink, we have $v \leq b_{ij}$, then the arc capacities are not constraining and the shortest path will give the solution. In general, however, this will not be the case. Formally, the min-cost-flow problem can be stated as

$$\text{Min} \quad \sum_i \sum_{j \neq i} c_{ij} x_{ij}$$

s.t.

$$\sum_{k \neq j} x_{jk} - \sum_{k \neq j} x_{kj} = \begin{cases} v & \text{if } j = \text{source} \\ 0 & \text{if } j \neq \text{source, sink} \\ -v & \text{if } j = \text{sink} \end{cases}$$

$$0 \leq x_{ij} \leq b_{ij}$$

14.4.4   The Max-Flow Problem

The problem is to find the maximum amount of flow that can be routed from a single source to a single sink in a network that has capacities on the arcs. Formally, the problem is

$$\text{Max} \quad v$$

s.t.

$$\sum_{k \neq j} x_{jk} - \sum_{k \neq j} x_{kj} = \begin{cases} v & \text{if } j = \text{source} \\ -v & \text{if } j = \text{sink} \\ 0 & \text{otherwise} \end{cases}$$

$$0 \leq x_{ij} \leq b_{ij}$$

where the above summations are over the nodes for which x_{ij} is defined.

This problem, along with the shortest-route problem, is of interest in its own right and also appears as a subproblem in solving numerous other more complicated models. For this reason, as well as because of the theoretic underpinnings, which we have obviously chosen to leave out of this section, it is often stated that these two problems (shortest-route and max-flow) are of central importance in network theory.

A key theoretic result in network theory is quite easily stated. It is called the *max-flow/min-cut theorem.* In order to state (but not prove) this theorem, it is necessary to define the notion of a *cut* and a *cut capacity.* Suppose we exhaustively partition the nodes into two disjoint classes, say C_1 and C_n, where the source is in C_1, and the sink is in C_n. Such a partition is called a cut. The cut capacity is defined as the sum of all the b_{ij} such that node i is in C_1 and j is in C_n. Then, the max-flow/min-cut theorem states that the maximum flow v in the network, from source to sink, is equal to the minimal cut capacity.

14.5 Multiple Objectives

In many applications, the planner has more than one objective. His different objectives may all be of equal importance or, at the very least, it may be difficult for the planner to compare the importance of one objective as opposed to another. We illustrated such a situation in Chapter 3, with the corporate president whose long-range goals were to

1 Maximize discounted profits
2 Maximize market share at the end of the planning period
3 Maximize existing physical capital at the end of the planning period

These goals are not commensurate, which means they cannot be *directly* compared. And yet, it is clear that there are **tradeoffs** in the sense that sacrificing the requirements on any one goal will tend to produce greater returns on the others.

In practice, the treatment of multiple objectives is a young but important area in applications. The analytic methods for handling these models are limited, and it is frequently the case that simulation models are applied to such situations. This is illustrated in Chapter 18, in the context of the above problem of the corporate president. In this section, we shall briefly mention two analytic approaches to the problem.

The Utility Formulation   Let $x = (x_1, ..., x_n)$ denote the decision variables for the problem at hand, and let $f_1(x), ..., f_p(x)$ denote the planner's multiple objective functions. It may be possible for the planner to construct a numerical measure of his preferences for all combinations of values $(f_1(x), ..., f_p(x))$, where x is presumably restricted to some set of constraints. Let U be a function of p variables that measures the planner's preference, and let S denote the set of feasible x values. Then, for any x in S, the number $U(f_1(x), ..., f_p(x))$ indicates the importance or the "utility" of the decision x in the sense of the associated return. The function U is called a **utility function.** Whether or not such a function exists conceptually and whether it can be practically constructed is a lengthy topic in itself. In case it can be, the problem is reduced to solving

$$\text{Max} \quad U[f_1(x), ..., f_p(x)]$$

s.t.

$$x \in S$$

In general, this would be a nonlinear programming model.

The Pareto Optimality Approach   In certain cases, it is possible to obtain more directly applicable analytic results. In particular, suppose we assume that the decision variables are subjected to *linear* constraints, say of the form

$$\sum_{j=1}^{n} a_{ij} x_j \le b_i, \, i = 1, ..., m$$

$$x_j \ge 0, j = 1, ..., n$$

Figure 14.14   *Pareto optimality*

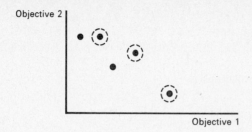

Let us also assume that there are p *different linear* objective functions. If the planner had her preferences, she would like to maximize all of these at the same time. However, this Panglossian dream cannot be realized, for in general, she will face the dilemma of having to trade off one objective for another.

One way of handling this problem is to seek a feasible point x^* that dominates all other feasible points in the following sense: there is no other feasible y^* at which all of the objective values are at least as good as at x^* and at which at least one objective value is better. Such a point x^* is termed a ***Pareto optimum.*** This concept is illustrated for two objectives in Figure 14.14. There are five feasible points in the underlying problem and the objective values at these points are shown in Figure 14.14. Each of the three encircled points corresponds to a Pareto optimum in the underlying problem. Though we shall omit the details, we note that it is possible to translate the problem of finding a Pareto optimum into a form that can be attacked with LP techniques.

A third possible way for treating multiple-objective problems is discussed in the next section.

14.6   Goal Programming

Goal programming is generally applied to linear problems; it is an extension of LP that enables the planner to come as close as possible to satisfying various goals and constraints. It is sometimes considered to be an attempt to put into a mathematical programming context the concept of *satisficing.* This term was coined to communicate the idea that individuals do not seek optimal solutions, but rather, they seek solutions that are "good enough" or "close enough." We shall illustrate the method of goal programming with an example. Suppose we have a model with decision variables (say, production quantities) x_1 and x_2. Assume that we have the following constraint on iron consumption:

$4x_1 + 3x_2 \leq 100$ (Iron consumption)

Suppose that there is a certain amount of flexibility on the amount of heat-treatment time used but that we would like to come as close as possible to using 150 hours. This condition is expressed as

$12x_1 + 29x_2 \cong 150$ (Heat treatment)

Imagine a similar constraint on fuel consumption, say

$19x_1 + 11x_2 \cong 30$ (Fuel consumption)

The heat treatment constraint is rewritten as

$12x_1 + 29x_2 + y_1 - z_1 = 150$

where y_1 and z_1 are nonnegative variables with the property that not both are positive. If y_1 is positive, then $12x_1 + 29x_2$ will be < 150. If z_1 is positive, then $12x_1 + 29x_2$ will be > 150. In order to make $12x_1 + 29x_2$ "nearly equal" to 150, we want y_1 to be small if it is positive, or z_1 to be small if it happens to be positive. Since only one of the two variables y_1, z_1 will be positive, it suffices to make the sum $y_1 + z_1$ small.

In a similar way, the fuel consumption constraint is written as

$19x_1 + 11x_2 + y_2 - z_2 = 30$

and in this case we want $y_2 + z_2$ to be small. Our complete (illustrative) model is now written as follows:

Min $y_1 + z_1 + y_2 + z_2$

s.t.

$$
\begin{aligned}
4x_1 + \ 3x_2 \quad\quad\quad\quad\quad\quad\quad &\le 100 \\
12x_1 + 29x_2 + y_1 - z_1 \quad\quad\quad &= 150 \\
19x_1 + 11x_2 \quad\quad + y_2 - z_2 &= \ 30
\end{aligned}
$$

$x_1, x_2, y_1, z_1, y_2, z_2 \ge 0$

This is an ordinary LP problem and can now be easily solved. The optimal decision variables will satisfy the iron consumption constraint. Also, it turns out that the simplex method (for technical reasons that we shall not dwell on) will guarantee that, at an optimal corner (basic) solution, $y_1^* z_1^* = 0$ (at least one of the variables is zero) and, similarly, $y_2^* z_2^* = 0$. Consequently, the optimal decision variables x_1^*, x_2^* will "come close to" using 150 hours of heat treatment time and 30 gallons of fuel.

The above model can be generalized in numerous ways. For example, weights w_1 and w_2 can be provided for the discrepancies from the preferred goals. In this case, the objective is

Min $w_1(y_1 + z_1) + w_2(y_2 + z_2)$

subject to the same conditions as specified above. More generally, four weights could be employed, a separate one for each of the variables y_1, z_1, y_2, z_2. Another area of generalization involves forcing a goal to lie within a particular interval of specified size. For example, in the above illustration we might have chosen to write the fuel consumption condition as

$29 \le 19x_1 + 11x_2 \le 31$

instead of

$$19x_1 + 11x_2 \cong 30$$

This type of formulation is termed *goal interval programming* and is treated in a similar way.

Goal programming has been applied to problems in salary evaluation, work-force planning, accounting, and environmental problems. It has become particularly important in the public policy area, where multiple objectives are often encountered.

14.7 Examples and Solutions

Example 1

Consider model (III) of Section 14.3.2. Suppose we wish to impose the additional constraint that at least three plant locations must be used, and a route from plant 1 to the first marketing district can be used only if plant 2 is also used. How can these conditions be imposed?

Solution to Example 1

Add the following constraints to the model:

$$\sum_{i=1}^{m} y_i \geq 3 \qquad \text{(At least three plants)}$$

$$z_{11} \leq y_2 \qquad \text{(Route 1-1 is used only if plant 2 is used)}$$

Example 2

Consider the following linear constraints. Construct the corresponding incidence matrix and the associated network diagram, labeling each arc with the flow variable and each node with its supply.

$$
\begin{aligned}
x_1 + x_2 \quad\quad\quad\ + x_5 \quad\quad\quad\quad\quad &= 2 \\
-x_2 + x_3 \quad\quad\quad\quad\quad\quad\quad &= 1 \\
-x_1 \quad\quad\quad + x_4 \quad\quad\quad\quad\quad\quad &= 0 \\
-x_3 \quad - x_5 + x_6 \quad\ + x_8 &= 0 \\
-x_4 \quad\quad\quad + x_7 - x_8 &= 0 \\
-x_6 - x_7 \quad\ &= -3
\end{aligned}
$$

$$x_j \geq 0, j = 1, \ldots, 8$$

Figure 14.15

Nodes	x_1	x_2	x_3	x_4	x_5	x_6	x_7	x_8	Supplies
				Arcs					
1	1	1			1				2
2		-1	1						1
3	-1			1					0
4			-1		-1	1		1	0
5				-1			1	-1	0
6						-1	-1		-3

Figure 14.16

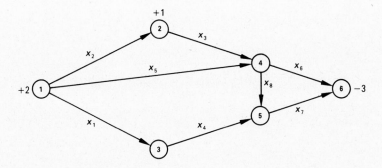

Solution to Example 2

The node-arc incidence matrix will have eight columns (equal to the number of variables) and six rows (equal to the number of constraints), as shown in Figure 14.15. We recall that each variable corresponds to an arc, with +1 denoting the node of origin and −1 the termination. The network diagram is shown in Figure 14.16.

Example 3

Write the linear constraints corresponding to the network in Figure 14.17. Use double subscript notation.

Figure 14.17

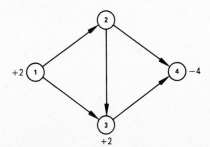

Solution to Example 3

Node 1: $x_{12} + x_{13} \qquad = \quad 2$

Node 2: $x_{24} + x_{23} - x_{12} = \quad 0$

Node 3: $x_{34} - x_{13} - x_{23} = \quad 2$

Node 4: $-x_{24} - x_{34} \qquad = -4$

Example 4

Consider the following four-period production model:

x_t = amount to be produced
   in period t
   (Decision variable)

d_t = demand in period t (Known data)

I_t = inventory at end of period t

h_t = per unit cost of holding inventory at end of period t

Assume demand in each period must be satisfied, so that

$$\left.\begin{array}{l} I_t = I_{t-1} + x_t - d_t \\ I_t \geq 0 \end{array}\right\} \quad t = 1, 2, 3, 4$$

where $I_0 = 0$. Let the cost of producing in period t be given by:

$$C_t(x_t) = \begin{cases} x_t & \text{if } x_t = 0 \\ C_t x_t + F_t & \text{if } x_t > 0 \end{cases}$$

Formulate the problem of determining a four-period production policy that satisfies demand at a minimum cost. (Hint: use 0/1 variables.)

Solution to Example 4

$$\text{Min} \quad \sum_{t=1}^{4} (C_t x_t + z_t F_t + h_t I_t)$$

s.t.

$$
\begin{array}{ll}
I_t = I_{t-1} + x_t - d_t & t = 1, 2, 3, 4 \\
x_t - z_t U \leq 0 & t = 1, 2, 3, 4 \\
x_t, I_t \geq 0 & t = 1, 2, 3, 4 \\
z_t = 0 \text{ or } 1 & t = 1, 2, 3, 4
\end{array}
$$

where $I_0 = 0$ and U is very large.

Example 5

Consider the goal programming problem

$$\text{Min} \quad \sum_{j=1}^{p} |f_j(x_1, ..., x_n) - t_j|$$

s.t.

$$\sum_{j=1}^{n} a_{ij} x_j \leq b_i \quad i = 1, ..., m$$

$$x_j \geq 0 \quad j = 1, ..., n$$

where the values t_j are known "targets" for the function values. Assume each f_j is a linear function. Formulate this problem as a linear program.

Solution to Example 5

For each j, introduce two new nonnegative variables u_j and v_j, and include a constraint

$$u_j - v_j = f_j(x_1, ..., x_n) - t$$

It was mentioned in the text that for a linear program, only one of the two variables u_j, v_j will be positive in an optimal basic solution. Hence, it is true that

$$u_j + v_j = |f_j(x_1, ..., x_n) - t_j| \quad \text{each } j$$

The complete formulation, then, is

$$\text{Min} \quad \sum_{j=1}^{p} (u_j + v_j)$$

s.t.

$$u_j - v_j \quad = f_j(x_1, ..., x_n) - t_j$$

$$\sum_{j=1}^{n} a_{ij} x_j \leq b_i \quad i = 1, ..., m$$

$$x_j, u_j, v_j \geq 0 \quad j = 1, ..., n$$

14.8 Summary of Key Concepts

There are two types of algorithms for solving IP problems. The "exact" algorithms, which are guaranteed to produce an optimal solution, are not comparable to the simplex algorithm for LP problems in terms of the size of the problems they can solve or the speed of solution. The "heuristic" algorithm is designed to efficiently produce a good, though not necessarily optimal, solution. From the viewpoint of the manager, a heuristic procedure may certainly be as acceptable as, and possibly even preferable to, a "more exact" algorithm that produces an optimal solution. The dominant considerations should be the amount of insight and guidance that the model can provide, and the cost of obtaining these. (Sections 14.1, 14.2)

There are two types of IP problems, which are quite different both in interpretation and in the way they are usually treated in practice.

1 In the first type of problem, the variables that are constrained to have integer values are physical quantities for which fractional values have no meaning. Such problems are typically treated in practice by ignoring the integrality conditions and solving the problem with continuous variables. The solution to the continuous problem is then implemented by rounding fractions to integers. In such situations it may be possible to place a bound on the potential error incurred by not solving the true integer model.

2 In the second type of problem, the variables represent logical conditions and they are constrained to the values 0/1. Such problems in practice are almost always treated with a formal IP model.
(Sections 14.1–14.3)

A very large variety of real-world problems that cannot be formulated with continuous variables can be put into IP form with 0/1 variables. (Section 14.3)

A network model is a special form of LP model that yields integer answers if the parameters in the model are integers. Special algorithms make it possible to solve extremely large network problems rapidly. (Section 14.4)

Goal programming is a mathematical programming approach to problems with multiple objectives. The objective is to minimize the weighted deviation of each objective from a stated goal. (Section 14.6)

14.9 Problems

1 Consider models (I) and (II) in Section 14.3.1.

a Suppose x^* is a solution to (I). Show that x^*, z^* must be a solution to (II), where, for each j

$$z_j^* = \begin{cases} 1 & \text{if } x_j^* > 0 \\ 0 & \text{if } x_j^* = 0 \end{cases}$$

b Suppose x^*, z^* is a solution to (II). Show that x^* must be a solution to (I).

2 Consider model (III) of Section 14.3.2.

a If there is a shipment from i to j, how do we know the route from i to j is paid for?

b How is it assured that if no routes are used from plant i, then plant i is not used?

c How do we know that if plant i is not used, then no routes from plant i will be used?

d How can you add to the model the specification that, at most, k plants and, at most, p routes can be used, where k is a known integer less than m, and p is a known integer between n and mn?

3 A method for satisfying at least k of m constraints was presented in Section 14.3.4. It included the constraints

$$\sum_{i=1}^{m} y_i \geq k$$

$$g_i(x_1, \ldots, x_n) \leq b_i y_i + (1 - y_i)U \qquad i = 1, \ldots, m$$

We know that, in general, if we replace an inequality constraint with an equality constraint, it may turn out that the optimal objective value will be impaired. Argue that the constraint

$$\sum_{i=1}^{m} y_i \geq k$$

in the above conditions can always be assumed to be active, and hence, in this situation it is harmless to replace the inequality with an equality.

4 Suppose the function $f(x_1, \ldots, x_n)$ is required to take on one of the values $v_1, \ldots, v_k$. Show how k 0/1 variables can be used to formulate this condition.

5 Consider the purchasing model discussed in Section 14.3.4. Incorporate in the model the following rule: Each supplier serves at least two districts, providing at least T units of total product to each of the two districts.

6 Consider the knapsack problem discussed in Section 14.3.5. Construct an example for which the method of ranking items according to value/weight will not lead to an optimal solution for the indivisible case.

7 In the transportation model of Section 14.4.1, assume that there are two origins and three destinations, and draw the schematic network representation.

8 Refer back to problem 19 in Chapter 4. Use a 0/1 variable to formulate the discount modification of part c.

9 Refer back to Chapter 4, problem 14, part b. Modify the problem as follows. Products A, B, and C are purely competitive, and any amounts made may be sold at respective per-pound prices of $5, $4, and $5. The first 20 pounds of products D and E produced per week can be sold at $4 each, and all made in excess of 20 can be sold at $6 each. Reformulate the model as modified, using the variables $M1$, $M2$, and $M3$, and two new 0/1 variables y and z, and new variables:

$D20$ = quantity of product D produced in excess of 20

$E20$ = quantity of product E produced in excess of 20

10 This question focuses on one particular aspect of the production process in one of the PROTRAC plants, namely the soaking of frames for units of E and F, called E-frames and F-frames, in a heat-treatment facility. In reality, the plant has four heat-treatment facilities. Two were constructed when the plant was built, and two were recently added. These latter facilities differ from the former in both capacity and effectiveness. In general, there is a difference in the heat-treatment requirements (in temperature and in hours of soaking) for E-frames and F-frames. Also, because the E-frames and F-frames differ in volume and shape, the capacity of a facility depends on which type of frame is being treated. Since requirements differ, not both E- and F-frames can be treated in the same facility at the same time. All four facilities are run off a central fuel supply system that provides only A_4 soaking hours each quarter. In the coming quarter, it has been determined that the total number of batches to be heat-treated is β, and each batch will consist of N_E E-frames and N_F F-frames (where β, N_E, and N_F are given). These frames are prepared for treatment and then simultaneously delivered in a batch to the heat-treatment plant. These batches of fixed size must always be treated immediately upon arrival, and, in particular, all the frames are treated simultaneously. For this reason, deliveries are staggered in such a way that the facilities are empty when each new batch arrives. The problem is to divide each batch among the four facilities in such a way as to minimize quarterly fuel costs. Note that this will be equivalent to minimizing the fuel cost per batch. Figure 14.18 gives data on fuel costs, capacities, and soaking times (heating hours) required for the various facility/frame combinations. (For example, the fuel cost of using facility 1 for E-frames is $700, the capacity of facility 1 if used for E-frames is 6, the

Figure 14.18

Frame	Fac 1	Fac 2	Fac 3	Fac 4
		Fuel Cost ($)		
E	700	700	1,200	1,200
F	600	600	1,000	1,000
		Capacities (frames)		
E	6	6	4	4
F	9	9	5	5
		Soaking Times (hr)		
E	13	13	10	10
F	16	16	12	12

soaking time of an E-frame in facility 1 is 13 hours, and so on.) Note that although the soaking times for E-frames are less than for F-frames, the fuel cost is more because higher temperatures are required.

a State the optimization problem that is implicit in the above discussion in the form of a mathematical program, expressing the objective function and each constraint in prose, not symbols.

b For each batch, let E_i and F_i denote the number of E-frames and F-frames, respectively, treated in facility i. Let y_i be a variable that has the value 1 if facility i is to be used for E-frames. Otherwise, the value of the variable is 0. Let z_i be similarly defined for F-frames. For each facility, write three constraints that express the capacity conditions for that facility. One such constraint should say that if y_i is zero, then E_i must also be zero. Another should make a similar statement for z_i and F_i. The third constraint should say that if facility i is used for either type of frame, then it cannot be used for the other.

c Suppose that, at most, three facilities can be used on a given batch. Write a constraint that says this.

d Write constraints that say that N_E E-frames and N_F F-frames must be heat-treated.

e Write a constraint that says the total number of soaking hours per batch does not exceed A_4/β.

f Write the total cost of treating a batch with the policy E_i, F_i, $i = 1, 2, 3, 4$.

g Write out the complete mathematical program as developed in parts b through d in the form of a cost-min model. Note the relationship between the problem as now stated in symbols and your answer to part a. How would you classify this model?

h Suppose that if facilities 1 and 2 are to be used at all, they must be prepared in advance and then relined at the end of the treatment. The combined cost of these operations is $1,000 per facility. Include this in the model.

i Suppose that no fewer than four E-frames can be soaked in facility 1. Express this constraint.

j Suppose that F-frames in facility 1 can be soaked only in multiples of three. Express the constraint.

k Suppose that because of temporary equipment alterations, facility 1 can be used only if facility 2 is used. Express this constraint.

l What is the total number of hours the soaking facilities are used for treating the batch with the plan E_i, F_i, $i = 1, 2, 3, 4$ in the model from part g? How would you determine the average hourly cost of heat treating the batch (in this same model)?

11 Discuss conditions under which a model with discrete activities might be treated as though the variables were continuous for the sake of approximation, with final policies obtained by rounding where integer values are required.

12 Consider the following constraints:

$$
\begin{aligned}
x_1 + x_2 + x_3 \quad\quad\quad\quad &= 1 \\
-x_1 \quad\quad\quad + x_4 \quad\quad &= 0 \\
-x_2 \quad - x_4 + x_5 &= 0 \\
-x_3 \quad\quad - x_5 &= -1
\end{aligned}
$$

Construct the corresponding incidence matrix and network diagram.

13 Write the linear constraints corresponding to the network in Figure 14.19. Use double subscript notation.

Figure 14.19

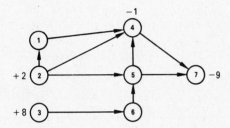

Part

Decisions under Uncertainty

2

15 Probability and Expected Utility: A Basic Model for Decisions under Uncertainty

This chapter introduces and illustrates the basic elements of any decision under uncertainty: probability and return. Sample spaces are introduced, and probabilities are treated as subjective assessments. Distinctions are made between the mathematical theory, the interpretation of probability in applications, and the actual numerical assessment. Utility is introduced, and monetary return is treated as a special case. The basic model of maximizing expected utility is presented. The role of risk and its incorporation in the utility structure are also discussed.

15.1 Introduction

Uncertainty about events in the future is a phenomenon that creates many management decision problems. Consider how the activities of the financial vice-president of an insurance company would change if she were to know exactly what changes would occur in the bond market.

Imagine the relief of the head buyer at Bloomingdale's if he were to know exactly how many full-length mink coats would be purchased in his store this year. This relief would be shared in part by the manufacturers of mink coats and even the operators of mink farms. On a broader scope, it is hard to believe that France would have built the Maginot Line or that the allied invasion of Normandy would have been so successful if the rulers of France and Germany had had a better vision of what the future would hold.

It seems clear that the effects of uncertainty are ubiquitous. It is also clear that those who deal effectively with uncertainty, through either skill or luck, are often handsomely rewarded for their accomplishments. In the first book of the Old Testament, Joseph is promoted from slave to assistant Pharaoh of Egypt by accurately forecasting seven years of feast and seven years of famine.[1]

Perhaps because of the omnipresence of uncertainty and the potential rewards for successfully dealing with it, there is a mind-boggling array of quantitative techniques to aid the manager in his efforts to cope with uncertainty. In management science, the models for dealing with decisions under uncertainty

---

1 As well as being an accurate forecaster, by virtue of his skill in successfully interpreting Pharaoh's dreams, Joseph has been called the first psychoanalyst. Less well known is the fact that Joseph was also the first management scientist. In anticipation of the famine, he advised Pharaoh to build storage facilities in order to hold inventories of grain. When it was all over and the famine had been survived, Joseph was asked how he had come to acquire such wisdom and knowledge. "Lean-year programming," was his reply.

are called *stochastic,* which means *probabilistic,* as opposed to the *deterministic* models discussed in the previous chapters of the text. Actually, a number of specific areas in management science are devoted to stochastic models. For example, there is a well-developed body of knowledge and an extensive literature in each of the three problem areas cited below.

Queuing Theory *Queuing theory* is the mathematical study of *queues,* or waiting lines. Conceptually, it is useful in describing the behavior of any system in which a number of items (people, autos, records of stock sales) arrive at a system for service. The analysis is complicated by the fact that the number of items that arrive in an interval of time and the service time per item are both uncertain. The list of examples is endless: airports, emergency rooms, toll bridges, defense systems. In some circumstances, it is possible to create a mathematical model that adequately describes the behavior of an interesting "queuing system" and to solve this model either to determine an optimal system design or an optimal operating policy. Unfortunately, in many if not most queuing systems, the model is extremely complicated and defies solution. In such cases, simulation can be used as a way of obtaining useful information about the system, and indeed simulation is probably the most commonly used approach for dealing with actual queuing problems. Simulation is discussed in some detail in Chapters 18 and 19, and queuing is discussed in Chapter 20.

Inventory Models The question of how much inventory a manufacturer or a retailer should hold in the face of uncertain demand has received a considerable amount of attention from scholars in management science, and inventory models have become important in applications. It turns out that a few basic models provide the rationale for most of the inventory control systems developed by individual firms or developed and sold by computer companies.

Reliability Theory *Reliability theory* considers the behavior of systems composed of more than one component. As observed by Ben Franklin, the failure of a simple component can mean the failure of an entire system and can thus imply dire consequences.[2] Reliability studies use information about the reliability of individual components and the relationship between these components to make inferences about the reliability of the overall system. Although it is possible to consider any type of system, including those cases where a component might be an individual or a department, most reliability studies deal with electronic or mechanical systems and are considered to be a part of engineering design.

Besides the models designed for the specific problem areas just presented, there are several more general mathematical techniques used to solve problems involving uncertainty. Several such techniques are dynamic programming, Markovian decision models, decision analysis, and simulation. Depending on the circumstances, any of these general techniques might be used to attack a particular problem.

---

2 "For want of a nail, the shoe is lost . . .," *Poor Richard's Almanac,* 1758. Originally due to George Herbert (1593–1632, English author), *Jacula Prudentum,* published 1640.

This abundance of models and techniques and the accompanying volumes of mathematical detail can certainly cause confusion about where to turn for a solution to one's problem. Thus, it is perhaps not surprising that a manager may choose to solve his problems involving uncertainty by substituting his best guess for the entity about which he is uncertain. Although this may be the appropriate action in some cases, it should not be adopted out of exasperation or confusion. There is no need to surrender. Just as in the case of constrained optimization, there are several basic concepts that the manager can use to guide his thinking. A good understanding of these concepts should change the way he thinks about certain problems and should enable him to understand the essence of any mathematical model involving uncertainty.

15.2 The Elements of a Decision Problem

In this book, a decision problem is considered to be a situation in which a manager must select one from a number of alternative actions (decisions). In the first part of this text, we considered problems where the set of allowable actions was defined by a collection of constraints. There was, however, no problem in comparing two allowable alternatives. A decision was always interpreted as an *n*-tuple of numbers, and the value of the objective function measured how attractive any decision would be. In other words, we knew what the return would be from any decision. We "simply" had to find an allowable decision that yielded the largest (smallest) value for the objective function.

Conceptually, a decision under uncertainty is more difficult because we are uncertain as to what return we will get from any particular decision. If the manager at Bloomingdale's orders 500 full-length mink coats to sell next season at $4,000 each, his return will depend on how many people will buy coats at that price. It will be known only after the fact.

In this setting, there are two basic elements that determine the attractiveness of a decision.

The two basic elements in making decisions under uncertainty are the likelihood associated with each possible outcome and the return associated with each possible outcome.

To illustrate this concept, consider the problem of a Las Vegas tourist deciding which of two slot machines to play. It costs $1 to play either slot machine. She will either win or not, and the size of the payoff from each slot machine is specified. Let us suppose her problem is illustrated in Figure 15.1. This

Figure 15.1 *Slot machine payoffs, case 1*

	Machine *A*	Machine *B*
Likelihood of Winning	Smaller	Larger
Payoff	Smaller	Larger

Figure 15.2   *Slot machine payoffs, case 2*

	Machine A	Machine B
Likelihood of Winning	Equal	Equal
Payoff	Smaller	Larger

Figure 15.3   *Slot machine payoffs, case 3*

	Machine A	Machine B
Likelihood of Winning	Smaller	Larger
Payoff	Equal	Equal

Figure 15.4   *Slot machine payoffs, case 4*

	Machine A	Machine B
Likelihood of Winning	Smaller	Larger
Payoff	Larger	Smaller

problem is trivial. Since the likelihood of winning and the payoff are both larger with slot machine B, she would of course decide to play slot machine B. Cases 2 and 3, as shown in Figures 15.2 and 15.3, are equally clear. In both these cases, the tourist would choose to play slot machine B. These cases illustrate the notions that all other things being equal, she would prefer a larger payoff, and all other things being equal she would prefer a larger likelihood of winning, respectively. As shown in Figure 15.4, however, case 4 is not so clear. With slot machine B she is more apt to win than she is with slot machine A, but the payoff will be smaller. Questions that naturally come to mind are:

1   How does one measure and quantify the likelihood of winning?
2   If there is a measure of the likelihood of winning, how does one combine that information with the magnitude of the payoffs in order to get a measure of the overall attractiveness of each alternative?

These questions are considered in the next two sections of this chapter.

15.3   Quantifying the Likelihood of an Uncertain Event

The word *likelihood*, as opposed to *probability*, has been used in our discussion up to this point in order to introduce the idea of decision making under uncertainty easily and informally, without beginning with a more careful technical discussion of probability. Probability theory is a branch of formal mathematics and, as such, many of the concepts and results have been developed within an abstract and purely formal framework. It is like Euclidean plane geometry in that sense. Although the topic was originally motivated by applied questions, the formal basis of geometry (points and lines) does not require any real-world analogue. The theorems and proofs exist within a system of axioms. In spite of this abstraction, and in spite of the fact that no portion of the earth is a perfect plane, it is obvious that plane geometry is extremely useful in certain real-world endeavors. The same statement can be made about probability. Our discussion of probability theory will be brief and introductory but detailed enough to serve our purpose in the decision-making context.

Working with the subject of probability, it is important to distinguish among three concepts:
1 *The mathematical probability framework*
2 *The interpretation of probability in applications*
3 *The actual numerical assessment of probabilities*

15.3.1   *The Mathematical Probability Framework*

A basic component of the mathematical theory of probability is the abstract notion of a *sample space S,* which consists of a set of objects that we shall call *elementary events.* In real-world applications, these events will be uncertain phenomena, and we will speak of "the probability of such and such an event." In the case of the Las Vegas tourist in the discussion of the previous section, there were two sample spaces, one associated with machine A, the other with machine B. In each case, the elementary events were the same—namely, win or lose. But the probabilities of these events depended on which space was being considered. As other applications of the concept of sample spaces, consider the following.

EXAMPLE 1

Let the elementary events be the possible outcomes of the roll of a six-sided die, where "outcome" denotes the upturned face when the die stops rolling. If we distinguish the faces in the obvious way, then the sample space S can be denoted as $S = \{1, 2, 3, 4, 5, 6\}$. Thus, we may speak of "the probability of the face 3," which means "the probability that the upturned face has three dots," and so on.

EXAMPLE 2

Let the elementary events be the possible outcomes of a major operation to remove a tumor from the brain of John Jones, where outcome is defined as "survives the operation" or "does not." Here, the sample space $S = \{Y, N\}$, where Y denotes "survives" and N denotes "does not." In this context, we may speak of "the probability that Jones will survive the operation," and so on.

EXAMPLE 3

Let the sample space S consist of two elementary events:

1 Shakespeare wrote the King James Version of the Bible.
2 He did not.

In the context of this sample space, we speak of "the probability that Shakespeare wrote the King James Version of the Bible," and so on.

As examples of other sample spaces, we have

1 The possible prices of the nearest soybeans futures contract on the Chicago Board of Trade at noon on the next day of trading
2 The number of full-length mink coats sold next season at Bloomingdale's after adopting a particular merchandising plan
3 The climatic conditions over Yankee Stadium next Saturday at noon, in terms of whether or not it will be raining

In some discussions, a sample space is considered to be the collection of possible outcomes of a well-defined experiment, but this need not be the case. For instance, with Example 1 above we could associate the experiment, "roll the die and then observe the number of dots on the upturned face." With Example 2 we can associate the experiment, "perform surgery on Jones and observe whether or not he survives." The outcomes of an experiment are regarded as *uncertain,* and "the probability of such and such an outcome" is a prior concept, that is, one that applies before the actual outcome of the experiment is known. In some cases, it may be difficult to integrate the concept of an underlying experiment with the sample space. As an illustration, it is not so easy to associate an underlying experiment with Example 3. One possible experiment might be, "perform a study to determine whether or not Shakespeare wrote the King James Version of the Bible." If the study is such that it is completely definitive, so that the only outcomes are the two possibilities "he did write it" or "he did not write it," then "the probability that Shakespeare wrote the King James Version of the Bible" would, in fact, coincide with the probability of one of the outcomes of the specified experiment. But suppose one of the possible outcomes of the experiment is, "it is extremely likely that Shakespeare wrote the King James Version of the Bible." How does the probability of this "extremely likely" statement relate to the probability that he actually wrote it? You can see that in this case the experiment interpretation leads to logical difficulty. One might then suggest making the study definitive, so that there are only two outcomes, but it may not be possible, in reality, to have a definitive study—and the discussion can go on and on. Because of difficulties such as this, we make no requirement that an experiment, even conceptual, underlie the sample space of interest.

In cases where the experiment interpretation is in fact applicable, a single performance of an experiment is called a *trial.* When an experiment can be performed more than once, one may employ the term *successive trials.* In the above illustrations, it is clear that we could speak of successive trials (successive rolls of the die) in Example 1, but this concept would have doubtful meaning for the patient in Example 2.

In order to present a precise mathematical definition of probability, the concept of sample space must be extended as follows. We wish to consider *all* subsets of S. Any such subset is referred to as an *event,* and together these subsets comprise what is called the *event space* [3], which we shall denote as $\tilde{S}$. In particular, the elementary events (being subsets of size 1) are themselves members of $\tilde{S}$.[4] Also, S itself is a member of $\tilde{S}$, as is the null set $\emptyset$ (the set with no elements). We now wish to define "the probability of event such and such." In formal terms, probability will be a function that assigns a number to every event in the event space $\tilde{S}$ and that satisfies several properties that we shall now specify.

A minimal amount of set theory will be required. Given two events, A and B, recall that each is by definition a subset of elementary events. The event containing all elementary events in *either* of the subsets A *or* B (or both) is called the *union* of A and B. This new event is denoted $A \cup B$. The event containing all elementary events in *both A and B* is called the *intersection* of A and B, and this new event is denoted $A \cap B$. If A and B have no elementary events in common, then the set $A \cap B$ is empty (that is, $A \cap B = \emptyset$), and we say that A and B are *mutually exclusive events.* It is now possible to give the formal mathematical definition of probability.

A probability function P is any function that assigns to each event A in the event space a real number, denoted P(A), and called the probability of that event, and that satisfies three axioms:

1 *For any event A, $P(A) \geq 0$.*
2 *$P(S) = 1$.*
3 *If A and B are mutually exclusive events then $P(A \cup B) = P(A) + P(B)$.*

These axioms provide the foundation of probability theory, and the logical consequences of these axioms comprise the subject matter of that theory. Some of the simple consequences of the axioms include

a $P(\emptyset) = 0$.
b $0 \leq P(A) \leq 1$ for every event A.
c If A is a subset of B then $P(A) \leq P(B)$.
d In general, $P(A \cup B) = P(A) + P(B) - P(A \cap B)$.
e Suppose $e_1, e_2, \ldots, e_k$ denotes the collection of elementary events that comprise event A; that is, $A = \{e_1, \ldots, e_k\} = \{e_1\} \cup \{e_2\} \ldots \cup \{e_k\}$. Then, since elementary events

---

3 More precisely, our definition applies only to a finite sample space S. In the more general nonfinite setting, an event space $\tilde{S}$ consists of any collection of subsets of S that contains $\emptyset$ (the empty set), and the set S itself, and that contains the complement of each subset included, and that contains all unions of the subsets included.

4 Here we consider that an elementary event e and the singleton set $\{e\}$ are one and the same.

are mutually exclusive, it follows from axiom 3 above that

$$P(A) = \sum_{i=1}^{k} P(e_i)$$

This means that the probability of any event can be obtained from a knowledge of only the probabilities of the elementary events.

As a specific illustration of the machinery thus far introduced, let us consider Example 1 above, the roll of a die. There are many assignments of probabilities to the associated sample space that satisfy the three axioms. How then should one make such an assignment? We shall return to this problem in the next section. For now, in conformance with our intuition about symmetry, and in the absence of other information about the die at hand, let us assign a probability of $\frac{1}{6}$ to each elementary event in the sample space. In accordance with item e above, the probability of any other event must be the sum of the probabilities of all elementary events that comprise that event. It is easy to verify that this will create a legitimate probability function, since axioms 1, 2, and 3 are satisfied. Now note that the event space associated with this example is the set of all subsets of $\{1, 2, 3, 4, 5, 6\}$. Thus, there are 64 possible events. We shall say that any event A occurs if the outcome of the roll is an element of A. Suppose the event A is "an even number turns up." Thus, $A = \{2, 4, 6\}$, and the event A "will occur" if a face with 2, 4, or 6 dots appears. It follows that

$$P(A) = \tfrac{1}{6} + \tfrac{1}{6} + \tfrac{1}{6} = \tfrac{3}{6}$$

We may also consider events $B = \{2, 3\}$, $C = \{2, 4, 6\}$, $D = B \cap C = \{2\}$, and $E = B \cup C = \{2, 3, 4, 6\}$. It follows that

$$P(B) = \tfrac{2}{6}$$
$$P(C) = \tfrac{3}{6}$$
$$P(D) = \tfrac{1}{6}$$
$$P(E) = \tfrac{4}{6}$$

Numerous other examples could be presented, but our goal has been merely to explain and illustrate the fact that probability has a rather simple, but very formal, mathematical definition. For our purposes, it will be more important to interpret rather than elaborate upon this formal definition.

As a concluding point, it can be formally demonstrated that the mathematical axioms must be satisfied in order to have a consistent or rational assignment of probabilities. Thus, the axioms provide not only a foundation for the mathematical development but a guide for the real applications as well. Accordingly, we shall always insist that a probability function satisfy the stated axioms.

15.3.2   Interpretation and Numerical Assessment of Probability

Although the formal mathematical definition of probability is straightforward, it is quite general, and we have already observed in the previous section that this formal definition does not completely specify the probability function for any particular event space of interest. It serves only as a guide, providing conditions that must not be violated. Consider the decision maker who is confronted by a number of uncertain events. He has carefully defined a sample space, whose subsets determine the associated event space, and now he wants to assess the probabilities of the events. But there will be numerous different ways to assign probabilities to events without violating the axioms. How, then, should he define the function P (that is, assign the probability values) in actual practice? What criterion and method should be used? In other words, we obviously need to distinguish between the formal mathematical definition of probability and the interpretation and numerical assessment of probabilities in applications. These latter topics involve considerable subtlety.

Consider an actual event of interest, such as "Jones will survive his brain surgery." Suppose the surgeon says, "The probability of Jones surviving is .6," (or he may say it is "about .6"). Intuitively, everyone has a loose idea about the meaning of the surgeon's assertion, though it may not be easy to express in a clear and noncircular fashion. At this point, you should spend some time analyzing your intuitive interpretation of the surgeon's meaning. How would you explain this meaning to a person who speaks only a language that is void of the words *probability, likelihood,* or *chance?*

In applications of probability theory to real decision-making problems, the event space will correspond to a collection of actual events of interest, and we shall want to choose the mathematical probability function in such a way as to reflect as closely as possible our intuitive feelings about the probabilities of occurrence of these various interesting events. In order to understand the mechanics of such a choice, it will be helpful to be as explicit as possible about the basis for our intuitive feelings about probability.

Let us then directly face the question of the surgeon's meaning when he says that the probability is .6 that Jones will survive. First of all, this statement reflects a *subjective expectation* or *estimate* about the outcome of the surgery. It means that if similar operations were performed on similar patients with similar tumors, then the surgeon's best estimate is that 6 out of 10 of the patients would survive. This assessment may be based on the surgeon's experience with past outcomes of similar surgery on people in Jones' condition. It may be based on operations he has performed or observed or read about. It may be based on theoretic knowledge and on the surgeon's feeling about his own ability. It is a subjective assessment based on the totality of the surgeon's experience up to this point in time.

One difficulty with probability assessments is that it is too easy to pick a number out of the air without adequate thought. How does Jones know whether he can trust the surgeon? Does the surgeon really believe in his own estimate? This question can be formally answered by setting up a particular type of elementary but ingenious choice situation. The surgeon must imagine that he has a choice between two lottery tickets. The first ticket entitles him to a very attractive prize if Jones survives. The second ticket entitles him to draw one (and only one) ball from an urn that contains 100 balls, 60 of them white and 40 of them red (or 10 balls, 6 of them white and 4 of them red). If his draw were to produce a white ball, then he would win the same prize. He must choose one and only one of the two tickets. If he is *indifferent* to the choice, then he has "correctly" or "consistently" identified his "intuitive feelings." For us, this means that he has correctly assessed the probability of Jones surviving.

This notion of *indifference,* exploited in the above lottery, is a primitive concept that provides a conceptual means for defining "equally probable" events and for assigning *numerical probabilities* to events of interest. The surgeon feels that if he were to draw from the urn *several times* (that is, perform the same experiment of drawing a single ball from the urn with 60 white balls and 40 red balls), then his *best estimate* of the outcomes is that a white ball would be obtained 60 percent of the time. If several similar operations were to be performed on patients like Jones, his *best estimate* is that 60 percent of the patients would survive. He has thus *conceptually* equated two repetitive concepts, and this example explains the basis for the meaning we intuitively assign to probability statements.

In this context, it is important to note that the word *several* does not imply a large number. The number of trials can be any number (large or small) for which our assertion makes sense. (For example, eight trials does not make sense because $(.6)(8) = 4.8$, and in our example it is not sensible to consider fractions of patients or balls.) If the surgeon assigns the probability .6 to the event Jones survives, then his *best estimate* is that 3 out of 5, or 6 out of 10, or 60 out of 100 patients who are "like" Jones would survive a similar operation. The surgeon is not saying that out of 5 operations *exactly* 3 patients will survive, or that *exactly* 600 white balls would result from 1,000 draws from the urn. He is merely saying that this is his best prior estimate of what will occur, and, at his point of indifference (60 percent white balls), the properties of the two processes are identical. If n balls are drawn, then his *best estimate* is that $.6n$ will turn out white. The number n need not be large. It is any number for which $.6n$ is an integer. If n operations are performed, then his *best estimate* is that $.6n$ survivors will be counted. In his future experiences, he may have occasion to be more or less surprised by the extent of observed departures from his estimate, taking "chance" into account, and he may or may not choose to revise his estimates as he obtains new information.

It should be mentioned that the notion of how to interpret and assess probability in applications has been historically controversial, even to a heated extent, and no doubt there are some probabilists and statisticians who would take exception with aspects of our approach. Books on probability and decision theory dwell at length on the issues in a more or less satisfactory way. To go much further into the topic would be too far afield for our purposes. However, the concept of *relative frequency* should be at least briefly mentioned.

In its usual meaning, the concept of *relative frequency* refers to sample spaces with an underlying experiment that can be repetitively performed at will, such as rolling a die, flipping a coin, drawing balls from an urn, and so on. Suppose such an experiment is performed n times. After each trial, we can observe whether or not some event of interest, say A, has occurred. After the n trials, let $k(n)$ be the total number of times A has occurred. Then $k(n)/n$ is called the relative frequency of the occurrence of A in the n trials. The performing of such an experiment may be used as a *guide* in the numerical assessment for the value $P(A)$. Thus, in relevant circumstances, relative frequency can be helpful in assessing a probability. But even a single trial of an experiment can be used as a guide. In fact, all information, experimental or otherwise, that the assessor considers pertinent should be so used, and there are formal methods in probability theory for updating prior assessments with new information. Some of these methods will be discussed in Chapter 16.

A number of writers, however, would reject the notion that relative frequency can serve only as a guide to assessing probabilities. They would actually base the concept of probability and the means for assessing probabilities on the notion of relative frequency, and that is where controversy arises. Such writers would assert that the intuitive concept of probability and the numerical value $P(A)$, should be the limiting value of $k(n)/n$ as the number of trials increases indefinitely. One serious difficulty with such an assertion is that the existence of the postulated value as an ordinary mathematical limit cannot be demonstrated.[5] Another difficulty is the dependence of this definition of probability on the performance of *numerous* trials of an experiment. Many management problems involve one-time decisions. In such a case, the notion of repetitive trials of an experiment does not seem conceptually meaningful. We prefer the position that although relative frequency may provide a useful *guide,* it seems overly restrictive to employ this notion exclusively to interpret or obtain a *specific* numerical value for the probability of an event.

Our approach might be considered a "relaxation" of the relative frequency attitude. Consider, for example, the statement, "The probability that Shakespeare wrote the King James Version of the Bible is .1." Such a statement has no clear meaning in an experimental or a relative frequency context. What it means to us is that under similar cases of doubtful authorship, with similar data, and taking all other experience into account, the assessor's best estimate is that one-tenth of the doubtful authors would actually turn out to be true authors. In this case, as in the case of all probability assessments, the veracity of the individual's assessment can be validated by employing the lottery device.

In summary, then:

In applications, probability is interpreted as a subjective assessment of the frequency with which a sufficiently similar event would occur under sufficiently similar circumstances.

There is no suggestion of "long-run" frequency in this interpretation. The actual numerical assessment can be obtained by using the lottery device. This assessment will be based on general experience and on specific data about past outcomes on what the assessor considers to be similar situations.

In concluding this section, it is to be noted that the lottery device does not have to be used in assessing probabilities. Probabilities can be assigned in any way that satisfies the three axioms. However, if the probabilities are deemed to be quite important, then considerable care should enter into the

---

5 This limit can be given a formal meaning, but not without using the concept of probability, and hence the logic becomes circular.

assessment. In such a circumstance, the decision maker may well resort to the lottery device as a useful mechanism to explore with honesty his own judgments and feelings. The use of such a device may not be simple. The surgeon would perhaps have little difficulty with his assessment when the urn contains, say, 10 rather than 100 balls. In such a case, he may feel quite comfortable with 6 white balls at his point of indifference. This means that his best judgment is more adequately reflected by .6 than by .5 or .7. But suppose the number of balls is 1,000. He may well have difficulty in deciding whether he is indifferent at the point of 600 white balls, as opposed to 599 or 601. There may well be an interval of indeterminacy in his ability to discriminate his own feelings between .599, .600, .601. At some level of precision, there will *certainly* be such an interval of *indeterminacy*—if not with an urn of 1,000 balls, then perhaps with one containing 1 million balls, in which case the assessor would have to discriminate between .599999, .600000, and .600001. Thus, the lottery experiment only provides a tool for determining one's best numerical estimate of the likelihood of an event. It is a useful tool, but it is limited by the assessor's own limitations. However, the existence of an interval of indeterminacy does not present a serious problem in using assessed probabilities for making decisions under uncertainty. Fortunately, our basic model will allow for different estimates or assessments for the probability of an event. There is no requirement to find the *exactly correct* value for a probability. In our decision model, the probabilities are parameters, just as a right-hand side for a particular constraint is a parameter in a mathematical programming model. In order to use the model, the decision maker must assign a probability (a specific number) to each event. This number will remain fixed while he solves the model to find the best or optimal decision. (In the next section, a precise meaning will be given for the term *optimal decision* in an uncertain environment.) After his model has been solved, the decision maker may wish to perform a sensitivity analysis to see how sensitive the solution is to the particular choice of probabilities that he used in the model. He may wish to solve the model again, using different probabilities. Suppose it turns out that small differences in assessed probabilities lead to significantly different optimal policies and payoffs. Suppose it is beyond the assessor's ability to discriminate this small difference with the use of the urn experiment. Then the only recourse of the experimenter is to gather more information with which to improve his assessments. However, he may well want to look at the sensitivity, even when he feels quite comfortable with his own assessments. Even in such a case, the implications of his assessments, in terms of model output, may not be consistent with his experience or expectations, to such an extent that he may wish to revise either these assessments or the model. In summary, then, a probability plays the same role as a parameter in a constrained optimization model.

15.4　Expected Return—A Criterion for Evaluating Alternatives

We are now in a good position to present our basic model for evaluating decisions under uncertainty. As an illustration, let us assume that the Las Vegas tourist has observed slot machines A and B for a complete day and has what she feels are good data on the relative frequency of winning on each machine. In terms of the formal framework presented in the previous section, a sample space is associated with each decision. The decision to play machine A produces the sample space {win, lose}. The sample space associated with machine B has the same elementary events, but the probabilities differ from one space to the other. Let $P_A(W)$ and $P_B(W)$ be her assessed probability of winning on slot machines A and B respectively. Her assessment is that $P_A(W) = \frac{1}{20} = .05$ and $P_B(W) = \frac{1}{10} = .1$. She also knows that slot machine A pays \$15 when she wins, and slot machine B pays \$8. In either case, the return is zero if she loses. Thus, to each elementary event in each sample space we have assigned a return as well as a probability. With the given assignments, neither machine obviously dominates the other. We are in the situation described in case 4 in Section 15.2, with probabilities and returns assigned, as shown in Figure 15.5. What she needs now is a criterion that will enable her to choose between these alternatives. That is, should she play A or B?

The criterion that is used is called the *expected return*. To calculate the expected return of a given alternative (decision):

1 For *each possible elementary event* in the sample space associated with that alternative, compute the product

Probability of the elementary event × return associated with the elementary event

2 Add all such products (one for each event). The result is called the *expected return* of the given alternative.

When using the terms *return* or *expected return*, it is implicitly assumed that we are dealing with *net returns*, and we shall frequently use these terms interchangeably.

Let us now apply these ideas to the above example, where there are two alternatives, slot machine A and slot machine B. Associated with the first alternative are two possible elementary events, winning and losing. Recalling that a \$1 fee is required to play, the expected net return for this alternative (slot machine A) is calculated according to the formula

Expected return = (probability of winning) × (net return if you win)
+ (probability of losing) × (net return if you lose)

Thus, we have

Figure 15.5 *Numerical probabilities and returns, case 4*

	Machine *A*	Machine *B*
Probability of Winning	.05	.1
Return	\$15	\$8

$$ER_A = P_A(W)(14) + [1 - P_A(W)](-1)$$
$$= .05(14) - .95 = -\$.25$$

Similarly, the expected return for slot machine B is

$$ER_B = .10(7) - .9(1) = -\$.20$$

Thus, if the Las Vegas tourist accepts the expected return criterion, she should play slot machine B.

A careful reader may wonder if this analysis is correct, since it seems to gloss over the fact that the expected returns are negative. The answer depends on the alternatives the Las Vegas gambler is going to consider. If she has already decided to play one machine or the other, the analysis is correct as it stands. She should play the machine with the smallest expected loss. If, however, the gambler is considering the alternative of not playing either machine, another analysis is called for. In this case, we must compare ER_A and ER_B with the expected net return associated with not playing, which is clearly zero. In this case then, the expected return criterion indicates that the correct decision is to abstain.

At this point, it has been stated that

The appropriate criterion for making a decision under uncertainty is to choose the decision that maximizes the expected net return. This statement defines an optimal decision in an uncertain environment.

We shall not offer a formal proof that maximization of expected return is indeed the correct procedure. Such a proof would be based on axioms such as the following:

---

1 *Comparability:* An individual can specify what is called a *complete preference ordering* over the sample space. This means that for any two events, say e_1 and e_2, he can say that he prefers e_1 to e_2, or that he prefers e_2 to e_1, or that he is indifferent.

2 *Transitivity:* The above ordering of outcomes must be completely transitive. This means that if the individual prefers e_1 to e_2 and e_2 to e_3, then he must prefer e_1 to e_3, and so on.

By using a set of reasonable axioms such as the above, it can be formally proved that the expected return is the appropriate criterion to use. A demonstration of this fact would lead us too far from our objectives. We therefore ask the reader to accept the appropriateness of the expected return criterion on faith.

We have used the Las Vegas tourist to illustrate the procedure for making a decision under uncertainty. This procedure can be stated in the following general (and more abstract) terms. Consider a decision problem with m possible decisions $d_1, d_2, ..., d_m$. With each decision is associated a sample space where, by assigning probabilities of zero as required, we may assume that each sample space contains the same elementary events $e_1, e_2, ..., e_n$. Consider the sample space associated with the decision d_j. We shall let $P_j(e_i)$ denote the probability of elementary event e_i and $R_j(e_i)$ denote the net return if event e_i occurs. Finally, let ER_j denote the expected net return associated with decision d_j. That is,

$$ER_j = \sum_{i=1}^{n} P_j(e_i)R_j(e_i)$$

Then d_k is said to be an optimal decision if

$$ER_k \geq ER_j \quad \text{for} \quad j = 1, ..., m$$

That is,

$$\sum_{i=1}^{n} P_k(e_i)R_k(e_i) \geq \sum_{i=1}^{n} P_j(e_i)R_j(e_i) \quad \text{for} \quad j = 1, ..., m$$

We therefore see that in order to find an optimal decision one must find a d_j for which the associated expected return

$$\sum_{i=1}^{n} P_j(e_i)R_j(e_i)$$

is a maximum.

In a general decision model, the expected net return associated with decision d_j is denoted ER_j and is defined by the summation

$$\sum_{i=1}^{n} P_j(e_i)R_j(e_i)$$

Although the notation and terminology associated with making a decision under uncertainty may be new, the concept of using expected return as a criterion in making decisions under uncertainty is extremely natural to anyone who has participated in gambling games. For example, suppose a friend pulls a 50¢ piece out of his pocket. He is about to flip this coin, and he offers to play the following game. You give him 20¢ and you call either heads or tails while his coin is in the air. If your prediction is correct, then you get the 50¢. If not, you get nothing. Will you play the game or not? Most people would quickly answer yes. Let us use the expected return criterion to see why.

The decisions are

d_1: Play and call heads

d_2: Play and call tails

d_3: Don't play

The sample space associated with each decision is {heads, tails}. Letting e_1 denote the elementary event heads, and e_2 tails, we find that the relevant probabilities[6] are

---

6 Since in this case the probabilities do not depend on the decisions, each $P_j(e_i)$ can be written more simply as $P(e_i)$.

$$P_1(e_1) = P_2(e_1) = P_3(e_1) = \tfrac{1}{2} = P(e_1)$$
$$P_1(e_2) = P_2(e_2) = P_3(e_2) = \tfrac{1}{2} = P(e_2)$$

If you don't play, your net return is zero, no matter how the coin lands. Therefore

$$R_3(e_1) = R_3(e_2) = 0$$

If you do play and call the coin correctly, you win 50¢ but you pay 20¢ to play. This yields a net return of 30¢. Therefore

$$R_1(e_1) = R_2(e_2) = 30$$

If you play and call the coin incorrectly, you merely lose 20¢. Therefore

$$R_2(e_1) = R_1(e_2) = -20$$

It follows that

$$ER_1 = P(e_1)R_1(e_1) + P(e_2)R_1(e_2) = \tfrac{1}{2}(30) + \tfrac{1}{2}(-20) = 5$$
$$ER_2 = P(e_1)R_2(e_1) + P(e_2)R_2(e_2) = \tfrac{1}{2}(-20) + \tfrac{1}{2}(30) = 5$$
$$ER_3 = P(e_1)R_3(e_1) + P(e_2)R_3(e_2) = 0$$

The above analysis shows that either d_1 or d_2 is an optimal decision, since either one produces a maximum value for the expected return.

At this point, a word of caution is appropriate. Notice that the expression for computing the expected return requires knowledge of the probability and the return associated with each elementary event. Often, however, returns may be originally specified in terms of events that are not necessarily elementary events. For example, consider a gambling game in which a card is drawn at random from a standard bridge deck (four suits, 13 cards per suit). The house pays $52 if a heart or an ace is drawn and $104 if the ace of hearts is drawn. What is the expected return to a player of this game?

One might be tempted to use the following *incorrect* approach to calculate the expected return. There are two events that yield a positive return. One is (heart or ace) and the other is (heart and ace). All other events yield a zero return. Hence, the expected return can be computed as

Expected return $= P$(heart or ace)$\$52 + P$(heart and ace)$\$104$

$$= \tfrac{16}{52}(52) + \tfrac{1}{52}(104) = \$18$$

This analysis is incorrect because the elementary event "the ace of hearts" is counted twice. A correct analysis can be obtained by more carefully identifying the return and the probability associated with each elementary event and using the usual formula. For this problem, the data on returns are summarized in Figure 15.6. All entries not explicitly shown are zero. The probability of each elementary event is $\tfrac{1}{52}$. Thus the correct answer is given as

Expected return $= \tfrac{15}{52}(52) + \tfrac{1}{52}(104) + \tfrac{36}{52}(0) = \$17$

In order to develop more familiarity with the basic decision model, we now present the following simplified but illustrative problem faced by PROTRAC.

Figure 15.6 *Data on returns for playing-card game*

Card Value	2	3	4	5	6	7	8	9	10	J	Q	K	A
Clubs													52
Diamonds													52
Hearts	52	52	52	52	52	52	52	52	52	52	52	52	104
Spades													52

A contractor is bidding on a job related to the Alaskan pipeline. If he gets the contract, he will need new heavy earth-moving equipment. Unfortunately, he doesn't know exactly how much equipment he will need until certain tests are made. These tests will not be completed until after the equipment must be shipped to Alaska. He has promised to buy as many E-9s from PROTRAC as he needs if they are immediately available on-site in Anchorage. If E-9s are not available, he will purchase the additional equipment from PROTRAC's competitor, EUCAR, who has a warehouse in Anchorage. PROTRAC estimates a net return of $5,000 on each E-9 sold and a net loss of $1,000 on each E-9 sent to Anchorage and not sold.

To use the model in making this decision, let

e_i = elementary event that the contractor wants i E-9s, $i = 0, ..., 4$

d_j = decision to send j E-9s, $j = 0, ..., 4$

$P(e_i)$ = probability that the contractor will buy exactly i E-9s[7]

$R_j(e_i)$ = net return if the contractor wants i E-9s and j have been sent

PROTRAC's consulting engineers estimate the following values for $P(e_i)$: $P(e_0) = \frac{10}{20}, P(e_1) = \frac{2}{20}, P(e_2) = \frac{4}{20}, P(e_3) = \frac{3}{20},$ and $P(e_4) = \frac{1}{20}$. Armed with this information, PROTRAC would like to determine how many E-9s to send to Anchorage.

The values for $R_j(e_i)$ and $P(e_i)$ are shown in Figure 15.7. To verify these

Figure 15.7 *Net returns and probabilities for the pipeline problem*

			Decision			
Event	d_0	d_1	d_2	d_3	d_4	Probability of e_i
e_0	0	−1,000	−2,000	−3,000	−4,000	$\frac{10}{20}$
e_1	0	5,000	4,000	3,000	2,000	$\frac{2}{20}$
e_2	0	5,000	10,000	9,000	8,000	$\frac{4}{20}$
e_3	0	5,000	10,000	15,000	14,000	$\frac{3}{20}$
e_4	0	5,000	10,000	15,000	20,000	$\frac{1}{20}$

---

7 Here again, since the probabilities do not depend on the decisions, each $P_j(e_i)$ is written more simply as $P(e_i)$.

figures, note that if the number demanded is greater than the number sent, then PROTRAC sells the number sent at a net return of $5,000 each. On the other hand, if the number sent is greater than the number demanded, PROTRAC sells the number demanded at a net return of $5,000 each and loses $1,000 on each extra E-9 sent. In symbolic notation,

$$R_j(e_i) = \begin{cases} 5{,}000j & \text{if } i \geq j \\ 5{,}000i - 1{,}000(j - i) & \text{if } i < j \end{cases}$$

To arrive at the optimal decision, PROTRAC must now calculate the expected return for every decision by using the expression

$$ER_j = \sum_{i=0}^{4} P(e_i) R_j(e_i)$$

These calculations are shown below.

$$ER_0 = \tfrac{10}{20}(0) + \tfrac{2}{20}(0) + \tfrac{4}{20}(0) + \tfrac{3}{20}(0) + \tfrac{1}{20}(0) = 0$$
$$ER_1 = \tfrac{10}{20}(-1{,}000) + \tfrac{10}{20}(5{,}000) = 2{,}000$$
$$ER_2 = \tfrac{10}{20}(-2{,}000) + \tfrac{2}{20}(4{,}000) + \tfrac{8}{20}(10{,}000) = 3{,}400$$
$$ER_3 = \tfrac{10}{20}(-3{,}000) + \tfrac{2}{20}(3{,}000) + \tfrac{4}{20}(9{,}000) + \tfrac{4}{20}(15{,}000) = 3{,}600$$
$$ER_4 = \tfrac{10}{20}(-4{,}000) + \tfrac{2}{20}(2{,}000) + \tfrac{4}{20}(8{,}000) + \tfrac{3}{20}(14{,}000) + \tfrac{1}{20}(20{,}000) = 2{,}900$$

The optimal decision is one for which the expected return is a maximum. The above calculations indicate that in this instance the optimal decision is d_3, which is to send three E-9s to Anchorage.

15.5 Money versus Utility as a Measure of Preference

The model used to make decisions under uncertainty involves a sample space and two basic quantities associated with that space, namely, the probability that an event will occur, and the return associated with that event. Combining this information via the calculation of an expected return is a general method for selecting the appropriate decision. There are, however, some other consider-ations that should be understood in order to cope with decisions under uncertainty. Note that in our previous discussion, returns have been set equal to the dollar amounts in the example problems. Under conditions in which dollar amounts are large compared with the assets of the decision maker, such a model may not be satisfactory. In such circumstances, the use of the expected return model with simple dollar amounts as returns can yield "optimal" decisions that the decision maker might, in actuality, be unwilling to accept. As an illustration, consider the following game. It costs you $5,000 to play. If you play, the integers from 1 to 1,000 are placed in a bowl and one is drawn at random (each number is drawn with probability $\tfrac{1}{1000}$). If the number 738 is drawn, you receive $5,100,000. If not, you receive nothing.

The expected net return from the decision to play the game is calculated with the usual formula

$$ER(\text{play}) = \tfrac{999}{1000}(-5{,}000) + \tfrac{1}{1000}(5{,}095{,}000)$$
$$= 100$$

Since $ER(\text{play}) = 100$ and $ER(\text{not play}) = 0$, the model claims you should play. Most individuals, however, would find this advice unacceptable. The overwhelming chance of losing \$5,000 and the effect it would have on one's life is simply too large to gamble on a small probability of being rich.

This example does not imply that the expected return model is an inappropriate way to analyze decisions under uncertainty. What it does imply is that one must be careful about selecting the units that are used to express the return associated with each event. The return must accurately reflect the relationships among the decision maker's preferences for each possible outcome. In order to better deal with examples such as the above, preferences are often conceptually thought of as being measured in some abstract units called *utility.* More specifically, consider any "desirable item." Most people prefer more rather than less, but *at a decreasing rate.* In such a case, if one plots utility, or "units of preference" for the item, against the amount of the item the individual possesses, the graph will assume the general shape shown in Figure 15.8. This graph assumes that the added or marginal utility for each additional unit of the given item is smaller than the added utility of the last unit; that is, the slope of the graph of the utility function is decreasing. Perhaps the easiest way to think about this concept is to ask yourself how much effort you would be willing to expend to earn an extra \$10,000 given your current income and how much effort you would be willing to expend if you were a millionaire. A person might typically feel that if he were a millionaire, then he would be willing to expend less energy for an additional \$10,000. This phenomenon is reflected in the graph in Figure 15.8, which, in this context, would represent the utility of money.

Suppose one uses the *utility of dollars* rather than dollars *per se* as the measure of the cost and return from playing the gambling game with 1,000 integers. Then it should be apparent that a different answer might occur. In particular, assume that the decision maker's utility for money is specified by the function *U,* and suppose *U* has the properties that $U(-5{,}000) = -5{,}200$,

Figure 15.8 *General shape of a typical utility function*

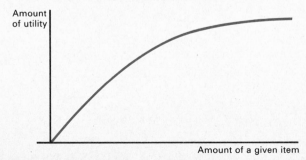

Amount of utility

Amount of a given item

$U(0) = 0$, and $U(5,095,000) = 5,000,000$. This function, then, has the general shape illustrated in Figure 15.8. Let us now employ utility in the basic model, rather than dollars, as a measure of return. The expected return becomes an expected utility, computed as follows:

$$.999\, U(-5,000) + .001\, U(5,095,000) = .999(-5,200) + .001(5,000,000) = -194.8$$

Since the dollar return of not playing is zero, and $U(0) = 0$, the expected utility of not playing is zero. Hence, by the criterion of maximizing expected *utility* (as opposed to dollar return), the optimal decision is not to play. This example helps to illustrate the potential importance of using the utility of money rather than money per se as a measure of return. More on this topic will appear in the discussion of risk in the next section. For now, we wish to provide a method for the decision maker to evaluate his utility for money. The common method uses what is called a ***standard gamble*** that is almost identical to the lottery method for assessing probabilities. Begin with the largest and smallest dollar amounts of interest. This would be the largest possible dollar loss and the largest possible dollar return—let us say, for example, -$20,000 and $1,000,000. Now assign *arbitrary* utilities to these numbers. Suppose these assignments are

$U(-20,000) = 0$

$U(1,000,000) = 1$

The numbers 0 and 1 could be replaced by -20,000 and 1,000,000 or by any other two arbitrary numbers, say a_1 and a_2, as long as $a_1 \le a_2$ (the utility of -$20,000 does not exceed the utility of $1 million). Now consider any intermediate number, such as 60,000. The utility of $60,000 is assessed by considering two lottery tickets. One ticket entitles you to $60,000 with certainty. The other ticket entitles you to $1,000,000 with probability P and -$20,000 with probability $(1 - P)$. The assessor must set the value of P at which he is indifferent between the two tickets. At such a value for P, his utility for each ticket will be the same. The expected utility of the second ticket is

$$(1 - P)\, U(-20,000) + P U(1,000,000)$$

Hence, it must be true at the P that creates indifference that

$$U(60,000) = (1 - P)\, U(-20,000) + P U(1,000,000)$$

Since all terms on the right of this equality are known, $U(60,000)$ has been determined. In this way, the decision maker can assess his utility for any monetary value between the limits -$20,000 and $1,000,000.

Although the concept of using a utility function to aid in making decisions under uncertainty is not difficult to understand, it can have a negative impact on someone considering using the expected return model as an aid in decision making under conditions of uncertainty. He might feel like the sales manager who was attempting to use this model to prepare a bid on a government contract. In great frustration he stated, "This is ridiculous. Not only do I have to play around with lotteries in order to come up with probabilities for an event that will occur only once, but I also have to dream up some numbers that reflect my happiness with the result. Instead of all that guessing, I might as well simply guess at the decision."

The frustration is understandable. The bidding problem he was facing, and many others like it, are intrinsically difficult. A manager is asked to make decisions in circumstances where there simply is not much information or historical data available. Unfortunately, the expected utility model does not make such decisions easy. It does, however, force a manager to consider the components of his decision separately and precisely. If one ignores the concept of expected utility, then an alternative that might yield an especially attractive but extremely unlikely result could receive undue attention. When a manager forces himself to be explicit about the likelihood of each event and the utility associated with it, he provides a framework for analyzing the model and for discussing the assumptions with his colleagues. Moreover, this approach provides an excellent opportunity to perform sensitivity analysis on the result. If a decision remains optimal for a wide range of probabilities and payoffs, management may feel much more comfortable about adopting that decision.

Finally, having discussed the expected utility concept, we wish to note the practical reality that organizations (as opposed to individuals) do not frequently resort to the use of utilities in the basic model. Rather, they more typically deal with dollar returns, per se. This is because all of the dollar amounts being considered are usually small by comparison with the total assets of the firm. In such a case, as indicated in the above discussion, monetary returns usually provide an adequate measure of the preferences of the firm. As an example, a major oil company was recently considering alternatives involving the entire design and expansion of its gasoline station system. It was eventually necessary to incorporate a utility measure into the problem in order to make the board of directors comfortable with the analysis. In spite of the fact that the management science group in this firm had analyzed many problems involving decisions under uncertainty using the basic expected return model, this was the first time that anyone could recall the use of utilities in such an analysis.

15.6 Risk

For many individuals, the notion of risk is synonymous with making decisions under uncertainty. For years "widows and orphans" were advised to buy blue-chip stocks because they could count on the dividend. There was little or no risk. On the other hand, growth stocks were to be avoided since they were too risky. Although there was the opportunity for large gains, there was considerable uncertainty about the future dividends and, worse yet, the possibility of losing the original investment was significant enough to be reckoned with. It is evident that the amount of uncertainty and in particular the probability of a "substantial" loss is an important factor in making decisions under uncertainty. Considerations such as these are generally referred to as risk.

One might well wonder, at this point, whether or not our basic model, as discussed above, incorporates the notion of risk. In this section, it will be seen that there are several ways to deal with risk.

Given a particular decision, d_j, our first goal will be to measure the amount of *variability,* or *dispersion,* or *scatter* in the possible values for the *returns* $R_j(e_i)$ as the elementary events e_i vary. This will indicate how closely the returns cluster about the *expected return* ER_j or, contrarily, how dispersed the returns are and, in this sense, will provide a measure of uncertainty.

The most common measure used to quantify variability is called the *variance.* Given the decision d_j, the variance of the return, $\text{Var}(R_j)$, is defined as

$$\text{Var}(R_j) = \sum_{i=1}^{n} P_j(e_i) \, [R_j(e_i) - ER_j]^2$$

where we recall that

$P_j(e_i)$ = probability of elementary event i given decision j

$R_j(e_i)$ = return associated with elementary event i given decision j

ER_j = expected return associated with decision j

To see intuitively that the variance provides a measure of dispersion, or scatter, think of ER_j as a number on the horizontal axis. Now note that the returns can be spread out further to the right and to the left of ER_j in such a way as to leave the value of ER_j unchanged. However, in widening this spread, the terms $[R_j(e_i) - ER_j]^2$ will increase, and thus the variance increases. In contrast, if each return $R_j(e_i)$ were to equal the expected return, ER_j, then the variance would clearly be zero.

To illustrate these ideas, we return to the Alaskan pipeline example. Let us recall from Section 15.4 that

e_i = event that the contractor wants i E-9s, $i = 0, ..., 4$

d_j = decision to send j E-9s, $j = 0, ..., 4$

$P(e_i)$ = probability of event i

$R_j(e_i)$ = (net) return if the contractor wants i E-9s and j have been sent

The values for $R_j(e_i)$ and $P(e_i)$ are shown in Figure 15.7. Let us use these data to compute the variance of the return associated with decision 2. First we compute the expected return and the variance as follows:

$$\begin{aligned}
ER_2 &= \sum_{i=0}^{4} P(e_i) R_2(e_i) \\
&= \tfrac{1}{2}(-2{,}000) + \tfrac{1}{10}(4{,}000) + \tfrac{1}{5}(10{,}000) + \tfrac{3}{20}(10{,}000) + \tfrac{1}{20}(10{,}000) \\
&= 3{,}400
\end{aligned}$$

$$\begin{aligned}
\text{Var}(R_2) &= \sum_{i=0}^{4} P(e_i) \, [R_2(e_i) - ER_2]^2 \\
&= \tfrac{1}{2}(-2{,}000 - 3{,}400)^2 + \tfrac{1}{10}(4{,}000 - 3{,}400)^2 + \tfrac{1}{5}(10{,}000 - 3{,}400)^2 \\
&\quad + \tfrac{3}{20}(10{,}000 - 3{,}400)^2 + \tfrac{1}{20}(10{,}000 - 3{,}400)^2 \\
&= \tfrac{10}{20}(-5{,}400)^2 + \tfrac{2}{20}(600)^2 + \tfrac{8}{20}(6{,}600)^2 \\
&= 32{,}040{,}000
\end{aligned}$$

Let us compare the variances associated with decisions d_2 and d_4. For decision d_4, the expected return is

$$ER_4 = \sum_{i=0}^{4} P(e_i) R_4(e_i)$$

$$= \tfrac{1}{2}(-4,000) + \tfrac{1}{10}(2,000) + \tfrac{1}{5}(8,000) + \tfrac{3}{20}(14,000) + \tfrac{1}{20}(20,000)$$

$$= 2,900$$

The variance is

$$\mathrm{Var}(R_4) = \sum_{i=0}^{4} P(e_i)\,[R_4(e_i) - ER_4]^2$$

$$= \tfrac{1}{2}(-4,000 - 2,900)^2 + \tfrac{1}{10}(2,000 - 2,900)^2 + \tfrac{1}{5}(8,000 - 2,900)^2$$

$$\quad + \tfrac{3}{20}(14,000 - 2,900)^2 + \tfrac{1}{20}(20,000 - 2,900)^2$$

$$= 62,190,000$$

As the calculations show,

Variance of the net return associated with decision d_2 = 32,040,000

Variance of the net return associated with decision d_4 = 62,190,000

According to this measure, then, since decision 4 has a greater variance, it would often be considered to be "riskier" than decision 2. That is, the possible returns associated with d_2 are less dispersed (more clustered) around the expected return ER_2 than is the case for d_4. This means there is *less uncertainty* associated with d_2. It is thus seen that variance can be used as a means for attempting to quantitatively measure the amount of risk.

In attempting to develop an intuitive feel for the variance, it is useful to plot possible returns on the horizontal axis and probabilities of those returns on the vertical axis. This is done in Figures 15.9 and 15.10 for decisions d_2 and d_4. The reader should be able to verify that these graphs are constructed from the data in Figure 15.7 as follows. For the decision d_2 there are three possible values for the returns: $-2,000$, $4,000$, and $10,000$. The return of $-2,000$ is associated with event e_0 and thus occurs with probability $\tfrac{10}{20}$. The return of $4,000$ is associated with event e_1 and thus occurs with probability $\tfrac{2}{20}$. The

Figure 15.9 *Probability versus return for decision d_2*

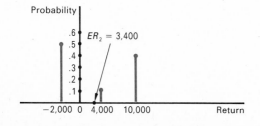

Figure 15.10 *Probability versus return for decision d_4*

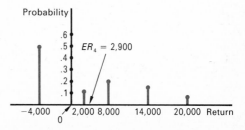

return of 10,000 is associated with events e_2, e_3, and e_4 and thus occurs with probability $\frac{4}{20} + \frac{3}{20} + \frac{1}{20}$, which equals $\frac{8}{20}$. The same type of analysis applies to decision d_4.

In viewing these figures, most people would feel comfortable with the visual impression that the returns associated with d_2 are more clustered around the expected return than the returns associated with d_4. Recall that the returns associated with d_2 had a smaller variance.

The square root of the variance is called the **standard deviation.** The standard deviation can also be employed to measure dispersion. These two measures, variance and standard deviation, are the most often used measures of risk.

Let us now consider, for example, two hypothetical investments, A and B. The possible returns from each investment and the probabilities of these returns are shown in Figure 15.11. The probability versus return is plotted for investment A and investment B in Figures 15.12 and 15.13, respectively.

The expected return of alternative A is

$$ER_A = \sum_{i=1}^{3} P_A(e_i) R_A(e_i) = (.3)(9) + (.4)(10) + (.3)(11) = 10$$

The expected return of alternative B is

$$ER_B = \sum_{i=1}^{5} P_B(e_i) R_B(e_i) = (.1)(8) + (.2)(9) + (.4)(10) + (.2)(11) + (.1)(12) = 10$$

Thus, each investment produces the same expected return. However, it can

Figure 15.11   *Returns and probabilities for investments A and B*

	Probability of Return	
Returns	Investment A	Investment B
8	0	.1
9	.3	.2
10	.4	.4
11	.3	.2
12	0	.1

Figure 15.12   *Probability versus return for investment A*

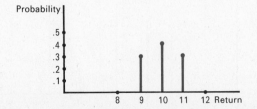

Figure 15.13   *Probability versus return for investment B*

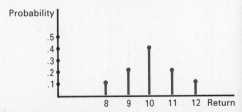

be noted that in investment B the revenue can equal 8, whereas for investment A all revenues are at least equal to 9. Thus it could loosely be stated that B has greater downside variability, where *downside* means to the left of the expected return. In other words, the probability of too large a loss (too small a return) is higher with B than with A. Also note that the potential gain with investment B is greater than with A. This means that B has greater upside potential (or upside variability) as well as downside risk. It should be clear that as the downside risk or the upside potential becomes greater, the variance will also increase. This is reflected in the fact that, for this particular example, the variance of investment A is .6, and the variance of B is 1.2.

It should be clear at this point that variance provides a way to measure the "width" of the scatter of returns about ER_j, and in this sense variance can be considered a measure of risk. But as we mentioned at the beginning of this section, risk is commonly thought of as the probability of "too large a loss." We have seen in the above example that variance reflects upside, as well as downside, potential, and hence variance is not a measure of loss potential per se. In this sense, it may seem to be somewhat less than an ideal measure of risk.

In any case, by now you may well be wondering, "How does all this fit in with the basic model that uses expected return as a decision-making criterion?" The answer to this question depends on whom you are talking to.

A first approach is to observe that the notion of "too large a loss" does not have a very well-defined meaning. For example, does it imply that the decision maker is unwilling to accept a loss larger than a specified amount but is willing to accept any loss up to that amount? Or, alternatively, does it imply that the total probability of a loss in excess of some specified amount must be less than a specified limit? Using the probabilities of specific returns (as, for example, in Figure 15.11), the above restrictions could be entered as constraints in the model, and one could then seek a decision that maximizes expected return subject to such loss-limiting constraints. This approach has several shortcomings, including the difficulty of *directly* assessing the meaning of "too large a loss" and of evaluating the sensitivity of the solution to the imposed constraint. These factors seriously limit the usefulness of this approach.

A second approach is to find a decision that maximizes expected return subject to a constraint that the variance must not exceed a specified value. Similarly, one could seek a decision that minimizes variance subject to a constraint that the expected return must exceed a specified value. This approach is commonly adopted in the field of finance and, in particular, in portfolio models. It is usually the case that a decision with relatively high expected return is also a decision with relatively high risk, which is often reflected in high variance. Thus, the portfolio model provides a way to select decisions under such circumstances.

The third approach provides the most general way to incorporate risk. It is based on the fact that

A decision maker's attitude toward risk is incorporated in his utility function.

Figure 15.14   *Three utility functions*

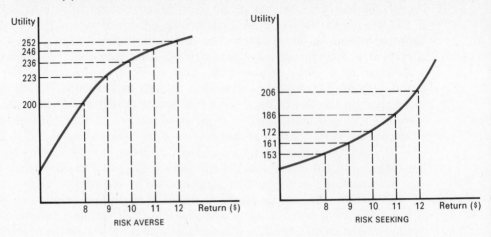

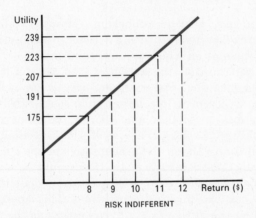

Consider the three general shapes for utility functions shown in Figure 15.14. The expected utility is calculated for the above two investments, *A* and *B*, using each of the utility functions shown in Figure 15.14 and the information about the investments contained in Figures 15.12 and 15.13.

The results are presented in Figure 15.15, and they illustrate the interesting fact that in properly defining his utility function, the decision maker will accommodate his feelings about the importance of risk. These preferences will be reflected in the expected utility (that is, the expected return as measured in units of utility).

We note that, for this particular example, if the typical concave utility

Figure 15.15   *Expected utilities*

Investment	Risk Averse	Risk Seeking	Risk Indifferent
A	235	172	207
B	233	174	207
Optimal	Investment A	Investment B	Indifferent

function (the curve labeled *Risk averse*) is used, the optimal decision is to select the investment with the smaller variance.[8] The concave utility function has the property that, starting from any point on the horizontal axis, a decrease of a specified amount in dollars yields a larger drop in utility than the rise in utility provided by an increase in dollars of the same amount. (Reading from the risk-averse graph in Figure 15.14 shows that decreasing from $10 to $9 decreases the utility by 13, whereas increasing from $10 to $11 increases the utility by 10.) It is in this sense that a risk-averse utility function protects against downside variability. In economic terms, risk aversion implies that the cost of a potential downside move is more important to the decision maker than the gain associated with a potential upside move of the same magnitude. This idea is, of course, consistent with the intuitive notion of risky investments discussed earlier.

The convex utility function of the risk seeker has exactly the opposite properties of the concave utility function of the risk-averse decision maker. Note that as dollar returns increase, the utility increases more rapidly than it decreases as dollar returns decrease. Thus, for the risk seeker, investment *B* is more attractive than investment *A*. For her, the opportunity to end up with a large gain of $12 more than outweighs the possibility of ending up with only $8.

The use of any linear utility function is equivalent to using the monetary returns per se, which corresponds to the specific case $U(x) = x$. In order to see this equivalence, first note that regardless of the shape of a utility function, it can be translated vertically without influencing the comparison between any pair of alternatives. That is, if decision d_j is preferred using $U(x)$, then d_j is also preferred using $U(x) + K$, where K is a fixed constant. This means that without loss of generality, any utility function can be translated so as to pass through the origin. Now consider a linear utility function that passes through the origin, but with arbitrary slope. Changing from this function to the linear function $U(x) = x$, with slope 1, can be interpreted as transforming into dollars from a different currency, where the slope of the original function is interpreted as the exchange rate. If a decision maker is indifferent between two alternatives when paid in francs, then he should also be indifferent between the two when paid in dollars. Thus, since the linear utility is equivalent to using dollars per se, and since the expected return in dollars between *A* and *B* is the same, the linear utility will show no preference for either investment over the other. This is why the decision maker with such a utility function is referred to as risk-indifferent.

---

[8] It should not be inferred that a risk-averse utility function will *always* lead to a selection of the decision with monetary returns having the smallest variance, even when expected returns are equal. In general, there will be tradeoffs between the magnitude of the various returns, the associated probabilities, and the precise shape of the utility function. A more correct inference would be the following. Given two decisions with equal expected monetary returns, a risk-averse utility function provides a way of choosing the decision with least *downside* variability. As an example, suppose $U(x) = ln\ x$. Alternative 1 has returns .05 and 1.95, with probabilities .5 each. Alternative 2 has returns .25 and 5, with probabilities $\frac{16}{19}$ and $\frac{3}{19}$, respectively. In each case, the expected return is 1. For alternative 1, the variance is .9025. For alternative 2, the variance is $\frac{49}{19}$. However, the expected utility for alternative 1 is -1.164, whereas it is $-.913$ for alternative 2. Hence, alternative 2, with more variance but less downside potential, is preferred. For certain special classes of utility functions, it can be shown that if two decisions have the same expected return, then utility maximization will also lead to a choice of the decision with smaller variance.

In summary, then, the above discussion indicates that the decision maker can take risk into account in the decision-making process in either of the following ways:

---

1   Adopt the portfolio model approach, which means minimizing variance subject to a constraint on expected return.
2   Maximize the expected utility of dollars, as opposed to expected monetary returns.

The first approach has the advantage that the utility function need not be explicitly defined. It can be implemented with the use of the data in the problem. However, as we have seen, variance need not be a good measure of downside risk (see footnote 8). The second approach is preferred in this respect, but in order to use it the decision maker must construct his utility function (employing, for example, a series of standard gambles). Under special circumstances, the two approaches are closely related. Establishing this point would require the presentation of more technical detail, and to do so would lead us too far from our objectives. From the theoretic point of view, the criterion of maximizing expected utility is preferred. The examples we have presented do not prove this statement. There is a substantial theoretical development required to establish this fact. Hopefully, however, the examples make the idea plausible and understandable to the potential user.

From this point on in our discussion, we shall often use the terms *expected return* and *expected utility* interchangeably. It is always assumed that the decision maker's predilection or aversion to risk is adequately reflected by the chosen measure of his preferences. Of course, the use of dollar returns implicitly assumes risk indifference. If the dollar amounts (in terms of potential losses) are sufficiently large so that the "risk indifference" assumption seems inappropriate to the reader, he should then think of the returns as being in units of utility.

15.7   How Do You Know a Good Decision When You See One?

In making decisions under uncertainty, the fact that you have made a good decision does not necessarily imply that you will have a better outcome than someone who has made a bad decision. This potentially ironic situation cannot arise (conceptually) with the deterministic constrained optimization models considered in Part 1 of the text. There, the measure of a decision was the value it produced for the objective function. The best decision yielded the largest (or smallest) value for the objective function. This is not so with decisions under uncertainty. It is intrinsic when dealing with uncertainty that the decision with the largest expected return may by chance produce a poor result. Unlikely events do occur, and thus a decision that seems bad because it has low expected return might just yield a good return. Examples from gambling and card games are easy to find. Betting to fill an inside straight is considered bad poker playing because the probability of filling it is so low. On occasion it does fill, however, and it could yield a big pot for the winner.

The quality of a decision maker facing problems under uncertainty should not be judged by a single decision. (As the promoters of the Edsel will testify, this advice is not always heeded.) The emphasis should be on the overall decision-making process, not on one particular outcome. If a number of people are making similar decisions, especially over a period of time, it is then possible to come up with objective measures of performance. When evaluated over a number of opportunities, a decision maker should not be consistently below the group average. If he is, there is evidence to believe that his analyses are not good, or that he is just very unlucky (if you believe in such things).

15.8 Examples and Solutions

Example 1

Consider an experiment in which a fair (perfectly symmetric) die is thrown and a fair coin is (say, simultaneously) flipped.
a List all of the *elementary events* in the sample space.
b Assign a probability to each elementary event. Let A be the event that a head occurs and B be the event that a number greater than or equal to 5 occurs. Obtain numerical values for each of the probabilities described in parts c, d, and e.
c $P(A)$
d $P(B)$
e $P(A \cap B)$
f Use the previous numerical results to verify that the following equality is satisfied: $P(A \cup B) = P(A) + P(B) - P(A \cap B)$.

Solution to Example 1

a The elementary events consist of all outcomes of the experiment, which means all possible combinations of coin side and die face. Thus, the elementary events are

$(H, 1), (H, 2), (H, 3), (H, 4), (H, 5), (H, 6)$

$(T, 1), (T, 2), (T, 3), (T, 4), (T, 5), (T, 6)$

where the first element of the pair is the result of flipping the coin and the second is the result of rolling the die.
b The problem states that the die and the coin are both fair. Thus it seems reasonable to assign equal probabilities to each elementary event. This implies that the probability of each elementary event is $\frac{1}{12}$.
c $P(A)$, the probability that a head occurs, can be found by adding the probabilities of all the elementary events in which a head occurs. That is, the event $A = \{(H,1), (H, 2), (H, 3), (H, 4), (H, 5), (H, 6)\}$ and hence

$P(A) = P(H, 1) + P(H, 2) + P(H, 3) + P(H, 4) + P(H, 5) + P(H, 6)$

$\quad = 6(\frac{1}{12}) = \frac{1}{2}$

d $P(B)$ can be found by adding the probabilities of all the elementary events in which a number greater than or equal to 5 appears on the die. That is, the event $B = \{(H, 5), (T, 5), (H, 6), (T, 6)\}$, and

$P(B) = P(H, 5) + P(T, 5) + P(H, 6) + P(T, 6)$

$\quad = 4(\frac{1}{12}) = \frac{1}{3}$

e $P(A \cap B)$ is the probability that A occurs and B occurs. That is, the event $A \cap B = \{(H, 5), (H, 6)\}$, and

$$P(A \cap B) = P(H, 5) + P(H, 6) = 2(\tfrac{1}{12}) = \tfrac{1}{6}$$

f The probability that either A occurs or B occurs or both occur is $P(A \cup B)$. Since $A \cup B = \{(H, 1), (H, 2), (H, 3), (H, 4), (H, 5), (H, 6), (T, 5), (T, 6)\}$, we obtain

$$P(A \cup B) = P(H, 1) + P(H, 2) + P(H, 3) + P(H, 4) + P(H, 5)$$
$$+ P(H, 6) + P(T, 5) + P(T, 6)$$
$$= 8(\tfrac{1}{12}) = \tfrac{2}{3}$$

From parts *c*, *d*, and *e* we know that

$$P(A) = \tfrac{1}{2} \quad P(B) = \tfrac{1}{3}, \quad P(A \cap B) = \tfrac{1}{6}$$

Thus

$$P(A) + P(B) - P(A \cap B) = \tfrac{6}{12} + \tfrac{4}{12} - \tfrac{2}{12} = \tfrac{8}{12} = \tfrac{2}{3}$$

and we have verified that in this case

$$P(A \cup B) = P(A) + P(B) - P(A \cap B)$$

Example 2

A firm is facing the problem of selecting between two marketing strategies. Strategy 1 requires an outlay of $15,000. Gross returns of $23,000, $21,000, $19,000, $16,000, $14,000, and $12,000 could occur. The probabilities associated with these outcomes are $\tfrac{4}{12}, \tfrac{1}{12}, \tfrac{1}{12}, \tfrac{1}{12}, \tfrac{2}{12}$, and $\tfrac{3}{12}$, respectively. Similarly, strategy 2 requires an outlay of $10,000. It yields possible gross returns of $16,000, $14,000, $13,000, $12,000, $10,000, and $7,000. The probabilities associated with these outcomes are $\tfrac{1}{12}, \tfrac{3}{12}, \tfrac{3}{12}, \tfrac{3}{12}, \tfrac{1}{12}$, and $\tfrac{1}{12}$, respectively.

a Use the notation presented in this chapter to formulate this problem as a decision under uncertainty.

b Using the criterion of maximizing expected return, select the better of the two strategies.

Solution to Example 2

a Let d_j be the decision to use strategy j, $j = 1, 2$. The *net* returns associated with d_1 are

$8,000, $6,000, $4,000, $1,000, -$1,000, -$3,000

The net returns associated with d_2 are

$6,000, $4,000, $3,000, $2,000, $0, -$3,000

We can think of the set of all possible outcomes from both strategies as constituting the sample space. There are thus nine elementary events in the sample space:

$e_1 = -\$3,000 \quad e_4 = \$1,000 \quad e_7 = \$4,000$

$e_2 = -\$1,000 \quad e_5 = \$2,000 \quad e_8 = \$6,000$

$e_3 = \$0 \qquad\quad e_6 = \$3,000 \quad e_9 = \$8,000$

Defining the sample space in this way implies

$R_j(e_i) = e_i$

for each decision d_j.

That is,

$R_1(-\$1,000) = R_2(-\$1,000) = -\$1,000$

$P_j(e_i)$ must be the probability that event i will occur if decision j is made. Thus,

$P_1(e_1) = \frac{3}{12} \qquad P_2(e_1) = \frac{1}{12}$

$P_1(e_2) = \frac{2}{12} \qquad P_2(e_2) = 0$

$P_1(e_3) = 0 \qquad P_2(e_3) = \frac{1}{12}$

$P_1(e_4) = \frac{1}{12} \qquad P_2(e_4) = 0$

$P_1(e_5) = 0 \qquad P_2(e_5) = \frac{3}{12}$

$P_1(e_6) = 0 \qquad P_2(e_6) = \frac{3}{12}$

$P_1(e_7) = \frac{1}{12} \qquad P_2(e_7) = \frac{3}{12}$

$P_1(e_8) = \frac{1}{12} \qquad P_2(e_8) = \frac{1}{12}$

$P_1(e_9) = \frac{4}{12} \qquad P_2(e_9) = 0$

The above data are summarized in Figure 15.16.

gure 15.16

		Probability	
Event	Return (Net)	Strategy 1	Strategy 2
e_1	−3,000	$\frac{3}{12}$	$\frac{1}{12}$
e_2	−1,000	$\frac{2}{12}$	0
e_3	0	0	$\frac{1}{12}$
e_4	1,000	$\frac{1}{12}$	0
e_5	2,000	0	$\frac{3}{12}$
e_6	3,000	0	$\frac{3}{12}$
e_7	4,000	$\frac{1}{12}$	$\frac{3}{12}$
e_8	6,000	$\frac{1}{12}$	$\frac{1}{12}$
e_9	8,000	$\frac{4}{12}$	0

b Using the rule for computing expected return, we obtain

$$ER_1 = \sum_{i=1}^{9} P_1(e_i) R_1(e_i)$$

$$= \frac{3}{12}(-3,000) + \frac{2}{12}(-1,000) + 0(0) + \frac{1}{12}(1,000) + 0(2,000) + 0(3,000)$$

$$+ \frac{1}{12}(4,000) + \frac{1}{12}(6,000) + \frac{4}{12}(8,000)$$

$$= 2,667$$

$$ER_2 = \sum_{i=1}^{9} P_2(e_i) R_2(e_i)$$

$$= \tfrac{1}{12}(-3,000) + 0(-1,000) + \tfrac{1}{12}(0) + 0(1,000) + \tfrac{3}{12}(2,000)$$

$$+ \tfrac{3}{12}(3,000) + \tfrac{3}{12}(4,000) + \tfrac{1}{12}(6,000) + 0(8,000)$$

$$= 2,500$$

The optimal decision is to select strategy 1.

At this point, we note that although the symbolic notation (that is, defining each e_i) is useful in describing the general model of Section 15.4, it seems to make the computations in specific cases such as the above unnecessarily complicated. (Students generally support the latter part of this statement.) Often it is true that with a minimum amount of thought, one can go directly from a problem statement to the calculations (such as those in part *b* of Example 2) without passing through the formal symbolism and the definition of the e_is.

Example 3

Assume that the firm in Example 2 has the utility function shown in Figure 15.17.
a The shape of this function describes what type of attitude toward risk?
b Based merely upon visual inspection of the data, which of the two strategies do you feel has more risk?
c Find the variance associated with the returns for each strategy. By this measure, which strategy has more risk?
d Calculate the expected utility associated with each strategy and select the

Figure 15.17

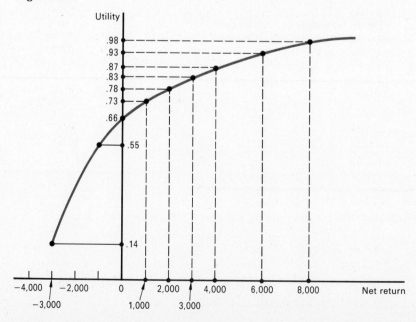

best strategy based on the criterion of maximizing expected utility. Why is the conclusion different from that in Example 2?

Solution to Example 3

a The utility function is concave; this indicates that management is *risk averse.*

b To answer this question, we create a table, shown in Figure 15.18, in which the returns and their associated probabilities are listed for each strategy. From this table, it seems reasonable to assess strategy 1 as being riskier than strategy 2 because strategy 1 has larger probabilities of losses. In particular, note that a loss of 3,000 occurs with probability $\frac{3}{12}$ in strategy 1 and only $\frac{1}{12}$ in strategy 2. Moreover, there is a positive probability of losing 1,000 with strategy 1, whereas this cannot happen with strategy 2.

c The variance of the returns from strategy 1 is defined by the expression

$$\text{Var} = \sum_{i=1}^{9} P_1(e_1) \, [R_1(e_i) - ER_1]^2$$

Thus for strategy 1

$$\begin{aligned}
\text{Var} &= \tfrac{4}{12}(8{,}000 - 2{,}667)^2 + \tfrac{1}{12}(6{,}000 - 2{,}667)^2 + \tfrac{1}{12}(4{,}000 - 2{,}667)^2 \\
&\quad + \tfrac{1}{12}(1{,}000 - 2{,}667)^2 + \tfrac{2}{12}(-1{,}000 - 2{,}667)^2 + \tfrac{3}{12}(-3{,}000 - 2{,}667)^2 \\
&= 21{,}056{,}000
\end{aligned}$$

For strategy 2,

$$\begin{aligned}
\text{Var} &= \tfrac{1}{12}(6{,}000 - 2{,}500)^2 + \tfrac{3}{12}(4{,}000 - 2{,}500)^2 + \tfrac{3}{12}(3{,}000 - 2{,}500)^2 \\
&\quad + \tfrac{3}{12}(2{,}000 - 2{,}500)^2 + \tfrac{1}{12}(0 - 2{,}500)^2 + \tfrac{1}{12}(-3{,}000 - 2{,}500)^2 \\
&= 4{,}750{,}000
\end{aligned}$$

By this measure we conclude that strategy 1 has more risk.

d To calculate the expected utilities, one must read the utility for each return off the graph in Figure 15.17. The data and results of the calculations are shown in Figure 15.19. Strategy 2 is thus preferred to strategy 1 on the basis of the criterion of maximizing expected utility. The preference has changed from 1 to 2 because 1 has more risk and the utility function is risk averse.

Figure 15.18

Strategy 1		Strategy 2	
Net Return	Probability	Net Return	Probability
8,000	$\frac{4}{12}$	6,000	$\frac{1}{12}$
6,000	$\frac{1}{12}$	4,000	$\frac{3}{12}$
4,000	$\frac{1}{12}$	3,000	$\frac{3}{12}$
1,000	$\frac{1}{12}$	2,000	$\frac{3}{12}$
−1,000	$\frac{2}{12}$	0	$\frac{1}{12}$
−3,000	$\frac{3}{12}$	−3,000	$\frac{1}{12}$

Figure 15.19

Strategy 1			Strategy 2		
Net Return	Utility	Probability	Net Return	Utility	Probability
8,000	.98	$\frac{4}{12}$	6,000	.93	$\frac{1}{12}$
6,000	.93	$\frac{1}{12}$	4,000	.87	$\frac{3}{12}$
4,000	.87	$\frac{1}{12}$	3,000	.83	$\frac{3}{12}$
1,000	.73	$\frac{1}{12}$	2,000	.78	$\frac{3}{12}$
−1,000	.55	$\frac{2}{12}$	0	.66	$\frac{1}{12}$
−3,000	.14	$\frac{3}{12}$	−3,000	.14	$\frac{1}{12}$

Expected Utility = 0.66　　　　　　　　　Expected Utility = 0.76

15.9　Summary of Key Concepts

The two basic elements in making decisions under uncertainty are the likelihood associated with each possible outcome and the return associated with each possible outcome. (Section 15.2)

In working with the subject of probability, it is important to distinguish among three concepts:
1 The mathematical probability framework
2 The interpretation of probability in applications
3 The actual numerical assessment of probabilities
(Section 15.3)

The mathematical framework treats a probability function P as any function that assigns to each event in the event space a real number, denoted P(A), and called the probability of event A. This function must satisfy the following three axioms:
1 For any event A, P(A) ≥ 0.
2 P(S) = 1, where S is the underlying sample space.
3 If A ∩ B = φ then P(A ∪ B) = P(A) + P(B).
(Section 15.3.1)

In applications, probability is interpreted as a subjective assessment of the frequency with which a sufficiently similar event would occur under sufficiently similar circumstances. (Section 15.3.2)

The actual numerical assessment of probabilities can be facilitated by using the lottery device. (Section 15.3.2)

The appropriate criterion for making a decision under uncertainty is to choose the decision that maximizes expected net return, defined, for the jth decision, as

$$\sum_{i=1}^{n} P_j(e_i) \, R_j(e_i)$$

where e_i is an elementary event. Such a maximizing decision is called an optimal decision in an uncertain environment. (Section 15.4)

A decision maker can take risk into account in either of the following ways:
1 Adopt the portfolio model approach, which means minimizing variance subject to a constraint on expected return.
2 Maximize expected utility of dollars rather than expected monetary returns.
(Section 15.6)

Concave, convex, and linear utility functions represent risk-averse, risk-seeking, and risk-indifferent preferences, respectively. **(Section 15.6)**

15.10 Problems

1 Suppose that you are working for a firm that manufactures detergents. The firm is attempting to decide whether or not it should introduce a new product. The cost analysis reveals that at least 150,000 units must be sold in the first year if the product is to be a success.
   a Is it meaningful to talk about the probability of success?
   b What information would you want to have access to in order to assess this probability?
   c How could you use a lottery device in assessing this probability?

2 Consider an experiment in which a ball is drawn at random from an urn; that is, each ball in the urn is equally likely to be drawn. Each ball in the urn is one of three colors, black, red, or yellow and has one of the integers 1, 2, 3 painted on it. At each trial both the color of the ball and the number are recorded. The elementary events in the sample space are shown below (that is, $B1$ is one elementary event, $B2$ is another, and so on). The number beside each color-number combination is the number of balls in the urn that have that particular combination.

$B1$ 14	$R1$ 15	$Y1$ 5
$B2$ 8	$R2$ 20	$Y2$ 7
$B3$ 3	$R3$ 10	$Y3$ 18

   Let A be the event that a red ball is drawn. Let B be the event that a number 2 is drawn.
   a Assign a probability to each elementary event in the sample space.
   b What is the probability that a red ball will be drawn?
   c What is the probability that a ball with a number 2 on it will be drawn?
   d What is the probability that a red ball with a number 2 on it will be drawn?
   e What is the probability that a red ball or a ball with the number 2 on it or both will be drawn?

3 A student has been observing a gambling game in which a six-sided die is rolled. There is no reason to believe that each side is equally likely. Let event A occur if one of the numbers 1, 2, or 3 shows. Event B occurs if either of the numbers 1 or 2 occurs, and event C occurs if either of the numbers 3 or 5 occurs. Payoffs for the game depend on the events A, B, and C. Currently, the student has assessed the following probabilities.

   $$P(A) = .6$$
   $$P(B) = .4$$
   $$P(C) = .1$$

   Comment on his assessments. (Hint: compute $P(5)$.)

4 The following situation is from the *Journal of Histrionics*. In order to investigate the

correspondence between sex, cigarette smoking, and the occurrence of fibromata, a group of doctors conceived of taking a random sample from a population of 1,000 patients suffering from a fibroma. In advance of the sampling, they subjectively assessed the following probabilities:

(1) Probability that the patient was female   = .3
(2) Probability that the patient smoked   = .6
(3) Probability that the patient was female and smoked = .4

Comment on these probability assessments. (Hint: compute the probability of a female nonsmoker.)

5 After additional training in probability, the doctors in problem 4 assessed the following probabilities:

(1) Probability that the patient was female   = .3
(2) Probability that the patient smoked   = .6
(3) Probability that the patient was female and smoked   = .2
(4) Probability that the patient was female, or smoked, or both = .95

Comment on these new assessments. (Hint: use the fact that $P(\text{female} \cup \text{smoke}) = P(\text{female}) + P(\text{smoke}) - P(\text{female} \cap \text{smoke})$.)

6 Consider the experiment described in Example 1 (a coin is flipped and a die is thrown). A gambler offers the following game. If a head occurs, he pays nothing. If a tail occurs, he pays $5 for each dot showing on the die (for example, if a tail and a 3 occur, he pays $15).

a What is the expected return from this game?
b What is the most you would be willing to pay to play the game if your utility function in dollars is linear over the range 0 to $1,000?

7 Consider the experiment described in Example 1. A gambler offers the following game. He will pay $10 if a head occurs or a number greater than or equal to 5 appears on the die. He will pay $20 if both a head occurs and a number greater than or equal to 5 appears on the die. What is the expected return associated with this game? (Note that in this problem the returns are specified in terms of *events* that are not *elementary events*. Be sure to heed the warning presented in Section 15.4.)

8 Consider the problem presented in Example 2. Suppose that in reviewing the decision, management decided that the revenue estimates were incorrect. In revising these estimates, $100 was added to each return associated with strategy 1 and $200 to each return associated with strategy 2. What is the expected return associated with each strategy in this revised problem?

9 Suppose that in reviewing the decision in Example 2, management decided that the data associated with strategy 2 were incorrect. For an outlay of $10,000 the possible revenues are changed to $16,000, $14,000, $13,000, $12,000, $11,000, $10,000, and $7,000 with probabilities of $\frac{3}{12}, \frac{3}{12}, \frac{1}{12}, \frac{1}{12}, \frac{1}{12}, \frac{1}{12}$, and $\frac{2}{12}$, respectively.

a What is the expected return now associated with strategy 2?
b If management adopts the utility function shown in Figure 15.17, what would you conjecture about the relation between the expected utility of the original version of strategy 2 (computed in Example 3) and that of the revised version? See if you can determine the answer by inspection of the data. Then calculate the expected utility to verify your answer.
c Find the variance of the returns associated with the revised version of strategy 2. How does it compare with the variance of the returns associated with the original version? Is this result consistent with your answer to part *b*?

10 In order to select the optimal strategy in Example 2, the following procedure was used:
(1) For each strategy, the net return (revenue minus cost) was calculated for each outcome.
(2) The net returns and their associated probabilities were used to calculate the expected return.
(3) The strategy with the largest expected net return was selected.

Suppose instead the following procedure was used:

(1) The expected revenue was calculated for each strategy by using the revenues and their associated probabilities.

(2) The difference between the expected revenue for a strategy and the cost of using that strategy was calculated for each strategy.

(3) The strategy that yielded the largest value in part (2) was selected. Would the two procedures yield the same decision? What is the relationship between the expected net return of a given strategy and the number calculated in part (2) of the second procedure for that same strategy?

11 This problem is the sequel to problem 10, but in this case utilities are used rather than returns. In order to select the optimal strategy in Example 3, the following procedure was used:

(1) For each strategy the utility of the net return was calculated for each outcome.

(2) These utilities and their associated probabilities were used to calculate the expected utility.

(3) The strategy with the largest expected utility was selected.

Suppose instead the following procedure was used:

(1) For each strategy, the utility of the revenue was calculated for each outcome.

(2) These utilities and their associated probabilities were used to calculate an expected utility of revenue for each strategy.

(3) The utility of the cost is determined for each strategy.

(4) For each strategy, the difference between the expected utility of the revenue and the utility of the cost is calculated.

(5) The strategy that yields the largest value in (4) is selected. Will the two procedures yield the same decision? Explain your answer.

16 Extending the Basic Model: Conditional Probabilities and Decision Trees

The basic model from Chapter 15 is extended in two ways. First, the framework is presented for incorporating new information via conditional probabilities. Second, sequential decision problems are treated. The use of decision trees is introduced, and illustrative examples are discussed.

16.1 Introduction

Chapter 15 presented the following basic model of a decision problem under uncertainty:

1. Define a sample space for the problem. (Recall that without loss of generality the same sample space can be used for all decisions, and this will be the case throughout our discussion.)
2. For each decision, assign a probability to each elementary event in the sample space.[1]
3. For each decision, assign a return (or utility) to each elementary event in the sample space.
4. Select the decision that maximizes the expected return (or utility).

This model is basic from the point of view of simplicity and by virtue of the fact that its rationale serves as a guiding principle for extensions to other models for use in a nondeterministic environment.

There are essentially two extensions of the basic model that we will consider in this chapter:

1. Models in which new information concerning the likelihood of the uncertain events becomes available
2. Models in which a *sequence* of decisions and uncertain events occur

In order to present these models in a clear and consistent manner, it will be convenient to utilize a graphical device known as a *decision diagram* or a *decision tree*. A *decision tree* is a means of graphically visualizing the

---

1. In general, the probability of an event e is dependent on the decision j; that is, $P_k(e)$ and $P_m(e)$ need not have the same value for different decisions k, m. In this chapter, however, we shall employ only examples for which the probabilities of events are independent of decisions. Hence the more cumbersome notation $P_j(e)$ will be replaced by $P(e)$.

interactions between decisions and uncertain events. In this chapter, decision trees will be used to exposit the similarities and differences among: the basic model; an extension of the basic model that incorporates new information; and a further extension involving a sequence of decisions and uncertain events. Each of these generalizations will be considered in the context of a marketing problem faced by the management of PROTRAC.

16.2 A Decision Tree for the Basic Model: The Home and Garden Tractor Problem

The design and product testing phase has just been completed for PROTRAC's new line of home and garden tractors. Top management is attempting to decide on the appropriate marketing and production strategy to use for this product. Three major alternatives are being considered. Each alternative is identified with a single word.

1 Aggressive (A): This strategy represents a major commitment of the firm to this product line. A major capital expenditure would be made for a new and efficient production facility. Large inventories would be built up to guarantee prompt delivery of all models. A major marketing campaign involving nationally sponsored television commercials and dealer discounts would be initiated.

2 Basic (B): In this plan, E–4 (the small crawler tractor) production would be moved from Joliet to Moline. This move would phase out the trouble-plagued department for adjustable pelican and excavator production. At the same time, the E–4 line in Joliet would be modified to produce the new home and garden product. Inventories would be held for only the most popular items. Headquarters would make funds available to support local or regional advertising efforts, but no national advertising campaign would be mounted.

3 Cautious (C): In this plan, excess capacity on several existing E–4 lines would be used to produce the new products. A minimum of new tooling would be developed. Production would be geared to satisfy demand, and advertising would be at the discretion of the local dealer.

Management decides to categorize the condition of the market (that is, the level of demand) for the new product line as either *strong* (S) or *weak* (W). The estimated net profit for each combination of strategy and market condition is given in Figure 16.1. In terms of the structure given in Chapter 15, the decisions are A, B, C, the sample space associated with the problem is $\{S, W\}$, and the entries in Figure 16.1 are the returns $R_j(i)$ associated with event i ($i = S$ or W) and decision j ($j = A$, B, or C). Note that these numbers

Figure 16.1 *Net profit data (millions of $) for the home and garden tractor problem*

Market Condition	Strategy		
	Aggressive (A)	Basic (B)	Cautious (C)
Strong (S)	30	20	5
Weak (W)	−8	7	15

Figure 16.2 *First step in creating a decision tree for the home and garden tractor problem*

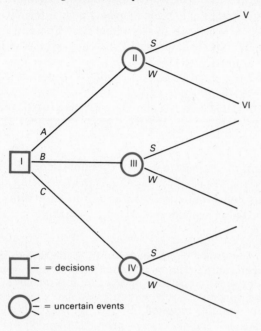

$R_j(i)$ represent the *net incremental change* in total profit to the firm for each combination of market condition and strategy. The fact that $R_C(S)$ is less than $R_C(W)$ is due to the fact that if there is a strong market for the new tractor and PROTRAC uses a cautious strategy, it will actually lose sales from its currently successful line of auxiliary products.

In order to use the basic model, the planner must assign a probability to each elementary event (weak and strong). As mentioned in footnote 1, this probability will be independent of the decision (A, B, or C). The optimal strategy is the one that yields the highest expected return. Suppose, for example, it is management's best judgment that the probability of a strong market condition is .45, that is, $P(S) = .45$. Then $P(W) = 1 - P(S) = .55$, and the expected returns associated with each of the decisions A, B, and C, respectively, would be calculated

$$ER_A = R_A(S)P(S) + R_A(W)P(W)$$
$$= 30\,(.45) + (-8)\,(.55) = 9.10$$
$$ER_B = 20\,(.45) + 7\,(.55) = 12.85$$
$$ER_C = 5\,(.45) + 15\,(.55) = 10.50$$

The *optimal* decision is to select the basic production and marketing strategy.

This marketing problem can also be represented by a diagram referred to as a *decision tree*. The first step in creating such a diagram is shown in Figure 16.2. In our exposition of decision trees, a *square node* will represent a point at which a decision must be made, and each line leading from a square will represent a possible decision. The *circular nodes* will represent encounters with uncertainty. As such, each node denoted as a circle has a sample space associated with it. Each line leading from a circle represents an occurrence of an elementary event in the sample space. The term *branches* will be employed for the lines emanating from the nodes, whether square or circular.

For the home and garden tractor problem, the decision tree in Figure 16.2 shows the initial node labeled I. Since it is square, a decision must be made. Thus management must choose one of the strategies A, B, or C. Depending on which decision is selected, a new position will be identified on the tree. For example, selecting strategy A brings about a transfer from node I to node II. Since node II, a circle, represents a sample space, the next branch to be followed depends on which of the events in the space will occur. If the market condition is strong, then position V is attained. If instead the market proves to be weak, then position VI will be attained. For obvious reasons, positions such as V and VI are referred to as *terminal positions*, and nodes II, III, and IV are called *terminal nodes*.

The part of a decision tree presented in Figure 16.2 provides an efficient way for management to visualize the interactions between decisions and uncertain events. However, if management wishes to use the decision tree to select an optimal decision, then some additional information must be appended to the diagram. In particular, one must find the return associated with each terminal position. This is called the *terminal value*. One must also assign a probability to each branch emanating from each circular node; in other words, a probability must be assigned to each elementary event in the sample space represented by such a node. For the basic model this is a simple task, and performing it yields the updated decision tree presented in Figure 16.3.

Figure 16.3 *Complete decision tree for home and garden tractor problem*

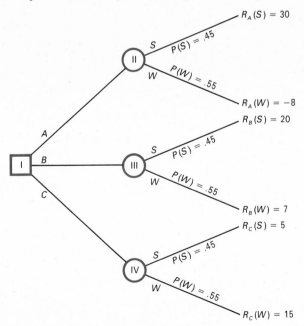

Completing the tree in this manner corresponds to the first three steps for analyzing a decision problem under uncertainty:

---

1 Define a sample space for the problem.
2 For each decision, assign a probability to each elementary event in the sample space.
3 For each decision, assign a return to each elementary event in the sample space.

Using a decision tree to find the optimal decision is called *solving the tree.* To solve a decision tree, one works backwards. First, the terminal branches (those which lead to terminal positions) are *eliminated* by calculating an *expected terminal value* for each terminal node. For example, consider node II in the home and garden tractor problem. The calculation to obtain the expected terminal value for this node is:

Expected terminal value = 30 (.45) + (−8)(.55) = 9.10

The branches emanating from the node are eliminated, and the expected terminal value of 9.10 is assigned to the node, as shown in Figure 16.4.

Figure 16.4 *Eliminating terminal branches*

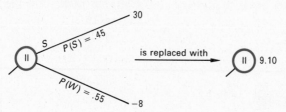

Performing the same calculations for nodes III and IV yields what is termed the *reduced decision tree,* which is shown in Figure 16.5 for the home and garden tractor problem.

Note that the expected terminal values on nodes II, III, and IV are identical to the expected returns computed earlier in this section for decisions. *A, B,* and *C,* respectively. Management now faces the simple problem of choosing the alternative that yields the highest expected terminal value. In this case, as we have seen earlier, the choice is alternative *B.*

This completes the analysis of the basic model in terms of a decision tree. Hopefully, it is clear that for the basic model a decision tree simply provides another more graphic way of viewing the same problem. Exactly the same information is utilized, and the same calculations are made whether one uses the steps described in Section 16.1 or one uses a decision tree to solve the problem.

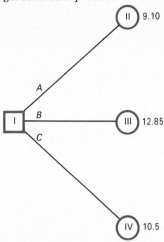

Figure 16.5 *Reduced decision tree for the home and garden tractor problem*

16.3 A Graphical Representation of the Expected Returns

Before proceeding to the next main topic, namely, a model in which new information becomes available concerning the likelihood of the uncertain events, it will be useful to consider again the expected return associated with each of the decisions in our previous example. We have already noted that to calculate the expected return of strategy A, one uses the relationship

$$ER_A = (30)\,P(S) + (-8)\,P(W)$$
$$= 30\,P(S) + (-8)\,[1 - P(S)]$$
$$= -8 + 38P(S)$$

This expected return is a linear function of the probability that the market response is strong.

A similar function can be found for alternatives B and C since

$$ER_B = 20P(S) + 7\,[1 - P(S)] = 7 + 13P(S)$$

and

$$ER_C = 5P(S) + 15\,[1 - P(S)] = 15 - 10P(S)$$

Each of these functions can now be plotted on the same set of axes, as illustrated in Figure 16.6. Since the criterion for making a decision is to select the decision that yields the highest expected return, Figure 16.6 clearly shows which decision is optimal for any particular value of $P(S)$. For example, it is seen that if $P(S)$ is larger than the value of $P(S)$ at which the graphs of ER_A and ER_B cross, then strategy A should be selected. The $P(S)$ value at which strategy

Figure 16.6   *Expected return as a function of P(S)*

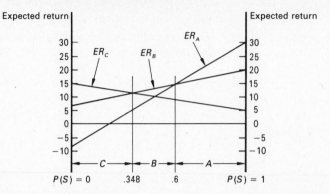

A becomes optimal can be found by setting ER_A equal to ER_B and solving for $P(S)$; that is,

$$ER_A = ER_B$$
$$-8 + 38P(S) = 7 + 13P(S)$$
$$25P(S) = 15$$
$$P(S) = .6$$

In a similar way, it is easily determined that the graphs of ER_C and ER_B cross when $P(S) = .348$, and Figure 16.6 indicates that PROTRAC should select the basic production and marketing strategy if $P(S)$ is larger than .348 and smaller than .6. The previous analysis, for the value $P(S) = .45$, prescribed the basic strategy, and this is consistent with Figure 16.6. However, the analysis of Figure 16.6 provides considerably more information than the previous analysis. It is now clear, for example, that the optimal decision in this case is not very sensitive to the assessment of the probability that the market is strong. The same strategy, B, remains optimal for an increase or decrease of more than .10 in the previously assessed probability, .45.

Although the diagram in Figure 16.6 is a useful pedagogical device for illustrating the sensitivity of the optimal solution to the assessment of probabilities, it should be clear that this device can only be used when there are two possible events in the sample space. If management had decided to categorize the market conditions as strong, *medium*, and weak, this graphical device could not be used.

16.4   Updating the Model: A Market Test for the Home and Garden Tractor

The management of PROTRAC's domestic tractor division was just on the verge of recommending the basic production and marketing strategy when the board of directors insisted that a market research study had to be performed. Only after such a study would the board be willing to approve the selection of a production and marketing strategy. As a result of the board's decision, management was constrained to consult the corporate marketing research group at PROTRAC headquarters. It was agreed that this group would perform a market research study and would report within a month on whether the study was encouraging, E, or discouraging, D. Thus, within a month the new-product planners would have this additional information with which to "update" the model. This new information should obviously be taken into account before making a decision on the marketing and production strategy. In particular, it should influence our assessment of the values $P(S)$ and $P(W)$. In this section, we shall discuss a formal technique for incorporating such new information into the decision process.

It is of course commonplace that new information concerning the likelihood of uncertain events becomes available in the course of the decision-making process. Indeed, many dollars are spent by management in both business and government in efforts to acquire additional information. Examples of such efforts are marketing research studies, quality-control tests, seismographic studies, opinion polls, account audits, pilot plants, and wire tapping.

Perhaps the most straightforward means of incorporating new information into the basic model is simply to reassess subjectively the probabilities assigned to the uncertain events, bearing the new information in mind, and proceed as before. To illustrate, suppose PROTRAC's management learns that the study performed by the market research group is encouraging, E. The original assessment $P(S)$ can now be replaced with the probability that the market is strong given the fact that the study is encouraging. The symbol $P(S|E)$ is used to denote this so-called *conditional probability* and is read "the probability of S, given E."

If the market test should turn out to be encouraging, management would construct the decision tree shown in Figure 16.7. Note that the only difference between this tree and the tree shown in Figure 16.3 is in the assessment of the probabilities assigned to the uncertain events. In Figure 16.7 the assessment is based on more information (the market test result) than in Figure 16.3.

As mentioned above, management could subjectively assess conditional probabilities like $P(S|E)$ directly, and in many circumstances that may be the best approach. There are, however, some formal theoretic relationships concerning conditional probabilities, and in some cases these relationships provide an approach more useful than direct assessment. Consequently, we shall turn to a discussion of these relationships before proceeding further with the analysis of Figure 16.7. As a final remark, it should be clear that if the result of the market test turns out to be D rather than E, then the conditional probabilities in Figure 16.7, $P(S|E)$ and $P(W|E)$, are replaced by $P(S|D)$ and $P(W|D)$.

16.4.1 Events and Conditional Probability

In order to more clearly understand the use of *conditional probability*, it is desirable to review our earlier discussion of *events*. Recall that in Chapter 15 *elementary events* were defined as the basic constituents of the sample space S. These elementary events are distinct entities. When the sample space S is produced by the possible outcomes of an experiment, then one and only one of these elementary events can occur. The probability of an elementary

Figure 16.7   *Home and garden tractor problem given that the test is encouraging*

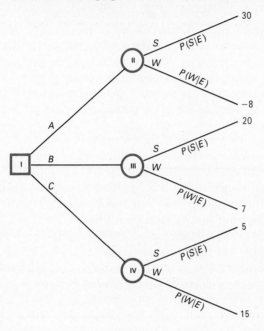

event is positive or zero, and the sum of the probabilities of all elementary events must equal one.

An *event* is a collection (subset) of elementary events. A trivial example of an event is an elementary event itself. That is, any particular elementary event is considered a subset of the set of all elementary events, and so the definition of an event fits.

As a more informative example, consider the sample space produced by the experiment consisting of a single throw of a fair die. Labeling the faces with the numbers 1 through 6 in the obvious way, the sample space is defined by the following set of elementary events:

{1, 2, 3, 4, 5, 6}

Our assumption that the die is fair means that we subjectively assess a probability of $\frac{1}{6}$ for each elementary event.

Now define the events A and B on the sample space as follows:

A occurs if an even number appears

B occurs if either of the numbers 2 or 4 appears

This means that A occurs if *any* elementary event in the set {2, 4, 6} occurs, and B occurs if *any* elementary event in the set {2, 4} occurs. Since A and B are each subsets of elementary events, they are each referred to as events. Thus

---

1 An event is a subset of elementary events.
2 An event is said to occur if any elementary event in the subset that defines it occurs.

It follows that

The probability of an event is the sum of the probabilities of the
constituent elementary events.

In the above example, it is easy to observe that the probability of A is $\frac{3}{6}$.
The probability of B is $\frac{2}{6}$.

In general, consider any sample space and let A and B be two events composed from elementary events in that space. We have defined the meaning of this statement and the meaning of "the probability of A" and "the probability of B." It is now desirable to sharpen and expand on the definition given in Chapter 15 of a new event called *A and B*, frequently denoted as AB, or $A \cap B$.

The event AB is the set of all elementary events belonging to both A and
B.

In the above example involving a single throw of a fair die, the event AB is the *intersection* of the sets $\{2, 4, 6\}$ and $\{2, 4\}$. Thus $AB = \{2, 4\}$. Since AB is an event, it has a probability, which is called the *joint probability* of A and B. This joint probability is computed by summing the probabilities of the elementary events comprising AB. Clearly then, $P(AB) = P(BA)$. In the above example

$$P(AB) = P(BA) = P(\{2, 4\}) = \tfrac{2}{6}$$

As already mentioned, an elementary event is a special case of an event. But if A and B are themselves elementary events, by definition they have no elementary events in common. In this special case, it must be true that the joint probability is zero.

With this view of probabilities and events it is now possible to give a formal definition for *conditional probability*. Let A and B be events from some specified experiment. The *conditional probability* of B, given that event A occurs, is denoted as $P(B|A)$ and is *defined* as follows:

$P(B|A) = \dfrac{P(BA)}{P(A)}$ *where* $P(A) > 0.$

Similarly, $P(A|B) = \dfrac{P(AB)}{P(B)}$ *where* $P(B) > 0.$

In our example with the die, the expression $P(B|A)$ is interpreted as the probability of a 2 or a 4 given that an even number appears. Applying the above formula for $A = \{2, 4, 6\}$, $B = \{2, 4\}$, we have

$$P(B|A) = \frac{P(BA)}{P(A)} = \frac{P(\{2, 4\})}{P(\{2, 4, 6\})} = \frac{2/6}{3/6} = \frac{2}{3}$$

In contrast, note that $P(B) = \frac{1}{3}$. Thus the probability of B and the probability of B given A are different in this case. The *knowledge* that A has occurred increases the *probability* that B has also occurred. For the same example with the die it is seen that

$$P(A|B) = \frac{P(AB)}{P(B)} = \frac{P(\{2, 4\})}{P(\{2, 4\})} = \frac{2/6}{2/6} = 1$$

As additional examples from the experiment with the die consider the following:

| EXAMPLE 1 | EXAMPLE 2 |

A = even number

A = even number

B = number 2

B = odd number

$P(A) \quad = \frac{3}{6}, P(B) = \frac{1}{6}, P(AB) = \frac{1}{6}$

$P(A) \quad = \frac{3}{6}, P(B) = \frac{3}{6}, P(AB) = 0$

$P(B|A) = \dfrac{P(BA)}{P(A)} = \dfrac{1/6}{3/6} = \frac{1}{3}$

$P(B|A) = \dfrac{P(BA)}{P(A)} = \dfrac{0}{3/6} = 0$

$P(A|B) = \dfrac{P(AB)}{P(B)} = \dfrac{1/6}{1/6} = 1$

$P(A|B) = \dfrac{P(AB)}{P(B)} = \dfrac{0}{3/6} = 0$

The above examples are simple and straightforward, but in many cases it is easy to be misled in thinking about conditional probabilities. It is a good general rule to write down the definition of the events and to use the definition of conditional probability to check your thinking. A case in point is provided by the following gambling game that supposedly has been associated with carnivals since medieval times. The gambler has three cards: the first is colored on both sides, the second is white on both sides, and the third is colored on one side and white on the other (see Figure 16.8). The player is blindfolded and then draws one of the three cards at random from a small barrel and places it on the table. The blindfold is then removed. The gambler bets that the color on the other side of the card is the same as the color showing. He pays you $1 if he is wrong. Otherwise you pay him $1. He argues the fairness of the game as follows: "After your blindfold is removed, you will see either white or color showing. Suppose you see a color. You now know [see Figure 16.8] that we have either card I or card III. If it is card I, I win. If it is Card III, you win. Since the cards are equally likely, the probability that you win is $\frac{1}{2}$. Thus we each have the same chance of winning."

Although history suggests that this argument is persuasive, you may already see that it is also incorrect. The error is in the assertion that if color

igure 16.8 *Cards for a gambling game*

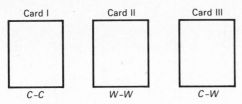

Card I   Card II   Card III

C–C   W–W   C–W

is showing then the probability of card I equals the probability of card III equals $\frac{1}{2}$.

To determine the true situation, it is helpful to use the definition of conditional probability. We wish to calculate P (color is down|color is showing). To do this, we number the faces of the cards as in Figure 16.9, where the number in the dotted circle indicates the back side of the card.

We now use this numbering scheme to define the sample space, S; $S = \{1, 2, 3, 4, 5, 6\}$. The fact that the side showing is drawn at random means that each of the six sides is equally likely to be showing. Hence, we assign the same probability to each elementary event, and $P(1) = P(2) = P(3) = P(4) = P(5) = P(6) = \frac{1}{6}$.

We now proceed to calculate P (color is down|color is showing) from the definition

$$P \text{ (color is down|color is showing)} = \frac{P \text{(color is down } and \text{ color is showing)}}{P \text{(color is showing)}}$$

Consider the individual terms in this expression:

1 The event "color is down *and* color is showing" means that side 1 or side 2 is showing; this is the event $\{1, 2\}$. Thus

$$P \text{(color is down } and \text{ color is showing)} = \frac{2}{6}$$

2 The event "color is showing" occurs if side 1, 2, or 5 is showing. Thus

$$P \text{(color is showing)} = \frac{3}{6}$$

Using the definition of conditional probability,

igure 16.9 *The cards revisited*

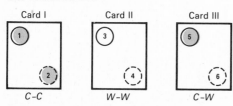

Card I   Card II   Card III

C–C   W–W   C–W

$$P(\text{color is down}|\text{color is showing}) = \frac{2/6}{3/6} = \frac{2}{3}$$

Now consider the outcome of the game to be an uncertain event. The sample space for the game has two elementary events, gambler wins and gambler loses $\{W, L\}$. From the previous discussion we assess $P(W) = \frac{2}{3}$ and $P(L) = \frac{1}{3}$. The net returns are $C(W) = 1.00$ and $C(L) = -1.00$. Thus

$$EC = 2/3(1.00) + 1/3(-1.00) = .66 - .33 = .33$$

Since the expected return to the gambler is 33¢ per trial, this is clearly a most desirable game from his point of view.

16.4.2 Bayes' Theorem

Let us now return to PROTRAC'S home and garden tractor problem to see how the definition of conditional probability can be used to update our earlier assessment $P(S)$ to a new assessment $P(S|E)$, which is the probability that the market will be strong given that the test results are encouraging. It is instructive to describe the home and garden tractor problem in terms of the discussion in Section 16.4.1. An experiment that produces the appropriate sample space for this problem can be described as follows:

1   Perform the market test and classify the result as E or D.
2   Distribute the new product, observe sales, and classify the result as S or W.

The elementary events in the sample space are found by creating all possible combinations of outcomes from steps 1 and 2. There are thus four elementary events in the sample space. In particular, the *elementary events* comprising the sample space are "encouraging *and* strong," ES; "encouraging *and* weak," EW; "discouraging *and* strong," DS; "discouraging *and* weak," DW.

We shall now use this sample space and appropriately assessed probabilities to update Figure 16.3 by replacing $P(S)$ with the value of $P(S|E)$, as in Figure 16.7. By definition,

$$P(S|E) = \frac{P(S \text{ and } E)}{P(E)} = \frac{P(SE)}{P(E)}$$

but this is not immediately useful since neither $P(E)$ nor $P(SE)$ is known. Management has at its disposal only its earlier assessment of $P(S)$, the probability that the market is strong, and $P(W)$, the probability that the market is weak. These earlier assessments $P(S)$ and $P(W)$ are referred to as *prior probabilities* since they are known prior to any information that the experiment may yield. The conditional probability $P(S|E)$ is also called the *posterior probability* of S. Certainly management must have beliefs in the reliability of the market research test. Otherwise it is doubtful that the results of the test could contribute much to a new assessment of market strength. This statement is true whether one assesses the conditional probability $P(S|E)$ subjectively or, alternatively, uses the formal definition. In this case it turns out that management's beliefs are formed from direct past experience with the use of the test in marketing other new products. In particular, the marketing research group is able to state the following indication of reliability: "The past results with our test have tended to be in the right direction. If a market has been strong, the test results have been encouraging 60 percent of the time. If a market has been weak, the test results have been discouraging 70 percent of the time." Management can use this information to assess the conditional probabilities of the test results given the market conditions. This assessment is:

$P(E|S) = .6 \quad P(E|W) = .3$

$P(D|S) = .4 \quad P(D|W) = .7$

Since $P(SE) = P(ES) = P(E|S)[P(S)]$ and we now know $(PE|S)$ from past data and $P(S)$ from our earlier assessment, we are in a position to calculate $P(SE)$, the numerator of the expression for $P(S|E)$. The denominator, $P(E)$, is the probability that the test is encouraging. In terms of the sample space, the event E will occur if any elementary event that includes an encouraging test result occurs. Thus,

$E = \{ES, EW\}$

From the definition of elementary events it follows that

$P(E) = P(ES) + P(EW)$

Other events of interest are

$D = \{DS, DW\}$

$S = \{ES, DS\}$

$W = \{EW, DW\}$

The process of calculating $P(S|E)$ is illustrated in Figure 16.10. This figure establishes the fact that

$$P(S|E) = \frac{P(E|S) \, P(S)}{P(E|S) \, P(S) + P(E|W) \, P(W)}$$

gure 16.10 *Calculating $P(S|E)$*

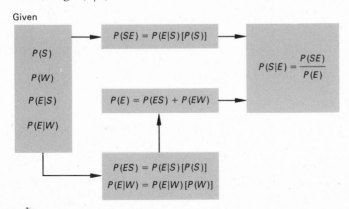

This relationship is a special case of the following result called **Bayes' theorem** after the English philosopher Thomas Bayes. Stated in general terms, suppose that $Z_1, ..., Z_n$ is a collection of pairwise disjoint events whose union is the entire sample space. Let A and B be any two events. Bayes' theorem states that

$$P(A|B) = \frac{P(B|A)\,P(A)}{\sum\limits_{i=1}^{n} P(B|Z_i)\,P(Z_i)}$$

Recalling in the above example that $P(S) = .45$, $P(W) = .55$, Bayes' theorem can now be applied to obtain

$$P(S|E) = \frac{.6(.45)}{.6(.45) + .3(.55)} = \frac{.270}{.435} = .621$$

Similarly, we can apply the theorem to obtain $P(W|E)$, as follows:

$$P(W|E) = \frac{P(WE)}{P(E)} = \frac{P(E|W)\,P(W)}{P(EW) + P(ES)} = \frac{P(E|W)\,P(W)}{P(E|W)\,P(W) + P(E|S)\,P(S)}$$

$$= \frac{(.3)(.55)}{(.3)(.55) + (.6)(.45)} = .379$$

Figure 16.11 *Home and garden tractor problem decision tree with posterior probabilities*

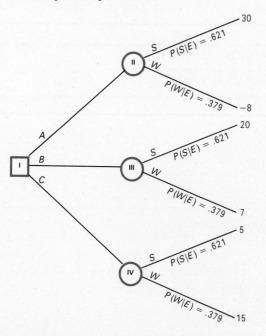

Figure 16.12 *Reduced decision tree with updated probabilities*

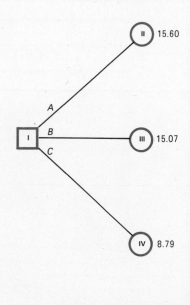

The availability of this information makes it possible to complete the decision tree for the home and garden tractor problem for the case in which the result of the market research test is encouraging. The results are shown in Figure 16.11. The reader should compare this with Figure 16.3.

It is now possible to employ the usual technique to determine *the optimal decision*. That is, computing the new expected terminal values we obtain the reduced decision tree shown in Figure 16.12. The optimal strategy is aggressive. In our earlier analysis using the prior probabilities (refer to Figures 16.3 and 16.5) the optimal strategy had been basic. Use of the new information in the form of posterior probabilities leads in this case to a new optimal decision. We might note that in this case Figure 16.6 can also be used to determine the optimal strategy. Since $P(S|E)$ is greater than .6, this figure also indicates that the appropriate decision is to adopt the aggressive strategy.

The same analysis can be applied to the case in which the result of the market research study is discouraging. The reader can verify that the optimal decision in this instance is to select the cautious marketing and production strategy. The results of these two analyses can be conveniently summarized in a *decision table* like the one in Figure 16.13.

Figure 16.13   *An optimal decision table*

Test Result	Optimal Decision
Encouraging, E	Aggressive, A
Discouraging, D	Cautious, C

16.5   Sequential Decisions: To Test or Not to Test

In the previous section, we assumed that the board of directors had decided to have a marketing research study done. We then considered the question of how the management of PROTRAC's domestic tractor division should use the information generated by the study to update the decision model. Let us step back for a moment, however. It seems clear that the decision to have a market research study done or not is no different in essence from the decision to adopt one marketing and production strategy or another. Management must carefully weigh the cost of performing the study against the gain that might result from having the information that the study would produce. It is also clear that the decision on whether or not to have a market research test is not an isolated decision. If the test is given, then management must still select one of the marketing and production strategies. Thus, the value of performing the test depends in part on how PROTRAC uses the information generated by the test. In other words, the value of an initial decision depends on a *sequence* of decisions and uncertain events that will follow the initial decision. This is called a *sequential decision problem.*

This is an extremely common type of management problem and is actually the kind of situation that decision trees are designed to handle. It is in cases where there are a number of interrelated decisions and uncertain events that the ability to display the problem graphically is especially useful. The decision tree for the decision to perform the market research test or not is presented in Figure 16.14.

With one exception, the notation and conventions used in this diagram are the same as those that have been employed earlier in this chapter. The exception concerns the notation used to denote the terminal values. This notation requires some comment. The term $R(E, S; T, A)$ is the actual *net* return to PROTRAC if the sequence of uncertain events and decisions described by the uppermost path of branches on the tree occurs, namely, if management decides to conduct a test (T), the result is encouraging (E), management chooses the aggressive (A) strategy, and the market is strong (S).

The terminal values, such as $R(E, S; T, A)$, are calculated by assigning to appropriate branches *net* cash flows as they occur and then summing along the sequence of branches leading to the terminal value. For illustrative purposes, assume that the cost of the test is $500,000. The net cash flows and the probabilities for the test or no-test problem are attached to the tree in Figure

Figure 16.14 *To test or not: the home and garden tractor problem*

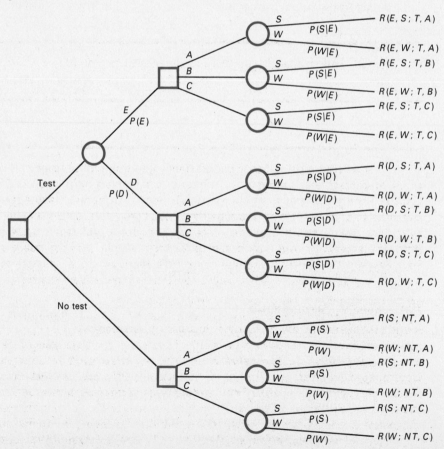

gure 16.15   *Test or no-test tree with returns and*
probabilities assigned

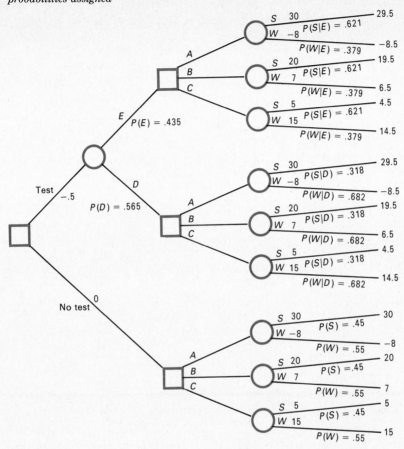

16.15. The cost of the test is written beside the branch labeled *Test*. It is negative because it is a cash outflow. The value of $R(E, S; T, A)$ in this figure is 29.5. This is obtained by summing the net cash flows along the uppermost sequence of branches of the tree, that is, the market return of 30 (refer to Figure 16.1) minus the test expenditure of .5. The probabilities $P(S|E)$ and $P(W|E)$ were computed in Section 16.4.2 for use in Figure 16.11. You should be able to derive the values for $P(S|D)$, $P(W|D)$, $P(E)$ and $P(D)$ from the data and discussion presented in Section 16.4.2.

Once each terminal value (net cash flow along each sequence of branches) and each probability is assigned, one solves the tree in the same manner as before; namely, by starting at the end of the tree and working backwards. Two types of steps are required:

1   A circular, or chance, node is reduced by calculating the expected return of the branches emanating from the node.

2   A square, or decision, node is reduced by selecting the decision associated with the branch that has the highest expected return.

Figure 16.16 *Solving the test or no-test tree, step 1*

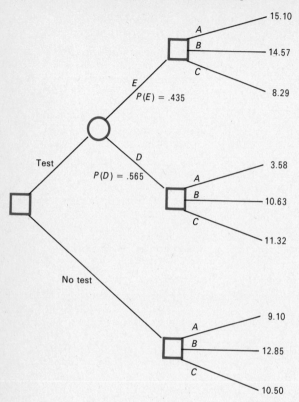

Figure 16.17 *Solving the test or no-test tree, step 2*

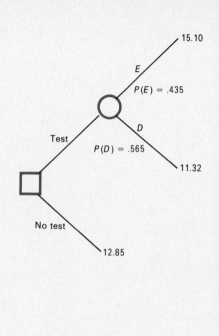

The step in item 1 is used to move from Figure 16.15 to Figure 16.16. For example, the top circular node at the end of the tree is replaced with the value $15.10 = (.621)(29.5) - (.379)(8.5)$. The step in item 2 is used to move from Figure 16.16 to Figure 16.17.

By repeating these steps as necessary, the original tree presented in Figure 16.15 is reduced to the tree shown in Figure 16.18. From this tree it is clear that the optimal decision is to have the test. In the process of arriving at this result we have already established (in Figure 16.13) what the optimal decisions will be after the test result is known. The optimal decision is A if the test result is E, and C if the test result is D.

In summary, then, the following overall optimal decision rule has been selected:

1 Have the market research test taken.
2 If the test results are encouraging, select the aggressive marketing and production strategy.
3 If the test results are discouraging, select the cautious marketing and production strategy.

This example demonstrates that problems involving a sequence of decisions and uncertain events can be solved by repeated applications of the techniques

Figure 16.18 *Solving the test or no-test tree, final step*

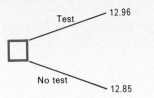

used to solve the basic tree. This example also completes the series of tasks described in Section 16.1. Decision trees have been used to analyze the basic model, the model with new information, and a model involving a sequence of decisions and uncertain events. The fundamental concepts of assigning probabilities to uncertain events, payoffs to combinations of decisions and uncertain events, and calculating expected returns have been applied in each of these models.

16.6 Examples and Solutions

Example 1

The customer service manager for PROTRAC is responsible for expediting late orders. To do his job effectively, when an order is late he must determine if the lateness is caused by an ordering error or a delivery error. If an order is late, one or the other of these two types of errors must have occurred. Because of the way in which this system is designed, both errors cannot occur on the same order. From past experience, he knows that an ordering error will cause 8 out of 20 deliveries to be late, whereas a delivery error will cause 8 out of 10 deliveries to be late. Historically, out of 1,000 orders, 30 ordering errors and 10 delivery errors have occurred.

Assume an order is late. If the customer service manager wishes to look first for the type of error that has the largest probability of occurring, should he look for an ordering error or a delivery error?

Solution to Example 1

Let

L = the event that an order is late

O = the event that an ordering error is made

D = the event that a delivery error is made

The problem is to find the maximum of $P(O|L)$ and $P(D|L)$. From the data in the problem it seems reasonable to assess the following probabilities:

$$P(O) = .03$$
$$P(D) = .01$$
$$P(L|O) = .40$$
$$P(L|D) = .80$$

From Bayes' theorem

$$P(O|L) = \frac{P(L|O)\,P(O)}{P(L|O)\,P(O) + P(L|D)\,P(D)}$$

$$P(D|L) = \frac{P(L|D)\,P(D)}{P(L|D)\,P(D) + P(L|O)\,P(O)}$$

Thus

$$P(O|L) = \frac{(.4)(.03)}{(.4)(.03) + (.8)(.01)} = .6$$

$$P(D|L) = \frac{(.8)(.01)}{(.8)(.01) + (.4)(.03)} = .4$$

Thus the customer service manager should first check on whether an ordering error has been made.

Example 2

This example is an abstraction and simplification of a decision problem faced by a nationally known chemical company. It seems that the firm was faced with two related law suits for patent infringement. For each suit, the firm had the option of going to trial or settling out of court. The trial date for one of the suits which we will cleverly identify as suit 1 was scheduled for July 15 and the second (suit 2, of course) was scheduled for January of the following year. Preparation costs for either trial are estimated at $10,000. However, if the firm prepares for both trials, the preparation costs of the second trial will only be $6,000. These costs can be avoided by settling out of court.

If the firm wins suit 1, it pays no penalty. If it loses, it pays a $200,000 penalty. Lawyers for the firm assess the probability of winning suit 1 as .5. The firm has the option to settle out of court for $100,000.

Suit 2 can be settled out of court for a cost of $60,000. Otherwise, a trial will result in one of three possible outcomes: (1) the suit is declared invalid and the firm pays no penalty; (2) the suit is found valid but with no infringement, and

Figure 16.19 *Probabilities for outcomes of suit 2 given the results of suit 1*

Outcomes	No Information Concerning Suit 1[a]	Firm Wins Suit 1	Firm Loses Suit 1
Invalid	.3	.7	.1
Valid, no infringement	.3	.2	.5
Valid, infringement	.4	.1	.4

[a]That is, suit 1 is settled out of court.

the firm pays a penalty of $50,000; (3) the suit is found valid with infringement, and the firm pays a penalty of $90,000.

The likelihood of these outcomes depends in general on the result of suit 1. The judge will certainly view suit 1 as an important precedent. The lawyers' assessment of the probability of the three possible outcomes of suit 2 under three sets of possible conditions (relating to suit 1) are presented in Figure 16.19.

a Represent the firm's problem with a decision tree.
b Solve the decision tree and find the optimal decision rule for the firm.
c What is the expected loss that the firm will incur if it follows the optimal strategy?
d What decisions would be made if the firm treated each suit independently, ignoring any interactions between the two? What is the expected savings from the decision analysis of this scenario?

Solution to Example 2

a The decision tree representing the firm's problem is shown in Figure 16.20. Since all numerical entries are costs, negative values need not be used.

Figure 16.20 *Decision tree for the lawsuit problem*

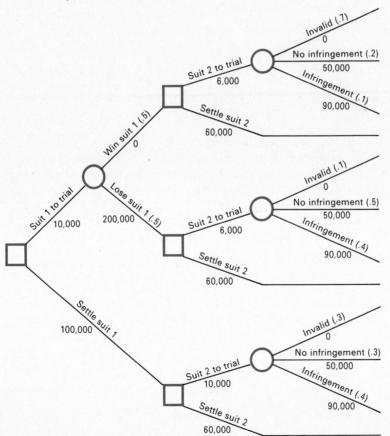

Figure 16.21   *Lawsuit problem with terminal values*

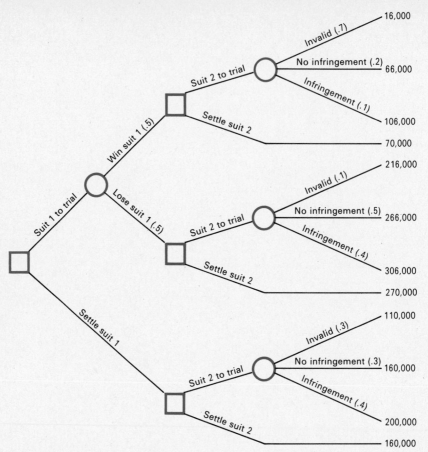

b   Solving the decision tree requires several steps. First, the value of each
terminal position is determined, as in Figure 16.21. Each circular terminal
node is then reduced by determining its expected cost. Figure 16.22 shows
the results. The decision that minimizes the expected cost is then made for
each terminal decision node. Figure 16.23 shows the results. Finally,
replacing the remaining circular node by its expected cost yields the end
result in Figure 16.24.

The optimal initial decision thus is to take suit 1 to trial. Figure 16.22 shows
that if the firm wins suit 1, then the second decision is to take suit 2 to trial.
If, on the other hand, the firm loses suit 1, then the second decision is to settle
suit 2 out of court.

c   The expected loss associated with the optimal strategy is $152,500.
d   For suit 1, the expected cost of taking the case to trial is
(.5)(210,000) + .5(10,000) = $110,000. The cost of settling out of court is
100,000, and thus this is the optimal decision. For suit 2 by itself, the
optimal decision is obtained by comparing $60,000, the cost of settling, with

ure 16.22 *Lawsuit problem after the first reduction*

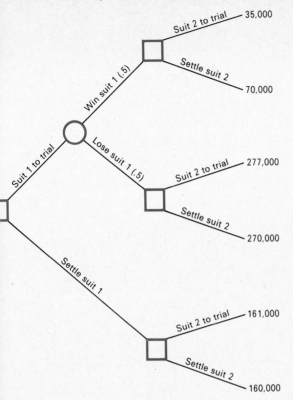

Figure 16.23 *Another reduction in the lawsuit problem*

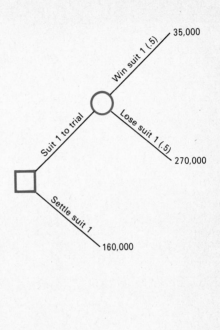

gure 16.24 *Final tree for the lawsuit problem*

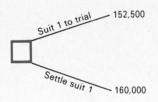

$61,000, the expected cost of a trial. Hence, the optimal decision is also to settle out of court. Treating cases independently, the expected total cost is thus 100,000 + 60,000 = $160,000, as opposed to an expected total cost of $152,500 associated with the optimal strategy. The expected savings due to the decision analysis is therefore $7,500.

16.7 **Summary of Key Concepts**

The use of conditional probabilities is a method of formally incorporating new information into the assessment of probabilities. The conditional probability of event B, given that event A has occurred, is defined as $P(B|A) = P(BA)/P(A)$. (Section 16.4.1)

Suppose that $Z_1, ..., Z_n$ is a collection of pairwise disjoint events whose union is the entire sample space. Let A and B be any two events. Bayes' theorem states that

$$P(A|B) = \frac{P(B|A)\,P(A)}{\displaystyle\sum_{i=1}^{n} P(B|Z_i)\,P(Z_i)}$$

(Section 16.4.2)

A general model for decision making under uncertainty involves a sequence (in time) of decisions and uncertain events. Such a model can be represented by a decision tree.
(Section 16.1)

Consider the generalized version of a single branch of a decision tree shown in Figure 16.25. This branch illustrates the following rules for constructing a decision tree.

Figure 16.25 *Generalized version of a single branch of a decision tree*

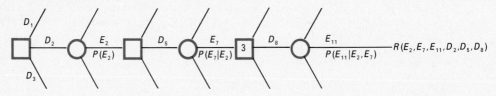

1 *Branches emanating from square nodes and labeled D_j represent decisions.*

2 *Branches emanating from circular nodes and labeled E_i represent uncertain events.*

3 *Probabilities are attached to each uncertain event. The probability of any specific event is conditional on the occurrence of all of the events that lead to the node from which the specific event emanates. For example, the probability that E_{11} occurs is conditional on the fact that events E_2 and E_7 have occurred.*

4 *$R(E_2, E_7, E_{11}, D_2, D_5, D_8)$ is the net cash flow that occurs along this particular branch. In a model involving both inflows and outflows, the outflows are represented by negative numbers. Cash flows are attached to decisions and/or chance events as appropriate and R( ) is calculated by summing along the branch.*
(Sections 16.2 and 16.5)

A decision tree is solved by working backward (from the terminal nodes) by using two techniques:

1 *A circular node is replaced by the expected value of the branches emanating from that node.*

2 *For each square node, the decision with the highest expected return is selected*

as part of the optimal policy. The node is then replaced with that expected return.
(Sections 16.2 and 16.5)

The solution to the decision tree consists of a sequential strategy of the following form:

1   Of the branches emanating from the first square node, suppose D_j has the highest expected return. Then D_j is the first decision to be implemented.

2   Observe the first uncertain event. Suppose it is E_i. This leads to a new square node and the associated decision (identified in item 2 immediately above). This is the next decision to be implemented.

3   Observe the next uncertain event. This will determine the next square node encountered. Continue in this fashion.
(Sections 16.2 and 16.5)

16.8 Problems

1 An urn contains 50 balls, as follows:
(1) Four sets of balls numbered 1 through 5, a total of 20 balls, are blue.
(2) Five sets of balls numbered 1 through 4, a total of 20 balls, are red.
(3) Two sets of balls numbered 1 through 5, a total of 10 balls, are white.
A ball is selected at random from the urn, and both the color of the ball and the number are recorded.
a What is the sample space for this experiment?
b Assign a probability to each elementary event.

c Let B = the event that a blue ball is drawn

R = the event that a red ball is drawn

W = the event that a white ball is drawn

i = the event that a ball with the number i is drawn

Find $P(B)$, $P(3)$, $P(B \cap 3)$, $P(B \cup 3)$, $P(B|3)$, $P(3|B)$.

2 The probability that a married man will vote in a presidential election is .6. However, the probability that a married woman will vote given that her husband votes is .9. What is the probability that a husband and wife both vote in the next presidential election?

3 A sociologist believes that married women are more apt to vote in a presidential election than married men. Assume the data in problem 2 are correct and let $P(W|\overline{H})$ equal the probability that a married woman will vote if her husband does not. What is the smallest value of $P(W|\overline{H})$ that would support the sociologist's belief?

4 Consider the following dice game. A pair of fair dice is rolled. The sum of the faces showing is called *the point*. The player now rolls the dice again. If the sum of the faces showing is less than or equal to the point, he wins. Otherwise, he loses.
a Suppose on the first throw he rolls a 4 (the point is 4). What is the probability that the player wins the game?
b The house offers to pay $10 if the player wins and $0 if he loses. Assuming that the player's utility is linear in dollars (he is risk indifferent), what is the most he should be willing to pay to play this game? (Assume this decision is made *before* the player establishes his point.)

5 A certain retail firm places applicants for credit into two categories, bad risks and good risks. Statistics indicate that 10 percent of the population would be classified as a bad risk by the firm's standards. The firm uses a credit-scoring device to decide whether or not credit should be granted to an applicant. Experience suggests that if a good risk applies, he will get credit 90 percent of the time. If a bad risk applies, he will get credit 20 percent of the time. Management believes that it is reasonable to assume that the persons who apply for credit are selected at random from the population. What is the probability that a person granted credit will be a bad risk? (Use Bayes' theorem.)

6 At PROTRAC's Moline plant, crankshafts are produced on each of two large automatic machines. The newer of the two machines is both faster and more reliable than the older machine. Out of a lot-size of 1,000 crankshafts, 600 would be produced on the new machine. The new machine produces defective crankshafts at the rate of 1 out of 100, whereas the old machine produces defects at the rate of 3 per 100. What is the probability that a defective piece selected at random was produced on the new machine?

7 A gambler has an opportunity to play the following two-stage game. At stage 1 he pays $10 and draws a ball at random from an urn containing 45 white and 55 red balls. The balls are identical except for color. The player may now quit or move on to play stage 2 at the cost of an additional $10. In stage 2, if a white ball was drawn in stage 1, the player draws a ball at random from a white urn that contains 70 blue and 30 green balls. If a red ball was drawn in stage 1, the player draws a ball at random from a red urn that contains 10 blue and 90 green balls.

If in stage 2 the player draws a blue ball, the house pays him $50. If he draws a green ball, the house pays him $0.

Use a decision tree to determine the optimal decision rule for the gambler. What is the maximum amount the gambler should be willing to pay to play the game with his optimal strategy?

8 Johnson's Metal, (JM), a small manufacturer of metal parts, is attempting to decide whether or not to enter the competition to be a supplier of transmission housings for PROTRAC. In order to compete, the firm must design a test fixture for the production process and produce 10 housings that PROTRAC will test. The cost of development, that is, designing and building the fixture and the test housings, is $50,000. If JM gets the order, an event estimated as occurring with probability .4, it will be possible to sell 10,000 items to PROTRAC for $50 each. If JM does not get the order, the development cost is essentially lost. In order to produce the housings, JM may either use its current machines or purchase a new forge. Tooling with the current machines will cost $40,000 and the per-unit production cost is $20. However, if JM uses its current machines, it runs the risk of incurring overtime costs. The relationship between overtime costs and the status of JM's other business is presented in Figure 16.26.

Figure 16.26   *Cost and probability data for Johnson's Metal problem*

Other Business	Probability	Overtime Cost to JM($)
Heavy	.2	200,000
Normal	.7	100,000
Light	.1	0

The new forge costs $260,000, including tooling costs for the transmission housings. However, with the new forge, JM would certainly not incur any overtime costs, and the production cost will be only $10 per unit.
Use a decision tree to determine the optimal set of actions for JM.

17 *Forecasting*

This chapter deals on a conceptual level with the topic of forecasting. Primary emphasis is placed on the rationale underlying the two main classes of forecasting models: piggyback models, which rely on other variables; and bootstrap models, which rely on the extrapolation of previous observations on the variable of interest. Some basic techniques, such as the method of least squares and exponential smoothing, are used to illustrate the two approaches to forecasting. A discussion of the importance of random walks and the role of historical data in testing models concludes the chapter.

17.1 Introduction

The date is June 15, 1941. Joachim von Ribbentrop, Hitler's special envoy, is meeting in Venice with Count Ciano, the Italian Foreign Minister, whereupon von Ribbentrop says, "My dear Ciano, I cannot tell you anything as yet because every decision is locked in the impenetrable bosom of the Führer. However, one thing is certain: if we attack, the Russia of Stalin will be erased from the map within eight weeks."[1] Seven days later, on June 22, Nazi Germany launched Operation Barbarossa and declared war on Russia. With this decision, a chain of events that led to the end of the Third Reich had been set in motion, and the course of history was dramatically changed.

Although few decisions are this significant, it is clearly true that many of the most important decisions made by individuals and organizations crucially depend on an assessment of the future. Predictions or forecasts with greater accuracy than that achieved by the German General Staff are thus fervidly hoped for and in some cases diligently worked for.

Economic forecasting considered by itself is an important activity. Government policies and business decisions are based on forecasts of the gross national product, the level of unemployment, the demand for refrigerators, and so on. Among the major insurance companies, it is difficult to find an investment department that does not have a contract with some expert or firm to obtain economic forecasts on a regular basis. Billions of dollars of investments in

---

1 Alan Louis Charles Bullock, *Hitler: A Study in Tyranny* (New York: Harper and Row, 1962), p. 648.

mortgages and bonds are influenced by these forecasts. Each year, over 2,000 people show up to hear the views of three economists on the economic outlook at a Forecast Luncheon sponsored by the University of Chicago. The data are overwhelming. Economic forecasting *is* important. Also, there is clearly a steady increase in the use of quantitative forecasting models by industry and government. In Chapter 13, we have already referred to the widespread use of inventory control programs that include a forecasting subroutine. For economic entities such as the GNP or exchange rates, many firms now rely on econometric models for their forecasts. These models, which consist of a system of statistically estimated equations, have made an important impact on the decision processes both in industry and government. According to the August 2, 1977 *Wall Street Journal,* "Although there isn't any solid evidence that model building produces much better predictions than any other forecasting method, businessmen in the current uncertain economy are highly curious about the future and how to plan for it. And they are relying more and more on econometrics."

Quantitative forecasting models possess two important and attractive features.

---

1 They are by definition expressed in mathematical notation. Thus, they establish an unambiguous record of how the forecast is made. This provides an excellent vehicle for communication about the forecast among those who are concerned. Furthermore, it provides an opportunity for systematic modification and improvement of the forecasting technique. In a quantitative model, coefficients can be modified and/or terms added until the model yields good results. (This assumes that the relationship expressed in the model is basically sound.)

2 With the use of computers, quantitative models can be based on an amazing quantity of data.

For example, a major oil company was considering a reorganization and expansion of its domestic marketing facilities (gasoline stations). Everyone understood that this was a pivotal decision for the firm. The size of the proposed capital investment alone, not to mention the possible effects on the revenue from gasoline sales, dictated that this decision be made by the board of directors. In order to evaluate the alternative expansion strategies, the board needed forecasts of the demand for gasoline in each of its more than 100 marketing regions for each of the next 15 years. Each of these 1,500 estimates was based on a combination of several factors including the population and the level of new construction in each region. Without the use of computers and quantitative models, a study involving this level of detail would generally be impossible. In a similar way, the inventory control systems that require forecasts that are updated on a monthly basis for literally thousands of items could not be constructed without quantitative models and computers.

The technical literature related to quantitative forecasting models is enormous, and a high level of technical sophistication is required to understand the intricacies of the models in certain areas. However, the models can be conveniently separated into two categories on the basis of their underlying approaches. These two categories, which we choose to call *piggyback models* and *bootstrap models* are discussed in the following two sections.

17.2 Piggyback Forecasting Models

In a *piggyback model,* the forecast for the quantity of interest "rides piggyback" on another quantity or set of quantities. In more precise terms, let y denote a value for some variable of interest, and let $\hat{y}$ denote a predicted or forecast value for that variable. Then, in a piggyback model,

$$\hat{y} = f(x_1, x_2, ..., x_n)$$

where f is a forecasting rule, or function, and $x_1, x_2, ..., x_n$ is a set of variables.

Consider the following examples:

1 If y is the demand for baby food, then x might be the number of children between 7 and 24 months old.
2 If y is the demand for plumbing fixtures, then x_1 and x_2 might be the number of housing starts and the number of existing houses, respectively.
3 If y is the traffic volume on a proposed expressway, then x_1 and x_2 might be the traffic volume on each of two nearby existing highways.
4 If y is the yield of usable material per pound of ingredients from a proposed chemical plant, then x might be the same quantity produced by a small-scale experimental plant.

In the representation $\hat{y} = f(x_1, ..., x_n)$, the x variables are often called independent variables. In order for a piggyback model to make sense, the independent variables must either be known in advance or it must be possible to forecast them more easily than y, the variable of interest. Knowing a functional relationship between the pounds of sauerkraut and the number of bratwurst sold in Milwaukee in the same year may be interesting to sociologists, but unless sauerkraut usage can be easily predicted, the relationship is of little value for anyone in the bratwurst forecasting business.

17.2.1 *The Method of Least Squares*

Suppose a manager believes there is a relationship between a knowable independent variable (say, traffic volume at an intersection) and a variable of interest (gasoline sales). In order to use a piggyback model, he still needs to find a functional relationship between these two variables. For illustrative purposes, consider a problem with one independent variable in which n previous observations are available. Let x denote the independent variable, y denote the variable to be predicted, also called the dependent variable. Finally, let x_i, y_i for $i = 1, 2, ..., n$ be the pairs of past observations. The problem then is:

Find a forecasting function f of a single independent variable so that each prediction $\hat{y}_i = f(x_i)$ is "close to" the true historical value y_i.

The *method of least squares* is a popular and relatively simple technique for "solving" this problem. The method consists of two steps:

1 Specify a general form for the function f. Typically, a linear function is selected, for example, for a single independent variable, let

$$\hat{y}_i = a + bx_i$$

2 Select the parameters (a and b above) to minimize

$$\sum_{i=1}^{n} (\hat{y}_i - y_i)^2$$

For the linear case, the rules of differential calculus can be used to find expressions for the optimal values of a and b (say a^* and b^*). They are

$$b^* = \frac{\displaystyle\sum_{i=1}^{n} x_i y_i - \left(\sum_{i=1}^{n} x_i \sum_{i=1}^{n} y_i\right)\bigg/ n}{\displaystyle\sum_{i=1}^{n} x_i^2 - \left(\sum_{i=1}^{n} x_i\right)^2 \bigg/ n}$$

$$a^* = \frac{\left(\displaystyle\sum_{i=1}^{n} y_i\right)}{n} - b^* \frac{\left(\displaystyle\sum_{i=1}^{n} x_i\right)}{n}$$

These expressions appear somewhat unwieldy; indeed, in the bad old days at a typical university, swarms of sweating statistics students would spend several stimulating sessions struggling with sums of squares and squares of sums on desk calculators simply to find a^* and b^* for relatively small problems. The revolution in computing has drastically changed this situation. Any self-respecting pocket calculator yields the values of a^* and b^* plus other statistical entities with relative ease. In general, one has only to enter the data and push specified keys to obtain the desired output. The same statement holds with more force for on-line computing facilities where statistical analysis packages are de rigueur.

There is an elegant and important statistical theory that underlies the method of least squares. *Regression theory,* as it is called, provides the basis for many of the forecasting and sophisticated econometric models now in use. Elements of the topic are usually studied in introductory statistics courses.

17.2.2   *A Geometric Representation: Curve Fitting*

A convenient geometric representation exists for a least squares problem with a single independent variable. Figure 17.1 shows a plot of the hypothetical data (that is, of the historical values for x_i and y_i). Such a plot is sometimes called a *scatter diagram.*

The problem of selecting a forecasting function, assuming the general form is linear, is equivalent to the problem of placing a line through the scatter diagram in such a way that the line lies "close to" the points. In Figure 17.2, line A–A seems to be a better candidate than either line B–B or line C–C.

In selecting a definition of "close to," most people are comfortable with the idea of using the distance between the actual value, y_i, and the value produced by the forecast function, $\hat{y}_i$, as a measure of closeness. Figure 17.3 indicates this distance for two different points. Squaring the arithmetic differences between $\hat{y}_i$ and y_i, that is, using $(\hat{y}_i - y_i)^2$, guarantees that a positive number will be associated with each distance. Minimizing the sum of the squared

Figure 17.1 *A scatter diagram*

deviations insures that the forecast function will lie roughly near all the points.

The general idea of finding a function whose graph lies close to the observed data, that is, curve fitting, is not restricted to situations in which the function is a straight line. In principle, any function might be advanced as a candidate. In practice, functions of the form

$$y = a_0 + a_1 x + a_2 x^2 + \ldots + a_n x^n$$

are often suggested. In this expression, a single independent variable has again been used for illustrative purposes. Such a function is called a *polynomial of degree n,* and it represents a broad and flexible class of functions. One can represent an amazing variety of configurations of points with polynomials, and thus they enjoy at least modest popularity with at least an occasional curve fitter. One must, however, proceed with caution when fitting data with a polynomial function. Under quite general conditions it is possible, for example, to find a $k - 1$-degree polynomial that will perfectly fit k data points. To be more specific, suppose we have on hand seven historical observations, denoted (x_i, y_i), $i = 1, 2, \ldots, 7$. It is possible to find a sixth-degree polynomial

$$y = a_0 + a_1 x + a_2 x^2 + \ldots + a_6 x^6$$

Figure 17.2 *Possible forecasting functions*

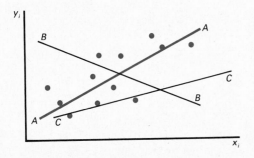

Figure 17.3 *A graphical representation of $\hat{y}_i - y_i$*

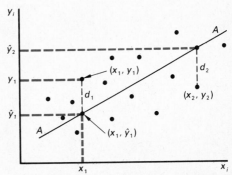

Figure 17.4   *A polynomial produces a perfect fit*

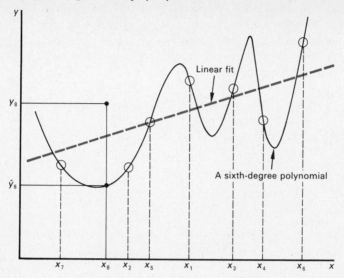

that exactly passes through each of these seven data points, as shown in Figure 17.4.

This perfect fit is deceptive, however, for it does not imply anything about the predictive value of the model. For example, refer again to Figure 17.4. When the independent variable (at some future time) assumes the value x_8, the true value of y might be given by y_8, whereas the predicted value is $\hat{y}_8$. Despite the previous perfect fit, the forecast is very inaccurate. In this situation a linear fit (a first-degree polynomial) such as the one indicated in Figure 17.4 might well provide more realistic forecasts for the future, though it does not fit the historical data nearly as well as the sixth-degree polynomial.

To be an effective forecasting device, the forecasting function must capture the essence of the true relationship between the independent variables and the variable being forecast. The above example shows that although the historical fit can be improved by adding additional (higher-order) terms to the polynomial, this certainly does not imply that a better predictive model has been produced.

Not only is it possible to consider functions other than straight lines as forecast functions, it is also reasonable to suggest criteria other than least squares to select parameters for a particular model. One criterion that is occasionally suggested is minimization of the sum of the absolute deviations between $\hat{y}_i$ and y_i; that is, one selects a and b in order to minimize

$$\sum_{i=1}^{n} \left| \hat{y}_i - y_i \right| = \sum_{i=1}^{n} \left| a + bx_i - y_i \right|$$

It can be shown that this problem is easily transformed to a linear program. However, rather than exploring in detail the formalities of this transformation, we shall move on to the second important class of forecasting models.

17.3 Bootstrap Forecasting Models

Bootstrap forecasts are produced by inspecting the past history of a particular single variable of interest, such as the demand for a particular item, or a particular market price, and using some technique to *extrapolate* the series of historical observations into the future. Figuratively, the series is being lifted into the future "by its own bootstraps."

In order to provide several examples of bootstrap methods, let us suppose that we have on hand the daily closing prices of a January soybean contract for the past 12 days, including today, and that from these past data we wish to predict tomorrow's closing price. Several possibilities come to mind:

1   If it is felt that all historical values are important, and that all have equal predictive power, we might take the *average* of the past 12 values as our best forecast for tomorrow.
2   If it is felt that today's value (the twelfth) is far and away the most important, then this value might be our best prediction for tomorrow.
3   It may be felt that in the current "fast-trending market" the first 6 values are too antiquated, but the most recent 6 are important and each has equal predictive power. We would then take the average of the most recent 6 values as our best estimate for tomorrow.
4   It may be felt that *all* past values contain useful information, but today's (the twelfth observation) is the most important of all, and, in succession, the eleventh, tenth, ninth, . . ., first observations have decreasing importance. In this case, we might take a *weighted average* of all 12 observations, with increasing weights assigned to each value in the order 1 through 12 and with the 12 weights summing to 1.
5   We might actually plot the 12 values on hand as a function of time, and then draw a linear *trend line* that lies close to these values. This line might then be used to predict tomorrow's value.

Let us now suppose that tomorrow's actual closing price is observed and consider our forecast for the day after tomorrow, using the 13 available historical values. The methods in items 1 and 2 can be applied in a straightforward manner. Now consider the method in item 3. In this case, we might take tomorrow's actual observed price along with today's and the previous four prices to obtain a new six-day average. This technique is called *a simple six-period moving average,* and it will be discussed in more detail in the following sections.

Let us now refer to the method in item 4. In this instance, since we employ all past values, we would be using 13 values rather than 12, with new weights assigned to these values. An important class of techniques called *exponential-smoothing models* operate in this fashion. These models will also be explored in the ensuing discussion.

Finally, we shall explore in more detail the technique mentioned in item 5. This provides another illustration of forecasting by a *curve-fitting method.*

We mention at this point that whenever we have values for a particular (single) variable of interest that can be plotted against time, these values are often termed a *time series,* and any method used to analyze and extrapolate such a series into the future falls within the general category of *time series analysis.* Thus, in fact, what we are calling *bootstrap models* would be called, in more austere terminology, *models for time series analysis.* This is currently a very active area of research in statistics and management science. We will barely be able to scratch the surface in terms of formal development. Nevertheless, some of the important concepts, from the manager's viewpoint, will be developed.

17.3.1   Curve Fitting

We have already touched upon this topic in the discussion of piggyback models. In using curve fitting in the bootstrap context, the main difference is that in this latter situation there is always only a single independent variable—namely, time. The historical observations on the dependent variable are plotted against time. A curve is then fitted to the existing historical data and extended into the future[2] to yield a forecast. Not surprisingly, a straight line is a commonly selected curve. This procedure is illustrated in Figure 17.5.

Figure 17.5   *Fitting a straight line*

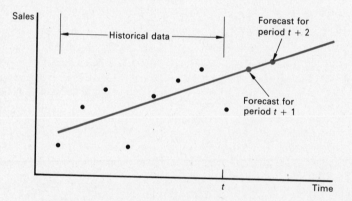

The curve is selected in such a way that it lies close to the existing data in the hope that the extrapolation will lie close to future values. To find such a curve, one might once again use the method of least squares with time playing the role of the independent variable. That is, one finds values a and b that minimize

$$\sum_{t=1}^{T} [y_t - (a + bt)]^2$$

It is possible to show that the equations presented in section 17.2.1 can be simplified by using the facts that

$$\sum_{t=1}^{T} a = aT, \quad \sum_{t=1}^{T} t = \frac{T(T+1)}{2}, \quad \sum_{t=1}^{T} t^2 = \frac{T(T+1)(2T+1)}{6}$$

---

2   Some readers may wonder at this point what it means to extend a curve. In the linear case, the meaning should be obvious. In the general case, it involves the identification of an equation that describes the curve and then evaluating the equation at future points in time.

However, we choose to spare you the joys of this algebraic manipulation.

The use of time as an independent variable has more serious implications than altering a few formulas, and a manager should understand the important difference between a piggyback model using curve fitting and a bootstrap model using curve fitting. The mathematical techniques for fitting the curves are identical, but the rationale behind the two models is basically quite different. To understand this difference, think of the values of y, the variable of interest, as being produced by a particular process or system. The piggyback model assumes that as the system changes to produce different values of y it will also produce corresponding differences in the independent variables. Thus, by knowing the independent variables, a good forecast of y can be deduced. The bootstrap model assumes that the system that produces y is essentially *stationary* (or *stable*) and will continue to act in the future as it has in the past. This means that time is a surrogate for many factors that may be difficult to measure but seem to vary in a consistent and systematic manner with time. If the system that produces y significantly changes (for example, because of changes in environment, technology, or government policy), then the assumption of a *stationary process* is invalid; consequently, a forecast based on time as an independent variable is apt to be badly in error.

Just as for piggyback models it is, of course, possible to use other than linear functions to extrapolate a series of observations (in other words, to forecast the future). As you might imagine, one alternative that is often suggested in practice is to assume that y_t is a higher-order polynomial in t; that is,

$$\hat{y} = b_0 + b_1 t + b_2 t^2 + \dots + b_K t^K$$

As before, appropriate values for the parameters b_0, b_1, ..., b_K must be mathematically derived from the values of previous observations. The high-order polynomial, however, suffers from the pitfalls described earlier. That is, it is possible to obtain perfect (or at least extremely good) historical fits with no predictive power.

17.3.2   *Moving Averages and Exponential Smoothing*

The assumption behind models of this type is that the average performance over the recent past is a good forecast of the future. It is perhaps surprising that these "naive" models are extremely important in applications. Almost all inventory control packages include a forecasting subroutine based on a particular type of moving average called *exponentially weighted moving averages*. On the basis of such a criterion as frequency of use, the method of moving averages is surely an important forecasting procedure.

It is convenient to introduce some notation at the outset. Let $\hat{y}_{t+r}$ be the estimate made in period t, after observing y_t (and earlier data), for the variable of interest r periods into the future. For example, we shall be particularly interested in predicting y_{t+1}, and this prediction is denoted $\hat{y}_{t+1}$. The simplest model in the moving-average category is the moving average of a selected number, say n, of the past observations. In this model

$$\hat{y}_{t+1} = \frac{1}{n}(y_t + y_{t-1} + \dots + y_{t-n+1})$$

This estimate is formally called a *simple n-period moving average.* The meaning of n period is that the estimate is always based upon only the last n observations. (You may wish to verify the fact that there are n terms in the above sum by, for example, setting $t = 5$, $n = 3$ and then writing out the sums.)

The simple moving average has two shortcomings, one philosophical and the other operational. The philosophical problem centers on the fact that in calculating the forecast ($\hat{y}_{t+1}$), the value y_t receives no more weight or importance than an older observation, such as y_{t-n+1}. Each of the last n observations is assigned to weight $1/n$. This procedure of assigning equal weights stands in opposition to one's intuition that in many instances the more recent data should tell us more than the older data about the likely value of y_{t+1}. This difficulty leads to the concept of a *weighted n-period moving average,* namely, a system in which

$$\hat{y}_{t+1} = \alpha_0 y_t + \alpha_1 y_{t-1} + \ldots + \alpha_{n-1} y_{t-n+1}$$

where the αs, which are called *weights,* are nonnegative numbers that are chosen so that smaller weights are assigned to more ancient data and all of the weights sum to one. In symbols,

$$\alpha_i > \alpha_{i+1} \qquad \text{and} \qquad \sum_{i=0}^{n-1} \alpha_i = 1$$

There are, of course, innumerable ways for selecting a set of αs to satisfy these criteria. One way would be to have the αs decreasing linearly. For example, if the weighted average is to include the last four observations (a weighted four-period moving average) one might set

$$\hat{y}_{t+1} = \tfrac{4}{10} y_t + \tfrac{3}{10} y_{t-1} + \tfrac{2}{10} y_{t-2} + \tfrac{1}{10} y_{t-3}$$

We referred above to the two shortcomings of a *simple* moving average. The first, *philosophic,* is to a large extent overcome by the concept of a *weighted* moving average. The second shortcoming, which is *operational,* is unfortunately shared by both types of models, the simple moving average and the weighted moving average. The operational difficulty is that if n observations are to be included in the moving average, then n pieces of data must be available, stored in some way, in order to calculate the forecast. This is not a serious problem when a small number of forecasts are involved. The situation is quite different for the firm that needs to forecast the demand for thousands of individual products on an item-by-item basis. In such a case, ease of computation and the extent of storage requirements become important factors in designing a forecasting and inventory control system.

Exponential smoothing, which is a shortened name for an exponentially weighted moving average, is another moving-average forecasting model, but one that avoids both of the problems just discussed. This model places the greatest weight on the most recent observations and requires that only a single number be stored for each variable being forecast. The "trick" that allows this savings in storage requirements consists of two steps. First, define a variable S_t, which is a "smoothed value" of the observation at time t and the observations at all previous times. Then set $\hat{y}_{t+1}$ (our forecast for y_{t+1}) equal to S_t. More precisely, S_t is defined by the expression

$$S_t = \alpha y_t + (1 - \alpha)S_{t-1} \quad \text{for } t \geq 1$$

where α is some user-specified value between zero and one. Note that when $t = 1$, the expression used to define S_1 is

$$S_1 = \alpha y_1 + (1 - \alpha)S_0$$

In this expression, S_0 is an initial value for the sequence of Ss. It must be preselected in order to get the forecasting model started. A reasonable way to do this would be to let S_0 denote one's best estimate for y_{t+1}, using all available data. Thus, if the model is started at $t = 1$ with only the single observation y_1 recorded, then one could take S_0 to equal y_1. If the model is initiated at $t = 6$ after $y_1, y_2, \ldots, y_6$ have been observed, then one might choose S_0 to be the mean of the past six values, or any other reasonable estimate for y_7. We shall soon see that as long as the choice of S_0 is reasonable, the model will be quite insensitive to the particular value chosen. First, however, let us examine some of the properties of the exponential smoothing model.

We note that it is possible to substitute $t - 1$ for t in the above definition for S_t to obtain

$$S_{t-1} = \alpha y_{t-1} + (1 - \alpha)S_{t-2} \qquad t \geq 2$$

Substituting this relationship into the original expression for S_t yields,

$$S_t = \alpha y_t + \alpha(1 - \alpha)y_{t-1} + (1 - \alpha)^2 S_{t-2} \qquad t \geq 2$$

By successively performing similar substitutions one is led to the following general expression for S_t,

$$S_t = \alpha y_t + \alpha(1 - \alpha)y_{t-1} + \alpha(1 - \alpha)^2 y_{t-2} + \ldots + \alpha(1 - \alpha)^{t-1}y_1 + (1 - \alpha)^t S_0$$

For example,

$$S_3 = \alpha y_3 + \alpha(1 - \alpha)y_2 + \alpha(1 - \alpha)^2 y_1 + (1 - \alpha)^3 S_0$$

Since $0 < \alpha < 1$, it follows that $0 < 1 - \alpha < 1$. We thus know that

$$\alpha > \alpha(1 - \alpha) > \alpha(1 - \alpha)^2 > \ldots > \alpha(1 - \alpha)^{t-1}$$

That is, the coefficients of the ys decrease as the data become older. It can also be shown that the sum of all of the coefficients (including the coefficient of S_0) is 1; for example, in the case of S_3

$$\alpha + \alpha(1 - \alpha) + \alpha(1 - \alpha)^2 + (1 - \alpha)^3 = 1$$

Thus the value of S_3, and hence $\hat{y}_4$ (which equals S_3), is a weighted average of y_1, y_2, y_3, and S_0 in which the weights on the y_i observations decrease as the age of the observation increases.

Let us now note the following points:

1   As t increases, the influence of S_0 on S_t (and hence on $\hat{y}_{t+1}$) decreases and in time becomes negligible. The coefficient of S_0 is $(1 - \alpha)^t$. Thus, the weight assigned to S_0 decreases exponentially with t. Even if α is small (which makes $(1 - \alpha)$ nearly 1), the value of $(1 - \alpha)^t$ decreases rapidly. For example, if $\alpha = .1$ and $t = 20$, then $(1 - \alpha)^t = .12$. If $\alpha = .1$ and $t = 40$, then $(1 - \alpha)^t = .014$. Thus, as soon as enough data have been observed, the value of $\hat{y}_{t+1}$ will be quite insensitive to the choice for S_0.

2   As noted previously, it is not uncommon to let $S_0 = y_1$. This implies that $S_1 = y_1$. The implication of this selection for S_0 is that for small values of t, more weight is placed on the oldest observation (y_1) than on any other observation. Even for large values of t, the coefficient of y_1 will be larger than the coefficients of several nearby terms (y_2, for example). Nevertheless, it remains true that for large values of t, the effect of *all* the older terms (and y_1 in particular) becomes negligible.

In summary, then, when the number of observations is small, the analyst should be aware of the influence of his choice for S_0 on S_t. With more data, the choice of S_0 is less important.

We have thus seen that the general value S_t is a weighted sum of *all* previous observations (including the last observed value, y_t) and that the weights sum to one and (except for the weight assigned to S_0) are decreasing as observations get older. In the spirit of weighted moving-average models, then, the smoothed value S_t is chosen as our best current forecast (where *current* means "in time period t, after observing y_t") for *any* future value. That is, for any integer $r \geq 1$, we set $\hat{y}_{t+r} = S_t$, and in particular, as stated earlier, $\hat{y}_{t+1} = S_t$.

It should now be noted that the assignment of relative importance to past values of y obviously depends directly on the value of α, which is a parameter input by the analyst. Figure 17.6 shows values for the weights when $\alpha = .1$, .3, and .5. You can see that for the larger values of α (for example, $\alpha = .5$), more relative weight is assigned to the more recent observations and the influence of older data is more rapidly diminished.

The above discussion shows that in order to obtain $\hat{y}_{t+1}$ (or $\hat{y}_{t+r}$) an exponential-smoothing model requires only two pieces of data, the value y_t

Figure 17.6   *Weights for different values of α*

Variable	Coefficient	$\alpha = .1$	$\alpha = .3$	$\alpha = .5$
y_t	α	.1	.3	.5
y_{t-1}	$\alpha(1 - \alpha)$	.09	.21	.25
y_{t-2}	$\alpha(1 - \alpha)^2$	.081	.147	.125
y_{t-3}	$\alpha(1 - \alpha)^3$	.07290	.1029	.0625
y_{t-4}	$\alpha(1 - \alpha)^4$	.06561	.07020	.03125
y_{t-5}	$\alpha(1 - \alpha)^5$	.05905	.04914	.01563
y_{t-6}	$\alpha(1 - \alpha)^6$	.05314	.03440	.00781
y_{t-7}	$\alpha(1 - \alpha)^7$	.04783	.02408	.00391
y_{t-8}	$\alpha(1 - \alpha)^8$	.04305	.01686	
y_{t-9}	$\alpha(1 - \alpha)^9$	.03874	.01180	
y_{t-10}	$\alpha(1 - \alpha)^{10}$	.03487	.00826	
Sum of the Weights		.68619	.97464	.99219

and the value S_{t-1}; and only the latter need be stored. The estimate $\hat{y}_{t+1}$ is therefore very easily computed. Moreover, more recent observations are automatically assigned greater weights. Consequently, the model is quite easy to use. However, it is important to note that the question of how to choose α must be faced by anyone attempting to use this technique. Qualitatively, the first answer to this question is that the choice depends on how responsive to recent observations the forecast should be. The data in Figure 17.6 illustrate the effect of choosing different values of α. In general, larger values of α put more weight on the most recent values and decrease the number of observations that have any real effect on the value of S_t. Note that when $\alpha = .5$, more than 95 percent of the weight is assigned to the first five terms, whereas when $\alpha = .1$, the total weight on the first five terms is only slightly greater than 40 percent.

To further illustrate the effect of choosing various values for α, that is, putting more or less weight on recent observations, we consider three specific cases.

CASE I

Suppose that at a certain point in time the underlying system experiences a rapid and radical change. How does the choice of α influence the way in which the exponential smoothing model will react? As an illustrative example, consider an extreme case in which

$$y_t = 0 \qquad \text{for } t = 1, 2, ..., 99$$
$$y_t = 1 \qquad \text{for } t = 100, 101, ...$$

This situation is illustrated in Figure 17.7. In this case, $S_{99} = 0$ for any value of α, and thus $\hat{y}(99 + 1) = 0$; that is, when t equals 99, the forecast of the next value of y is 0. In fact, our best forecast (at $t = 99$) for *any* future value

Figure 17.7 *A system change when* $t = 100$

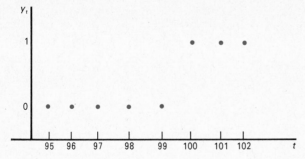

of y, such as y_{101} or y_{102}, is also 0, whereas all such actual values of y will be 1. The question is, how quickly will the system respond as time passes and the information that the system has changed becomes available? We note that

$$S_{100} = \alpha(1) + (1 - \alpha)S_{99} = \alpha$$

$$S_{101} = \alpha(1) + \alpha(1 - \alpha)(1) + (1 - \alpha)^2 S_{99} = \alpha + \alpha(1 - \alpha)$$

$$S_{102} = \alpha(1) + \alpha(1 - \alpha)(1) + \alpha(1 - \alpha)^2 (1) + (1 - \alpha)^3 S_{99} = \alpha + \alpha(1 - \alpha) + \alpha(1 - \alpha)^2$$

$$\vdots$$

$$S_{99+r} = \alpha + \alpha(1 - \alpha) + \alpha(1 - \alpha)^2 + \dots + \alpha(1 - \alpha)^{r-1} \qquad r \geq 1$$

The rate at which the values S_{99+r} approach 1 provides a good measure of how quickly the exponential smoothing model responds to a rapid system change. For example, when $\alpha = .5$ and $r = 5$ (after five observations of the value 1), $S_{104} = .96875$ and the difference between S_{104} and y_{104} is only .03125. However, when $\alpha = .1$ and $r = 21$ (after 21 observations of the value 1), $S_{120} = .89058$ and the difference is .10942. The values of S_{t+r} are plotted in Figure 17.8 to illustrate graphically how quickly the forecasts respond when $\alpha = .1$ and when $\alpha = .5$.

Figure 17.8   *Response to a unit change in y_t*

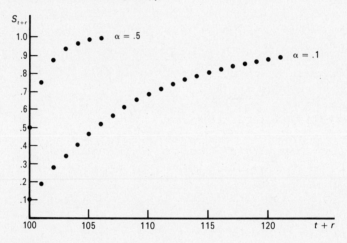

CASE II

As opposed to the rapid and radical change investigated in Case I, suppose now that a system experiences a *steady* change in the value of y. How then will the exponential smoothing model respond, and how will this response be affected by the choice of α? Consider, for example, a case in which

$$y_{t+1} = y_t + \delta \qquad \text{for all } t$$

This steady growth pattern is called a ***linear ramp*** and is illustrated in Figure 17.9.

An exact expression for S_{t+r} could be derived and its value compared to y_{t+r} to obtain a precise measure of the responsiveness of the model. However, the general relationship can easily be deduced. Since $\hat{y}_{t+1} = S_t$ and S_t is a weighted sum of terms, each of which is smaller than y_{t+1}, it follows that $\hat{y}_{t+1}$ will always be smaller than y_{t+1}. Also, $\hat{y}_{t+1}$ will decrease with decreasing values of α since

Figure 17.9 *Steadily increasing values of* y_t

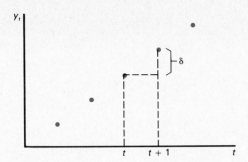

this implies less weight on the more recent (and hence larger) values of y. Thus, the forecast will become worse as α decreases.

It should now be evident that if a significant and identifiable trend (such as the above linear ramp) actually exists in the data, then the exponential-smoothing model as discussed above is not a very good predictor of future values. This is especially true if one wishes to forecast a number of periods into the future. The discussion of this topic is continued in the next example, Case III.

CASE III

Suppose that a system experiences a regular *seasonal pattern* in y (such as would be the case if y represents, for example, the demand in the city of Chicago for bathing suits). How then will the exponential-smoothing model respond, and how will this response be affected by the choice of α? Consider, for example, the seasonal pattern illustrated in Figure 17.10.

When y_t has a seasonal pattern, and when it is desirable to forecast several periods forward, say to specify $\hat{y}_{t+1}$, $\hat{y}_{t+2}$, $\hat{y}_{t+3}$, and so on, all based only on data through period t, then the exponential-smoothing model is inadequate to the task of producing good forecasts. If a small value of α is chosen, S_t will closely resemble a simple moving average of a number of terms. In this case, the future predictions $\hat{y}_{t+r}$ will all lie somewhere near the average of the past observations. The forecast thus essentially ignores the seasonal pattern. If a large value of α is chosen, S_t will more nearly track the movement of

Figure 17.10 *A seasonal pattern in* y_t

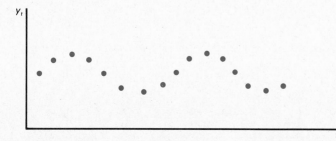

y_t. Unfortunately, this does not imply that a better forecast will occur. The fact that S_t (that is, $\hat{y}_{t+r}$) is close to the current value of y_t implies that it will most likely be far away from values of y_{t+r} when $t + r$ lies in some other part of the seasonal pattern. Suppose y_t is the sales of bathing suits in month t. With a large value of α, the value of S_t in June might be a good forecast of what will happen next June, but it may not be very useful as a forecast of sales in November.

The exponential-smoothing model $S_t = \alpha y_t + (1 - \alpha)S_{t-1}$ is intended for situations in which the behavior of the variable of interest is essentially stable, in the sense that deviations over time have nothing to do with *time*, per se, but are caused by *random effects*, which do not follow a regular pattern. This is what we have termed the ***stationarity*** assumption. Not surprisingly, then, the above model has various shortcomings when it is used in situations (such as bathing suit demand) that do not fit this prescription. Although this statement may be true, it is not very constructive. What approach should a manager take when the exponential-smoothing model as described above is not appropriate? In the case of a seasonal pattern, a naive approach would be to use the exponential-smoothing model on "appropriate" past data. For example, to forecast sales in June one might take a smoothed average of sales in previous Junes. This approach has two problems. First, it ignores a great deal of useful information. Certainly, sales from last July through this May should provide some information about the likely level of sales this June. Secondly, if the cycle is very long, say a year, this approach means that very old data must be used to get a reasonable sample size. The bootstrap models are based on the assumption that the system or process that produces the variable of interest is essentially *stationary* over time. This assumption becomes more tenuous when the span of time covered by the data becomes quite large.

If the manager is convinced that there is a trend or a seasonal effect in the variable being predicted, then a better approach is to develop modified exponential-smoothing models that incorporate a linear trend or seasonal effects. References to models of this sort exist in the technical literature, and the models are not exceptionally complicated. Presentation of these developments, however, carries us too far into the realm of a quite special technique and too far from our goal in this chapter of presenting mainly the basic concepts.

17.3.3   *The Random Walk*

The above discussed moving-average techniques are examples of what are called time series models. Recently, much more sophisticated methods for time series analysis have become available. These methods, primarily based on developments by G. E. P. Box and G. M. Jenkins[3] in the late 1960s, have already made an important impact on the practice of forecasting, and indeed the Box-Jenkins approach is incorporated in certain computer packages.

These time series forecasting techniques are based on the assumption that the true values of the variable of interest, y_t, are generated by a stochastic (probabilistic) model. Introducing enough of the theory of probability to enable

---

3   Box, G. E. P., and G. M. Jenkins, *Time Series Analysis, Forecasting and Control* (San Francisco: Holden-Day, Inc., 1970).

us to discuss these models in any generality seems inappropriate at this time. One special but very important (and very simple) stochastic process is called a *random walk*. This process serves as a nice illustration of a stochastic model. Here the variable y_t is assumed to be produced by the relationship

$$y_t = y_{t-1} + \epsilon$$

where the value of ϵ is determined by a random event. To illustrate this process even more explicitly, let us consider a man standing at a street corner on a north-south street. He flips a fair coin. If it lands with a head showing he walks one block north. If it lands with a tail showing he walks one block south. When he arrives at the next corner (whichever one it turns out to be), he repeats the process. This is the classic example of a random walk. To put this example in the form of the model, label the original corner 0. We shall call this the value of the first observation, y_1. Starting at this point, label successive corners going north $+1$, $+2$, ... Also starting at the original corner, label successive corners going south -1, -2, ... (see Figure 17.11). These labels that describe the location of our random walker are the y_ts.

In the model, $y_t = y_{t-1} + \epsilon$ where (assuming a fair coin) $\epsilon = 1$ with probability .5 and $\epsilon = -1$ with probability .5. If our walker observes the sequence H, H, H, T, T, H, T, T, T, he will follow the path shown in Figure 17.11.

Suppose that after our special agent has flipped the coin nine times (that is, he has moved nine times, and we have, starting with corner 0, ten observations of corners), we would like to forecast where he will be after another move. This is the typical forecasting problem in the bootstrap context. That is, we have observed $y_1, y_2, \ldots, y_{10}$, and we need a good forecast $\hat{y}_{11}$ of the forthcoming variable y_{11}. In this case, for a soon-to-be-mentioned reasonable criterion, the best value for $\hat{y}_{11}$ is the *conditional expected value* of the random quantity y_{11}. In other words, the best forecast is the expected value of y_{11} given that we know $y_1, y_2, \ldots, y_{10}$. From the model, we know that y_{11} will equal $y_{10} + 1$ with a probability equal to .5 and y_{11} will equal $y_{10} - 1$ with a probability equal to .5. Thus $E(y_{11}|y_1, \ldots, y_{10})$, the conditional expected value of y_{11} given $y_1, y_2, \ldots, y_{10}$, is calculated as follows:

$$E(y_{11}|y_1, \ldots, y_{10}) = .5(y_{10} + 1) + .5(y_{10} - 1) = y_{10}$$

Figure 17.11 *The classic random walk*

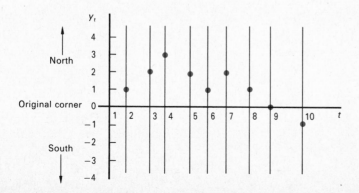

Thus we see that for this model the data y_1, ..., y_9 are irrelevant, and the best forecast of the random walker's position one move from now is his current position. We note that, in fact, y_{11} will never equal y_{10}. It turns out, mathematically, that this forecast is the best according to the following criterion; select $\hat{y}_{11}$ in order to minimize

$$E\left[(y_{11} - \hat{y}_{11})^2\right]$$

It is interesting to observe that the best forecast of y_{12} given y_1, ..., y_{10} is also y_{10}. Indeed, the best forecast for any future value of y, given this particular model, is its current value.

 This example is not as silly as it may seem at first glance. Indeed, there is a great deal of evidence that supports the idea that stock prices behave like a random walk and that the best forecast of a future stock price is its current value. Not surprisingly, this conclusion is not warmly accepted by research directors and technical chartists who make their living forecasting stock prices. One reason for this fact is the almost universal human tendency when looking at a set of data to observe certain patterns or regularities no matter how the data are produced. Consider the time series data plotted in Figure 17.12. It does not seem unreasonable to believe that the data are following a sinusoidal pattern as suggested by the smooth curve in the figure and thus that at time 60 or so, the value of y_t (by extrapolation) would be somewhere around -5. Actually, these data were generated by the random walk model presented earlier in this section. Since, at each step, the series is as likely to increase by one as it is to decrease by one, and since y_{50} has the value 0, it is easily deduced that by time 60 the series is just as apt to assume a value of $+5$ as it is a value of -5.

 In concluding this section we should stress that it is *not* a general conclusion of time series analysis that the best estimate of the future is the present, that is, that $\hat{y}(t + r) = y_t$. This result holds for the particular random walk model presented above. The result depends crucially on the assumption that the expected or mean value of ϵ, the random component, is 0. If the probability

Figure 17.12 *Time series data*

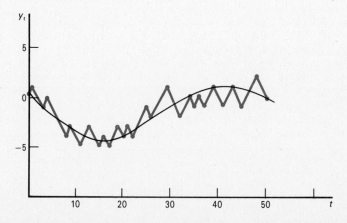

that ϵ equals 1 had been .6 and the probability that ϵ equals -1 had been .4, then the best forecast of y_{t+r} would not have been y_t. To find this forecast, one would have had to find $E(y_{t+r}|y_1, \ldots, y_t)$. Such a model is called *a random walk with a trend*.

17.4 The Role of Historical Data: Divide and Conquer

Historical data play a critical role in the construction and testing of forecasting models. Hopefully, a rationale precedes the construction of a forecasting model. There may be theoretical reasons for believing that a relationship exists between some independent variables and the variable to be forecast and thus that a piggyback model is appropriate. Or one may take the more deterministic and, at times, pessimistic view that the past is a good indication of the future. Nevertheless, in almost all cases the parameters of the model must be selected. In particular:

1 In a piggyback model using a linear forecasting function, $\hat{y}_i = a + bx_i$, the values of a and b must be specified.
2 In a bootstrap model using a weighted n-period moving average, $\hat{y}_{t+r} = \alpha_0 y_t + \alpha_1 y_{t-1} + \ldots + \alpha_{n-1} y_{t-n+1}$, the number of terms, n, and the values for the weights, $\alpha_0, \alpha_1, \ldots, \alpha_{n-1}$, must be specified.
3 In a bootstrap model using exponential smoothing, $S_t = \alpha y_t + (1 - \alpha) S_{t-1}$, the value of α must be specified.

In any of these models, in order to specify the parameter values one typically must make use of historical data. A useful guide in seeking to use such data effectively is to divide and conquer. More directly, this means that it is often a useful practice to use part of the data to estimate the parameters and the rest of the data to test the model.

For example, suppose that a firm has weekly sales data on a particular product for the last two years and plans to use an exponential-smoothing model to forecast demand for this product. The firm might use the following procedure:

1 Use data on the first 75 weeks to find a value of α so that S_t is a "good" forecast of the future sales over the appropriate forecasting horizon. Suppose the firm is interested in forecasting 4 weeks ahead. The analyst would then pick a particular α and compare the values of S_t (which is our prediction for y_{t+1}, y_{t+2}, and so on) [4] and y_{t+4} for $t = 25$ to 75. (The first 24 values are not compared so as to negate any initial or "start-up" effect.) The analyst then would continue to select different values of α until the model produces a satisfactory fit.
2 Test the model derived in step 1 on the remaining 29 pieces of data. That is, using the best value of α from item 1, compare the values of S_t and y_{t+4} for $t = 76$ to 104.

---

4 Throughout the discussion of this chapter, it has been stated either explicitly or implicitly that, given data up through period t, $\hat{y}_{t+1} = \hat{y}_{t+r}$ for all $r > 1$. This is based on an assumption that the underlying probabilistic process that generates the data is stationary in time. In particular, there can be no trend or seasonality in the process.

If the model does a good job of forecasting values for the last part of the historical data, then there is some reason to believe that it will also do a good job with the future. On the other hand, if by using the data from weeks 1–75 the model cannot perform well in predicting the demand in weeks 76–104, the prospects for predicting the future with the same model seem dubious.

The same type of divide-and-conquer strategy can be used with any of the forecasting techniques we have presented, and indeed this type of simulation is a popular method of testing models. It should be stressed, however, that this procedure represents what is termed a *null test*. If the model fails on historical data, the model probably is not appropriate. If the model succeeds on historical data, one cannot be sure that it will work in the future. Who knows, the underlying system that is producing the observations may change. It is this type of sober experience that causes certain forecasters to be less so.

17.5 Examples and Solutions

Example 1

Consider the set of data values in Figure 17.13

Figure 17.13

x	y	x	y
100	57	60	46
70	43	50	45
30	35	20	26
40	33	10	26
80	56	90	53

a Plot a scatter diagram of these data.
b Fit a straight line to these data "by eye."
c Find the equation of the line selected in part b.
d Fit a straight line to the data using the method of least squares.
e Use the function derived in part d to forecast a value for y when x = 120.

Solution to Example 1

Parts a and b are solved in Figure 17.14.
c The intercept of the line fit "by eye" is 20; thus a = 20. The line increases $61 - 20 = 41$ units in y while x is increasing by 100 units; thus the slope of the line is $\frac{41}{100}$, or .41, and b = .41.
d From Section 17.2.1 we know that

$$b^* = \frac{\sum_{i=1}^{n} x_i y_i - \sum_{i=1}^{n} x_i \sum_{i=1}^{n} y_i \Big/ n}{\sum_{i=1}^{n} x_i^2 - \left(\sum_{i=1}^{n} x_i\right)^2 \Big/ n}$$

Figure 17.14

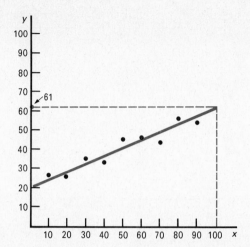

$$a^* = \frac{\sum\limits_{i=1}^{n} y_i}{n} - b^* \frac{\sum\limits_{i=1}^{n} x_i}{n}$$

For these data,

$\Sigma x_i y_i = 26{,}120$

$\Sigma x_i = 550$

$\Sigma y_i = 420$

$\Sigma x_i^2 = 38{,}500$

Thus

$b^* = 0.3661$

$a^* = 21.86$

e $\hat{y} = a^* + b^*(120)$

$= 21.86 + 0.3661(120)$

$= 65.79$

Example 2

Consider the data presented in Example 1. Now assume that the variable referred to as x is really time and that we associate the x values 10, 20, 30, and so on with the t values 1, 2, 3, and so on.

a Would you expect the exponential-smoothing model $S_t = \alpha y_t + (1 - \alpha)S_{t-1}$ to produce a good fit for these data? Why?

b What relationship would you expect to hold between S_t and y_t?

c Suppose α were originally set equal to .5. Would you increase or decrease α to get a better fit?

Solution to Example 2

a The scatter diagram in Figure 17.14 shows that y appears to increase with t. Since the model $S_t = \alpha y_t + (1 - \alpha)S_{t-1}$ is designed for systems in which variations in y_t occur at random (that is, where there is not a regular pattern of change), the model will probably not produce a very good fit.

b One would expect S_t to be smaller than y_t, because S_t is a weighted sum of terms, most of which are less than or equal to y_t.

c One would expect a better fit by increasing the value of α since this puts more weight on the most recent, and thus larger, values of y.

Example 3

Consider a random walk model in which

$$y_t = y_{t-1} + \epsilon$$

Let $f(x)$ be the probability that ϵ equals x where

$$f(-1) = .3$$
$$f(1) \quad = .7$$
$$f(x) \quad = 0 \quad \text{all other } x$$

and suppose $y_{10} = 50$.

a Find the best estimate of y_{11} and y_{15} using observed values $y_1, \ldots, y_{10}$.

b Suppose an exponential-smoothing model with $\alpha = .3$ were to be used on this time series. What relationship would you expect to obtain between $\hat{y}_{t+1}$ and y_{t+1}?

c What is the probability that y_{12} equals 52?

Solution to Example 3

By definition

$$y_{11} = y_{10} + \epsilon$$

Since the value of y_{10} is 50, the expected value of y_{11} can be derived as follows:

$$E(y_{11}) = 50 + E(\epsilon)$$

where $E(\epsilon)$ denotes the expected value (the mean) of ϵ. This quantity $E(\epsilon)$ can be calculated in the usual way,

$$E(\epsilon) = P(\epsilon = 1)(1) + P(\epsilon = -1)(-1) = .7(1) + .3(-1) = .4$$

Thus $E(y_{11}) = 50.4$, and this is the best estimate for y_{11} at time 10. Similarly,

$$y_{12} = y_{11} + \epsilon$$

Thus, by substitution,

$$y_{12} = y_{10} + \epsilon + \epsilon$$

Continuing in the same manner yields

$$y_{15} = y_{10} + \epsilon + \epsilon + \epsilon + \epsilon + \epsilon$$

Since the expected value of a sum equals the sum of the expected values, we obtain

$$E(y_{15}) = y_{10} + E(\epsilon) + E(\epsilon) + E(\epsilon) + E(\epsilon) + E(\epsilon) = 50 + 5(.4) = 52$$

which is the best estimate for y_{15}.

b This particular random walk model suggests that the time series is apt to increase, because the expected value of the series increases by .4 each step. Since S_t is a weighted sum of past values, S_t is likely to be less than y_t. Since $\hat{y}_{t+1} = S_t$, the estimate is likely to be low.

c The variable y_{12} can equal 52 if and only if the next two changes in the random walk are +1, that is, if the values of y_{10}, y_{11} and y_{12} are 50, 51, and 52, respectively. The probability that $y_{11} = 51$ is .7. The conditional probability that $y_{12} = 52$ given that $y_{11} = 51$ is .7. Thus the probability that $y_{12} = 52$ is .49.

17.6 Summary of Key Concepts

Quantitative forecasting models establish an unambiguous record of how the forecast is made. This provides a vehicle for communication about the forecast and a device for systematic modification and improvement of the forecasting technique. (Section 17.1)

With the use of computers, quantitative models can be based on large quantities of data. (Section 17.1)

In piggyback models, the forecast for the variable of interest is based on another variable or set of variables. Such models are often based on a linear regression analysis and more general curve-fitting methods. (Section 17.2)

A forecasting model based on polynomial functions can be made to perfectly fit any set of historical data simply by adding higher-order terms to the function. This does not imply anything about the predictive value of the model. (Section 17.2.2)

In bootstrap models, also called models for time series analysis, the forecast for the variable of interest is based on earlier observations of the same variable. Such models are often based on curve-fitting methods. Particularly popular approaches include simple n-period moving averages, with or without weights, and exponential-smoothing techniques. (Sections 17.3)

The exponential-smoothing model $S_t = \alpha Y_t + (1 - \alpha) S_{t-1}$ is intended for situations in which the behavior of the variable of interest is essentially stable. (Section 17.3.2)

The random walk is a basic stochastic model in which the change between two successive values of the variable of interest is assumed to be the realization of an independent random variable. (Section 17.3.3)

It is a common and useful practice to select parameter values for a forecasting model by using only a portion of a set of data and then to test the goodness of the model on the rest of the data. (Section 17.4)

17.7   Problems

1   Write the formulas for:
  a A simple n period moving average.
  b A weighted n period moving average.
  c An exponentially-weighted moving average.

2   Describe the differences between the formulas in parts a, b, and c in Problem 1 with regard to
  a Relative importance of old versus recent observations.
  b Storage space required in order to perform the calculations.

3   Describe how one might use historical data to aid in the specification of parameter values in each of these models.

4   Consider the set of data in Figure 17.15.

Figure 17.15

x	y	x	y
180	213	40	284
80	257	60	265
100	252	140	226
20	296	120	238
200	194	160	225

  a Plot a scatter diagram of these data.
  b Draw a straight line approximation to these data in such a way that the line passes through the points (0, 301) and (200, 199).
  c Find the equation of the line selected in part b.
  d Fit a straight line to the data using the method of least squares.
  e Use the function derived in part d to forecast the y value corresponding to an x value of 230.

5   Consider the set of data in Figure 17.16

Figure 17.16

t	y	t	y
1	50	6	36
2	55	7	24
3	45	8	33
4	43	9	32
5	57	10	27

  a Plot y_t versus t.
Now use the exponential smoothing model

$$S_0 = 50$$
$$S_t = \alpha y_t + (1 - \alpha) S_{t-1} \qquad t \geq 1$$

Set $\alpha = .3$.
b Find S_{10}.
c Forecast y_{12}.
d Approximate the data with a straight line through the points $(0,67.5)$ and $(10,24.5)$.
e Find the equation of this line.
f Forecast y_{12} by extrapolating the line found in parts *d* and *e*.
g Which forecasting model do you prefer, the exponential-smoothing or the linear extrapolation? Why?

6 Consider the set of data in Figure 17.17. To forecast y_{20}, which of the following methods would you prefer?

Figure 17.17

t	*y*	*t*	*y*	*t*	*y*
1	200	6	33	11	36
2	47	7	44	12	32
3	38	8	45	13	48
4	42	9	39	14	41
5	35	10	42	15	37

a Fit a straight line to these data by the method of least squares and extrapolate it.
b Use an exponential smoothing model with $\alpha = .3$.

7 Consider a random walk model in which

$$y_t = y_{t-1} + \epsilon$$

Let $f(x)$ be the probability that ϵ equals x.
If

$$f(-2) = .3$$
$$f(-1) = .1$$
$$f(0) \ = .2$$
$$f(1) \ = .1$$
$$f(2) \ = .3$$

and

$$y_{10} = 40$$

then
a What is the best estimate of y_{11} and y_{15} given the values $y_1, \ldots, y_{10}$?
b If you fit a least squares line to many observations from the above model, what would you expect the slope of that line to be?

8 Consider the random walk model described in the text in Section 17.3.3. Imagine that, starting at time zero, the process continues ad infinitum.
a Use your intuition to assess (at time zero) the probability that the walker will at some point find himself at least 1 million blocks from the initial corner.
b Does your answer to part *a* change if you are given the following fact? The probability is 1 that the walker will at some point find himself at least three blocks from the initial corner.

9 In order for a piggyback model of the form $\hat{y}_i = f(x_i)$ to be useful must there necessarily be a causal relationship between y and x? That is, must it be the case that a change in

y is caused by a related change in x? Think of the following cases in constructing your answer:
(1) Let

y = pork prices in January

x = number of new hogs in July of the previous year

(2) Let

y = total donations to the community during its fund-raising drive in March

x = total expenditures on liquor during the previous six months

10 Suppose that a technician used a computer program to fit a straight line by the method of least squares to the data presented in Example 1. Unfortunately, he accidently interchanged x_1 and y_1 while entering the data; that is, he set $x_1 = 57$ and $y_1 = 100$.
a Find the values of a^* and b^* that he would obtain. (Note that it isn't necessary to find all the sums from scratch. The values in Example 1 can be used to reduce the amount of computation required. For example:

$$\Sigma x_i = (\Sigma x_i \text{ in Example 1}) - 100 + 57 = 550 - 43 = 507$$

b Plot a scatter diagram of the data and the line found in part a.
c Use the function to forecast a value for y if $x = 120$.
d-f Now assume that the technician entered the first data point as $x_1 = 100$, $y_1 = 100$. Repeat parts a, b, and c.
g Comment on the sensitivity of the least squares technique to "extreme values" and the implications of your observation for the use of the least squares technique in practice.

11 In the exponential-smoothing model, the variables are indexed according to the order in which they occur, that is, $y_1, y_2, y_3, \ldots$. In cases (1) and (2) below, determine whether or not it is important that the interval between observations be the same. In other words, is it important that the interval between y_1 and y_2, say a month, be the same as the interval between y_2 and y_3?
(1) The accumulated sales between observation i and observation $i - 1$ is y_i.
(2) The interval between observations is more than a week, and y_i is the amount sold during the previous week.

18 *Simulation Models*

A number of examples are used to illustrate various roles of simulation models in applied work. These examples will help to explain some of the mechanics of the construction of simulation models. Advantages and pitfalls of these models are discussed. Simulation and optimization models are compared.

18.1 Introduction

Any discussion of models in managerial decision making, no matter how broad, is pointedly incomplete without some reasonable amount of attention to the topic of simulation. If you would select at random a practitioner of management science or an analyst from a corporate planning department, the chances are high that he would be working with a simulation model. Our goal in this chapter is to develop a reasonable understanding of how such models work and where they fit into the spectrum of applications.

At the outset, it is important to recognize that simulation is one of those words that means different things to different people. The president of PROTRAC uses a simulation model to assist in long-range corporate planning. This is a strategic planning model. A project director at NASA uses a simulation model to assist in planning the next trip to Mars. Simulation models are used by the Federal Reserve Board in economic planning and by the Department of Defense in military planning. A simulation model is used by a commodities speculator to test her latest theory on how to profit in futures trading in the soybean market. A job-shop scheduler uses a simulation model to help plan the acquisition of new machinery.

All of these models have little in common, and yet they are all referred to as "simulation." The concept of simulation applies to any situation in which someone is interested in the behavior of a particular system.

The basic idea of a simulation is to build an experimental device that will "act like" (simulate) the system of interest in certain important respects.

This approach has a long history in the applied physical and engineering sciences. Consider the following examples:

1 Models of yachts to be built for the America's Cup race are tested in a tow tank at MIT. Towing the model through the tank *simulates* the flow of the water over the hull of the actual ship.

2 Models of planes are tested in wind tunnels to test the aerodynamic properties of the plane. The wind tunnel experience *simulates* actual flight.

3 Pilots train in models of actual airplane cabins under *simulated* conditions.

4 Pilot plants are used to *simulate* the behavior of chemical processes in order to reduce the risk associated with the construction of the actual processor.

5 New products are subjected to tests that *simulate* the conditions they will later encounter.

In spite of its popularity in other fields, simulation is a relatively new technique for studying management systems. Its popularity and growth have coincided with the availability and the computational power of digital computers. Computers provide the student of management with a device that can work through amazingly complicated logical structures unerringly, rapidly, and at a reasonable cost. Thus, with the aid of a computer it is possible to describe the logical operation of a management system and to experiment with it.

In the following sections, several examples will be presented to illustrate the different meanings of simulation. These examples will give some understanding of how simulation models are constructed and how they can be properly and improperly used.

18.2 Simulation and Random Numbers

18.2.1 *The Use of Random Numbers*

Simulation is an important tool for analyzing problems in which there are elements of uncertainty. This importance stems in no small part from the fact that it is difficult to get analytic results for many interesting and important problems when uncertainty is present. This is particularly true of the so-called queuing or waiting-line models. In fact, apparently enough people are interested in simulating queuing situations that more than one supplier of computer software has found it to be an advantage to introduce general purpose simulation packages for queuing systems. In this section, we consider several applications of simulation to problems that have the flavor of a queuing model. The discussion of these applications will underscore the use of random numbers in simulation models.

Random numbers are used, in the simulation context, to generate uncertain events.

To focus more clearly on what is meant by a random number, let us consider an experiment in which a set of identical balls is numbered from 0 through 99 and placed in an urn. A ball is then drawn from the urn at random; that is, each ball is equally likely to be drawn. The number on the ball is recorded, the ball is returned to the urn, and the experiment is repeated. Suppose that this experiment is repeated 400 times and the results are recorded in a table.

The sequence of 400 numbers shown in Figure 18.1 was created by a computer using a device conceptually equivalent to the procedure just described.

To understand how such a table can be used in a simulation, consider simulating a coin-flipping game in which the house pays $2 if a head occurs and nothing if a tail occurs. Suppose you wanted to obtain a better feeling for the potential sequence of outcomes of this game. This can be done by simulation as follows. Adopt the convention that if the random number that is chosen

Figure 18.1   *Table of random digits*

	1	2	3	4	5	6	7	8	9	10
1	97	95	12	11	90	49	57	13	86	81
2	02	92	75	91	24	58	39	22	13	02
3	80	67	14	99	16	89	96	63	67	60
4	66	24	72	57	32	15	49	63	00	04
5	96	76	20	28	72	12	77	23	79	46
6	55	64	82	61	73	94	26	18	37	31
7	50	02	74	70	16	85	95	32	85	67
8	29	53	08	33	81	34	30	21	24	25
9	58	16	01	91	70	07	50	13	18	24
10	51	16	69	67	16	53	11	06	36	10
11	04	55	36	97	30	99	80	10	52	40
12	86	54	35	61	59	89	64	97	16	02
13	24	23	52	11	59	10	88	68	17	39
14	39	36	99	50	74	27	69	48	32	68
15	47	44	41	86	83	50	24	51	02	08
16	60	71	41	25	90	93	07	24	29	59
17	65	88	48	06	68	92	70	97	02	66
18	44	74	11	60	14	57	08	54	12	90
19	93	10	95	80	32	50	40	44	08	12
20	20	46	36	19	47	78	16	90	59	64
21	86	54	24	88	94	14	58	49	80	79
22	12	88	12	25	19	70	40	06	40	31
23	42	00	50	24	60	90	69	60	07	86
24	29	98	81	68	61	24	90	92	32	68
25	36	63	02	37	89	40	81	77	74	82
26	01	77	82	78	20	72	35	38	56	89
27	41	69	43	37	41	21	36	39	57	80
28	54	40	76	04	05	01	45	84	55	11
29	68	03	82	32	22	80	92	47	77	62
30	21	31	77	75	43	13	83	43	70	16
31	53	64	54	21	04	23	85	44	81	36
32	91	66	21	47	95	69	58	91	47	59
33	48	72	74	40	97	92	05	01	61	18
34	36	21	47	71	84	46	09	85	32	82
35	55	95	24	85	84	51	61	60	62	13
36	70	27	01	88	84	85	77	94	67	35
37	38	13	66	15	38	54	43	64	25	43
38	36	80	25	24	92	98	35	12	17	62
39	98	10	91	61	04	90	05	22	75	20
40	50	54	29	19	26	26	87	94	27	73

is any integer from 00 through 49, we will say that a head has occurred, and if the random number is any integer from 50 through 99, a tail occurs. Note that since each integer from 00 through 99 is equally likely, the probability that a head occurs is the sum of the probabilities that each of the integers from 00 through 49 occurs. Since each of these probabilities is $\frac{1}{100}$, the probability of a head occurring must be $\frac{50}{100} = \frac{1}{2}$.

Now one simply starts at a random position in the table of random numbers and reads them consecutively (down columns) in order to simulate the game. Suppose the simulation starts with the integer in column 3, row 16. For ten trials, the results are recorded in Figure 18.2.

Figure 18.2   *Simulating a coin flip*

Trial	Random Number	Event	Return ($)
1	41	H	2
2	48	H	2
3	11	H	2
4	95	T	0
5	36	H	2
6	24	H	2
7	12	H	2
8	50	T	0
9	81	T	0
10	02	H	2

Total Return	$14.00
Average Return	$ 1.40

Based on these results, our estimate of average return is $1.40. It can also be noted that after 20 trials the total return is $22.00, which gives an average return of $1.10 per trial. Thus, based on this larger sample of 20 trials, one might conclude that $1.10 would be a reasonable sum to pay to play this game. Actually, in this example it is a trivial analytic matter to calculate that the expected return of the game is $1.00, and hence you should be willing to pay the house a fee of up to $1.00 per flip of the coin in order to play the game. We thus see that in this case, as the number of trials increased the results became more accurate, and a simulation of only 20 observations provided a good estimate of the expected return.

In many real-world problems, it is difficult if not impossible to calculate the expected return associated with the various alternatives. The hope is that just as in the coin-flipping example, a simulation will provide a good estimate of the returns. We now illustrate the way in which a simulation works by considering a simple queuing problem.

18.2.2   *A Simple Hand Simulation*

The following problem is faced by the manufacturing superintendent at PRO-TRAC's Moline plant. One of his most expensive pieces of capital equipment is called a *frame-processing machine*. This machine performs a number of machining operations on the frame for the E–9 and the F–9. After this machining is completed, the frame is transported to inventory at the head of the assembly line. Plant engineering is proposing to install an overhead monorail crane system that would remove the frame from the machining operation and move it to the assembly line. This monorail crane, however, would also serve other functions in the plant. The crane would move along its track visiting each of a number of different locations in the plant where it has specific tasks to perform. The frame-processing machine would represent one such location. Should there be a completed frame waiting at this location when the crane arrives, the frame would be picked up by the crane. If no frame is ready, however, the crane operator would not wait. The situation is represented in Figure 18.3.

Figure 18.3 *A transportation system for frames*

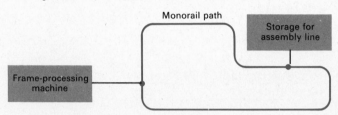

The time required to process the frames varies greatly, depending on the amount of straightening required and on the surface condition of the frame. The time between visits of the crane at the frame-processing machine also varies, depending on what other tasks it encounters as it makes its rounds. Any idle time on the frame-processing machine has a significant opportunity cost to PROTRAC since this machine is a major bottleneck in the overall processing operation.

After a group of four frames has been completed, the processor is shut down in order to readjust the tools. Since the crane is used in the final part of this readjustment operation, it turns out that as part of its regular routine the crane begins its rounds from the frame-processing machine as soon as that machine is ready to begin operating again. In other words, both the processing machine and the crane begin at the same time. The industrial engineering department has provided the estimates of operating data shown in Figure 18.4.

The production superintendent would like to know how much idle time he will have on the average during a production run of four frames. With the data in Figure 18.4 and the table of random numbers provided in Figure 18.1, he decides to simulate the behavior of the E–9 frame-processing machine.

Figure 18.4 *Data for E–9 frame production*

Time on the Frame-Processing Machine (min)	Probability	Time between Arrivals for the Crane (min)	Probability
45	$\frac{1}{5}$	10	$\frac{1}{4}$
60	$\frac{3}{5}$	15	$\frac{2}{4}$
75	$\frac{1}{5}$	20	$\frac{1}{4}$

He first defines the following variables:

$P(N)$ = processing time of frame N

$R(M)$ = time required for round M by the crane

$T(N)$ = time at which the processing of frame N will be complete

$S(M)$ = time at which the crane will complete its Mth round and arrive at the frame-processing machine

With the aid of this notation, he develops the flow chart shown in Figure 18.5. Before the superintendent can use this flow chart, the boxes labeled *Determine* $P(N)$ and *Determine* $R(M)$ must be specified. The idea, of course, is to select processing times and route times according to the probabilities shown in Figure 18.4. This idea is implemented by using the table of random numbers provided in Figure 18.1. For example, since the probability is $\frac{1}{5}$ that the processing time is 45 minutes, we assign the random digits 00 through 19 to this event.

Figure 18.5 *Flow diagram for E–9 frame-processing simulation*

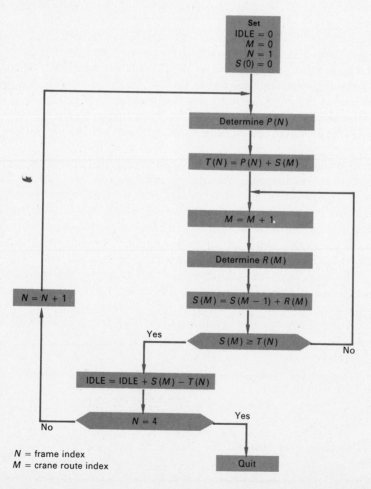

N = frame index
M = crane route index

Figure 18.6 *Using random digits*

Processing Time (min)	Probability	Random Digits
45	$\frac{1}{5}$	00–19
60	$\frac{3}{5}$	20–79
75	$\frac{1}{5}$	80–99

Route Time (min)	Probability	Random Digits
10	$\frac{1}{4}$	00–24
15	$\frac{2}{4}$	25–74
20	$\frac{1}{4}$	75–99

In other words, if a 16 is selected, we will say that the processing time is 45 minutes. The function that defines the relationship between the random digits and the actual event is shown in Figure 18.6. The function that defines the relationship between the random digits and the route times is also presented in this figure.

The superintendent can now start his simulation. Suppose that he starts with the digit from column 9, row 33 in Figure 18.1. Since this number is 61, the time to process the first frame is 60 minutes. Since the next number (column 9, row 34) is 32, he knows that the crane will complete its first route in 15 minutes and arrive at the frame-processing machine at time 15. Since the first frame is still being processed, the crane moves on. More route times will be generated until the first frame can be picked up. The entire simulation for four frames is shown in Figure 18.7. The notation used corresponds to the notation in the flow chart (Figure 18.5). Each processing time and route time is recorded in the appropriate box. The other two numbers in each box are the random number that was drawn to generate the value for the processing time or route time and which random number it is in the overall sequence of draws. This latter figure is included to allow you to follow the development of the simulation in the order in which it occurred. We recommend that you follow this development closely in order to understand better how a simulator works.

This particular run proceeded as follows:

1 Random number 61 was chosen. This implied that $P(1) = 60 = T(1)$.
2 Random number 32 was chosen, so $R(1) = 15$. Now $S(1) = 15 + 0 = 15$. Thus $S(1) < T(1)$.
3 With $S(1) < T(1)$, another random number, 62, was chosen. This implied that $R(2) = 15$. Then, since $S(2) = R(2) + S(1)$, it follows that $S(2) = 30$.
4 Since $S(2) < T(1)$, another random number, 67, was drawn. Thus $R(3) = 15$. Now $S(3) = R(3) + S(2) = 45$.
5 Since $S(3) < T(1)$, another random number, 25, was drawn. Now $S(5) = 60$, which equals $T(1)$. Thus, the first frame was completed with no idle time.
6 To start the next frame, another random number, 17, was drawn, and so $P(2) = 45$.

Figure 18.7   *A simulation of processing four frames*

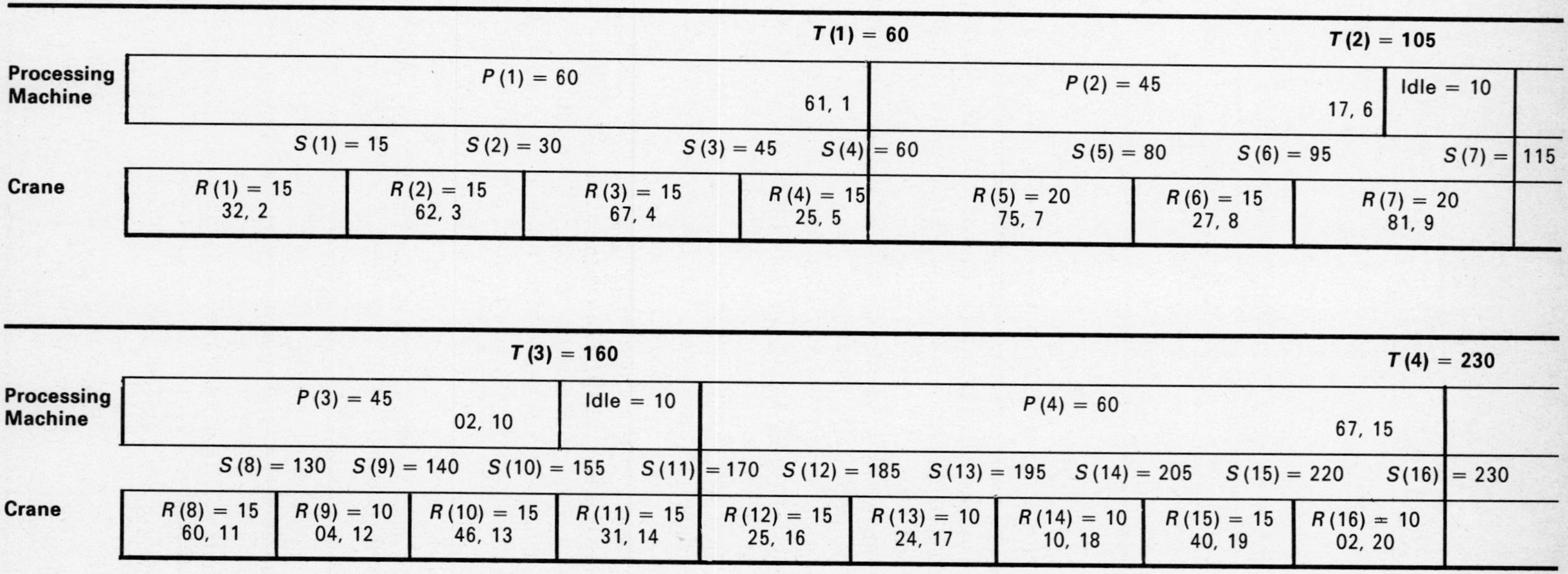

$T(1) = 60$ $T(2) = 105$

Processing Machine: $P(1) = 60$ $P(2) = 45$ Idle $= 10$

Crane:
$S(1) = 15$ $S(2) = 30$ $S(3) = 45$ $S(4) = 60$ 61, 1 $S(5) = 80$ $S(6) = 95$ $S(7) = 115$ 17, 6

$R(1) = 15$ 32, 2
$R(2) = 15$ 62, 3
$R(3) = 15$ 67, 4
$R(4) = 15$ 25, 5
$R(5) = 20$ 75, 7
$R(6) = 15$ 27, 8
$R(7) = 20$ 81, 9

$T(3) = 160$ $T(4) = 230$

Processing Machine: $P(3) = 45$ Idle $= 10$ $P(4) = 60$

Crane:
$S(8) = 130$ $S(9) = 140$ $S(10) = 155$ $S(11) = 170$ 02, 10 $S(12) = 185$ $S(13) = 195$ $S(14) = 205$ $S(15) = 220$ $S(16) = 230$ 67, 15

$R(8) = 15$ 60, 11
$R(9) = 10$ 04, 12
$R(10) = 15$ 46, 13
$R(11) = 15$ 31, 14
$R(12) = 15$ 25, 16
$R(13) = 10$ 24, 17
$R(14) = 10$ 10, 18
$R(15) = 15$ 40, 19
$R(16) = 10$ 02, 20

By following the complete development, it should be clear that a total of 20 minutes of idle time and 16 rounds of the crane occurred during this particular processing of four frames. The idle time, in general, is a chance phenomenon, and in another run it could turn out to be some other number. Suppose, for example, that the last random number (the twentieth) chosen in this run was 84 (rather than 02). In this case, the final route time would have been 20 minutes and the fourth frame would have had to wait 10 minutes to be picked up. Under this set of circumstances, the total idle time would have been 30 rather than 20 minutes.

It is easy to see that the logical operations and the bookkeeping associated with a simulation can become complicated and burdensome as the complexity of the system under consideration increases. Even for the extremely simple system presented here, the prospect of accurately completing many runs by hand is hardly encouraging. Unfortunately, for most simulations large samples are required to produce good estimates of the quantities of interest. Thus, except for very simple systems, hand simulation is not really a viable tool for analysis. The frame-processing example has been presented for its pedagogical value. To understand and interpret the results of a simulation accurately, one must understand the concept of using random numbers to generate uncertain events. The frame-processing example clearly illustrates this concept and, accordingly, the role of random numbers in creating a simulation model. This example provides a good idea of how many simulation models actually work. The problems at the end of the chapter provide additional experience in the creation and operation of simple simulation models.

At this point, a word of warning is probably appropriate. Simulation is an appealing concept that is deceptively simple in appearance. The idea of having a device that can be used to evaluate alternative decisions without employing higher mathematics is typically appealing to a manager. The fact of the matter, however, is that using a simulator as an aid to decision making in any reasonably complicated environment is anything but a trivial task. The modeling problem remains as formidable as ever. That is, one must still find a selective representation of reality that captures the essence of the real problem. Furthermore, in order to arrive at valid conclusions one must design appropriate experiments and analyze the resulting data. This often involves formal statistical methods, as will be illustrated in detail in the next chapter. The remainder of this chapter is devoted to discussing other types of simulation models. The PROTRAC strategic planning model will provide some insight into the complexities of simulation models.

18.3 Simulating the Future: Strategic Planning in PROTRAC

18.3.1 Background

As part of the annual budgeting procedure at PROTRAC, the planning department is required to assist in the preparation of a budget for the president. The president's task is to decide on the following quantities:

1 Amount of money to borrow
2 Amount of existing debt to pay
3 Amount of dividend to pay
4 Amount of money to allocate to production
5 Amount of money to allocate to research
6 Amount of money to allocate to marketing
7 Amount of money to allocate to capital investment in production and research facilities, respectively

These decisions will be referred to as the "presidential decisions."

Even in this simplified framework it is clear that the complexities are numerous. For example, according to the elementary theory of the firm, production should continue to the point that marginal cost equals marginal revenue. However, in any operational form this simple prescription is bound to ignore many important factors. A complication to be considered is that allocations to marketing and research create better products and more demand in future years, thereby making it possible to produce in the future for greater profits. On the other hand, existing plants deteriorate. Without capital investments, there will not be the facilities with which to carry on future production. The dollars allocated to production in the current year will decrease the availability of dollars for marketing and research and for capital investment in new facilities. To some extent, this will detract from potential future profits. It would seem desirable to be able somehow to predict the future returns from alternative current allocations to production, marketing, research, and capital investment. This presupposes the ability to capture the key interactions between these activities, present and future.

The president has attempted to conceptualize his problem in an optimization framework. He realizes that expenditures today must be motivated by the desire to enhance future as well as current returns. Therefore he must take a "long-term" viewpoint. Thinking in terms of, for example, a 15-year time period, he wants to make his decisions in such a way that the 15-year profits will be high but also so that the future prospects for the firm, at the end of 15 years, are good. Consequently, his goals are three-fold; namely,

1 To maximize the discounted stream of profits during the time horizon
2 To maximize the firm's market share *at the end* of the time horizon
3 To maximize the firm's physical capital in the form of production and research facilities; that is, maximize the capital existing *at the end* of the time horizon

The president realizes that enhancing any one of these objectives can only leave a smaller budget to further the other two objectives. It is thus clear that, given a budget constraint, he cannot literally try to maximize all three simultaneously. In order to conceptualize his problem as an optimization model, he must distinguish between objectives and constraints. He must identify one of the goals as an objective and try to attain his other goals through the use of constraints. He decides, we shall suppose, that his long-run objective is to maximize discounted profits, but he wants to set targets at the end of the time horizon for minimal threshold levels on market share and physical capital. Accordingly, his conceptual model is to

Maximize   Total discounted 15-year profits

s.t.

Market share at end of 15 years $\geq M$

Physical capital at end of 15 years $\geq C$

where M and C are parameters. These parameters may be set at various levels to determine their effects on the optimal objective value. He may then finally decide on the values to specify for his targets as policy objectives.

It is clear that the above model would be very difficult to explicitly construct and solve. There are many variables, many interactions and uncertainties, and many of the required functional forms could only be estimated. For example, revenue depends on the level of production, but the amount we decide to produce depends on our forecast for future demand. Currently, this forecast is obtained from a forecasting model. Inputs to this model include:

1   Decision variables such as the level of marketing activity, the price level and the retail credit policy
2   *Exogenous parameters* (those that are external to the model) such as the current interest rate, the GNP, the level of government loans for farmers, and the current rate of inflation.

Pictorially, the situation can be represented as in Figure 18.8.

Figure 18.8   *The current system for determining production quantities*

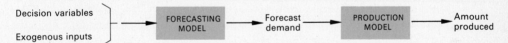

The current system utilizes two models to convert the inputs (decision variables and exogenous inputs) into production quantities, but we cannot algebraically write out the explicit functional relationship between the amount produced and the inputs to the forecasting model. Certainly the optimization approach, even in this complex framework, can be conceptually useful. But in a complex problem such as this, it could well be the case that the optimization model would have little chance of being brought to fruition. It is in such situations, often as "a last resort," that the simulation approach is adopted.

In our scenario, in order to assist the president, the planning department has been asked to develop a strategic corporate planning model. This model operates by simulating the president's problem on a period-by-period basis (for example, year by year). The output of one year's activities forms part of the input for the next year. This general idea is illustrated in Figure 18.9. As this figure shows, the simulator can be thought of as a black box that receives inputs and generates outputs. In any one year (say t) it receives the following inputs:

Figure 18.9 *The general flows in a strategic corporate planning model*

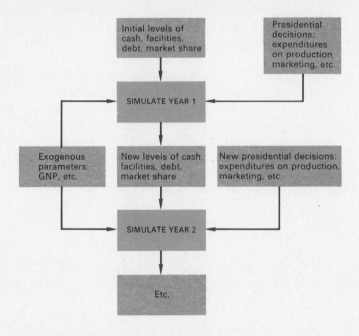

1 **External inputs**
   a The set of exogenous parameters
   b The set of presidential decisions
2 The simulated output from the previous year $(t - 1)$

Since year 0 doesn't exist, it is obvious that an initial set of "outputs" must be provided to do the simulation in year 1. The simulator itself contains models (a simulation model is often a collection of submodels) that reproduce and update pertinent aspects of the PROTRAC environment. These models use the inputs to make various ***endogenous decisions*** like price and the quantity produced.

The overall model then simulates the behavior of the system under the conditions that would exist if these inputs and endogenous decisions had actually occurred. It does so by using random numbers to select an "actual demand" from a statistical distribution and then by determining what would happen if this demand had occurred. The appropriate distribution of demand is itself determined by some combination of external inputs (exogenous parameters and presidential decisions), and endogenous decisions. For example, the distribution of demand might be determined by the general state of the economy (an exogenous parameter), the level of marketing activity (a presidential decision), and the price (an endogenous decision). Given the price, quantity produced, and "the actual demand," the simulator can calculate the gross revenue and profits. These quantities determine PROTRAC's new financial position, which is part of the internally generated input to the next period of activity. In this next period, new values for the exogenous parameters are input. Financial results from the previous time period, augmented possibly by a decision to borrow at the beginning of this new period, are now used to determine the available funds for a new set of budget allocations. The model continues to operate in this manner over a sequence of time periods. Thus, with a given sequence of exogenous parameters and presidential decisions, the model unfolds the future, and discounted future profits over any given time horizon can be obtained. In this way, the model is used as a tool to explore some of the interactions between various presidential policies and exogenous conditions.

Some of the major relationships to be captured by the model are shown in Figure 18.10. This figure reveals interactions in the firm in the sense of

Figure 18.10 *Flows of influence and dollars*

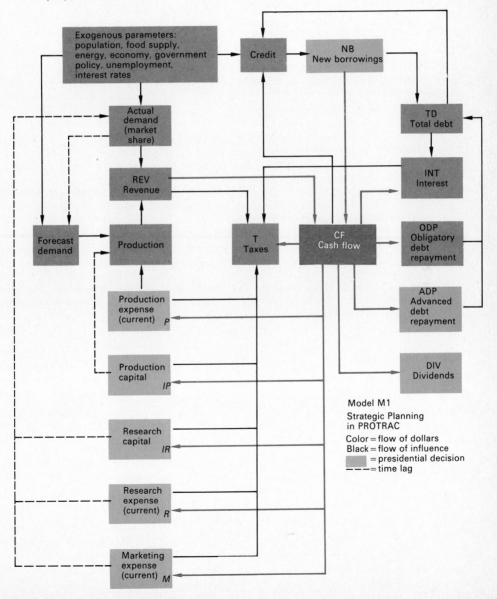

the cash flow between various activities and the direction of influence between activities. For example, the colored arrow from the *Cash Flow* box to the *Interest* box indicates that dollars flow into interest payments. The black arrow from the *Total Debt* box to the *Interest* box indicates that the amount or level of total debt influences the amount of interest to be paid. Similarly, dollars flow into taxes, and interest payments influence taxes.

Figure 18.10 shows how each presidential decision explicitly affects the cash flow and how each decision influences the state of the firm in terms of credit, total debt, market share, and physical capital. In particular, we note the following:

1 The effect of borrowing is to increase debt. This increases the size of the current pot available for expenditures, but at the added cost of future interest payments.
2 Accelerating the payment of current debt (via the advanced debt repayment decision) has an effect opposite to that cited in item 1.
3 Paying dividends decreases the size of the pot available for other expenditures (marketing, investment in new facilities, current production budget) and raises the immediate cash receipts of the stockholders. This increases the stockholders' income (as distinguished from wealth).
4 Production expense represents expenditures devoted to current production. These expenditures play a major role in determining the quantity produced. Clearly then, this allocation directly affects near-term revenues and profits.
5 Research expense represents current expenditures on research. Developments in future products and future production processes depend on the current research programs supported with these funds. Thus, the demand for products in the future and the cost of supplying this demand are directly affected by this allocation. We note that because of discounting (a dollar tomorrow is worth less than a dollar today), a dollar of future profit becomes increasingly less attractive with time than a dollar of profit today.
6 Marketing expense represents funds that are used to *estimate demand* with market research and to *stimulate demand* with promotional schemes. Since demand along with supply determines sales, the effect of this allocation on the president's objective function is clear. It should also be stressed that coordination between production and marketing expenditures is necessary. Supply without demand, or vice versa, can obviously be inefficient.
7 Investments in production capital involve the creation of new plants, warehouses, and so on. These funds are thus used either to maintain or expand capacity, making it possible to satisfy future demands or to modernize production equipment, thereby reducing production costs. The main idea is to be able to continue to produce efficiently in the future and thereby acquire greater future profits.
8 Investments in research capital are used to make it possible for the firm to continue to conduct research activities in the future. This involves the creation of new research facilities, laboratories, equipment, and so on.

With the aid of Figure 18.10, we are now in a good position to focus more clearly on some of the specifics of the actual simulation model for this problem. Before doing this, however, it will be useful to compare a simulation model with an optimization model.

18.3.2 Simulation versus Optimization

In each type of model, the user inputs parameters as data. In each case, a certain amount of useful information is created by the model and printed as output. In the optimization model, the output includes decisions (optimal values of the decision variables), the OV (the optimal value of the objective function), and the values of the constraint functions at the optimal solution. A simulation model does not have the formal structure of an objective function and constraints. The output may include the values of numerous functions of interest, such as yearly profits, total 15-year discounted profits, yearly sales, final market share, and so on. A major difference between the two types of models is this:

In a simulation model, the decisions of primary interest are input by the user. In an optimization model, the decisions of interest are produced by the model.

This assertion must be taken in the proper context, for in earlier discussions in the text we saw applications in which, in some sense, one could input a decision to an optimization model, but that is not an accurate description of what was going on. For example, in Chapter 12 we saw a study in which a capacity decision could be input as a value for an RHS parameter. By assigning a sequence of possible RHS values, we generated the optimal value function, and this function became the tool for determining the optimal capacity level. This process of running the optimization model many times, with a sequence of differing capacity levels, casts the model into a "what if" type of scenario. Explicitly, we were saying, "If the capacity is b_1 then what is the OV, and if the capacity is b_2 then what is the OV?" In this instance, the decision of *primary interest* was the capacity. Possible values of the capacity were being input to a simulation. The simulation consisted of running a linear program. Thus, it is reasonable to assert that the key concept above provides the main distinction between simulation and optimization. That is, in a simulation model the decision variables of interest are input by the user. The model then *describes* what happens under the assumption that those decisions are made. The simulator may "make" endogenous decisions in order to describe what happens, but these are not the decisions being studied. The optimization model may take as an input a value for a decision variable of interest, but then the decisions produced by the model are not the ones of major interest, and the optimization model is really a component of a simulation.

For the above reasons, simulation models are often called *descriptive* models. In particular, let us note that in the PROTRAC strategic planning model, *all* the presidential decisions are input. The model says, "If you make such and such decisions, then here is the effect of those decisions." By varying his decisions and "playing" the model many times, the president or his staff analyst may sharpen his judgment and improve his understanding of how the annual budgeting may interact with the environment of the future.

18.3.3 *The PROTRAC Model in more Detail*

Let us now describe in more detail the actual structure, or "nuts and bolts," of the strategic planning model shown in Figure 18.10. One of the purposes of this figure is to show the flow of cash in a given time period t. This flow is represented in the simulation model, and in the computer, by the following equation:

$$REV(t) + NB(t) = INT(t) + ODP(t) + ADP(t) + DIV(t) + P(t) + I_P(t) +$$
$$I_R(t) + R(t) + M(t)$$

where the variables correspond to activities as indicated in Figure 18.10. The above equation states that in period t the inflow of cash must equal the outflow. It is easy to verify that the equation is correct by considering the box labeled *Cash Flow* in Figure 18.10. The variables on the left-hand side of the above equation flow into this square, and those on the right flow out. Note there is no cash inventory or reserve of retained earnings in this particular model.

Another equation in the model deals with the total debt in period t. The status of the total debt is expressed with the following type of accounting identity:

$$TD(t) = TD(t-1) + NB(t) - ODP(t) - ADP(t)$$

This equation states that the total debt in period t equals the total debt in period $(t-1)$ plus new borrowing in period t minus debt payments in period t.

Another equation, or series of equations, in the model determine taxes as a function of interest payments, revenue, and total expenses. Thus the simulation model contains, as another component, a tax model. This tax model is a relation of the form

$$T = f(INT, REV, P, I_P, I_R, R, M)$$

But *INT* and *REV* are other quantities determined in the simulation. For example,

$$INT = g(NB, TD)$$

and

$$REV = h \quad \text{(Actual demand, production)}$$

where g and h represent either specified functions or additional submodels. Thus we have the schematic relations shown in Figure 18.11.

The above discussion illustrates the point that the simulation model provides a dynamic description of the PROTRAC environment and its interfaces with the external world. This description occurs via a linkage of flow equations, accounting identities, and submodels.

Figure 18.11 *Some linkages in the simulation model*

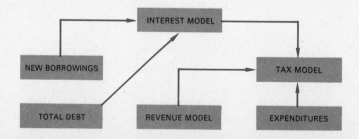

A very important aspect of a simulation model can be illustrated by referring to the revenue calculation. We saw above that revenue is determined as a function of two quantities, actual demand and production. For simplicity of exposition, let us suppose there is a single product and that the functional relation is

$$REV(t) = p(t)\min \text{ [actual demand } (t), \text{ quantity produced } (t)]$$

where $p(t)$ is the price of the product in period t. In this particular model price must either be one of the exogenous input parameters or be produced endogenously by the simulator, since it is not one of the presidential decisions. The above expression produces a figure for revenue as follows:

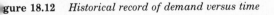

1   Suppose that the quantity produced is 50 units and that the actual demand (the quantity that could be sold if the units were available) is 120 units. Since only the 50 units that have been produced can be sold, the revenue is $p(t)50$.

2   Suppose that the quantity produced is 100 units and that the actual demand is 75 units. In this case, the entire actual demand of 75 units will be sold, and the revenue is $p(t)75$.

Thus, in order to determine revenue it is necessary to determine actual demand and quantity produced and then multiply the minimum of these values by the price.

Now consider the quantity produced. Figure 18.10 indicates that production depends on the current budget allocated to production (P), on the current status (current level) of production capital (I_p), and on forecast demand. It seems reasonable that the firm's expectations (in the sense of a forecast) concerning the level of demand will influence the amount to be produced. In any realistic situation, the forecast demand might come out of a forecasting model that could have numerous inputs such as income levels, the unemployment rate, crop conditions, marketing activity (in this and previous time periods) and actual demand in previous time periods. The point we wish to make can be developed just as well by simplifying the forecast to make it a function only of time. Such a forecasting model is shown in Figure 18.12, where previous annual demand is plotted against time.

gure 18.12   *Historical record of demand versus time*

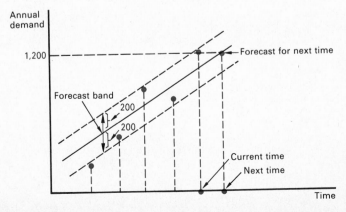

The straight line in Figure 18.12 represents a linear approximation to the past actual demand data. Our forecast for one period into the future is obtained by extrapolating along this line. As shown in the figure, this produces a forecast demand of 1,200. The computer now takes this forecast, enters it into the production model along with current values for P and I_p, and out of the production model comes quantity produced. The next step is to compare quantity produced with actual demand in order to obtain revenue. But since we are projecting into the future, how can we obtain actual demand? The computer cannot know what the actual demand will really be, but it must find a way to simulate this quantity in the model. You may feel that we should use our forecast of 1,200 for this purpose, but that would not be very realistic. It would be most unusual for the actual demand to exactly equal the forecast. Life is simply too uncertain for forecasting to be that accurate. The model requires a method of producing an actual demand that maintains a more realistic relationship between the forecast and the actual demand. One way to accomplish this is to use the statistics produced in the forecast model associated with Figure 18.12. The statistics associated with such a model might tell us, for example, that 95 percent of the time the true observed historical demand was in a specified band about the forecast line. Suppose that band is of width 400 units (200 units on each side of the forecast line), as shown in Figure 18.12. Then we might expect the actual demand in the next time period to be between 1,000 and 1,400 with probability of .95. The computer can be instructed to draw a random number in such a way that any integer between 1,000 and 1,400 is equally likely. The value of this number will be the model's representation (the simulated value) of the actual demand. This number is compared with quantity produced. The minimum of the two numbers is multiplied by price, and revenue is thereby obtained. These interactions are shown in Figure 18.13. In this figure, the forecast demand model is shown to be more complex than in the above exposition, but the random number enters conceptually in an analogous way. It is to be emphasized that all the above-described models and all these linkages are programmed into the computer. The simulation model is the totality of these submodels and linkages, and all the operations and flows from one model to another are carried out within the computer.

The above discussion leads us to the following important point. The simulation model can be executed two times in succession, using identical inputs for parameters and decisions, and each execution will produce a different output. The reason for this is that in each execution a different random number will be drawn for actual demand. Different numbers will thus be created in the internal working of the model.

Thus, we again see that the generation of random numbers is the computer's way of simulating uncertainty in the real world. This phenomenon is a useful aspect of the simulation approach, for it allows the user to perceive some of the impact of this uncertainty. The user may, for example, run the model many times with identical inputs in order to observe the distribution of output values. He will be interested in computing the average of these values and in measuring the variation of these values about the average. The more the variation, the greater the impact of uncertainty.

Figure 18.13   *A random aspect of the simulation model*

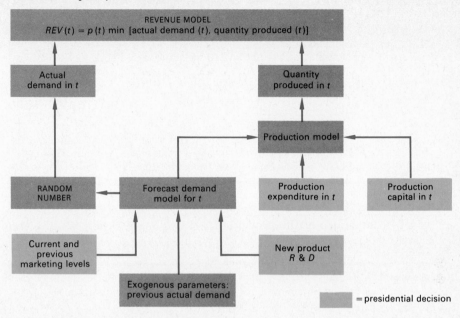

18.3.4   *Suboptimization in the Model*

The basic characteristic of our corporate planning model is that for any particular set of decision variables, the model yields values for quantities the decision maker is interested in. The decision variables in this model are the set of presidential decisions, and the model produces values for such quantities as gross revenue, share of market, rate of capital growth, and others, for each time period. The model can then be used to compare alternative policies (sets of decisions), but it cannot be used to produce a best or optimal policy.

There are however, a variety of potential places for optimization *submodels* within the corporate planning model. These models are optimization models in the sense that they yield an optimal solution for a particular component of the overall system. Usually, the optimization would be constrained by a specified set of inputs that are either generated by other sections of the model or are directly input by the decision maker. The submodels are not optimization models in the sense of being part of a solution that yields the best solution for the larger overall problem. This discussion lies in the area of what is often referred to as *suboptimization,* a topic that was considered in Chapter 10.

Three of the many possible opportunities for suboptimization, in our current context, are presented below for illustrative purposes.

Production Planning Model   The basic question in this model is how much of each product to produce in each plant in each period. It has the following characteristics:

1 Inputs
a The capacity of the plants in each period. This is determined by factors such as current work force and previous capital investment.
b The cost of producing a given quantity of each product in each period.
c The cost of accumulating inventory and the physical limitations on holding inventory (if any).
d The forecast demand for the various products in each time period.
e The revenue per item.
2 Objective: Typically, one might use an objective of maximizing total net revenue, which is gross revenue minus costs. The model might or might not include transportation costs, depending on the circumstances and on the ability of the analyst to devise a model that can be solved, that is, a model for which a mathematical technique is available to find an optimal decision.

Media Planning (A Marketing Strategy Model)   The basic question in this model is how much of the promotion budget should be allocated to the various promotional devices.

1 Inputs
a An exhaustive list of the promotional devices under consideration.
b The size of the budget to be allocated.
c Response functions for each promotional device, that is, functions that show the dollars of final product demanded for any specific expenditure in a given promotional device. To be realistic, such functions would require a time-lag factor; that is, promotional expenditures in a given period (say t) would have an effect on demand in later periods (perhaps $t + 1$ or $t + 2$).
2 Objective: In this case, the goal might be to find an allocation of dollars to media in such a way as to maximize the total dollar value of final demand for the specified promotional budget. It is clear that it would be attractive to build a model incorporating both the media planning and production planning models. By linking these two models, one can reasonably worry about total net revenue as an objective. Using the models separately, one faces the possibility of generating a large total dollar volume of final demand for products that cannot be produced because of capacity constraints or for products with low net revenue yields.

Debt Management   The basic question considered in this model is what type of debt instruments should be used by the firm. It should be noted that for any activity in either the debt or investment markets, there are typically costs for making a transaction, plus an interest payment (either income or expenditure).

1 Inputs
a A capital expenditures plan over some reasonably long horizon.
b A forecast of cash flows over the same horizon.
c A list of the debt instruments that are available and their associated costs.
d Investments available in the money markets with their associated costs and returns.
2 Objective: In such a model, a reasonable objective is to minimize the total cost (transactions costs plus interest expenditures minus interest income) of meeting the given capital expenditure plan.

18.3.5 *Use of the Strategic Planning Model: Comparing Policies*

Different evaluations of present and future conditions and different expectations based on these evaluations can lead to quite different strategic policies. As an example, let us imagine that the president's task is to choose between two basic policies. The following description of these policies will also help to convey an appreciation for the importance of the exogenous parameters in the model.

POLICY 1

This policy deemphasizes current production in favor of capital expansion abroad and the expectation of large future profits in foreign markets. This policy reflects pessimism about the strength of current domestic demand. Weak demand, combined with high labor costs and possibly even a price freeze, might provide a dim picture for current profits. The emphasis on foreign capital expansion reflects confidence in predictions for rapid growth in overseas markets. It also reflects a support for arguments to put overseas business on a sound footing. Factors that help to support an optimistic outlook for the future of overseas markets include: (1) evidence of substantial agricultural investment in developing countries that are currently net importers of food grains; (2) reduction of trade barriers by industrialized countries; (3) predictions for continuing growth of foreign populations; and (4) evidence that agricultural investment and specialization in foreign countries tend to be going in a direction that will not compete with PROTRAC's heavy farm machinery products. (For example, the foreign emphasis might be on fertilizer production, land development, irrigation, and so on.)

POLICY 2

This policy places emphasis on maximizing current domestic profits at the expense of expansion. This policy reflects more concern for future uncertainties and places more reliance on, and confidence in, the immediacy of the present. Support for this policy may be based on a belief in the fundamental strength of domestic demand, even in a period of recession. Advocates of this policy argue that world grain supplies are in a current state of shortage and that recent government policy has been to encourage international sales of grain. This stimulates grain prices and encourages the American farmer, as a profit-maximizing entrepreneur, to produce more, and this in turn stimulates domestic demand for PROTRAC equipment. Thus, those planners who support policy 2 look for high profits in the short run at home.

Let us now consider how the strategic planning model might be used to evaluate and compare these two policies. First, each policy must be formulated in quantitative terms. That is, presidential decisions must be made that are consistent with each policy. For example, it might be expected that the ratio

$$\frac{\text{Dollars allocated to foreign investment and marketing}}{\text{Dollars allocated to domestic production}}$$

would be larger for policy 1 than for policy 2. After a reasonable set of decisions is quantified for each of the policies, the model is then run with each set of presidential decisions over a comparable time horizon. The outputs will give some insight into the relative merits of each policy. Clearly, the assumed values of the inputs for the exogenous parameters (those that describe the condition of the "real world") strongly affect the output.

Of course, if the world is not as predicted, the relative performances of the two policies in the model may not correspond at all to their relative performances if they were to be used in the real world. Thus, in order to strengthen the credibility of the output, it is desirable to run the model a number of times for each policy, where with each run a different set of exogenous parameters is chosen. This gives a "spectrum" of outputs that might be obtained from each policy.

As discussed in the previous section, there is yet another reason for running the model many times. Some of the quantities, such as actual (as opposed to forecast) product demand, are drawn from statistical distributions. Thus, even if the model is run twice with exactly the same exogenous inputs and the same set of presidential decisions, different outputs would be expected because of statistical variations. This is typical of simulation models, and it is important to obtain a series of runs in order to determine the magnitude of the possible statistical variations.

It should be emphasized that variability in the output of a simulation is intrinsically neither good nor bad. The important fact is that the simulation should do a reasonable job of reproducing the amount of variability that actually occurs in the system being simulated. For example, if in the real world there is a large degree of variability between forecast demand and actual demand, then the same condition should exist in the simulation model. If in the real world there is a high degree of correspondence between the forecast for an event and the realization of that event, then this high degree of correspondence should also hold true in the simulation model.

This requirement for corresponding degrees of variability may pose a real dilemma for the designer of a simulation. In order to build a model of manageable size, it is frequently necessary to "aggregate" reality. This means that the model might include three aggregated classes of products rather than 500 individual products. A typical model for delivery times of finished goods might be based on aggregated point-of-origin and point-of-destination data. It may be true, however, that delivery times for finished goods in the real situation heavily depend on whether the items are shipped by the firm's own trucks or whether they must use a common carrier.

If the variability within the model significantly differs from one's perception of the real-world variability, it is necessary to make the model more realistic. This usually means one must disaggregate. In the above examples, this would mean increasing the number of specific products to be considered or including the type of carrier in the model. This pressure for more realism tends to encourage the designers of simulators to build models that are very large and hence expensive to program and execute.

Let us now illustrate another situation where the model can be used to compare and evaluate alternative policies. Suppose that the president has directed several of his key executives to give him projected budget requests on a yearly basis for ten years into the future, along with a justification for that request. For example, he has made such requests of the vice-president in charge of production and the vice-president in charge of marketing and research. He has also requested a plan for debt management from the corporate treasurer. Of course, each executive makes recommendations to strengthen his own position and power in the firm, and it turns out that there is no single plan that will satisfy both vice-presidents and the treasurer simultaneously. In order to satisfy the requests of both vice-presidents (their recommended allocations to both investment and operations in their respective areas), the debt becomes larger than that which the treasurer would recommend. It follows that in order to adopt the treasurer's plan it would be necessary to cut the recommendations elsewhere.

In any case, based on the information he has received, and after considering all the arguments, the president and his staff have worked out five different policies, all of potential interest for the next ten-year period. Each policy dictates a yearly set of presidential decisions, given the output of the previous year. For example, policy 1 might be stated as follows.

STATEMENT OF POLICY 1

1 Over the ten-year horizon there will be no net addition to research capital. Each year, the amount of investment in research capital will be just enough to replace the previous year's depreciation in existing capital. Production capital increases at the rate of 5 percent per year.
2 In no year for which the interest rate exceeds 4 percent will there be any dollars allocated to prepayment of existing debt. Only obligatory debt payments are made.
3 Current dividend policy is unchanged.
4 If the interest rate falls below 6 percent, funds are borrowed to make the obligatory debt payment. Otherwise, this payment comes out of gross revenue. Funds are borrowed for no other purpose, unless the interest rate falls to 4 percent, in which case funds are borrowed for the investment allocation specified in item 1. In addition, in any year in which the interest rate falls to 4 percent, the existing debt will be refinanced (money will be borrowed to pay it all off).
5 Gross revenue, possibly depleted by an obligatory debt payment and by investment allocations (as stipulated above), is then used for allocations to production, marketing, and research on a 60-percent, 30-percent, 10-percent basis.

The other four policies are specified in a similar way. In addition to these five policies, the president has approved three different exogenous scenarios as alternative forecasts for the relevant time horizon. Essentially, these have to do with domestic economic expectations in terms of money supply, interest rates, employment levels, and GNP, and with expectations concerning foreign markets. The three different exogenous scenarios are referred to as XS1, XS2, XS3.

The president has directed his management science department to perform this study. The department's report to the president takes the form of the table shown in Figure 18.14 (appended to which would be many pages of explanation, documentation, and speculation).

It can be seen in this figure that in all three scenarios, policy 3 behaves uniformly more poorly than the other policies. Since policy 3 is dominated

Figure 18.14 *Summary of simulation results for the president's five-policy decision*

	Policy	5-year totals							10-year totals						
		TDP	DPC	FPC	RC	GR	MS	TD	TDP	DPC	FPC	RC	GR	MS	TD
XS1	1	321	455	60	20	8.1	49	89	510	405	51	20	17	53	72
	2	321	460	30	16	8.8	49	30	660	330	42	12	14	75	95
	3	320	450	30	15	7.6	48	90	500	300	40	10	13	52	110
	4	331	452	45	16	7.7	50	80	502	312	48	11	15	80	105
	5	360	451	35	18	9	49	64	570	302	60	13	19	60	80
XS2	1	320	460	32	15	8	46	60	488	340	39	12	16	56	40
	2	314	444	40	16	7	50	74	484	324	58	16	13	52	45
	3	310	440	20	14	6	46	75	480	320	38	11	12	51	60
	4	312	450	30	18	10	48	50	482	328	55	17	18	60	55
	5	316	470	25	22	9	49	62	486	321	40	13	14	53	50
XS3	1	330	430	30	13	9	60	69	472	295	42	15	11.2	52	60
	2	313	425	35	14	7	63	70	490	330	50	10	14	70	82
	3	312	420	25	13	6.5	52	80	471	290	42	9	9	48	82
	4	340	426	40	13	11	64	71	475	300	61	11	10.5	50	81
	5	320	440	45	15	10	65	75	480	310	70	10	9.2	60	40

TDP = total discounted profits (millions)
DPC = domestic production capital (10^3 ft^2)
FPC = foreign production capital (10^3 ft^2)
RC = research capital (10^3 ft^2)
GR = gross revenues (billions)
MS = market share (percentage)
TD = total debt (millions)

by all the others, it might seem appropriate to eliminate it from the list of alternatives. However, it might also be possible that policy 3 has some importance or special significance to the president that stems from considerations not adequately built into the model. All that can be said with certainty is that within the context of the model policy 3 can be rejected as clearly undesirable.

The uses that the president might make of this report could be any of the following:

1 He may request information on the statistical variation of the numbers in the table. (Recall that two runs of the model with identical inputs will lead to different outputs because certain entities are drawn from statistical distributions.) In particular, he may want to know whether the results in the table are based on single runs or whether they are averaged over many runs. If they are averaged, how much did the individual results deviate from the average?

2 He may use the information in the table to derive new policies that he sends back to the management science department as a new set of inputs. Or, he may wish to examine a different exogenous scenario with the same previous policies.

3 He may wish to see the model rerun with the same policies, but with a number of specified changes in the model.

4 Finally, he may accept the results of the model. From these results he may select a policy that seems to him to be the most reasonable to implement. This perception would depend on the executive's nature and on a number of judgments. For example, he might pick a policy that never does extremely well but leads to a modest or

acceptable level of performance by his judgment under all of the exogenous scenarios. Alternatively, he might pick a policy that does "best" in the scenario he considers most likely. He might measure "best" in terms of a single criterion, such as TDP over 10 years, but he may also insist that certain threshold levels be attained in regard to DPC, FPC, and MS. Thus, out of the five policies, he might seek one that, for a specified scenario, maximizes ten-year TDP, subject to DPC $\geq K_1$, FPC $\geq K_2$, and MS $\geq K_3$, where K_1, K_2, and K_3 are constants that he has chosen.

18.3.6 The Role of Judgment in Using the Model

Judgment plays a major role in the construction and use of the strategic planning model. First, the president's perception of the future delimits the types of policies he will want to consider. The president's knowledge of the firm, his executive ability, his relation to the board of directors, his awareness of internal politics, all of these factors lead to judgmental evaluations and serve to further focus his interest on smaller subsets of policies. Also, keep in mind that this model is one that tends to provide guidance for the development of a long-range strategic policy as opposed to short-run answers. Considerable judgment can be exercised in knowing which of the exogenous parameters are most important in the long run and the extent to which they should be varied in attempting to determine more credible information. Also, consider the fact that the model is run over a sequence of time periods. How long should this time horizon be? What should be the existing capital at the end of the horizon? These are certainly at least in part matters of judgment.

For example, one way of looking at the model is as an instrument that measures the effects of different rates of capital consumption. Suppose at the end of a 15-year time horizon a certain "desired state of capital" is stipulated. Two broadly different ways to achieve this target are as follows:

1 Emphasize current production for as long as possible, then place large amounts of funds into plant and equipment late in the horizon.

2 Invest large amounts in plant and equipment early in the horizon, produce more later.

In general, the two policies would tend to produce different total discounted profits. By using the model, we could compare these two policies and select the better. However, the judgmental role is crucially important since the answer is very dependent on the length of the horizon and the desired target.

On the output side, there are also numerous ways in which judgment becomes involved in leading to a presidential decision. Some policies may be rejected out of hand because although the president felt that he had chosen reasonable inputs he knows that the board would not approve of the type of performance the model predicts. On the other hand, he may have enough confidence in his own judgment to know that his inputs, in reality, could not possibly lead to the results predicted by the model. Consequently, he may reject the model on the basis of judgment, requesting modifications or even seeking other assistance. Finally, not everything can be built into a model. Consequently, the president might use the model to find certain policies that satisfy other requirements that, for one reason or another, have not been built in. Then, finally, out of some suitable set of policies he will choose one that appeals most to his own taste, and this too might be considered a judgmental influence.

18.3.7 *The Management Scientist's Role*

Chapter 3 included a number of comments about the role of the management scientist or the professional model builder in the construction and use of optimization models. Most of the same comments apply in the context of simulation modeling as well. In particular, as soon as the management scientist begins, or is expected, to recommend solutions he is in for trouble by allowing a confusion between his own role and that of the actual decision maker. Even with an optimization model, the most he can do is state that, given such and such assumptions in such and such a model, then such and such decisions are optimal. He must never fail to emphasize (1) the assumptions and (2) the nature of the model. In some cases, the assumptions may determine the nature of the model (for example, certain assumptions lead to an LP model), but even within the context of a given type of model there may be room for many different kinds of assumptions (concerning data, parameters, specific constraints, and so on). In this context we have repeatedly emphasized that not even an optimization model can be expected to provide a client with the best decision for his real problem. Such a model can provide only the best decision within the context of the model. If the model is quite realistic, this decision might be a very good one for the client, but even if the model is a terrible approximation it could, by chance, produce a very good decision (though probably a very bad one next year). In any case, in order to obtain the best results consistently, it is clearly desirable for the management scientist to make his model as realistic as possible, and this must be done in close consultation with the client. Moreover, only the client can pass final judgment on the realism achieved; and let the user beware, for ultimately judgments on realism are his responsibility. The major responsibilities of the modeler may be stated as follows:

1 To be clearly aware of the assumptions
2 To state the assumptions clearly to the client
3 To make certain that the mathematics is correct and that the model does what the modeler says (and thinks) it does

We note that, concerning judgments on realism, it is a major goal of our approach to teach you, as the client, enough about models and modelers to make such judgments and to better evaluate the claims of those you may employ.

From all of the above we conclude that certainly the management scientist should do all he can *not* to create a profile of "recommending allocations" or providing "best answers." However, this is not intended to detract from the importance or potential usefulness of his work. To the contrary, a proper understanding of his role should enhance the potential value of his services.

18.3.8 *Advantages and Limitations*

The main advantage of corporate planning simulation models is that they handle a large number of interactions in a consistent but adjustable manner and in this way allow for a consistent evaluation of alternative policies. As with models in general, another advantage is the explicit identification and specification of the relations of interest. Human beings are not particularly good at consistently tracing through the implications of a decision that must interact with numerous other decisions or exogenous variables before its impact is realized.

Another advantage is that after the fact it is possible to observe the deviations between the results predicted by the model and the actual events. These observations can be used to modify the model and hopefully improve its performance in the next decision period. If one does not record the assumptions and calculations that lead to a particular decision, it is difficult to learn much from experience. Simulation modeling is another systematic way of specifying and recording the important interactions.

At least two limitations should be mentioned. The first might be identified as the size of the model. This is closely related to the problem of not knowing exactly which variables one must work with to capture the essence of the problem. Big models are expensive to build and operate. A common error when people first begin to build models is to make them too realistic and too comprehensive. The number of interactions that must be specified is large, and the data required to make these specifications in a reasonable manner are both expensive and time-consuming to obtain. Often, attempts to model a complicated situation are stillborn because the projects are simply too ambitious. In addition, a large simulation model with many parameters will require many, many executions in order to study variability and to test the sensitivity of the output to parameter values. This can be prohibitively expensive.

A second limitation, beyond sheer size, is that often no one understands the interactions and the relationships well enough to build even a simulation model that works effectively. Simple extrapolations of policies that have worked well in the past for reasons not well understood may be more useful than recommendations from elaborate models based on dubious relationships. For example, there are many people who have more confidence in the economic forecasts made by "experts" combining facts in a heuristic manner than in the forecasts emanating from large simulation models.

18.4 Simulating the Past

We have just discussed a model that simulates the future. In this section we want to illustrate types of analyses that simulate the past. You may wonder why anyone would wish to simulate something that is already known with complete certainty. Simulating the past is a device commonly used by modelers to gain some measure for the credibility of a model. The general notion of simulating the past applies to models that attempt to predict real-world phenomena or prescribe decisions to be made in some particular context. Such a model may be tested on historical data in two steps:

1   First, decisions (in the past) are made by the model as they would have been made if the model had been available at that time.

2   Then the model is evaluated by comparing its performance on past data with the actual historical data. One can thereby determine the costs (or savings) that would have been incurred if the model actually had been used.

This provides a type of null test. If the model did not perform well on historical data, it is often difficult to believe that it will perform well in the future. Unfortunately, the fact that it *did* work well on historical data does not prove that it will work well in the future. Assessing how well it will work in the future involves a great deal of judgment. This judgment should rest on an understanding of why the model worked in the past and how stable the system is. In other words, the model captures a particular logical structure or collection of relationships that appear to explain the reality of the past. How likely is it that the reality of the future will be explained by the same collection of relationships? That is what we mean by judging the stability of the system. The following specific example is intended to illustrate and clarify the general statements made in this paragraph.

A commodities speculator has developed a set of quantitative rules for buying and selling futures contracts on frozen pork bellies. These rules are based on historical price relationships that existed during the past 15 years between the various contract months. Historical storage charges and interest rates also entered into the development of his rules. In this case, then, the speculator's mathematical theory, along with an analysis of historical data, has lead to his trading model. In order to use his model on any given day, he must input the closing prices for each contract on the previous day. He also inputs the 30-day interest rate and the current storage charges. The model then tells him which contracts to buy or sell, and respective quantities thereof.

In order to evaluate his model with a simulation, the trader might typically employ the past data as follows. Beginning, for example, in 1965, he acts as though he were actually trading with his model. He takes the actual daily closing prices from then to the present, along with the then-current interest rates and storage charges, inputs this data to the computer, and has the computer execute his trading rules and compute yearly profits, losses, margin requirements, and so on. If he is disappointed in the results, he may modify some of the rules and then repeat the simulation in the hope of achieving a better past performance. Thus, he simulates the past to develop more confidence in the way his model might perform if he uses it today, in the present, with real dollars.

There are two points worth noting about the above procedure. First, as was previously stated, the fact that his model performed very well on past data is no guarantee that it will perform well in the future. Storage charges may have been relatively important up until about two years ago. Since that time their significance may have dwindled. The overall past performance of the model may be good, but because the economic relationships are in a significant state of change the future prognosis is terrible. As a second point worth noting, we have said that the trader's rules were based on historical price relationships. This need not have been the case. The trader may simply have been given the rules, or he may have found them written on a wall, or he may have personally created them out of sheer brilliance, with no use of historical data. So-called technical traders frequently acquire their rules in such ways. One can nevertheless simulate the application of these rules by using past data. Thus, the use of the past to create rules should be distinguished from the use of the past to simulate and test rules, regardless of their origin.

You may have already had the following thought: If past data were used to create the rules, then how could these rules fail to perform quite well when they are applied to this very same data? As an extreme example, suppose the past data were used as follows:

1   For each day in each January of the past 15 years the pork belly prices for the nearest contract are obtained.
2   All these prices are then averaged to obtain an *average January price.*
3   This procedure is repeated for each of the remaining months of the year, to obtain an *average February price,* and so on.

Based on these historical monthly averages the trader devises the following rules:

1   Look at the price of the nearest contract on the first trading day of the month. If this price is between 10 and 20 percent lower than this month's historical average, then buy one contract.
2   If it is between 20 and 50 percent lower, then buy two contracts, and so on.

Thus, the trader has used past data to create his rules and yet experience has shown that such rules, when simulated with the actual past data, yield disastrous financial results.

The idea of simulating the past is important in numerous and diverse applications. For example, a large government agency was recently concerned about the effect of money supply on the rate of inflation. Some of the analysts in the agency were thus working with a *conditional* forecasting model that would predict the national inflation rate five quarters into the future as a function of the global and domestic money supplies.

The model was based on two factors:

1   The strongly held belief on the part of the economists for the agency that the global and domestic money supplies are primary determinants of the rate of inflation.
2   A very successful one-period forecasting model.

This model used data in the current quarter to predict the rate of inflation in the next quarter. Inputs were the rate of inflation, the global money supply, and the domestic money supply in the current quarter, and the output was the rate of inflation in the next quarter. In particular, the model was a system of equations, and the parameters in the equations were estimated by using standard statistical techniques on past data, starting with the first quarter of 1965 through the present. Such models are often called *econometric models,* and many such models have been developed for macroeconomic forecasting. This model was a "good fit" in the sense that there was close correspondence between each quarter's actual inflation rate and that quarter's predicted inflation rate (based upon the previous quarter's actual inflation rate and the previous quarter's actual money supplies).

The analysts hoped to transform this one-quarter forecasting model into the desired *conditional* forecasting model. As different values for the money supply were input into this proposed model, different rates of inflation would be produced, and hence the effect of such policy changes (in the money supply) could be studied. In essence, the analyst's model was a function machine like

Figure 18.15   *A model for predicting inflation*

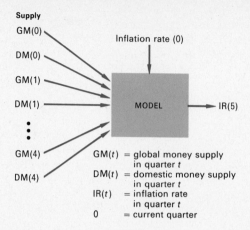

the one shown in Figure 18.15. Since this agency could influence the domestic money supply, this model could be tremendously useful in determining the policies to be supported.

This particular model was designed to operate as follows. The model accepts the actual global and domestic money supplies and the actual rate of inflation during the current quarter (say $t = 0$) as *inputs* and yields a predicted rate of inflation for next quarter as intermediate output. This *predicted* value of the rate of inflation for next quarter along with an *assigned* level for the money supplies during the next quarter would then lead to a *prediction* of the inflation rate two quarters into the future. Continuing to iterate in this way, the model could presumably predict the inflation rate five quarters into the future ($t = 5$), *conditional* upon the assigned intermediate money supply values. Of course, there is no particular importance to time periods 0 and 5. The important point is that, given data on money supply for a particular quarter and rate of inflation for that quarter, and given hypothetical money supply values for four succeeding quarters, then the inflation rate in the fifth succeeding quarter is estimated. Thus, for example, one could take the data in quarter 3 as given, and predict the inflation rate in quarter 8, and so on.

The analysts and the economists for the agency were convinced that the proposed model would yield accurate results. After all, they had a well-developed theory and the impressive statistics of the one-period forecasting model to support their position. Nevertheless, the client, being rather cautious, wanted to test this model somehow. The model purports to estimate reasonably well the inflation rate that will be produced by various money supply levels in the five preceding periods. One obvious test would be to look at past money supply levels and see if the model's prediction was close to the actual past rates of inflation. This procedure is called *simulating the model's performance with past data.*

The client began with the first quarter of 1965 ($t = 0$), inputting the then-current actual money supplies and the actual rate of inflation at that time and allowing the model to predict the rate of inflation during the second quarter ($t = 1$). He then took the *actual* money supply during the second quarter and the *predicted* (rather than actual) rate of inflation to predict the rate of inflation in the third quarter. This process is continued on into quarter 5, where the predicted inflation rate and actual inflation rate are then compared. Next, the client began with the second quarter of 1965 ($t = 1$), inputting the then-current actual money supplies and the actual rate of inflation at that time. The actual money supplies for the next five quarters were then used to obtain an estimated inflation rate for quarter 6, and this was compared with the actual value in quarter 6. Continuing the simulation in this way, it soon became apparent that the model's predictions were enormously different from the rates of inflation that actually existed. This caused the client considerable discomfort. Had the correspondence between actual and predicted inflation been good, nothing would have been proved, for this would not imply that an equally good correspondence would have been obtained if the data had been different. Nevertheless, the simulation run by the client was really the only test available, and good results would at least have given a sort of null test for the model. As it was, the results of this simulation left the model on very shaky ground. The client's attitude was the following: "I don't care how good the statistics are. I don't even want to look at them. Our job is to predict the future. Give me a model that is not ridiculous at predicting the past and I will use it. I don't care what the theoretic justification is."

This type of pragmatic response is not unusual among those who must live with a decision to be made on the basis of a model. A decision maker (especially in the government in terms of macroeconomic planning problems) frequently has to choose between a theory in which he believes intellectually but which simulates the past poorly and a set of equations of unexplainable economic origin that appear to track the past more closely.

The above discussion concludes our introductory treatment of simulation models. In the next chapter we shall pursue the topic on a more detailed and somewhat more advanced level. The discussion will be in the context of a simulation approach to the problem of designing a dock facility for an oil refinery. Although the analysis will be more complicated and extensive, the simulator itself is designed from the same point of view as the frame-processing simulator discussed in Section 18.2.2. It will be seen that the complications arise in attempting to properly analyze and interpret the data produced by the simulation. In this respect, the next chapter provides you with an opportunity to study simulation in a fairly realistic application.

18.5 Summary of Key Concepts

The basic idea of a simulation is to build an experimental device that will "act like" (simulate) the system of interest in certain important respects. (Section 18.1)

Random numbers are used in simulation to generate the occurrence of uncertain events. (Section 18.2.1)

The large number of logical and bookkeeping operations associated with most simulation models implies that computers are essential to the process of experimenting with these models. (Section 18.2.2)

In a simulation model, the decisions of primary interest are input by the user. These are called exogenous decisions. In an optimization model, the decisions of interest are produced by the model. **(Section 18.3.2)**

There are two main reasons to "run" a simulation model a number of times with the same set of exogenous decisions:
1 To test the robustness of the decisions to changes in the exogenous parameters
2 To better understand the variability of the outcomes for any decision-parameter combination
(Sections 18.3.3 and 18.3.4)

Simulating the past is a device commonly used by modelers to gain some measure for the credibility of a model. **(Section 18.4)**

Simulating the past provides a null test of a model. If the model does not work well on historical data, it is difficult to believe that it will perform well in the future. Furthermore, even if the model works well on historical data, it still may not perform well in the future. **(Section 18.4)**

18.6 Problems

1 A gambler plays the following game: a regular bridge deck (4 suits, 13 cards each) is shuffled, and a card is drawn at random. If a heart is drawn he pays $10. If a club or a spade is drawn he pays $20. If a diamond is drawn he pays $0. Assume that you wished to use the random numbers in Figure 18.1 to simulate the play of this game. What random numbers would you assign to each event?

2 An urn contains 20 red, 30 blue, and 50 white balls. A gambler has the opportunity to play the following game: a ball is selected at random. If a red ball is drawn he wins $20. If a blue ball is drawn he wins $30. If a white ball is drawn he wins $2.

   a Start with the random number in row 10, column 6 of Figure 18.1 and simulate 10 trials of this game. Make the correspondence between numbers and colors as follows:

Red	0–19
Blue	20–49
White	50–99

   Calculate the average return.

   b Repeat part *a* starting where you left off in the sequence of random numbers. Are the average returns the same? Is this a surprise?

   c Use the data from the 20 trials to calculate the average return.

   d Find the expected return associated with this game.

   e Compare the answers between parts *a* and *d*, parts *b* and *d*, and between parts *c* and *d*. Does the relationship surprise you? Why?

3 A gambler has the opportunity to play the following game: a card is drawn at random from a standard bridge deck (4 suits, 13 cards per suit).

   (1) If a club or a diamond is drawn a fair coin is flipped. If a head appears the gambler wins $10. If a tail appears he wins $0.

   (2) If a heart is drawn a fair die is thrown. If a 1 or a 2 appears the gambler wins $30. Otherwise he wins $0.

   (3) If a spade is drawn the card is returned to the deck, the deck is shuffled, and

another card is drawn at random. If a spade is drawn again the gambler wins $40. Otherwise he wins $0.

a Make a flow chart for a simulator for this game.

b Starting with the number in row 5, column 5 of the random numbers in Figure 18.1, find the average return from playing this game ten times.

c Find the expected return associated with a single play of this game.

d How much should the gambler be willing to pay to participate in a single play of this game?

4 Use the flow chart in Figure 18.5 to simulate the processing of four E–9 frames. Determine the idle time. Start where the example in the text ended, namely, with the number in row 13, column 10, of Figure 18.1. (This number is 39.)

5 Comment on the following statement: In order for a mathematical model to be a simulation, the model must include random elements and thus employ random numbers in its operation.

6 A major oil company has a complicated nonlinear programming model that finds an optimal production schedule, including optimal quantities of each of several crude oils to use in the refining process, as a function of both the sales price and demand for the firm's retail products. The objective of this model is to maximize profits. The marketing department is attempting to develop a solid program for next year. The department manager must select a strategy in which both the promotional effort and product prices are specified. Given any strategy, the manager believes that he can accurately forecast the demand for retail products (perhaps using another model). There are currently three strategies he is thinking of using, and he plans to use the model to select the best of these.

Describe the sense in which the marketing department manager, although using an optimization model, is actually employing a simulation approach.

7 In Sections 18.2.1 and 18.2.2 we have seen that in a simulation model containing random elements, it is typically necessary to run a simulator a number of times for the same decision in order to get a good estimate of the true cost (or benefit) of the decision under consideration. Can you think of another reason for running a number of trials for the same decision?

8 Comment on the following statement: Variability is a natural enemy of simulation. Simulations should be designed to keep variability to a reasonably low level so that accurate estimates of the effectiveness of alternative policies can be arrived at with a reasonable number of simulation trials.

9 Consider the inflation model discussed in Section 18.4. The analyst defends his rejected model as follows:

The test you have applied is unfair. You assume that the actual values for GM(t) and DM(t) $t = 0, \ldots, 4$ are available but that IR(t) is not. That is nonsense. Either you know the values from period t or you don't. Why assume that you only know some of them? The model will yield excellent results if we put the true values for GM(t), DM(t) and $\underline{\text{IR}}(t)$ into the model, rather than using the predicted values for the inflation rate, say $\widehat{\text{IR}}(t)$, as you've done in your test. You should change your mind and adopt the model.

Discuss the difference between this point of view and the one taken in the text.

10 Section 17.4 considered the role of historical data in constructing forecasting models. A "divide-and-conquer" approach was suggested. In this approach, one used the first half of the data to select parameter values so that the model fit the data. The ability of the model to forecast was then tested on the second half of the data. In Section 18.4, a commodity-pricing example was given in which a model was both derived and tested on the same set of historical data.

Is the advice given in these two sections contradictory? Try to specify some general guidelines to use in deciding when one should "divide and conquer" and when one can both derive and test a model on the same set of data. Is the "divide-and-conquer" rule applicable to the model described by the analyst in question 9 above?

19 Simulation and Sample Statistics

A particular simulation study is analyzed as a statistical experiment. The underlying concepts that are introduced include random variable, probability mass function, expected value and variance, random sampling, and independence. The sample mean is discussed as an estimate of the population mean, and confidence intervals are introduced. These concepts are employed in the analysis of a specific problem within the firm. The design of the experiment, along with the sequence of computer runs, is discussed and developed in considerable detail, and the results are presented.

19.1 Introduction

In the previous chapter we saw that a simulation study consists of four main steps:

1 A model is built and parameter values are specified.
2 The model is run on the computer.
3 Data are gathered.
4 Conclusions regarding the real problem are drawn.

By virtue of steps 2 and 3, a simulation study is often formally regarded as a statistical experiment. This implies that the model is aimed at real-world situations in which the outcomes are uncertain events. The "occurrence" of these uncertain events can be simulated with the use of a computer and its random number generator. In such studies, the experiment is performed many times and the collection of occurrences thereby produced is called a *sample.* Alternatively, one might say that the set of all possible outcomes of the experiment is the sample space of interest.

The field of statistics includes a well-developed theory for analyzing samples. Thus, by thinking of a simulation as a statistical experiment, one can use the tools and theories of statistics to analyze the data that result from the simulation. The likelihood of drawing valid inferences from the data, to use in aiding the decision process, is greatly enhanced by the use of formal statistical methods, whereas the use of untrained intuition on experimental results often produces notoriously erroneous conclusions.

The statistical approach is particularly common in the analysis of so-called queuing or waiting line problems. In this chapter, a decision problem with this flavor will be analyzed with a carefully developed simulation study. In order to understand the approach and the plan of attack, a number of important and useful statistical concepts must be introduced. This material is conceptually more difficult than that in the preceding chapters of Part 2 of this text. However, a careful study should produce a good understanding for the use of simulation at a rather sophisticated level of application. The concepts in this chapter will also give the reader a well-motivated introduction to statistics.

19.2 The Scenario

PROTRAC Engineering is a wholly owned subsidiary of PROTRAC that designs and builds large construction projects. A current study involves the design of a docking facility for an oil company. The facility can handle one 500,000 barrel tanker at a time. The refinery served by the docking facility can accept oil at the rate of 250,000 barrels per day. This is termed the *pipeline capacity.* By using new high-speed pumps, the tankers can unload at the rate of 400,000 barrels per day. For this reason, the oil company is considering the use of a storage tank so that tankers can unload at the faster rate. The company is motivated by the fact that it is charged demurrage fees if a tanker has to wait too long before it is able to start unloading its oil. In particular, a demurrage fee of $1,000 per day is charged if a tanker must wait more than two days to start unloading. The charge is a pro-rata charge so that, for example, if a tanker waits 3.5 days before the start of unloading, then the fee is $1,500.

With a storage tank, oil would be unloaded from the tanker and would enter the tank at the rate of 400,000 barrels per day. The oil would be pumped out of the tank at the rate of 250,000 barrels per day. When the tank is full, then the rate at which the ship is unloaded would decrease to 250,000 barrels per day.

Rather than owning the oil tank, the oil company would have to pay a dock fee to the owner of the dock property for each ship that arrives at the facility. The agreement is that the owner of the dock property will build any size tank that the oil company wants. However, the size of the dock fee will depend on the size of the tank. In particular, the dock fee *per tanker* will be calculated so that the owner of the property receives, on the average, a total dollar-amount *per day* equal to (.0005)(tank size in barrels). *Assuming then that the oil company can define an average number of ships that will arrive per day,* the dock fee per ship will be assessed by the following formula:

$$\text{Dock fee per ship} = \frac{(.0005)(\text{tank size in barrels})}{\text{average number of ships arriving per day}}$$

A diagram of the system is shown in Figure 19.1.

The tradeoffs in the problem are clear. The larger the tank, the greater the dock fee. But for a larger tank we would anticipate smaller demurrage costs; that is, the larger the tank, the smaller the average demurrage cost

Figure 19.1 *The docking facility*

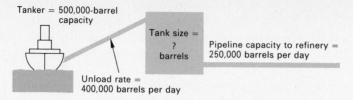

Tanker = 500,000-barrel capacity

Tank size = ? barrels

Pipeline capacity to refinery = 250,000 barrels per day

Unload rate = 400,000 barrels per day

per tanker.[1] The problem faced by the analysts at PROTRAC Engineering is to recommend an optimal tank size. A problem of this type, which focuses on arrivals of objects and waiting times, is called a *queuing* problem.

A quantity of interest in this problem is the *interarrival time*, or the time between arrivals of two ships. We shall use the symbol T to denote this quantity. It seems clear that if the time between arrivals of any two ships tends to be large, then there will be little or no waiting and hence a small tank (or no tank) will be required. As T becomes smaller, a larger tank size will be optimal. Unfortunately, because of weather conditions, crew efficiency, and so on, the value of T is not constant (that is, the value of T differs for different pairs of ships). Thus, T is an uncertain quantity and it must be treated as such. Based on historical data and their intimate knowledge of the current state of the art in scheduling tankers, the analysts at PROTRAC Engineering have determined that it is appropriate to use the following expression for the probability that T is less than or equal to any specified number, a:

$$P(T \leq a) = \begin{cases} 0 & \text{if } a \leq 0 \\ 1 - e^{-.4a} & \text{if } a \geq 0 \end{cases}$$

In the following development, the arrivals of ships, the waiting times, and the unloading will all be simulated. The role of the above expression for $P(T \leq a)$ will be to help simulate arrivals as follows. Suppose a ship has just arrived. The computer now draws a random number x between 0 and 1. It then determines the number y with the property that $P(T \leq y) = x$. This number will be used to denote the interarrival time to the next ship (that is, the next ship will arrive y days later). The process is then repeated. It is worth noting that, in the language of Chapter 15, the possible values for the interarrival time define a sample space S. In this case, since T can take on a continuum of values (that is, the values are real numbers), we have what is termed a *continuous* sample space. The situations discussed in Chapter 15 involved only *discrete* (in fact, *finite*) sample spaces. In order to deal with continuous sample spaces in a detailed and satisfactory way, the tools of calculus are required. However, for our purposes, there should be no difficulty, for the

---

1   If the tankers arrive at the facility "too fast" there will not be a well-defined average waiting time per tanker, since in this case the length of the line of waiting tankers will continue to grow and grow with time. This means that the *average* period of time per tanker over which a demurrage fee will have to be paid will keep increasing, and this means that a stable value for the average demurrage cost per tanker cannot be obtained. That is, the "long-run" average demurrage cost per tanker will be unbounded.

interarrival times T are used mainly by the computer, as described above, to simulate tanker arrivals. Only one analytic result is required, and that we ask the reader to accept on faith. This result follows from the properties of the chosen expression for $P(T \le a)$, as displayed above. The theory of statistics enables one to deduce from this expression that the tankers arrive at an average rate of .4 per day; that is, one tanker arrives every 2.5 days on the average. From this fact and the dock fee assessment formula given above, it follows that

$$\text{Dock fee per ship} = \frac{(.0005)(\text{tank size in barrels})}{.4}$$

$$= (.00125)(\text{tank size in barrels})$$

A graph of the function $F(a) = P(T \le a)$ is shown in Figure 19.2.

Figure 19.2   *Graph of P(T ≤ a) versus a*

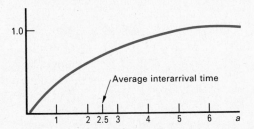

Upon a little reflection, it may appear that no storage tank is needed since the average interarrival time is 2.5 days. This fact implies that *on the average,* 500,000 barrels of oil arrive every 2.5 days, whereas in the same period of time the refinery can receive 625,000 barrels. (The latter figure is calculated by taking the daily rate of 250,000 barrels times 2.5 days.) Thus, it appears that the average value of T may be large enough to essentially eliminate waiting. However, the fact that the average arrival rate (.4 ships, or 200,000 barrels per day) is less than the average service rate (250,000 barrels per day) does not imply that the optimal tank size is zero. It only implies that the waiting line (queue) of tankers will not increase without limit. That is, the tankers do not arrive "too fast" (see footnote 1). In this instance, even with no tank, the long-run average demurrage cost of this system will not be unbounded.

19.3   The Underlying Model

The dock facility problem can be conveniently analyzed within the framework of the basic model presented in Chapter 15. The decision to be made in this problem is the tank size. The analysts decide that the appropriate criterion is to minimize the expected total cost (dock fee plus demurrage cost) incurred by an *arbitrarily selected* tanker. The term *arbitrarily selected* may mean, for example, the one-thousand forty-third tanker to be unloaded after the facility is built (or any other arbitrarily, or *randomly*, selected tanker). The analysts wish to select a tank size to minimize the expected total cost incurred by this tanker.

Let us now consider the two cost components. As mentioned earlier, the dock fee per tanker is given by

Dock fee per tanker = $(.00125)j$

where j denotes the tank capacity in barrels. The demurrage fee for an arbitrarily selected tanker will depend on its waiting time. The waiting time, however, is an uncertain quantity. Let W be the waiting time in days. Then the demurrage fee is calculated as follows:

$$\text{Demurrage fee} = \begin{cases} 0 & W \le 2 \\ \$1{,}000\,(W - 2) & W \ge 2 \end{cases}$$

The total cost C_j incurred by the arbitrarily selected tanker, given a tank size j, is calculated by the expression

C_j = dock fee per tanker + demurrage fee

The problem faced by the analysts is exactly analogous to the problem faced by PROTRAC when deciding how many E-9s to send to Anchorage (see Chapter 15). Note that

1 The possible waiting times, W_i, *for an arbitrarily selected tanker* form a sample space. That is, the possible waiting times are elementary events. In order not to worry about continuous sample spaces (that is, a sample space in which the waiting time can assume any real number in an interval, say, $0 \le W \le 100$), imagine that we have a sample space with a finite number of elementary events. This is easily justified by envisioning that the waiting time for any ship is measured only to five decimal places and that it can vary between 0 and, say, 100 days. Thus, the totality of possible waiting times per tanker is finite.
2 For a given decision (a chosen tank size j), there are probabilities $P_j(W_i)$ associated with each elementary event.
3 For a given decision, there is a total cost (rather than a return) associated with each elementary event. The cost is $C_j(W_i)$.

In order to solve the problem, one must:

1 Assess the appropriate probabilities, namely $P_j(W_i)$.
2 Calculate the expected total cost EC_j associated with each decision (each tank size j). Thus, given tank size j,

$$EC_j = \sum_i C_j(W_i) P_j(W_i)$$

is the expected total cost incurred by an arbitrarily selected tanker.
3 Select the tank size that yields the smallest value of EC_j.

To quote one of the analysts, "That's easy for you to say, Jack." In contrast to the situation concerning the interarrival times, T, the analysts have had little experience that will allow them to confidently assess the probabilities $P_j(W_i)$. Although they have designed many docking facilities, the parameters (number of docks, unload rate, pipeline capacity, and so on) have varied widely. They thus have very little feeling for the way in which the waiting time will depend on the tank size at this particular facility. Unfortunately, there is also no analytic model that will answer the question for them. The waiting time clearly depends on the interarrival time, T. The probability that T will assume its various possible values is known. Consequently, one might hope to be able to produce a mathematical expression for the probability that W will assume its various values. Unfortunately, this is not possible.

In view of this difficulty, the project manager at PROTRAC Engineering decides that a management conference is in order. He wants to determine whether his analysts should simply assess the probabilities for W to the best of their ability and go ahead or whether they should construct a simulation model to aid them in their decision. The simulation analysis would create considerable additional expenses. However, management must consider the reaction of the oil company to the final report, with and without simulation results. In particular, the effect of that reaction on current and future business must be taken into account. Finally, the ability to perform the study within the allowable time and the likelihood of getting good results must also be taken into account. In this particular situation, the case for constructing and using a simulation model seems very strong, and it is decided to proceed in that direction.

19.4 Sampling

19.4.1 *Random Variables and Random Samples*

Before describing the simulator and the efforts of PROTRAC Engineering's analysts to use it in "optimizing" the tank size, it is necessary to digress briefly to discuss a topic in statistics called *sampling.*

Consider a sample space $\{e_1, ..., e_n\}$. Corresponding to each decision d_j are the probabilities $P_j(e_i)$ and the returns $R_j(e_i)$. Let us imagine that the decision is fixed (that is, that the value of j is fixed and only the events e_i vary). In the terminology of statistics, the return $R_j(e_i)$ is called a *random variable.* Informally, a random variable is a number whose value is uncertain. Formally,

---

A random variable is a real-valued function defined on a sample space to which probabilities have been assigned.

For any random variable defined on a finite sample space, it is conceptually easy to specify the probability that that random variable takes on a particular value. For example, consider the toss of a die and let the sample space consist of the possible upturned faces, that is, $S = \{1, 2, ..., 6\}$. Also assume that a probability of $\frac{1}{6}$ is assigned to each of these points. Finally, suppose R is a random variable defined on S as follows: $R(6) = 10$, $R(5) = 6$, $R(4) = 5$, $R(3) = 5$, $R(2) = 4$, $R(1) = 0$. Let $P_R(r)$ denote the probability that R equals r, that is, the probability that after the die is rolled R will have the value r. Then it is easy to see that

$P_R(10) = \frac{1}{6}$

$P_R(6) = \frac{1}{6}$

$P_R(5) = \frac{2}{6}$

$P_R(4) = \frac{1}{6}$

$P_R(0) = \frac{1}{6}$

$P_R(x) = 0$ otherwise

Note that $P_R(r)$ is a function that specifies the probability that the random variable R takes on the value r. Such a function is often called a *probability mass function*, denoted *pmf*. This function describes the way in which the values of the random variable are "distributed," or what is often called the *distribution* of R. Associated with the distribution of a random variable are numerous parameters. Two of special interest to us are the expected value and the variance.

The *expected value* of a random variable R, denoted $E(R)$, is defined by the expression:

$$E(R) = \sum_r P_R(r)(r) \quad \textit{where } P_R(r) \textit{ is the pmf.}$$

In terms of the above example, the expected value of R is calculated as follows:

$E(R) = \frac{1}{6}(10) + \frac{1}{6}(6) + \frac{2}{6}(5) + \frac{1}{6}(4) + \frac{1}{6}(0) = \frac{30}{6} = 5$

Note that we can also interpret the values of R as a return, and we may then calculate the *expected return* ER in the manner prescribed in Chapter 15. That is,

$$ER = \sum_{i=1}^{n} R(e_i) P(e_i)$$

For the above example

$$ER = \sum_{i=1}^{6} R(e_i) P(e_i) = R(1) P(1) + R(2) P(2) + \dots + R(6) P(6)$$

$$= 0(\tfrac{1}{6}) + 4(\tfrac{1}{6}) + 5(\tfrac{1}{6}) + 5(\tfrac{1}{6}) + 6(\tfrac{1}{6}) + 10(\tfrac{1}{6})$$

$$= \tfrac{30}{6} = 5$$

Thus, in a general decision problem, treating $R_j(e_i)$ as in Chapter 15, we are interested in ER_j, the *expected return*. Treating $R_j(e_i)$ as a random variable, we are interested in $E(R_j)$, the *expected value*. The above example illustrates the fact that, for finite sample spaces,

$$ER_j = E(R_j)$$

In Chapter 15 we also spoke about the *variance* of the return. Analogously, the *variance* of a random variable R is a measure of the dispersion of its values and is defined by the expression

$$\text{Var}(R) = \sum_r P_R(r)\,[r - E(R)]^2$$

For the above example, the variance is calculated as follows:

$$\text{Var}(R) = \tfrac{1}{6}(10 - 5)^2 + \tfrac{1}{6}(6 - 5)^2 + \tfrac{2}{6}(5 - 5)^2 + \tfrac{1}{6}(4 - 5)^2 + \tfrac{1}{6}(0 - 5)^2$$

$$= \tfrac{1}{6}(25) + \tfrac{1}{6}(1) + \tfrac{2}{6}(0) + \tfrac{1}{6}(1) + \tfrac{1}{6}(25)$$

$$= \tfrac{52}{6} = 8.67$$

Now in a general sense consider any sample space S. Assume that an experiment is performed to generate one of the uncertain events in the space S. Let R be a random variable defined on S, and let $P_R(r)$ be the *pmf* of R. Now suppose the experiment is performed n times, and that we think of R_1 as being the random variable R associated with the first trial, R_2 the random variable R associated with the second trial, and so on. Thus, R_1 is a random variable, as is R_2, and so on. These random variables R_i are said to be *identically distributed* (since each has the same *pmf* as R). Let r_1 denote the observed value of R_1 (the value of R after the first trial), r_2 the observed value of R_2 (the value of R after the second trial), and so on. The *sample value r_i* is termed a *realization* of the random variable R_i. We shall assume that the trials of the experiment are *independent* in the sense that the result of one trial has no effect on the result of any other trial. In the language of statistics, the results from these n independent trials are said to comprise a *random sample* of the random variable R, and the random variables R_i are said to be *independent*.

The physical experiment associated with this terminology can be easily illustrated in terms of the following example.

Consider an urn with six balls that are identical except for the numbers painted on them. One ball is painted with the number 10, one with 6, two with 5, one with 4, and one with 0. On each trial, a ball is selected from the urn in such a way that each ball is equally likely to be selected. After each trial, the ball is returned to the urn. This experiment is equivalent to the die-throwing experiment that originally determined the value of the random variable R. In this situation, the balls in the urn are often referred to as the *population* being sampled. The phrase "expected value of a population" is used to denote the expected value of the random variable that determines the population.

We are now in a position to make our first statement concerning a quantity that is calculated from a random sample. The quantity is the *sample mean*, denoted $\bar{r}$, and defined by

$$\bar{r} = \frac{1}{n} \sum_{i=1}^{n} r_i$$

The mean of a random sample is important because it is generally regarded as the *best estimator* of the expected value of the population from which the sample is drawn, that is, the expected value of the random variable R. In other words, the sample mean $\bar{r}$ is considered a good estimate of $E(R)$. There is an exact and formal definition of the sense in which $\bar{r}$ is a *best estimator* of $E(R)$, but to pursue this in great detail would take us outside the intended scope of this book. Nevertheless, we can provide some convincing indication of "how good" $\bar{r}$ actually is as an estimate of $E(R)$.

19.4.2   Confidence Intervals

The use of a **confidence interval** makes it possible to make a statement like, "We are 95-percent confident that $L \leq E(R) \leq U$," where L and U are specified numbers. We shall see that the sample mean $\bar{r}$ will be used to compute the values of L and U.

To understand the meaning (and derivation) of a confidence statement, let us consider a sample space with an underlying experiment. Each outcome of the experiment provides an observation or realization of the random variable R. Consider two independent trials of that experiment, which generate a *random sample* of size 2. Let R_1 and R_2 be the independent random variables associated with the first and second trials, respectively.[2] Now define a new quantity $\bar{R}$ as

$$\bar{R} = \frac{(R_1 + R_2)}{2}$$

Since R_1 and R_2 are random variables, so is $\bar{R}$. (In fact, any function of a random variable is also a random variable.) More generally, suppose we observe n different values r_i, $i = 1, \ldots, n$ and then calculate

$$\bar{r} = \frac{1}{n} \sum_{i=1}^{n} r_i$$

This value $\bar{r}$ can now be thought of as a single observation from the population of the new random variable $\bar{R}$, where

$$\bar{R} = \frac{1}{n} \sum_{i=1}^{n} R_i$$

and where the R_is are independent, identically-distributed random variables.

Statistical theory tells us that the distribution of $\bar{R}$ has several important properties that provide information on the quality of the numerical value $\bar{r}$ as an estimate of $E(R)$:

---

2   Since R_1 and R_2 are independent random variables each of which has the same *pmf*, they are referred to as IID, shorthand for independent, identically distributed.

$$E(\bar{R}) = E(R)$$

$$Var(\bar{R}) = \frac{Var(R)}{n}$$

Let $\bar{r}$ be a single observation, or realization, (that is, a sample of size 1) of the random variable $\bar{R}$. (The value $\bar{r}$ is the mean of a sample of size n of the random variable R.) The above two properties partially indicate a sense in which $\bar{r}$ is considered a good estimate for $E(R)$, at least when n is large. In particular, since $Var(R)$ is a constant (independent of n), we see that when the sample size n is large, $Var(\bar{R})$ is small. This means that $\bar{r}$ would generally be close to $E(\bar{R})$ and hence close to $E(R)$ in value. Moreover, it is known from statistical theory that for n large enough (100 is certainly "large enough"), the distribution of the sample mean is approximately normal. It is thus usually assumed that $\bar{R}$ is, in fact, normally distributed, and it then follows that

The probability is .95 that $E(R) - 1.96 \sqrt{\dfrac{Var(R)}{n}} \leq \bar{R} \leq$
$E(R) + 1.96 \sqrt{\dfrac{Var(R)}{n}}.$

By simple algebra,

The probability is .95 that $\bar{R} - 1.96 \sqrt{\dfrac{Var(R)}{n}} \leq E(R) \leq$
$\bar{R} + 1.96 \sqrt{\dfrac{Var(R)}{n}}.$

Notice that this is a probability statement about the value of a random variable $\bar{R}$. Given $\bar{r}$, a *realization* of $\bar{R}$, the above probability statements motivate the statement

We are 95-percent confident that $\bar{r} - 1.96 \sqrt{\dfrac{Var(R)}{n}} \leq E(R) \leq$
$\bar{r} + 1.96 \sqrt{\dfrac{Var(R)}{n}}.$

This is a **confidence statement** rather than a probability statement, because it refers to numbers rather than random variables. It is in this sense that we have constructed a confidence interval about $E(R)$.

Unfortunately, this confidence interval cannot be directly computed because $Var(R)$ is not known. It is possible, however, to use sample data once again to estimate the needed quantity. The **sample variance**, s^2, is calculated with the following expression:

$$s^2 = \sum_{i=1}^{n} \frac{(r_i - \bar{r})^2}{n-1}$$

If the sample is large enough (100 or more), then s^2 is a good estimate for $\text{Var}(R)$ and hence can be substituted directly for $\text{Var}(R)$ in the previous expression for the confidence interval. In other words,

---

We are 95-percent confident that $\bar{r} - 1.96 \sqrt{\dfrac{s^2}{n}} \leq E(R) \leq$

$\bar{r} + 1.96 \sqrt{\dfrac{s^2}{n}}$.

19.4.3   The Dock Facility Problem

Returning now to the dock facility problem, the discussion in Section 19.3 indicated that the analysts are concerned with the expected total cost, EC_j, for an arbitrarily selected tanker, given tank size j. In the context of the discussion on sampling, the total cost, C_j, for an arbitrary tanker can be thought of as a random variable with an unknown *pmf*. The analysts would like to estimate the expected value $E(C_j)$, which, as we have already discussed (Section 19.4.1), is the same as EC_j. Thus, using the terminology from the sampling discussion, the analysts would like to:

---

1 Draw a random sample of the total costs for an arbitrary tanker (the possible values of the random variable C_j).
2 Calculate the sample mean $\bar{c}_j$, the sample variance s_j^2, and form a confidence interval for $E(C_j)$.
3 Select a tank size j^*, for which $\bar{c}_{j^*} \leq \bar{c}_j$ for all decisions j.

The relationship $\bar{c}_{j^*} < \bar{c}_j$ between sample means does not, per se, mean that $EC_{j^*} < EC_j$. In other words, the danger to be reckoned with is the possibility that for two tank sizes, say i and k,

$\bar{c}_i < \bar{c}_k$ whereas $EC_i > EC_k$

This is the case when two specific sample means *by chance* do not reflect the true relationship between the expected costs. Let s_i^2 and s_k^2 be the sample variances associated with the samples whose means are $\bar{c}_i$ and $\bar{c}_k$, respectively. Suppose that

$\bar{c}_i + 1.96\sqrt{s_i^2/n} < \bar{c}_k - 1.96\sqrt{s_k^2/n}$

Note that if the sample size is large, we are *at least* 95-percent confident that

$EC_i \leq \bar{c}_i + 1.96\sqrt{s_i^2/n}$

Also, we are *at least* 95-percent confident that

$\bar{c}_k - 1.96\sqrt{s_k^2/n} \leq EC_k$

In this case then, it is clearly most unlikely that

$$EC_k < EC_i$$

Thus, if the 95-percent confidence intervals for the expected costs do not overlap, the analysts can feel comfortable in assuming that the tank size that yields the smallest sample mean is optimal.

Notice that the size of the confidence interval is $3.82\sqrt{s^2/n}$. Consider what happens as n, the sample size, increases. The number 3.82 obviously remains constant. The sample variance s^2 is an estimate of the population variance Var (C_j), which is constant, and hence s^2 will remain relatively constant for reasonably large samples. Thus, the size of the confidence interval decreases as n increases. By taking a large enough sample it is possible to make the 95-percent confidence interval arbitrarily small. Thus, if EC_i is not really equal to EC_k, it is possible to take a large enough sample so that the above confidence intervals for these two entities are very small and hence do not overlap. In cases where a sufficiently large sample is not obtained, and overlapping occurs, we shall see in Section 19.9.3 that there are more effective ways to compare the two sizes.

The analysts at PROTRAC Engineering plan to use a simulator to generate the sample data (values of C_j) for the dock facility problem. A description of this simulator is presented in the next section.

19.5 A Simulation Model

The decision is made to build a simulator for a single tanker docking facility that will accept fairly general specifications for the parameters: pipeline capacity, tank size and so on. Some computer output from this simulator is shown in Figure 19.3. Note that the parameters that have been input for this particular run are exactly those that describe the problem PROTRAC Engineering is considering. For example, a tanker size of 500,000 barrels has been specified. By inspecting the input it should be clear that this run describes the behavior of the system during the arrival of the first six tankers, with a storage tank of 100,000 barrels being used. The last item of the input, INPUT A STARTING RANDOM NUMBER? 3457, is perhaps unfamiliar. The importance of a starting random number will be discussed later.

To understand how the system works, it is instructive to follow the behavior of the first few tankers in Figure 19.3. Note that the first tanker arrives at time 0.00 and departs at time 1.60. To arrive at this latter figure, note that oil will accumulate in the tank at the rate of 150,000 (400,000 − 250,000) barrels per day until the tank is full. Since a 100,000-barrel tank has been specified, the tank will be full in

$$\frac{100,000 \text{ barrels}}{150,000 \text{ barrels per day}} = .667 \text{ days}$$

if the tanker is big enough to continue to supply oil during this time. The tanker unloads at the rate of 400,000 barrels per day until the tank is full.

Figure 19.3   *A sample simulation run*

```
INPUT PIPELINE CAPACITY IN BARRELS PER DAY?  250000
INPUT TANK CAPACITY IN BARRELS?  100000
INPUT UNLOAD RATE IN BARRELS PER DAY?  400000
INPUT TANKER SIZE IN BARRELS?  500000
INPUT AVERAGE NUMBER OF TANKERS TO ARRIVE EACH DAY?  .4
INPUT DEMURRAGE LIMIT IN DAYS?  2
INPUT DOLLAR AMOUNT PER DAY TO BE CHARGED FOR EXCEEDING LIMIT?  1000
INPUT NO. OF SHIP UNLOADINGS TO SIMULATE?  6
INPUT A STARTING RANDOM NUMBER?  3457
```

#			
1	TANKER ARRIVES AT TIME	0.00	0 TANKERS WAITING
2	TANKER DEPARTS AT TIME	1.60	0 TANKERS WAITING
3	TANK WAS FULL .933334	DAYS	
4	TANKER ARRIVES AT TIME	4.34609	0 TANKERS WAITING
5	TANK HAS BEEN EMPTY 2.34609	DAYS	
6	TANKER ARRIVES AT TIME	5.09976	1 TANKERS WAITING
7	TANKER ARRIVES AT TIME	5.69024	2 TANKERS WAITING
8	TANKER DEPARTS AT TIME	5.94609	2 TANKERS WAITING
9	TANK WAS FULL .933333	DAYS	
10	TANKER DEPARTS AT TIME	7.94609	1 TANKERS WAITING
11	TANK WAS FULL 2	DAYS	
12	TANKER DEPARTS AT TIME	9.94609	0 TANKERS WAITING
13	TANK WAS FULL 2	DAYS	
14	TANKER ARRIVES AT TIME	10.235	0 TANKERS WAITING
15	TANKER ARRIVES AT TIME	10.2998	1 TANKERS WAITING
16	TANKER ARRIVES AT TIME	11.0847	2 TANKERS WAITING
17	TANKER ARRIVES AT TIME	11.3785	3 TANKERS WAITING
18	TANKER DEPARTS AT TIME	11.9461	3 TANKERS WAITING
19	TANK WAS FULL 1.22966	DAYS	
20	TANKER ARRIVES AT TIME	12.211	3 TANKERS WAITING
21	TANKER ARRIVES AT TIME	13.3246	4 TANKERS WAITING
22	TANKER DEPARTS AT TIME	13.9461	4 TANKERS WAITING
	TANK WAS FULL 2 DAYS		

```
END OF SIMULATION AT TIME 13.9461

6  TANKERS WERE UNLOADED
AVERAGE TIME IN PORT WAS  2.60994
4  TANKERS WERE WAITING AT END OF SIMULATION
4.7485  DAYS WERE SPENT WAITING
255.851  DOLLARS IN FEES WERE CHARGED
TANK WAS EMPTY  2.346 DAYS
TANK WAS FULL  9.0963 DAYS
```

Thus, after .667 days, (.667)(400,000) = 266,667 barrels have been unloaded. The remaining oil in the tanker (233,333 barrels) is unloaded at the reduced rate of 250,000 barrels per day. Thus, the tanker must remain at the dock another

$$\frac{233,333 \text{ barrels}}{250,000 \text{ barrels per day}} = .933 \text{ days}$$

At time 1.60 (calculated .667 + .933 = 1.60) the first tanker departs the system. When the first tanker departs, the tank is full. The tank continues to empty at the rate of 250,000 barrels per day. The tank thus becomes empty at 100,000/250,000 = .4 days later, or at time 2.0. It remains empty until time 4.34609, when the second tanker arrives. The system records that the tank was empty for 2.34609 days at that moment. The first five lines on the computer output have now been explained. The simulation continues in this way.

PROTRAC Engineering is particularly interested in the total demurrage fees, since the goal is to balance demurrage fees with the dock fee in such a way as to minimize expected total cost for an arbitrarily selected tanker.

Figure 19.4 *Calculation of demurrage fees*

Tanker	Arrives	Departs	Service Starts	Waiting	Waiting > 2	Demurrage Charge
1	0.00000	1.60000	0.00000	0	0	0
2	4.34609	5.94609	4.34609	0	0	0
3	5.09976	7.94609	5.94609	.84633	0	0
4	5.69024	9.94609	7.94609	2.25585	.25585	$255.85
5	10.23500	11.94610	10.23500	0	0	0
6	10.29980	13.94610	11.94610	1.64630	0	0

Figure 19.4 illustrates the way in which the simulator obtains the demurrage charge.

The total demurrage fee of $255.85 corresponds to the amount under DOLLARS IN FEES WERE CHARGED in the summary data in Figure 19.3. Thus, for the above sample of tankers 1 through 6, the mean demurrage fee per tanker is 255.85/6 = $42.64. Of course these six tankers do not comprise a *random* sample. This is an important point that will now be considered in detail.

19.6 Estimating The Expected Cost with a Random Sample

In the previous section, we have seen that the analysts at PROTRAC Engineering have at their disposal a simulator that reproduces the interactions between tank size and waiting lines and calculates the total demurrage charge. The question is how to use this device to help select the optimal tank size.

The discussion in Section 19.4.3 provided the following possible way to proceed for a given tank size j:

---

1 Draw a random sample from the population of possible total costs for an *arbitrarily selected* tanker.
2 Calculate the sample mean $\bar{c}$ and the sample variance s_j^2.
3 Select a tank size j^* for which $\bar{c}_{j^*} \leq \bar{c}_j$ for all j.
4 Use confidence intervals as an aid in determining whether an optimal tank size was selected.

The only problem associated with implementing this procedure is in determining how to use the simulator to draw a random sample of the total cost incurred on an *arbitrarily* selected tanker. Recall that for a random sample the result of one trial should not be influenced by the result of any other trial. This implies that the individual costs incurred by each of two *consecutive* tankers that arrive at the dock cannot be part of a random sample. To see this, think of the individual total costs incurred by the forty-first and forty-second tankers to arrive at the dock. If tanker 41 incurs a large demurrage charge, the queue was clearly large when it arrived. This means it is more likely that the queue will also be large when tanker 42 arrives and hence that it will also incur a high demurrage charge. The fact that this inference can be drawn implies that the sample is not random. Conceptually, this difficulty may be overcome as follows. Suppose the tankers are selected in such a manner that "enough" tankers (say *at least* 200) arrive between any two tankers to be observed[3] (for example, the first "arbitrary" ship is number 201, the next is number 429, and so on). This procedure yields an approximately random sample and will produce a legitimate estimate and confidence interval for $E(C_j)$. The approach might be termed a naive application of basic sampling theory to a simulation. Intuitively, it seems like a wasteful process, since data are gathered from only one out of every several hundred simulated arrivals. It seems that a high price is being paid to obtain a random sample, and indeed it is.

Another alternative involves using all the data after they have been partitioned into groups. Although there are no precise or formal guidelines on exactly how to do this, a considerable amount of empirical work suggests that this is a good general approach to adopt. This is, in fact, the approach adopted by the PROTRAC Engineering analysts, as described in the next section.

19.7 An Alternative Procedure for Estimating the Expected Cost

Using a simulator as an aid in decision making can be an expensive and time-consuming process. Without careful planning, a large computer bill can be run up with little gained in return. In particular, it is important to get as much information as possible out of every computer run. Unfortunately, at this time there is no universally agreed-upon method for designing effective simulation experiments. However, a number of studies reported in the literature support an approach that involves the *grouping of data.*

Recall that our objective is to obtain the best possible estimate for $E(C_j)$. Suppose we are willing to use as much computer time as is required to simulate 8,000 consecutive tankers. One approach would be to identify a random subset, as discussed in the above section. For example, one might consider the sequence consisting of ship numbers 400, 800, 1,200, ..., which would produce a random sample of 20 tankers. Or one might instead consider every twentieth ship, feeling that this is enough separation to produce randomness. One would then have a random sample of 400 observations. Or one might use the random number generator to select an arbitrary sequence of tankers, such as 46, 298, 316, 681, and so on. In all of these cases, one would use the sample mean as an estimate for $E(C_j)$. Since each of these suggestions involves the simulation of 8,000 consecutive tankers, it seems at least intuitively plausible that we would be better off using all 8,000 observations to compute a sample mean, even though these observations are consecutive and hence not random. In order to understand how and why this can be done, let us refer back to our discussion of sample means. Suppose that the random variables C_{ji} (the total cost for ship i when the tank size is j) all have the same *pmf* as C_j (the total cost for an arbitrarily selected ship), so that for each ship i, $E(C_{ji}) = E(C_j)$.

---

3 The theory of statistics provides tests for randomness of a stream of data and hence can be used to determine whether or not 200 is enough.

In this case,

$$E\left(\frac{1}{n}\sum_{i=1}^{n}C_{ji}\right) = E(C_j)$$

whether or not the sample is random (that is, whether or not the C_{ji}s are independent). We assume that the physical process being modeled does indeed justify the assumption that, ignoring the initial tankers (which will be discussed later), the random variables C_{ji} are identically distributed (but not independent). This means we have no reason to believe that the *pmf* associated with, say, ship 1043 is any different than the *pmf* associated with, say, ship 2269 or ship 2270. Thus, the analysts can indeed use the total cost incurred by each consecutive ship in estimating $E(C_j)$, and the sample mean

$$\bar{c}_j = \sum_{i=1}^{8,000}\frac{c_{ji}}{8,000}$$

is an excellent estimate of $E(C_j)$, the expected total cost of an arbitrarily selected tanker. However, in the absence of a random sample, it is *incorrect* to state the following:

---

1 The variance of the sample mean equals $\text{Var}(C_j)/n$.
2 The sample variance calculated by the expression

$$s_j^2 = \sum_{i=1}^{8,000}\frac{(c_{ji} - \bar{c}_j)^2}{7,999}$$

is a good estimate of $\text{Var}(C_j)$.

Thus, if the sample is not random, we are unable to obtain a confidence interval for our estimate. Although the sample mean is in fact an estimate of $E(C_j)$, we have no way of measuring the goodness of the estimate. Nevertheless, the theory of statistics can be used to show that the variance will be smaller for samples of larger size, even though we cannot precisely state that the variance equals $\text{Var}(C_j)/n$. Thus, a sample mean from a sample of size 8,000 would be expected to be closer to $E(C_j)$ than a sample mean from a smaller sample. For these reasons, it is certainly advantageous to use all 8,000 observations in estimating $E(C_j)$.

The method for using all observations and for circumventing the confidence-interval difficulty involves the use of sample means from grouped data. The grouping of data refers to the process of dividing a long simulation of many trials into a number of sections and then calculating a sample mean for each section. In our example, the analysts decided that for each tank size the data would be grouped into 20 consecutive batches of 400 tankers each. The mean cost per tanker would be calculated for each of the 20 batches. The scheme is illustrated in Figure 19.5.

The number $\bar{g}_{j\alpha}$ is a specific realization of a new random variable $\bar{G}_{j\alpha}$, where

Figure 19.5   *Using grouped data*

$$\tilde{G}_{j\alpha} = \frac{1}{400} \sum_{i=\alpha}^{\alpha+399} C_{ji}$$

Thus,

$$\tilde{g}_{j\alpha} = \frac{1}{400} \sum_{i=\alpha}^{\alpha+399} c_{ji}$$

and, for example, $\tilde{g}_{j1}$ is the sample mean for the first batch (ships 1–400), $\tilde{g}_{j401}$ is the sample mean for the second batch (ships 401–800), and so on. The analysts assumed that the sample means shown in Figure 19.5 are each a *random* observation of the random variable $\tilde{G}_{j\alpha}$. This is based on the assumption that the number of tankers in each batch is sufficiently large that the means of successive batches can be considered to be independent. Thus, we assume that we have a *random sample* of size 20.

Let us now define the random variable

$$\tilde{G}_{j} = \frac{1}{20}(\tilde{G}_{j1} + \tilde{G}_{j401} + \tilde{G}_{j801} + \ldots + \tilde{G}_{j7,601})$$

$$= \frac{1}{20}\left(\frac{1}{400}\sum_{i=1}^{400} C_{ji} + \frac{1}{400}\sum_{i=401}^{800} C_{ji} + \frac{1}{400}\sum_{i=801}^{1,200} C_{ji} + \ldots + \frac{1}{400}\sum_{i=7,601}^{8,000} C_{ji}\right)$$

$$= \frac{1}{8,000}\sum_{i=1}^{8,000} C_{ji}$$

Let $\tilde{g}_{j}$ denote a specific realization of $\tilde{G}_{j}$. That is,

$$\tilde{g}_{j} = \frac{1}{20}(\tilde{g}_{j1} + \tilde{g}_{j401} + \ldots + \tilde{g}_{j7,601}) = \frac{1}{8,000}\sum_{i=1}^{8,000} c_{ji}$$

Since the C_{ji} are assumed to be identically distributed,

$$E(\tilde{G}_{j}) = E(C_{ji}) = E(C_{j})$$

In other words $\tilde{g}_{j}$, the mean of the 8,000 observations, provides an estimate of $E(C_{j})$. Of course, this is a fact we have already stated. The more cogent motive for the grouping is the following. If we assume that $\tilde{G}_{j1}, \tilde{G}_{j401}, \ldots, \tilde{G}_{j7,601}$ are independent and identically distributed, as seems reasonable in our context, then

$$Var(\tilde{G}_{j}) = \tfrac{1}{20} Var(\tilde{G}_{j\alpha})$$

In accordance with the results stated in Section 19.4.2, the facts displayed above mean we are 95-percent confident that

$$\bar{g}_j - 1.96\sqrt{\frac{\text{Var}(\bar{G}_{j\alpha})}{20}} \leq E(C_j) \leq \bar{g}_j + 1.96\sqrt{\frac{\text{Var}(\bar{G}_{j\alpha})}{20}}$$

Actually, this result is an approximation that depends on the number of observations used to calculate the mean. With a sample size of 20, it is quite a good approximation.

Of course, the quantity $\text{Var}(\bar{G}_{j\alpha})$ is not known. However, since the sample observations $\bar{g}_{j\alpha}$ are considered random, the sample variance s_G^2 can be used to approximate the population variance $\text{Var}(\bar{G}_{j\alpha})$. Thus we have

$$s_G^2 = \tfrac{1}{19}[(\bar{g}_{j1} - \bar{g}_j)^2 + (\bar{g}_{j401} - \bar{g}_j)^2 + \ldots + (\bar{g}_{j7,601} - \bar{g}_j)^2] \approx \text{Var}(\bar{G}_{j\alpha})$$

The sample variance can now be substituted into the expression for the confidence interval, but since the sample is small, a new coefficient is required.[4] With a sample of 20, the modified expression for the confidence interval becomes

$$\bar{g}_j - 2.09\sqrt{s_G^2/20} \leq E(C_j) \leq \bar{g}_j + 2.09\sqrt{s_G^2/20}$$

The analysts have thus arrived at a statistical procedure for using all of the data to estimate $E(C_j)$ and to obtain a measure for the goodness of that estimate. However, they must still proceed carefully. Once again, without care a needless amount of analyst time and computer time can be expended in attempting to arrive at a decision.

19.8 Additional Considerations in Planning a Simulation

There is more to running an efficient simulation study than simply devising the statistical procedure to be used. Before presenting the results of the dock facility simulation, it will be useful to consider some additional general guidelines to be followed in working with a simulation model. This section considers some of these guidelines.

19.8.1 The Use of Analytic Results

Before you start simulating, be sure to

Impose reasonable simplifying assumptions and use any analytic results that are thereby obtainable.

In the dock facility problem, the analysts at PROTRAC Engineering are able to make an assumption that allows them to obtain a good idea of the general shape of the graph of the total cost per tanker as a function of tank size, even before any simulations are performed. Since the dock fee is a linear

---

4   This coefficient is taken from the t distribution, whereas the former coefficient of 1.96 is taken from the normal distribution. Additional discussion of the t distribution is included in Section 19.9.3, and a table of this distribution is presented in Figure 19.13.

function of tank size, and since the expected demurrage fee per tanker will decrease as a function of tank size, it is reasonable to hypothesize a function of the type shown in Figure 19.6.

Figure 19.6   *Graph of the expected total cost for an arbitrary tanker*

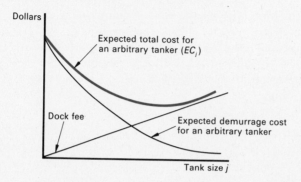

Employing a cost curve of this type eliminates the concern about finding a local minimum that is not a global minimum. If EC_j were, in fact, to have a shape like that shown in Figure 19.7, the task of finding the tank size with the minimum expected total cost would be considerably more difficult. In a case in which EC_j has a unique minimum, as in Figure 19.6, the search procedure is fairly straightforward. One must simply find a tank size (say j^*) for which the expected total cost is greater for a tank slightly bigger than j^* (say, $EC_{j^*+\Delta} > EC_{j^*}$) and the expected total cost is also greater for a tank slightly smaller than j^* (say, $EC_{j^*-\Delta} > EC_{j^*}$).

Figure 19.7   *A hypothetical EC_j function*

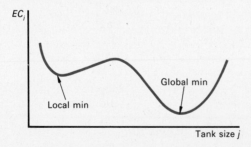

There is yet another useful analytic result available to PROTRAC Engineering. Having an estimate of EC_0 (the expected total cost for the case when there is no tank) makes it possible to specify an upper bound on the size of the tank to be considered. Clearly, it would never pay to spend more for a dock fee per tanker than the expected demurrage charge for that tanker if there were no tank. Thus, for any tank size of interest, and for an arbitrary tanker, it should be true that:

Dock fee ≤ expected demurrage fee with no tank

or

.00125 (maximum tank size) $\leq$ expected demurrage fee with no tank

or, finally, we need only consider those tank sizes that satisfy

$$\text{Tank size} \leq \frac{E(C_0)}{.00125} \approx \frac{\bar{c}_0}{.00125}$$

In a later discussion, we will show how the analysts at PROTRAC Engineering used this fact and an estimate for the expected demurrage fee with no tank to specify an upper bound on the tank sizes to be considered.

19.8.2 Representative Sampling

Another general principle for the experimentor is that

The data produced by the simulation must reflect the actual operation of the system.

At one level this statement seems silly. This, of course, is the whole rationale of a simulation. By improper use, however, even a good model can produce results that badly distort the true interactions being studied. An example of this fact concerns the situation in the simulator at the time one starts gathering data.

For example, if PROTRAC Engineering is interested in the behavior of the docking facility over the long run, the data gathered from the start of a simulation run (no tankers waiting and an empty tank) do not accurately reflect the operation of the system. To observe this fact, consider the output presented in Figure 19.3. Notice that the number of tankers waiting tends to increase throughout the simulation. On this basis, it would seem reasonable that the average demurrage cost of $42.64 per tanker (255.85 dollars/6 tankers) would be an underestimate of the expected demurrage cost for an arbitrarily selected tanker over the long run. It follows from this observation that if one were to compare the costs associated with two tank sizes and include the data from the start of the simulation, the results would be biased in favor of the smaller tank. At the start of the simulation, the smaller tank simply would not produce the higher demurrage charges that it would in the long run. Because of such "startup distortions" it is often the case that the initial results of a simulation are discarded.

Other similar types of distortions can occur. The experimentor and the potential user of the information must carefully consider the questions they wish to answer with a simulation and make sure that the data produced by the simulator accurately reflect the operation of the system in question.

19.8.3 Selecting the Sequence of Experiments

Plan your simulation experiments sequentially.

Information obtained from a series of simulations can often be used to help determine the appropriate set of parameters to specify for the next run. In the example problem, PROTRAC Engineering decided that, rather than running a total of 8,000 observations for many different tank sizes, it would be more sensible to run relatively smaller samples (1,000 observations for each tank size) in order to locate an approximate value for the optimal tank size first. The following procedure was used:

1 Specify a zero tank size (set $j = 0$).
2 Run an initial sample of 400 ships and discard the data. This helps to remove the "initial bias" from the system.
3 Continue the simulation by taking 1,000 additional *consecutive* observations and computing $\bar{c}_j$, the mean total cost per tanker for this sample of a thousand tankers, given a tank of size j.
4 Use the data from $j = 0$ to calculate an upper bound on the tank size.
5 Repeat steps 2 and 3 for a select sequence of tank sizes j between 0 and the upper bound. This produces the mean values $\bar{c}_j$, and the smallest of these will suggest an approximate optimal tank size.

Note that there is no confidence interval determination, and hence no grouping, in this initial part of the study.

Having performed the above initial analysis, the PROTRAC Engineering analysts then implement their previously described grouping plan as follows:

1 Select a tank size near the above approximate optimum.
2 Run a sample of 20 groups of 400 observations each, computing sample means and a variance as described in Section 19.7.
3 Repeat step 2 for a select group of tank sizes until a tank size j^* is obtained, with the property that j^* is optimal to within 100,000 barrels. That is, using confidence intervals, we would like j^* to have the property that

$$\bar{g}_{j^*} + 2.09\sqrt{s_G^2/20} \le \bar{g}_{j^*-100,000} - 2.09\sqrt{s_G^2/20}$$
$$\bar{g}_{j^*} + 2.09\sqrt{s_G^2/20} \le \bar{g}_{j^*+100,000} - 2.09\sqrt{s_G^2/20}$$

19.8.4 *Reducing Variability*

The analysts at PROTRAC Engineering are now ready to start performing simulations and producing data according to the procedure outlined above. In doing so, the analysts naturally want to perform their experiments in such a way as to obtain the maximum possible amount of information. In general, this means eliminating extraneous sources of *variability* from the experiment. Variability is the archenemy of experimentors, and they will go to great lengths to eliminate extraneous effects from their experiments. An agronomist who wishes to compare the yields from two strains of corn will attempt to eliminate variability in yield introduced by factors such as soil fertility, weather, methods of cultivation, and so on. The famous study by Cyril Burt concerning the relative importance of heredity and environment on intelligence attempted to eliminate extraneous variability by using data from sets of identical twins who had been raised in different environments. This study, now under question, provided the rationale for the organization of the English educational system.

Simulation presents a perhaps unique opportunity for eliminating extraneous variability. Since the random events in a simulation are generated by the simulator itself, it is possible to control the experiment carefully by comparing different decision rules on exactly the same sequence of random events. In particular, in the problem being considered by PROTRAC Engineering, one can evaluate the effects of two different tank sizes on the demurrage cost by using exactly the same sequence of arrival times for the tankers. Suppose that this were not possible and that we would wish to compare the total cost of the system with a tank of size A to the total cost of the system with a tank of size B. The analysis might proceed as follows: Tank B had a smaller mean total cost per tanker than tank A, but while using tank A more tankers arrived and some of the arrivals were very close together. I don't know if we would have done better with tank B under that same set of circumstances. Using the same sequence of tanker arrival times eliminates this problem. Given the specified sequence of arrivals, any difference in costs will be attributable only to the difference in tank size. There remains, of course, the question of whether or not the lower-cost tank size will change when a different sequence of arrival times is used. Our use of a large sample (8,000 observations) diminishes the possibility of such a change. This will be discussed in more detail in Section 19.9.

Use the same sequence of random numbers when comparing alternatives.

Fortunately, this advice is easy to implement. In most simulation packages, the sequence of random numbers is generated deterministically from a user-supplied input called a *root*, or a *base*, or an *initial random number*. Once this input is specified, the random number generator produces a fixed sequence of random numbers. To obtain the same sequence of random numbers, one merely has to specify the same input. The simulator written by the analysts at PROTRAC Engineering to study the dock facility problem includes this feature. One of the parameters that must be input along with the pipeline capacity, the tanker size, and so on, is a starting random number. (As shown in Figure 19.3, this number was 3,457.) By specifying the same starting random number, the analysts can use the same sequence of random numbers to compare total cost per tanker for various tank sizes.

19.9 Performing the Experiment

Armed with a statistical procedure and a planned series of computer runs, the analysts commenced to attack the dock facility problem.

19.9.1 *Phase 1: A Sequence of Small Experiments*

The first phase of the study was to use a sequence of small samples (1,000 observations) to locate a tank size j for which EC_j is an approximate minimum. In order to obtain an upper bound on the tank size of interest, the analysts

Figure 19.8   *The first simulation (tank size = 0)*

```
INPUT PIPELINE CAPACITY IN BARRELS PER DAY?250000
INPUT TANK CAPACITY IN BARRELS?0
INPUT UNLOAD RATE IN BARRELS PER DAY?400000
INPUT TANKER SIZE IN BARRELS?500000
INPUT AVERAGE NUMBER OF TANKERS TO ARRIVE EACH DAY?.4
INPUT DEMURRAGE LIMIT IN DAYS?2
INPUT DOLLAR AMOUNT PER DAY TO BE CHARGED FOR EXCEEDING LIMIT?1000
INPUT NO. OF SHIP UNLOADINGS TO SIMULATE?400
INPUT A STARTING RANDOM NUMBER?3457
WANT INTERMEDIATE OUTPUT?N
WANT OUTPUT ON FILE?N



END OF SIMULATION AT TIME 1089.12

 400   TANKERS WERE UNLOADED
AVERAGE TIME IN PORT WAS 4.34008
 4      TANKERS WERE WAITING AT END OF SIMULATION
 936.026      DAYS WERE SPENT WAITING
 472635.      DOLLARS IN FEES WERE CHARGED
TANK WAS EMPTY 289.122
TANK WAS FULL 800.004
WANT TO SIMULATE MORE?Y
HOW MANY MORE SHIPS?1000


END OF SIMULATION AT TIME 3479.5

 1000      TANKERS WERE UNLOADED
AVERAGE TIME IN PORT WAS 7.03569
 1      TANKERS WERE WAITING AT END OF SIMULATION
 5035.63      DAYS WERE SPENT WAITING
 3.59013E+06   DOLLARS IN FEES WERE CHARGED
TANK WAS EMPTY 390.375
TANK WAS FULL 2000.02
WANT TO SIMULATE MORE?N
```

initially ran an experiment for a tank size of zero barrels. First, a batch of 400 tankers was run to initialize the system. After this "start-up" batch, for which the data were discarded, they then ran a batch of 1,000 consecutive tankers and calculated the sample mean of the total cost incurred by each tanker. The value 3,457 was arbitrarily selected for the random number to be input by the user (and, as mentioned in Section 19.8.4, this value was used in all runs). The results are shown in Figure 19.8. Since the tank size is zero, there is no dock fee. Hence, the total cost, $\bar{c}_0$, in this case is simply the demurrage cost. It follows that $\bar{c}_0$ is obtained by dividing the amount found under DOLLARS IN FEES WERE CHARGED by 1,000. Thus

$$\bar{c}_0 = \frac{3,590,130}{1,000} = \$3,590.13$$

Our previous discussion described how this information could be used to find an upper bound on the tank size. From that discussion, we recall that

Tank size $\leq \dfrac{\bar{c}_0}{(.00125)}$

or

Tank size $\leq \dfrac{3,590}{.00125} = 2,872,104$ barrels

The analysts at PROTRAC Engineering then ran a sequence of experiments in an attempt to locate an approximate minimum tank size. They used the same format that they used for tank size 0: the starting random number was 3,457; 400 tankers were used to initialize the system; and 1,000 consecutive tankers were then simulated to obtain a sample mean. The calculations are shown in Figure 19.9.

Figure 19.9 *A summary of experimental results with small samples*

Experiment	Tank Size (hundred-thousands of barrels)	Total Demurrage Fees for 1000 Tankers ($)	Demurrage Fees per Tanker ($)	Dock Fee per Tanker ($)	Sample Mean (total cost per Tanker, $)
1	10	1,937,240	1,937.24	1,250.00	3,187.24
2	15	1,444,410	1,444.41	1,875.00	3,319.41
3	13	1,624,190	1,624.19	1,625.00	3,249.19
4	7	2,314,790	2,314.79	875.00	3,189.79
5	8	2,181,240	2,181.24	1,000.00	3,181.24
6	9	2,055,320	2,055.32	1,125.00	3,180.32

Since the total cost per tanker for the 900,000-barrel tank is smaller (if only slightly) than the total cost per tanker with either the 800,000- or the 1 million-barrel tank, the analysts have found what appears to be an approximate minimum with this first sequence of experiments. They then turned to more lengthy grouping experiments designed to establish a confidence interval for the expected total cost per tanker.

19.9.2 *Phase 2: A Sequence of Larger Experiments with Grouped Data*

The first sequence of experiments has given an indication of the tank size that would yield a minimum value for $E(C_j)$, the expected total cost for an arbitrary tanker. Having narrowed their search, the analysts were now prepared to do more extensive experimentation to determine the optimal tank size with greater precision and to produce a confidence interval for the expected total cost per tanker.

The analysts ran 21 batches of 400 tankers each for each tank size of interest. The data from the first 400 tankers were discarded, and the data from the remaining 8,000 tankers were treated by the method previously described. That is, all 8,000 observations were used to form $\bar{g}_j$, an estimate of $E(C_j)$, and the 20 sample means $\bar{g}_{j1}, \bar{g}_{j401}, \ldots$, and so on, were used to compute the sample variance

$$s_G^2 = \tfrac{1}{19}[(\bar{g}_{j1} - \bar{g}_j)^2 + (\bar{g}_{j401} - \bar{g}_j)^2 + \ldots + (\bar{g}_{j7,601} - \bar{g}_j)^2]$$

The 95-percent confidence interval

$$\bar{g}_j - 2.09\sqrt{s_G^2/20} \leq E(C_j) \leq \bar{g}_j + 2.09\sqrt{s_G^2/20}$$

was then established. The analysts began with a tank size of 900,000 barrels and continued the analysis to the point of determining an optimal tank size to within 100,000 barrels. That is, they located a tank size that produced a smaller total cost per tanker than a tank either 100,000 barrels larger or 100,000 barrels smaller. The data are summarized in Figure 19.10.

Figure 19.10   *Experimental results with large samples of grouped data*

Experiment	Tank Size (hundred-thousands of barrels)	Mean of the 20 Group Means for Demurrage Cost per Tanker[a] ($)	$\bar{g}_j$ Mean of the 20 Group Means for Total Cost per Tanker[a] ($)	s_G Standard Deviation of the 20 Group Means
1	9	1,266.28	2,391.28	796.68
2	10	1,174.38	2,424.38	772.55
3	8	1,367.05	2,367.05	821.40
4	7	1,475.43	2,350.43	846.20
5	6	1,594.25	2,344.25	871.53
6	5	1,724.03	2,349.03	896.53

[a]8,000 observations

The results in Figure 19.10 are called "experimental results with large samples of grouped data because the total cast of 8,000 tankers (20 batches of 400 each) was used to estimate the value $E(C_j)$. The smallest estimator is achieved with a tank size of 600,000 barrels. Recall that our initial estimate (after Phase 1) was at 900,000 barrels. Thus, the use of larger samples caused the analysts to revise their initial opinion of the optimal size. The 95-percent confidence interval for $E(C_{600,000})$ is calculated to be

$$\bar{g}_{600,000} - 2.09\sqrt{s_G^2/20} \leq E(C_{600,000}) \leq \bar{g}_{600,000} + 2.09\sqrt{s_G^2/20}$$

$$2,344.25 - 2.09\left(\frac{871.53}{\sqrt{20}}\right) \leq E(C_{600,000}) \leq 2,344.25 + 2.09\left(\frac{871.53}{\sqrt{20}}\right)$$

$$1,936.95 \leq E(C_{600,000}) \leq 2,751.55$$

The data in Figure 19.10 show that a graph of the total cost per tanker as a function of tank size is very flat in the region around the minimum. For example, the difference between the sample means for the 700,000- and the 600,000-barrel tanks (that is, $\bar{g}_{700,000} - \bar{g}_{600,000}$) is only about $6. Clearly the confidence intervals for $E(C_{700,000})$ and $E(C_{600,000})$ will overlap greatly (as will the intervals for all tank sizes in Figure 19.10) and in such circumstances it is not yet clear whether $E(C_{600,000})$ really is smaller than $E(C_{700,000})$ or whether the sample results just happened (by chance) to give this indication. The analysts could of course take larger samples (that is, run more than 20 batches of 400 each or partition the data into more than 20 batches and hope that the independence of the groups is not too seriously damaged) in order to obtain smaller confidence intervals. There is, however, another technique that they can use to get a better estimate of $E(C_{700,000}) - E(C_{600,000})$ with the data they already have. This technique is discussed in the next section.

19.9.3   Selecting the Best of Two Alternative Tank Sizes

The basic idea behind the technique for estimating the difference in expected total cost per tanker for two tank sizes is to

Use paired comparisons to reduce variability.

The technique used to implement this idea can be illustrated with the following simple example.

Let us suppose that a new tool is being designed and the decision maker is confronted with the problem of whether to make the tool of material A or material B. In order to obtain some data on which material will suffer less wear, 20 prototypes are produced, 10 of each material. On day 1, ten workers are given the material A tools and each worker is given the same task to perform. On day 2, the same ten workers are given the material B tools and given the same task to perform. The wear on each tool is measured in units of 1 to 1000, with higher values denoting more wear. These data are shown in Figure 19.11, along with the differences.

Figure 19.11   *Data for the wear on materials A and B*

	Material		
Workers	***A***	***B***	***A − B***
1	42	37	5
2	300	295	5
3	600	591	9
4	200	196	4
5	800	792	8
6	760	754	6
7	610	601	9
8	432	420	12
9	180	171	9
10	96	89	7
Mean	402	394.6	7.4
Standard Deviation	277.6	276.8	2.5

One way to analyze these data would be in a manner analogous to the procedure suggested for the tank sizes. That is, we would calculate the mean wear for material A and for material B and then form a confidence interval for the expected wear in each case. Let

$E(A)$ = expected wear with material A

$E(B)$ = expected wear with material B

$\bar{X}_A$ = sample mean wear with material A

$\bar{X}_B$ = sample mean wear with material B

S_A = sample standard deviation with material A

S_B = sample standard deviation with material B

The 95-percent confidence intervals for $E(A)$ and $E(B)$ are formed as follows:

$$\bar{X}_A - 2.26 \frac{S_A}{\sqrt{20}} \le E(A) \le \bar{X}_A + 2.26 \frac{S_A}{\sqrt{20}}$$

$$\bar{X}_B - 2.26 \frac{S_B}{\sqrt{20}} \le E(B) \le \bar{X}_B + 2.26 \frac{S_B}{\sqrt{20}}$$

The value 2.26 once again comes from the t distribution (see Figure 19.13), in this case with nine degrees of freedom.

Since

$\bar{X}_A = 402$

$\bar{X}_B = 394.6$

$S_A = 277.6$

$S_B = 276.8$

the data indicate that material B is better, but the confidence intervals overlap so greatly that it is not clear whether this result occurred by chance or not.

A closer inspection of the data in Figure 19.11 indicates that much of the variation is due to the worker who used the tool rather than to the material. The third column of this table shows that taking the difference of the wear measurements for each worker eliminates much of the variability and gives a better indication of which material wears more. The $A - B$ column makes it clear that material B is the preferred choice.

In the context of the tank-size analysis, let us consider the series of experiments when the tank size is 600,000 barrels and when it is 700,000 barrels. The mean for each batch of 400 tankers for each tank size is shown in the table in Figure 19.12. In inspecting these data, recall that the same sequence of arrival times for the tankers is used in both cases. Clearly, the costs associated with the two tank sizes move together. When a particular batch produces a relatively large cost with the 700,000-barrel tank, it also produces a relatively large cost with the 600,000-barrel tank. For example, note that the third batch produces the largest cost for both tank sizes. The variability between batches (that is, the variability of the data in each of columns 2 and 3 of Figure 19.12) may be due to a variety of factors in the experiment. The major source of this variation is no doubt due to the particular sequence of random numbers that was drawn. When the differences of these data are considered, the cause of this variability tends to cancel out. This can be verified by noting that the standard deviation in the difference column is only 29.89,

Figure 19.12 *Estimating the difference in expected total cost per tanker*

	1	2	3	4
	Batch Number	Batch Mean 700,000-Barrel Tank	Batch Mean 600,000-Barrel Tank	Difference (column 2 − column 3)
	0	1,281.95	1,228.40	53.55
	1	2,277.15	2,265.85	11.30
	2	2,608.10	2,639.20	−31.10
	3	4,493.45	4,543.50	−50.05
	4	1,952.80	1,950.43	2.37
	5	2,850.73	2,880.00	−29.27
	6	2,355.55	2,381.30	−25.75
	7	2,434.53	2,405.80	28.73
	8	3,218.23	3,233.95	−15.72
	9	2,865.03	2,868.43	− 3.40
	10	1,271.95	1,213.55	58.40
	11	1,786.38	1,772.20	14.18
	12	3,283.15	3,301.98	−18.83
	13	1,660.88	1,633.45	27.43
	14	2,024.60	2,016.18	8.42
	15	2,112.80	2,097.23	15.57
	16	1,146.18	1,085.08	61.10
	17	1,644.80	1,618.95	25.85
	18	1,526.03	1,487.08	38.95
	19	1,860.88	1,844.65	16.23
	20	3,635.20	3,646.43	−11.23
Mean		2,350.42	2,344.26	6.16
Standard Deviation		846.20	871.54	29.89

as compared to a value of 871.54 for the standard deviation in column 3. The effect of this reduction in the standard deviation will be to decrease the size of our confidence interval and, accordingly, to increase our confidence in the optimality of the 600,000-barrel tank. This point will become clear in the following discussion.

To formally treat the differencing of costs on a batch-by-batch basis, it is helpful to create a new random variable. For two different tank sizes, say j and k, let

$$D_{jk\alpha} = \bar{G}_{j\alpha} - \bar{G}_{k\alpha}$$

and

$$d_{jk\alpha} = \bar{g}_{j\alpha} - \bar{g}_{k\alpha}$$

Recall that $\bar{g}_{j\alpha}$ is the mean for a sample of 400 consecutive tankers, beginning with tanker number α. That is,

$$\bar{G}_{j\alpha} = \frac{1}{400} \sum_{i=\alpha}^{\alpha+399} C_{ji}$$

and $E(\bar{G}_{j\alpha}) = E(C_j)$. From the theory of statistics, it is also true that

$$E(D_{jk\alpha}) = E(\bar{G}_{j\alpha}) - E(\bar{G}_{k\alpha}) = E(C_j) - E(C_k)$$

We are now in a very familiar position. The analysis at this point follows the same grouping strategy as before. First, define a new random variable

$$\bar{D}_{jk} = \frac{1}{20}(D_{jk1} + D_{jk401} + \ldots + D_{jk\,7,601}) = \frac{1}{8,000} \sum_{i=1}^{8,000} (C_{ji} - C_{ki})$$

The term $\bar{d}_{jk}$ will denote a specific realization of $\bar{D}_{jk}$. Hence

$$\bar{d}_{jk} = \frac{1}{8,000} \sum_{i=1}^{8,000} (c_{ji} - c_{ki})$$

Also, $E(\bar{D}_{jk}) = E(C_j) - E(C_k)$. If $E(\bar{D}_{jk}) > 0$ then it follows that $E(C_j) > E(C_k)$. Letting 7 denote the 700,000-barrel tank, and 6 denote the 600,000-barrel tank, we shall be interested in determining the probability that $E(\bar{D}_{76}) > 0$, which is the probability that $E(C_7) > E(C_6)$.

We can assume that the random variables D_{jk1}, D_{jk401}, ... are independent (the sample d_{jk1}, d_{jk401}, ..., is a *random* sample from $D_{jk\alpha}$). Consequently, we can state that $\mathrm{Var}(\bar{D}_{jk}) = \mathrm{Var}(D_{jk\alpha})/20$, and a good estimate of $\mathrm{Var}(D_{jk\alpha})$ is the sample variance

$$s_{jk}^2 = \tfrac{1}{19}\,[(d_{jk1} - \bar{d}_{jk})^2 + (d_{jk\,401} - \bar{d}_{jk})^2 + \ldots + (d_{jk7,601} - \bar{d}_{jk})^2]$$

Although we are basically interested in the difference $\bar{D}_{jk}$, and in determining the probability that $E(\bar{D}_{jk}) > 0$, it is useful to work with a standardized version of this random variable, say T_{jk}, where

$$T_{jk} = \frac{\bar{D}_{jk} - E(\bar{D}_{jk})}{\sqrt{s_{jk}^2/20}}$$

From the laws of statistics we know that T_{jk} has the t distribution with 19 degrees of freedom. Thus, by using the table of that distribution shown in Figure 19.13, we are able to make probability statements about this random variable. In this table, $P(T_{jk} \leq t_s) = s$. Entries in the table are the values of t_s for different degrees of freedom. For example, reading across the 19-degrees-of-freedom row and letting $t_s = 1.33$, it is seen that $P(T_{jk} \leq 1.33) = .90$, and $P(T_{jk} \leq -2.09) = .025$ (using table footnote a). We have seen in Figure 19.12 that $\bar{d}_{76} = 6.16$ and $s_{76} = 29.89$. What we really want to know is whether $E(C_7) - E(C_6) > 0$, which is the same as asking whether $E(\bar{D}_{76}) > 0$. Noting that $6.16 = 0.92 s_{76}/\sqrt{20}$, it is true that $\bar{d}_{76} - 0.92 s_{76}/\sqrt{20} = 0$. By interpolating in Figure 19.13, we see that

.81 = probability that $T_{76} \leq 0.92$

   = probability that $\dfrac{\bar{D}_{76} - E(\bar{D}_{76})}{\sqrt{s_{76}^2/20}} \leq 0.92$

   = probability that $\bar{D}_{76} - .92\sqrt{s_{76}^2/20} \leq E(\bar{D}_{76}) = E(C_7) - E(C_6)$

Using 6.16 for a realization of $\bar{D}_{76}$, the above probability statements mean that we have 81-percent confidence that $E(C_7) - E(C_6) > 0$. Thus, we have

Figure 19.13 *Percentiles of the t-distribution*

Degrees of Freedom	$t_{.55}$[a]	$t_{.60}$	$t_{.65}$	$t_{.70}$	$t_{.75}$	$t_{.80}$	$t_{.85}$	$t_{.90}$	$t_{.95}$	$t_{.975}$	$t_{.99}$	$t_{.995}$	$t_{.9995}$
1	.158	.325	.510	.727	1.00	1.38	1.96	3.08	6.31	12.7	31.8	63.7	637
2	.142	.289	.445	.617	.816	1.06	1.39	1.89	2.92	4.30	6.96	9.92	31.6
3	.137	.277	.424	.584	.765	.978	1.25	1.64	2.35	3.18	4.54	5.84	12.9
4	.134	.271	.414	.569	.741	.941	1.19	1.53	2.13	2.78	3.75	4.60	8.61
5	.132	.267	.408	.559	.727	.920	1.16	1.48	2.01	2.57	3.36	4.03	6.86
6	.131	.265	.404	.553	.718	.906	1.13	1.44	1.94	2.45	3.14	3.71	5.96
7	.130	.263	.402	.549	.711	.896	1.12	1.42	1.90	2.36	3.00	3.50	5.40
8	.130	.262	.399	.546	.706	.889	1.11	1.40	1.86	2.31	2.90	3.36	5.04
9	.129	.261	.398	.543	.703	.883	1.10	1.38	1.83	2.26	2.82	3.25	4.78
10	.129	.260	.397	.542	.700	.879	1.09	1.37	1.81	2.23	2.76	3.17	4.59
11	.129	.260	.396	.540	.697	.876	1.09	1.36	1.80	2.20	2.72	3.11	4.44
12	.128	.259	.395	.539	.695	.873	1.08	1.36	1.78	2.18	2.68	3.06	4.32
13	.128	.259	.394	.538	.694	.870	1.08	1.35	1.77	2.16	2.65	3.01	4.22
14	.128	.258	.393	.537	.692	.868	1.08	1.34	1.76	2.14	2.62	2.98	4.14
15	.128	.258	.393	.536	.691	.866	1.07	1.34	1.75	2.13	2.60	2.95	4.07
16	.128	.258	.392	.535	.690	.865	1.07	1.34	1.75	2.12	2.58	2.92	4.02
17	.128	.257	.392	.534	.689	.863	1.07	1.33	1.74	2.11	2.57	2.90	3.96
18	.127	.257	.392	.534	.688	.862	1.07	1.33	1.73	2.10	2.55	2.88	3.92
19	.127	.257	.391	.533	.688	.861	1.07	1.33	1.73	2.09	2.54	2.86	3.88
20	.127	.257	.391	.533	.687	.860	1.06	1.32	1.72	2.09	2.53	2.84	3.85
21	.127	.257	.391	.532	.686	.859	1.06	1.32	1.72	2.08	2.52	2.83	3.82
22	.127	.256	.390	.532	.686	.858	1.06	1.32	1.72	2.07	2.51	2.82	3.79
23	.127	.256	.390	.532	.685	.858	1.06	1.32	1.71	2.07	2.50	2.81	3.77
24	.127	.256	.390	.531	.685	.857	1.06	1.32	1.71	2.06	2.49	2.80	3.74
25	.127	.256	.390	.531	.684	.856	1.06	1.32	1.71	2.06	2.48	2.79	3.72
26	.127	.256	.390	.531	.684	.856	1.06	1.32	1.71	2.06	2.48	2.78	3.71
27	.127	.256	.389	.531	.684	.855	1.06	1.31	1.70	2.05	2.47	2.77	3.69
28	.127	.256	.389	.530	.683	.855	1.06	1.31	1.70	2.05	2.47	2.76	3.67
29	.127	.256	.389	.530	.683	.854	1.05	1.31	1.70	2.04	2.46	2.76	3.66
30	.127	.256	.389	.530	.683	.854	1.05	1.31	1.70	2.04	2.46	2.75	3.65
∞	.126	.253	.385	.524	.674	.842	1.04	1.28	1.64	1.96	2.33	2.58	3.29

[a]For the lower percentiles, use the relation $t_a = -t_{1-a}$. In particular, $t_{.50} = -t_{.50} = 0$. For example, for 6 degrees of freedom, $t_{.35} = -t_{.65} = -.404$.

This table is taken from Table III of Fisher and Yates, *Statistical Tables for Biological, Agricultural and Medical Research*, published by Longman Group Ltd., London, (previously published by Oliver and Boyd, Edinburgh), and by permission of the authors and publishers.

used the differencing technique to perform an analysis to aid in the choice between *two tank sizes*, the 600,000-barrel tank, the apparent optimum after the large sample run, and a close competitor, the 700,000-barrel tank.

At this point, an important caveat should be stated. The tools of classical statistics are not directly suited to choosing the better of two alternatives. Different schools of statisticians would use different approaches. The approach we have suggested can be implemented relatively simply, it has some intuitive appeal, and very importantly for our purposes, it is used in practice. Other approaches could well produce confidence intervals different from the one derived above.

19.9.4　*Selecting the Best of K Alternative Tank Sizes*

Naturally, the analysts aren't only interested in the 600,000-barrel and the 700,000-barrel tanks. The data in Figure 19.10 suggest that the 500,000–800,000-barrel tanks are all candidates for the optimum. The comments at the end of the previous section regarding the difficulty of selecting the better of two alternatives hold with even more force when the problem is to select the best of K alternatives. Once again, we shall present a relatively simple and pragmatic approach.

Since the 600,000-barrel tank is currently our best guess at the optimum size, our goal is to obtain a confidence statement that *all* of the following are true:

$$E(C_6) \le E(C_7)$$
$$E(C_6) \le E(C_5)$$
$$E(C_6) \le E(C_8)$$

The approach to be taken is based on the *Bonferroni t statistic*. To use this statistic it is useful to introduce the following three statements:

$$S_1 : \{\bar{D}_{76} - 0.92 \sqrt{s_{76}^2/20} \le E(C_7) - E(C_6)\}$$
$$S_2 : \{\bar{D}_{56} - 0.84 \sqrt{s_{56}^2/20} \le E(C_5) - E(C_6)\}$$
$$S_3 : \{\bar{D}_{86} - 2.78 \sqrt{s_{86}^2/20} \le E(C_8) - E(C_6)\}$$

We realize that the origin of these statements may be unclear at the moment. The variables $\bar{D}_{76}$ and so on are, of course, the differences that interest us. The Figure 19.14 data show the derivation of the numbers 0.92 and so on.

Figure 19.14　*Data for the multiple comparisons test*

Tank Size j, k	$\bar{d}_{jk}$	s_{jk}
7,6	6.18	29.89
5,6	4.78	25.34
8,6	22.80	36.72

Using the t distribution and the approach presented in Section 19.9.3, the analysts calculated the following probabilities

$$P(S_1) = P\{\bar{D}_{76} - 0.92\sqrt{s_{76}^2/20} \le E(C_7) - E(C_6)\} = .81$$
$$P(S_2) = P\{\bar{D}_{56} - 0.84\sqrt{s_{56}^2/20} \le E(C_5) - E(C_6)\} = .79$$
$$P(S_3) = P\{\bar{D}_{86} - 2.78\sqrt{s_{86}^2/20} \le E(C_8) - E(C_6)\} = .99$$

What we wish to ascertain is the probability that all three of the statements S_1, S_2, and S_3 are true. Though we are unable to obtain the exact value, we can produce bounds. For example, the probability that all three are true is surely less than .79. This gives an upper bound. Of more interest is a lower bound, obtained as follows. The probability that all three statements are true is equal to 1 minus the probability that at least one is false. Also

$$P(\text{at least 1 is false}) \le \sum_{j=1}^{3} P(S_j \text{ is false})$$

This can be illustrated by considering only two statements. Let

A = the event that S_1 is false

B = the event that S_2 is false

Then

$$P(\text{at least 1 is false}) = P(A \cup B) = P(A) + P(B) - P(A \cap B) \le P(A) + P(B)$$

If A and B are not independent, then $P(A \cap B) > 0$ and the above inequality is strict. In the tanker context, it is clear that the events A, B are not independent. For example, if the statement identified as S_1 is false, it could be due to the fact that the mean cost of the sample for the 600,000-barrel tank ($\bar{c}_6$) is small, which would imply there is also a good chance that S_2 is false. These arguments lead to the conclusion that

$$P(\text{all 3 are true}) \ge 1 - \sum_{j=1}^{3} P(S_j \text{ is false}) = 1 - (.19 + .21 + .01) = .59$$

This is the confidence statement the analysts were looking for. They can be *at least* 59-percent confident that the 600,000-barrel tank is better than the 500,000-, 700,000-, and 800,000-barrel tanks.

At this point, the analysts at PROTRAC Engineering were pretty comfortable about the decision to select a tank with a 600,000-barrel capacity. The data supported the fact that the model yields a minimum cost when the tank size is 600,000 barrels. Further, the fact that the cost function is so flat in the region of optimality leads them to believe that they can't go too wrong with this decision.

19.10 A Concluding Overview

The analysts at PROTRAC Engineering finally decided to recommend a 600,000-barrel tank. In concluding our analysis of their simulation study, there are several important points to make. For a manager with little or no experience with quantitative techniques, simulation is an especially appealing device for analyzing management problems. The idea of building a model that will enable her to get "experience" with the system in question without incurring the actual costs of trying out new policies is certainly attractive. Using simulation *seems* to allow the manager the opportunity to use a "quantitative approach" while eliminating the problem of mastering the mathematics necessary to understand other analytic models. Simulation also *seems* simple. The staff analysts write a computer program that simulates the behavior of the system in question. The manager then simply runs a few experiments and selects the set of decisions that yields the best result.

Unfortunately, this simple-minded view of the use of simulation is quite naive. The truth of the matter is:

1   Developing a model for a simulation study typically requires the same skill, judgment, and careful analysis that are demanded in creating an analytic model. Almost all real problems include so many factors and interactions that attempting to duplicate the behavior of the real system on the computer is out of the question. Only an abstract version of the problem can be studied. The analyst and the managers must isolate the important factors in a problem and specify the proper interactions among them. This task requires skill in the use of analytic modeling techniques. Symbols must be used to represent decisions and parameters. Functions must be used to specify the relationships between decisions and parameters. Indeed, standard management science models (such as an LP model) may be an integral part of a simulation model. Thus, if a manager is going to really understand what is happening in a simulation model, he will have to be able to understand the way in which quantitative models are used. It is typically no easier to understand a simulation model than an analytic model of corresponding levels of detail. It is true that there may be a lot of difficult mathematical theory that lies behind *solving* the analytic model, but the consistent point of view of this text is that this theory need not be a concern of the manager.

2   Hopefully, the dock facility problem has already dispelled the notion that using a simulator is simply a matter of "running a few experiments and selecting the best decision." Using a simulator effectively to obtain valid results requires careful planning and the appropriate use of conceptually difficult statistical techniques. Suppose that one can construct a simulator that accurately models the system in question and that one has an unlimited computing budget. Then it is certainly possible to obtain precise estimates of quantities of interest (costs, and so on) and arrive at good decisions. In real situations, however, there is usually a limit on both the time and the budget available for performing the analysis pursuant to a management decision. In general, a manager cannot afford the luxury of solving a problem by employing an overwhelming number of computer runs.

The analysis of the docking-facility problem may have seemed reasonably complicated to the reader. In reality, however, as simulations go, it is quite simple. In particular:

1   The decision consisted of selecting the best value for a single decision variable, the tank size. More typically, the decision would involve a selection of values for a number of decision variables. In the context of the dock facility problem, one can think of situations in which quantities that are parameters in the current version of the problem become decision variables. It is certainly plausible that quantities such as the size of the tankers, their arrival rate, the pipeline and unloading rates, and so on, could all be variables in the model. In such a setting, it is not hard to imagine that the number of possible solutions could become enormous. For example, suppose there are

ten decision variables, each of which can assume five different values. If all possible combinations are feasible, there are 5^{10} (about 9.7 million) different possible decisions to consider.

2 The general shape of the cost function as a function of the decision variable was easy to specify. In a problem with a number of decision variables, this usually is not the case. When the general shape of the cost function is unknown, the process of searching for an optimal decision becomes more difficult. To illustrate this idea, suppose for a moment that you have the following problem:

Max $f(x_1, x_2, x_3)$

s.t.

$0 \le x_i \le 200$ $i = 1, 2, 3$

x_i integer valued

Also assume that you know nothing about the general shape of the function f. You may, however, sequentially specify 100 different sets of decision variables (100 sets of triples) and observe the value of f. You might work with a table of the type shown in Figure 19.15. What strategy would you use in selecting the values of x_i in order to obtain as large a value of f as possible? Note that you can only observe 100 out of the possible $200^3 = 8$ million possible decisions.

Figure 19.15   *Decision table*

Specified Values of x_i			
x_1	x_2	x_3	$f(x_1, x_2, x_3)$
3	9	27	1,008
16	40	82	93

This is essentially the problem being faced by the manager attempting to use a simulator to find the optimal decision. It is extreme in the sense that we have assumed that you know nothing about f. It is simple in the sense that you get to see the true value of f, not an estimate of f based on a sample. It captures the essence of the manager's problem in the sense that a sequence of trials can be performed in an effort to find a good (or optimal) decision.

3 The dock facility problem was also simple in that the cost of obtaining simulated results was low. The simulator itself is a fairly simple computer program. There are only a few items in the system (the tankers and the oil in the tank) that need to be monitored. Contrast this situation to a more complicated model. A good example is provided by the problem of determining the appropriate mix of personnel to assign to a hospital floor and determining a schedule of activities for each individual. It is not necessary to go into the details of such a problem to see that there is a substantial challenge in creating a model that reasonably simulates the behavior of such a system. Gathering experimental data for any given set of decision variables in such a problem would be significantly more time-consuming and expensive than using the dock facility simulator. The analyst using such a system is under increased pressure to plan his experiments carefully and to make maximum use of the data he obtains.

We have just pointed out a number of ways in which the dock facility problem is particularly simple. There is, however, one way in which it is quite difficult. This has to do with the fact that the oil company is concerned with a system that will run continuously over a long period of time. One thus needs a decision (a tank size) that produces good results in the long run, and this makes the analysis more difficult. Many experimental problems are caused by the difficulty of obtaining a random sample of the total cost for "an arbitrarily selected tanker." There are, however, many problems in which one is interested in the behavior of the system over some specific period of time. For example, consider simulating the pattern of airplane arrivals and departures at Chicago's O'Hare field. It is quite a good approximation to assume that the airport is empty and idle at about 4:00 A.M., which means that the scenario is "restarted" at 4:00 A.M. each day. In other words, the analyst can conveniently think of simulating the airport on a day-by-day basis. In cases like this, the analysis is much easier. The question of initialization essentially disappears, and long-run considerations are eliminated. The net effect of all this is that the task of achieving a random sample to use in a statistical analysis is more straightforward.

There is a strong tendency for simulation models to grow during the formulation process. Spurred by the desire to have a realistic model and aided by the fact that additional ideas can usually be appended to the logical structure of a simulation model without a great deal of difficulty, the model grows. The wise manager realizes that creating an effective simulation model involves more than specifying the appropriate logical structure. Producing a useful simulation model also involves writing the computer program and testing it to make sure that it does indeed faithfully reproduce the behavior of the system in question. One must then perform the proper experiments and analyze the data. Keeping this entire process in mind can help the manager and the analyst arrive at a parsimonious and useful model.

In summary, then, simulation is a popular and important way to attack management problems. To use it effectively, a manager must use good judgment in the creation of the simulation model, in the design of the study, and in the analysis of the output.

19.11   Statistical and Notational Summary

C_j = the random variable denoting the total cost for an *arbitrary* tanker given the decision j (lease a tank of size j).

In other words,

C_j = dock fee + demurrage cost

c_j = a particular realization or value for C_j

$E(C_j)$ = the expected value of C_j

$$E(C_j) = \Sigma\ c_j P_{C_j}(c_j)$$

where each term in the sum corresponds to a possible value for C_j, and P_{C_j} is the *pmf* for C_j.

EC_j = the expected total cost associated with an arbitrary tanker given the decision j.

$$EC_j = \sum_i P_j(W_i)\, C_j(W_i)$$

where the elementary events W_i are waiting times for an arbitrary tanker given decision j, $C_j(W_i)$ is the total cost of waiting time W_i, given decision j, and $P_j(W_i)$ is the associated probability.

$$EC_j = E(C_j)$$

C_{ji} = the random variable denoting the total cost for the ith ship observed, given decision j.

c_{ji} = a particular realization for C_{ji}.

Assuming C_{ji} and C_j are identically distributed, for all i,

$$E(C_{ji}) = E(C_j) \text{ and } \text{Var}(C_{ji}) = \text{Var}(C_j)$$

$\bar{C}_j$ = the random variable $1/n \sum_I C_{ji}$, where I denotes an index set for i, say
$\{i_1, i_2, \dots, i_n\}$.

$\bar{c}_j$ = a particular realization for $\bar{C}_j$, called a *sample mean*.

$$\bar{c}_j = \frac{1}{n} \sum_I c_{ji}$$

$$E(\bar{C}_j) = E(C_j)$$

Suppose $C_{ji_1}, C_{ji_2}, \dots, C_{ji_n}$ are independent as well as identically distributed. Then

$$\text{Var}(\bar{C}_j) = \frac{\text{Var}(C_j)}{n}$$

Also, the .95 confidence interval for $E(C_j)$ is given by

$$E(\bar{C}_j) - 1.96 \sqrt{\frac{\text{Var}(C_j)}{n}} \le E(C_j) \le \bar{c}_j + 1.96 \sqrt{\frac{\text{Var}(C_j)}{n}}$$

Since $\text{Var}(C_j)$ is unknown, we use the fact that

$$\text{Var}(C_j) \approx s_j^2 = \frac{1}{n-1} \sum_I (c_{ji} - \bar{c}_j)^2$$

For a suitably large sample (say 100 or so) the confidence interval becomes

$$\bar{c}_j - 1.96 \sqrt{s_j^2/n} \le E(C_j) \le \bar{c}_j + 1.96 \sqrt{s_j^2/n}$$

Consecutive Groupings of 400

$\bar{G}_{j\alpha}$ = the random variable $\dfrac{1}{400} \displaystyle\sum_{i=\alpha}^{\alpha+399} C_{ji}$, where α identifies an arbitrary tanker.

$\bar{g}_{j\alpha}$ = a specific realization of $\bar{G}_{j\alpha}$.

$\bar{G}_j$ = the random variable $\frac{1}{20}(\bar{G}_{j1} + \bar{G}_{j401} + \bar{G}_{j801} + \dots + \bar{G}_{j7,601})$

$$\bar{G}_j = \frac{1}{8,000} \sum_{i=1}^{8,000} C_{ji}$$

$\bar{g}_j$ = a specific realization of $\bar{G}_j = \dfrac{1}{8,000} \displaystyle\sum_{i=1}^{8,000} c_{ji}$

$E(\bar{G}_j) = E(C_j)$

Assuming $\bar{G}_{j1}, \bar{G}_{j401}, \ldots, \bar{G}_{j7,601}$ are independent and identically distributed,

$\operatorname{Var}(\bar{G}_j) = \frac{1}{20} \operatorname{Var}(\bar{G}_{j\alpha})$

A .95 confidence interval for $E(C_j)$ is given by

$$\bar{g}_j - 1.96 \sqrt{\frac{\operatorname{Var}(\bar{G}_{j\alpha})}{20}} \le E(C_j) \le \bar{g}_j + 1.96 \sqrt{\frac{\operatorname{Var}(\bar{G}_{j\alpha})}{20}}$$

Since $\operatorname{Var}(\bar{G}_{j\alpha})$ is unknown, we use the fact that

$$\operatorname{Var}(\bar{G}_{j\alpha}) \approx s_G^2 = \tfrac{1}{19} \left[(\bar{g}_{j1} - \bar{g}_j)^2 + (\bar{g}_{j401} - \bar{g}_j)^2 + \ldots + (\bar{g}_{j7,601} - \bar{g}_j)^2 \right].$$

For a sample of size 20, the .95 confidence interval becomes

$$\bar{g}_j - 2.09 \sqrt{s_G^2/20} \le E(C_j) \le \bar{g}_j + 2.09 \sqrt{s_G^2/20}$$

The value 2.09 (rather than 1.96) is used because of the small sample size.

DIFFERENCING

$D_{jk\alpha}$ = $\bar{G}_{j\alpha} - \bar{G}_{k\alpha} = \dfrac{1}{400} \displaystyle\sum_{i=\alpha}^{\alpha+399} (C_{ji} - C_{ki})$

$d_{jk\alpha}$ = $\bar{g}_{j\alpha} - \bar{g}_{k\alpha}$ = a specific realization of $D_{jk\alpha}$

$E(D_{jk\alpha})$ = $E(C_j) - E(C_k)$

$\bar{D}_{jk}$ = $\dfrac{1}{20} (D_{jk1} + D_{jk401} + \ldots + D_{jk7,601}) = \dfrac{1}{8,000} \displaystyle\sum_{i=1}^{8,000} (C_{ji} - C_{ki})$

$\bar{d}_{jk}$ = a specific realization of $\bar{D}_{jk}$

$E(\bar{D}_{jk})$ = $E(C_j) - E(C_k)$

$\operatorname{Var}(\bar{D}_{jk})$ = $\dfrac{\operatorname{Var}(D_{jk\alpha})}{20}$

A .95 confidence interval for $E(\bar{D}_{jk})$ is given by

$$\bar{d}_{jk} - 1.96 \sqrt{\frac{\operatorname{Var}(D_{jk\alpha})}{20}} \le E(\bar{D}_{jk}) \le \bar{d}_{jk} + 1.96 \sqrt{\frac{\operatorname{Var}(D_{jk\alpha})}{20}}$$

For a sample of size 20, the .95 confidence interval becomes

$$\bar{d}_{jk} - 2.09 \sqrt{s_{jk}^2/20} \le E(\bar{D}_{jk}) \le \bar{d}_{jk} + 2.09 \sqrt{s_{jk}^2/20}$$

where

$$s_{jk}^2 = \frac{1}{19} \left[(d_{jk1} - \bar{d}_{jk})^2 + (d_{jk401} - \bar{d}_{jk})^2 + \ldots + (d_{jk7,601} - \bar{d}_{jk})^2 \right]$$

and the value 2.09 is again used because of the small sample.

19.12 Problems

1   What does it mean to say that in many instances one can formally think of a simulation as a statistical experiment?

2   In the problem being considered by PROTRAC, when will oil be pumped from the tanker at a rate determined by the pipeline capacity?

3   If there is no tank, what condition is sufficient to guarantee that the waiting line will not increase without limit?

4   In the current model, it is assumed that one tanker arrives every 2.5 days, on the average. What happens to the dock fee per ship if all other parameters (including the tank size) remain the same and tankers begin to arrive more rapidly? For example, assume that one tanker arrives every 1.25 days on the average.

5   Consider an urn with six balls that are identical except for the numbers painted on them. One ball is painted with the number 10, one with 6, two with 5, one with 4, and one with 0. The following experiment is performed:
   (1) A ball is chosen at random from the urn. Its number is recorded. The ball is discarded.
   (2) Another ball is chosen at random from the five balls that remain in the urn. Its number is recorded. The ball is returned to the urn. Let R_1 be the first number recorded and R_2 be the second number recorded.
   a Is R_1 a random variable? If so, specify its pmf.
   b Is R_2 a random variable? If so, specify its pmf.
   c Are R_1 and R_2 independent?
   d Find $P(R_1 = 10)$ and $P(R_2 = 10 \mid R_1 = 10)$. Are the results of these calculations consistent with your answer to part c?

6   Is it possible to have two random variables, say R_1 and R_2, that are independent but are not identically distributed?

7   Let R_i be a sequence of independent, identically distributed random variables for which $E(R_i) = E(R)$ and $\text{Var}(R_i) = \text{Var}(R)$. A random sample of 100 items is taken, and a confidence interval is created using the sample mean ($\bar{r}$) and the sample variance s^2. A confidence interval of a certain total length (say L) is obtained. Assuming that the estimate of s^2 remains unchanged, how large a sample would be required to obtain a confidence interval with a total length of $L/2$?

8   Consider the output shown in Figure 19.3 and the discussion that follows it. It is shown that the first tanker to arrive unloads in 1.60 days. Why then does the fourth tanker to arrive require 2.00 days to unload?

9   In Figure 19.3, what will happen to the value under DOLLARS IN FEES WERE CHARGED if the value under DOLLAR AMOUNT PER DAY TO BE CHARGED FOR EXCEEDING LIMIT is doubled?

10   In Figure 19.3, what will happen to the value under DOLLARS IN FEES WERE CHARGED if the value under DEMURRAGE LIMIT IN DAYS is doubled?

11   Comment on the following statement: In the tanker simulation experiment, the primary motivation for grouping data in analyzing the output of a simulation (for example, the reason for working with $\bar{g}_{j\alpha}$ rather than just C_{ji}) is to obtain a better estimate of the expected total cost of an arbitrarily selected tanker, $E(C_j)$.

12   What is the relationship between the dock fee associated with the optimal tank size and the expected demurrage charge when the tank size is zero (for an arbitrarily selected tanker)? (Recall that the dock fee is a function of tank size.)

13   In the tanker simulation, it was argued that the data from the first group of tankers were not representative of the behavior of the docking facility over the long run, and thus the data should be discarded. Since no more tankers will arrive after the last group, is the last group also nonrepresentative? Why or why not?

14   Why do the analysts at PROTRAC follow the two-step procedure described in Section

19.8.3 rather than simply running a sample of 20 groups of 400 tankers to estimate the expected cost and establish a confidence interval for that cost for any tank size in which they are interested?

15 What is the common motivation underlying the following two simulation techniques recommended in the text?

    (1) Use the same sequence of random numbers when comparing alternatives.

    (2) Use paired comparisons to reduce variability.

20 Stochastic Inventory Management and Queuing Problems

This chapter applies previously developed concepts to two specific types of stochastic problems. In particular, with a progressive development of the newsboy problem, stochastic inventory models are discussed from the point of view of general forms for optimal operating policies and implications of these policies for management. Queuing models are also discussed, with the emphasis placed on the structural components of queuing systems and illustrations of typical results.

20.1 Introduction

This final chapter of the text concludes our considerations of decisions under uncertainty. In the following pages two important types of management questions will be considered:

1 Stochastic inventory management, or how much inventory should a firm hold in what locations in order to "best" satisfy *uncertain* future demands.
2 Queuing problems, or how much should management invest in capital and labor in order to "best" balance the cost of producing a good or service with the cost of waiting to receive that good or service.

The discussion of these topics will draw heavily on material that has been developed earlier. In fact, one can view this chapter as just another application of the basic concept of the maximization of expected utility as a criterion for making decisions under uncertainty.

Even though this view is correct, it does not imply that the development is superfluous. Two points should be made.

1 The specific problems under consideration are practically universal in their occurrence and clearly major in their significance.
2 An enormous amount of time, energy, and expertise has in the past been devoted to analyzing these problems and to creating quantitative models to aid management in dealing with them.

It thus seems useful to attempt to distill and understand the basic features (perhaps we should call them miniconcepts) of the analysis and models in these areas.

Hopefully, it is clear by now that

It is indeed an unusual set of circumstances in which one can find a textbook model that will exactly fit a real problem.

That is certainly true of the models presented in this chapter. These models, however, are prototypes that provide the basis for the analysis of inventory and queuing problems. With appropriate modifications and expansions, they will often apply to specific real-world problems. In some cases, these same models form the basis of essentially automated decision systems.

Inventory is a very general concept. It can consist of anything from machine-piece parts to jars of jelly, from water behind a dam to cash on hand, from a railroad's rolling stock to the number of lieutenants in the army. The concept of a queue (a waiting line) is equally general. Queues form at service counters, in traffic (called *jams*), in computer facilities, and in telephone exchanges. It is simply difficult to avoid encountering the types of problems to be considered in this chapter. It follows that numerous opportunities should arise for you to exploit your understanding of the "miniconcepts" that relate to these models.

20.2   Stochastic Inventory Models

Chapter 13 (Section 13.2) deals with the topic of managing the inventory function. In particular, the reasons for holding inventories and the conceptual components of mathematical inventory models are discussed in some detail. This discussion provides essential background for understanding stochastic inventory models. It should be reviewed before proceeding. The new wrinkle in this section is that it is explicitly recognized that, in many interesting situations, the heart of the inventory problem is the fact that management is not sure what the future demand will actually turn out to be.

Stochastic inventory models deal with this problem by assuming that demand is a random variable; that is, that there is a known probability mass function (*pmf*) for the future demand. Taken at face value, this statement implies that in order to implement such models it may be necessary for management to attempt to estimate the pmf from past data. Some of the problems of estimating future values from past values were discussed in Chapter 17, "Forecasting." Suffice it to say at this point that the magnitude of this problem could well be sufficient to seriously diminish the interest of a manager. However, it will be seen that some of the models to be discussed will have the advantage of significantly reducing the associated information requirements and, accordingly, the estimation task. Such considerations are important and will be emphasized in the sequel.

20.2.1   *The Newsboy Problem*

The basic one-period stochastic inventory model is generally called the newsboy problem. It has on occasion been called the Christmas tree problem. The scenario proceeds as follows. A vendor (the newsboy) may purchase as many items as he wishes for c dollars (say \$.15) each. He will then attempt to sell the items for r dollars (say \$.25) each. Unfortunately, he faces an uncertain demand for the item. It is assumed, however, that he knows the probability with which various demands will occur. (This means that he knows the *pmf* of the demand.) In this chapter, we will use the notation $p(\ )$ to indicate probability. Thus $p(d)$ is the probability that the random variable under consideration takes on the value d and $p[d \leq y]$ means the probability that the random variable takes on a value less than or equal to y. In the newsboy example, the random variable is the quantity demanded, and $p(d)$ will denote the probability that the quantity demanded turns out to be d units. As a particular illustration, assume that the possible values for d and the associated probabilities are as given in Figure 20.1.

From previous chapters we know that the newsboy should buy a quantity of papers that maximizes his *expected utility*. Let us assume that his utility function is linear in dollars over the range of possible money values for this problem. Then, as discussed in Chapter 15, the newsboy can equivalently maximize his *expected dollar return*. Let $R(y)$ be the newsboy's expected dollar return if he decides to purchase y papers. Then it can be deduced that

$$R(y) = \sum_{d=0}^{y} r\, d\, p(d) + \sum_{d=y+1}^{\infty} r\, y\, p(d) - cy$$

Note that the first term includes all the cases (that is, values for demand) in which the newsboy has purchased enough papers to satisfy demand. The second term includes all cases in which demand exceeds the number of papers ordered, which means that the newsboy sells exactly the number of papers he purchased. The last term is the cost of purchasing the y papers.

The newsboy's problem, then, is to select the value y so that $R(y)$ is maximized. We shall call such a value of y *the optimal value of y* and will use the symbol S to denote such a value. For a particular numerical problem (with discrete units), one could determine S simply by calculating $R(y)$ for each appropriate value of y and then selecting the y value that maximizes $R(y)$. As an example, let $c = .15$, $r = .25$, and let d and $p(d)$ be as given in Figure 20.1. The resulting values for $R(y)$ are presented in Figure 20.2.

It can be seen that the optimal decision is to purchase 23 papers. Thus far, nothing new has been introduced. The newsboy problem exactly fits the general model for decisions under uncertainty discussed in Chapter 15.

Figure 20.1   *Probabilities for various demands*

Demand (d)	$p(d)$
21	.1
22	.2
23	.4
24	.2
25	.1
Otherwise	0

Figure 20.2   *Values for the expected return*

y	$R(y)$
21	2.100
22	2.175
23	2.200
24	2.125
25	2.000

20.2.2 *Optimal S Policies*

It turns out that much of the theoretical work on stochastic inventory models is *not* devoted to finding a numerical solution to a particular inventory management problem. Rather, the goal is to find the general formula for the optimal operating policy for a wide class of problems. To understand what this means, it is convenient to consider the newsboy problem with a small modification. Let us suppose that the newsboy currently has x papers on hand. In other words, x is a parameter that will, of course, have a particular value in a particular instance, but our development will be for a general unspecified value of x. Now assume that the newsboy may purchase as many additional papers as he wishes. Let y be the number of papers the newsboy has on hand at the beginning of the period *after* he makes his purchase; that is, he orders $y - x$. This problem is clearly a generalization of the former, in which case the value of x was zero. For each different value of x, the newsboy faces a different problem. Thus, we have created a general class of problems, and we shall obtain a formula for the optimal policy for any problem in this class.

At the outset, note that the problem can be expressed as a constrained optimization model, as follows. The newsboy wishes to find a solution to

$$\text{Max} \quad \sum_{d=0}^{y} r\,d\,p(d) + \sum_{d=y+1}^{\infty} r\,y\,p(d) - c(y - x)$$

s.t.

$$y \geq x$$

Using the previous definition of $R(y)$, this problem becomes

$$\text{Max} \quad R(y) + cx$$

s.t.

$$y \geq x$$

where, as defined above, x represents some fixed numerical value (the number of papers currently on hand) and y is the decision variable (the number of papers on hand after ordering). Fortunately, the function $R(y)$ has certain characteristics that make this a particularly easy problem to solve. Figure 20.3 shows a typical $R(y)$. We have chosen to show $R(y)$ as a continuous function

Figure 20.3 *A typical R(y)*

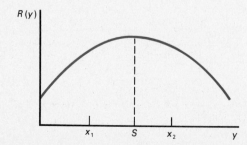

in order to have a clearer graphical representation.[1] In the discussion, of course, $R(y)$ is defined only for integer values of y and is thus discrete. The rules of calculus can be used to show that, under any set of reasonable assumptions about $p(d)$, the function $R(y)$ does indeed have this "typical shape," namely, that it is concave and that a maximum exists. As before, the symbol S will be used to denote a value of y that maximizes $R(y)$.

Now back to the newsboy problem, which is

Max $R(y) + cx$

s.t.

$y \geq x$

Since x is a parameter with a fixed value, the term cx in the objective function is a constant and can therefore be ignored in the optimization. Thus, the newsboy's optimal policy is determined by the value of y that maximizes $R(y)$ over a specified region, and such a policy can be easily deduced from Figure 20.3. In particular, if $x \leq S$ (like x_1), then the optimal policy is to purchase $(S - x)$ papers; that is, the newsboy should order *up to* the point S. If $x > S$ (like x_2), then the optimal policy is to purchase zero papers. An optimal policy of this general form is termed an *S policy*. Thus, an S policy has the form

---

If $x \leq S$, the newsboy should purchase $(S - x)$ papers. If $x > S$, the newsboy should not purchase any papers.

This value S, which maximizes the expected return $R(y)$, can be rather easily computed. In particular, it can be shown that S is the smallest value of y for which

$$\frac{r - c}{r} \leq p[d \leq y]$$

As an example, let us show how this computation can be applied to the specific problem presented in Section 20.2.1. Note that

$$\frac{r - c}{r} = \frac{.25 - .15}{.25} = .4$$

Also

$$p[d \leq 22] = .3$$

and

$$p[d \leq 23] = .7$$

---

1   This implies that $R(y)$ would be defined with integrals rather than sums, but for our purposes this technicality can be ignored.

Thus, 23 is the smallest y such that

$$p[d \le y] \ge .4$$

For this example, then,

$$S = 23$$

From the above general formula for the optimal operating policy, it follows that if the newsboy has zero papers on hand, as in the earlier example, he should order 23 papers, and indeed this is the optimal solution presented in Section 20.2.1. Thus we have solved the problem without explicitly computing each $R(y)$, as was done to obtain the results presented in Figure 20.2. If, more generally, the newsboy is assumed to have x papers on hand, then the general formula tells us that if x is less than 23, he should purchase enough to bring his inventory up to 23. If x is greater than or equal to 23, then the newsboy should order zero.

Let us now consider several advantageous implications of the above results for management.

IMPLICATION 1

With a simple calculation, the solution is immediately available for any stochastic one-period inventory model in which the only relevant financial considerations are the purchase price, c, and the sales revenue, r. In other words, as illustrated above, the need to compute $R(y)$ for each value of y is eliminated. As another example, consider the PROTRAC Alaskan pipeline problem discussed in Section 15.4. This problem can be interpreted as a newsboy problem. The problem states that PROTRAC realizes a net gain of $5,000 for each E–9 sold and loses $1,000 for each E–9 delivered and not sold. It is equivalent to think of the number of E–9s sent to Alaska as the number of E–9s purchased at a cost, c, of $1,000 and to assume that the returns are created by an r of $6,000. With this interpretation, S E–9s should be sent to Alaska where S is the smallest y such that

$$\frac{6,000 - 1,000}{6,000} = .833 \le p[d \le y]$$

The problem states that

$$p[d = 0] = .50$$
$$p[d = 1] = .10$$
$$p[d = 2] = .20$$
$$p[d = 3] = .15$$
$$p[d = 4] = .05$$

thus $S = 3$. This solution procedure, as compared to the procedure presented in Chapter 15, presents a striking example of the value of knowing the general formula for the optimal operating policy.

IMPLICATION 2

In previous sections of the text, it has been emphasized that in real-world applications the problems associated with data collection and parameter estimation are often so difficult that, by themselves, they can lead to failure of the modeling effort. Thus, it is important to eliminate the need for data collection to the greatest extent possible. The above formula for computing S is a step in this direction, since it means that the estimation task required of management has been substantially reduced. For example, consider the two cases:

1 Using the general formula for the optimal operating policy, it is only necessary to specify the smallest y such that

$$\frac{r - c}{r} \leq p\,[d \leq y]$$

For example, if $r - c/c$ turns out to be .7, the analyst simply needs an answer to the question, "What is the minimum number of items we need on hand so that 70 percent of the time we will not run out?"

2 If one does not use the general formula, it is necessary to estimate the entire pmf for the demand in order to compute $R(y)$ for each value of y. This estimation may not be a trivial task. In any case, it should generally be true that estimating an answer to the question in item 1 should be easier.

20.2.3   Optimal (s, S) Policies

One of the best-known results in stochastic inventory management concerns the optimality of the so-called (s, S) *policies*. For such policies the optimal operating rule is

If $x < s$, order $(S - x)$ items. If $x \geq s$, do not order.

Here x again refers to the amount on hand, and S is again the quantity that maximizes the expected return. The added feature of this type of policy is the introduction of a new parameter, s. Clearly, if $s = S$, then the above formula gives us the previous S policy. Thus, the (s, S) policy is a generalization of the S policy, and we shall see that it applies to an even broader class of models. In particular, let us further expand the newsboy problem by allowing a *fixed cost* component in the ordering cost function. This means that the cost of ordering z items is given by the expression

$$C(z) = \begin{cases} K + c(z) & \text{if } z > 0 \\ 0 & \text{if } z = 0 \end{cases}$$

where K is a new parameter denoting a specified fixed or lumpy cost. For the special case of $K = 0$, we have the cost function already dealt with. This more general cost function $C(z)$ is commonly employed in both stochastic and deterministic inventory models (see Sections 13.2.3 and 13.2.4).

Now, in analyzing this expanded model, let $R(y)$ be defined as it was in Section 20.2.1, namely,

$$R(y) = \sum_{d=0}^{y} r\,d\,p(d) + \sum_{d=y+1}^{\infty} r\,y\,p(d) - cy$$

In the current version of the problem (x items on hand and a lumpy cost), the newsboy may choose to purchase nothing, in which case his return is

$$\sum_{d=0}^{x} r\,d\,p(d) + \sum_{d=x+1}^{\infty} r\,x\,p(d) = R(x) + cx$$

Or, he may choose to purchase $y - x$ units, with $y > x$, in which case the expected return is given by

$$\sum_{d=0}^{y} r\,d\,p(d) + \sum_{d=y+1}^{\infty} r\,y\,p(d) - [K + c(y-x)] = R(y) + cx - K$$

The question of whether or not the newsboy should purchase additional papers can be easily analyzed by referring to a plot of $R(y)$, as shown in Figure 20.4.

Figure 20.4 $R(y)$

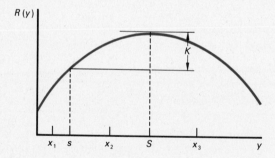

Let us now examine three cases.

CASE 1

Assume $x \geq S$ (like x_3). In this region, purchasing (moving to $y > x_3$) can only decrease the expected return and thus the newsboy should not order.

CASE 2

Assume $s \leq x < S$ (like x_2), where s is defined by the relations $s < S$ and $R(s) = R(S) - K$, as illustrated in Figure 20.4. In this region, an increase in return would be obtained if the number on hand at the beginning of the period were larger, but this increase is not large enough to cover the lumpy cost of placing an order. The newsboy will again not order.

CASE 3

Assume $x \leq s$ (like x_1). In this region it pays to purchase $(S - x)$ units, that is, to start the period with S units on hand.

It is also clear from this analysis that the optimal policy has the (s, S) form. As pointed out earlier, if $s = S$ then the (s, S) policy reduces to an S policy. It is the presence of the fixed cost K that necessitates the discrepancy between s and S.

It should also be noted that since S is the value of y that maximizes $R(y)$, we again have the result that

---

S is the smallest y such that $\dfrac{r - c}{r} \leq p\,[d \leq y]$.

As this rule indicates, S is rather easily determined. Unfortunately, however, solving for s in a real problem can present a considerable computational challenge. To find s one must know $R(y)$ and thus the *pmf* $p(d)$, at least over part of its domain. We have already commented that in real problems it may be difficult to acquire this information. This does not, however, imply that there is no value in knowing the form of the optimal policy. Quite to the contrary, the fact that (s, S) policies are optimal for the newsboy problem with lumpy ordering costs has had a significant effect on actual inventory management practice. This topic is considered in more depth in the next section.

20.2.4 *Dynamic Problems: Practical Considerations*

An important feature of the newsboy problem is that it is only one period long. In particular, this means that whether or not all items are sold, the problem ends at the end of the single period. This model is obviously not appropriate for many situations. In many real-world problems, there is an ongoing nature to the inventory situation. This means that items not presently sold may be available for sale in the future. Demand retains its uncertain nature in the sense that the quantity demanded over any interval of time is a random variable. Such problems are termed *dynamic stochastic inventory problems*.

In attempting to deal with dynamic *deterministic* problems, we saw in Chapter 13 that management typically uses one of two possible types of inventory control systems. The same is true for dynamic *stochastic* problems. One type of system is a *periodic review model*, in which ordering decisions are made at regular predetermined intervals, say at the first of each month. The other possibility is a *continuous review model*, in which the inventory level is constantly monitored and an ordering decision can be made at any point in time. Although both types of systems rely on the same basic approach, there are important differences in applications that a manager must take into account.

Figure 20.5 illustrates a typical periodic review inventory system. In this figure,

I_t = inventory on hand at time t

Q_t = quantity ordered at time t

Figure 20.5   *A periodic review inventory system*

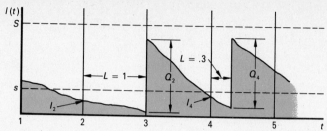

L = lead time, the amount of time that elapses between placing and receiving an order.

We have assumed in Figure 20.5 that the firm is using an s, S policy. Thus, at time 2 when $I_2 < s$, an order for $S - I_2$ items is placed. That is,

$$Q_2 = S - I_2$$

At this point we have assumed that there is a one-period lag in getting orders filled ($L = 1$) and thus the quantity ordered at $t = 2$ is not available to satisfy demand until $t = 3$.

If a firm chooses to use this type of policy, its inventory control problem reduces to a problem of choosing s and S. In essence,

---

The parameter s protects against stockouts, and S − s determines how many times orders will be placed.

It is important to realize that s must protect the firm against stockouts over a time period whose length is the sum of the length of the inspection period plus the lead time. For example, in Figure 20.5, observe that when $t = 1$ the inventory is slightly greater than s, and thus no order is placed. The first time that the inventory level can increase is after it has been observed to be below s (at $t = 2$ in the figure) and the order placed at that time has time to arrive (at $t = 3$ in the figure). Thus, in this example the level of s must provide protection against stockouts between $t = 1$ and $t = 3$. Figure 20.5 also illustrates a case when $L = .3$. In this case, the order placed at $t = 4$ arrives three-tenths of an inspection period later, and consequently s must provide stockout protection for only 1.3 periods.

The quantity s is often selected on the basis of intuitive arguments. Management may endorse a policy that the probability of a stockout should equal P, where P, for example, is set equal to .05 or some other small number. The value for P presumably is selected by intuitively balancing holding costs and penalty costs. In this case, let d denote the demand over the appropriate interval (the inspection period plus the lead time). Then s is selected so that

$$p \, [d \leq s] = 1 - P$$

Members of management may feel more comfortable in selecting a value of

s by this intuitive procedure than in using a more rigorous analysis involving a choice of s that minimizes expected penalty and holding costs. A pertinent question is, Just how good is one's intuition in selecting "good values" for P? This question is typically unanswered.

We note that the choice of S determines the quantity ordered; that is, $Q_t = S - I_t$. In practice, S itself may vary over time. Let S_t be the value of S at time t. This quantity might then be selected in such a way that, when the order placed at time t arrives, the number of items on hand equals the safety stock, s, plus enough items to satisfy the expected demand for some specified number of periods, say three. It is convenient to describe such a system in terms of a *reorder point, s*, and a *reorder quantity, Q*. Clearly, either or both of these quantities could vary with time. In some circumstances, the reorder point is called a *trigger inventory*, for obvious reasons.

All of the inventory control systems mentioned above are suboptimal in the sense that none purports to be a model of the entire system or to produce a "truly optimal" operating policy. Each system, however, uses quantitative models along with computers to help management control ordering, holding, and penalty costs in a consistent and economically advantageous manner.

Let us now turn to the second of the above mentioned models for dynamic problems. This is the *continuous review* type of system. In such systems, (s, Q) operating policies are typically used, where s denotes reorder point and Q denotes reorder quantity.

Figure 20.6 provides an example. Note that in this system, as soon as the inventory level reaches s, an order for Q units is placed. After a lead time of L, the number of units that was ordered arrives.

Figure 20.6   *A continuous review inventory system*

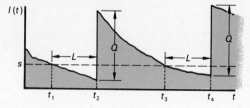

It is important to note that in a continuous review system, s has to protect against a stockout over the lead time, as opposed to the periodic review systems, which require protection against stockouts over the lead time plus the interval between decisions. It follows, then, that s in a periodic review system should be greater than s in a continuous review system for any given level of uncertainty in the demand pattern. At first glance, one might think that a compensating tradeoff exists between the higher costs of monitoring the system for continuous review systems and a higher holding cost (that is, a larger value of s) for periodic review systems. This is not necessarily correct. Note that in order to implement an (s, Q) continuous review system, it is not really necessary to know what $I(t)$ is at every moment. It is sufficient to know when $I(t) = s$. In many sets of circumstances, it is possible to obtain this information by using a *two-bin inventory system.* In this system, bin 1 contains s items and bin 2 contains all additional items. Items from bin 2 are used first. As soon as the first item from bin 1 is used, a signal is activated to place an order for Q items. Such a design clearly simplifies the continuous monitoring process.

There are a variety of methods used to specify s and Q. The choice depends on the information available and the importance of the decision. The quantity Q, for example, might be derived with the EOQ formula by using the expected demand in place of the known deterministic demand. A manager can expect to see any of a variety of methods either currently in place or being proposed by analysts. Armed with a solid understanding of the models we have considered, the manager should be able to understand whether or not the inventory control system under consideration seems reasonable in the given context.

20.3 Queuing Models

Time waits for no man. Unfortunately, the reverse statement does not hold. Waiting and efforts to avoid waiting constitute an important part of both personal and professional life. Customers wishing to purchase goods typically wait. Shoppers wait in supermarket lines. Swingers wait for a table at Arnie's. Contractors wait for a shipment of insulation. Furniture dealers wait for at least three months, and builders of new homes who want to burn natural gas may wait forever.

For those wishing to purchase services, the situation is the same. For tradesmen, such as plumbers, the waiting time is merely long. For health services it is a national scandal.

In a seemingly endless list of applications, managers are faced with the problem of balancing capital and/or labor costs against the costs of waiting. In some cases, they have turned to quantitative models to aid them in this process. The term *queuing models* comes from the British word *queue,* which refers to a line of waiting people. The term is used to describe the large set of models in this area. These queuing models, then, are the subject of the ensuing sections of this chapter.

20.3.1 Components of Queuing Systems

The technical literature concerned with queuing is enormous. A bibliography prepared by Bell Laboratories lists 628 research papers published on the subject for the period from 1960 through 1970. It is, however, possible to identify certain common components in these models. The basic components of a queuing system are:

1 Arrivals who want service and wait to receive it
2 A service facility that dispenses the desired service

As an illustration of the simplest queuing system, consider a single-chair barbershop that gives only haircuts. Patrons arrive, form a line, and are served on a first-come–first-served basis by the barber. This system, which is illustrated in Figure 20.7, can be completely described by specifying:

Figure 20.7 *A simple queuing system*

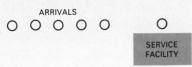

ARRIVALS

SERVICE FACILITY

---

1 The *interarrival time*; that is, the time between arrivals
2 The *service time*; that is, the time required to give a haircut

---

It is typically appropriate to assume that the interarrival time (say, A) and the service time (say, S) are random variables and that the *pmf* is known for each of these quantities. A variable of substantial interest to management, then, is the *waiting time* (say, W) for a typical arrival to the system. In this setting, W is also a random variable. In the most general terms, management is often interested in influencing W by taking actions that change either the interarrival time or the service time.

For those students who are not using this text in a barber college, it will be useful to consider generalizations of the simple model just discussed. Generalizations may take place in the ways discussed below.

The Arrival Process   Arrivals might appear in batches, like a bus unloading at McDonalds, rather than one at a time. Or, perhaps not all arrivals join the queue. For example, you can consider a system in which no arrival joins the queue if some specified number of people are already waiting.

The Service Process   Here, management options abound. How about increasing the number of servers? Suppose there is more than one server. Should arrivals form a single queue and go to the first open server (like passport control in London's Heathrow Airport), or should there be separate queues at each server, as in a typical grocery store? What is the tradeoff between introducing faster servers (decreasing the expected value of the service time) and increasing the number of servers? This list of possibilities for intervention is limited only by imagination.

The Queue Discipline   Why should arrivals be served on a first-come-first-served basis? It has, for example, been shown that in certain instances selecting the job with the shortest service time is a policy with desirable properties. Finally, management can attempt to obtain "better results" by simultaneously changing both the service process and queue discipline. Establishing express lanes on city expressways and using special gift-return centers after Christmas are common examples.

20.3.2   *Queuing Results and Management Action*

The previous sections indicate that the language and general structure of queuing models can be used in a seemingly endless list of applications, from designing gasoline service stations and operating an international airport to determining the staffing requirements and operating procedures for a hospital operating room. Given this fact, it is perhaps not surprising that there are almost no general quantitative results that apply to all situations. The interactions between the arrival process, the service process, and the queue discipline must, in general, be considered on a model-by-model basis. It may be more surprising to realize that for many interesting problems it is impossible to derive useful mathematical expressions for the behavior of a queuing system.

Simulation is, however, an enormously useful technique to use in analyzing queuing systems, and indeed it is easy to find examples of ongoing simulation studies of queuing systems in many firms. Since simulation has been discussed in great detail in Chapters 18 and 19, further discussion seems unnecessary here. It is worth noting, however, that the tanker simulation problem that is the basis of Chapter 19 is an analysis of a queuing system.

One system that yields useful analytic results is the simple queuing system illustrated in Figure 20.7. This comment is especially true if it is reasonable to assume that A, the interarrival time, is a random variable with an *exponential distribution*. Presenting the details of this distribution requires the use of calculus, which is off-limits for this text. Thus, let it suffice to say that the exponential distribution is a good description of observed interarrival times in many actual applications. There is a theoretically-based argument as to why this should be true, but we will also ignore that. Consider, then, a simple queuing system in which

1 A, the interarrival time, has an exponential distribution.
2 S, the service time, has a known distribution.

For this system,

$$
E(W) = \begin{cases} \left(\dfrac{\mathrm{Var}\, S + E(S)^2}{E(A)} \right) \dfrac{1}{2\{1 - [E(S)/E(A)]\}} & \text{if } E(S) < E(A) \\[3ex] \infty & \text{if } E(S) \geq E(A) \end{cases}
$$

where the symbol Var denotes variance, E denotes expected value, and, as previously defined, W is the waiting time. A number of intuitively appealing results can be confirmed or inferred (depending on the status of your intuition) with the use of this result. For example, the expected value of the waiting time, $E(W)$, increases as $E(S)$, the average service time, increases from zero to $E(A)$. In fact, there is a "two-pronged attack." When $E(S)$ increases, the numerator of the first term increases, and simultaneously the denominator of the second term decreases.

Some of the effects of randomness on the system can also be analyzed with this expression. For example, note that $E(W)$ increases with the variance of S. In other words, a system with more consistent service times (less variance) might produce a lower expected waiting time even at the cost of an increase in the expected service time. For another look at the effects of randomness, compare the following two cases:

CASE 1

A is a constant, namely   1,000 minutes.
S is a constant, namely   999 minutes.

CASE 2

A has an exponential distribution, and $E(A) = 1,000$ minutes.
S is a constant, namely 999 minutes.

The difference in the two cases is that in Case 1, the time between arrivals is constant, whereas in Case 2 it is a random variable.

For Case 1, since the service time is less than the interarrival time, it is clear that no arrival will have to wait. Thus, the waiting time for each arrival is 0, and $E(W) = 0$. Note that in this case the above-discussed formula for $E(W)$ does not apply because A does not have an exponential distribution.

For Case 2, $E(W)$ is given by the expression

$$E(W) = \left(\frac{0 + (999)^2}{1000} \right) \frac{1}{2[1 - (999/1,000)]}$$

or

$$E(W) = \frac{(999)^2}{2} = 499,000.5$$

In this "heavily loaded" system, the effects of randomness in the arrivals are indeed profound.

This example illustrates the power of analytic results in queuing situations and demonstrates why such results should be considered before turning to simulation. The following problems will illustrate additional analysis involving analytic expressions such as the above formula for $E(W)$.

20.4 Examples and Solutions

Example 1

Historical data have been used to estimate the *pmf* for d_1, the demand over a one-week interval, and for d_2, the demand over a two-week interval. The values for these functions are shown in Figures 20.8 and 20.9, respectively.

Figure 20.8 *Demand for one week, d_1*

d_1	$p(d_1)$[a]	d_1	$p(d_1)$[a]
96	1	101	4
97	2	102	3
98	3	103	2
99	4	104	1
100	5		

[a]Numbers in these columns must be divided by 25 to yield the probability.

Figure 20.9 *Demand for two weeks, d_2*

d_2	$p(d_2)^a$	d_2	$p(d_2)^a$
192	1	201	80
193	4	202	68
194	10	203	52
195	20	204	35
196	35	205	20
197	52	206	10
198	68	207	4
199	80	208	1
200	85		

[a] Numbers in these columns must be divided by 625 to yield the probability.

Assume the system is inspected every Monday morning and there is a one-week lead time for these items. Management plans to place an order for Q items anytime it is observed that the inventory on hand is $\leq s$.

a Select the smallest possible s so that the probability of a stockout is no greater than .07.

b In an intuitive effort to balance holding and ordering costs, management decides to choose Q in such a way that there will be *approximately* 13 orders placed each year. According to this criterion, what should the value of Q be?

Solution to Example 1

a Since there is a one-week period between inspections and a one-week lead time, s must be chosen to protect against stockouts over a two-week interval. Thus, s is the smallest m such that

$$p[d_2 > m] \leq .07$$

If $m = 203$, Figure 20.9 shows that

$$p[d_2 > 203] = \frac{70}{625} = 0.112$$

and if $m = 204$,

$$p[d_2 > 204] = \frac{35}{625} = .056$$

Thus, s must equal 204.

b If we wish to order 13 times a year, each order must, on the average, cover the demand for four weeks. From $p(d_1)$ it follows that $E(d_1)$, the expected demand per week, is 100 units. Thus, setting Q equal to 400 units should yield approximately 13 orders per year.

Example 2

Consider the simple queuing system illustrated in Figure 20.7. Assume that
(1) A, the interarrival time, has an exponential distribution.
(2) S, the service time, has a known distribution.

Suppose this system is modified by letting each arrival be a batch of B jobs, where the service time for each job is S. Then for this system,

$$E(W) = \begin{cases} \left(\dfrac{B\,[\mathrm{Var}\,S + E(S)^2]}{E(A)}\right) \dfrac{1}{2\{1 - [BE(S)/E(A)]\}} & \text{if } B\,[E(S)] < E(A) \\[2em] \infty & \text{if } B\,[E(S)] > E(A) \end{cases}$$

Assume that S is a constant whose value is $.2E(A)$. Compare the effect on expected waiting time of the following two situations:

a $B = 1$ but S is doubled to $.4E(A)$.
b B is doubled to 2 but S remains at $.2E(A)$.

Solution to Example 2

a If $B = 1$ and $S = .4E(A)$, then $E(S) = .4E(A)$, $\mathrm{Var}\,S = 0$, and

$$E(W) = \frac{1\{0 + [.4E(A)]^2\}}{E(A)} \left(\frac{1}{2\{1 - [.4E(A)/E(A)]\}}\right)$$

$$= 0.16\,E(A)\left(\frac{1}{1.2}\right)$$

$$E(W) = 0.133E(A)$$

b If $B = 2$ and $S = .2E(A)$, then $E(S) = .2E(A)$, $\mathrm{Var}\,S = 0$, and

$$E(W) = \frac{2\{0 + [.2E(A)]^2\}}{E(A)} \left(\frac{1}{2\{1 - [.4E(A)/E(A)]\}}\right)$$

$$= 0.08\,E(A)\left(\frac{1}{1.2}\right)$$

$$E(W) = 0.067E(A)$$

These results show that doubling the service time for an individual job has twice the effect on the expected waiting time as doubling the number of identical jobs that arrive with each arrival. In less precise language, it might be said that in this case, doubling the time for a job has twice the effect on the expected waiting time as doubling the amount of work to be done. To the extent that this statement is understandable, it is certainly counterintuitive. This illustrates the importance of knowing precisely what you are talking about in a queuing system and the power of quantitative results when they are available.

20.5 Summary of Key Concepts

In theoretical work on stochastic inventory models, it is typically assumed that demand is a random variable with a known pmf. In practice, it is seldom necessary to specify the entire pmf in order to use the model. **(Section 20.2)**

The theoretical work on stochastic inventory models is typically devoted to finding the general form for the optimal operating policy for a wide class of problems. The policies so derived are then modified and adapted for use in specific applications. (Section 20.2.2)

Let x be the inventory on hand. Then, for an S policy, the optimal operating rule is: If x < S, order S − x items. If x ≥ S, order no items. (Section 20.2.2)

Let x be the inventory on hand. Then, for an (s, S) policy the optimal operating rule is: If x < s, order (S − x) items. If x ≥ s, do not order. The discrepancy between s and S is due to the presence of a fixed-cost term in the cost function. (Section 20.2.3)

Optimal operating policies for dynamic stochastic inventory problems typically involve a reorder point and a reorder quantity or an order-up-to level. The review system may be either periodic or continuous. (Section 20.2.4)

In dynamic stochastic inventory models, the reorder point protects against stockouts, and the reorder quantity or order-up-to level determines how many times orders will be placed during a year. (Section 20.2.4)

The basic components of a queuing system are:
1 Arrivals who want service and wait to receive it.
2 A service facility that dispenses the desired service.
(Section 20.3.1)

The waiting time for service, W, is a quantity of substantial interest to management. In the most general terms, management is interested in influencing W by taking actions that change either the arrival process or the service process. (Section 20.3.1)

20.6 Problems

1   Assume that a newstand can buy copies of the Sunday *Times* for $.50 and that they are sold for $1. At 10:30 A.M. the vendor has 44 copies on hand. The vendor assumes that demand for this paper for the remainder of the day is a random variable with the following *pmf:*

$$p(d) = \tfrac{1}{20} \qquad d = 40, 41, ..., 59$$
$$= 0 \qquad \text{otherwise}$$

The delivery truck will be stopping in a few minutes. The vendor must decide whether or not to buy any more papers and, if so, how many. What is the optimal policy for this problem?

2   Let

$$R(y) = \sum_{d=0}^{y} r \, d \, p(d) + \sum_{d=y+1}^{\infty} r \, y \, p(d) - cy$$

For the data presented in problem 1, a reasonable amount of algebra yields the fact that

$$R(y) = -\frac{y^2}{40} + \frac{99}{40}y - 39 \qquad \text{for } 40 \le y \le 59$$

Figure 20.10 shows $R(y)$ for all interesting values of y.

Figure 20.10

y	R(y)	y	R(y)
40	20.00	50	22.25
41	20.45	51	22.20
42	20.85	52	22.10
43	21.20	53	21.95
44	21.50	54	21.75
45	21.75	55	21.50
46	21.95	56	21.20
47	22.10	57	20.85
48	22.20	58	20.45
49	22.25	59	20.00

Now assume that if the vendor wants the delivery truck to stop, it will be necessary to pay a delivery charge of $1.
a What is the general form of the optimal operating policy, and what are the optimal values for the parameters that describe that policy for this problem?
b Given the answer to part *a*, what action should the vendor take?

3 Assume that you do not have at your disposal the numerical values for $R(y)$ that were presented in problem 2. Given the answer to problem 1, show how to determine the appropriate action for the vendor in problem 2 by evaluating $R(y)$ at only two points.

4 Consider the following one-period inventory problem. A vendor can buy as many items as he wishes for c dollars each. He plans to sell them for r dollars each. He believes that his inventory carrying cost throughout the period is proportional to the number of items he has on hand after his order arrives at the beginning of the period. He thus will assign a cost of $h\,y$ dollars to this project if he starts the period with y items on hand. Any items that are unsold at the end of the period can be sold in another market for a price of $r/2$ dollars. Let $p(d)$ be the probability that d items are demanded during the period. Assume that the vendor currently has x items on hand before his order arrives. Find an expression for $R(y)$, the expected return as a function of y, the inventory on hand after his order arrives.

5 In Section 20.2.1, the expected return for the newsboy problem was given by the expression

$$R(y) = \sum_{d=0}^{y} r\,d\,p(d) + \sum_{d=y+1}^{\infty} r\,y\,p(d) - cy$$

a Can the expected return in problem 4 be written in this form? That is, can it assume the form

$$R(y) = \sum_{d=0}^{y} A\,d\,p(d) + \sum_{d=y+1}^{\infty} A\,y\,p(d) - By$$

where A and B are constants whose values depend on the cost and revenue parameters in problem 4. (Hint: see the equation below.)

$$\sum_{d=0}^{y} \frac{ry}{2} p(d) = \frac{ry}{2} - \sum_{d=y+1}^{\infty} \frac{ry}{2} p(d)$$

b Given the answer to part *a*, can you define the optimal operating policy for the problem posed in problem 4 and specify a general formula for finding the value of the parameter(s) of this policy?

Problems 6 and 7 consider the following dynamic inventory situation. Demand per week is a random variable with the *pmf* presented in problem 1. This implies that for a two-week interval, demand is a random variable with the probability mass function shown in Figure 20.11.

Figure 20.11

d	p(d)ᵃ	d	p(d)ᵃ	d	p(d)ᵃ	d	p(d)ᵃ
80	1	90	11	100	19	110	9
81	2	91	12	101	18	111	8
82	3	92	13	102	17	112	7
83	4	93	14	103	16	113	6
84	5	94	15	104	15	114	5
85	6	95	16	105	14	115	4
86	7	96	17	106	13	116	3
87	8	97	18	107	12	117	2
88	9	98	19	108	11	118	1
89	10	99	20	109	10		

ᵃEach entry in this column must be divided by 400 to obtain the probability.

6 Management plans to use a periodic review system in which the inventory level is determined every Monday morning. One week elapses between the time when items are ordered and when they arrive and are available to satisfy demand. Management wants to use an (s, Q) policy, that is, a policy with the operating rule if

$I(t) \leq s$ order Q items

$I(t) > s$ order 0 items

Assume that K, the cost of placing an order, is $8 and h, the cost of holding a unit of inventory one week, is $.02. Choose s so that the probability of a stockout over the appropriate interval is approximately .05.

7 Management wishes to use a continuous review system with parameters s and Q. Choose s so that the probability of a stockout over the appropriate interval is .05. Determine Q by using the cost parameters in problem 6, by using the expected rate of demand, and by applying the EOQ model (Section 13.2.4).

8 An aircraft carrier has a single repair crew. Planes requiring repair are serviced on a first-come-first-served basis. Historical data show that the time between arrivals at the repair shop can be approximated by a random variable, with an exponential distribution for which the expected value is 2 weeks. The expected value of the service time is 1.3 weeks, but the distribution has a variance of .5.
a Use results from this chapter to estimate the expected waiting time for a plane.
b In addition to the approximations inherent in estimating the distributions of the interarrival and the service times, in what sense is the result used in part *a* an approximation?
c As captain of the carrier, what criteria might you use to judge the effectiveness of the repair shop? Comment on the suggested queue discipline from this point of view.

Problems 9 and 10 consider the following queuing system. The system has c servers. The service time for each server is an exponential random variable, S, and $E(S)$ is known. The interarrival time for the system is also an exponential random variable, A, and $E(A)$ is also known. Arrivals form a single queue and proceed in a first-come-first-served manner to the first open server. Let N be the number of items in the system at a random point in time. N includes those waiting and those being served. A general expression for $E(N)$ is available for this system. It is shown for $c = 1$ and $c = 2$ below. When $c = 1$ there is one server, and

$$E(N) = \frac{E(S)}{E(A) - E(S)} \quad \text{if } E(S) < E(A)$$

When $c = 2$ there are two servers and

$$E(N) = \frac{2\,[E(S)/2E(A)]^3}{1 - [E(S)/2E(A)]^2} + \frac{E(S)}{E(A)} \quad \text{if } E(S) < 2E(A)$$

9 In the current system, $c = 1$ and $E(S) = .7E(A)$. Management has the option of either adding a second server or leasing special equipment for the current server that will cut $E(S)$ in half. The annual cost of the two options is about the same. If management's goal is to minimize $E(N)$, which of these two options should be selected?

10 Assume that the system under consideration is a tool crib in a factory, and that the "items" arriving are machinists who need new tools. If machinists are paid \$8 per hour and tool crib attendants are paid \$5 per hour, does it pay to add a second attendant if $E(S)/E(A) = .8$? [Hint: Estimate the total expected cost (that is, waiting costs for machinists plus attendant costs) for any period of time (an hour or a day) for each system, and compare.]

Appendixes

Supplementary Mathematical Topics

1, 2, 3

1 *Notation of Sums*

A1.1 Introduction

Summation notation, used at times in the present text, and, in fact, in many quantitative discussions, is reviewed in this appendix.

A1.2 Single Sums

Suppose that the manager of a 60-product-line firm has a list of the revenues obtained last year from the sales of each individual product. In order to obtain the total revenue from the sale of all 60 products, he must, of course, add the 60 individual revenues. In symbols, we can express this fact as follows. Let

r_1 = revenue from product 1

r_2 = revenue from product 2

and so on. Then

Total revenue = $r_1 + r_2 + r_3$ + etc.

where *etc.* means "keep adding on up through r_{60}." A more precise and concise symbolic representation is

Total revenue = $r_1 + r_2 + \ldots + r_{60}$

This is more precise since it explicitly shows how far to continue the process of addition.

An even more concise way to represent this sum is to use the summation operator, Σ, which is a Greek letter, the capital sigma. Using this notation, one would write

$$\text{Total revenue} = \sum_{i=1}^{60} r_i$$

The expression on the right of the equality sign is read:

"The summation from $i = 1$ to 60 of r sub i"

Note that the subscript i, called the ***index of summation***, is merely a place marker. One might just as well have used a different subscript, such as j, k, t, or any symbol whatsoever. For example, the total revenue could equally well have been written

$$\sum_{j=1}^{60} r_j \quad \text{or} \quad \sum_{t=1}^{60} r_t \quad \text{or} \quad \sum_{A=1}^{60} r_A \quad \text{or} \quad \sum_{\theta=1}^{60} r_\theta$$

for each of these forms is a shorthand representation for

$r_1 + r_2 + \ldots + r_{60}$

In all cases, the first term in the sum is r_1, the revenue from product 1. The second term in each sum is r_2. The eleventh term in each sum is r_{11}, and so on. Clearly, then, all of the sums must yield the same value for total revenue.

This summation notation is widely used in a variety of contexts, and so it will be useful to broaden our understanding. Generally speaking, then, suppose E_i is any expression depending on an *integer i,* such as i^2, or $(i + 4)/i$, or $2^i - 1$, and let N denote a *specified* integer. Then

$$\sum_{i=1}^{N} E_i$$

is read:

"The summation from $i = 1$ to N of E sub i"

In other words,

$$\sum_{i=1}^{N} E_i$$

is shorthand notation for the sum $E_1 + E_2 + ... + E_N$. Again, note that the choice of the symbol i is unimportant, and we might just as well have used j, k, or any other symbol.

A1.3   Examples

As specific illustrations of this notation, consider the following examples.

1 $\displaystyle\sum_{i=1}^{4} i^2 = 1^2 + 2^2 + 3^2 + 4^2 = 1 + 4 + 9 + 16 = 30$

2 $\displaystyle\sum_{t=1}^{4} t^2 = 1^2 + 2^2 + 3^2 + 4^2 = 1 + 4 + 9 + 16 = 30$

3 $\displaystyle\sum_{t=0}^{4} t^2 = 0^2 + 1^2 + 2^2 + 3^2 + 4^2 = 0 + 1 + 4 + 9 + 16 = 30$

4 $\displaystyle\sum_{j=1}^{3} \frac{j + 4}{j} = \frac{1 + 4}{1} + \frac{2 + 4}{2} + \frac{3 + 4}{3} = 5 + 3 + \frac{7}{3} = 10\frac{1}{3}$

5 $\displaystyle\sum_{k=0}^{4} (2^{k-1} + 1) = (2^{-1} + 1) + (2^0 + 1) + (2^1 + 1) + (2^2 + 1) + (2^3 + 1)$

$$= 1\frac{1}{2} + 2 + 3 + 5 + 9 = 20\frac{1}{2}$$

That is, when $k = 0$, $2^{k-1} + 1 = 2^{-1} + 1$, when $k = 1$, $2^{k-1} + 1 = 2^0 + 1$, and so on.

6 $\displaystyle\sum_{k=1}^{3} k = 1 + 2 + 3 = 6$

7 $\displaystyle\sum_{k=1}^{3} 1 = 1 + 1 + 1 = 3$

8 $\displaystyle\sum_{k=1}^{3} (k + 1) = (1 + 1) + (2 + 1) + (3 + 1) = 2 + 3 + 4 = 9$

9 $\displaystyle\sum_{k=1}^{3} k + 1 = 1 + 2 + 3 + 1 = 7$

Note the difference between Examples 8 and 9. Also compare Examples 6, 7, and 8 to see that

$$\sum_{k=1}^{3} (k + 1) = \sum_{k=1}^{3} k + \sum_{k=1}^{3} 1$$

10 $\sum_{k=1}^{3} (k-1) + \sum_{j=0}^{2} \frac{j}{2} + \sum_{x=1}^{4} (-1)^x x^2 = (0+1+2) + \left(0+\frac{1}{2}+1\right) + (-1+4-9+16)$

$$= 3 + 1\frac{1}{2} + 10 = 14\frac{1}{2}$$

11 $\sum_{k=2}^{4} k^2 = 4 + 9 + 16 = 29$

12 $\sum_{k=3}^{3} 2^k = 8$

A1.4 Exercises

In order to test your understanding, work the following problems.

1 $\sum_{i=1}^{K} 2^i =$

2 $\sum_{i=1}^{K} 2^{2i-1} =$

3 $\sum_{i=1}^{K} x^i =$

4 $\sum_{k=1}^{3} \frac{x^k}{2k-1} =$

5 $\sum_{k=1}^{3} 2^k - \sum_{k=3}^{5} (2k-1) =$

6 Show that $\sum_{i=1}^{3} (a_i + b_i) = \sum_{i=1}^{3} a_i + \sum_{i=1}^{3} b_i$.

A1.5 Double Sums

Suppose that the manager of the 60-product-line firm has a list of the *weekly* revenues for the past year from the sales of each individual product. In order to obtain the total revenue from the sale of all products in the past year, he must add $60(52) = 3,120$ terms. In symbols, we can conveniently use double subscripts to express the process, as follows. Let

r_{11} = revenue from product 1 in week   1

r_{12} = revenue from product 1 in week   2

$\vdots$ $\vdots$

$r_{1,52}$ = revenue from product 1 in week   52

r_{21} = revenue from product 2 in week   1

$\vdots$ $\vdots$

$r_{2,52}$ = revenue from product 2 in week   52

$\vdots$ $\vdots$

$r_{60,1}$ = revenue from product 60 in week   1

$\vdots$ $\vdots$

$r_{60,52}$ = revenue from product 60 in week   52

Then

$$\text{Total revenue} = (r_{11} + r_{12} + \dots + r_{1,52}) + (r_{21} + r_{22} + \dots + r_{2,52})$$
$$+ \dots + (r_{60,1} + \dots + r_{60,52})$$

More concisely, this sum can be represented in *double summation notation* as follows:

$$\sum_{i=1}^{60} \sum_{j=1}^{52} r_{ij} \quad \text{or equivalently,} \quad \sum_{j=1}^{52} \sum_{i=1}^{60} r_{ij}$$

This is read

"The double sum of r sub ij, where i goes from 1 to 60 and j goes from 1 to 52"

Thus, the first subscript denotes the particular product and the second denotes the week. Again, note that the choice of i and j is not important. *It is the definition of the first and second subscripts that matters.* For example, if the first subscript has value 3 (regardless of whether it is denoted by i or j or k or t) and the second subscript has value 2, then the term r_{32} is identified, and according to the definition (that is, according to our chosen convention), this denotes the revenue from product 3 in week 2. Thus the expression

$$\sum_{i=1}^{60} \sum_{j=1}^{52} r_{ij}$$

is the same as

$$\sum_{j=1}^{60} \sum_{i=1}^{52} r_{ji}$$

which is the same as

$$\sum_{s=1}^{60} \sum_{t=1}^{52} r_{st}$$

If you have difficulty in seeing this, simply verify that in each expression the first subscript on r runs from 1 to 60 regardless of whether it is called i, j, or s, and the second subscript on r runs from 1 to 52. Hence, the first and second subscripts take on the same values in the expansion of each expression, and therefore the sums must be identical. However, you should convince yourself that

$$\sum_{i=1}^{60} \sum_{j=1}^{52} r_{ij}$$

is not the same as

$$\sum_{j=1}^{52} \sum_{i=1}^{60} r_{ji}$$

We finally observe that we could have initially adopted the different convention of letting the first subscript denote the week and the second denote the product. The initial choice is arbitrary, but once made it must be followed consistently.

As a further illustration of the notation, verify that

1   The total revenue in week 1 is $\displaystyle\sum_{i=1}^{60} r_{i1}$.

2   The total revenue in week 3 is $\displaystyle\sum_{j=1}^{60} r_{j3}$.

3 The total revenue in week k is $\displaystyle\sum_{i=1}^{60} r_{ik}$ where k is any integer between 1 and 52.

4 The total year's revenue from product 1 is $\displaystyle\sum_{t=1}^{52} r_{1t}$.

5 The total year's revenue from product 19 is $\displaystyle\sum_{j=1}^{52} r_{19,j}$.

6 The total revenue from products 22 through 30 for the first 26 weeks is $\displaystyle\sum_{i=22}^{30}\sum_{j=1}^{26} r_{ij}$.

7 The total year's revenues for *each* of the 60 products is $\displaystyle\sum_{j=1}^{52} r_{ij} \qquad i = 1, ..., 60.$

Note that there are 60 separate sums represented by this expression.

8 The 52 total weekly revenues are given by $\displaystyle\sum_{i=1}^{60} r_{ij} \qquad j = 1, ..., 52.$

Here there are 52 separate sums represented.

A convenient rule for expanding a double sum is the following:

For each value of the subscript under the first summation symbol, beginning with the first allowable value, exhaust all allowable values for the subscript under the second summation symbol.

Thus, for a sum

$$\sum_{i=1}^{10}\sum_{j=1}^{5} r_{ij}$$

one would hold i at 1 and let j go from 1 to 5, then move i to 2, hold it there, and let j go from 1 to 5, eventually moving i to 10 and letting j go from 1 to 5, at which point the process is finished (all the terms are added together). An expansion in this order is called *lexicographic* since it is the same order in which two-letter words would appear in a dictionary (with the first letter ranging through the ten letters A through J, and the second letter ranging through the five letters A through E).

A1.6 Examples

1 $\displaystyle\sum_{i=1}^{6}\sum_{j=1}^{100} x_{ij} = \sum_{j=1}^{100} x_{1j} + \sum_{j=1}^{100} x_{2j} + ... + \sum_{j=1}^{100} x_{6j} =$
$(x_{11} + ... + x_{1,100}) + ... + (x_{61} + ... + x_{6,100})$

Note that there are $6\,(100) = 600$ terms being added.

2 $\displaystyle\sum_{j=1}^{100}\sum_{i=1}^{6} x_{ij} = \sum_{i=1}^{6} x_{i1} + \sum_{i=1}^{6} x_{i2} + ... + \sum_{i=1}^{6} x_{i,100} =$
$(x_{11} + x_{21} + ... + x_{61}) + (x_{12} + x_{22} + ... + x_{62}) + ... + (x_{1,100} + x_{2,100} + ... + x_{6,100})$

Note that Examples 1 and 2 show that $\displaystyle\sum_{i=1}^{6}\sum_{j=1}^{100} x_{ij} = \sum_{j=1}^{100}\sum_{i=1}^{6} x_{ij}$

3 $\displaystyle\sum_{i=1}^{M}\sum_{k=1}^{N} x_{ik} = (x_{11} + ... + x_{1,N}) + ... + (x_{M1} + ... + x_{MN})$

Note that there are M times N terms being added.

4 $\displaystyle\sum_{i=1}^{3}\sum_{j=1}^{2} i(j-1)^2 = 1(0) + 1(1) + 2(0) + 2(1) + 3(0) + 3(1) = 6$

5 $\displaystyle\sum_{i=1}^{3}\sum_{j=1}^{2} ja_i = a_1(1+2) + a_2(1+2) + a_3(1+2) = 3a_1 + 3a_2 + 3a_3$

6 $\displaystyle\sum_{k=1}^{2}\sum_{j=1}^{3} a_k b_j = a_1(b_1 + b_2 + b_3) + a_2(b_1 + b_2 + b_3)$

7 $\displaystyle\sum_{k=1}^{2}\sum_{j=1}^{3} a_{kj} b_j = a_{11} b_1 + a_{12} b_2 + a_{13} b_3 + a_{21} b_1 + a_{22} b_2 + a_{23} b_3$

8 $\displaystyle\sum_{k=1}^{2}\sum_{j=1}^{3} a_{kj} b_{jk} = a_{11} b_{11} + a_{12} b_{21} + a_{13} b_{31} + a_{21} b_{12} + a_{22} b_{22} + a_{23} b_{32}$

9 Suppose that two products are made on three machines. A unit of product 1 uses 2 hours on machine 1, 3 hours on machine 2, and 4 hours on machine 3. A unit of product 2 uses 1 hour on machine 1, 2 hours on machine 2, and 0 hours on machine 3. Suppose that x_1 units of product 1 and x_2 units of product 2 are made. Then

Total time used on machine 1 $= 2x_1 + x_2$

Total time used on machine 2 $= 3x_1 + 2x_2$

Total time used on machine 3 $= 4x_1$

More generally, suppose a unit of product j uses a_{ij} hours on machine i, $i = 1, 2, 3$; $j = 1, 2$. Then

Total time used on machine 1 $= \displaystyle\sum_{j=1}^{2} a_{1j} x_j$

Total time used on machine 2 $= \displaystyle\sum_{j=1}^{2} a_{2j} x_j$

Total time used on machine 3 $= \displaystyle\sum_{j=1}^{2} a_{3j} x_j$

Thus, total time used on machine i, for $i = 1, 2,$ or 3, is given by $\displaystyle\sum_{j=1}^{2} a_{ij} x_j$.

The total time used on all machines is $\displaystyle\sum_{i=1}^{3}\sum_{j=1}^{2} a_{ij} x_j$.

The total machine time used by product 1 is $\displaystyle\sum_{i=1}^{3} a_{i1} x_1$.

The total machine time used by product 2 is $\displaystyle\sum_{i=1}^{3} a_{i2} x_2$.

The total machine time used by product j, for $j = 1$ or 2, is given by $\displaystyle\sum_{i=1}^{3} a_{ij} x_j$.

10 Suppose that in Example 8 above, we wish to express in symbols the specification that the amount of products 1 and 2 produced should satisfy the condition that the total time used on machine i cannot exceed b_i hours, for $i = 1, 2, 3$. We would write

$$\sum_{j=1}^{2} a_{ij} x_j \le b_i \qquad i = 1, 2, 3$$

A1.7 Higher Order Sums

Higher order sums such as

$$\sum_{i=1}^{M} \sum_{j=1}^{N} \sum_{k=1}^{K}$$

should not be difficult to expand if the rule for double sums is understood. The same type of lexicographic (dictionary order) expansion can be used. Thus, suppose E_{ijk} is some expression involving the symbols $i, j,$ and k. Then

$$\sum_{i=1}^{2} \sum_{j=1}^{2} \sum_{k=1}^{3} E_{ijk}$$

can be expanded in dictionary order, as follows:

$i = 1, j = 1$	$i = 1, j = 2$	$i = 2, j = 1$	$i = 2, j = 2$
$k = 1, 2, 3$	$k = 1, 2, 3$	$k = 1, 2, 3$	$k = 1, 2, 3$

$$\overbrace{E_{111} + E_{112} + E_{113}} + \overbrace{E_{121} + E_{122} + E_{123}} + \overbrace{E_{211} + E_{212} + E_{213}} + \overbrace{E_{221} + E_{222} + E_{223}}$$

Note that there are $(2)(2)(3) = 12$ terms in the sum.

A1.8 Exercises

1 There are 36 numbers denoted a_{ij} where i runs from 1 to 3 and j runs from 1 to 12. Let $x_j, j = 1, \ldots, 12$, denote 12 numbers. Expand the expressions

$$\sum_{j=1}^{12} a_{ij} x_j = b_i \qquad i = 1, 2, 3$$

How many equations are there? How many terms are being added on the left side of each equality?

2 Expand the following expressions.

a $\sum_{i=1}^{3} \sum_{j=1}^{4} (-1)^i (j)^{i-1}$

b $\sum_{i=1}^{3} \sum_{j=1}^{4} (-1)^j (j)^{i-1}$

c $\sum_{i=1}^{3} \sum_{j=1}^{2} a_{ij} b_{ij}$

d $\sum_{i=1}^{3} \sum_{k=1}^{2} a_{ik} b_{ik}$

e $\sum_{i=1}^{3} \sum_{j=1}^{2} b_{ij} a_{ji}$

f $\sum_{j=0}^{4} \frac{C_j}{(1+r)} j$

g $\sum_{t=0}^{T} \frac{C_j}{(1+r)} t$

h $\sum_{i=1}^{5} (i+1)^2 x_{2i-1}$

3 For $i = 1, 2$ and $j = 1, 2, 3$, expand

$$\sum_{k=1}^{4} a_{ik} b_{kj}$$

How many sums are there? How many terms are being added in each sum?

4 Let r_{ij} denote the amount of revenue from product i in week j, $i = 1, ..., 60$, $j = 1, ...,$ 52. Write the total revenue from all products as a double sum. Now let r_{ij} denote the amount of revenue in week i from product j, $i = 1, ..., 52$, $j = 1, ..., 60$. Write the total revenue from all products as a double sum.

5 Show that

$$\sum_{i=1}^{60} \sum_{j=1}^{52} r_{ij} = \sum_{j=1}^{52} \sum_{i=1}^{60} r_{ij}$$

and that, in general, double sums can be interchanged. That is,

$$\sum_{i=1}^{M} \sum_{j=1}^{N} a_{ij} = \sum_{j=1}^{N} \sum_{i=1}^{M} a_{ij}$$

6 Show that

$$\sum_{i=1}^{M} \sum_{j=1}^{N} a_{ij}$$

is not, in general, equal to

$$\sum_{i=1}^{M} \sum_{j=1}^{N} a_{ji}$$

When are the two expressions equal?

7 Suppose that we have a single product made in three plants and sold in four marketing districts. Assume that everything produced is sent to the marketing districts and sold. Let x_{ij} denote the quantity of product sent from plant i to be sold in marketing district j. Using notation of sums, express the following conditions.
a The amount of product sent from plant 2 to marketing district 4 is 3,000 units.
b The total amount of product produced in plant 2 is 6,000 units.
c The total amount of product produced (in all plants) is 10,000 units.

8 In the above scenario, let x_{ijt} denote the amount of product made in plant i and sent to marketing district j in time period t, $t = 1, ..., 52$. Express the following conditions.
a The amount of product sent from plant 2 to marketing district 4 in period 3 is 3,000 units.
b The total amount of product sent in all time periods from plant 2 to marketing district 4 is 3,000 units.
c The total amount of product produced in all plants in all time periods is 10,000 units.
d The total amount of product sent to district 4 in time period 2 is 10,000 units.
e The total amount of product sent from plant 2 to district 3 plus the amount sent from plant 3 to district 4 in the first 26 time periods is 10,000 units.

A1.9 Solutions to Exercises

SECTION A1.4

1 $\displaystyle\sum_{i=1}^{K} 2^{i} = 2^{1} + 2^{2} + 2^{3} + ... + 2^{K}$

2 $\displaystyle\sum_{i=1}^{K} 2^{2i-1} = 2^1 + 2^3 + 2^5 + \dots + 2^{2K-1}$

3 $\displaystyle\sum_{i=1}^{K} x^i = x^1 + x^2 + x^3 + \dots + x^K$

4 $\displaystyle\sum_{k=1}^{3} \frac{x^k}{2k-1} = \frac{x^1}{1} + \frac{x^2}{3} + \frac{x^3}{5}$

5 $\displaystyle\sum_{k=1}^{3} 2^k - \sum_{k=3}^{5}(2k-1) = 2^1 + 2^2 + 2^3 - (5+7+9) = -7$

6 $\displaystyle\sum_{i=1}^{3}(a_i + b_i) = a_1 + b_1 + a_2 + b_2 + a_3 + b_3 = a_1 + a_2 + a_3 + b_1 + b_2 + b_3$

$$= \sum_{i=1}^{3} a_i + \sum_{i=1}^{3} b_i$$

SECTION A1.8

1 $\displaystyle\sum_{j=1}^{12} a_{ij}x_j = b_i, \quad i = 1, 2, 3$ is expanded as

$$a_{11}x_1 + a_{12}x_2 + \dots + a_{1,12}x_{12} = b_1$$
$$a_{21}x_1 + a_{22}x_2 + \dots + a_{2,12}x_{12} = b_2$$
$$a_{31}x_1 + a_{32}x_2 + \dots + a_{3,12}x_{12} = b_3$$

There are three equations, with 12 terms being added on the left side of each equality.

2 a $\displaystyle\sum_{i=1}^{3}\sum_{j=1}^{4}(-1)^i (j)^{i-1} = (-1)^1 [(1)^0 + (2)^0 + (3)^0 + (4)^0]$

$$+ (-1)^2 [(1)^1 + (2)^1 + (3)^1 + (4)^1] + (-1)^3 [(1)^2 + (2)^2 + (3)^2 + (4)^2]$$
$$= -4 + 10 - 30 = -24$$

b $\displaystyle\sum_{i=1}^{3}\sum_{j=1}^{4}(-1)^j (j)^{i-1} = [(-1)^1 (1)^0 + (-1)^2 (2)^0 + (-1)^3 (3)^0 + (-1)^4 (4)^0]$

$$+ [(-1)^1 (1)^1 + (-1)^2 (2)^1 + (-1)^3 (3)^1 + (-1)^4 (4)^1]$$
$$+ [(-1)^1 (1)^2 + (-1)^2 (2)^2 + (-1)^3 (3)^2 + (-1)^4 (4)^2]$$
$$= (-1 + 1 - 1 + 1) + (-1 + 2 - 3 + 4) + (-1 + 4 - 9 + 16)$$
$$= 12$$

c $\displaystyle\sum_{i=1}^{3}\sum_{j=1}^{2} a_{ij}b_{ij} = \sum_{j=1}^{2} a_{1j}b_{1j} + \sum_{j=1}^{2} a_{2j}b_{2j} + \sum_{j=1}^{2} a_{3j}b_{3j}$

$$= a_{11}b_{11} + a_{12}b_{12} + a_{21}b_{21} + a_{22}b_{22} + a_{31}b_{31} + a_{32}b_{32}$$

d $\displaystyle\sum_{i=1}^{3}\sum_{k=1}^{2} a_{ik}b_{ik} = \sum_{k=1}^{2} a_{1k}b_{1k} + \sum_{k=1}^{2} a_{2k}b_{2k} + \sum_{k=1}^{2} a_{3k}b_{3k}$

$$= a_{11}b_{11} + a_{12}b_{12} + a_{21}b_{21} + a_{22}b_{22} + a_{31}b_{31} + a_{32}b_{32}$$

e $\displaystyle\sum_{i=1}^{3}\sum_{j=1}^{2} b_{ij}a_{ji} = \sum_{j=1}^{2} b_{1j}a_{j1} + \sum_{j=1}^{2} b_{2j}a_{j2} + \sum_{j=1}^{2} b_{3j}a_{j3}$

$$= b_{11}a_{11} + b_{12}a_{\cdot 1} + b_{21}a_{12} + b_{22}a_{22} + b_{31}a_{13} + b_{32}a_{23}$$

f $\displaystyle\sum_{j=0}^{4} \frac{C_j}{(1+r)^j} = \frac{C_0}{(1+r)^0} + \frac{C_1}{(1+r)^1} + \frac{C_2}{(1+r)^2} + \frac{C_3}{(1+r)^3} + \frac{C_4}{(1+r)^4}$

g $\displaystyle\sum_{t=0}^{T} \frac{C_j}{(1+r)^t} = \frac{C_0}{(1+r)^0} + \frac{C_1}{(1+r)^1} + \frac{C_2}{(1+r)^2} + \frac{C_3}{(1+r)^3} + \frac{C_4}{(1+r)^4}$

h $\displaystyle\sum_{i=1}^{5} (i+1)^2 x_{2i-1} = 2^2 x_1 + 3^2 x_3 + 4^2 x_5 + 5^2 x_7 + 6^2 x_9$

$$= 4x_1 + 9x_3 + 16x_5 + 25x_7 + 36x_9$$

3 $\displaystyle\sum_{k=1}^{4} a_{ik} b_{kj}, \quad i = 1, 2, \quad j = 1, 2, 3,$ is expanded as

$$
\begin{array}{ll}
a_{11}b_{11} + a_{12}b_{21} + a_{13}b_{31} + a_{14}b_{41} & (i=1, j=1) \\
a_{11}b_{12} + a_{12}b_{22} + a_{13}b_{32} + a_{14}b_{42} & (i=1, j=2) \\
a_{11}b_{13} + a_{12}b_{23} + a_{13}b_{33} + a_{14}b_{43} & (i=1, j=3) \\
\\
a_{21}b_{11} + a_{22}b_{21} + a_{23}b_{31} + a_{24}b_{41} & (i=2, j=1) \\
a_{21}b_{12} + a_{22}b_{22} + a_{23}b_{32} + a_{24}b_{42} & (i=2, j=2) \\
a_{21}b_{13} + a_{22}b_{23} + a_{23}b_{33} + a_{24}b_{43} & (i=2, j=3)
\end{array}
$$

There are six sums, with each sum containing four terms.

4 Total revenue from all products is

$$\sum_{i=1}^{60} \sum_{j=1}^{52} r_{ij}$$

where i = product, j = week. If i = week, j = product, then total revenue from all products is

$$\sum_{i=1}^{52} \sum_{j=1}^{60} r_{ij}$$

5 $\displaystyle\sum_{i=1}^{M} \sum_{j=1}^{N} a_{ij} = \sum_{j=1}^{N} a_{1j} + \sum_{j=1}^{N} a_{2j} + \ldots + \sum_{j=1}^{N} a_{Mj}$

$$= (a_{11} + a_{12} + \ldots + a_{1N}) + (a_{21} + a_{22} + \ldots + a_{2N})$$
$$+ \ldots + (a_{M1} + a_{M2} + \ldots + a_{MN})$$
$$= (a_{11} + a_{21} + \ldots + a_{M1}) + (a_{12} + a_{22} + \ldots + a_{M2})$$
$$+ \ldots + (a_{1N} + a_{2N} + \ldots + a_{MN})$$
$$= \sum_{i=1}^{M} a_{i1} + \sum_{i=1}^{M} a_{i2} + \ldots + \sum_{i=1}^{M} a_{iN}$$
$$= \sum_{j=1}^{N} \sum_{i=1}^{M} a_{ij}$$

6 In showing that

$$\sum_{i=1}^{M} \sum_{j=1}^{N} a_{ij}$$

is not, in general, equal to

$$\sum_{i=1}^{M} \sum_{j=1}^{N} a_{ji}$$

one need only observe that in the first expression the first subscript of a runs up to M while in the second expression it runs up to N. In the general case, M and N are not equal, and one will be larger. For example, taking $M = 20$, $N = 12$, the first expression will involve terms such as $a_{20,1}, a_{20,2}, \ldots$, etc., while the second will not. The two expressions will be equal if M and N are equal, for in that case

$$\sum_{i=1}^{M} \sum_{j=1}^{N} a_{ij} = \sum_{j=1}^{M} \sum_{i=1}^{N} a_{ji} = \sum_{j=1}^{N} \sum_{i=1}^{M} a_{ji} = \sum_{i=1}^{M} \sum_{j=1}^{N} a_{ji}$$

7   **a** $x_{24} = 3{,}000$

    b $\displaystyle\sum_{j=1}^{4} x_{2j} = 6{,}000$

    c $\displaystyle\sum_{i=1}^{3} \sum_{j=1}^{4} x_{ij} = 10{,}000$

8   **a** $x_{243} = 3{,}000$

    b $\displaystyle\sum_{t=1}^{52} x_{24t} = 3{,}000$

    c $\displaystyle\sum_{i=1}^{3} \sum_{j=1}^{4} \sum_{t=1}^{52} x_{ijt} = 10{,}000$

    d $\displaystyle\sum_{i=1}^{3} x_{i42} = 10{,}000$

    e $\displaystyle\sum_{t=1}^{52} x_{23t} + \sum_{t=1}^{26} x_{34t} = 10{,}000$

2 *Plotting Point Sets, Equalities, and Inequalities*

A2.1 Introduction

The ability to plot points and sets of points usually makes it much easier to understand the quantitative concepts and tools used in managerial decision making. It is often possible to construct a diagram or a picture that illustrates the concept or technique under consideration by plotting points and sets of points, and one picture can, indeed, be worth 1,000 words. In addition, students will discover that their ability to construct geometric illustrations can provide a quick tool for resolving confusion and answering many of their questions.

All the discussions and examples in this appendix concern two-dimensional space. The concepts are applicable in any finite space, however.

A2.2 The Coordinate System

Two *axes* are introduced (see Figure A2.1). One is horizontal, the other is vertical. The horizontal is labeled the *first axis.* The vertical is labeled the *second axis.* Each axis is now marked with a numerical scale (see Figure A2.2). The point of reference for this numerical scale is the point of intersection of the two axes, and this point is called the *origin.* Note that there is a numerical scale on each axis. On the first axis, by convention, all numbers to the left of the origin are negative and all to the right are positive. On the second axis, all numbers below the origin are negative and all above are positive. In this way, all integers and fractions, positive and negative, have a location on each axis. The space containing the two axes is called a *two-dimensional space,* and the two labeled axes form what is called a *coordinate system.*

Figure A2.1   *Two axes*

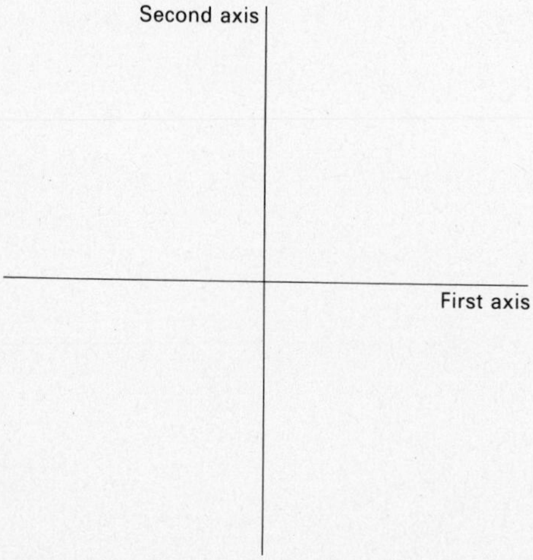

Figure A2.2   *The coordinate system*

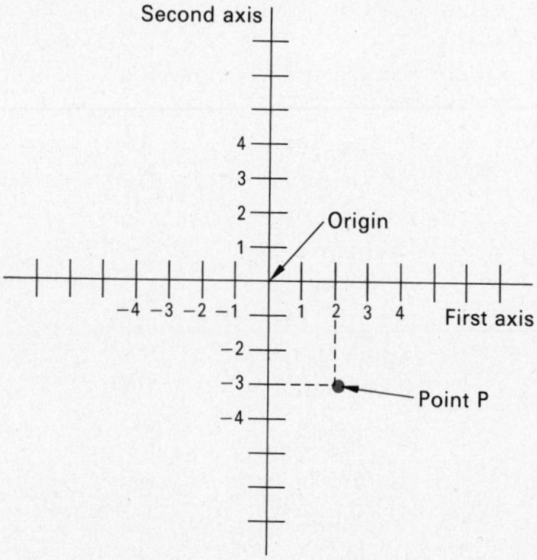

A2.3 Depicting Points in the Coordinate System

The two axes enable us to plot points in two dimensional space. For example, the dot labeled *Point P* in Figure A2.2 is described by the symbol $(2, -3)$. This means that point P is reached by moving from the origin two units horizontally and three units vertically. The horizontal movement is to the right because the 2 is positive and the vertical movement is down because the 3 is negative. As illustrations of point plotting, Figure A2.3 depicts the points $(1, 1)$, $(-1\frac{1}{2}, 3)$, $(-2\frac{1}{4}, -1)$, $(4, -1)$.

It is easy to see that each ***ordered pair*** of numbers corresponds to a point in the coordinate system, and each point in the coordinate system corresponds to an ordered pair of numbers. We use the term *ordered pair* because the order is important. That is, when we plot $(1, 2)$ and $(2, 1)$ we obtain two *different* points. These are *different* ordered pairs.

gure A2.3   *Plotting points*

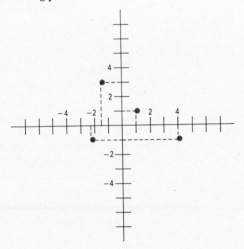

A2.4 Abstract Representation of Points

It has been shown above that points and ordered pairs amount to the same thing. Given any ordered pair, we can plot a point. Given any point, we can identify it as an ordered pair. That much is simple enough, but you must be cautious, for in mathematical literature points (and, hence, ordered pairs) are symbolically represented in a variety of ways. You will recall from algebra that any symbol such as x or y or t could be used to represent a number. Similarly, any symbol can be used to represent a point. Thus, if x stands for a point, it must also stand for a specific ordered pair of numbers. If we denote the first number by the symbol a and the second by b, then

$x = (a, b)$

As in algebra, we can use any symbol for a pair and any symbol for a number. Thus, we could let P denote the point and let x and y denote the pair of numbers for which

$P = (x, y)$

For example, in Figure A2.2 the point P corresponds to the ordered pair $(2, -3)$, or, in other words, $x = 2$ and $y = -3$.

It is fairly common to conform to a practice of letting x represent the first number in an ordered pair and y the second number. Thus, the ordered pair frequently is denoted (x, y). In keeping with this practice, the first axis is frequently called the x axis and the second the y axis. However, it is equally frequent that the symbol x_1 is used to denote the first number in an ordered pair and x_2 the second. In such a case, the ordered pair is denoted (x_1, x_2). In terms of this notation the first axis would be called the x_1 axis and the second the x_2 axis. Unfortunately for the student, there are endless variations on this theme and ordered pairs can be represented as (u, v), (s, t), (w_1, w_2), (y_1, y_2), (z, w), (k_1, k_2), ad infinitum. Moreover, in addition to having x denote one number in an ordered pair, such as (x, y), we could, as mentioned above, let x denote the entire pair. Thus, for example, we might have $x = (a, b)$ or $x = (x_1, x_2)$, or $x = (p_1, p_2)$. Examples of notation similar to all of these are likely to be encountered. Though this may seem confusing, a little thought about the context should make any reasonable notation clear. As you become more familiar with abstract notation, it tends to become more easily readable *if it is correct*. In contrast, notation such as $x = (x, y)$ is horrendously incorrect, for the same symbol, x, is being used to represent both an ordered pair of numbers and a number. When you encounter such notation (and you will), it is wise to give up on its author.

A2.5   Plotting Sets of Points

It should be clear that several points can be plotted as easily as one. For example, let us plot $(1, 1)$, $(2, 2)$, $(3, 3)$, as shown in Figure A2.4. For each of these three points, the first and second numbers are the same.

Suppose we wish to plot *the set of all points* with this property. Let us conform to the frequently used notation that x denotes the first number in the ordered pair and y denotes the second. Then we can easily describe all ordered pairs with the property that the first and second numbers are the same. That is, such ordered pairs are precisely those that satisfy the condition $y = x$. The plot of these points is shown in Figure A2.5.

Figure A2.4   *The points (1, 1), (2, 2), (3, 3)*

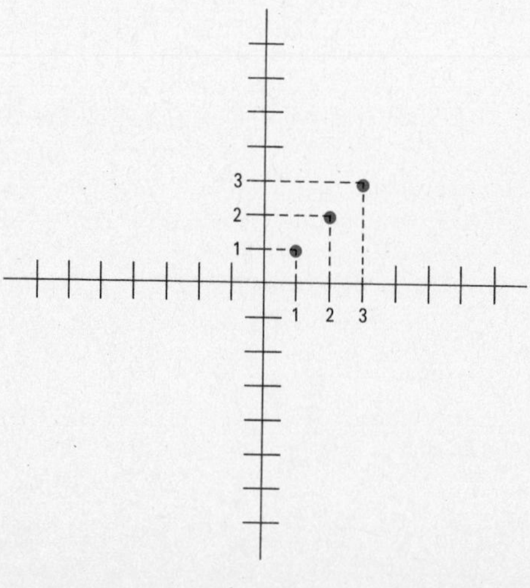

Figure A2.5   *The points for which x = y*

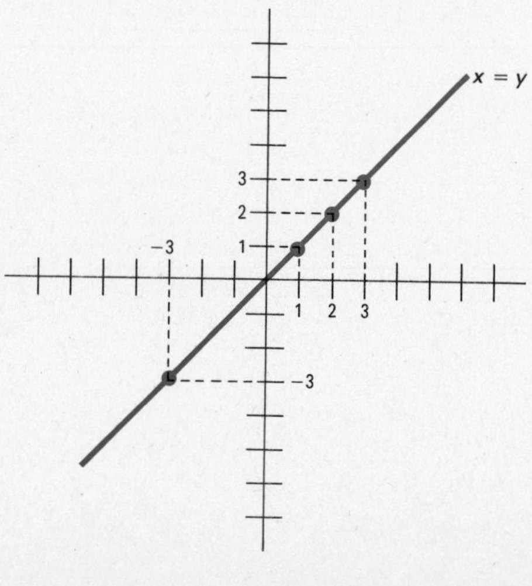

Using the same notation, (x,y), for an ordered pair, suppose we wish to plot the set of all points for which the second number, y, equals the square of the first number, x. In other words, $y = x^2$. We obtain the plot shown in Figure A2.6.

As further examples, consider the following plots:

1 All (x,y) for which $y = 2x$ (see Figure A2.7)
2 All (x,y) for which $y = 2x + 1$ (see Figure A2.8)
3 All (x,y) for which $x = 1$ (see Figure A2.9)
4 All (x,y) for which $y = 2$ (see Figure A2.10)
5 All (x,y) for which $x^2 + y^2 = 4$ (see Figure A2.11)

Figure A2.6   *The points for which $y = x^2$*

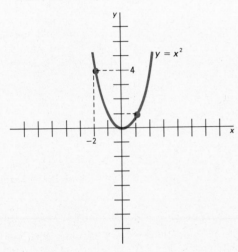

Figure A2.7   *The points for which $y = 2x$*

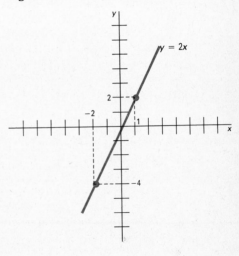

Figure A2.8   *The points for which $y = 2x + 1$*

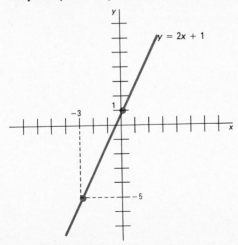

Figure A2.9   *The points for which $x = 1$*

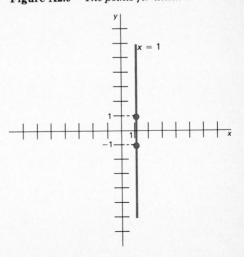

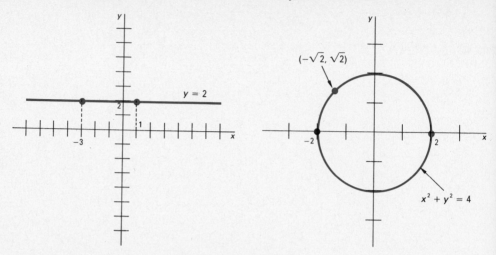

Figure A2.10   *The points for which y = 2*

Figure A2.11   *The points for which* $x^2 + y^2 = 4$

A2.6   Plots of Points Derived from Word Problems

In any real problem, symbols such as x and y will represent the quantities of certain entities (called *variables*) of interest. Consider the following examples.

Suppose item 1 sells for $10 per unit and item 2 sells for $5 per unit. Let x be the number of units of item 1 sold next month and y be the number of units of item 2 sold next month. Plot all the possible sales results (values of x and y) for next month for which the total revenue is $50.

If x units of item 1 and y units of item 2 are sold, total revenue (in dollars) is $10x + 5y$. Our problem, then, is to plot all (x, y) for which the equation $10x + 5y = 50$ holds; that is, all (x, y) for which $y = 10 - 2x$. Since negative sales are not meaningful, we shall further require that $x \geq 0$ and $y \geq 0$. The result is pictured in Figure A2.12.

For the next example, use the same definition for x and y given in the scenario above, and assume that item 1 requires one-third hour of production time and item 2 requires one-half hour of production time. Plot all the possible sales results for next month for which the revenue per production hour is $24.

As before, total revenue (in dollars) is given by the expression

$10x + 5y$

Similarly, total production time (in hours) is given by the expression

$\dfrac{1}{3}x + \dfrac{1}{2}y$

Thus, revenue per production hour is total dollars of revenue divided by total hours of production, which is

$$\frac{10x + 5y}{1/3x + 1/2y}$$

Our problem, then, is to plot all (x, y) for which

$$\frac{10x + 5y}{1/3x + 1/2y} = 24$$

or all (x, y) for which

$$10x + 5y = 8x + 12y$$
$$2x = 7y$$
$$\frac{2}{7}x = y$$

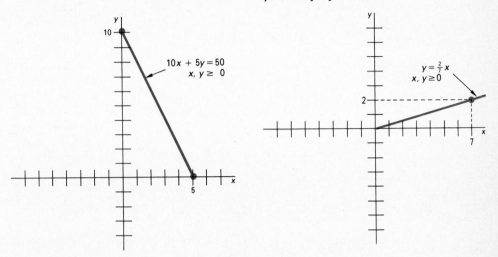

gure A2.12 *All sales results for which total revenue is $50*

Figure A2.13 *All sales results that give $24 of revenue per production hour*

We also want to require $x \geq 0$ and $y \geq 0$. The resulting plot is shown in Figure A2.13.

A2.7 Plotting Point Sets Defined by Inequalities

In many situations, management is more concerned that certain boundaries not be exceeded or that certain quotas be met than with exact relationships of the type just presented. Management may well wish to know the various production plans that can be followed *without exceeding* the capacity of a certain production facility or what combinations of sales will guarantee that profit is *at least* equal to a specified level. The answers to such questions can be expressed in mathematical notation as *inequalities,* and these inequalities can be represented by point sets.

Suppose, for example, that you want to plot all (x,y) for which $y \leq x$ (read "y is less than or equal to x"). When plotting sets of points described by an inequality, the first step is to plot the *equality*. Therefore, plot all (x,y) for which $y = x$. Then choose an arbitrary point and see if it satisfies the inequality. If it does, then everything on the same side of the equality line will also satisfy the inequality. To illustrate, in plotting all (x,y) for which $y \leq x$, let us select the point $(4,-4)$. Since this point satisfies the inequality $y \leq x$ (that is, $-4 \leq 4$), we know that every point below the equality line will satisfy the inequality. On the other hand, suppose we had selected the point $(2,4)$. This point does not satisfy the inequality, since $4 > 2$ or $y > x$. Thus, all the points on the same side of the equality line (above it) will *not* satisfy the inequality. All this is shown in Figure A2.14.

Consider another example of this technique. Plot all (x,y) for which $x^2 + y^2 \leq 4$. First, plot $x^2 + y^2 = 4$. (This was done in Figure A2.11.) Now choose the origin $(0,0)$ to see if it satisfies the inequality $x^2 + y^2 = 4$. If $x = 0$ and $y = 0$, then

$$x^2 + y^2 = 0^2 + 0^2 = 0 < 4$$

We see that $(0,0)$ satisfies the inequality, and thus all points on and inside the circle

Figure A2.14 *All (x,y) for which y ≤ x*   **Figure A2.15** *All (x,y) for which $x^2 + y^2 \leq 4$*

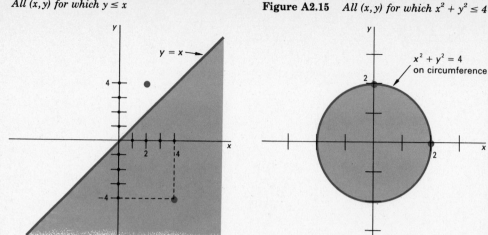

will satisfy $x^2 + y^2 \leq 4$. (All points inside the circle satisfy $x^2 + y^2 < 4$.) The result is shown in Figure A2.15.

Having seen how to plot sets of points described by equalities and inequalities, it is now possible to plot more complicated sets of points described by several conditions. As examples, consider the following plots:

1 All (x,y) for which $y \geq x$, $x \leq 2$, and $x \geq 0$ (see Figure A2.16)
2 All (x,y) for which $y \geq x$, $x \leq 2$, $y \leq 3$, and $x \geq 0$ (see Figure A2.17)
3 All (x,y) for which $x^2 + y^2 \leq 4$ and $y - x \geq 0$ (see Figure A2.18)
4 All (x,y) for which $x^2 + y^2 \leq 4$ or $x \geq 6$ (see Figure A2.19)
5 All (x,y) for which $x^2 + y^2 \leq 4$ or $y \geq x$ (see Figure A2.20)

Note that the word *and* between two (or more) conditions means that both (all) conditions must be satisfied. When this is the case, the points must satisfy both (all) conditions.

Figure A2.16 *All (x,y) for which y ≥ x, x ≤ 2, and x ≥ 0*   **Figure A2.17** *All (x,y) for which y ≥ x, x ≤ 2, y ≤ 3, and x ≥ 0*

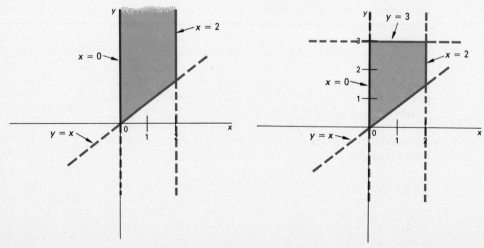

Figure A2.18 *All (x, y) for which $x^2 + y^2 \leq 4$ and $y - x \geq 0$*

Figure A2.19 *All (x, y) for which $x^2 + y^2 \leq 4$ or $x \geq 6$*

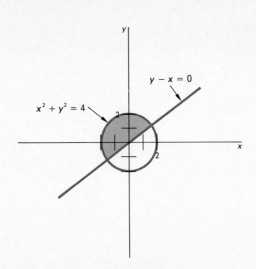

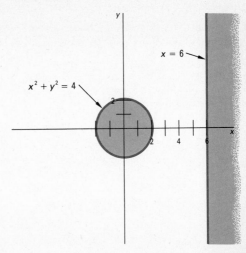

Figure A2.20 *All (x, y) for which $x^2 + y^2 \leq 4$ or $y \geq x$*

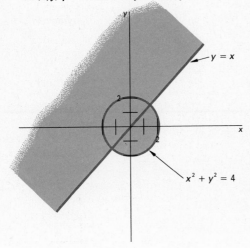

The word *or*, as in item 4 above, means one condition or the other must be true, and possibly but not necessarily both. Hence, when you see *or*, you know the points must satisfy at least one of the conditions, and possibly both.

The ability to define point sets using the logical operators *and* and *or* makes it possible to characterize sets with a variety of attributes. Some of the exercises in the following section illustrate this point.

A2.8 Exercises

1 Consider a firm whose labor force includes individuals from 18 to 65 years of age with a varying number of years of work experience. Refer to the plot in Figure A2.21. The shaded area is a graphic representation of a set *A* that *contains* all employees. Note

Figure A2.21

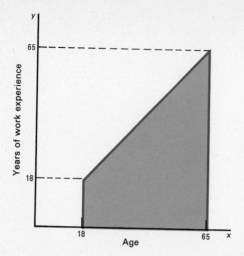

that no employee is younger than 18 and no employee's work experience is greater than his or her age. Letting x denote *age* and y denote *years of work experience*, the set A is given by the following inequalities:

$$18 \leq x \leq 65, \quad y \leq x$$

In parts *a–f* of this problem, give an inequality representation of the point sets associated with the various groups of special interest to the personnel department. Also give a graphic representation of each set.

a Apprentice tool and die makers must be between 18 and 25 years of age when they are hired, in addition to having at least 2 years of work experience. Indicate the smallest point set (based on the given data) that includes all newly hired apprentice tool and die makers.

b Assume henceforth that it is impossible for an 18-year old to have more than 2 years of work experience. Use this assumption and now indicate the smallest point set that includes all newly hired apprentice tool and die makers.

c Assume henceforth that each year in the apprentice program is also a year of work experience. It requires 4 years to complete the apprentice program for tool and die makers. Indicate the smallest point set that shows the age and experience of all tool and die makers currently in the apprentice program.

d An individual who successfully completes the apprentice program becomes a journeyperson tool and die maker. An individual remains at this position for 7 years. Indicate the smallest point set that shows the age and experience of all currently employed journeypersons. A year as a journeyperson is also a year of work experience.

e Indicate the smallest point set that shows the age and experience satisfying both the apprentice and the journeyperson requirements.

f Show the smallest point set of all individuals who satisfy the age and experience requirements for either the apprentice or the journeyperson position.

2 Plot the set of all points (x,y) satisfying the following conditions:

a $y \geq x^2$, $\quad x \leq 2$
b $y \geq x + 1$, $\quad y \leq 2$
c $y \geq x$, $\quad x = 2$
d $y \leq -x$ or $y \leq -1$
e $y = x^2$ or $y = x$

3 Plot the set of all points (x,y) such that $y - 3x = 2$. What happens to this plot as the number 2 varies? For example, plot $y - 3x = 3$, $y - 3x = 1$.

4 Plot the set of all points (x,y) such that $y - 3x \leq 2$ and $x + y \leq 3$.

5 Plot the set of all points satisfying the conditions in problem 4 plus the added conditions $x \geq 0$, $y \geq 0$.

6 Plot the set of all points satisfying $xy - 1 \leq 0$, $x + y \geq 3$, $x \geq 0$, $y \geq 0$. That is, plot the points that simultaneously satisfy *all* these conditions.

A2.9 Solutions to Exercises

1 **a** The inequality representation of the point set is $18 \leq x \leq 25$, $y \geq 2$, $y \leq x$. The graphic representation is shown in Figure A2.22.

  b The inequality representation of the point set is $x \leq 25$, $y \geq 2$, $y \leq x - 16$. The graphic representation is shown in Figure A2.23.

  c The inequality representation of the point set is $x \leq 29$, $y \geq 2$, $y \leq x - 16$, $y \geq x - 23$. The graphic representation is shown in Figure A2.24.

Figure A2.22

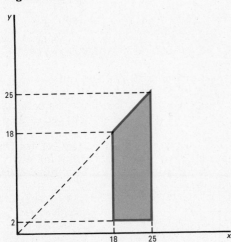

Figure A2.23

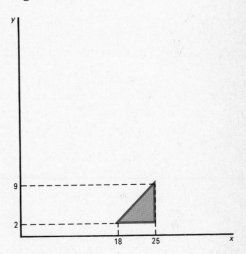

Figure A2.24

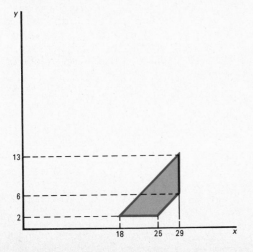

Figure A2.25

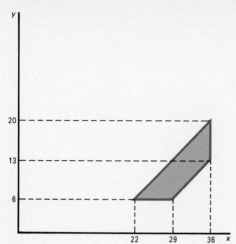

Figure A2.26

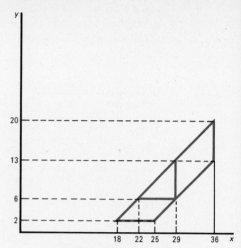

Figure A2.27

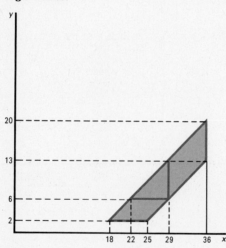

Figure A2.28

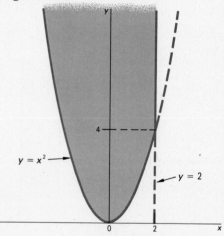

Figure A2.29

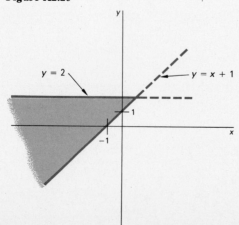

d The inequality representation of the point set is $x \le 36$, $y \ge 6$, $y \le x - 16$, $y \ge x - 23$. The graphic representation is shown in Figure A2.25.
e The inequality representation of the point set is $x \le 29$, $y \le x - 16$, $y \ge 6$. The graphic representation is shown in Figure A2.26.
f The inequality representation of the point set is $y \ge 2$, $y \le 36$, $y \ge x - 23$, $y \le x - 16$. The graphic representation is shown in Figure A2.27.

2 **a** The point set for $y \ge x^2$, $x \le 2$ is shown in Figure A2.28.
  b The point set for $y \ge x + 1$, $y \le 2$ is shown in Figure A2.29.
  c The point set for $y \ge x$, $x = 2$ is shown in Figure A2.30.
  d The point set for $y \le -x$ or $y \le -1$ is shown in Figure A2.31.
  e The point set for $y = x^2$ or $y = x$ is shown in Figure A2.32.

3 The point sets for $y - 3x = 2$, $y - 3x = 3$, and $y - 3x = 1$ are shown in Figure A2.33.

Figure A2.30

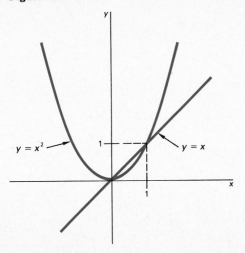

Figure A2.31

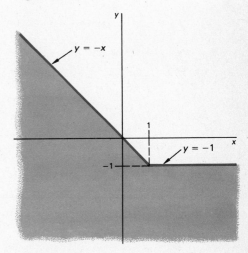

Figure A2.32

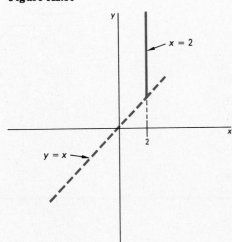

Figure A2.33

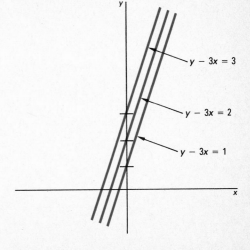

4 The point set for $y - 3x \leq 2$ and $x + y \leq 3$ is shown in Figure A2.34.

5 The point set for $y - 3x \leq 2$ and $x + y \leq 3$ plus the added conditions $x \geq 0$, $y \geq 0$ is shown in Figure A2.35.

6 The point set for $xy - 1 \leq 0$, $x + y \geq 3$, $x \geq 0$, $y \geq 0$ is shown in Figure A2.36.

Figure A2.34

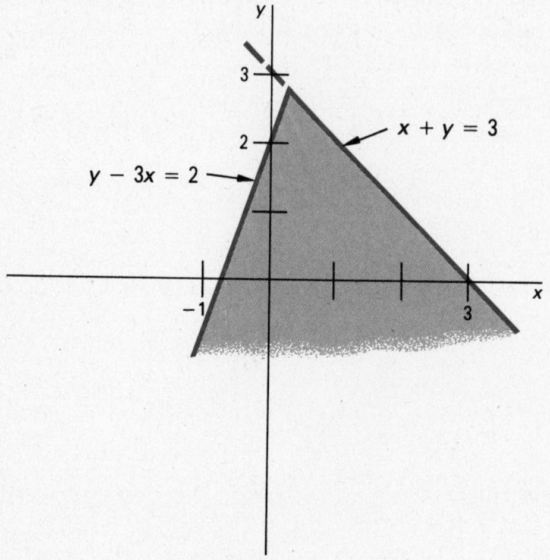

Figure A2.35

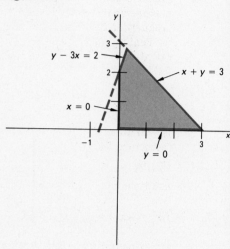

Figure A2.36

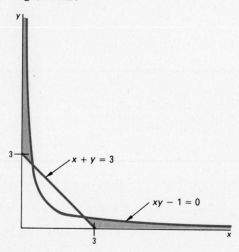

3 *The Language of Linear Algebra*

A3.1 Introduction

Linear algebra is so important to the mathematical study of science, economics, and management that a special language has been developed to facilitate its use. That language is the subject of this appendix. Linear algebra provides a notational framework for dealing with the study of linear functions and of systems of linear equalities (also called *linear equations*) and inequalities. Examples of these mathematical structures follow.

LINEAR FUNCTIONS

Linear functions have a very special form, or, in the jargon of mathematics, a special "structure." For example,

$$f(x_1, x_2, x_3, x_4) = 2x_1 - x_2 - 13x_3 + 12x_4 \qquad\qquad \text{(I)}$$

is a linear function of four variables.

$$f(x_1, ..., x_n) = \sum_{i=1}^{n} c_i x_i = c_1 x_1 + c_2 x_2 + ... c_n x_n \qquad\qquad \text{(II)}$$

is a linear function of n variables. (The c_i terms are constants, or coefficients, and the x_i terms are the variables.)

SYSTEMS OF LINEAR EQUALITIES

An example of a system of three linear equalities in four unknowns is

$$\begin{array}{rcrcrcrcr} -6x_1 & + & x_2 & + & 3x_3 & + & x_4 & = & 9 \\ 2x_1 & - & x_2 & + & 14x_3 & - & 2x_4 & = & -1 \\ 3x_1 & + & x_2 & + & x_3 & + & 16x_4 & = & 2 \end{array} \qquad\qquad \text{(III)}$$

The general representation of a system of m linear equalities in n unknowns is

$$\begin{array}{rcrcrcrcl} a_{11}x_1 & + & a_{12}x_2 & + & ... & + & a_{1n}x_n & = & b_1 \\ a_{21}x_1 & + & a_{22}x_2 & + & ... & + & a_{2n}x_n & = & b_2 \\ \vdots & & & & & & \vdots & & \\ a_{m1}x_1 & + & a_{m2}x_2 & + & ... & + & a_{mn}x_n & = & b_m \end{array} \qquad\qquad \text{(IV)}$$

in which m and n are any positive integers, the x_is are variables, and the a_{ij}s and b_is are constants.

SYSTEMS OF LINEAR INEQUALITIES

A system of four linear inequalities in three unknowns is given by

$$\begin{array}{rcrcrcl} -6x_1 & + & x_2 & + & 3x_3 & \le & 11 \\ 2x_1 & - & x_2 & + & 14x_3 & \le & 6 \\ 3x_1 & + & x_2 & + & x_3 & \ge & -2 \\ 4x_1 & - & x_2 & - & x_3 & \le & 1 \end{array} \qquad\qquad \text{(V)}$$

The general representation of a system of m linear inequalities in n unknowns is

$$
\begin{aligned}
a_{11}x_1 + a_{12}x_2 + \ldots + a_{1n}x_n &\leq b_1 \\
a_{21}x_1 + a_{22}x_2 + \ldots + a_{2n}x_n &\leq b_2 \\
\vdots \qquad\qquad\qquad \vdots \\
a_{m1}x_1 + a_{m2}x_2 + \ldots + a_{mn}x_n &\leq b_m
\end{aligned}
\qquad\text{(VI)}
$$

MIXED SYSTEMS OF EQUALITIES AND INEQUALITIES

A mixed linear system of equalities and inequalities in four unknowns is given by

$$
\begin{aligned}
2x_1 + x_2 - x_3 + x_4 &= 16 \\
3x_1 - 13x_2 + x_3 - 12x_4 &= 12 \\
8x_1 + x_2 \qquad\qquad &\geq 3 \\
4x_1 + 2x_2 + 3x_3 + x_4 &\leq -8 \\
3x_1 - x_2 \qquad + 4x_4 &\leq 10
\end{aligned}
\qquad\text{(VII)}
$$

The subject of linear algebra deals with both the theory and the notation of the special mathematical systems or structures illustrated above. The notation involves the use of a special set of symbols, called **vectors** and **matrices,** and the rules for manipulating these symbols. The use of such symbols in applications is common, and the language of linear algebra is encountered in a variety of decision-making models. This is the case because most of the popular statistical models (such as linear regression) and the most popular optimization model (linear programming) are linear models. As a result, the language of linear algebra appears in the econometric models used by long-range planning groups, in the discriminate analysis and factor analysis models used in many marketing research projects, in the forecasting models used by the financial sections, and in solving many operating problems. It is possible to explain the assumptions and results of these studies without using vector and matrix notation (that is, without using the language of linear algebra). However, the facts of life are that this language provides an extremely convenient shorthand notation, and for this reason it is commonly employed by both the builders and consumers of quantitative models. The manager who understands the language will not be put off by unfamiliar symbols and jargon. Instead of anguishing over the language, such managers will spend their time on the important parts of a model: the assumptions, the logic, and the conclusions. In this appendix we will introduce vector and matrix notation for the potential manager who either has not seen it previously or who needs a refresher. We provide enough experience in manipulating these entities to make you a more effective user of many types of models.

Thus far we have talked in such terms as "shorthand," "notation," and "language." Here is precisely what we mean. It will be shown in the following sections of this chapter that

---

1   The function $c_1x_1 + \ldots + c_nx_n$ in (II) above can be written in shorthand form as

$$cx$$

where c and x are n-dimensional vectors, c is a vector of constants, and x is a vector of variables.

2   The system of equations in (IV) above can be written in shorthand form as

$$Ax = b$$

where A is an $m \times n$ matrix, x is an n-dimensional vector, and b is an m-dimensional vector.

3 Similarly, m linear inequalities in n unknowns, as in (VI) above, can be written in the shorthand form of

$$Ax \leq b$$

where, again, A is an $m \times n$ matrix, x is an n-dimensional vector, and b is an m-dimensional vector.

A3.2 Vector Notation

An n-dimensional vector is an ordered set of n symbols. The symbols can be either numbers or variables that represent numbers. Such a vector is also called an n-tuple, or a point.

For example,

$(1, 2, -1)$	is a three-dimensional vector
(x_1, x_2, x_3)	is a three-dimensional vector
(x, y, z)	is a three-dimensional vector
$(x_1, x_2, ..., x_n)$	is an n-dimensional vector

Just as was the case with representing points, an n-dimensional vector is often conveniently represented with a single symbol, such as x. Thus, if the symbol x is used to denote a four-dimensional vector, then there are four numbers, say, x_1, x_2, x_3, x_4, such that $x = (x_1, x_2, x_3, x_4)$. These four numbers are called the four *components* of the vector x (or, equally correctly, the four *coordinates* of the point x). Similarly, for an n-dimensional vector x it is true that $x = (x_1, ..., x_n)$, where x_i is the ith *component* of x.

It will now be useful to define four operations on vectors: addition, subtraction, scalar multiplication, and the product.

VECTOR ADDITION

In order to add two vectors, each must be of the same dimension. The sum is the new vector obtained by adding the components. For example,

$$(1, 3, -2) + (2, 1, 2) = (3, 4, 0)$$
$$(x_1, x_2, ..., x_n) + (y_1, y_2, ..., y_n) = (x_1 + y_1, x_2 + y_2, ..., x_n + y_n)$$
$$(x_1, x_2) + (y_1, y_2) + (z_1, z_2) = (x_1 + y_1 + z_1, x_2 + y_2 + z_2)$$

VECTOR SUBTRACTION

This operation is the same as addition except that components are subtracted. Again, both vectors must be of the same dimension. Thus,

$$(1, -2, -3) - (1, 3, -3) = (0, -5, 0)$$

MULTIPLICATION BY A SCALAR

Loosely called *scalar multiplication,* this refers to the operation of a scalar (that is, a constant) times a vector. It is easily illustrated:

$6(1, 3, -2) = (6, 18, -12)$

$-3(x_1, x_2) = (-3x_1, -3x_2)$

Thus, multiplying a scalar times a vector gives a new vector.

VECTOR MULTIPLICATION

Here we define a way of multiplying two vectors so that the result is a scalar, *not* a vector. For this reason the rule is sometimes called the *scalar product.* It is also called the *inner product* or *dot product.* In order to multiply two vectors, each must be of the same dimension.

The rule for the product of two vectors is: multiply components and add.

For example,

$(1, 2) \cdot (4, 1) = 1 \cdot 4 + 2 \cdot 1 = 4 + 2 = 6$

$(1, 3, -2) \cdot (1, 1, 2) = 1 \cdot 1 + 3 \cdot 1 - 2 \cdot 2 = 1 + 3 - 4 = 0$

$$xy = (x_1, x_2, ..., x_n) \cdot (y_1, y_2, ..., y_n) = x_1 y_1 + x_2 y_2 + ... + x_n y_n = \sum_{i=1}^{n} x_i y_i$$

$$cx = (c_1, c_2, ..., c_n) \cdot (x_1, x_2, ..., x_n) = c_1 x_1 + c_2 x_2 + ... + c_n x_n = \sum_{i=1}^{n} c_i x_i$$

Note that the last example above shows that the linear function

$$\sum_{i=1}^{n} c_i x_i$$

can be written compactly as the product cx, where c is the vector of numbers $(c_1, ..., c_n)$ and x is the vector of variables $(x_1, ..., x_n)$.

Example 1

Consider a firm that sells four products from two locations. Data on these products are given in Figure A3.1. For an individual product and location

Figure A3.1

Product	Price per Unit	Location 1		Location 2	
		Initial Inventory	Sales	Initial Inventory	Sales
1	15	500	300	80	50
2	5	400	250	140	90
3	10	130	85	250	180
4	8	94	64	320	270

$$\text{Revenue} = \text{price} \times \text{sales}$$

$$\text{Value of final inventory} = (.6 \times \text{price})[\text{initial inventory} - \text{sales} - .1(\text{initial inventory} - \text{sales})]$$

The firm has determined that the per-unit value of its final inventory is adequately approximated by multiplying the price by 0.6. Hence, the value of its final inventory equals (.6 × price) times the amount of the final inventory. Ten percent of the unsold items spoil, and consequently final inventory is found by subtracting the sales and the spoilage from the initial inventory.

Define vectors and use vector operations to symbolically express:

a Total revenue

b Total value of final inventory where the totals are taken over both locations and all products

Solution to Example 1

Let I_i be the vector whose components are initial inventories at location i:

$I_1 = (500, 400, 130, 94)$

$I_2 = (80, 140, 250, 320)$

Let S_i be the vector whose components are sales at location i:

$S_1 = (300, 250, 85, 64)$

$S_2 = (50, 90, 180, 270)$

Let P be the vector whose components are the product prices:

$P = (15, 5, 10, 8)$

Then

$$\text{Total revenue} = P(S_1 + S_2)$$

$$\text{Total value of final inventory} = .6P\{.9[(I_1 - S_1) + (I_2 - S_2)]\}$$

$$= .54P[(I_1 + I_2) - (S_1 + S_2)]$$

A3.3 Matrix Notation

An $m \times n$ (read "m by n", not "m times n") matrix is a rectangular array of mn (that is, m times n) numbers, where the array has m rows and n columns and the dimension is said to be "m by n." The numbers in a matrix are called "entries."

For example,

$$\begin{bmatrix} 1 & 6 \\ -4 & 2 \end{bmatrix} \text{ is a } 2 \times 2 \text{ matrix}$$

$$\begin{bmatrix} 1 & 6 & 2 \\ 4 & 1 & 1 \end{bmatrix} \text{ is a } 2 \times 3 \text{ matrix}$$

$$\begin{bmatrix} 1 & 2 \\ 4 & 2 \\ 1 & 1 \end{bmatrix} \text{ is a } 3 \times 2 \text{ matrix}$$

In order to represent a general $m \times n$ matrix we need a way to represent each term.

For example, recall that with vectors we can equally correctly use either the symbol x or the symbols $(x_1, x_2, ..., x_n)$ to represent a general n-dimensional vector. In either case it is understood that x_i represents the ith component of the vector.

For matrices the proper analogy is to have notation that will identify every entry. This is conveniently accomplished with double subscript notation. That is, we let a symbol such as a_{ij} denote the number in the ith row and j^{th} column of the matrix. (It could equally well be the symbol x_{ij} or b_{ij} or t_{ij}, etc.) Then the general $m \times n$ matrix can be represented as:

$$\begin{bmatrix} a_{11} & a_{12} & \cdots & a_{1n} \\ a_{21} & a_{22} & \cdots & a_{2n} \\ \vdots & & & \\ a_{m1} & a_{m2} & \cdots & a_{mn} \end{bmatrix}$$

It is important to note and memorize the following almost universal convention:

The first subscript refers to row, and the second subscript refers to column.

It is often convenient to use a single symbol to denote the *entire* matrix (all mn entries). In this case it is most common to employ a capital letter. Thus, the symbol A might be used to denote the $m \times n$ matrix whose entries are a_{ij}. Similarly, B or Γ (capital gamma) might be used to denote matrices with entries b_{ij} or γ_{ij} (lower case gamma), respectively.

It is now appropriate to define for matrices the operations of addition, subtraction, multiplication by a scalar, and multiplication of two matrices.

MATRIX ADDITION

Matrices can be added if and only if they are of the same dimension. In this case the sum is a new matrix of the same dimension. The entries are obtained by summing the entries in the matrices being added. For example,

$$\begin{bmatrix} 1 & 2 & -4 \\ 3 & 1 & 1 \end{bmatrix} + \begin{bmatrix} 2 & 0 & 1 \\ 1 & 1 & 1 \end{bmatrix} = \begin{bmatrix} 1+2 & 2+0 & -4+1 \\ 3+1 & 1+1 & 1+1 \end{bmatrix} = \begin{bmatrix} 3 & 2 & -3 \\ 4 & 2 & 2 \end{bmatrix}$$

$$\begin{bmatrix} a_{11} & a_{12} \\ a_{21} & a_{22} \end{bmatrix} + \begin{bmatrix} b_{11} & b_{12} \\ b_{21} & b_{22} \end{bmatrix} = \begin{bmatrix} a_{11}+b_{11} & a_{12}+b_{12} \\ a_{21}+b_{21} & a_{22}+b_{22} \end{bmatrix}$$

MATRIX SUBTRACTION

Subtraction is the same as addition except that entries are subtracted. For example,

$$\begin{bmatrix} 1 & 2 \\ 1 & 1 \\ 3 & 4 \end{bmatrix} - \begin{bmatrix} -1 & 2 \\ 4 & 1 \\ 2 & 1 \end{bmatrix} = \begin{bmatrix} 1-(-1) & 2-2 \\ 1-4 & 1-1 \\ 3-2 & 4-1 \end{bmatrix} = \begin{bmatrix} 2 & 0 \\ -3 & 0 \\ 1 & 3 \end{bmatrix}$$

MULTIPLICATION BY A SCALAR

This operation refers to the product of a scalar (that is, a constant) times a matrix. This gives a new matrix. The rule is easily demonstrated:

$$2 \begin{bmatrix} 1 & 3 & 2 \\ 4 & 1 & 1 \\ 1 & 0 & 0 \end{bmatrix} = \begin{bmatrix} 2 & 6 & 4 \\ 8 & 2 & 2 \\ 2 & 0 & 0 \end{bmatrix}$$

$$c \begin{bmatrix} a_{11} & a_{12} & \cdots & a_{1n} \\ a_{21} & a_{22} & \cdots & a_{2n} \end{bmatrix} = \begin{bmatrix} ca_{11} & ca_{12} & \cdots & ca_{1n} \\ ca_{21} & ca_{22} & \cdots & ca_{2n} \end{bmatrix}$$

where c is a scalar.

MATRIX MULTIPLICATION

Suppose A and B are two matrices:

The product AB is defined if and only if the number of columns of A equals the number of rows of B.

In this case the product is a new matrix. The rule for obtaining the entry in the ith row and j^{th} column of the product can be stated as follows. Think of the ith row of the first matrix and the jth column of the second matrix as though they were vectors:

The product of these two vectors gives the number in the ith row and j^{th} column of the product.

For example, suppose we wish to compute AB, where

$$A = \begin{bmatrix} 1 & 0 & 1 \\ 2 & 1 & 0 \end{bmatrix} \quad \text{and} \quad B = \begin{bmatrix} 2 & 0 & 2 \\ 0 & 1 & 1 \\ 1 & 0 & 1 \end{bmatrix}$$

Then, since the columns of A are equal in number to the rows of B (A has three columns, B has three rows), the product will be defined. If we let C denote the new matrix (that is, $C = AB$) then, according to the above rule:

$c_{11} = (1, 0, 1)(2, 0, 1) = 2 + 0 + 1 = 3$

$c_{12} = (1, 0, 1)(0, 1, 0) = 0 + 0 + 0 = 0$

$c_{13} = (1, 0, 1)(2, 1, 1) = 2 + 0 + 1 = 3$

$c_{21} = (2, 1, 0)(2, 0, 1) = 4 + 0 + 0 = 4$

$c_{22} = (2, 1, 0)(0, 1, 0) = 0 + 1 + 0 = 1$

$c_{23} = (2, 1, 0)(2, 1, 1) = 4 + 1 + 0 = 5$

Thus we have

$$C = \begin{bmatrix} 3 & 0 & 3 \\ 4 & 1 & 5 \end{bmatrix}$$

It follows from the definition of the product that
1 The number of rows of the product AB = the number of rows of A.
2 The number of columns of the product AB = the number of columns of B.

We note the order "A times B" is important in matrix multiplication since the product is defined if and only if the number of columns of A equals the number of rows of B. In the example just considered, AB is defined since A has three columns and B has three rows. However, the product BA is not defined (B has three columns but A has two rows). The definition of product is illustrated in the following examples.

Example 1

Suppose

$$A = \begin{bmatrix} 1 & 0 & 1 \\ 1 & 1 & 0 \end{bmatrix} \quad \text{and} \quad B = \begin{bmatrix} 1 & 4 \\ 3 & 7 \end{bmatrix}$$

Then AA is not defined. However, since B is *square* (this means that m and n are the same), BB is defined and has the same dimension as B. Also note that AB is not defined, but BA is defined.

Example 2

Suppose

$$A = \begin{bmatrix} a_{11} & a_{12} & a_{13} \\ a_{21} & a_{22} & a_{23} \end{bmatrix} \quad \text{and} \quad X = \begin{bmatrix} x_1 \\ x_2 \\ x_3 \end{bmatrix}$$

Then AX is defined but XA is not.

$$AX = \begin{bmatrix} a_{11}x_1 + a_{12}x_2 + a_{13}x_3 \\ a_{21}x_1 + a_{22}x_2 + a_{23}x_3 \end{bmatrix} \qquad (AX \text{ is } 2 \times 1)$$

Example 3

Suppose

$$A = \begin{bmatrix} a_{11} & a_{12} & a_{13} \\ a_{21} & a_{22} & a_{23} \end{bmatrix} \quad \text{and} \quad X = [x_1, x_2]$$

Then XA is defined but AX is not.

$$XA = [a_{11}x_1 + a_{21}x_2 a_{12}x_1 + a_{22}x_2 \quad a_{13}x_1 + a_{23}x_2] \qquad (XA \text{ is } 1 \times 3)$$

Example 4

Suppose

$$X = [x_1, x_2] \quad \text{and} \quad Y = \begin{bmatrix} y_1 \\ y_2 \end{bmatrix}$$

Then

$$XY = [x_1 y_1 + x_2 y_2] \qquad (XY \text{ is } 1 \times 1)$$

$$YX = \begin{bmatrix} y_1 x_1 & y_1 x_2 \\ y_2 x_1 & y_2 x_2 \end{bmatrix} \qquad (YX \text{ is } 2 \times 2)$$

A3.4 Relations between Numbers, Vectors, and Matrices

If we think of a number as a one-dimensional vector, or a 1×1 matrix, then it is clear that the operations defined for vectors and matrices (addition, subtraction, multiplication by a scalar, and the product) reduce to the usual operations on numbers. If we think of an n-dimensional vector as either a $1 \times n$ matrix or an $n \times 1$ matrix, then the matrix operations of addition, subtraction and multiplication by a scalar coincide with the corresponding vector operations. A $1 \times n$ matrix is often called a *row vector* (there is a single row) and an $n \times 1$ matrix is a *column vector* (there is a single column).

Let us now see whether or not the rule for multiplying two vectors can be considered a special case of the rule for multiplying two matrices. Suppose, for example, that x and y are n-dimensional vectors. Then we know that the vector product

$$xy = \sum_{i=1}^{n} x_i y_i$$

The vector product xy can be interpreted as a matrix product if we interpret x as a $1 \times n$ matrix (a row vector) and y as an $n \times 1$ matrix (a column vector).

Thus, thinking of x and y as matrices, we would write

$$xy = [x_1, ..., x_n] \begin{bmatrix} y_1 \\ \vdots \\ y_2 \end{bmatrix} = \sum_{i=1}^{n} x_i y_i$$

That is, the same result is obtained by applying either the matrix multiplication rule or the vector multiplication rule, as long as we think of the first vector as a row and the second as a column. This association is of interest because it gives a natural way to define two other useful products: namely, a matrix times a vector and a vector times a matrix. In either case it must be specified as to whether or not the vector is a row or a column. The matrix product rule can then be applied.

For example, suppose A is 2×3 and x is a three-dimensional column vector. Then Ax is interpreted as the product of the 2×3 matrix A and the 3×1 matrix x. In this case xA would not make sense because the number of columns of x and the number of rows of A are not the same. Note that even if x is considered a row vector, the product xA would not be defined. However, if x is a two-dimensional vector then xA makes sense if we consider x to be a row vector (that is, 1×2). In this case Ax makes no sense. If A is a square matrix (say, $n \times n$) and x is an n-dimensional vector, then both Ax and xA can be sensibly interpreted. In the first case x is $n \times 1$. In the second case x is $1 \times n$. It will soon be shown that even when Ax and xA are both defined it could be the case that $Ax \neq xA$.

In the student's first exposure to linear algebra the distinction between row and column vectors is often a point of confusion. A given n-dimensional vector, by itself, can be arbitrarily considered to be a row or a column. Calling it one or the other does not change the vector. For example, the vector

$(1, 2)$ is the same as the vector $\begin{pmatrix} 1 \\ 2 \end{pmatrix}$

which is the same as

$[1 \quad 2]$ or $\begin{bmatrix} 1 \\ 2 \end{bmatrix}$

In this sense it is irrelevant to distinguish between row and column or to identify a vector as one or the other. The time when such a distinction is meaningful is when we are multiplying a matrix times a vector or a vector times a matrix. Then it is important to identify a vector as a row or a column, for different results are obtained in either case. There will be no confusion if the proper identification is always made. It is *almost* always the case that, in a product, a vector following a matrix is a column, and a vector preceding a matrix is a row. In any case, the person who creates the system is obligated to make clear the use of the symbols.

The following examples illustrate the mechanics of multiplications involving matrices and vectors. A careful study of these examples will clarify many of the above points.

Example 1

Let

$$A = \begin{bmatrix} 1 & 0 & 2 \\ -1 & 0 & 1 \end{bmatrix} \quad \text{and} \quad x = \begin{bmatrix} 1 \\ 2 \\ 2 \end{bmatrix}$$

Then

$$Ax = \begin{bmatrix} 1 & 0 & 2 \\ -1 & 0 & 1 \end{bmatrix} \begin{bmatrix} 1 \\ 2 \\ 2 \end{bmatrix} = \begin{bmatrix} 1 + 0 + 4 \\ -1 + 0 + 2 \end{bmatrix} = \begin{bmatrix} 5 \\ 1 \end{bmatrix}$$

Note that xA is not defined because x has one column and A has two rows.

Example 2

Let

$$A = \begin{bmatrix} 1 & 0 & 2 \\ -1 & 0 & 1 \end{bmatrix} \quad \text{and} \quad x = [1 \quad 1]$$

Then

$$xA = [1, \quad 1] \begin{bmatrix} 1 & 0 & 2 \\ -1 & 0 & 1 \end{bmatrix} = [1 - 1 \quad 0 + 0 \quad 2 + 1] = [0 \quad 0 \quad 3]$$

Note that Ax is not defined because A has three columns and x has one row.

Example 3

Suppose

$$A = \begin{bmatrix} 1 & 0 \\ 2 & -1 \end{bmatrix} \quad \text{and} \quad x = (1, \quad 3) = [1 \quad 3]$$

Then

$$xA = [1 \quad 3] \begin{bmatrix} 1 & 0 \\ 2 & -1 \end{bmatrix} = [7 \quad -3] = (7, \quad -3)$$

Example 4

Take A and x as in Example 3 but change x from a row to a column. Then

$$Ax = \begin{bmatrix} 1 & 0 \\ 2 & -1 \end{bmatrix} \begin{bmatrix} 1 \\ 3 \end{bmatrix} = \begin{bmatrix} 1 \\ -1 \end{bmatrix}$$

Thus, Examples 3 and 4 show that even when Ax and xA are both defined it may not be the case that the two products give the same vector.

Example 5

Suppose

$$x = [1, 1], \qquad A = \begin{bmatrix} 0 & 1 & 1 \\ 1 & 1 & 1 \end{bmatrix}, \qquad y = \begin{bmatrix} 2 \\ 1 \\ 0 \end{bmatrix}$$

Let us compute xAy. This can be interpreted as x times Ay, that is, $x(Ay)$, or xA times y, that is, $(xA)y$. The same result is obtained in either case. Let us compute $x(Ay)$. First, we obtain

$$Ay = \begin{bmatrix} 1 \\ 3 \end{bmatrix}$$

Hence,

$$x(Ay) = \begin{bmatrix} 1 & 1 \end{bmatrix} \begin{bmatrix} 1 \\ 3 \end{bmatrix} = 4$$

Alternatively, we can compute $(xA)y$. First we obtain

$$xA = \begin{bmatrix} 1 & 2 & 2 \end{bmatrix}$$

Hence,

$$(xA)y = \begin{bmatrix} 1 & 2 & 2 \end{bmatrix} \begin{bmatrix} 2 \\ 1 \\ 0 \end{bmatrix} = 4$$

Example 6

Let

$$A = \begin{bmatrix} 1 & 0 & 2 \\ -1 & 0 & 1 \end{bmatrix} \qquad \text{and} \qquad x = \begin{bmatrix} x_1 \\ x_2 \\ x_3 \end{bmatrix}$$

Then

$$Ax = \begin{bmatrix} 1 & 0 & 2 \\ -1 & 0 & 1 \end{bmatrix} \begin{bmatrix} x_1 \\ x_2 \\ x_3 \end{bmatrix} = \begin{bmatrix} x_1 + 2x_3 \\ -x_1 + x_3 \end{bmatrix}$$

Example 7

Let

$$A = \begin{bmatrix} a_{11} & a_{12} \\ a_{21} & a_{22} \end{bmatrix} \quad \text{and} \quad x = \begin{bmatrix} x_1 \\ x_2 \end{bmatrix}$$

Then

$$Ax = \begin{bmatrix} a_{11} & a_{12} \\ a_{21} & a_{22} \end{bmatrix} \begin{bmatrix} x_1 \\ x_2 \end{bmatrix} = \begin{bmatrix} a_{11}x_1 + a_{12}x_2 \\ a_{21}x_1 + a_{22}x_2 \end{bmatrix}$$

Example 8

Let

$$A = \begin{bmatrix} a_{11} & a_{12} \\ a_{21} & a_{22} \end{bmatrix} \quad \text{and} \quad x = [x_1, x_2]$$

Then

$$xA = [x_1, x_2] \begin{bmatrix} a_{11} & a_{12} \\ a_{21} & a_{22} \end{bmatrix} = [a_{11}x_1 + a_{21}x_2 \quad a_{12}x_1 + a_{22}x_2]$$

Compare this result with that in Example 7. Note that the resulting vectors are the same if and only if $a_{12} = a_{21}$.

Example 9

Let A denote a general $m \times n$ matrix and x denote an n-dimensional column vector (that is, x is $n \times 1$). Then

$$Ax = \begin{bmatrix} a_{11} & \cdots & a_{1n} \\ \vdots & & \vdots \\ a_{m1} & \cdots & a_{mn} \end{bmatrix} \begin{bmatrix} x_1 \\ \vdots \\ x_n \end{bmatrix} = \begin{bmatrix} a_{11}x_1 + \ldots + a_{1n}x_n \\ \vdots & & \vdots \\ a_{m1}x_1 + \ldots + a_{mn}x_n \end{bmatrix}$$

Example 10

Consider three products and three locations. Let S be a 3×3 matrix where S_{ij} is the quantity of product i sold at location j and P be a three-dimensional vector where P_i is the sales price per unit of product i.

If we think of P as a row vector then PS is defined. Letting R denote this product, we can write

$$R = PS$$

where R is a row vector. An entry R_j in R is the revenue of location j since

$$R_j = \sum_{i=1}^{3} P_i S_{ij}$$

Alternatively, if we think of P as a column vector then SP is also defined. Letting Q denote this product, we can write

$$Q = SP$$

where Q is a column vector. An entry Q_i does not have any economic meaning. For example,

$$Q_1 = \sum_{j=1}^{3} S_{1j} P_j$$

Note that when $j = 2$, S_{12} is the quantity of product 1 sold at location 2 and we are multiplying this by the sales price of product 2.

A3.5 Matrix Representation of Linear Equations and Inequalities

At this point in the discussion, it is appropriate to assign a formal meaning to the assertion that "one vector equals another," or "one matrix equals another." We say that

---

Two vectors are equal if they have the same dimension and corresponding components are equal.

Thus, if x and y are n-dimensional vectors, we say that $x = y$ if and only if $x_i = y_i$ for each $i = 1, \ldots, n$. Also, if x and y are of the same dimension, we say that $x \le y$ if and only if $x_i \le y_i$ for each i. For example, $x \ge 0$ means $(x_1, \ldots, x_n) \ge (0, \ldots, 0)$, which means $x_i \ge 0$, $i = 1, \ldots, n$. We say that

---

Two matrices are equal if they have the same dimension and corresponding entries are equal.

Thus, if A and B are matrices of the same dimension, $A = B$ means $a_{ij} = b_{ij}$ for all i and j.

It is now an easy matter to demonstrate the shorthand notation for systems of linear equations or inequalities. Let us begin with system (III) in Section A3.1:

$$
\begin{aligned}
-6x_1 + x_2 + \ 3x_3 + \ \ x_4 &= \ \ 9 \\
2x_1 - x_2 + 14x_3 - \ 2x_4 &= -1 \\
3x_1 + x_2 + \ \ x_3 + 16x_4 &= \ \ 2
\end{aligned}
$$

The rules for representing such a system are the following. Let A denote the matrix of coefficients of the variables in this system, where the coefficients are "lifted" directly from the system. That is,

$$
A = \begin{bmatrix} -6 & 1 & 3 & 1 \\ 2 & -1 & 14 & -2 \\ 3 & 1 & 1 & 16 \end{bmatrix}
$$

Let b denote the column vector comprising the terms on the right-hand side of the equalities. That is,

$$
b = \begin{bmatrix} 9 \\ -1 \\ 2 \end{bmatrix}
$$

Finally, let x be a column vector. That is,

$$
x = \begin{bmatrix} x_1 \\ x_2 \\ x_3 \\ x_4 \end{bmatrix}
$$

Then the above system is written in shorthand as

$Ax = b$

To show that this assertion is correct, we shall expand $Ax = b$. Thus, $Ax = b$ is literally the same as

$$\begin{bmatrix} -6 & 1 & 3 & 1 \\ 2 & -1 & 14 & -2 \\ 3 & 1 & 1 & 16 \end{bmatrix} \begin{bmatrix} x_1 \\ x_2 \\ x_3 \\ x_4 \end{bmatrix} = \begin{bmatrix} 9 \\ -1 \\ 2 \end{bmatrix}$$

Carrying out the multiplication on the left, we obtain

$$\begin{bmatrix} -6x_1 + x_2 + 3x_3 + x_4 \\ 2x_1 - x_2 + 14x_3 - 2x_4 \\ 3x_1 + x_2 + x_3 + 16x_4 \end{bmatrix} = \begin{bmatrix} 9 \\ -1 \\ 2 \end{bmatrix}$$

On each side of this equality we have a three-dimensional column vector. According to our definition of equality of vectors (or equality of matrices), this equality means that corresponding components are equal, which means

$-6x_1 + x_2 + 3x_3 + x_4 = 9$

$2x_1 - x_2 + 14x_3 - 2x_4 = -1$

$3x_1 + x_2 + x_3 + 16x_4 = 2$

We have thus shown that the above system is the same as the system $Ax = b$, with A, x, and b defined in the way we indicated. If you understand this special case then you will be able to easily demonstrate for yourself that (IV), the general system of linear equations in (Section A3.1,) can be written in the form

$Ax = b$

where

$$A = \begin{bmatrix} a_{11} & a_{12} & \cdots & a_{1n} \\ a_{21} & a_{22} & \cdots & a_{2n} \\ \vdots & \vdots & & \vdots \\ a_{m1} & a_{m2} & \cdots & a_{mn} \end{bmatrix} \quad \text{and} \quad x = \begin{bmatrix} x_1 \\ x_2 \\ \vdots \\ x_n \end{bmatrix} \quad \text{and} \quad b = \begin{bmatrix} b_1 \\ b_2 \\ \vdots \\ b_m \end{bmatrix}$$

Also, (VI), the general system of linear inequalities in Section A3.1, can be represented as

$Ax \le b$

where A, x, and b are the same as above.

As an illustration of these ideas, suppose a warehousing superintendant has four warehouses under his authority. Each warehouse can ship stainless rod to each of three marketing depots. Suppose that next month the minimum requirements shown in Figure A3.2 must be sent to the depots. If x_{ij} is the amount to be sent from warehouse i to depot j, then the following conditions must be satisifed:

$$\begin{aligned} x_{11} + x_{21} + x_{31} + x_{41} & & \ge 100 \\ x_{12} + x_{22} + x_{32} + x_{42} & & \ge 125 \\ x_{13} + x_{23} + x_{33} + x_{43} & \ge 75 \\ x_{ij} & \ge 0 \quad \text{all } i, j \end{aligned}$$

Figure A3.2

Depot	Minimal Amount of Stainless Rod
1	100 tons
2	125 tons
3	75 tons

In matrix notation this is written as $Ax \geq b$ where

$$A = \begin{bmatrix} 1 & 1 & 1 & 1 & 0 & 0 & 0 & 0 & 0 & 0 & 0 & 0 \\ 0 & 0 & 0 & 0 & 1 & 1 & 1 & 1 & 0 & 0 & 0 & 0 \\ 0 & 0 & 0 & 0 & 0 & 0 & 0 & 0 & 1 & 1 & 1 & 1 \end{bmatrix} \quad \text{and}$$

$$x = \begin{bmatrix} x_{11} \\ x_{21} \\ x_{31} \\ x_{41} \\ x_{12} \\ x_{22} \\ x_{32} \\ x_{42} \\ x_{13} \\ x_{23} \\ x_{33} \\ x_{43} \end{bmatrix} \quad \text{and} \quad b = \begin{bmatrix} 100 \\ 125 \\ 75 \end{bmatrix}$$

As a final illustration, consider a production process where each of two products must be processed on each of two machines. The amount of time (in hours) required to process a unit of each product on each machine is given in Figure A3.3. Suppose the total hours available next month on machine 1 is 27 and on machine 2 is 48. If x_1 denotes the number of units of product 1 to be made next month and x_2 the number of units of product 2, then the following conditions must be satisfied:

$$9x_1 + 3x_2 \leq 27$$

$$8x_1 + 12x_2 \leq 48$$

In matrix form this is written as $Ax \leq b$ where

$$A = \begin{bmatrix} 9 & 3 \\ 8 & 12 \end{bmatrix} \quad \text{and} \quad x = \begin{bmatrix} x_1 \\ x_2 \end{bmatrix} \quad \text{and} \quad b = \begin{bmatrix} 27 \\ 48 \end{bmatrix}$$

Figure A3.3

	Product	
Machine	1	2
1	9	3
2	8	12

A3.6 The Transpose and Symmetry

The *transpose* of an $m \times n$ matrix A is the new $n \times m$ matrix obtained by interchanging rows and columns. This new matrix, the transpose of A, is denoted as A^T or A'. Thus, the ith row of A' is the ith column of A, and vice versa. For example, if

$$A = \begin{bmatrix} 0 & 1 & -2 \\ 3 & 1 & 2 \end{bmatrix}$$

then

$$A' = \begin{bmatrix} 0 & 3 \\ 1 & 1 \\ -2 & 2 \end{bmatrix} \quad \text{and} \quad A'' = A$$

In the special case when A and A' are the same matrix, A is said to be *symmetric*. This is equivalent to stating that $a_{ij} = a_{ji}$ for all $i \neq j$. For example, suppose

$$A = \begin{bmatrix} 2 & 3 & 1 \\ 3 & 6 & 4 \\ 1 & 4 & 5 \end{bmatrix}$$

Then $a_{12} = a_{21} = 3$, $a_{13} = a_{31} = 1$, $a_{23} = a_{32} = 4$, and A is symmetric.

Let us suppose that the product matrix AB is defined. Then it can be shown that $(AB)' = B'A'$. Thus, if A is $m \times n$ and x is $n \times 1$, then $(Ax)' = x'A'$.

In discussions involving vector and matrix notation, it is often implicitly assumed that all "unprimed" vectors are to be interpreted as columns, and primes are rows. Thus, if A is a matrix and x is a vector, then in the expression Ax it is assumed that x is a column. In the expression $x'A$ it is assumed that x' is a row. Also, using the same convention, the scalar product xy would be unambiguously written as a row times a column, that is, $x'y$.

A3.7 Exercises

1 Suppose

$$A = \begin{bmatrix} 1 & 2 & 1 \\ 1 & 1 & 0 \end{bmatrix} \quad \text{and} \quad B = \begin{bmatrix} 1 & 0 \\ 2 & 0 \\ 1 & 1 \end{bmatrix}$$

   a Compute AB.
   b Compute BA.

2 In each of the following cases, tell whether A times B is defined, and if it is give the dimension of the product matrix.
   a A is 64×129, B is 64×129.
   b A is 19×80, B is 80×30.
   c A is 1×10, B is 10×990.
   d A is 10×20, B is 900×20.
   e A is 1×3, B is 3×1.

3 Let

$$A = \begin{bmatrix} 1 & 0 & 1 & 2 \\ 2 & 2 & 1 & 4 \end{bmatrix} \quad \text{and} \quad b = \begin{bmatrix} -1 \\ 12 \end{bmatrix} \quad \text{and} \quad x = \begin{bmatrix} x_1 \\ x_2 \\ x_3 \\ x_4 \end{bmatrix}$$

Expand $Ax = b$. That is, write out the system of equations that $Ax = b$ represents.

4   Let x and y be n-dimensional *vectors*.
   a Show that $x + y = y + x$.
   b Show that $xy = yx$.

5   If c is a scalar and x is a vector, then the operation cx has been defined. Suppose we define xc to be the same as cx. Now choose three two-dimensional vectors x, y, and z that demonstrate that $(xy)z \neq x(yz)$.

6   Suppose x_1, x_2, x_3, x_4 are each three-dimensional vectors. Let x_{ij} denote the jth component of x_i. Write out each of the components of $x_1 + x_2 - x_3 + 2x_4$.

7   Define

$$A = \begin{bmatrix} 1 & 3 & 0 \\ 2 & 4 & 1 \end{bmatrix} \quad \text{and} \quad x = \begin{bmatrix} 1 \\ 0 \\ 1 \end{bmatrix} \quad \text{and} \quad B = Ax$$

Compute B and B' and show that $B' = x'A'$.

8   Consider three products and three locations. Define S as a 3×3 matrix where S_{ij} is the quantity of product i sold at location j and P is a three-dimensional column vector where P_i is the sales price per unit of product i. Write an expression using S' to find a vector R where R_i is the total revenue accrued at location i.

9   Suppose

$$A = \begin{bmatrix} 12 \\ 21 \end{bmatrix} \quad \text{and} \quad x = \begin{bmatrix} 1 \\ 3 \end{bmatrix}$$

Show that Ax and $x'A$ have the same components.

10 Suppose A and B are square matrices of the same dimension and both symmetric. Show with an example that AB and BA may not be the same. What is the relationship between AB and BA?

11 Suppose A is $m \times n$ and x is an n-dimensional column vector. It should be clear that Ax and $x'A$ are both defined only if $m = n$. Let us now suppose that this is the case; that is, A is $n \times n$.
   a Show that Ax and $x'A'$ have the same components.
   b Show that if A is symmetric as well as square then Ax and $x'A$ have the same components.

12 A general quadratic function of two variables can be represented

$$f(x_1, x_2) = ax_1^2 + bx_1x_2 + cx_2^2 + dx_1 + ex_2 + k$$

Show that this quadratic function can be represented in matrix notation

$$f(x_1, x_2) = x'Qx + Lx + k$$

where

$$x = \begin{bmatrix} x_1 \\ x_2 \end{bmatrix} \quad \text{and} \quad x' = [x_1 \quad x_2]$$

$$Q = \begin{bmatrix} a & b/2 \\ b/2 & c \end{bmatrix} \quad \text{and} \quad L = [d \quad e]$$

This turns out to be a special case of the fact that a general quadratic function of n variables has the form $x'Ax + Lx + k$ where A is an $n \times n$ symmetric matrix, L is a vector, and k a scalar. For this reason, much in the study of quadratic functions reduces to the study of properties of matrices.

13 Suppose a single product is made in three plants and sold in four marketing districts. Assume everything produced is sent to the marketing districts and sold. Let x_{ij} denote the quantity of product sent from plant i to be sold in marketing district j. Let X be the

matrix whose entries are x_{ij}. Let S be a three-dimensional column vector such that S_i is the total amount sent from plant i. Let D be a four-dimensional column vector such that D_i is the total amount sold in district i. In each of the following cases, define vectors e and $\hat{e}$ so that the stated conditions are satisfied:

a $S = Xe$. Write each component of S in summation notation.

b $D = X'e$. Write each component of D in summation notation.

c The total amount sent from all plants $= \hat{e}'Xe$. Use summation notation to represent $\hat{e}'Xe$.

d The total amount sold in all districts $= \hat{e}'X'e$. Use summation notation to represent $\hat{e}'X'e$.

e What is the relation between the quantities in parts c and d?

A3.8 Solutions to Exercises

1 **a** $AB = \begin{bmatrix} 6 & 1 \\ 3 & 0 \end{bmatrix}$

b $BA = \begin{bmatrix} 1 & 2 & 1 \\ 2 & 4 & 2 \\ 2 & 3 & 1 \end{bmatrix}$

This shows that even when AB and BA are both defined, it is generally not true that $AB = BA$.

2 **a** Undefined
b 19×30
c 1×990
d Undefined
e 1×1

3 $x_1 \qquad + x_3 + 2x_4 = -1$
$2x_1 + 2x_2 + x_3 + 4x_4 = 12$

4 **a** $(x_1, ..., x_n) + (y_1, ..., y_n) = (x_1 + y_1, ..., x_n + y_n)$
$$= (y_1 + x_1, ..., y_n + x_n)$$
$$= (y_1, ..., y_n) + (x_1, ..., x_n)$$

b $xy = \displaystyle\sum_{i=1}^{n} x_i y_i = \sum_{i=1}^{n} y_i x_i = yx$

5 $x = (1, 1)$, $y = (1, 2)$, $z = (-1, 1)$
$xy = 3$, $yz = 1$
$(xy)z = (-3, 3)$, $x(yz) = (yz)x = (1, 1)$
Hence, $(xy)z \neq (yz)x$.

6 The first component is $x_{11} + x_{21} - x_{31} + 2x_{41}$. The second component is $x_{12} + x_{22} - x_{32} + 2x_{42}$. The third component is $x_{13} + x_{23} - x_{33} + 2x_{43}$.

7 $B = \begin{bmatrix} 1 & 3 & 0 \\ 2 & 4 & 1 \end{bmatrix} \begin{bmatrix} 1 \\ 0 \\ 1 \end{bmatrix} = \begin{bmatrix} 1 \\ 3 \end{bmatrix}$

$B' = \begin{bmatrix} 1 & 3 \end{bmatrix}$

$$[1 \quad 0 \quad 1]A' = [1 \quad 0 \quad 1]\begin{bmatrix} 1 & 2 \\ 3 & 4 \\ 0 & 1 \end{bmatrix} = [1 \quad 3] = B'$$

8 $R = S'P' = \begin{pmatrix} s_{11} & s_{21} & s_{31} \\ s_{12} & s_{22} & s_{32} \\ s_{13} & s_{23} & s_{33} \end{pmatrix}\begin{pmatrix} P_1 \\ P_2 \\ P_3 \end{pmatrix}$

so

$$R_j = \sum_{i=1}^{3} S_{ij} P_i$$

9 Since

$$A = \begin{bmatrix} 1 & 2 \\ 2 & 1 \end{bmatrix} \quad \text{and} \quad A' = \begin{bmatrix} 1 & 2 \\ 2 & 1 \end{bmatrix}$$

and $A = A'$,

$$Ax = \begin{bmatrix} 1 & 2 \\ 2 & 1 \end{bmatrix}\begin{bmatrix} 1 \\ 3 \end{bmatrix} = \begin{bmatrix} 7 \\ 5 \end{bmatrix}$$

$$x'A = [1 \quad 3]\begin{bmatrix} 1 & 2 \\ 2 & 1 \end{bmatrix} = [7 \quad 5]$$

and hence the components are the same.

10 $A = \begin{bmatrix} 1 & 2 \\ 2 & 3 \end{bmatrix} \quad \text{and} \quad B = \begin{bmatrix} 0 & 3 \\ 3 & 1 \end{bmatrix} \quad \text{and}$

$$AB = \begin{bmatrix} 6 & 5 \\ 9 & 9 \end{bmatrix} \quad \text{and} \quad BA = \begin{bmatrix} 6 & 9 \\ 5 & 9 \end{bmatrix}$$

$$AB = ((AB)')' = (B'A')' = (BA)'$$

11 **a** The ith component of Ax is

$$\sum_{j=1}^{n} a_{ij} x_j$$

This is also the ith component of $x'A'$.

b If A is symmetric, $A = A'$. In this case, $(Ax)' = x'A$. Thus, Ax and $x'A$ have the same components.

12 $x'Qx + Lx + k = [x_1 \quad x_2]\begin{bmatrix} a & b/2 \\ b/2 & c \end{bmatrix}\begin{bmatrix} x_1 \\ x_2 \end{bmatrix} + [d \quad e]\begin{bmatrix} x_1 \\ x_2 \end{bmatrix} + k$

$$= [x_1 \quad x_2]\begin{bmatrix} ax_1 + bx_2/2 \\ bx_1/2 + cx_2 \end{bmatrix} + [d \quad e]\begin{bmatrix} x_1 \\ x_2 \end{bmatrix} + k$$

$$= ax_1^2 + (bx_1x_2/2) + (bx_1x_2/2) + cx_2^2 + dx_1 + ex_2 + k$$

$$= ax_1^2 + bx_1x_2 + cx_2^2 + dx_1 + ex_2 + k$$

13

$$\begin{matrix} & & \text{District 2} \\ & & \downarrow \\ X = & & \begin{bmatrix} x_{11} & x_{12} & x_{13} & x_{14} \\ x_{21} & x_{22} & x_{23} & x_{24} \\ x_{31} & x_{32} & x_{33} & x_{34} \end{bmatrix} \\ \text{Plant 2} \nearrow & & \end{matrix}$$

a $S = Xe = $ [total sent from plant 1, total sent from plant 2, total sent from plant 3]
where

$$e = \begin{bmatrix} 1 \\ 1 \\ 1 \\ 1 \end{bmatrix} \qquad S_i = \sum_{j=1}^{4} x_{ij}, \qquad i = 1, 2, 3$$

b $D' = e'X$, where $e' = [1, 1, 1]$. Hence $D = (e'X)' = X'e$
where

$$e = \begin{bmatrix} 1 \\ 1 \\ 1 \end{bmatrix}$$

$$D_j = \sum_{i=1}^{3} x_{ij}, \qquad j = 1, 2, 3, 4.$$

c $\hat{e}' = [1, 1, 1]$ $\qquad e = \begin{bmatrix} 1 \\ 1 \\ 1 \\ 1 \end{bmatrix}$ $\qquad \hat{e}' Xe = \sum_{i=1}^{3} \sum_{j=1}^{4} x_{ij}$

d $\hat{e}' = [1, 1, 1, 1]$ $\qquad e = \begin{bmatrix} 1 \\ 1 \\ 1 \end{bmatrix}$ $\qquad e' X' e = \sum_{j=1}^{4} \sum_{i=1}^{3} x_{ij}$

e They are the same.

Bibliography

Here is a brief bibliography for the major topics covered in this text. Works that contain substantial amounts of introductory material are identified by a bullet.

THE MEANING, USE, AND RELEVANCE OF MODELS

● 1 Ackoff, R. L., "Some Ideas on Education in the Management Sciences," *Management Science, Appl. Series,* **17**, no. 2, October 1970.

● 2 Bedow, B., "The Ten Natural Laws of Operations Analysis," *Interfaces,* **7**, no. 3, May 1977.

● 3 Caywood, T. E., "How Can We Improve Operations Research," *Operations Research,* **18**, no. 4, July–August 1970.

● 4 Churchman, C. W., "Operations Research as a Profession," *Management Science, Appl. Series,* **17**, no. 2, October 1970.

● 5 Churchman, C. W., "Perspectives of the Systems Approach," *Interfaces,* **4**, no. 4, August 1974.

● 6 Churchman, C. W., "Reliability of Models in the Social Sciences," *Interfaces,* **4**, no. 1, November 1973.

● 7 Eilon, S., "What Is a Decision?," *Management Science, Appl. Series,* **16**, no. 4, December 1969.

● 8 Fromm, Erich, "Thoughts on Bureaucracy," *Management Science, Appl. Series,* **16**, no. 12, August 1970.

● 9 Geoffrion, Arthur, M., "The Purpose of Mathematical Programming Is Insight, not Numbers," *Interfaces,* **7**, no. 1, November 1976.

●10 Graham, Robert J., "Is Management Science Arcane?," *Interfaces,* **7**, no. 2, February 1977.

●11 Greenberger, Martin, Matthew A. Crenson, and Brian L. Crissey, *Models in The Policy Process.* New York: Russell Sage Foundation, 1976.

●12 Gruber, W. H., and J. S. Niles, "Problems in the Utilization of Management Science/Operations Research: A State of the Art Survey," *Interfaces,* **2**, no. 1, November 1971.

●13 Jensen, A., "International Aspects of Operations Research and the Future of Our Industrial Society," *Interfaces,* **4**, no. 4, August 1974.

●14 Johnson, E. A., "The Long-Range Future of Operational Research," *Operations Research,* **8**, no. 1, January 1960.

●15 King, W. R., "On the Nature and Form of Operations Research," *Operations Research,* **15**, no. 6, November–December 1967.

●16 "Lawrence Klein and His Forecasting Machine," *Fortune,* **XCI**, no. 3, March 1975.

●17 Lazarus, M., "The Elegance and the Relevance of Mathematics," from "Point of View," *The Chronicle of Higher Education,* **XI**, no. 12, December 1, 1975.

●18 Littauer, S. B., "What's OR-MS?" *Management Science, Appl. Series,* **17**, no. 2, October 1970.

●19 Little, J. D. C., "Models and Managers: The Concept of a Decision Calculus," *Management Science,* **16**, no. 8, April 1970.

●20 Magee, J. F., "Progress in the Management Sciences," *Interfaces,* **3**, no. 2, February 1973.

●21　Martin, Michael J. C., and Raymond A. Denison, *Case Exercises In Operations Research.* London: John Wiley & Sons, Ltd., 1971.

●22　Morris, W. T., "On the Art of Modeling," *Management Science,* **13**, no. 12, August 1967.

●23　"Piercing Future Fog," *Business Week,* **I**, no. 2378, April 28, 1975.

●24　Saaty, T. L., "The Future of Operations Research in the Government," *Interfaces,* **2**, no. 2, February 1972.

●25　Simon, Herbert A., *The New Science of Management Decision.* Englewood Cliffs, N.J.: Prentice-Hall, Inc., 1960.

●26　Simon, Leonard S., "What is a Management Scientist?," *Interfaces,* **1**, no. 2, February 1971.

●27　Starr, M. K., "The Politics of Management Science," *Interfaces,* **1**, no. 4, June 1971.

●28　"Three-Pronged Service Strategy Helps DRI Customers Forecast," *Computerworld,* **IX**, no. 10, March 5, 1975.

●29　Urban, G. L., "Building Models for Decision Makers," *Interfaces,* **4**, no. 3, May 1974.

●30　von Lanzenauer, Christoph H., *Cases in Operations Research.* London, Ontario: The University of Western Ontario, 1975.

●31　Wagner, Harvey M., "The ABC's of OR," *Operations Research,* **19**, no. 6, December 1969.

●32　Zeleny, M., "Managers Without Management Science?," *Interfaces,* **5**, no. 4, August 1975.

LINEAR PROGRAMMING, THEORY, APPLICATIONS, AND SENSITIVITY ANALYSIS

1　Charnes, A., and W. W. Cooper, *Management Models and Industrial Applications of Linear Programming,* vols. I and II. New York: John Wiley & Sons, Inc., 1961.

2　Dantzig, George B., *Linear Programming and Extensions.* Princeton, N.J.: Princeton University Press, 1963.

● 3　Driebeek, Norman J., *Applied Linear Programming.* Reading, Mass.: Addison-Wesley Publishing Company, 1969.

4　Gass, Saul I., *Linear Programming: Methods and Applications,* 3rd ed., New York: McGraw-Hill Book Company, 1969.

5　Hadley, G., *Linear Programming.* Reading, Mass.: Addison-Wesley Publishing Company, Inc. 1962.

6　Hays-Orchard, William, *Advanced Linear-Programming Computing Techniques.* New York: McGraw-Hill Book Company, 1968.

● 7　Hillier, Frederick S., and Gerald J. Lieberman, *Operations Research.* San Francisco: Holden-Day, Inc., 1967.

● 8　Simmons, Donald M., *Linear Programming for Operations Research.* San Francisco: Holden-Day, Inc., 1972.

9　Spivey, Allen W., and Robert M. Thrall, *Linear Optimization.* New York: Holt, Rinehart and Winston, Inc., 1970.

●10　Wagner, Harvey, M., *Principles of Operations Research.* Englewood Cliffs, N.J.: Prentice-Hall, Inc., 1969.

NONLINEAR PROGRAMMING

1　Avriel, Mordecai, *Nonlinear Programming: Analysis and Methods.* Englewood Cliffs, N.J.: Prentice-Hall, Inc., 1976.

2　Beltrami, Edward J., *An Algorithmic Approach to Nonlinear Analysis and Optimization.* New York: Academic Press, Inc., 1970.

3 Bradley, Stephen P., Arnoldo C. Hax, and Thomas L. Magnanti, *Applied Mathematical Programming.* Reading, Mass.: Addison-Wesley Publishing Company, 1977.

4 Fiacco, Anthony V., and Garth P. McCormick, *Nonlinear Programming and Sequential Unconstrained Minimization Techniques.* New York: John Wiley & Sons, Inc., 1968.

5 Hadley, G., *Nonlinear and Dynamic Programming.* Reading, Mass.: Addison-Wesley Publishing Company, Inc., 1964.

6 Lasdon, Leon S., *Optimization Theory for Large Systems.* New York: The Macmillan Company, 1970.

7 Mangasarian, Olvi L., *Nonlinear Programming.* New York: McGraw-Hill Book Company, 1969.

8 Polak, E., *Computational Methods in Optimization.* New York: Academic Press, Inc., 1971.

9 Vajda, S., *Theory of Linear and Non-Linear Programming.* London: Longman Group Ltd., 1974.

●**10** Wagner, Harvey M., *Principles of Operations Research.* Englewood Cliffs, N.J.: Prentice-Hall, Inc., 1969.

●**11** Zangwill, Willard I., *Nonlinear Programming: A Unified Approach.* Englewood Cliffs, N.J.: Prentice-Hall, Inc., 1969.

PRODUCTION AND INVENTORY MODELS

1 Arrow, K., S. Karlin, and H. Scarf, *Studies in the Mathematical Theory of Inventory and Production.* Stanford, Calif.: Stanford University Press, 1958.

● **2** Brown, Robert G., *Decision Rules for Inventory Management.* New York: Holt, Rinehart and Winston, Inc., 1967.

● **3** Buffa, E., *Production-Inventory Systems: Planning and Control.* Homewood, Ill.: Richard D. Irwin, Inc., 1968.

4 Conway, Richard W., William L. Maxwell, and Louis W. Miller, *Theory of Scheduling.* Reading, Mass.: Addison-Wesley Publishing Company, 1967.

5 Hadley, G. and T. M. Whitin, *Analysis of Inventory Systems.* Englewood Cliffs, N.J.: Prentice-Hall, Inc., 1963.

6 Johnson, L., and Douglas C. Montgomery, *Operations Research in Production Planning, Scheduling, and Inventory Control.* New York: John Wiley & Sons, Inc., 1974.

● **7** Naddor, Eliezer, *Inventory Systems.* New York: John Wiley & Sons, Inc., 1966.

● **8** Orlicky, Joseph, *Material Requirements Planning.* New York: McGraw-Hill, Inc., 1975.

INTEGER PROGRAMMING, NETWORK MODELS, AND PERT

1 Berge, Claude, *The Theory of Graphs.* London: Methuen & Co., Ltd., 1962.

2 Christofides, Nicos, *Graph Theory.* London: Academic Press, Ltd., 1975.

3 Garfinkel, Robert S., and George L. Nemhauser, *Integer Programming.* Canada: John Wiley & Sons, Inc., 1972.

4 Greenberg, Harold, *Integer Programming.* New York: Academic Press, Inc., 1971.

5 Hu, T. C., *Integer Programming and Network Flows.* Reading, Mass.: Addison-Wesley Publishing Company, 1969.

6 Thesen, Arne, *Computer Methods in Operations Research.* New York: Academic Press, Inc., 1978.

● **7** Wagner, Harvey M., *Principles of Operations Research.* Englewood Cliffs, N.J.: Prentice-Hall, Inc., 1969.

8 Zionts, Stanley, *Linear and Integer Programming.* Englewood Cliffs, N.J.: Prentice-Hall, Inc., 1974.

PROBABILITY MODELS

●1   Freund, John E., *Statistics*. Englewood Cliffs, N.J.: Prentice-Hall, Inc., 1970.

2   Hadley, G., *Introduction to Probability and Statistical Decision Theory*. San Francisco: Holden-Day, Inc., 1967.

3   Parzen, Emanuel, *Modern Probability Theory and Its Applications*. New York: John Wiley & Sons, Inc., 1960.

4   Ross, Sheldon M., *Applied Probability Models With Optimization Applications*. San Francisco: Holden-Day, Inc., 1970.

●5   Sasaki, Kyohei, *Statistics for Modern Business Decision Making*. Belmont, Calif.: Wadsworth Publishing Company, Inc., 1969.

●6   Schlaifer, Robert, *Probability and Statistics for Business Decisions*. New York: McGraw-Hill, Inc., 1959.

DECISION ANALYSIS AND UTILITY

●1   Chernoff, Herman, and Lincoln E. Moses, *Elementary Decision Theory*. London: John Wiley & Sons, Inc., 1959.

2   Howard, Ronald A., *Dynamic Probabilistic Systems*. Canada: John Wiley & Sons, Inc., 1971.

3   Pratt, John W., Howard Raiffa, and Robert Schlaifer, *Introduction to Statistical Decision Theory*. New York: McGraw-Hill, Inc., 1965.

4   Raiffa, Howard and Robert Schlaifer, *Applied Statistical Decision Theory*. Boston: Division of Research, Harvard Business School, 1961.

●5   Raiffa, Howard, *Decision Analysis*. Reading, Mass.: Addison-Wesley, Inc., 1970.

6   Schlaifer, Robert, *Analysis of Decisions Under Uncertainty*. New York: McGraw-Hill, Inc., 1969.

FORECASTING

1   Box, G. E. P., and G. M. Jenkins, *Time Series Analysis, Forecasting and Control.* San Francisco: Holden-Day, 1970.

2   Brown, Robert, *Statistical Forecasting for Inventory Control*. New York: McGraw-Hill Book Company, 1959.

●3   Granger, C. W. J. and Paul Newbold, *Forecasting Economic Time Series*. New York: Academic Press, 1977.

QUEUING MODELS

1   Conway, R. W., W. L. Maxwell, and L. W. Miller, *Theory of Scheduling*. Reading, Mass.: Addison-Wesley Publishing Company, Inc., 1967.

●2   Cooper, Robert B., *Introduction to Queuing Theory*. New York: The Macmillian Company, 1972.

3   Cox, D. R., and Walter L. Smith, *Queues*. London: Methuen & Co., Ltd., 1961.

●4   Kleinrock, Leonard, *Queueing Systems*. New York: John Wiley & Sons, Inc., 1975.

5   Saaty, Thomas L., *Elements of Queueing Theory*. New York: McGraw-Hill Book Company, Inc., 1961.

SIMULATION

1 Fishman, George S., *Concepts and Methods in Discrete Event Digital Simulation.* New York: John Wiley & Sons, Inc., 1973.

●2 Gordon, Geoffrey, *System Simulation,* 2nd ed., Englewood Cliffs, N.J.: Prentice-Hall, Inc., 1978.

●3 Schrieber, Albert N., ed., *Corporate Simulation Models.* Seattle: The University of Washington Printing Plant, 1970.

4 Thesen, Arne, *Computer Methods in Operations Research.* New York: Academic Press, 1978.

Glossary

ABC classification scheme A scheme for partitioning items held in inventory into three categories on the basis of their contribution to the total cost of carrying inventory. Typically, a small proportion of the items (the A items) contributes a large proportion of the total cost.

Active constraint In a constrained optimization model, an inequality constraint for which the slack variable associated with the constraint has a zero value in the optimal solution; also called a *binding, effective,* or *tight constraint.*

Activity analysis The process of determining the changes in the current optimal solution that would be necessary to produce a particular dual price or reduced cost.

Aggregated data Data that are summed across several subcategories.

Algorithm A numerical method for solving a specified problem.

Alternative optima The existence of more than one set of optimal values for the decision variables; that is, the optimal solution is not unique.

Arc The entity connecting two nodes in a network model.

Arrival process A model describing the arrival of units to a queuing system.

Backlogging In inventory models, the assumption that fulfillment of demand can be delayed.

Basic variables The positive variables at a nondegenerate corner in an LP problem.

Basis The set of basic variables.

Batch processing A mode of running jobs on a computer in which the entire set of instructions is submitted at one time. See also *Conversational mode.*

Binding constraint See *Active constraint.*

Bootstrap forecast A forecast based on an extrapolation of a series of historical observations of the variable of interest.

Branch A line emanating from a node in a decision tree.

Circular node A component of a decision tree representing an uncertain event.

Combinatorial algorithms Solution techniques for IP problems. These techniques eliminate possible decisions without having to evaluate them explicitly.

Complementary slackness The relationship whereby the dual variable that corresponds to

an inactive constraint in any optimal solution to an LP problem will be zero in any optimal solution to the dual of that problem.

Completion time A specifically assigned time that is necessary for the completion of an event in a PERT network.

Concave function A function with an umbrella shape. Such a function, when representing increasing returns, exhibits diminishing marginal returns.

Concave program A max model with a concave objective function and a convex constraint set.

Conditional probability The probability of an event (say, B) given that another event (say, A) occurs; denoted $P(B|A)$ and defined $P(B|A) = P(B \text{ and } A)/P(A)$.

Confidence interval A statistical concept that provides an indication of the goodness of an estimate.

Constant Part of the data for a model, a number (for example, π) whose value never changes from one run of a model to another. See also *Parameter.*

Constrained optimization Finding a best decision when restrictions are placed on the possible decisions that can be made; also called *mathematical programming.*

Constraint A condition that restricts the decisions that can be made.

Constraint function Part of the mathematical expression of a limiting condition in a decision problem. A constraint is expressed mathematically by an inequality or an equality, and the function on the left is the constraint function. For example, in the constraint $g(x) \leq b$, $g(x)$ is the constraint function.

Constraint set The set of all values of the decision variables that satisfies all the constraints in a constrained optimization problem; the set of allowable decisions. Also called the *feasible set.*

Continuous review An inventory control system in which the status of the system (the number of items on hand and on order) is known at all times and the opportunity to make an order for replenishment items is always present.

Contour of a function The set of all arguments (that is, values for the independent variables) for which the function assumes a specified value.

Conversational mode A mode of computer usage in which the user and the computer engage in a dialogue; also called *interactive mode.*

Convex function A function with a bowl shape. When representing increasing cost, such a function exhibits increasing marginal costs.

Convex program A min model with a convex objective function and a convex constraint set.

Convex set of points A set in which the straight line segment joining any two points in the set also lies entirely in the set.

Corner A colloquial word for an extreme point or a vertex of an LP constraint set. If an LP problem has a solution, there is always a solution at a corner.

Critical path A sequence of activities that determines the minimum time in which an entire project can be completed.

Critical path method (CPM) A method for planning and controlling projects composed of a number of interrelated activities with precedence relationships that must be satisfied. See also *Precedence relationships.*

Cut A way to partition the nodes in a network into two disjoint classes.

Cut capacity In a network partitioned by a cut, the maximal possible flow from one class to the other.

Decision tree A means of graphically visualizing the interactions among decisions, uncertain events, and possible outcomes.

Decision variable A variable in a decision model whose value can be selected by the decision maker. It is the quantitative expression of some action or activity to be taken.

Definitional variable A variable defined in terms of other decision variables. Typically used in a problem for ease of formulation and interpretation.

Degeneracy A situation in which the optimal solution to an LP model has a smaller number of positive variables than constraints. Such a solution is called *degenerate.*

Dependent variable In a functional relationship, a variable whose value is determined by the arguments of the function. For example, in the expression $y = f(x_1, \ldots, x_n)$, the y variable is a dependent variable.

Descriptive model A class of models in which decisions are input and consequences are output; for example, a simulation model is a descriptive model.

Destination In the context of a network, a node that requires more units of flow to enter than to leave; also called a *sink.*

Deterministic inventory model An inventory model in which it is assumed that demand is known.

Deterministic model A general term that encompasses any model in which all components of the model are known with certainty.

Dual feasible A term used to describe a set of values assigned to the dual problem variables that satisfies the constraints (including the sign conditions) of the dual problem.

Dual price A value associated with a constraint in an LP problem. It specifies the rate of improvement in the optimal value of the objective function as the RHS of the constraint is increased. Also called a *shadow price.*

Dual pricing A study of the changes in the optimal value of the objective function as a function of changes in the RHS of a constraint.

Dual problem An LP problem derived from another LP problem, using the same data, and related to the original problem in a special way. See also *Primal problem.*

Dual variable One of the decision variables in the dual to an LP problem. It specifies the rate of change in the optimal value of the objective function as the RHS of the associated constraint is increased.

Dynamic lot-size model A multiperiod inventory model with deterministic demand, a cost of production including a fixed and a proportional component, and a linear holding cost.

Dynamic model A multiperiod model in which decisions made in a given period affect not only the returns in that period but the allowable decisions and returns in future periods as well.

Earliest start time In a PERT network, the earliest moment at which an event can occur; specifically assigned to each event.

Economic order quantity (EOQ) model An inventory model characterized by a continuous review system, deterministic and constant rate of demand, a cost of ordering including a fixed and a proportional component and a linear holding cost.

Effective constraint See *Active constraint.*

Elementary events The elements of a sample space.

Endogenous Developed from within; used to describe decisions of parameters internally produced by a model, often a simulation model.

Event Any subset of a sample space or, equivalently, any collection of elementary events.

Event space The collection of all events or, equivalently, the set of all subsets of the sample space.

Exogenous Originating externally; used to describe parameters or decisions that are input to a model, often a simulation model.

Expected return   The expected value of the return when the return is interpreted as a random variable.

Expected value of a random variable   An indication of the central location of a random variable. If $P_R(r)$ is the probability that the random variable R takes on the r, then the expected value of R, denoted $E(R)$, is defined by the expression $E(R) = \sum_r rP_R(r)$.

Extreme point   See *Corner*.

Feasible   A word used to describe a set of decision variable values for a given model that satisfies the constraints and sign requirements specified by the model. A problem is said to be feasible when the constraint set is nonempty.

Feasible set   See *Constraint set*.

Fixed cost   A component of total cost that is incurred if a particular activity is selected, but whose value is independent of the level of that activity. Mathematically typically expressed by a term like K in a function of the form

$$C(x) = K + cx \qquad x > 0$$
$$\quad\quad\ = 0 \qquad\qquad x = 0$$

Flow balance equations   Constraints that describe the relationship between the flow into and out of each node in a network model.

Flow chart   A diagram showing the appropriate relationships among operations for a task that consists of a sequence of operations.

Heuristic algorithm   A problem-solving method based on common sense or rules of thumb; usually designed to produce "good," rather than optimal, solutions.

Inactive constraint   In a constrained optimization model, an inequality constraint for which the slack variable associated with the constraint has a nonzero value in the optimal solution.

Inconsistent problem   A constrained optimization problem for which there is no point that satisfies all the constraints; also called an *infeasible problem*.

Independent variables   The variables in the argument of the function in a functional relationship. For example, in the functional relationship $y = f(x_1, ..., x_n)$, the x variables are independent variables.

Infeasible problem   See *Inconsistent problem*.

In-process inventory   Inventory of intermediate or unfinished items in a manufacturing process.

Integer programming (IP) problem   A constrained optimization problem in which at least some of the variables are constrained to be integers.

Interactive mode   See *Conversational mode*.

Interarrival time   The time between arrivals to a queuing system.

Intersection   A logical operation on sets. Given two sets A and B, a set consisting of all elements that are members of both A and B; denoted $A \cap B$.

Inventory equation   An equation that expresses the relationship between the inventory on hand at the end of a period as a function of the inventory on hand at the end of the previous period.

Inventory theory   The study of systems in which some entity is held in inventory in anticipation of future demand.

Isocost lines   Contours of a cost function.

Isoprofit lines   Contours of a profit function.

Knapsack model   An IP problem with a single constraint and all coefficients nonnegative in both the objective function and the constraint. Such a problem can be interpreted as maximizing the total utility gained by placing various items into a knapsack of fixed size, where each item has a specified utility and size.

Lagrange multiplier   A term often used to describe the dual variable in a nonlinear programming model.

Latest start time   In a PERT network, the latest moment at which an event can occur without delaying completion of the entire process; specifically assigned to each event.

Lead time   The time that elapses between the placement and receipt of an order in an inventory model.

Least squares   A method of fitting a curve to a collection of points by minimizing squared deviations.

Linear programming (LP) problem   A constrained optimization problem with a linear objective function and linear constraints.

Load leveling   The practice of producing at a relatively steady level rather than completely adjusting production to variations in demand.

Mathematical programming   See *Constrained optimization*.

Mixed integer programming problem   A constrained optimization problem in which some, but not all, of the variables are required to be integers.

Model   A selective representation of reality.

Multiechelon models   Inventory models in which items may be stored in a hierarchy of warehouses and outlets.

Multiple objectives problem   A constrained optimization model in which the decision maker actually has numerous incommensurate objectives (that is, objectives that lack a common standard of comparison).

Network models   A class of LP models with a

special structure, such as the fact that all the a_{ij}s are zero or one. Network models can be represented with nodes and arcs.

Node   A component in a network model.

Nonbasic variables   The zero variables at a nondegenerate corner.

Null test   A test that can be used to establish that a hypothesis is false but not that it is true.

Objective function   A component in a mathematical programming model. The goal is to maximize or minimize the value of this function. Also called *payoff function* or *return.*

Opportunity cost   A cost incurred because assigning a resource to one activity precludes alternative uses of that resource. For example a cost of holding inventory deriving from the fact that funds invested in inventory cannot be used for other revenue-producing ventures.

Optimal decision   That decision (set of values of the decision variables) that yields the maximum (or minimum) value of the objective function; also called the *optimal solution.*

Optimal objective value   The maximum (or minimum) value of the objective function.

Optimal solution   See *Optimal decision.*

Optimal value function   The optimal objective value as a function of a parameter in the programming model; for example, the RHS of a constraint.

Origin   A network node with the property that more units of flow are required to leave than to enter; also called a *source.*

Parameter   Part of the data for a model, a number whose value remains fixed for a specified solving of the problem but whose value can be changed in subsequent runnings of the problem. See also *Constant.*

Parametric analysis   An investigation of the changes in the optimal objective value as a function of changes in the value of a specific parameter; also called *postoptimality analysis* or *sensitivity analysis.*

Partial enumeration   A solution technique for a combinatorial problem requiring inspection of less than the total number of possible solutions.

Payoff function   See *Objective function.*

Periodic review   An inventory control system in which the status of the system (the number of items on hand and on order) is assessed at certain predetermined points in time, and the opportunity to order replenishment items can occur only at these points in time.

Piecewise linear function   A function that consists of linear segments joined at the ends.

Piggyback forecast   A forecast based on the observed values of other variables thought to be related to the variable of interest.

Pivoting operation   An arithmetic operation in the simplex algorithm for solving LP problems.

Planning horizon   An initial time interval in a dynamic problem that can be planned optimally with less than complete information for the entire duration of the problem. For example, in a 10-period problem, period 5 is a planning horizon if one can find the optimal operating plan for periods 1 through 4 with less than complete information on periods 6 through 10.

Portfolio problem   The mathematical programming problem of selecting a collection of securities in order to minimize risk, subject to linear constraints, including one that requires the achievement of a specified minimal level of expected return.

Posterior probability   A reassessed probability. The reassessment combines the prior probabilities and new information with Bayes' law.

Postoptimality analysis   See *Parametric analysis.*

Precedence relationships   Relationships that express the fact that certain events must occur before other events can occur during the progress of a project.

Prescriptive models   A class of models in which the outputs consist of decisions. An optimization model is a prescriptive model.

Primal feasible   A term used to describe a set of values assigned to the primal problem variables that satisfies the constraints (including sign conditions) of the primal problem.

Primal problem   One problem of a pair of LP problems that exhibit a special symmetric and reflexive relationship. See also *Dual problem.*

Prior probabilities   The originally assessed values for probabilities.

Probability mass function (pmf)   A function that assigns probabilities to the possible values of a random variable.

Program evaluation review technique (PERT)   A method for planning and controlling projects composed of a number of interrelated activities with precedence relationships that must be satisfied. See also *Precedence relationships.*

Pure integer program   A mathematical programming problem with all the variables required to be integers.

Queue discipline   The rule that determines which of the items in a queue will be selected for service.

Queuing model   A mathematical model that describes waiting lines.

Random number   A number selected from a specified set of numbers (say, 00–99), where every number of the specified set is equally likely to be selected.

Random sample The result of n independent observations of a random variable.

Random variable A real-valued function defined on a sample space to which probabilities have been assigned.

Random walk A stochastic process in which the value of the process at time t equals the value at time $t - 1$ plus a random variable.

Redundant constraint A constraint that can be removed without changing the feasible region of a mathematical programming problem (for a particular set of parameter values).

Regression theory The statistical theory that underlies the method of least squares.

Relative frequency The ratio of the number of times that a specific event has occurred to the total number of observations.

Reorder point A parameter in a dynamic inventory policy that indicates when an order should be placed.

Reorder quantity A parameter in a dynamic inventory policy that indicates the number of units to be ordered when an order is placed.

Replenishment decision A decision about how many units to order (possibly zero) as part of an inventory control system.

Right-hand side (RHS) The parameters that appear on the right of equalities or inequalities defining constraints.

Roundoff error Numerical error in a computer produced by sequential operations and due to the fact that computer arithmetic is not exact.

s, S policy An inventory control policy that compares inventory on hand (say, x) to a value s. If $x < s$, then $S - x$ items are ordered. If $x \geq s$, no items are ordered.

S policy An inventory control policy that states if the inventory on hand (say, x) is less than S, $S - x$ units are ordered.

Sample A set of realizations or observations of a random variable.

Sample mean The average of the values in a sample, with each value weighted by the number of times it occurs. Denoting the sample mean $\bar{x}$, if x_i are the n observations for a sample of size n, then

$$\bar{x} = \frac{1}{n} \sum_{i=1}^{n} x_i$$

Sample space A set of objects called *elementary events* and providing a basis for the axiomatic development of probability theory.

Sample variance A measure of dispersion in a sample. Denoting the sample variance s^2, if x_i are the observations for a sample of size n,

then

$$s^2 = \sum_{i=1}^{n} \frac{(x_i - \bar{x})^2}{n - 1}$$

where $\bar{x}$ is the sample mean.

Satisficing An expression of the concept that individuals do not seek optimal solutions but rather that they accept solutions that are "good enough" or "better than before."

Scatter diagram A plot of the values of one variable (say, y_i) against another (say, x_i).

Sensitivity analysis See *Parametric analysis.*

Sequential decision problem A decision problem that involves a series of decisions and uncertain events.

Service process A component of a queuing model that determines the manner in which arrivals to the system will be served.

Service time The time required for service in a queuing system; typically a random variable.

Shadow price See *Dual price.*

Simplex method An algorithm for solving an LP problem.

Simulation An analysis of a problem or an environment with an experimental device that "acts like" the phenomenon of interest in certain important respects.

Sink See *Destination.*

Slack variable A nonnegative variable added to the left side of a $\leq$ constraint in an LP problem for the purpose of converting an inequality to an equality constraint. See also *Surplus variable.*

Solution Used in common practice and this text as a synonym for *optimal solution.*

Source See *Origin.*

Square node A node showing a marked lack of social development and abusively used in certain decision tree diagrams.

Standard deviation A parameter used to describe the dispersion of a random variable. Typically denoted σ, σ^2 is defined for the random variable X by the expression $\sigma^2 = E\{ [X - E(X)]^2 \}$, where E is the expected value.

Standard equality-constraint form The form of an LP problem with all constraints converted to equalities and all variables nonnegative. An LP problem must be put into this form before it can be solved with the simplex algorithm.

Standard gamble A device used by a decision maker to evaluate a personal utility for money.

Stationarity The condition that a series of observations is essentially stable over time, which means that variation does not depend on time but is due to random causes.

Stochastic inventory model An inventory model in which the assumption is that demand is a random quantity generated by a known stochastic process.

Stochastic model A general term that encompasses any model including a random element; also called a *probabilistic model*.

Suboptimization The process of optimizing a subcomponent or subproblem of an overall system.

Successive trials Repeated performances of an experiment for which the possible outcomes are a chance event.

Surplus variable A nonnegative variable subtracted from the left side of a $\geq$ constraint in an LP problem for the purpose of converting an inequality to an equality constraint. See also *Slack variable*.

Surrogate A substitute; used in this context to describe an objective function used in place of the true, but unquantifiable, objective.

Terminal node A node in a decision tree that is not succeeded by other nodes.

Terminal position The end of a branch emanating from a terminal node.

Terminal value The net return associated with a terminal node.

Tight constraint See *Active constraint*.

Time series A sequence of values for a particular (single) variable that can be plotted against time.

Time series analysis Any method used to analyze and extrapolate a time series into the future, generally for the purpose of forecasting.

Trend line A line fitted to a time series and then extrapolated to obtain a prediction for a future value.

Trial The performance of an experiment for which the possible outcomes are the result of a chance event.

Trigger inventory An inventory level at the observation of which an order is placed.

Two-bin inventory system An inventory system in which inventory is held in two bins, all orders are originally filled from bin 1, and as soon as the first item is removed from bin 2, an order is placed.

Unbounded A numerical quantity that can be made arbitrarily large, or arbitrarily small, or both.

Unbounded constraint set A constraint set in which at least one decision variable can be made arbitrarily large (or small) in value.

Unbounded problem A constrained optimization problem in which the optimal objective value can be made either arbitrarily large or arbitrarily small.

Unconstrained optimization An optimization problem in which no explicit constraints are placed on the decision variables.

Underling problem A constrained optimization problem in which a subordinate is able to add a constraint to the problem in order to influence the final decision in a personally advantageous way, generally at the expense of the overall objective.

Union A logical operation on sets. Given two sets A and B, the union of A and B consists of all elements that are members of A or B or both; denoted $A \cup B$.

Unique solution A situation in which there is one and only one optimal solution to a problem.

Utility An abstract and subjective measure used to quantify the relative desirability of the possible results of alternative decisions.

Variance The square of the standard deviation.

Waiting time The amount of time a unit spends in a queuing system between the time it arrives and the time service begins.

Index